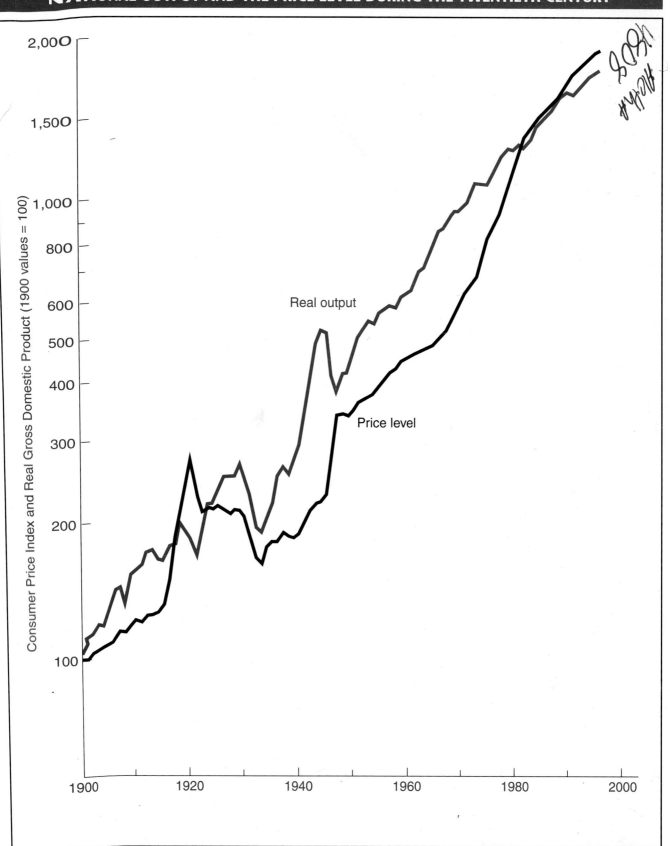

W9-AKY-822

Consumer Price Index and Real Gross Domestic Product (1900 values = 100)

Real output

Price level

1900 1920 1940 1960 1980 2000

MACROECONOMICS

Seventeenth Edition

PAUL A. SAMUELSON
Institute Professor Emeritus
Massachusetts Institute of Technology

WILLIAM D. NORDHAUS
A. Whitney Griswold Professor of Economics
Yale University

McGraw-Hill
Irwin

Boston Burr Ridge, IL Dubuque, IA Madison, WI New York San Franscisco St. Louis
Bangkok Bogotá Caracas Kuala Lumpur Lisbon London Madrid Mexico City
Milan Montreal New Delhi Santiago Seoul Singapore Sydney Taipei Toronto

McGraw-Hill Higher Education

A Division of The McGraw·Hill Companies

MACROECONOMICS

Published by McGraw-Hill, an imprint of The McGraw-Hill Companies, Inc. 1221 Avenue of the Americas, New York, NY, 10020. Copyright © 2001, 1998, 1995, 1992, 1989, 1985, 1980, 1976, 1973, 1970, 1967, 1964, 1961, 1958, 1955, 1951, 1948, by The McGraw-Hill Companies, Inc. All rights reserved. No part of this publication may be reproduced or distributed in any form or by any means, or stored in a data base or retrieval system, without the prior written consent of The McGraw-Hill Companies, Inc., including, but not limited to, in any network or other electronic storage or transmission, or broadcast for distance learning. Some ancillaries, including electronic and print components, may not be available to customers outside the United States.

This book is printed on acid-free paper.

domestic 1 2 3 4 5 6 7 8 9 0   VNH/VNH   0 9 8 7 6 5 4 3 2 1 0
international 1 2 3 4 5 6 7 8 9 0   VNH/VNH   0 9 8 7 6 5 4 3 2 1 0

ISBN 0072314893

Vice president/Editor-in-chief: *Michael W. Junior*
Executive editor: *Lucille Sutton*
Marketing manager: *Marty W. Quinn*
Senior project manager: *Mary Conzachi*
Production supervisor: *Debra R. Sylvester*
Designer: *Amy Feldman*
Senior supplement coordinator: *Becky Szura*
Media technology producer: *Adelaide A. Rogula*
Cover design: *Amy Feldman*
Cover image: *3D Spherical Jigsaw Puzzle™ World Globe made in USA by Buffalo Games, Inc.*
Compositor: *York Graphics Services, Inc.*
Typeface: *10/12 New Baskerville*
Printer: *Von Hoffmann Press, Inc.*

Library of Congress Cataloging-in-Publication Data

Samuelson, Paul Anthony, 1915-
    Macroeconomics / Paul A. Samuelson, William D. Nordhaus.–17th ed.
        p. cm.
    Includes index.
    ISBN 0-07-231478-3 (alk. paper)
    1. Macroeconomics. I. Nordhaus, William D. II. Title.

HB172.5 .S255 2001
339–dc21   00-062473

INTERNATIONAL EDITION ISBN 0071180656
Copyright © 2001. Exclusive rights by The McGraw-Hill Companies, Inc. for manufacture and export.
This book cannot be re-exported from the country to which it is sold by McGraw-Hill.
The International Edition is not available in North America.

www.mhhe.com

PAUL A. SAMUELSON, founder of the renowned MIT graduate department of economics, was trained at the University of Chicago and Harvard. His many scientific writings brought him world fame at a young age, and in 1970 he was the first American to receive a Nobel Prize in economics. One of those rare scientists who can communicate with the lay public, Professor Samuelson wrote an economics column for *Newsweek* for many years and was economic adviser to President John F. Kennedy. He testifies often before Congress and serves as academic consultant to the Federal Reserve, the U.S. Treasury, and various private, nonprofit organizations. Professor Samuelson, between researches at MIT and tennis games, is a visiting professor at New York University. His six children (including triplet boys) have contributed 15 grandchildren.

WILLIAM D. NORDHAUS is one of America's eminent economists. Born in Albuquerque, New Mexico, he was an undergraduate at Yale, received his Ph.D. in economics at MIT, and is now the A. Whitney Griswold Professor of Economics at Yale University and on the staff of the Cowles Foundation for Research in Economics. His economic research has spanned a wide variety of topics—including the environment, price measurement, energy, technological change, economic growth, and trends in profits and productivity. In addition, Professor Nordhaus takes a keen interest in economic policy. He served as a member of President Carter's Council of Economic Advisers from 1977 to 1979, serves on many government advisory boards and committees, and writes occasionally for the *New York Times* and other periodicals. He regularly teaches the Principles of Economics course at Yale. Professor Nordhaus lives in New Haven, Connecticut, with his wife, Barbara, and his golden retriever, Pandora. Two of them share enthusiasms for music, hiking, travel, and skiing.

To
Our
Children
and
Students

Contents in Brief

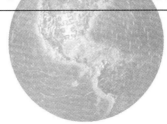

Preface   xiv
Economics and the Internet   xxi

Contents

PART TWO
MACROECONOMICS: THE STUDY OF ECONOMIC GROWTH AND BUSINESS CYCLES
65

**PART THREE
ECONOMIC GROWTH AND
MACROECONOMIC POLICY
219**

**PART FOUR
UNEMPLOYMENT, INFLATION, AND
ECONOMIC POLICY
313**

Preface

As humanity welcomes the new century, economics as a science and as a subject continues to be central to concerns around the globe. The twentieth century witnessed a spectacular change in the living standards of most of the world, particularly those in the affluent countries of North America, Western Europe, and East Asia. While the first half of the century was marked by two world wars and one great depression, the last half has been one of virtually uninterrupted growth of living standards and the spread of free markets, democracy, and personal freedoms to many corners of the globe. The central question for the years ahead is, "Will the good fortune spread from the affluent minority to the poor majority?"

Fifty Years of Economics

Over the past two decades, there have been dramatic changes in both attitudes and in economic institutions. Dozens of countries have rejected socialist and collectivist approaches and adopted market systems. Strong economic growth has been experienced in countries as diverse as Ireland, Botswana, and the Philippines. At no time in recorded history have so many enjoyed such a sustained period of economic growth as they have during the Great Peace of the past half century.

You might think that prosperity would lead to a declining interest in economic affairs, but paradoxically, an understanding of the enduring truths of economics has become even more vital in the affairs of people and nations. The United States grappled with slow growth in living standards and large government budget deficits; but by the turn of the century budget deficits had turned to surpluses, productivity growth turned up, and real incomes were increasing at a healthy pace.

In the larger scene, the world has become increasingly interconnected as computers and communications create an ever-more-competitive global marketplace. Developing countries and countries like Russia and Poland, all of which are trying to develop the institutions of mature capitalism, need a firm understanding of the institutions of a market economy if they are to attain the living standards of the affluent. At the same time, there is growing concern about international environmental problems and the need to forge agreements to preserve our precious natural heritage. All these fascinating changes are part of the modern drama that we call economics.

Fifty Years of ECONOMICS

For more than half a century, this book has served as the standard bearer for the teaching of introductory economics in classrooms in America and throughout the world. Each new edition has distilled the best thinking of economists about how markets function and about what society can do to improve people's living standards. But economics has changed profoundly since the first edition of this text appeared in 1948. And because economics is above all a living and evolving organism, the need to keep *Economics* at the frontier in the rapidly evolving world economy affords the authors an exciting opportunity to present the latest thinking of modern economists and to show how the subject can contribute to a more prosperous world.

Our task then is this: We want to present a clear, accurate, and interesting introduction to the principles of modern economics and to the institutions of the American and world economies. Our primary goal is to survey economics, and in doing this we emphasize the basic economic principle that will endure beyond today's headlines.

THE SEVENTEENTH EDITION

Economics is a dynamic science—changing to reflect the shifting trends in economic affairs, in the environment, in the world economy, and in society at large. As economics and the world around it evolve, so does this book. These nine features differentiate this edition from other books:

1. The Core Truths of Economics. Often, economics appear to be an endless procession of new puzzles, problems, and difficult dilemmas. But as experienced teachers have learned, there are a few basic concepts that underpin all of economics. Once these basic concepts have been mastered, learning is much quicker and more enjoyable. *We have therefore chosen to focus on the central core of economics—on those endur-*

ing truths that will be just as important in the twenty-first century as they were in the twentieth. Microeconomic concepts such as scarcity, efficiency, the gains from specialization, and the principle of comparative advantage will be crucial concepts as long as scarcity itself exists. Moreover students of macroeconomics must receive a firm grounding in the concepts of aggregate supply and demand and must understand the role of national and international monies. Students will learn the widely accepted theory of economic growth, but they should also understand the controversial theories of the business cycle.

2. *Innovation in the Economy.* One of the striking features of the modern economy is the rapidity of innovations in virtually every sector. We are accustomed to the dizzying speed of invention in computers, where new products and software appear monthly. The Internet is revolutionizing communications and making inroads into commerce. Nowhere in recorded history do we find such a rapid rate of improvement as has been seen for computers over the past three decades. But other sectors are also witnessing rapid innovation—we run in athletic equipment made of miraculous new materials and relax while listening to music from crystal-clear audio equipment. Our understanding of economic trends and policies must reflect this rapid change in our societies.

Economics is increasingly attentive to rapid innovation. In macroeconomics, new growth theories emphasize the importance of technology, invention, and human capital in the growth process. In microeconomics, we have included a new section on the economics of information, showing how externalities in the production of information and new technologies lead to market failures. And a case study of the economics of the Internet explores the dilemmas of pricing information.

3. *Innovation in Economics.* In addition, we emphasize innovations in economics itself. Economists are tinkerers, innovators, and inventors in their own way. History shows that economic ideas can produce tidal waves when they are applied to real-world problems. Among the important innovations studied here is the application of economics to our environmental problems through "emissions trading" plans. Other im-

portant economic innovations discussed are improved regulatory mechanisms and the radical new step of European monetary unification. One of the most influential economic innovations of the last few years involves the measurement of consumer prices. We introduce the important notion of "network economics" and show how it affects economic efficiency and market power, and how it has entered into the debate about breaking up Microsoft. One of the most important innovations for our common future is dealing with global public goods like climate change, and we analyze new approaches to dealing with international environmental problems such as the Kyoto Protocol.

4. *Small Is Beautiful.* Economics has increased its scope greatly over the past half-century. The flag of economics flies over its traditional territory of the marketplace, but it also covers the environment, legal studies, statitiscal and historical methods, art, gender and racial discrimination, and even family life. But at its core, economics is the science of choice, which means that we, as authors, have to choose the most important and enduring issues for this text. In a survey, as in a meal, small is beautiful because it is digestible.

Choosing the subjects for this text required many hard choices. To select these topics, we continually survey teachers and leading scholars to determine the ones most crucial for an informed citizenry and a new generation of economists. We drew up a list of key ideas and bid adieu to many appendices and sections. *At every stage, we asked whether the material was, as best we could judge, necessary for a student's understanding of the economics of the twenty-first century.* Only when a subject passed this test was it included. The result of this campaign is a book that has lost more than one-quarter of its weight in the last two editions. Farming, labor unions, and Marxian economics have been trimmed to make room for environmental economics, network economics, and real business cycles.

5. *Policy Issues at Century's Dawn.* Each generation of economists finds new challenges to contend with in the attempt to understand evolving economic policy problems. Two areas that have been at the forefront of economics in the past decade have received expanded treatment in the seventeenth edition. As human societies grow, they begin to overwhelm the environment and ecosystems of the natural world. Environmental economics, presented in Chapter 18, helps students understand the externalities associated with economic activity and then analyzes different approaches to making human economies compatible with natural systems. A second important area is international economics. We have completely reorganized our treatment of international economics by integrating the theory of comparative advantage into the microeconomics sections while reorganizing and restructuring the macroeconomic sections. The new organization will allow students to get an appreciation of the global economy at an earlier stage in their studies.

6. *The Incredible Shrinking Globe.* A century ago, the leading military strategist of the age, Captain A. T. Mahan, declared in his important book *The Influence of Sea Power on History*, "Whether they will or no, Americans must now begin to look outward." President William Jefferson Clinton echoed these words when he wrote about economic affairs, "There is simply no way to close our borders and return to the insular days. To try to do so would be an exercise in futility, doomed not only to fail but to lower living standards in the process."

Americans are learning that no nation is an island. Immigration and international trade have profound effects on the goods that are available, the prices we pay, and the wages we earn. Labor economists have found that the surge of uneducated immigrants over the last two decades has been an important contributor to the declining real wages of unskilled workers. Development economists have found striking results regarding the impact of economic openness on economic growth. No complete understanding of modern economics is possible without a thorough grounding in the world economy. The seventeenth edition continues to increase the material devoted to international economics and the interaction between international trade and domestic economic events.

7. *Advances in Modern Macroeconomics.* One of the major obstacles to understanding modern economics is the proliferation of contesting schools of macroeconomics. Teachers often wonder how students can understand the subject when macroecon-

omists themselves are so divided. While many fret about the divisiveness of modern macroeconomics, we think it is a sign of health and prefer lively debate to complacent consensus.

The seventeenth edition analyzes all major schools of modern macroeconomics within the clear organizing synthesis of aggregate supply and demand. We show how macroeconomics of the Keynesian, old and new classical, supply-side, and monetarist varieties can be understood as emphasizing different aspects of expectations, market clearing, and aggregate demand. Each school is clearly presented and compared with its competitors in a balanced and evenhanded way. For each, the empirical evidence is presented and evaluated. The major schools are presented in a chapter entitled "The Warring Schools of Macroeconomics." But we also emphasize the importance of the *policy implications* of the different approaches. And we also have reorganized and integrated the open-economy issues into the core chapters.

Although much macroeconomic combat is devoted to arguing about the sources of the business cycle, one of the major recent developments in economics has been the resurgence of attention to the forces underlying long-run economic growth. Economists are increasingly examining the determinants of long-run economic growth, the slowdown and recent rebound in productivity growth, and the generation of innovation and new technological knowledge. Putting economic growth front and center is necessary if students are to understand modern debates about the role of government debt and deficits. The seventeenth edition reflects this revival by synthesizing growth theories and findings into the central section on macroeconomics. We include growth theory as an integral part of aggregate supply and potential output and have revised and moved the chapter on economic development to follow the material on economic growth theory.

8. *Emphasis on History and Policy.* Students study economics to understand the rapidly changing world around them. For this reason, economics is at its core an empirical science. It first aims to explain the world around us and then helps us devise economic policies, based on sound economic principles, that can enhance the living standards of people at home and abroad.

Drawing upon history, economic chronicles, and the experience of the authors, the seventeenth edition continues to emphasize the use of case studies and empirical evidence to illustrate economic theories. The dilemmas involved in combating poverty become real when we understand the 1996 welfare reforms or the problems of the current health-care system. Our appreciation of macroeconomic analysis increases when we see how government deficits in the 1980s lowered national saving and how the current budget surpluses are increasing national saving. Macroeconomics can help explain the American economic miracle of the late 1990s.

The microeconomic chapters draw upon case studies, economic history, business decisions, and real-world experience to illustrate the fundamental principles. Examples such as network economics, the Microsoft antitrust case, the flat tax, and the Kyoto Protocol on global warming, the economics of addictive substances, the minimum-wage debate, trading pollution permits, and the history of stock markets help bring the theorems of microeconomics to life. Game theory becomes serious—and has striking implications—when applied to pollution or winner-take-all games.

This "hands-on" approach to economics allows students to understand better the relevance of economic analysis to real-world problems. The abstract notion of scarcity becomes concrete when we see its implications for whether we have a good job, a healthy environment, adequate health care, and a secure nest egg for our retirement.

9. Clarity. Although there are many new features in the seventeenth edition, the pole star for our pilgrimage in preparing this edition has been to present economics clearly and simply. Students enter the classroom with a wide range of backgrounds and with many preconceptions about the way the world works. Our role is not to change their values, but to help them to understand the enduring economic principles and then to be able to apply them to make the world a better place for them, their families, and their communities. Nothing aids understanding better than clear, simple exposition. We have labored over every page to improve this survey of introductory economics. We have received thousands of comments and suggestions from teachers and students

and have incorporated their counsel in the seventeenth edition.

Optional Matter

Economics courses range from one-quarter surveys to year-long intensive honors courses. This textbook has been carefully designed to meet all situations. The more advanced materials have been put in separate appendices or specially designated sections. These will appeal to curious students and to students in demanding courses that survey the entire discipline thoroughly. We have included advanced questions for discussion to test the mettle of the most dedicated student.

If yours is a fast-paced course, you will appreciate the careful layering of the more advanced material. Hard-pressed courses can skip the advanced sections, covering the core of economic analysis without losing the thread of the economic reasoning. This book will challenge the most advanced young scholar. Indeed, many of today's leading economists have written to say they've relied upon *Economics* all along their pilgrimage to the Ph.D.

Format

The seventeenth edition employs a greatly expanded set of in-text logos and material to help illustrate the central topics. You will find three distinctive logos: warnings for the fledgling economist, examples of economics in action, and biographical material on the great economists of the past and present. But these central topics are not drifting off by themselves in unattached boxes. Rather, they are integrated right into the chapters so that students can read them without breaking their train of thought. Keep these logos in mind as you read through the text:

 is a warning that students should pause to ensure that they understand a difficult or subtle point.

 is an interesting example or application of the analysis, and often it represents one of the major innovations of modern economics.

 presents biographies of important economic figures. Sometimes these are famous economists like Adam Smith, while at other times they are people who introduced economics into public policy.

New features in this edition include fresh end-of-chapter questions, with a special accent upon short problems that reinforce the major concepts surveyed in the chapter. Terms printed in bold type in the text mark the first occurrence and definition of the most important words that constitute the language of economics.

But these many changes have not altered one bit the central stylistic beacon that has guided *Economics* since the first edition: to use simple sentences, clear explanations, and concise tables and graphs.

For Those Who Prefer Macro First

Although, like the previous edition, this new edition has been designed to cover microeconomics first, many teachers continue to prefer beginning with macroeconomics. They may think that the beginning student finds macro more approachable and will more quickly develop a keen interest in economics when the issues of macroeconomics are encountered first. We have taught economics in both sequences and find both work well.

Whatever your philosophy, this text has been carefully designed for it. Instructors who deal with microeconomics first can move straight through the chapters. Those who wish to tackle macroeconomics first should skip from Part One directly to Part Five, knowing that the exposition and cross-references have been tailored with their needs in mind.

In addition, for those courses that do not cover the entire subject, the seventeenth edition is available in two paperback volumes, *Microeconomics* (Chapters 1 to 19 of the full text) and *Macroeconomics* (Chapters 1 to 3 and 20 to 34 of the full text).

Auxiliary Teaching and Study Aids

Students of this edition will benefit greatly from the *Study Guide*. This carefully designed supplement was prepared by Kathryn Nantz and Laurence Miners of Fairfield University who worked in close collaboration with us in our revision. When used alongside classroom discussions and when employed independently for self-study, the *Study Guide* has proved to be an impressive success. There is a full-text *Study Guide*, as well as micro and macro versions.

In addition, instructors will find both the *Instructor's Resource Manual* and the *Test Bank* useful for planning their courses and preparing multiple sets of test questions in both print and computerized formats. Moreover, McGraw-Hill/Irwin has designed a beautiful set of two-color overhead transparencies for presenting the tabular and graphical material in the classroom. The graphs and figures in this edition can also be viewed electronically as PowerPoint slides. The slides can be downloaded from our website (www. mhhe.com/economics/samuelson). The website also contains self-grading, practice quizzes, interactive diagrams of key graphs, and the websites suggested for further research found at the end of each chapter. These items can all be obtained by contacting your local McGraw-Hill/Irwin sales representative.

Economics in the Computer Age

The electronic age has revolutionized the way that scholars and students can access information. In economics, the information revolution allows us quick access to economic statistics and research. An important feature of the seventeenth edition is the section "Economics and the Internet," which appears just before Chapter 1. This little section provides a road map for the state of economics on the Information Superhighway.

In addition, each chapter has a new section at the end with suggestions for further reading and a set of websites that can be used to deepen student understanding or find data and case studies.

Students can also purchase *The Power of Macroeconomics* and *The Power of Microeconomics*, which contain lessons directly tied to this text. These programs are lively combinations of PowerPoints with audio designed to reinforce economics concepts. They allow students to move at their own pace and engage students with questions during the presentation. *The Power of Macroeconomics* and *The Power of Microeconomics* were developed by Peter Navarro at the University of California at Irvine, Graduate School of Management. A complete description of this supplement can be found at www.powerofeconomics. com.

Acknowledgments

This book has two authors but a multitude of collaborators. We are profoundly grateful to colleagues, reviewers, students, and McGraw-Hill's staff for contributing to the timely completion of the seventeenth edition of *Economics*. Colleagues at MIT, Yale, and elsewhere who graciously contributed their comments and suggestions include William C. Brainard,

E. Cary Brown, John Geanakoplos, Robert J. Gordon, Lyle Gramely, Paul Joskow, Alfred Kahn, Richard Levin, Robert Litan, Barry Nalebuff, Merton J. Peck, Gustav Ranis, Herbert Scarf, Robert M. Solow, James Tobin, Janet Yellen, and Gary Yohe.

In addition, we have benefited from the tireless devotion of those whose experience in teaching elementary economics is embodied in this edition. We are particularly grateful to the reviewers of the seventeenth edition. They include:

John Brennan, *Ana Maria College*
Adhip Chaudhuri, *Georgetown University*
Stephen Erfle, *Dickinson College*
Margaret Fogarty, *Skidmore College*
Richard Fox, *Madonna University*
James Gale, *Michigan Technological University*
Gypsy Gallardo, *Eckerd College*
Steven Hackett, *Humboldt State University*
Joyce Jacobsen, *Wesleyan University*
Philip LeBel, *Montclair State University*
Patrick Mann, *West Virginia University*
Ibrahaim M. Oweiss, *Georgetown University*
John Rapczak, *Community College of Rhode Island*
Virginia Shingleton, *Valparaiso University*
Leanne Smith, *Massey University*—New Zealand
Chaitram J. Talele, *Columbia State University*
Richard Tiffin, *University of Durham*
Michael Meng-Hua Ye, *St. Mary's College of Maryland*

Students at MIT, Yale, and other colleges and universities have served as an "invisible college." They constantly challenge and test us, helping to make this edition less imperfect than its predecessor. Although they are too numerous to enumerate, their influence is woven through every chapter. The statistical and historical material was prepared and double-checked by Andrew Pearlman. Nancy King and Glena Ames provided help in word processing. Marnie Wiss and Grace Profatilov coordinated the editorial process at the authors' end.

This project would have been impossible without the skilled team from McGraw-Hill who nurtured the book at every stage. We particularly would like to thank, in chronological order to their appearance on the scene, Economics Editor Lucille Sutton, Developmental Editor Shoshannah Flach, Project Manager Mary Conzachi, Production Manager Debra Sylvester, and Marketing Manager Martin Quinn. This group of skilled professionals turned a pile of diskettes and a mountain of paper into a finely polished work of art.

A WORD TO THE SOVEREIGN STUDENT

You have read in the history books of revolutions that shake civilizations to their roots—religious conflicts, wars for political liberation, struggles against colonialism and imperialism. A decade ago, economic revolutions in Eastern Europe, in the former Soviet Union, in China, and elsewhere tore those societies apart. Young people battered down walls, overthrew established authority, and agitated for democracy and a market economy because of discontent with their centralized socialist governments.

Students like yourselves are marching, and even going to jail, to win the right to study radical ideas and learn from Western textbooks like this one in the hope that they may enjoy the freedom and economic prosperity of democratic market economies.

The Intellectual Marketplace

Just what is the market that students in repressed societies are agitating for? In the pages that follow, you will learn about the markets for stocks and bonds, Mexican pesos and European Euros, unskilled labor and highly trained neurosurgeons. You have probably read in the newspaper about the gross domestic product, the consumer price index, the stock market, and the unemployment rate. After you have completed a thorough study of the chapters in this textbook, you will know precisely what these words mean. Even more important, you will also understand the economic forces that influence and determine them.

There is also a marketplace of ideas, where contending schools of economists fashion their theories and try to persuade their scientific peers. You will find in the chapters that follow a fair and impartial review of the thinking of the intellectual giants of our profession—from the early economists like Adam Smith, David Ricardo, and Karl Marx to modern-day titans like John Maynard Keynes, Milton Friedman, and Robert Solow.

Skoal!

As you begin your journey into the land of markets, it would be understandable if you are somewhat anxious. But take heart. The fact is that we envy you, the beginning student, as you set out to explore the exciting world of economics for the first time. This is a thrill that, alas, you can experience only once in a lifetime. So, as you embark, we wish you bon voyage!

Paul A. Samuelson
William D. Nordhaus

For the Student: Economics and the Internet

The Information Age is revolutionizing our lives. The impact on scholars and students has been particularly profound because it allows inexpensive and rapid access to vast quantities of information. The Internet, which is a huge and growing public network of linked computers and information, is changing the way we study, shop, share our culture, and communicate with our friends and family.

In economics, the Internet allows us quick access to economics statistics and research. With just a few clicks of a mouse, we can find out about the most recent unemployment rate, track down information on poverty and incomes, or investigate the intricacies of our banking system. A few years ago, it might have taken weeks to dig out the data necessary to analyze an economic problem. Today, with a computer and a little practice, that same task can be done in a few minutes.

This book is not a manual for driving on the Information Superhighway. That skill can be learned in classes on the subject or from informal tutorials. Rather, we want to provide a road map that shows the locations of economic data and research. With this map and some rudimentary navigational skills, you can explore the various sites and find a rich array of data, information, studies, and chat rooms.

This introduction provides an overview of the Internet and describes some of the most important websites in economics. Additionally, at the end of each chapter there is a list of useful websites that can be used to follow up the major themes of that chapter.

Note that some of these sites may be free, some may require a registration or be available through your college or university, and others may require paying a fee. Pricing practices change rapidly, so while we have attempted to include primarily free sites, we have not excluded high-quality sites that may charge during 2000.

Data and Institutions. The Internet is an indispensable source of useful data and other information. Since most economic data are provided by governments, the first place to look is the Web pages of government agencies and international organizations. The starting point for U.S. government statistics, www.fedstats.gov, provides one-stop shopping for Federal statistics with links to over 70 government agencies that produce statistical information. Sources are organized by subject or by agency, and the contents are fully searchable. Another good launching site into the federal statistical system is the Economic Statistics Briefing Room at www.whitehouse.gov/fsbr/esbr.html. Additionally, the Commerce Department operates a huge database at www.stat-usa.gov, but use of parts of this database requires a subscription (which may be available at your college or university). A portal for government data in many sectors can be found at www.lib.umich.edu/libhome/Documents.center/stats.html.

The best single statistical source for data on the United States is *The Statistical Abstract of the United States*, published annually. It is available online at www.census.gov/statab/www. If you want an overview of the U.S. economy, you can read *The Economic Report of the President* at w3.access.gpo.gov/eop and www.whitehouse.gov/WH/EOP/CEA/html/index.html.

Most of the major economic data is produced by specialized agencies. One place to find general data is the Department of Commerce, which encompasses the Bureau of Economic Analysis (BEA) (www.bea.doc.gov) and the Census Bureau (www.census.gov). The BEA site includes all data and articles published in the *Survey of Current Business*, including the national income and product accounts, international trade and investment flows, output by industry, economic growth, personal income and labor series, and regional data.

The Census site goes well beyond a nose count of the population. It also includes the economic census as well as information on housing, income and poverty, government finance, agriculture, foreign trade, construction, manufacturing, transportation, and retail and wholesale trade. In addition to making Census publications available, the Census site allows users to create custom extracts of popular microdata sources including the Survey of Income and Program Participation, Consumer Expenditure Survey, Current Population Survey, American Housing Survey, and, of course, the most recent census.

The Bureau of Labor Statistics (at www.bls.gov) provides easy access to commonly requested labor data, including employment and unemployment, prices and living conditions, compensation, productivity, and technology. Also available are labor-force data from the Current Population Survey and payroll statistics from the Current Employment Statistics Survey.

A useful source for financial data is the website of the Federal Reserve Board at www.federalreserve.gov. This site provides historical U.S. economic and financial data, including daily interest rates, monetary and business indicators, exchange rates, balance-of-payments data, and price indices. In addition, the Office of Management and Budget at www.gpo.gov/usbudget/index.html makes available the federal budget and related documents.

International statistics are often harder to find. The World Bank at www.worldbank.org has information on its programs and publications at its site, as does the International Monetary Fund, or IMF at www.imf.org. The United Nations website (www.unsystem.org) is slow and confusing but has links to most international institutions and their databases. Another good source of information about high-income countries is the Organisation for Economic Cooperation and Development, or OECD, at www.oecd.org. The OECD's website contains an array of data on economics, education, health, science and technology, agriculture, energy, public management, and other topics.

Economic Research and Journalism. The Internet is rapidly becoming the world's library. Newspapers, magazines, and scholarly publications are increasingly posting their writing in electronic form. Most of these present what is already available in the paper publications. Some interesting sources can be found at the *Economist* at www.economist.com and *The Financial Times* (www.ft.com). *The Wall Street Journal* at www.wsj.com is currently expensive and not recommended. Current policy issues are discussed at www.policy.com. The online magazine *Slate* at www.slate.com occasionally contains excellent essays in economics.

For scholarly writings, many journals are making their contents available online. WebEc at www.helsinki.fi/WebEc contains a listing of websites for many economic journals. The archives of many journals are available at www.jstor.org.

There are now a few websites that bring many resources together in one place. One place to start is *Resources for Economists on the Internet*, sponsored by the American Economic Association and edited by Bill Goffe at www.rfe.org. Also see *WWW Resources in Economics*, which has links to many different branches of economics at netec.wustl.edu/WebEc/WebEc.html. Another site with much entertaining and useful information is www.economics.miningco.com/finance/economics. These sites also offer a comprehensive list of links to economics journals. For working papers, the National Bureau of Economic Research (NBER) website at www.nber.org contains current economic research. The NBER site also contains general resources, including links to data sources and the official U.S. business-cycle dates.

An excellent site that archives and serves as a depository for working papers is located at econwpa.wustl.edu/wpawelcome.html. This site is particularly useful for finding background material for research papers.

Did someone tell you that economics is the dismal science? You can chuckle over economist jokes (mostly at the expense of economists) at www.netec.wustl.edu/JokEc.html.

A Word of Warning. Note that, because of rapid technological change, this list will soon be out of date. New sites with valuable information and data are appearing every day . . . and others are disappearing almost as rapidly.

Before you set off into the wonderful world of the Web, we would pass on to you some wisdom from experts. Remember the old adage, you only get what you pay for:

> **Warning: Be careful to determine that your sources and data are reliable. The Internet and other electronic media are notoriously easy to use and equally easy to abuse.**

The Web is the closest thing in economics to a free lunch. But you must select your items carefully to ensure that they are palatable and digestible.

MACROECONOMICS

PART ONE

Basic Concepts

CHAPTER

1

The Fundamentals of Economics

The Age of Chivalry is gone; that of sophisters, economists, and calculators has succeeded.

Edmund Burke

As you begin your studies, you are probably wondering, Why study economics? In fact, people do it for a number of reasons.

Many study economics because they hope to make money. Some people worry that they will be considered illiterate if they cannot understand the laws of supply and demand.

Others are interested in learning about how computers and the information revolution are shaping our society or why inequality in the distribution of income in the United States has risen so sharply in recent years.

For Whom the Bell Tolls

All these reasons, and many more, make good sense. Still, as we have come to realize, there is one overriding reason for learning the basic lessons of economics: All your life—from cradle to grave and beyond—you will run up against the brutal truths of economics. As a voter, you will make decisions on issues that cannot be understood until you have mastered the rudiments of this subject. Without a study of economics, you cannot be fully informed about international trade, the economic impact of the Internet, or the trade-off between inflation and unemployment.

Choosing your life's occupation is the most important economic decision you will make. Your future depends not only on your own abilities but also on how economic forces beyond your control affect your wages. Also, your knowledge of economics may help you invest the nest egg you save from your earnings. Of course, studying economics cannot make you a genius. But without economics the dice of life are loaded against you.

There is no need to belabor the point. We hope you will find that, in addition to being useful, economics is a fascinating field in its own right. Generations of students, often to their surprise, have discovered how stimulating economics can be.

SCARCITY AND EFFICIENCY: THE TWIN THEMES OF ECONOMICS

What is economics? Over the last half-century, the study of economics has expanded to include a vast range of topics. What are the major definitions of these growing subjects?[1] The important ones are that economics

- analyzes how a society's institutions and technology affect prices and the allocation of resources among different uses.
- explores the behavior of the financial markets, including interest rates and stock prices.
- examines the distribution of income and suggests ways that the poor can be helped without harming the performance of the economy.
- studies the business cycle and examines how monetary policy can be used to moderate the swings in unemployment and inflation.
- studies the patterns of trade among nations and analyzes the impact of trade barriers.
- looks at growth in developing countries and proposes ways to encourage the efficient use of resources.
- asks how government policies can be used to pursue important goals such as rapid economic growth, efficient use of resources, full employment, price stability, and a fair distribution of income.

This list is a good one, yet you could extend it many times over. But if we boil down all these definitions, we find one common theme:

Economics is the study of how societies use scarce resources to produce valuable commodities and distribute them among different people.

Behind this definition are two key ideas in economics: that goods are scarce and that society must use its resources efficiently. Indeed, economics is an important subject because of the fact of scarcity and the desire for efficiency.

Consider a world without scarcity. If infinite quantities of every good could be produced or if hu-man desires were fully satisfied, what would be the consequences? People would not worry about stretching out their limited incomes because they could have everything they wanted; businesses would not need to fret over the cost of labor or health care; governments would not need to struggle over taxes or spending or pollution because nobody would care. Moreover, since all of us could have as much as we pleased, no one would be concerned about the distribution of incomes among different people or classes.

In such an Eden of affluence, all goods would be free, like sand in the desert or seawater at the beach. All prices would be zero, and markets would be unnecessary. Indeed, economics would no longer be a useful subject.

But no society has reached a utopia of limitless possibilities. Ours is a world of **scarcity,** full of **economic goods.** A situation of scarcity is one in which goods are limited relative to desires. An objective observer would have to agree that, even after two centuries of rapid economic growth, production in the United States is simply not high enough to meet everyone's desires. If you add up all the wants, you quickly find that there are simply not enough goods and services to satisfy even a small fraction of everyone's consumption desires. Our national output would have to be many times larger before the average American could live at the level of the average doctor or big-league baseball player. Moreover, outside the United States, particularly in Africa and Asia, hundreds of millions of people suffer from hunger and material deprivation.

Given unlimited wants, it is important that an economy make the best use of its limited resources. That brings us to the critical notion of efficiency. **Efficiency** denotes the most effective use of a society's resources in satisfying people's wants and needs. By contrast, consider an economy with unchecked monopolies or unhealthy pollution or unwarranted government interferences. Such an economy may produce less than would be possible without these factors, or it may produce a disorted bundle of goods that leaves consumers worse off than they otherwise could be—either situation is an inefficient allocation of resources.

In economics, we say that an economy is producing efficiently when it cannot make anyone economically better off without making someone else worse off.

---

[1] This list contains several specialized terms from economics. To master the subject, you will need to understand its vocabulary. If you are not familiar with a particular word or phrase, you should consult the Glossary at the back of this book. The Glossary contains most of the major technical economic terms used in this book. All terms printed in boldface are defined in the Glossary.

The essence of economics is to acknowledge the reality of scarcity and then figure out how to organize society in a way which produces the most efficient use of resources. That is where economics makes its unique contribution.

Microeconomics and Macroeconomics

Adam Smith is usually considered the founder of the field of **microeconomics,** the branch of economics which today is concerned with the behavior of individual entities such as markets, firms, and households. In *The Wealth of Nations* (1776), Smith considered how individual prices are set, studied the determination of prices of land, labor, and capital, and inquired into the strengths and weaknesses of the market mechanism. Most important, he identified the remarkable efficiency properties of markets and saw that economic benefit comes from the self-interested actions of individuals. These remain important issues today, and while the study of microeconomics has surely advanced greatly since Smith's day, he is still cited by politicians and economists alike.

The other major branch of our subject is **macroeconomics,** which is concerned with the overall performance of the economy. Macroeconomics did not even exist in its modern form until 1935, when John Maynard Keynes published his revolutionary *General Theory of Employment, Interest and Money*. At the time, England and the United States were still stuck in the Great Depression of the 1930s, with over one-quarter of the American labor force unemployed. In his new theory Keynes developed an analysis of what causes business cycles, with alternating spells of high unemployment and high inflation. Today, macroeconomics examines a wide variety of areas, such as how total investment and consumption are determined, how central banks manage money and interest rates, what causes international financial crises, and why some nations grow rapidly while others stagnate. Although macroeconomics has progressed far since his first insights, the issues addressed by Keynes still define the study of macroeconomics today.

The two branches—microeconomics and macroeconomics—converge to form the core of modern economics.

THE LOGIC OF ECONOMICS

Economic life is an enormously complicated hive of activity, with people buying, selling, bargaining, investing, persuading, and threatening. The ultimate purpose of economic science and of this text is to understand this complex undertaking. How do economists go about their task?

Economists use the *scientific approach* to understand economic life. This involves observing economic affairs and drawing upon statistics and the historical record. For complex phenomena like the impacts of budget deficits or the causes of inflation, historical research has provided a rich mine of insights.

Often, economics relies upon analyses and theories. Theoretical approaches allow economists to make broad generalizations, such as those concerning the advantages of international trade and specialization or the disadvantages of tariffs and quotas.

In addition, economists have developed a specialized technique known as *econometrics*, which applies the tools of statistics to economic problems. Using econometrics, economists can sift through mountains of data to extract simple relationships.

Budding economists must also be alert to common fallacies in economic reasoning. Because economic relationships are often complex, involving many different variables, it is easy to become confused about the exact reason behind events or the impact of policies on the economy. The following are some of the common fallacies encountered in economic reasoning:

- *The post hoc fallacy.* The first fallacy involves the inference of causality. *The post hoc fallacy occurs when we assume that, because one event occurred before another event, the first event caused the second event.*[2] An example of this syndrome occurred in the Great Depression of the 1930s in the United States. Some people had observed that periods of business expansion were preceded or accompanied by rising prices. From this, they concluded that the appropriate remedy for depression was to raise wages and prices. This idea led to a host of legislation and regulations to prop up wages and prices in an inefficient manner. Did these measures promote economic recovery? Almost surely not. Indeed, they probably slowed recovery, which did not occur until total spending

---

[2] "Post hoc" is shorthand for *post hoc, ergo propter hoc*. Translated from the Latin, the full expression means "after this, therefore necessarily because of this."

began to rise as the government increased military spending in preparation for World War II.

- *Failure to hold other things constant.* A second pitfall is failure to hold other things constant when thinking about an issue. For example, we might want to know whether raising tax rates will raise or lower tax revenues. Some people have put forth the seductive argument that we can eat our fiscal cake and have it too. They argue that cutting tax rates will at the same time raise government revenues and lower the budget deficit. They point to the Kennedy-Johnson tax cuts of 1964, which lowered tax rates sharply and were followed by an increase in government revenues in 1965. Hence, they argue, lower tax rates produce higher revenues.

  What is wrong with this reasoning? This argument overlooks the fact that the economy grew from 1964 to 1965. Because people's incomes grew during that period, government revenues also grew, even though tax rates were lower. Careful studies indicate that revenues would have been even higher in 1965 had tax rates not been lowered in 1964. Hence, this analysis fails to hold other things (namely, total incomes) constant.

  Remember to hold other things constant when you are analyzing the impact of a variable on the economic system.

- *The fallacy of composition.* Sometimes we assume that what holds true for part of a system also holds true for the whole. In economics, however, we often find that the whole is different from the sum of the parts. *When you assume that what is true for the part is also true for the whole, you are committing the fallacy of composition.*

  Here are some true statements that might surprise you if you ignored the fallacy of composition: (1) If one farmer has a bumper crop, she has a higher income; if all farmers produce a record crop, farm incomes will fall. (2) If one person receives a great deal more money, that person will be better off; if everyone receives a great deal more money, the society is likely to be worse off. (3) If a high tariff is put on the product of a particular industry, the producers in that industry are likely to profit; if high tariffs are put on all industries, most producers and consumers will be worse off.

These examples contain no tricks or magic. Rather, they are the results of systems of interacting individuals. Often the behavior of the aggregate looks very different from the behavior of individual people.

We mention these fallacies only briefly in this introduction. Later, as we introduce the tools of economics, we will provide examples of how inattention to the logic of economics can lead you to false and sometimes costly errors. When you reach the end of this book, you can look back to see why each of these paradoxical examples is true.

COOL HEADS AT THE SERVICE OF WARM HEARTS

Economics has, over the last century, grown from a tiny acorn into a mighty oak. Under its spreading branches we find explanations of the gains from international trade, advice on how to reduce unemployment and inflation, formulas for investing your retirement funds, and even proposals for selling the rights to pollute. Throughout the world, economists are laboring to collect data and improve our understanding of economic trends.

You might well ask, What is the purpose of this army of economists measuring, analyzing, and calculating? The ultimate goal of economic science is to improve the living conditions of people in their everyday lives. Increasing the gross domestic product is not just a numbers game. Higher incomes mean good food, warm houses, and hot water. They mean safe drinking water and inoculations against the perennial plagues of humanity.

Higher incomes mean even more. They allow governments to build schools so that young people can learn to read and develop the skills necessary to invent new technologies like artificial intelligence. As incomes rise further, nations can afford deep scientific inquiries into biology and discover still more vaccines against still more diseases. With the resources freed up by economic growth, talented artists have the opportunity to write poetry and compose music, while others have the leisure time to read, to listen, and to perform. Although there is no single pattern of economic development, and the evolution of culture will differ around the world, freedom from hunger, disease, and the elements is a universal human aspiration.

But centuries of human history also show that warm hearts alone will not feed the hungry or heal the sick. A free and efficient market will not necessarily produce a distribution of income that is socially acceptable. Determining the best route to economic progress or an equitable distribution of society's output requires cool heads, ones that objectively weigh the costs and benefits of different approaches, trying as hard as humanly possible to keep the analysis free from the taint of wishful thinking. Sometimes, economic progress will require shutting down an outmoded factory. Sometimes, as when the formerly socialist countries adopted market principles, things get worse before they get better. Choices are particularly difficult in the field of health care, where limited resources literally involve life and death.

You may have heard the saying, "From each according to his ability, to each according to his need." Governments have learned that no society can long operate solely on this utopian principle. To maintain a healthy economy, governments must preserve incentives for people to work and to save. Societies can support the unemployed for a while, but when unemployment insurance covers too much for too long, people come to depend upon the government and stop looking for work. If they begin to believe that the government owes them a living, this may dull the sharp edge of enterprise. Just because government programs derive from lofty purposes does not mean that they should be pursued without care and efficiency.

Society must find the right balance between the discipline of the market and the compassion of government social programs. By using cool heads to inform our warm hearts, economic science can do its part in ensuring a prosperous and just society.

B. THE THREE PROBLEMS OF ECONOMIC ORGANIZATION

Every human society—whether it is an advanced industrial nation, a centrally planned economy, or an isolated tribal nation—must confront and resolve three fundamental economic problems. Every society must have a way of determining *what* commodi-

ties are produced, *how* these goods are made, and *for whom* they are produced.

Indeed, these three fundamental questions of economic organization—*what, how,* and *for whom*—are as crucial today as they were at the dawn of human civilization. Let's look more closely at them:

- *What* commodities are produced and in what quantities? A society must determine how much of each of the many possible goods and services it will make and when they will be produced. Will we produce pizzas or shirts today? A few high-quality shirts or many cheap shirts? Will we use scarce resources to produce many consumption goods (like pizzas)? Or will we produce fewer consumption goods and more investment goods (like pizza-making machines), which will boost production and consumption tomorrow.
- *How* are goods produced? A society must determine who will do the production, with what resources, and what production techniques they will use. Who farms and who teaches? Is electricity generated from oil, from coal, or from the sun? Will factories be run by people or robots?
- *For whom* are goods produced? Who gets to eat the fruit of economic activity? Is the distribution of income and wealth fair and equitable? How is the national product divided among different households? Are many people poor and a few rich? Do high incomes go to teachers or athletes or autoworkers or Internet entrepreneurs? Will society provide minimal consumption to the poor, or must people work if they are to eat?

Positive economics versus normative economics

In thinking about economic questions, we must distinguish questions of fact from questions of fairness. Positive economics describes the facts of an economy, while normative economics involves value judgments.

Positive economics deals with questions such as: Why do doctors earn more than janitors? Does free trade raise or lower the wages of most Americans? What is the impact of computers on productivity? Although these are difficult questions to answer, they can all be resolved by reference to analysis and empirical evidence. That puts them in the realm of positive economics.

Normative economics involves ethical precepts and norms of fairness. Should poor people be required to work if they are to get government assistance? Should unemployment be raised to ensure that price inflation does not become too rapid? Should the United States break up Microsoft because it has violated the antitrust laws? There are no right or wrong answers to these questions because they involve ethics and values rather than facts. They can be resolved only by political debate and decisions, not by economic analysis alone.

MARKET, COMMAND, AND MIXED ECONOMIES

What are the different ways that a society can answer the questions of *what, how,* and *for whom?* Different societies are organized through *alternative economic systems,* and economics studies the various mechanisms that a society can use to allocate its scarce resources.

We generally distinguish two fundamentally different ways of organizing an economy. At one extreme, government makes most economic decisions, with those on top of the hierarchy giving economic commands to those further down the ladder. At the other extreme, decisions are made in markets, where individuals or enterprises voluntarily agree to exchange goods and services, usually through payments of money. Let's briefly examine each of these two forms of economic organization.

In the United States and most democratic countries, most economic questions are solved by the market. Hence their economic systems are called market economies. A **market economy** is one in which individuals and private firms make the major decisions about production and consumption. A system of prices, of markets, of profits and losses, of incentives and rewards determines *what, how,* and *for whom.* Firms produce the commodities that yield the highest profits (the *what*) by the techniques of production that are least costly (the *how*). Consumption is determined by individuals' decisions about how to spend the wages and property incomes generated by their labor and property ownership (the *for whom*). The extreme case of a market economy, in which the

government keeps its hands off economic decisions, is called a **laissez-faire** economy.

By contrast, a **command economy** is one in which the government makes all important decisions about production and distribution. In a command economy, such as the one which operated in the Soviet Union during most of the twentieth century, the government owns most of the means of production (land and capital); it also owns and directs the operations of enterprises in most industries; it is the employer of most workers and tells them how to do their jobs; and it decides how the output of the society is to be divided among different goods and services. In short, in a command economy, the government answers the major economic questions through its ownership of resources and its power to enforce decisions.

No contemporary society falls completely into either of these polar categories. Rather, all societies are **mixed economies,** with elements of market and command. There has never been a 100 percent market economy (although nineteenth-century England came close).

Today most decisions in the United States are made in the marketplace. But the government plays an important role in overseeing the functioning of the market; governments pass laws that regulate economic life, produce educational and police services, and control pollution. Most societies today operate mixed economies.

✳ C. SOCIETY'S TECHNOLOGICAL POSSIBILITIES

Every gun that is made, every warship launched, every rocket fired signifies, in the final sense, a theft from those who hunger and are not fed.

President Dwight D. Eisenhower

Each economy has a stock of limited resources—labor, technical knowledge, factories and tools, land, energy. In deciding *what* and *how* things should be produced, the economy is in reality deciding how to allocate its resources among the thousands of different possible commodities and services. How much land will go into growing wheat? Or into housing the population? How many factories will produce computers? How many will make pizzas? How many children will grow up to play professional sports or to be professional economists or to program computers?

Faced with the undeniable fact that goods are scarce relative to wants, an economy must decide how to cope with limited resources. It must choose among different potential bundles of goods (the *what*), select from different techniques of production (the *how*), and decide in the end who will consume the goods (the *for whom*).

INPUTS AND OUTPUTS

To answer these three questions, every society must make choices about the economy's inputs and outputs. **Inputs** are commodities or services that are used to produce goods and services. An economy uses its existing *technology* to combine inputs to produce outputs. **Outputs** are the various useful goods or services that result from the production process and are either consumed or employed in further production. Consider the "production" of pizza. We say that the eggs, flour, heat, pizza oven, and chef's skilled labor are the inputs. The tasty pizza is the output. In education, the inputs are the time of the faculty, the laboratories and classrooms, the textbooks, and so on, while the outputs are informed, productive, and well-paid citizens.

Another term for inputs is **factors of production.** These can be classified into three broad categories: land, labor, and capital.

- *Land*—or, more generally, natural resources—represents the gift of nature to our productive processes. It consists of the land used for farming or for underpinning houses, factories, and roads; the energy resources that fuel our cars and heat our homes; and the nonenergy resources like copper and iron ore and sand. In today's congested world, we must broaden the scope of natural resources to include our environmental resources, such as clean air and drinkable water.
- *Labor* consists of the human time spent in production—working in automobile factories, tilling

the land, teaching school, or baking pizzas. Thousands of occupations and tasks, at all skill levels, are performed by labor. It is at once the most familiar and the most crucial input for an advanced industrial economy.

- *Capital* resources form the durable goods of an economy, produced in order to produce yet other goods. Capital goods include machines, roads, computers, hammers, trucks, steel mills, automobiles, washing machines, and buildings. As we will see later, the accumulation of specialized capital goods is essential to the task of economic development.

Restating the three economic problems in terms of inputs and outputs, a society must decide (1) *what* outputs to produce, and in what quantity; (2) *how* to produce them—that is, by what techniques inputs should be combined to produce the desired outputs; and (3) *for whom* the outputs should be produced and distributed.

THE PRODUCTION-POSSIBILITY FRONTIER

Societies cannot have everything they want. They are limited by the resources and the technology available to them. Take defense spending as an example. Countries must decide how much of their limited resources goes to their military and how much goes into other activities (such as new factories or education). Some countries, like Japan, allocate only 1 percent of their national output to their military. The United States spends 4 percent of its national output on defense, while a fortress economy like North Korea spends up to 20 percent of its national output on the military. The more output that goes for defense, the less there is available for consumption and investment.

Let us dramatize this choice by considering an economy which produces only two economic goods, guns and butter. The guns, of course, represent military spending, and the butter stands for civilian spending. Suppose that our economy decides to throw all its energy into producing the civilian good, butter. There is a maximum amount of butter that can be produced per year. The maximal amount of butter depends on the quantity and quality of the economy's resources and the productive efficiency

Alternative Production Possibilities		
Possibilities	**Butter** (millions of pounds)	**Guns** (thousands)
A	0	15
B	1	14
C	2	12
D	3	9
E	4	5
F	5	0

TABLE 1-1. Limitation of Scarce Resources Implies the Guns-Butter Tradeoff

Scarce inputs and technology imply that the production of guns and butter is limited. As we go from A to B . . . to F, we are transferring labor, machines, and land from the gun industry to butter and can thereby increase butter production.

produce 15,000 guns of a certain kind if no butter is produced.

These are two extreme possibilities. In between are many others. If we are willing to give up some butter, we can have some guns. If we are willing to give up still more butter, we can have still more guns.

A schedule of possibilities is given in Table 1-1. Combination F shows the extreme, where all butter and no guns are produced, while A depicts the opposite extreme, where all resources go into guns. In between—at E, D, C, and B—increasing amounts of butter are given up in return for more guns.

How, you might well ask, can a nation turn butter into guns? Butter is transformed into guns not physically but by the alchemy of diverting the economy's resources from one use to the other.

We can represent our economy's production possibilities more vividly in the diagram shown in

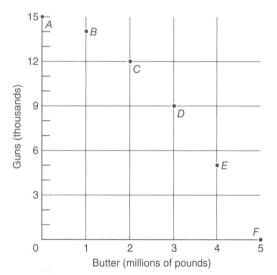

FIGURE 1-1. The Production Possibilities in a Graph

This figure displays the alternative combinations of production pairs from Table 1-1.

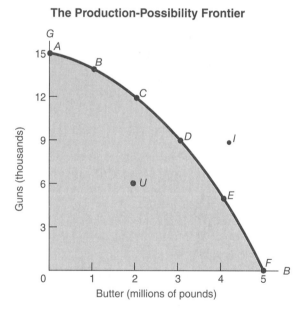

FIGURE 1-2. A Smooth Curve Connects the Plotted Points of the Numerical Production Possibilities

This frontier shows the schedule along which society can choose to substitute guns for butter. It assumes a given state of technology and a given quantity of inputs. Points outside the frontier (such as point *I*) are infeasible or unattainable. Any point inside the curve, such as *U*, indicates that the economy has not attained productive efficiency, as is the case, for instance, when unemployment is high during severe business cycles.

with which they are used. Suppose 5 million pounds of butter is the maximum amount that can be produced with the existing technology and resources.

At the other extreme, imagine that all resources are instead devoted to the production of guns. Again, because of resource limitations, the economy can produce only a limited quantity of guns. For this example, assume that the economy can

Figure 1-1. This diagram measures butter along the horizontal axis and guns along the vertical one. (If you are unsure about the different kinds of graphs or about how to turn a table into a graph, consult the appendix to this chapter.) We plot point *F* in Figure 1-1 from the data in Table 1-1 by counting over 5 butter units to the right on the horizontal axis and going up 0 gun units on the vertical axis; similarly, *E* is obtained by going 4 butter units to the right and going up 5 gun units; and finally, we get *A* by going over 0 butter units and up 15 gun units.

If we fill in all intermediate positions with new blue-colored points representing all the different combinations of guns and butter we have the continuous blue curve shown as the *production-possibility frontier,* or *PPF,* in Figure 1-2.

The **production-possibility frontier** (or *PPF*) shows the maximum amounts of production that can be obtained by an economy, given its technological knowledge and quantity of inputs available. The *PPF* represents the menu of goods and services available to society.

Putting the PPF to Work

The *PPF* in Figure 1-2 was drawn for guns and butter, but the same analysis applies to any choice of goods. Thus the more resources the government uses to build public goods like highways, the less will be left to produce private goods like houses; the more we choose to consume of food, the less we can consume of clothing; the more society decides to consume today, the less can be its production of capital goods to turn out more consumption goods in the future.

The graphs in Figures 1-3 to 1-5 present some important applications of *PPF*s. Figure 1-3 shows the effect of economic growth on a country's production possibilities. An increase in inputs, or improved technological knowledge, enables a country to produce more of all goods and services, thus shifting out the

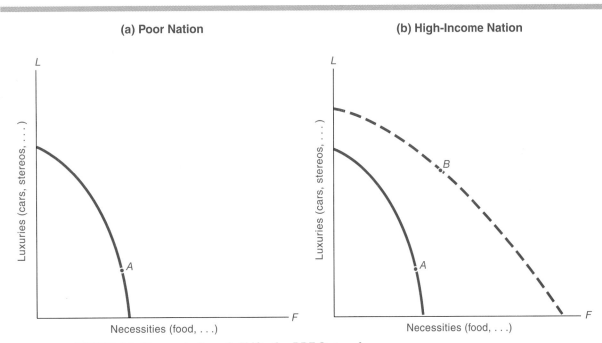

(a) Poor Nation

(b) High-Income Nation

FIGURE 1-3. Economic Growth Shifts the *PPF* Outward

(a) Before development, the nation is poor. It must devote almost all its resources to food and enjoys few comforts. **(b)** Growth of inputs and technological change shift out the *PPF*. With economic growth, a nation moves from *A* to *B*, expanding its food consumption little compared with its increased consumption of luxuries. It can increase its consumption of both goods if it desires.

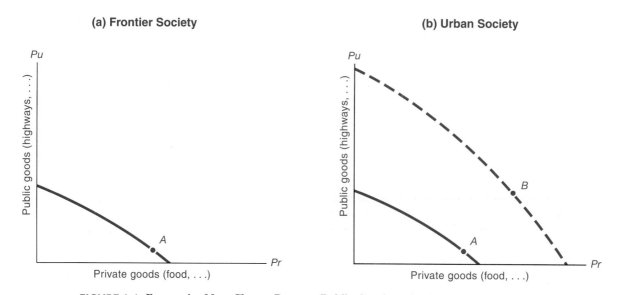

FIGURE 1-4. Economies Must Choose Between Public Goods and Private Goods

(a) A poor frontier society lives from hand to mouth, with little left over for public goods like highways or public health. **(b)** A modern urbanized economy is more prosperous and chooses to spend more of its higher income on public goods and government services (roads, environmental protection, and education).

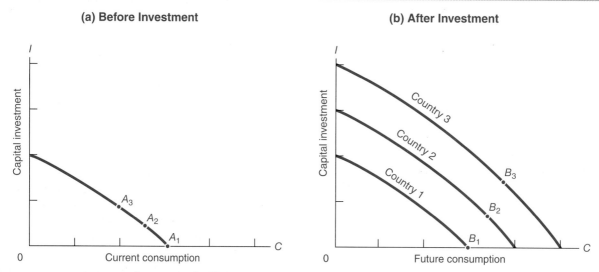

FIGURE 1-5. Investment for Future Consumption Requires Sacrificing Current Consumption

A nation can produce either current-consumption goods (pizzas and concerts) or investment goods (pizza ovens and concert halls). **(a)** Three countries start out even. They have the same *PPF*, shown in the panel on the left, but they have different investment rates. Country 1 does not invest for the future and remains at A_1 (merely replacing machines). Country 2 abstains modestly from consumption and invests at A_2. Country 3 sacrifices a great deal of current consumption and invests heavily. **(b)** In the following years, countries that invest more heavily forge ahead. Thus thrifty Country 3 has shifted its *PPF* far out, while Country 1's *PPF* has not moved at all. Countries that invest heavily have higher investment and consumption in the future.

PPF. The figure also illustrates that poor countries must devote most of their resources to food production while rich countries can afford more luxuries as productive potential increases.

Figure 1-4 depicts the electorate's choice between private goods (bought at a price) and public goods (paid for by taxes). Poor countries can afford little of public goods like public health and scientific research. But with economic growth, public goods as well as environmental quality take a larger share of output.

Figure 1-5 portrays an economy's choice between (*a*) current-consumption goods and (*b*) investment or capital goods (machines, factories, etc.). By sacrificing current consumption and producing more capital goods, a nation's economy can grow more rapidly, making possible more of *both* goods (consumption and capital) in the future.

The trade-off of time

The production-possibility frontier can also show the crucial economic notion of trade-offs. One of the most important decisions all people make is how to use their time. People have limited time available to pursue different activities. For example, as a student, you might have 10 hours to study for upcoming tests in both economics and history. If you study only history, you will get a high grade there and do poorly in economics, and vice versa. Treating the grades on the two tests as the "output" of your studying, sketch out the *PPF* for grades, given your limited time resources. Alternatively, if the two student commodities are "grades" and "fun," how would you draw this *PPF*? Where are you on this frontier? Where are your lazy friends?

Opportunity Costs

Life is full of choices. Because resources are scarce, we must always consider how to spend our limited incomes or time. When you decide whether to study economics, buy a car, or go to college, in each case you must consider how much the decision will cost in terms of forgone opportunities. The cost of the forgone alternative is the *opportunity cost* of the decision.

The concept of opportunity cost can be illustrated using the *PPF.* Examine the frontier in Figure 1-2, which shows the trade-off between guns and butter. Suppose the country decides to increase its gun purchases from 9000 guns at *D* to 12,000 units at *C*. What is the opportunity cost of this decision? You might calculate the cost in dollar terms. But in economics we always need to "pierce the veil" of money to examine the *real* impacts of alternative decisions. On the most fundamental level, the opportunity cost of moving from *D* to *C* is the butter that must be given up to produce the extra guns. In this example, the opportunity cost of the 3000 extra guns is 1 million pounds of butter forgone.

Or consider the real-world example of the cost of opening a gold mine near Yellowstone National Park. The developer argues that the mine will have but a small cost because Yellowstone's revenues will hardly be affected. But an economist would answer that the dollar receipts are too narrow a measure of cost. We should ask whether the unique and precious qualities of Yellowstone might be degraded if a gold mine were to operate, with the accompanying noise, water and air pollution, and degradation of amenity value for visitors. While the dollar cost might be small, the opportunity cost in lost wilderness values might be large indeed.

In a world of scarcity, choosing one thing means giving up something else. The **opportunity cost** of a decision is the value of the good or service forgone.

Efficiency

All of our explanations up to now have implicitly assumed that the economy is producing efficiently—that is, it is on, rather than inside, the production-possibility frontier. Remember that efficiency means that the economy's resources are being used as effectively as possible to satisfy people's needs and desires. One important aspect of overall economic efficiency is productive efficiency.

Productive efficiency occurs when an economy cannot produce more of one good without producing less of another good; this implies that the economy is on its production-possibility frontier.

Let's see why productive efficiency requires being on the *PPF.* Start in the situation shown by point

D in Figure 1-2. Say the market calls for another million pounds of butter. If we ignored the constraint shown by the *PPF*, we might think it possible to produce more butter without reducing gun production, say, by moving to point *I*, to the right of point *D*. But point *I* is outside the frontier, in the "infeasible" region. Starting from *D*, we cannot get more butter without giving up some guns. Hence point *D* displays productive efficiency, while point *I* is infeasible.

One further point about productive efficiency can be illustrated using the *PPF*: Being on the *PPF* means that producing more of one good inevitably requires sacrificing other goods. When we produce more guns, we are substituting guns for butter. Substitution is the law of life in a full-employment economy, and the production-possibility frontier depicts the menu of society's choices.

Unemployed Resources and Inefficiency. Even casual observers of modern life know that society has unemployed resources in the form of idle workers, idle factories, and idled land. When there are unemployed resources, the economy is not on its production-possibility frontier at all but, rather, somewhere *inside* it. In Figure 1-2, point *U* represents a point inside the *PPF*; at *U*, society is producing only 2 units of butter and 6 units of guns. Some resources are unemployed, and by putting them to work, we can increase our output of all goods; the economy can move from *U* to *D*, producing more butter and more guns, thus improving the economy's efficiency. We can have our guns and eat more butter too.

One source of inefficiency occurs during business cycles. From 1929 to 1933, in the Great Depression, the total output produced in the United States declined by almost 25 percent. This occurred not because the *PPF* shifted in but because various shocks reduced spending and pushed the economy inside its *PPF*. Then the buildup for World War II expanded demand, and output grew rapidly as the economy pushed back to the *PPF*. Similar forces were at work in much of the industrial world between 1990 and 1996 as macroeconomic factors pushed Europe and Japan inside their *PPFs*.

Business-cycle depressions are not the only reason why an economy might be inside its *PPF*. One

of the most dramatic declines in production occurred during the early 1990s after countries threw off their socialist planning systems and adopted free markets. Because of the disruptions to organizations and production patterns, output fell and unemployment rose as firms responded to changing markets and the new rules of capitalism. No period of peacetime history saw such sustained declines in output as the "real business cycles" of the postsocialist economies.

However, economists expect that this downturn will be but a temporary setback. Already, the economies that have made the most thorough reforms—such as Poland and the Czech Republic—have turned the corner and are beginning to recover. Their *PPFs* are once again shifting outward, and their incomes are likely to surpass the incomes of countries like Ukraine or Belarus, which have been reluctant reformers.

As we close this introductory chapter, let us return briefly to our opening theme, Why study economics? Perhaps the best answer to the question is a famous one given by Keynes in the final lines of *The General Theory of Employment, Interest and Money:*

> The ideas of economists and political philosophers, both when they are right and when they are wrong, are more powerful than is commonly understood. Indeed the world is ruled by little else. Practical men, who believe themselves to be quite exempt from any intellectual influences, are usually the slaves of some defunct economist. Madmen in authority, who hear voices in the air, are distilling their frenzy from some academic scribbler of a few years back. I am sure that the power of vested interests is vastly exaggerated compared with the gradual encroachment of ideas. Not, indeed, immediately, but after a certain interval; for in the field of economic and political philosophy there are not many who are influenced by new theories after they are twenty-five or thirty years of age, so that the ideas which civil servants and politicians and even agitators apply to current events are not likely to be the newest. But, soon or late, it is ideas, not vested interests, which are dangerous for good or evil.

To understand how the powerful ideas of economics apply to the central issues of human societies—ultimately, this is why we study economics.

SUMMARY

A. Introduction

1. What is economics? Economics is the study of how societies choose to use scarce productive resources that have alternative uses, to produce commodities of various kinds, and to distribute them among different groups. We study economics to understand not only the world we live in but also the many potential worlds that reformers are constantly proposing to us.

2. Goods are scarce because people desire much more than the economy can produce. Economic goods are scarce, not free, and society must choose among the limited goods that can be produced with its available resources.

3. Microeconomics is concerned with the behavior of individual entities such as markets, firms, and households. Macroeconomics views the performance of the economy as a whole. Through all economics, beware of the fallacy of composition and the post hoc fallacy, and remember to keep other things constant.

B. The Three Problems of Economic Organization

4. Every society must answer three fundamental questions: *what, how,* and *for whom? What* kinds and quantities are produced among the wide range of all possible goods and services? *How* are resources used in producing these goods? And *for whom* are the goods produced (that is, what is the distribution of income and consumption among different individuals and classes)?

5. Societies answer these questions in different ways. The most important forms of economic organization today are *command* and *market*. The command economy is directed by centralized government control; a market economy is guided by an informal system of prices and profits in which most decisions are made by private individuals and firms. All societies have different combinations of command and market; all societies are mixed economies.

C. Society's Technological Possibilities

6. With given resources and technology, the production choices between two goods such as butter and guns can be summarized in the *production-possibility frontier (PPF)*. The *PPF* shows how the production of one good (such as guns) is traded off against the production of another good (such as butter). In a world of scarcity, choosing one thing means giving up something else. The value of the good or service forgone is its opportunity cost.

7. Productive efficiency occurs when production of one good cannot be increased without curtailing production of another good. This is illustrated by the *PPF*. When an economy is on its *PPF*, it can produce more of one good only by producing less of another good.

8. Production-possibility frontiers illustrate many basic economic processes: how economic growth pushes out the frontier, how a nation chooses relatively less food and other necessities as it develops, how a country chooses between private goods and public goods, and how societies choose between consumption goods and capital goods that enhance future consumption.

9. Societies are sometimes inside their production-possibility frontier. When unemployment is high or when revolution or inefficient government regulations hamper economic activity, the economy is inefficient and operates inside its *PPF*.

CONCEPTS FOR REVIEW

Fundamental Concepts

scarcity and efficiency
free goods vs. economic goods
macroeconomics and microeconomics
normative vs. positive economics
fallacy of composition, post hoc fallacy
"keep other things constant"
cool heads, warm hearts

Key Problems of Economic Organization

what, how, and *for whom*
alternative economic systems: command vs. market
laissez-faire
mixed economies

Choice Among Production Possibilities

inputs and outputs
production-possibility frontier (*PPF*)
productive efficiency and inefficiency
opportunity cost

FURTHER READING AND INTERNET WEBSITES

Further Reading

Robert Heilbroner, *The World Philosophers*, Seventh Edition, 1999, Touchstone Books provides a lively biography of the great economists along with their ideas and impact. The authoritative work on the history of economic analysis is Joseph Schumpeter, *History of Economic Analysis* (McGraw-Hill, New York, 1954).

Websites

One of the greatest books of all economics is Adam Smith, *The Wealth of Nations* (many publishers, 1776). Every economics student should read a few pages to get the flavor of his writing. *The Wealth of Nations* can be found at www.bibliomania.com/NonFiction/Smith/Wealth/index. html.

Log onto one of the Internet reference sites for economics such as *Resources for Economists on the Internet* (www.rfe.org or rfe.wustl.edu/EconFAQ.html). Browse through some of the sections to familiarize yourself with the site. You might want to look up your college or university, look at recent news in a newspaper or magazine, or check some economic data.

Two sites for excellent analyses of public policy issues in economics are those of the Brookings Institution (www.brook.edu) and of the American Enterprise Institute (www.aei.org and www.aei.org/eo/eofront.htm). Each of these publishes books and has policy briefs on line.

QUESTIONS FOR DISCUSSION

1. The great English economist Alfred Marshall (1842–1924) invented many of the tools of modern economics, but he was most concerned with the application of these tools to the problems of society. In his inaugural lecture, Marshall wrote:

   > It will be my most cherished ambition to increase the numbers who Cambridge University sends out into the world with cool heads but warm hearts, willing to give some of their best powers to grappling with the social suffering around them; resolved not to rest content till they have opened up to all the material means of a refined and noble life. [*Memorials of Alfred Marshall*, A. C. Pigou, ed. (MacMillan and Co., London, 1925), p. 174, with minor edits.]

   Explain how the cool head might provide the essential positive economic analysis to implement the normative value judgments of the warm heart. Do you agree with Marshall's view of the role of the teacher? Do you accept his challenge?

2. The late George Stigler, an eminent conservative Chicago economist, wrote as follows:

   > No thoroughly egalitarian society has ever been able to construct or maintain an efficient and progressive economic system. It has been universal experience that some system of differential rewards is necessary to stimulate workers. [*The Theory of Price*, 3d ed. (Macmillan, New York, 1966), p. 19.]

   Are these statements positive or normative economics? Discuss Stigler's view in light of Alfred Marshall's quote in question 1. Is there a conflict?

3. Define each of the following terms carefully and give examples: *PPF*, scarcity, productive efficiency, inputs, outputs.

4. As people become wealthier, time becomes their major scarce resource. Suppose that you are very rich but have only a few hours a week of spare time. Give some examples of steps you can take to economize on your use of time. Compare time use of a wealthy person with that of a poor person.

5. Assume that Econoland produces haircuts and shirts with inputs of labor. Econoland has 1000 hours of labor available. A haircut requires $\frac{1}{2}$ hour of labor, while a shirt requires 5 hours of labor. Construct Econoland's production-possibility frontier.

6. Assume that scientific inventions have doubled the productivity of society's resources in butter production without altering the productivity of gun manufacture. Redraw society's production-possibility frontier in Figure 1-2 to illustrate the new trade-off.

7. Many scientists believe that we are rapidly depleting our natural resources. Assume that there are only two inputs (labor and natural resources) producing two goods (concerts and gasoline) with no improvement in society's technology over time. Show what would

happen to the *PPF* over time as natural resources are exhausted. How would invention and technological improvement modify your answer? On the basis of this example, explain why it is said that "economic growth is a race between depletion and invention."

8. Say that Diligent has 10 hours to study for upcoming tests in economics and history. Draw a *PPF* for grades, given Diligent's limited time resources. If Diligent studies inefficiently by listening to loud music and chatting with friends, where will Diligent's grade "output" be relative to the *PPF*? What will happen to the grade *PPF* if Diligent increases study inputs from 10 hours to 15 hours?

Appendix 1

HOW TO READ GRAPHS

A picture is worth a thousand words.
Chinese Proverb

Before you can master economics, you must have a working knowledge of graphs. They are as indispensable to the economist as a hammer is to a carpenter. So if you are not familiar with the use of diagrams, invest some time in learning how to read them—it will be time well spent.

What is a *graph?* It is a diagram showing how two or more sets of data or variables are related to one another. Graphs are essential in economics because, among other reasons, they allow us to analyze economic concepts and examine historical trends.

You will encounter many different kinds of graphs in this book. Some graphs show how variables change over time (see, for example, the inside of the front cover); other graphs show the relationship between different variables (such as the example we will turn to in a moment). Each graph in the book will help you understand an important economic relationship or trend.

THE PRODUCTION-POSSIBILITY FRONTIER

The first graph that you encountered in this text was the production-possibility frontier. As we showed in the body of this chapter, the production-possibility frontier, or *PPF*, represents the maximum amounts of a pair of goods or services that can both be produced with an economy's given resources, assuming that all resources are fully employed.

Let's follow up an important application, that of choosing between food and machines. The essential data for the *PPF* are shown in Table 1A-1, which is very much like the example in Table 1-1. Recall that each of the possibilities gives one level of food production and one level of machine production. As the quantity of food produced increases, the production of machines falls. Thus, if the economy produced 10 units of food, it could produce a maximum of 140 machines, but when the output of food is 20 units, only 120 machines can be manufactured.

Production-Possibility Graph. The data shown in Table 1A-1 can also be presented as a graph. To construct the graph, we represent each of the table's pairs of data by a single point on a two-dimensional plane. Figure 1A-1 displays in a graph the relationship between

Alternative Production Possibilities		
Possibilities	Food	Machines
A	0	150
B	10	140
C	20	120
D	30	90
E	40	50
F	50	0

TABLE 1A-1. The Pairs of Possible Outputs of Food and Machines

The table shows six potential pairs of outputs that can be produced with the given resources of a country. The country can choose one of the six possible combinations.

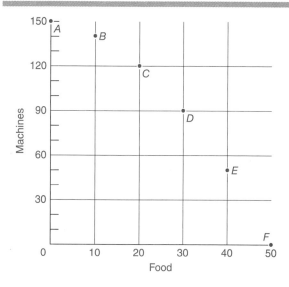

FIGURE 1A-1. Six Possible Pairs of Food-Machines Production Levels

This figure shows the data of Table 1A-1 in graphical form. The data are exactly the same, but the visual display presents the data more vividly.

the food and machines outputs shown in Table 1A-1. Each pair of numbers is represented by a single point in the graph. Thus the row labeled "A" in Table 1A-1 is graphed as point A in Figure 1A-1, and similarly for points B, C, and so on.

In Figure 1A-1, the vertical line at left and the horizontal line at bottom correspond to the two variables—food and machines. A **variable** is an item of interest that can be defined and measured and that takes on different values at different times or places. Important variables studied in economics are prices, quantities, hours of work, acres of land, dollars of income, and so forth.

The horizontal line on a graph is referred to as the *horizontal axis,* or sometimes the *X axis.* In Figure 1A-1, food output is measured on the black horizontal axis. The vertical line is known as the *vertical axis,* or *Y axis.* In Figure 1A-1, it measures the number of machines produced. Point *A* on the vertical axis stands for 150 machines. The lower left-hand corner, where the two axes meet, is called the *origin.* It signifies 0 food and 0 machines in Figure 1A-1.

A Smooth Curve. In most economic relationships, variables can change by small amounts as well as by the large increments shown in Figure 1A-1. We therefore generally draw economic relationships as continuous curves. Figure 1A-2 shows the *PPF* as a smooth curve in which the points from *A* to *F* have been connected.

By comparing Table 1A-1 and Figure 1A-2, we can see why graphs are so often used in economics. The smooth *PPF* reflects the menu of choice for the economy. It is a visual device for showing what types of goods are available in what quantities. Your eye can see at a glance the relationship between machine and food production.

Slopes and Lines. Figure 1A-2 depicts the relationship between maximum food and machine production. One important way to describe the relationship between two variables is by the slope of the graph line.

The **slope** of a line represents the change in one variable that occurs when another variable changes. More precisely, it is the change in the variable *Y* on the vertical axis per unit change in the variable *X* on the horizontal axis. For example, in Figure 1A-2, say that food production rose from 25 to 26 units. The slope of the curve in Figure 1A-2 tells us the precise

change in machinery production that would take place. *Slope is an exact numerical measure of the relationship between the change in* Y *and the change in* X.

We can use Figure 1A-3 to show how to measure the slope of a straight line, say, the slope of the line between points *B* and *D*. Think of the movement from *B* to *D* as occurring in two stages. First comes a horizontal movement from *B* to *C* indicating a 1-unit increase in the *X* value (with no change in *Y*). Second comes a compensating vertical movement up or down, shown as *s* in Figure 1A-3. (The movement of 1 horizontal unit is purely for convenience. The formula holds for movements of any size.) The two-step movement brings us from one point to another on the straight line.

Because the *BC* movement is a 1-unit increase in *X*, the length of *CD* (shown as *s* in Figure 1A-3) indicates the change in *Y* per unit change in *X*. On a graph, this change is called the *slope* of the line *ABDE*.

Often slope is defined as "the rise over the run." The *rise* is the vertical distance; in Figure 1A-3, the rise is the distance from *C* to *D*. The run is the horizontal distance; it is *BC* in Figure 1A-3. The rise over the run in this instance would be *CD* over *BC*. Thus the slope of *BD* is *CD/BC*.

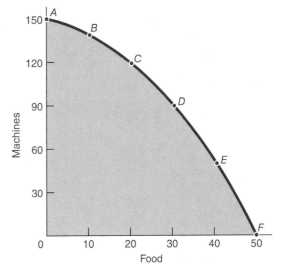

The Production-Possibility Frontier

FIGURE 1A-2. A Production-Possibility Frontier

A smooth curve fills in between the plotted pairs of points, creating the production-possibility frontier.

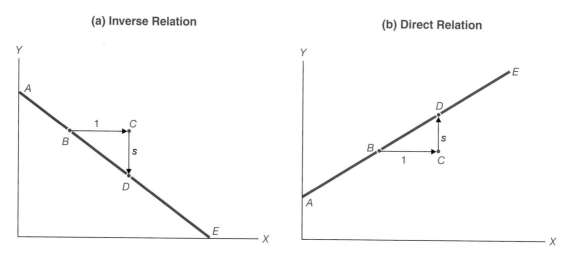

FIGURE 1A-3. Calculation of Slope for Straight Lines

It is easy to calculate slopes for straight lines as "rise over run." Thus in both **(a)** and **(b)**, the numerical value of the slope is rise/run = $CD/BC = s/1 = s$. Note that in **(a)**, CD is negative, indicating a negative slope, or an inverse relationship between X and Y.

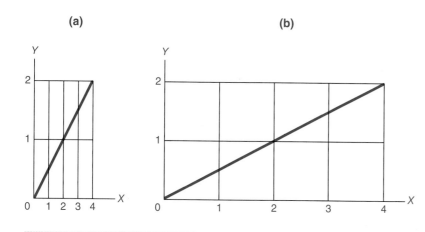

FIGURE 1A-4. Steepness is not the Same as Slope

Note that even though **(a)** looks steeper than **(b)**, they display the same relationship. Both have a slope of $1/2$ but the X axis has been stretched out in **(b)**.

The key points to understand about slopes are the following:

1. The slope can be expressed as a number. It measures the change in Y per unit change in X, or "the rise over the run."
2. If the line is straight, its slope is constant everywhere.
3. The slope of the line indicates whether the relationship between X and Y is direct or inverse. *Direct relationships* occur when variables move in the same direction (that is, they increase or decrease together); *inverse relationships* occur when the variables move in opposite directions (that is, one increases as the other decreases).

Thus a negative slope indicates the X-Y relation is inverse, as it is in Figure 1A-3(*a*). Why? Because an increase in X calls for a decrease in Y.

People sometimes confuse slope with the appearance of steepness. This conclusion is often but not always valid. The steepness depends on the scale of the graph. Panels (*a*) and (*b*) in Figure 1A-4 both portray exactly the same relationship. But in (*b*), the horizontal scale has been stretched out compared with (*a*). If you calculate carefully, you will see that the slopes are exactly the same (and are equal to $\frac{1}{2}$).

Slope of a Curved Line. A curved or nonlinear line is one whose slope changes. Sometimes we want to know the slope at *a given point,* such as point *B* in Figure 1A-5. We see that the slope at point *B* is positive, but it is not obvious exactly how to calculate the slope.

To find the slope of a smooth curved line at a point, we calculate the slope of the straight line that just touches, but does not cross, the curved line at the point in question. Such a straight line is called a *tangent* to the curved line. Put differently, the slope of a curved line at a point is given by the slope of the straight line that is tangent to the curve at the given point. Once we draw the tangent line, we find the slope of the tangent line with the usual right-angle measuring technique discussed earlier.

To find the slope at point *B* in Figure 1A-5, we simply construct straight line *FBJ* as a tangent to the curved line at point *B*. We then calculate the slope of the tangent as *NJ/MN*. Similarly, the tangent line *GH* gives the slope of the curved line at point *D*.

Another example of the slope of a nonlinear line is shown in Figure 1A-6. This shows a typical microeconomics curve, which is dome-shaped and has a maximum at point *C*. We can use our method of slopes-as-tangents to see that the slope of the curve is always positive in the region where the curve is rising and negative in the falling region. At the peak or maximum of the curve, the slope is exactly zero. A zero slope signifies that a tiny movement in the X variable around the maximum has no effect on the value of the Y variable.[1]

---

[1] For those who enjoy algebra, the slope of a line can be remembered as follows: A straight line (or linear relationship) is written as $Y = a + bX$. For this line, the slope of the curve is b, which measures the change in Y per unit change in X.

A curved line or nonlinear relationship is one involving terms other than constants and the X term. An example of a nonlinear relationship is the quadratic equation $Y = (X - 2)^2$. You can verify that the slope of this equation is negative for $X < 2$ and positive for $X > 2$. What is its slope for $X = 2$?

For those who know calculus: A zero slope comes where the derivative of a smooth curve is equal to zero. For example, plot and use calculus to find the zero-slope point of a curve defined by the function $Y = (X - 2)^2$.

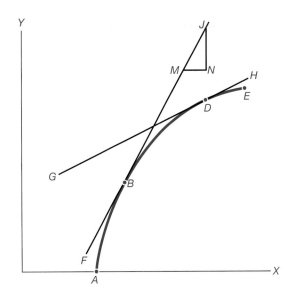

FIGURE IA-5. Tangent as Slope of Curved Line

By constructing a tangent line, we can calculate the slope of a curved line at a given point. Thus the line *FBMJ* is tangent to smooth curve *ABDE* at point *B*. The slope at *B* is calculated as the slope of the tangent line, that is, as *NJ/MN*.

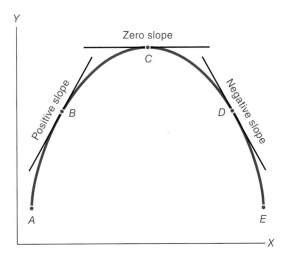

FIGURE IA-6. Different Slopes of Nonlinear Curves

Many curves in economics first rise, then reach a maximum, then fall. In the rising region from *A* to *C* the slope is positive (see point *B*). In the falling region from *C* to *E* the slope is negative (see point *D*). At the curve's maximum, point *C*, the slope is zero. (What about a U-shaped curve? What is the slope at its minimum?)

Shifts of and Movement Along Curves. An important distinction in economics is that between shifts of curves and movement along curves. We can examine this distinction in Figure 1A-7. The inner production-possibility frontier reproduces the *PPF* in Figure 1A-2. At point *D* society chooses to produce 30 units of food and 90 units of machines. If society decides to consume more food with a given *PPF*, then it can *move along* the *PPF* to point *E*. This movement along the curve represents choosing more food and fewer machines.

Suppose that the inner *PPF* represents society's production possibilities for 1990. If we return to the same country in 2000, we see that the *PPF* has *shifted* from the inner 1990 curve to the outer 2000 curve. (This shift would occur because of technological change or because of an increase in labor or capital available.) In the later year, society might choose to be at point *G*, with more food and machines than at either *D* or *E*.

The point of this example is that in the first case (moving from *D* to *E*) we see movement along the curve, while in the second case (from *D* to *G*) we see a shift of the curve.

Some Special Graphs. The *PPF* is one of the most important graphs of economics, one depicting the relationship between two economic variables (such as food and machines or guns and butter). You will encounter other types of graphs in the pages that follow.

Time Series. Some graphs show how a particular variable has changed over time. Look, for example, at the graphs on the inside front cover of this text. The left-hand graph shows a time series, since the American Revolution, of a significant macroeconomic variable, the ratio of the federal government debt to total gross domestic product, or *GDP*— this ratio is the *debt-GDP ratio*. Time-series graphs have time on the horizontal axis and variables of interest (in this case, the debt-GDP ratio) on the vertical axis. This graph shows that the debt-GDP ratio has risen sharply during every major war.

Scatter Diagrams. Sometimes individual pairs of points will be plotted, as in Figure 1A-1. Often, combinations of variables for different years will be plotted. An important example of a scatter diagram from macroeconomics is the *consumption function,* shown in Figure 1A-8. This scatter diagram shows the nation's total disposable income on the horizontal axis and total consumption (spending by households on goods like food, clothing, and housing) on the vertical axis. Note that consumption is very closely linked to income, a vital clue for understanding changes in national income and output.

Diagrams with More Than One Curve. Often it is useful to put two curves in the same graph, thus obtaining a "multicurve diagram." The most important example is the *supply-and-demand diagram,* shown in Chapter 3 (see page 47). Such graphs can show two different relationships simultaneously, such as how consumer purchases respond to price (demand) and how business production responds to price (supply). By graphing the two relationships together, we can determine the price and quantity that will hold in a market.

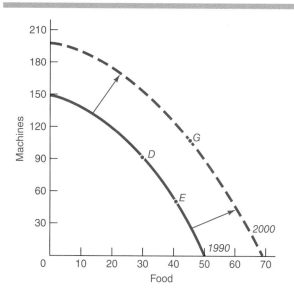

FIGURE IA-7. Shift of Curves Versus Movement Along Curves

In using graphs, it is essential to distinguish *movement along* a curve (such as from high-investment *D* to low-investment *E*) from a *shift* of a curve (as from *D* in an early year to *G* in a later year).

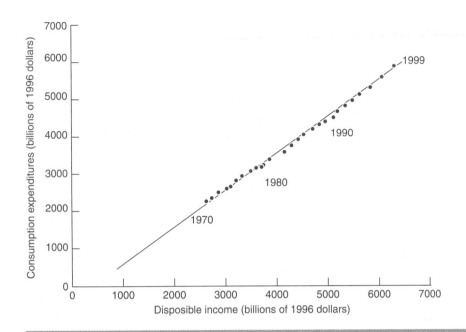

FIGURE 1A-8. Scatter Diagram of Consumption Function Shows Important Macroeconomic Law

Observed points of consumption spending fall near the *CC* line, which displays average behavior over time. Thus, the blue-colored point for 1999 is so near the *CC* line that it could have been quite accurately predicted from that line even before the year was over. Scatter diagrams allow us to see how close the relationship is between two variables.

This concludes our brief excursion into graphs. Once you have mastered these basic principles, the graphs in this book, and in other areas, can be both fun and instructive.

SUMMARY TO APPENDIX

1. Graphs are an essential tool of modern economics. They provide a convenient presentation of data or of the relationships among variables.

2. The important points to understand about a graph are: What is on each of the two axes (horizontal and vertical)? What are the units on each axis? What kind of relationship is depicted in the curve or curves shown in the graph?

3. The relationship between the two variables in a curve is given by its slope. The slope is defined as "the rise over the run," or the increase in *Y* per unit increase in *X*. If it is upward- (or positively) sloping, the two variables are directly related; they move upward or downward together. If the curve has a downward (or negative) slope, the two variables are inversely related.

4. In addition, we sometimes see special types of graphs: time series, which show how a particular variable moves over time; scatter diagrams, which show observations on a pair of variables; and multicurve diagrams, which show two or more relationships in a single graph.

CONCEPTS FOR REVIEW

Elements of Graphs

horizontal, or *X*, axis
vertical, or *Y*, axis
slope as "rise over run"
slope (negative, positive, zero)
tangent as slope of curved line

Examples of Graphs

time-series graphs
scatter diagrams
multicurve graphs

QUESTIONS FOR DISCUSSION

1. Consider the following problem: After your 8 hours a day of sleep, you have 16 hours a day to divide between leisure and study. Let leisure hours be the *X* variable and study hours be the *Y* variable. Plot the straight-line relationship between all combinations of *X* and *Y* on a blank piece of graph paper. Be careful to label the axes and mark the origin.

2. In question 1, what is the slope of the line showing the relationship between study and leisure hours? Is it a straight line?

3. Let us say that you absolutely need 6 hours of leisure per day, no more, no less. On the graph, mark the point that corresponds to 6 hours of leisure. Now consider a *movement along the curve:* Assume that you decide that you need only 4 hours of leisure a day. Plot the new point.

4. Next show a *shift of the curve:* You find that you need less sleep, so you have 18 hours a day to devote to leisure and study. Draw the new (shifted) curve.

5. Keep a record of your leisure and study for a week. Plot a time-series graph of the hours of leisure and study each day. Next plot a scatter diagram of hours of leisure and hours of study. Do you see any relationship between the two variables?

CHAPTER

2

Markets and Government in a Modern Economy

Every individual endeavors to employ his capital so that its produce may be of greatest value. He generally neither intends to promote the public interest, nor knows how much he is promoting it. He intends only his own security, only his own gain. And he is in this led by an invisible hand to promote an end which was no part of his intention. By pursuing his own interest he frequently promotes that of society more effectually than when he really intends to promote it.

Adam Smith, *The Wealth of Nations* (1776)

In medieval times, the aristocracy and town guilds directed much of the economic activity in Europe and Asia. However, about two centuries ago, governments began to exercise less and less power over prices and production methods. Feudalism gradually gave way to markets, or what we call the "market mechanism" or "competitive capitalism."

In most of Europe and North America, the nineteenth century became the age of **laissez-faire.** This doctrine, which translates as "leave us alone," holds that government should interfere as little as possible in economic affairs and leave economic decisions to the private marketplace. Many governments espoused this economic philosophy in the middle of the nineteenth century.

Nevertheless, by the end of the century, the unbridled excesses of capitalism led the United States and the industrialized countries of Western Europe to retreat from full laissez-faire. Government's role expanded steadily as it regulated monopolies, levied income taxes, and began to provide a social safety net with support for the elderly. This new system, called the **welfare state,** is one in which markets direct the detailed activities of day-to-day economic life while government regulates social conditions and provides pensions, health care, and other necessities for poor families.

Then, around 1980, the tides shifted again, as conservative governments in many countries began to reduce taxes and deregulate government's control over the economy. Particularly influential was the "Reagan revolution" in the United States, which changed public attitudes about taxes and government and reversed the trends in U.S. federal spending on civilian programs. Even Democratic president William Clinton held that "the era of big government is over."

The most dramatic turn toward the market came in Russia and the socialist countries of Eastern Europe. After decades of extolling the advantages of a government-run command economy, these countries scrapped central planning and made the difficult transition to a decentralized, market economy. China, while still run by the dictatorship of the Communist party, has enjoyed an economic boom in the last two decades by allowing competition to operate within its borders. Developing countries like Taiwan, Singapore, and Chile have enjoyed rapid income growth by embracing capitalism and reducing the role of government in their economies.

This capsule history of the shifting balance between state and market raises many questions. What exactly is a market economy, and what makes it so powerful? What is the "capital" in "capitalism"? What government controls are needed to make markets function effectively? Why do societies redefine the roles of government and market from time to time? The time has come to understand the principles that lie behind the market economy and to review government's role in economic life.

A. WHAT IS A MARKET?

In a country like the United States, most economic decisions are resolved through the market, so we begin our systematic study there. Who solves the three fundamental questions—*what, how,* and *for whom*—in a market economy? You may be surprised to learn that *no one individual or organization or government is responsible for solving the economic problems in a market economy.* Instead, millions of businesses and consumers engage in voluntary trade, intending to improve their own economic situations, and their actions are invisibly coordinated by a system of prices and markets.

To see how remarkable this is, consider the city of New York. Without a constant flow of goods into and out of the city, New Yorkers would be on the verge of starvation within a week. For New York to thrive, many kinds of goods must be provided. From the surrounding counties, from 50 states, and from the far corners of the world, goods travel for days and weeks with New York as their destination.

How is it that 10 million people can sleep easily at night, without living in mortal terror of a breakdown in the elaborate economic processes upon which they rely? The surprising answer is that, without coercion or centralized direction by anyone, these economic activities are coordinated through the market.

Everyone in the United States notices how much the government does to control economic activity: it places tolls on bridges, polices the streets, regulates drugs, levies taxes, sends armies to Europe, and so forth. But we seldom think about how much of our ordinary economic life proceeds without government intervention. Thousands of commodities are produced by millions of people every day, willingly, without central direction or master plan.

Not Chaos, but Economic Order

The market looks like a jumble of different sellers and buyers. It seems almost a miracle that food is produced in suitable amounts, gets transported to the right place, and arrives in a palatable form at the dinner table. But a close look at New York or other economies is convincing proof that a market system is neither chaos nor miracle. It is a system with its own internal logic. And it works.

A market economy is an elaborate mechanism for coordinating people, activities, and businesses through a system of prices and markets. It is a communication device for pooling the knowledge and actions of billions of diverse individuals. Without central intelligence or computation, it solves problems of production and distribution involving billions of unknown variables and relations, problems that are far beyond the reach of even today's fastest supercomputer. Nobody designed the market, yet it functions remarkable well. In a market economy, no single individual or organization is responsible for production, consumption, distribution, and pricing.

How do markets determine prices, wages, and outputs? Originally, a market was an actual place where buyers and sellers could engage in face-to-face bargaining. The *marketplace*—filled with slabs of butter, pyramids of cheese, layers of wet fish, and heaps of vegetables—used to be a familiar sight in many villages and towns, where farmers brought their goods to sell. In the United States today there are still important markets where many traders gather together to do business. For example, wheat and corn are traded at the Chicago Board of Trade, oil and platinum are traded at the New York Mercantile Exchange, and gems are traded at the Diamond District in New York City.

In a general sense, markets are places where buyers and sellers interact to set prices and exchange goods and services. There are markets for almost everything. You can buy artwork by old masters at auction houses in New York, or pollution permits at the Chicago Board of Trade, or legal drugs from delivery serivces in many large cities. A market may be centralized, like the stock market. It may be decentralized, as in the case of labor. Or it may exist only electronically, as is increasingly the case with "e-commerce" on the Internet.

A **market** is a mechanism through which buyers and sellers interact to set prices and exchange goods and services.

In a market system, everything has a **price,** which is the value of the good in terms of money (the role of money will be discussed in Section B of this chapter). Prices represent the terms on which people and firms voluntarily exchange different commodities. When I agree to buy a used Ford from a dealer for $4050, this agreement indicates that the Ford is worth at least $4050 to me and that the $4050 is worth at least as much as the Ford to the dealer. The used-car market has determined the price of a used Ford and, through voluntary trading, has allocated this good to the person for whom it has the highest value.

In addition, prices serve as *signals* to producers and consumers. If consumers want more of any good, the price will rise, sending a signal to producers that more supply is needed. When a terrible disease reduces beef production, the supply of beef decreases and raises the price of hamburgers. The higher price encourages farmers to increase their production of beef and, at the same time, encourages consumers to substitute other foods for hamburgers and beef products.

What is true of the markets for consumer goods is also true of markets for factors of production, such as land or labor. If more computer programmers are needed to run Internet businesses, the price of computer programmers (their hourly wage) will tend to rise. The rise in relative wages will attract workers into the growing occupation.

Prices coordinate the decisions of producers and consumers in a market. Higher prices tend to reduce consumer purchases and encourage production. Lower prices encourage consumption and discourage production. Prices are the balance wheel of the market mechanism.

Market Equilibrium. At every moment, some people are buying while others are selling; firms are inventing new products while governments are passing laws to regulate old ones; foreign companies are opening plants in America while American firms are selling their products abroad. Yet in the midst of all this turmoil, markets are constantly solving the *what, how,* and *for whom.* As they balance all the forces operating on the economy, markets are finding a **market equilibrium of supply and demand.**

A market equilibrium represents a balance among all the different buyers and sellers. Depending upon the price, households and firms all want to buy or sell different quantities. The market finds the equilibrium price that simultaneously meets the desires of buyers and sellers. Too high a price would mean a glut of goods with too much output; too low a price would produce long lines in stores and a deficiency of goods. Those prices for which buyers desire to buy exactly the quantity that sellers desire to sell yield an equilibrium of supply and demand.

How Markets Solve the Three Economic Problems

We have just described how prices help balance consumption and production (or demand and supply) in an individual market. What happens when we put all the different markets together—beef, cars, land, labor, capital, and everything else? These markets work simultaneously to determine a general equilibrium of prices and production.

By matching sellers and buyers (supply and demand) in each market, a market economy simultaneously solves the three problems of *what, how,* and *for whom.* Here is an outline of a market equilibrium:

1. *What* goods and services will be produced is determined by the dollar votes of consumers—not every 2 or 4 years at the polls, but in their daily purchase decisions. The money that they pay into businesses' cash registers ultimately provides the payrolls, rents, and dividends that consumers, as employees, receive as income.

    Firms, in turn, are motivated by the desire to maximize profits. **Profits** are net revenues, or the difference between total sales and total costs. Firms abandon areas where they are losing profits; by the same token, firms are lured by high profits into production of goods in high demand. Some of the most profitable activities today are producing and marketing legal drugs—drugs for depression, anxiety, impotence, and all other manner of human frailty. Lured by the high profits, companies are investing billions in research to come up with yet more new and improved chemicals.

2. *How* things are produced is determined by the competition among different producers. The best way for producers to meet price competition and maximize profits is to keep costs at a minimum by adopting the most efficient methods of production. Sometimes change is incremental and consists of little more than tinkering with the machinery or adjusting the input mix to gain a cost advantage, which can be very important in a competitive market. At other times there are drastic shifts in technology, as with steam engines displacing horses because steam was cheaper per unit of useful work, or airplanes replacing railroads as the most efficient mode for long-distance travel. Right now we are in the midst of just such a transition to a radically different technology, with computers revolutionizing many tasks in the workplace, from the checkout counter to the drafting table.

3. *For whom* things are produced—who is consuming and how much—depends, in large part, on the supply and demand in the markets for factors of production. Factor markets (i.e., markets for factors of production) determine wage rates, land rents, interest rates, and profits. Such prices are called *factor prices*. The same person may receive wages from a job, dividends from stocks, interest on a bond, and rent from a piece of property. By adding up all the revenues from factors, we can calculate the person's market income. The distribution of income among the population is thus determined by the quantity of factor services (person-hours, acres, etc.) and the prices of the factors (wage rates, land rents, etc.).

Be warned, however, that incomes reflect more than the rewards for sweaty labor or frugal living. High incomes can come from large inheritances, good luck, and skills highly prized in the marketplace. Those with low incomes are often pictured as lazy, but the truth is that low incomes are generally the result of poor education, discrimination, or living where jobs are few and wages are low. When we see someone on the unemployment line, we should remember, "There, but for the grace of supply and demand, go I."

Monarchs of the Marketplace

Who rules a market economy? Do giant companies like Microsoft and AT&T call the tune? Or perhaps Congress and the president? Or the advertising moguls from Madison Avenue? All these entities can affect us, but the core determinants of the shape of our economy are the dual monarchs of *tastes* and *technology*. Innate and acquired tastes—as expressed in the dollar votes of consumer demands—direct the uses of society's resources. They pick the point on the production-possibility frontier (*PPF*).

But consumers alone cannot dictate *what* goods will be produced. The available resources and technology place a fundamental constraint on their choices. The economy cannot go outside its *PPF.* You can fly to Hong Kong, but there are no flights to Mars. An economy's resources, along with the available science and technology, limit the candidates for the dollar votes of consumers. Consumer demand has to dovetail with business supply of goods. So business cost and supply decisions, along with consumer demand, help determine what is produced.

You will find it helpful to recall the dual monarchy when you wonder why some technologies fail in the marketplace. From the Stanley Steamer—a car that ran on steam—to the Premiere smokeless cigarette, which was smokeless but also tasteless, history is full of products that found no markets. How do useless products die off? Is there a government agency that pronounces upon the value of new products? No such agency is necessary. Rather, they become extinct because there is no consumer demand for the products at the going market price. These products earn losses rather than profits. This reminds us that profits serve as the rewards and penalties for businesses and guide the market mechanism.

Like a farmer using a carrot and a stick to coax a donkey forward, the market system deals out profits and losses to induce firms to produce desired goods efficiently.

A Picture of Prices and Markets

We can picture the circular flow of economic life in Figure 2-1 on page 29. The diagram provides an overview of how consumers and producers interact to determine prices and quantities for both inputs and outputs. Note the two different kinds of markets in the circular flow. At the top are the product markets, or the flow of outputs like pizza and shoes; at the bottom are the markets for inputs or factors of production like land and labor. Further, see how de-

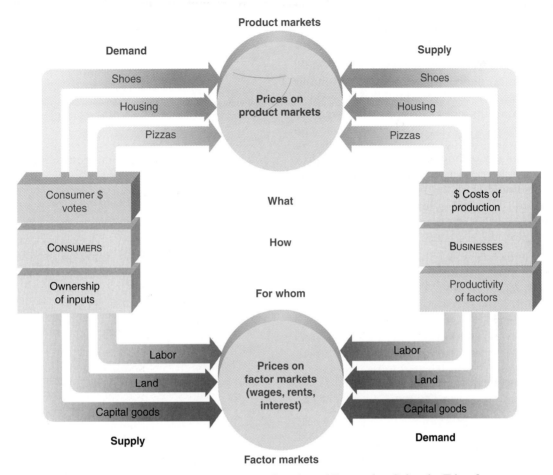

FIGURE 2-1. The Market System Relies on Supply and Demand to Solve the Trio of Economic Problems

We see here the circular flow of a market economy. Dollar votes of consumers (households, governments, and foreigners) interact with business supply in the product markets at top, helping to determine *what* is produced. Business demand for inputs meets the supply of labor and other inputs in the factor markets below to help determine wage, rent, and interest payments; incomes thus influence *for whom* goods are delivered. Business competition to buy factor inputs and sell goods most cheaply determines *how* goods are produced.

cisions are made by two different entities, consumers and businesses.

Consumers buy goods and sell factors of production; businesses sell goods and buy factors of production. Consumers use their income from the sale of labor and other inputs to buy goods from businesses; businesses base their prices of goods on the costs of labor and property. Prices in goods markets are set to balance consumer demand with business

supply; prices in factor markets are set to balance household supply with business demand.

All this sounds complicated. But it is simply the total picture of the intricate web of interdependent supplies and demands, interconnected through a market mechanism to solve the economic problems of *what, how,* and *for whom.* Look at Figure 2-1 carefully. A few minutes spent studying it will surely help you understand the workings of a market economy.

The Invisible Hand

The order contained in a market economy was first recognized by Adam Smith. In one of the most famous passages of all economics, quoted from *The Wealth of Nations* at the opening of this chapter, Smith saw the harmony between private profit and public interest. He argued that even though every individual "intends only his own security, only his own gain, . . . he is led by an invisible hand to promote an end which was no part of his intention. By pursuing his own interest he frequently promotes that of society more effectually than when he really intends to promote it."

Pause for a moment to consider these paradoxical words, written in 1776. That same year was also marked by the American Declaration of Independence. It is no coincidence that both ideas appeared at the same time. Just as the American revolutionaries were proclaiming freedom from tyranny, Adam Smith was preaching a revolutionary doctrine emancipating trade and industry from the shackles of a feudal aristocracy. Smith held that in this best of all possible worlds, government interference with market competition is almost certain to be injurious.

Smith's insight about the functioning of the market mechanism has inspired modern economists—both the admirers and the critics of capitalism. Economic theorists have proved that under limited conditions a perfectly competitive economy is efficient (remember that an economy is producing efficiently when it cannot increase the economic welfare of anyone without making someone else worse off).

After two centuries of experience and thought, however, we recognize the limited scope of this doctrine. We know that there are "market failures," that markets do not always lead to the most efficient outcome. One set of market failures concerns monopolies and other forms of imperfect competition. A second failure of the "invisible hand" comes when there are spillovers or externalities outside the marketplace—positive externalities such as scientific discoveries and negative spillovers such as pollution.

A final reservation comes when the income distribution is politically or ethically unacceptable. When any of these elements occur, Adam Smith's invisible-hand doctrine breaks down and government may want to step in to mend the flawed invisible hand.

In summary:

Adam Smith discovered a remarkable property of a competitive market economy. Under perfect competition and with no market failures, markets will squeeze as many useful goods and services out of the available resources as is possible. But where monopolies or pollution or similar market failures become pervasive, the remarkable efficiency properties of the invisible hand may be destroyed.

Adam Smith: Founding father of economics

"For what purpose is all the toil and bustle of this world? What is the end of avarice and ambition, of the pursuit of wealth, of power, and pre-eminence?" Thus wrote Adam Smith (1723–1790), of Scotland, who glimpsed for the social world of economics what Isaac Newton recognized for the physical world of the heavens. Smith answered his questions in *The Wealth of Nations* (1776), where he explained the self-regulating natural order by which the oil of self-interest lubricates the economic machinery in an almost miraculous fashion. Smith believed that the toil and bustle had the effect of improving the lot of the common man and woman. "Consumption is the sole end and purpose of all production."

Smith was the first apostle of economic growth. At the dawn of the Industrial Revolution, he pointed to the great strides in productivity brought about by specialization and the division of labor. In a famous example, he described the specialized manufacturing of a pin factory in which "one man draws out the wire, another straightens it, a third cuts it," and so it goes. This operation allowed 10 people to make 48,000 pins in a day, whereas if "all wrought separately, they could not each of them make twenty, perhaps not one pin a day." Smith saw the result of this division of labor as "universal opulence which extends itself to the lowest ranks of the people." Imagine what he would think if he returned today to see what two more centuries of economic growth have produced!

Smith wrote hundreds of pages railing against countless cases of government folly and interference. Consider the seventeenth-century guild master who was attempting to improve his weaving. The town guild decided, "If a cloth weaver intends to process a piece according to his own invention, he should obtain permission from the judges of the town to employ the number and length of threads that he desires after the question has been considered by four of the oldest merchants and four of the oldest weavers of the guild." Smith argued that such restrictions—whether imposed by government or by monopolies, whether on production or on foreign trade—limit the proper workings of the market system and ultimately hurt both workers and consumers.

None of this should suggest that Smith was an apologist for the establishment. He had a distrust of all entrenched power, private monopolies as much as public monarchies. He was for the common people. But, like many of the great economists, he had learned from his research that the road to waste is paved with good intentions.

Above all, it is Adam Smith's vision of the self-regulating "invisible hand" that is his enduring contribution to modern economics.

B. TRADE, MONEY, AND CAPITAL

Since the time of Adam Smith, market economies have evolved enormously. Advanced capitalist economies, such as the United States, Western Europe, and Japan, have three distinguishing features: trade and specialization, money, and capital.

- An advanced economy is characterized by an elaborate network of *trade*, among individuals and countries, that depends on great *specialization* and an intricate division of labor.
- Modern economies today make extensive use of *money*, or the means of payment. The flow of money is the lifeblood of our system. Money provides the yardstick for measuring the economic value of things and for financing trade.
- Modern industrial technologies rest on the use of vast amounts of *capital:* precision machinery, large-scale factories, and stocks of inventories. Capital goods leverage human labor power into a much more efficient factor of production and allow productivity many times greater than that possible in an earlier age.

TRADE, SPECIALIZATION, AND DIVISION OF LABOR

As compared to the economies of the 1700s, today's economies depend heavily on the specialization of individuals and firms, connected by an extensive network of trade. Western economies have enjoyed rapid economic growth as increasing specialization has allowed workers to become highly productive in particular occupations and to trade their output for the commodities they need.

Specialization occurs when people and countries concentrate their efforts on a particular set of tasks—it permits each person and country to use to its best advantage its specific skills and resources. One of the facts of economic life is that, rather than have everyone do everything in a mediocre way, it is better to establish a *division of labor*—dividing production into a number of small specialized steps or tasks. A division of labor permits tall people to play basketball, numerate people to teach, and persuasive people to sell cars. It sometimes takes many years to receive the training for particular careers—it usually takes 14 postgraduate years to become a certified neurosurgeon.

Capital and land are also highly specialized. Land can be specialized, as in the vineyard lands of California and France, which it has taken decades to cultivate. The computer software that went along with the labor to write this textbook took over a decade to be developed, but it is useless at managing an oil refinery or solving large numerical problems. One of the most impressive examples of specialization is the computer chip that manages automobiles, increases their efficiency, and can even serve as a "black box" to record accident data.

The enormous efficiency of specialization allows the intricate network of trade among people and nations that we see today. Very few of us produce a single finished good; we make but the tiniest fraction of what we consume. We might teach a small part of one college's curriculum, or empty coins from parking meters, or separate the genetic material of fruit flies. In exchange for this specialized labor, we will receive an income adequate to buy goods from all over the world.

The idea of *gains from trade* forms one of the central insights of economics. Different people or countries tend to specialize in certain areas; they then engage in the voluntary exchange of what they produce for what they need. Japan has grown enormously productive by specializing in manufacturing goods such as automobiles and consumer electronics; it exports much of its manufacturing output to pay for imports of raw materials. By contrast, countries which have tried the strategy of becoming self-sufficient, attempting to produce most of what they consume, have discovered that this is the road to stagnation. Trade can enrich all nations and increase *everyone's* living standards.

To summarize:

Advanced economies engage in specialization and division of labor, which increase the productivity of their resources. Individuals and countries then voluntarily trade goods in which they specialize for others' products, vastly increasing the range and quantity of consumption and having the potential to raise everyone's living standards.

Globalization

You can hardly open a newspaper today without reading about the most recent trends in "globalization." What exactly does this term mean? How can economics contribute to understanding the issues?

Globalization is a popular term that is used to denote an increase in *economic integration among nations*. Increasing integration is seen today in the dramatic growth in the flows of goods, services, and capital across national borders.

One major component of globalization is the spectacular increase in the share of national output devoted to imports and exports. With a continuous drop in transportation and communication costs, along with declining tariffs and other barriers to trade, the share of trade in U.S. national output has more than doubled over the last half-century. Domestic producers now compete with producers from around the world in their prices and design decisions.

The increased share of trade has been accompanied by increased specialization in the production process itself as different stages of production are "outsourced" to different countries. A typical example is the production of Barbie dolls:

The plastic and hair come from Taiwan and Japan. Assembly used to be done in those countries but has now migrated to lower-cost locations in Indonesia, Malaysia, and China. The molds themselves come from the United States, as do the paints used in decorating. China supplies labor and the cotton cloth used for dresses. The dolls sell for $10, of which 35 cents covers Chinese labor, 65 cents covers foreign materials, $1 covers Hong Kong profits and transportation, and the rest is Mattel profit, marketing, and transportation expenses in the United States.[1]

Evidence indicates that this process of slicing up the productive process is typical of manufacturing activities in the United States and other high-income countries.

A second component of globalization is the increasing integration of financial markets. Financial integration is seen in the accelerated pace of lending and borrowing among nations as well as in the convergence of interest rates among different countries. The major causes of financial market integration have been the dismantling of restrictions on capital flows among nations, cost reductions, and innovations in financial markets, particularly the use of new kinds of financial instruments.

Financial integration among nations has undoubtedly led to gains from trade, as nations with productive uses for capital can borrow from countries with excess saving. In the last two decades, Japan has served as the world's major lending country. Surprisingly, the United States has been the world's largest borrower—partly because of its low national savings rate and partly because of the technological dynamism of its computer, telecommunication, and biotechnology industries.

Integration of goods and financial markets has produced impressive gains from trade in the form of lower prices, increased innovation, and more rapid economic growth. But these gains have been accompanied by painful side effects.

One consequence of economic integration is the unemployment and lost profits that occur when low-cost foreign producers displace domestic production. The unemployed textile worker, the bankrupt soybean farmer —they find little solace in the fact that consumers are enjoying lower prices for food and clothing. Those who lose from increased international trade have become tireless advocates of "protectionism" in the form of tariffs and quotas on international trade.

---

[1] See Feenstra in the Further Reading section at the end of this chapter.

A second consequence comes when financial integration triggers international financial crises. In the late 1990s, problems in Thailand, Mexico, and Russia spilled over into stock and bond markets around the world. The contagion arising from small disturbances is a direct result of closely linked markets. American investors put their funds into Thailand, seeking higher returns. But these same investors are likely to pull out their funds when they smell trouble, and that can lead to a financial crisis as countries attempt to prop up exchange rates or financial institutions in the face of a massive speculative attack.

Globalization raises many new issues for policymakers. Are the gains from trade worth the domestic costs in terms of social disruption and dislocation? Should countries prevent investors from moving funds in and out so rapidly that domestic markets are threatened? Does integration lead to greater inequality? Should international institutions become lenders of last resort for countries in financial difficulties? These questions are on the minds of policymakers around the world who are attempting to deal with globalization.

MONEY: THE LUBRICANT OF EXCHANGE

If specialization permits people to concentrate on particular tasks, money then allows people to trade their specialized outputs for the vast array of goods and services produced by others. What is money? **Money** is the means of payment—the currency and checks that we use when we buy things. But more than that, money is a lubricant that facilitates exchange. When everyone trusts and accepts money as payment for goods and debts, trade is facilitated. Just imagine how complicated economic life would be if you had to barter goods for goods every time you wanted to buy a pizza or go to a concert. What services could you offer Sal's Pizza? And what about your education—what could you barter with your college for tuition that it needs? Because everyone accepts money as the medium of exchange, the need to match supplies and demands is enormously simplified.

Governments control the money supply through their central banks. But like other lubricants, money can get overheated and damage the economic engine. It can grow out of control and cause a hyperinflation, in which prices increase very sharply. When that happens, people concentrate on spending their money quickly, before it loses its value, rather than investing it for the future. That's what happened to several Latin American countries in the 1980s, and many former socialist economies in the 1990s, when they had inflation rates exceeding 1000 percent or even 10,000 percent per year. Imagine getting your paycheck and having it lose 20 percent of its value by the end of the week!

Money is the medium of exchange. Proper management of the money supply is one of the major issues for government macroeconomic policy in all countries.

CAPITAL

An advanced industrial economy like the United States uses an enormous number of buildings, machines, computers, software, and so on. These are the factors of production called **capital**—a produced factor of production, a durable input which is itself an output of the economy.

Most of us do not realize how much our daily activities depend upon capital, including our houses, the highways on which we drive, and the wires that bring electricity and cable TV to our homes. The total net private capital stock in the U.S. economy is more than $19 trillion—including government-owned, business, and residential capital. On average, this is $70,000 per person.

As we have seen, capital is one of the three major factors of production. The other two, land and labor, are often called *primary factors of production.* That means their supply is mostly determined by noneconomic factors, such as the fertility rate and the country's geography. Capital, by contrast, has to be produced before you can use it. For example, some companies build textile machinery, which is then used to make shirts; some companies build farm tractors, which are then used to help produce corn.

Use of capital involves time-consuming, roundabout methods of production. People learned long ago that indirect and roundabout production techniques often are more efficient than direct methods of production. For example, the most direct method of catching fish is to wade into a stream and grab fish with your hands, but this yields more frustration than fish. By using a fishing rod (which is capital equipment), fishing time becomes more productive in terms of fish caught per day. By using even more capital, in the form of nets and fishing boats, fishing becomes productive enough to feed many people and provide a good living to those who operate the specialized nets and equipment.

Growth from the Sacrifice of Current Consumption. If people are willing to save—to abstain from present consumption and wait for future consumption—society can devote resources to new capital goods. A larger stock of capital helps the economy grow faster by pushing out the *PPF.* Look back at Figure 1-5 to see how forgoing current consumption in favor of investment adds to future production possibilities. High rates of saving and investment help explain how Taiwan, China, and other Asian countries have grown so fast over the last three decades. By comparison, many poor countries save and invest little—they start the economic race at the back and fall further behind because they cannot accumulate productive capital.

Is there no limit to the amount of useful capital? Should we continue to boost productivity by adding more capital, by replacing all direct processes with more productive, roundabout ones and all roundabout processes with still more roundabout processes? While this seems sensible, it has a high cost because too much roundabout investment would cause too great a reduction in today's consumption. Investing resources to give every worker an advanced degree, to remove 99.9 percent of pollution, and to build a subway system under every town and hamlet would certainly increase productivity. But the payoff would not be worth the enormous cost in reducing consumption.

We summarize as follows:

Economic activity involves forgoing current consumption to increase our capital. Every time we invest—building a new factory or road, increasing the years or quality of education, or increasing the stock of useful technical knowledge—we are enhancing the future productivity of our economy and increasing future consumption.

Capital and Private Property

In a market economy, capital typically is privately owned, and the income from capital goes to individuals. Every patch of land has a deed, or title of ownership; almost every machine and building belongs to an individual or corporation. *Property rights* bestow on their owners the ability to use, exchange, paint, dig, drill, or exploit their capital goods. These capital goods also have market values, and people can buy and sell the capital goods for whatever price the goods will fetch. *The ability of individuals to own and profit from capital is what gives capitalism its name.*

However, while our society is one built on private property, property rights are limited. Society determines how much of "your" property you may bequeath to your heirs and how much must go in inheritance and estate taxes to the government. Society determines how much your factory can pollute and where you can park your car. Even your home is not your castle: you must obey zoning laws and, if necessary, make way for a road.

Interestingly enough, the most valuable economic resource, labor, cannot be turned into a commodity that is bought and sold as private property. Since the abolition of slavery, it has been against the law to treat human earning power like other capital assets. You are not free to sell yourself; you must rent yourself at a wage.

Property rights for capital and pollution
Property rights define the ability of individuals or firms to own, buy, sell, and use the capital goods and other property in a market economy. These rights are enforced through the legal framework, which constitutes the set of laws within which an economy operates. An efficient and acceptable legal framework for a market economy includes the definition of property rights, the laws of contract, and a system for adjudicating disputes.

As the ex-communist countries are discovering, it is very difficult to have a market economy when there are no laws enforcing contracts or guaranteeing that a company can keep its own profits. And when the legal framework breaks down, as in the former Yugoslavia or in drug-producing countries like Colombia, people begin to fear for their lives and have little time or inclination to make long-term investments for the future. Production falls and the quality of life deteriorates. Indeed, many of the most horrifying African famines were caused by civil war and the breakdown in the legal order, not by bad weather.

The environment is another example where poorly designed property rights harm the economy. Water and air are generally open-access resources, meaning that no one owns and controls them. As the saying goes, "Everyone's business is nobody's business." As a result, people do not weigh all the costs of their actions. Someone might throw trash into the water or emit smoke into the air because the costs of dirty water or foul air are borne by other people. By contrast, people are less likely to throw trash on their own lawn or burn coal in their own living room because they themselves will bear the costs.

In recent years, economists have proposed extending property rights to environmental commodities by selling or auctioning permits to pollute and allowing them to be traded on markets. Preliminary evidence suggests that this extension of property rights has given much more powerful incentives to reduce pollution efficiently.

Specialization, trade, money, and capital form the key to the productiveness of an advanced economy. But note as well that they are closely interrelated. Specialization creates enormous efficiencies, while increased production makes trade possible. Use of money allows trade to take place quickly and efficiently. Without the facility for trade and exchange that money provides, an elaborate division of labor would not be possible. Money and capital are related because the funds for buying capital goods are funneled through financial markets, where people's savings can be transformed into other people's capital.

✾

C. THE ECONOMIC ROLE OF GOVERNMENT

An ideal market economy is one in which all goods and services are voluntarily exchanged for money at market prices. Such a system squeezes the maximum benefits out of a society's available resources without

government intervention. In the real world, however, no economy actually conforms totally to the idealized world of the smoothly functioning invisible hand. Rather, every market economy suffers from imperfections which lead to such ills as excessive pollution, unemployment, and extremes of wealth and poverty.

For that reason, no government anywhere in the world, no matter how conservative, keeps its hands off the economy. In modern economies governments take on many tasks in response to the flaws in the market mechanism. The military, the police, the national weather service, and highway construction are all typical areas of government activity. Socially useful ventures such as space exploration and scientific research benefit from government funding. Governments may regulate some businesses (such as banking and drugs) while subsidizing others (such as education and health care). Governments also tax their citizens and redistribute some of the proceeds to the elderly and needy.

How do governments perform their functions? Governments operate by requiring people to pay taxes, obey regulations, and consume certain collective goods and services. Because of its coercive powers, the government can perform functions that would not be possible under voluntary exchange. This coercion increases the freedoms and consumption of those who benefit while reducing the incomes and opportunities of those who are taxed or regulated.

But for all the wide range of possible activities, governments have three main economic functions in a market economy. These functions are increasing efficiency, promoting equity, and fostering macroeconomic stability and growth.

1. Governments increase *efficiency* by promoting competition, curbing externalities like pollution, and providing public goods.
2. Governments promote *equity* by using tax and expenditure programs to redistribute income toward particular groups.
3. Governments foster *macroeconomic stability and growth*—reducing unemployment and inflation while encouraging economic growth—through fiscal policy and monetary regulation.

We will examine briefly each function.

EFFICIENCY

Adam Smith recognized that the virtues of the market mechanism are fully realized only when the checks and balances of perfect competition are present. What is meant by **perfect competition?** This is a technical term that refers to a market in which no firm or consumer is large enough to affect the market price. For example, the wheat market is perfectly competitive because the largest wheat farm, producing only a minuscule fraction of the world's wheat, can have no appreciable effect upon the price of wheat.

The invisible-hand doctrine applies to economies in which all the markets are perfectly competitive. Perfectly competitive markets will produce an efficient allocation of resources, so the economy is on its production-possibility frontier. When all industries are subject to the checks and balances of perfect competition, as we will see later in this book, markets will produce the bundle of outputs most desired by consumers using the most efficient techniques and the minimum amount of inputs.

Alas, there are many ways that markets can fall short of efficient perfect competition. The three most important involve imperfect competition, such as monopolies; externalities, such as pollution; and public goods, such as national defense and lighthouses. In each case, market failure leads to inefficient production or consumption, and government can play a useful role in curing the disease.

Imperfect Competition

One serious deviation from an efficient market comes from *imperfect competition* or *monopoly* elements. Whereas under perfect competition no firm or consumer can affect prices, **imperfect competition** occurs when a buyer or seller can affect a good's price. For example, if the telephone company or a labor union is large enough to influence the price of phone service or labor, respectively, some degree of imperfect competition has set in. When imperfect competition arises, society may move inside its *PPF.* This would occur, for example, if a single seller (a monopolist) raised the price to earn extra profits. The output of that good would be reduced below the most efficient level, and the efficiency of the economy would thereby suffer. In such a situation, the invisible-hand property of markets may be violated.

What is the effect of imperfect competition? Imperfect competition leads to prices that rise above cost and to consumer purchases that are reduced below efficient levels. The pattern of too high price and too low output is the hallmark of the inefficiencies associated with imperfect competition.

In reality, almost all industries possess some measure of imperfect competition. Airlines, for example, may have no competition on some of their routes but face several rivals on others. The extreme case of imperfect competition is the *monopolist*—a single supplier who alone determines the price of a particular good or service. For example, Microsoft has been a monopolist in the production of Windows operating systems.

Over the last century, most governments have taken steps to curb the most extreme forms of imperfect competition. Governments sometimes regulate the price and profits of monopolies such as local water, telephone, and electric utilities. In addition, government antitrust laws prohibit actions such as price fixing and agreeing to divide up markets. The most important check to imperfect competition, however, is the opening of markets to competitors, whether they be domestic or foreign. Few monopolies can long withstand the attack of competitors unless governments protect them through tariffs or regulations.

Externalities

A second type of inefficiency arises when there are spillovers or externalities, which involve involuntary imposition of costs or benefits. Market transactions involve voluntary exchange in which people exchange goods or services for money. When a firm buys a chicken to make frozen drumsticks, it buys the chicken from its owner in the chicken market, and the seller receives the full value of the hen. When you buy a haircut, the barber receives the full value for time, skills, and rent.

But many interactions take place outside markets. While airports produce a lot of noise, they generally do not compensate the people living around the airport for disturbing their peace. On the other hand, some companies which spend heavily on research and development have positive spillover effects for the rest of society. For example, researchers at AT&T invented the transistor and launched the electronic revolution, but AT&T's profits increased by only a small fraction of the global social gains. In each case, an activity has helped or hurt people outside the market transaction; that is, there was an economic transaction without an economic payment.

Externalities (or spillover effects) occur when firms or people impose costs or benefits on others outside the marketplace.

Governments are generally more concerned with negative externalities than positive ones. As our society has become more densely populated and as the production of energy, chemicals, and other materials increases, negative externalities or spillover effects have grown from little nuisances into major threats. This is where governments come in. Government *regulations* are designed to control externalities like air and water pollution, damage from strip mining, hazardous wastes, unsafe drugs and foods, and radioactive materials.

In many ways, governments are like parents, always saying no: Thou shalt not expose thy workers to dangerous conditions. Thou shalt not pour out poisonous smoke from thy factory chimney. Thou shalt not sell mind-altering drugs. Thou shalt not drive without wearing thy seat belt. And so forth. Finding the precisely correct regulations is a difficult task that requires complex science and economics and is subject to heavy political pressure, but few today would argue for returning to the unregulated economic jungle where firms would be allowed to dump pollutants like plutonium wherever they wanted.

Public Goods

While negative externalities like pollution or global warming command most of the headlines, positive externalities may well be economically more significant. Important examples of positive externalities are construction of a highway network, operation of a national weather service, support of basic science, and provision of measures to enhance public health. These are not goods which can be bought and sold in markets. Adequate private production of these public goods will not occur because the benefits are so widely dispersed across the population that no single firm or consumer has an economic incentive to provide the service and capture the returns.

The extreme example of a positive externality is a public good. **Public goods** are commodities for which the cost of extending the service to an addi-

tional person is zero and which it is impossible to exclude individuals from enjoying. The best example of a public good is national defense. When a nation protects its freedoms and way of life, it does so for all its inhabitants, whether they want the protection or not and whether they pay for it or not.

Because private provision of public goods is generally insufficient, the government must step in to encourage the production of public goods. In buying public goods like national defense or lighthouses, the government is behaving exactly like any other large spender. By casting sufficient dollar votes in certain directions, it causes resources to flow there. Once the dollar votes are cast, the market mechanism then takes over and channels resources to firms so that the lighthouses or tanks get produced.

Are lighthouses public goods?

For many years, lighthouses were used to illustrate the notion of public goods. They save lives and cargoes. But lighthouse keepers cannot reach out to collect fees from ships; nor, if they could, would it serve an efficient social purpose for them to exact an economic penalty on ships who use their services. The light can be provided most efficiently free of charge, for it costs no more to warn 100 ships than to warn a single ship of the nearby rocks.

This view became controversial when Nobel Prize-winning economist Ronald Coase reviewed the history of lighthouses in England and Wales and determined that these had been *privately* operated. Coase found that English lighthouses operated profitably under licenses purchased from the Crown and were financed by government-authorized "light duties" levied on ships which used nearby ports. From this history, Coase concluded that "contrary to the belief of many economists, a lighthouse service can be provided by private enterprise." Some have even concluded that lighthouses are not public goods.

But let's look carefully here. The two key attributes of a public good are that the cost of extending the service to an additional person is zero ("nonrivalry") and that it is impossible to exclude individuals from enjoying it ("nonexcludability"). Both these characteristics are applicable to lighthouses.

But a "public" good is not necessarily publicly provided. Often, it is provided by no one. Moreover, just because it is privately provided does not indicate that it is efficiently provided or that a market mechanism can pay for the lighthouse. The English example shows the interesting case where, *if* provision of the public good can be tied to another good or service (in this case, vessel tonnage), and *if* the government gives private persons the right to collect what are essentially taxes, then an alternative mechanism for *financing* the public good can be found. Such an approach would work poorly where the fees could not be easily tied to tonnage (such as in international waterways). And it would not work at all if the government refused to privatize the right to collect light duties on shipping.

America shows quite a different experience. From its earliest days, the United States believed that navigational aids should be government-provided. Indeed, one of the first acts of the first Congress, and America's first public-works law, provided that "the necessary support, maintenance, and repairs of all lighthouse, beacons, [and] buoys . . . shall be defrayed out of the Treasury of the United States."

But, like many public goods, lighthouses were provided meager funding, and it is interesting to note what happened in the absence of navigational aids. A fascinating case lies off the east coast of Florida, which is a treacherous waterway with a 200-mile reef lying submerged a few feet below the surface in the most active hurricane track of the Atlantic Ocean. This heavily used channel was prime territory for storm, shipwreck, and piracy.

There were no lighthouses in Florida until 1825, and no private-sector lighthouses were ever built in this area. The market responded vigorously to the perils, however. What arose from the private sector was a thriving "wrecking" industry. Wreckers were ships that lurked near the dangerous reefs waiting for an unfortunate boat to become disabled. The wreckers would then appear, offer their help in saving lives and cargo, tow the boat into the appropriate port, and then claim a substantial part of the value of the cargo. Wrecking was the major industry of south Florida in the mid-nineteenth century and made Key West the richest town in America at that time.

While wreckers probably had positive value added, they provided none of the public-good attributes of lighthouses. Indeed, because many cargoes were insured, there was significant "moral hazard" involved in navigation. Connivance between wreckers and captains often enriched both at the expense of owners and insurance companies.

It was only when the U.S. Lighthouse Service, financed by government revenues, began to build lighthouses through the Florida channel that the number of shipwrecks began to decrease—and the wreckers were gradually driven out of business.

Lighthouses are no longer a central issue of public policy today and are mainly of interest to tourists. They have been largely replaced by the satellite-based Global Positioning System (GPS), which is also a public good provided free by the government. But the history of lighthouses reminds us of the problems that can arise when public goods are inefficiently provided.

Taxes. The government must find the revenues to pay for its public goods and for its income-redistribution programs. Such revenues come from taxes levied on personal and corporate incomes, on wages, on sales of consumer goods, and on other items. All levels of government—city, state, and federal—collect taxes to pay for their spending.

Taxes sound like another "price"—in this case the price we pay for public goods. But taxes differ from prices in one crucial respect: taxes are not voluntary. Everyone is subject to the tax laws; we are all obligated to pay for our share of the cost of public goods. Of course, through our democratic process, we as citizens choose both the public goods and the taxes to pay for them. However, the close connection between spending and consumption that we see for private goods does not hold for taxes and public goods. I pay for a hamburger only if I want one, but I must pay my share of the taxes used to finance defense and public education even if I don't care a bit for these activities.

EQUITY

Our discussion of market failures like monopoly or externalities focused on defects in the allocative role of markets—imperfections that can be corrected by judicious intervention. But assume for the moment that the economy functioned with complete efficiency—always on the production-possibility frontier and never inside it, always choosing the right amount of public versus private goods, and so forth. Even if the market system worked perfectly, it might still lead to a flawed outcome.

Markets do not necessarily produce a fair distribution of income. A market economy may produce inequalities in income and consumption that are not acceptable to the electroate.

Why might the market mechanism produce an unacceptable solution to the question *for whom?* The reason is that incomes are determined by a wide variety of factors, including effort, education, inheritance, factor prices, and luck. The resulting income distribution may not correspond to a fair outcome. Moreover, recall that goods follow dollar votes and not the greatest need. A rich man's cat may drink the milk that a poor boy needs to remain healthy. Does this happen because the market is failing? Not at all, for the market mechanism is doing its job— putting goods in the hands of those who have the dollar votes. If a country spends more fertilizing its lawns than feeding poor children, that is a defect of income distribution, not of the market. Even the most efficient market system may generate great inequality.

Often the income distribution in a market system is the result of accidents of birth. Every year *Forbes* magazine lists the 400 richest Americans, and it's impressive how many of them either received their wealth by inheritance or used inherited wealth as a springboard to even greater wealth. Would everyone regard that as necessarily right or ideal? Probably not. Should someone be allowed to become a billionaire simply by inheriting 5000 square miles of rangeland or the family's holding of oil wells? That's the way the cookie crumbles under laissez-faire capitalism.

For most of American history, economic growth was a rising tide that lifted all boats, raising the incomes of the poor as well as those of the rich. But over the last two decades, changes in family structure and declining wages of the less skilled and less educated have reversed the trend. With a return to greater emphasis on the market has come greater homelessness, more children living in poverty, and deterioration of many of America's central cities.

Income inequalities may be politically or ethically unacceptable. A nation does not need to accept the outcome of competitive markets as predetermined and immutable; people may examine the distribution of income and decide it is unfair. If a democratic society does not like the distribution of dollar votes under a laissez-faire market system, it can take steps to change the distribution of income.

Let's say that voters decide to reduce income inequality. What tools could the government use to implement that decision? First, it can engage in *progressive taxation,* taxing large incomes at a higher rate than small incomes. It might impose heavy taxes on wealth or on large inheritances to break the chain of privilege. The federal income and inheritance taxes are examples of such redistributive progressive taxation.

Second, because low tax rates cannot help those who have no income at all, governments can make *transfer payments,* which are money payments to people. Such transfers today include aid for the elderly, blind, and disabled and for those with dependent children, as well as unemployment insurance for the jobless. This system of transfer payments provides a "safety net" to protect the unfortunate from privation. And, finally, governments sometimes subsidize consumption of low-income groups by providing food stamps, subsidized medical care, and low-cost housing—though in the United States, such spending comprises a relatively small share of total spending.

These programs have become increasingly unpopular in the last two decades. As the real wages of the middle class have stagnated, people naturally ask why they should support the homeless or able-bodied people who do not work. What can economics contribute to debates about equality? Economics as a science cannot answer such normative questions as how much of our market incomes—if any—should be transferred to poor families. This is a political question that can be answered only at the ballot box.

Economics can, however, analyze the costs or benefits of different redistributive systems. Economists have devoted much time to analyzing whether different income-redistribution devices (such as taxes and food stamps) lead to social waste (e.g., people working less or buying drugs rather than food). They have also studied whether giving poor people cash rather than goods is likely to be a more efficient way of reducing poverty. Economics cannot answer questions of how much poverty is acceptable and fair, but it can help design more effective programs to increase the incomes of the poor.

MACROECONOMIC GROWTH AND STABILITY

Since its origins, capitalism has been plagued by periodic bouts of inflation (rising prices) and recession (high unemployment). Since World War II, for example, there have been nine recessions in the United States, some putting millions of people out of work. These fluctuations are known as the *business cycle*.

Today, thanks to the intellectual contribution of John Maynard Keynes and his followers, we know how to control the worst excesses of the business cycle. By careful use of fiscal and monetary policies, governments can affect output, employment, and inflation. The *fiscal policies* of government involve the power to tax and the power to spend. *Monetary policy* involves determining the supply of money and interest rates; these affect investment in capital goods and other interest-rate-sensitive spending. Using these two fundamental tools of macroeconomic policy, governments can influence the level of total spending, the rate of growth and level of output, the levels of employment and unemployment, and the price level and rate of inflation in an economy.

Governments in advanced industrial countries have successfully applied the lessons of the Keynesian revolution over the last half-century. Spurred on by active monetary and fiscal policies, the market economies witnessed a period of unprecedented economic growth in the three decades after World War II.

In the 1980s, governments became more concerned with also designing macroeconomic policies to promote long-term objectives, such as economic growth and productivity. (*Economic growth* denotes the growth in a nation's total output, while *productivity* represents the output per unit input or the efficiency with which resources are used.) For example, tax rates were lowered in most industrial countries in order to improve incentives for saving and production. Many economists emphasized the importance of public saving through smaller budget deficits as a way to increase national saving and investment.

Macroeconomic policies for stabilization and economic growth include fiscal policies (of taxing and spending) along with monetary policies (which affect interest rates and credit conditions). Since the development of macroeconomics in the 1930s, governments have succeeded in curbing the worst excesses of inflation and unemployment.

Table 2-1 summarizes the economic role played by government today. It shows the important governmental functions of promoting efficiency, achiev-

Failure of Market Economy	Government Intervention	Current Examples of Government Policy
Inefficiency:		
Monopoly	Encourage competition	Antitrust laws, deregulation
Externalities	Intervene in markets	Antipollution laws, antismoking ordinances
Public goods	Encourage beneficial activities	Build lighthouses, provide public education
Inequality:		
Unacceptable inequalities of income and wealth	Redistribute income	Progressive taxation of income and wealth
		Income-support or transfer programs (e.g., food stamps)
Macroeconomic problems:		
Business cycles (high inflation and unemployment)	Stabilize through macroeconomic policies	Monetary policies (e.g., changes in money supply and interest rates)
		Fiscal policies (e.g., taxes and spending programs)
Slow economic growth	Stimulate growth	Invest in education
		Raise national savings rate by reducing budget deficit or increasing budget surplus.

TABLE 2-1. Government Can Remedy the Shortcomings of the Market

ing a fairer distribution of income, and pursuing the macroeconomic objectives of economic growth and stability. In all advanced industrial societies we find some variant of a **mixed economy**, in which the market determines output and prices in most individual sectors while government steers the overall economy with programs of taxation, spending, and monetary regulation.

TWILIGHT OF THE WELFARE STATE?

In 1942, the great Austria-born Harvard economist Joseph Schumpeter argued that the United States was "capitalism living in an oxygen tent" on its march to socialism. Capitalism's success would breed alienation and self-doubt, sapping its efficiency and innovation. But he was wrong. The next half-century saw sustained growth in government's involvement in the economies of North America and Western Europe along with the *most impressive economic performance ever recorded.*

Rapid economic growth has been accompanied by increased skepticism about government's role. Critics of government say that the state is overly intrusive; governments create monopoly; government failures are just as pervasive as market failures; high taxes distort the allocation of resources; social security threatens to overload workers in the decades ahead; environmental regulation dulls the spirit of enterprise; government attempts to stabilize the economy must fail at best and increase inflation at worst. In short, for some, government is the problem rather than the solution.

Guardians of economic freedom: Friedrich Hayek and Milton Friedman

Economists, being human, are subject to fluctuations in opinions and ideology. Because government policies seemed so successful in mobilizing the U.S. and U.K. war economies for military victory over Germany and Japan during World War II, and because active macroeconomic policies seemed to succeed in conquering the Great Depression, conservative laissez-faire ideologies came to represent only minority opinion among most free-world professional economists.

Two eminent scholars never wavered in their skepticism about the merits of heavy government intervention in the economy. Friedrich Hayek (1899–1992), of Vienna, London, and Chicago, and Milton Friedman (1912–), of the University of Chicago and the Hoover Library at Stanford, received Nobel Prizes in economics for their scientific innovations. Their work is today highly regarded by conservative and "libertarian" economic thinkers.

Hayek's most influential work examined the efficiency of different forms of economic organization. The 1920s and 1930s witnessed a great debate as to whether resources could be efficiently organized under socialism. Oskar Lange and Abba Lerner argued that a socialist firm could use capitalist-style pricing and thereby emulate a market economy without the monopolistic tendencies of capitalism. Hayek provided an important rebuttal. He pointed out that costs and production possibilities are not known. Only with the incentives of a private, free-enterprise system could the information dispersed among the millions of economic agents be effectively mobilized and used. No system can generate innovations without the carrot of profits and the stick of bankruptcy. Modern economics, with its emphasis on dispersed and asymmetrical information, owes much to the brilliant insights of Hayek.

Hayek's best-seller, and the book that most captured the attention of the broader public, was *The Road to Serfdom.* In this work he warned that the road to the hell of totalitarian tyranny and economic inefficiency was paved by the good intentions of modest interferens with free markets and private enterprises.

Friedman's statistical and analytic researches have ranged widely. He documented how small the differences are between the saving rates of rich and poor in the long run after adjusting saving for temporary ups and downs in income. This led to the permanent-income theory of consumption (which is discussed in the macroeconomic sections of this text). Together with Anna Schwartz, Friedman authored the definitive *Monetary History of the United States, 1876–1960* (1993). This book launched the monetarist revolution and led to an appreciation among macroeconomists of how the money supply can affect aggregate spending, prices, and output. Friedman helped convince economists that monetary policy definitely matters for overall economic activity.

During the last half of the twentieth century, everywhere—in the United States, Western Europe, and Asia, as well as in Stalin's Soviet Union and Mao's China—there has been a significant swing back toward the competitive-market pole and away from the centralized-command pole. No one within the economist guild has been more important, both as an architect and as an expositor of this shift, than Milton Friedman. His classic book, *Capitalism and Freedom* (1962), argues why a rational thinker might, along with advocating free international trade and maximal deregulation, deplore the minimum wage, state licensing of surgeons, and prohibition of drugs like heroin and cocaine. All thoughtful economists should study his arguments carefully.

In weighing the relative merits of state and market, public debate often oversimplifies the complex choices that societies face. Markets have worked miracles in some countries. But without the right kind of legal and political structure, and without the social overhead capital that promotes trade and private investment, markets have also produced corrupt capitalism with great inequality, pervasive poverty, and declining living standards.

In economic affairs, success has many parents, while failure is an orphan. The success of market economies may lead us to overlook the many successes of collective action over the last century, as the case of the lighthouse reminds us. Collective action has helped reduce malnutrition and conquered many terrible diseases like smallpox. Government programs have increased literacy and life expectancy. Macroeconomic successes have reduced the sting of inflation and unemployment, while government transfer programs have brought health care to the poor and improved the quality of life for the aged. State-supported science has penetrated the atom, discovered the DNA molecule, and explored outer space.

Of course, these successes do not belong to governments alone. Governments harnessed private ingenuity through the market mechanism to help achieve these social aims. And, in some cases, governments were like orators who didn't know when enough was enough.

The debate about government's successes and failures demonstrates again that drawing the boundary between market and government is an enduring problem. The tools of economics are indispensable to help societies find the golden mean between laissez-faire market mechanisms and democratic rules of the road. The good mixed economy is, perforce, the limited mixed economy. But those who would reduce government to the constable plus a few lighthouses are living in a dream world. An efficient and humane society requires both halves of the mixed system—market and government. Operating a modern economy without both is like trying to clap with one hand.

SUMMARY

A. What Is a Market?

1. In an economy like the United States, most economic decisions are made in markets, which are mechanisms through which buyers and sellers meet to trade and to determine prices and quantities for goods and services. Adam Smith proclaimed that the *invisible hand* of markets would lead to the optimal economic outcome as individuals pursue their own self-interest. And while markets are far from perfect, they have proved remarkably effective at solving the problems of *how, what,* and *for whom.*

2. The market mechanism works as follows to determine the *what* and the *how:* The dollar votes of people affect prices of goods; these prices serve as guides for

the amounts of the different goods to be produced. When people demand more of a good, its price will increase and businesses can profit by expanding production of that good. Under perfect competition, a business must find the cheapest method of production, efficiently using labor, land, and other factors; otherwise, it will incur losses and be eliminated from the market.

3. At the same time that the *what* and *how* problems are being resolved by prices, so is the problem of *for whom.* The distribution of income is determined by the ownership of factors of production (land, labor, and capital) and by factor prices. People possessing fertile land or the ability to hit home runs will earn many dollar

votes to buy consumer goods. Those without property or with skills, color, or sex that the market undervalues will receive low incomes.

B. Trade, Money, and Capital

4. As economies develop, they become more specialized. Division of labor allows a task to be broken into a number of smaller chores that can each be mastered and performed more quickly by a single worker. Specialization arises from the increasing tendency to use roundabout methods of production that require many specialized skills. As individuals and countries become increasingly specialized, they tend to concentrate on particular commodities and trade their surplus output for goods produced by others. Voluntary trade, based on specialization, benefits all.

5. Trade in specialized goods and services today relies on money to lubricate its wheels. Money is the universally acceptable medium of exchange—including primarily currency and checking deposits. It is used to pay for everything from apple tarts to zebra skins. By accepting money, people and nations can specialize in producing a few goods and can then trade them for others; without money, we would waste much time negotiating and bartering.

6. Capital goods—produced inputs such as machinery, structures, and inventories of goods in process—permit roundabout methods of production that add much to a nation's output. These roundabout methods take time and resources to get started and therefore require a temporary sacrifice of present consumption in order to increase future consumption. The rules that define how capital and other assets can be bought, sold, and used are the system of property rights. In no economic system are private-property rights unlimited.

C. The Economic Role of Government

7. Although the market mechanism is an admirable way of producing and allocating goods, sometimes market failures lead to deficiencies in the economic outcomes. The government may step in to correct these failures. Its role in a modern economy is to ensure efficiency, to correct an unfair distribution of income, and to promote economic growth and stability.

8. Markets fail to provide an efficient allocation of resources in the presence of imperfect competition or externalities. Imperfect competition, such as monopoly, produces high prices and low levels of output. To combat these conditions, governments regulate businesses or put legal antitrust constraints on business behavior. Externalities arise when activities impose costs or bestow benefits that are not paid for in the marketplace. Governments may decide to step in and regulate these spillovers (as it does with air pollution) or provide for *public goods* (as in the case of public health).

9. Markets do not necessarily produce a fair distribution of income; they may spin off unacceptably high inequality of income and consumption. In response, governments can alter the pattern of incomes (the *for whom*) generated by market wages, rents, interest, and dividends. Modern governments use taxation to raise revenues for transfers or income-support programs that place a financial safety net under the needy.

10. Since the development of macroeconomics in the 1930s, the government has undertaken a third role: using fiscal powers (of taxing and spending) and monetary policy (affecting credit and interest rates) to promote long-run economic growth and productivity and to tame the business cycle's excesses of inflation and unemployment. Since 1980, the blend of the mixed economy called the welfare state has been on the defensive in the enduring struggle over the boundary between state and market.

CONCEPTS FOR REVIEW

The Market Mechanism

market, market mechanism
markets for goods and for factors of
    production
prices as signals
market equilibrium
perfect and imperfect competition
Adam Smith's invisible-hand doctrine

Features of a Modern Economy

specialization and division of labor
money
factors of production (land, labor,
    capital)
capital, private property, and property rights

Government's Economic Role

efficiency, equity, stability
inefficiencies: monopoly and externalities
inequity of incomes under markets
macroeconomic policies:
fiscal and monetary policies
stabilization and growth

FURTHER READING AND INTERNET WEBSITES

Further Reading

A useful discussion of globalization is contained in "Symposium on Globalization in Perspective," *Journal of Economic Perspectives,* fall 1998.

For examples of the writings of libertarian economists, see Milton Friedman, *Capitalism and Freedom* (University of Chicago Press, 1963), and Friedrich Hayek, *The Road to Serfdom* (University of Chicago Press, 1994).

A strong defense of government interventions in the economy can be found in Robert Kuttner, *Everything for Sale: The Virtues and Limits of the Market* (University of Chicago Press, 1999) and in Anne Alstott and Bruce Ackerman, *The Stakeholder Economy* (Yale University Press, New Haven, CT, 1999).

A fascinating example of how a small economy is organized without money is found in R. A. Radford, "The Economic Organization of a P.O.W. Camp," *Economica,* vol. 12, November 1945, pp. 189–201.

Websites

You can explore recent analyses of the economy along with a discussion of major economic policy issues in the *Economic Report of the President* at w3.access.gpo.gov/eop/. See www.whitehouse.gov for federal budget information and as an entry point into the useful Economic Statistics Briefing Room.

Major issues are presented from a conservative or libertarian economic perspective at the website of the Cato Institute, www.cato.org/.

QUESTIONS FOR DISCUSSION

1. What determines the composition of national output? In some cases, we say that there is "consumer sovereignty," meaning that consumers decide how to spend their incomes on the basis of their tastes and market prices. In other cases, decisions are made by political choices of legislatures. Consider the following examples: transportation, education, police, energy efficiency of appliances, health-care coverage, television advertising. For each, describe whether the allocation is by consumer sovereignty or by political decision. Would you change the method of allocation for any of these goods?

2. When a good is limited, some means must be found to ration the scarce commodity. Some examples of rationing devices are auctions, ration coupons, and first-come, first-served systems. What are the strengths and weaknesses of each? Explain carefully in what sense a market mechanism "rations" scarce goods and services.

3. This chapter discusses many "market failures," areas in which the invisible hand guides the economy poorly, and describes the role of government. Is it possible that there are, as well, "government failures," government attempts to curb market failures that are worse

than the original market failures? Think of some examples of government failures. Give some examples in which government failures are so bad that it is better to live with the market failures than to try to correct them.

4. Consider the following cases of government intervention: regulations to limit air pollution, income support for the poor, and price regulation of a telephone monopoly. For each case, (1) explain the market failure, (2) describe a government intervention to treat the problem, and (3) explain how "government failure" (see the definition in question 3) might arise because of the intervention.

5. The circular flow of goods and inputs illustrated in Figure 2-1 has a corresponding flow of dollar incomes and spending. Draw a circular-flow diagram for the dollar flows in the economy, and compare it with the circular flow of goods and inputs. What is the role of money in the dollar circular flow?

6. Give three examples of specialization and division of labor. In what areas are you and your friends thinking of specializing? What might be the perils of overspecialization?

Major Expenditure Categories for Federal Government	
Budget category	**Federal spending, 2001 ($, billion)**
Social security	426
Health care and Medicare	387
National defense	291
Income security	260
Interest on public debt	208
Natural resources and environment	25
International affairs	20

Source: Office of Management and Budget, *Budget of the United States Government,* Fiscal Year 2001.

7. "Lincoln freed the slaves. With one pen stroke he destroyed much of the capital the South had accumulated over the years." Comment.

8. The table opposite shows some of the major expenditures of the federal government. Explain how each one relates to the economic role of government.

3

Basic Elements of Supply and Demand

What is a cynic? A man who knows the price of everything and the value of nothing.

Oscar Wilde

Like the weather, markets are dynamic, subject to periods of storm and calm, and constantly evolving. Yet, as with weather forecasting, a careful study of markets will reveal certain forces underlying the apparently random movements. To forecast prices and outputs in individual markets, you must first master the analysis of supply and demand.

Take the example of gasoline prices, illustrated in Figure 3-1 on page 47. (This graph shows the "real gasoline price," or the price corrected for movements in the general price level.) Demand for gasoline and other oil products rose sharply after World War II as people fell in love with the automobile and moved increasingly to the suburbs. Next, in the 1970s, supply restrictions, wars among producers, and political revolutions reduced production, with the consequent price spikes seen after 1973 and 1979. In the years that followed, a combination of energy conservation, smaller cars, the growth of the information economy, and expanded production around the world led to falling oil prices. The real price of gasoline fell from over $2.50 per gallon in 1980 to around $1.00 per gallon in 1999. The most recent turn came when production cutbacks by the oil cartel and booming demand led to a sharp spike in oil prices in early 2000, angering truckers and motorists and putting upward pressure on inflation.

What lay behind these dramatic shifts? Economics has a very powerful tool for explaining such changes in the economic environment. It is called the *theory of supply and demand.* This theory shows how consumer preferences determine consumer demand for commodities, while business costs are the foundation of the supply of commodities. The increases in the price of gasoline occurred either because the demand for gasoline had increased or because the supply of oil had decreased. The same is true for every market, from Internet stocks to diamonds to land: changes in supply and demand drive changes in output and prices. If you understand how supply and demand work, you have gone a long way toward understanding a market economy.

This chapter introduces the notions of supply and demand and shows how they operate in competitive markets for *individual commodities.* We begin with demand curves and then discuss supply curves. Using these basic tools, we will see how the market price is determined where these two curves intersect—where the forces of demand and supply are just in balance. It is the movement of prices—the price mechanism—which brings supply and demand into balance or equilibrium. This chapter closes with some examples of how supply-and-demand analysis can be applied.

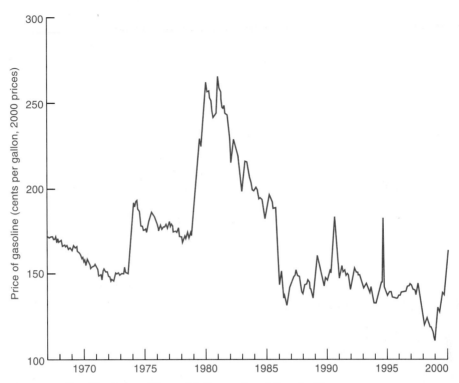

FIGURE 3-1. Gasoline Prices Move with Demand and Supply Changes

Gasoline prices have fluctuated wildly over the last four decades. Supply reductions in the 1970s produced two dramatic "oil shocks," which provoked social unrest and calls for increased regulation. Reductions in demand from new energy-saving technologies led to the long decline in price after 1980. When the oil cartel reduced supply in late 1999, oil prices once again shot up sharply. The tools of supply and demand are crucial for understanding these trends. (Source: U.S. Departments of Energy and Labor. The price of gasoline has been converted into 2000 prices using the consumer price index.)

A. THE DEMAND SCHEDULE

Both common sense and careful scientific observation show that the amount of a commodity people buy depends on its price. The higher the price of an article, other things held constant,[1] the fewer units consumers are willing to buy. The lower its market price, the more units of it are bought.

There exists a definite relationship between the market price of a good and the quantity demanded of that good, other things held constant. This relationship between price and quantity bought is called the **demand schedule,** or the **demand curve.**

Let's look at a simple example. Table 3-1 presents a hypothetical demand schedule for cornflakes. At each price, we can determine the quantity of cornflakes that consumers purchase. For example, at $5 per box, consumers will buy 9 million boxes per year.

At a lower price, more cornflakes are bought. Thus, at a price of $4, the quantity bought is 10 million boxes. At yet a lower price (P) equal to $3, the quantity demanded (Q) is still greater, at 12 million. And so forth. We can determine the quantity demanded at each listed price in Table 3-1.

---

[1] Later in this chapter we discuss the other factors that influence demand, including income and tastes. The term "other things held constant" simply means we are varying the price without changing any of these other determinants of demand.

Demand Schedule for Cornflakes		
	(1) Price ($ per box) P	(2) Quantity demanded (millions of boxes per year) Q
A	5	9
B	4	10
C	3	12
D	2	15
E	1	20

TABLE 3-1. The Demand Schedule Relates Quantity Demanded to Price

At each market price, consumers will want to buy a certain quantity of cornflakes. As the price of cornflakes falls, the quantity of cornflakes demanded will rise.

THE DEMAND CURVE

The graphical representation of the demand schedule is the *demand curve.* We show the demand curve in Figure 3-2, which graphs the quantity of cornflakes demanded on the horizontal axis and the price of cornflakes on the vertical axis. Note that quantity and price are inversely related; that is, Q goes up when P goes down. The curve slopes downward, going from northwest to southeast. This important property is called the *law of downward-sloping demand.* It is based on common sense as well as economic theory and has been empirically tested and verified for practically all commodities—cornflakes, gasoline, college education, and illegal drugs being a few examples.

Law of downward-sloping demand: When the price of a commodity is raised (and other things are held constant), buyers tend to buy less of the commodity. Similarly, when the price is lowered, other things being constant, quantity demanded increases.

Quantity demanded tends to fall as price rises for two reasons. First is the **substitution effect.** When the price of a good rises, I will substitute other similar goods for it (as the price of beef rises, I eat more chicken). A second reason why a higher price reduces quantity demanded is the **income effect.** This comes into play because when a price goes up, I find myself somewhat poorer than I was before. If gaso-

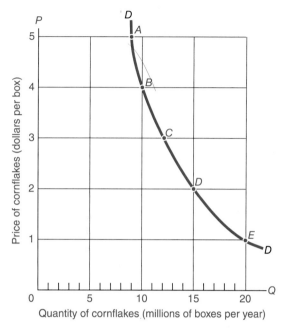

FIGURE 3-2. A Downward-Sloping Demand Curve Relates Quantity Demanded to Price

In the demand curve for cornflakes, price (P) is measured on the vertical axis while quantity demanded (Q) is measured on the horizontal axis. Each pair of (P, Q) numbers from Table 3-1 is plotted as a point, and then a smooth curve is passed through the points to give us a demand curve, *DD.* The negative slope of the demand curve illustrates the law of downward-sloping demand.

line prices double, I have in effect less real income, so I will naturally curb my consumption of gasoline and other goods.

Market Demand

Our discussion of demand has so far referred to "the" demand curve. But whose demand is it? Mine? Yours? Everybody's? The fundamental building block for demand is individual preferences. However, in this chapter we will always focus on the *market demand,* which represents the sum total of all individual demands. The market demand is what is observable in the real world.

The market demand curve is found by adding together the quantities demanded by all individuals at each price.

Does the market demand curve obey the law of downward-sloping demand? It certainly does. If prices drop, for example, the lower prices attract new customers through the substitution effect. In addition, a price reduction will induce extra purchases of goods by existing consumers through both the income and the substitution effects. Conversely, a rise in the price of a good will cause some of us to buy less.

The explosive growth in computer demand

We can illustrate the law of downward-sloping demand for the case of personal computers (PCs). The prices of the first PCs were high, and their computing power was relatively modest. They were found in few businesses and even fewer homes. It is hard to believe that just 20 years ago students wrote most of their papers in longhand and did most calculations by hand or with simple calculators.

But the prices of computing power fell sharply over the last two decades. As the prices fell, new buyers were enticed to buy their first computers. PCs came to be widely used for work, for school, and for fun. In the late 1990s, as the value of computers increased with the development of the Internet, yet more people jumped on the computer bandwagon. Worldwide, PC sales totaled about 100 million in 1999.

Figure 3-3 shows the prices and quantities of computers and peripheral equipment in the United States as calculated by government statisticians. The prices reflect the cost of purchasing computers with constant quality—that is, they take into account the rapid quality change of the average computer purchased. You can see how falling prices along with improved software, increased utility of the Internet and e-mail, and other factors have led to an explosive growth in computer output.

Forces behind the Demand Curve

What determines the market demand curve for cornflakes or gasoline or computers? A whole array of factors influences how much will be demanded at a given price: average levels of income, the size of the population, the prices and availability of related goods, individual and social tastes, and special influences.

- The *average income* of consumers is a key determinant of demand. As people's incomes rise, indi-

viduals tend to buy more of almost everything, even if prices don't change. Automobile purchases tend to rise sharply with higher levels of income.

- The *size of the market*—measured, say, by the population—clearly affects the market demand curve. California's 32 million people tend to buy 32 times more apples and cars than do Rhode Island's 1 million people.

- The prices and availability of *related goods* influence the demand for a commodity. A particularly important connection exists among substitute goods—ones that tend to perform the same function, such as cornflakes and oatmeal, pens and pencils, small cars and large cars, or oil and natural gas. Demand for good A tends to be low if the price of substitute product B is low. (For example, if the price of computers falls, will that increase or decrease the demand for typewriters?)

- In addition to these objective elements, there is a set of subjective elements called *tastes* or *preferences*. Tastes represent a variety of cultural and historical influences. They may reflect genuine psychological or physiological needs (for liquids, love, or excitement). And they may include artificially contrived cravings (for cigarettes, drugs, or fancy sports cars). They may also contain a large element of tradition or religion (eating beef is popular in America but taboo in India, while curried jellyfish is a delicacy in Japan but would make many Americans gag).

- Finally, *special influences* will affect the demand for particular goods. The demand for umbrellas is high in rainy Seattle but low in sunny Phoenix; the demand for air conditioners will rise in hot weather; the demand for automobiles will be low in New York, where public transportation is plentiful and parking is a nightmare. In addition, expectations about future economic conditions, particularly prices, may have an important impact on demand.

The determinants of demand are summarized in Table 3-2, which uses automobiles as an example.

Shifts in Demand

As economic life evolves, demand changes incessantly. Demand curves sit still only in textbooks.

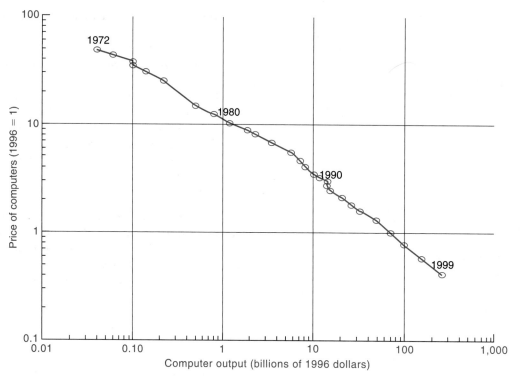

FIGURE 3-3. Declining Computer Prices Have Fueled an Explosive Growth in Computer Power

The prices of computers and peripheral devices such as printers are measured in terms of the cost of purchasing a given bundle of characteristics (such as memory or speed of calculations). The price of computer power has fallen more than a hundred-fold since 1972. Falling prices along with higher incomes and a growing variety of uses has led to a 5000-fold growth in the quantity of computers produced. (Source: Department of Commerce estimates of real output and prices. Note that the data are plotted on ratio scales.)

Factors affecting the demand curve	Example for automobiles
1. **Average income**	As incomes rise, people increase car purchases.
2. **Population**	A growth in population increases car purchases.
3. **Prices of related goods**	Lower gasoline prices raise the demand for cars.
4. **Tastes**	Having a new car becomes a status symbol.
5. **Special influences**	Special influences include availability of alternative forms of transportation, safety of automobiles, expectations of future price increases, etc.

TABLE 3-2. Many Factors Affect the Demand Curve

Why does the demand curve shift? Because influences other than the good's price change. Let's work through an example of how a change in a nonprice variable shifts the demand curve. We know that the average income of Americans rose sharply during the long economic boom of the 1990s. Because there is a powerful income effect on the demand for automobiles, this means that the quantity of automobiles demanded at each price will rise. For example, if average incomes rose by 10 percent, the quantity demanded at a price of $10,000 might rise from 10 million to 12 million units. This would be a shift in the demand curve because the increase in quantity demanded reflects factors other than the good's own price.

The net effect of the changes in underlying influences is what we call an *increase in demand*. An increase in the demand for automobiles is illustrated in Figure 3-4 as a rightward shift in the demand curve. Note that the shift means that more cars will be bought at every price.

You can test yourself by answering the following questions: Will a warm winter shift the demand curve for heating oil leftward or rightward? Why? What will happen to the demand for baseball tickets if young people lose interest in baseball and watch basketball instead? What will a sharp fall in the price of personal computers do to the demand for typewriters? What happens to the demand for a college education if wages are falling for blue-collar jobs while salaries for college-educated investment bankers and computer scientists are rising rapidly?

When there are changes in factors other than a good's own price which affect the quantity purchased, we call these changes shifts in demand. Demand increases (or decreases) when the quantity demanded at each price increases (or decreases).

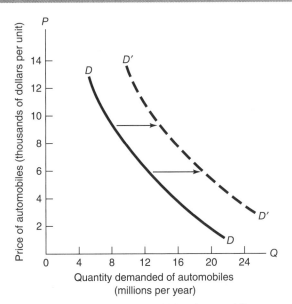

FIGURE 3-4. Increase in Demand for Automobiles

As elements underlying demand change, the demand for automobiles is affected. Here we see the effect of rising average income, increased population, and lower gasoline prices on the demand for automobiles. We call this shift in the demand curve an increase in demand.

Movements along curves versus shifts of curves

Do not confuse movement along curves with shift of curves. Great care must be taken not to confuse a change in demand (which denotes a shift of the demand curve) with a change in the quantity demanded (which means moving to a different point on the same demand curve after a price change).

A change in demand occurs when one of the elements underlying the demand curve shifts. Take the case of pizzas. As incomes increase, consumers will want to buy more pizzas even if pizza prices do not change. In other words, higher incomes will increase demand and shift the demand curve for pizzas out and to the right. This is a shift in the demand for pizzas.

Distinguish this from a change in quantity demanded that occurs because consumers tend to buy more pizzas as pizza prices fall, all other things remaining constant. Here, the increased purchases result not from an increase in demand but from the price decrease. This change represents a *movement along* the demand curve, not a *shift of* the demand curve. A movement along the demand curve means that other things were held constant when price changed.

✳ B. THE SUPPLY SCHEDULE

Let us now turn from demand to supply. The supply side of a market typically involves the terms on which businesses produce and sell their products. The supply of tomatoes tells us the quantity of tomatoes that will be sold at each tomato price. More precisely, the supply schedule relates the quantity supplied of a good to its market price, other things constant. In considering supply, the other things that are held constant include costs of production, prices of related goods, and government policies.

The **supply schedule** (or **supply curve**) for a commodity shows the relationship between its market price and the amount of that commodity that producers are willing to produce and sell other things held constant.

THE SUPPLY CURVE

Table 3-3 shows a hypothetical supply schedule for cornflakes, and Figure 3-5 plots the data from the table in the form of a supply curve. These data show that at a cornflakes price of $1 per box, no cornflakes at all will be produced. At such a low price, breakfast cereal manufacturers might want to devote their factories to producing other types of cereal, like bran flakes, that earn them more profit than cornflakes. As the price of cornflakes increases, ever more cornflakes will be produced. At ever-higher cornflakes prices, cereal makers will find it profitable to add more workers and to buy more automated cornflakes-stuffing machines and even more cornflakes factories. All these will increase the output of cornflakes at the higher market prices.

Figure 3-5 shows the typical case of an upward-sloping supply curve for an individual commodity. One important reason for the upward slope is "the law of diminishing returns" (a concept we will learn more about later). Wine will illustrate this important law. If society wants more wine, then additional labor will have to be added to the limited land sites suitable for producing wine grapes. Each new worker will be adding less and less extra product. The price needed to coax out additional wine output is there-

Supply Schedule for Cornflakes		
	(1) Price ($ per box) P	(2) Quantity supplied (millions of boxes per year) Q
A	5	18
B	4	16
C	3	12
D	2	7
E	1	0

TABLE 3-3. Supply Schedule Relates Quantity Supplied to Price

The table shows, for each price, the quantity of cornflakes that cereal makers want to produce and sell. Note the positive relation between price and quantity supplied.

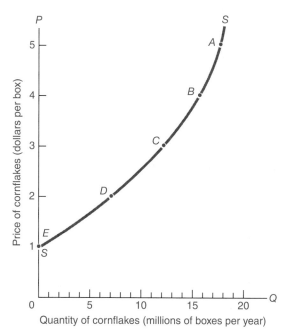

FIGURE 3-5. Supply Curve Relates Quantity Supplied to Price

The supply curve plots the price and quantity pairs from Table 3-3. A smooth curve is passed through these points to give the upward-sloping supply curve, *SS*.

fore higher. By raising the price of wine, society can persuade wine producers to produce and sell more wine; the supply curve for wine is therefore upward-sloping. Similar reasoning applies to many other goods as well.

Forces behind the Supply Curve

In examining the forces determining the supply curve, the fundamental point to grasp is that producers supply commodities for profit and not for fun or charity. One major element underlying the supply curve is the *cost of production*. When production costs for a good are low relative to the market price, it is profitable for producers to supply a great deal. When production costs are high relative to price, firms produce little, switch to the production of other products, or may simply go out of business.

Production costs are primarily determined by the *prices of inputs* and *technological advances*. The prices of inputs such as labor, energy, or machinery obviously have a very important influence on the cost of producing a given level of output. For example, when oil prices rose sharply in the 1970s, the increase raised the price of energy for manufacturers, increased their production costs, and lowered their supply. By contrast, as computer prices fell over the last three decades, businesses increasingly substituted computerized processes for other inputs, as for example in payroll or accounting operations; this increased supply.

An equally important determinant of production costs is *technological advances,* which consist of changes that lower the quantity of inputs needed to produce the same quantity of output. Such advances include everything from scientific breakthroughs to better application of existing technology or simply reorganization of the flow of work. For example, manufacturers have become much more efficient over the last decade or so. It takes far fewer hours of labor to produce an automobile today than it did just 10 years ago. This advance enables car makers to produce more automobiles at the same cost. To give another example, if Internet commerce allows purchasers more easily to compare the prices of necessary inputs, that will lower the cost of production.

But production costs are not the only ingredient that goes into the supply curve. Supply is also influenced by the *prices of related goods,* particularly goods that are alternative outputs of the production process. If the price of one production substitute rises, the supply of another substitute will decrease. For example, auto companies typically make several different car models in the same factory. If there's more demand for one model, and its price rises, they will switch more of their assembly lines to making that model, and the supply of the other models will fall. Or if the demand and price for trucks rise, the entire factory can be converted to making trucks, and the supply of cars will fall.

Government policy also has an important impact on the supply curve. Environmental and health considerations determine what technologies can be used, while taxes and minimum-wage laws can significantly raise input prices. In the local electricity market, government regulations influence both the number of firms that can compete and the prices they charge. Government trade policies have a major impact upon

Factors affecting the supply curve	Example for automobiles
1. **Technology**	Computerized manufacturing lowers production costs and increases supply.
2. **Input prices**	A reduction in the wage paid to autoworkers lowers production costs and increases supply.
3. **Prices of related goods**	If truck prices fall, the supply of cars rises.
4. **Government policy**	Removing quotas and tariffs on imported automobiles increases total automobile supply.
5. **Special influences**	Internet shopping allows consumers to compare the prices of different dealers more easily and drives high-cost sellers out of business.

TABLE 3-4. Supply Is Affected by Production Costs and Other Factors

supply. For instance, when a free-trade agreement opens up the U.S. market to Mexican footwear, the total supply of footwear in the United States increases.

Finally, *special influences* affect the supply curve. The weather exerts an important influence on farming and on the ski industry. The computer industry has been marked by a keen spirit of innovation, which has led to a continuous flow of new products. Market structure will affect supply, and expectations about future prices often have an important impact upon supply decisions.

Table 3-4 highlights the important determinants of supply, using automobiles as an example.

Shifts in Supply

Businesses are constantly changing the mix of products and services they provide. What lies behind these changes in supply behavior?

When changes in factors other than a good's own price affect the quantity supplied, we call these shifts in supply. Supply increases (or decreases) when the amount supplied increases (or decreases) at each market price.

When automobile prices change, producers change their production and quantity supplied, but the supply and the supply curve do not shift. By contrast, when other influences affecting supply change, supply changes and the supply curve shifts.

We can illustrate a shift in supply for the automobile market. Supply would increase if the introduction of cost-saving computerized design and manufacturing reduced the labor required to produce cars, if autoworkers took a pay cut, if there were lower production costs in Japan, or if the government repealed environmental regulations on the industry. Any of these elements would increase the supply of automobiles in the United States at each price. Figure 3-6 illustrates an increase in the supply of automobiles.

To test your understanding of supply shifts, think about the following: What would happen to the world supply curve for oil if a revolution in Saudi Arabia led to declining oil production? What would happen to the supply curve for clothing if tariffs were slapped on Chinese imports into the United States? What happens to the supply curve for computers if Intel introduces a new computer chip that dramatically increases computing speeds?

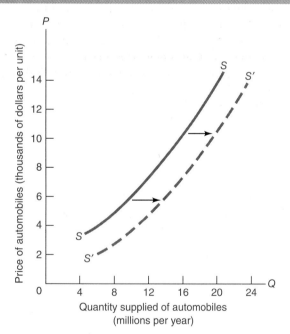

FIGURE 3-6. Increased Supply of Automobiles

As production costs fall, the supply of automobiles increases. At each price, producers will supply more automobiles, and the supply curve therefore shifts to the right. (What would happen to the supply curve if Congress were to put a restrictive quota on automobile imports?)

> **Reminder on shifts of curves versus movements along curves**
>
> As you answer the questions above, make sure to keep in mind the difference between moving along a curve and a shift of the curve. Look back at the gasoline-price curve in Figure 3-1 on page 47. When the price of oil rose and the production of oil declined because of political disturbances in the 1970s, these changes resulted from an inward shift in the supply curve. When sales of gasoline declined in response to the higher price, that was a movement along the demand curve.
>
> Does the history of computer prices and quantities shown in Figure 3-3 on page 50 look more like shifting supply or shifting demand? (Question 8 at the end of this chapter explores this issue further.)
>
> How would you describe a rise in chicken production that was induced by a rise in chicken prices? What about the case of a rise in chicken production because of a fall in the price of chicken feed?

EQUILIBRIUM OF SUPPLY AND DEMAND

C. EQUILIBRIUM OF SUPPLY AND DEMAND

Up to this point we have been considering demand and supply in isolation. We know the amounts that are willingly bought and sold at each price. We have seen that consumers demand different amounts of cornflakes, cars, and computers as a function of these goods' prices. Similarly, producers willingly supply different amounts of these and other goods depending on their prices. But how can we put both sides of the market together?

The answer is that supply and demand interact to produce an equilibrium price and quantity, or a market equilibrium. The **market equilibrium** comes at that price and quantity where the forces of supply and demand are in balance. At the equilibrium price, the amount that buyers want to buy is just equal to the amount that sellers want to sell. The reason we call this an equilibrium is that, when the forces of supply and demand are in balance, there is no reason for price to rise or fall, as long as other things remain unchanged.

Let us work through the cornflakes example in Table 3-5 to see how supply and demand determine a market equilibrium; the numbers in this table come from Tables 3-1 and 3-3. To find the market price and quantity, we find a price at which the amounts desired to be bought and sold just match. If we try

a price of $5 per box, will it prevail for long? Clearly not. As row A in Table 3-5 shows, at $5 producers would like to sell 18 million boxes per year while demanders want to buy only 9. The amount supplied at $5 exceeds the amount demanded, and stocks of cornflakes pile up in supermarkets. Because too few consumers are chasing too many cornflakes, the price of cornflakes will tend to fall, as shown in column (5) of Table 3-5.

Say we try $2. Does that price clear the market? A quick look at row D shows that at $2 consumption exceeds production. Cornflakes begin to disappear from the stores at that price. As people scramble around to find their desired cornflakes, they will tend to bid up the price of cornflakes, as shown in column (5) of Table 3-5.

We could try other prices, but we can easily see that the equilibrium price is $3, or row C in Table 3-5. At $3, consumers' desired demand exactly equals producers' desired production, each of which is 12 units. Only at $3 will consumers and suppliers both be making consistent decisions.

A **market equilibrium** comes at the price at which quantity demanded equals quantity supplied. At that equilibrium, there is no tendency for the price to rise or fall. The equilibrium price is also called the **market-clearing price.** This denotes that all supply and demand orders are filled, the books are "cleared" of orders, and demanders and suppliers are satisfied.

	(1) Possible price ($ per box)	(2) Quantity demanded (millions of boxes per year)	(3) Quantity supplied (millions of boxes per year)	(4) State of market	(5) Pressure on price
		Combining Demand and Supply for Cornflakes			
A	5	9	18	Surplus	↓Downward
B	4	10	16	Surplus	↓Downward
C	3	12	12	Equilibrium	Neutral
D	2	15	7	Shortage	↑Upward
E	1	20	0	Shortage	↑Upward

TABLE 3-5. Equilibrium Price Comes Where Quantity Demanded Equals Quantity Supplied

The table shows the quantities supplied and demanded at different prices. Only at the equilibrium price of $3 per box does amount supplied equal amount demanded. At too low a price there is a shortage and price tends to rise. Too high a price produces a surplus, which will depress the price.

EQUILIBRIUM WITH SUPPLY AND DEMAND CURVES

We often show the market equilibrium through a supply-and-demand diagram like the one in Figure 3-7; this figure combines the supply curve from Figure 3-5 with the demand curve from Figure 3-2. Combining the two graphs is possible because they are drawn with exactly the same units on each axis.

We find the market equilibrium by looking for the price at which quantity demanded equals quantity supplied. *The equilibrium price comes at the intersection of the supply and demand curves, at point* C.

How do we know that the intersection of the supply and demand curves is the market equilibrium? Let us repeat our earlier experiment. Start with the initial high price of $5 per box, shown at the top of the price axis in Figure 3-7. At that price, suppliers

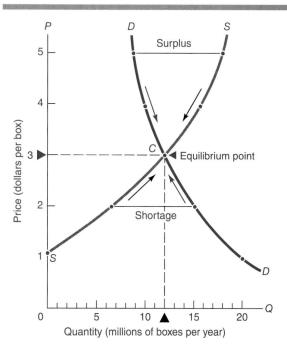

FIGURE 3-7. Market Equilibrium Comes at the Intersection of Supply and Demand Curves

The market equilibrium price and quantity come at the intersection of the supply and demand curves. At a price of $3, at point C, firms willingly supply what consumers willingly demand. When the price is too low (say, at $2), quantity demanded exceeds quantity supplied, shortages occur, and the price is driven up to equilibrium. What occurs at a price of $4?

want to sell more than demanders want to buy. The result is a *surplus,* or excess of quantity supplied over quantity demanded, shown in the figure by the black line labeled "Surplus." The arrows along the curves show the direction that price tends to move when a market is in surplus.

At a low price of $2 per box, the market shows a *shortage,* or excess of quantity demanded over quantity supplied, here shown by the black line labeled "Shortage." Under conditions of shortage, the competition among buyers for limited goods causes the price to rise, as shown in the figure by the arrows pointing upward.

We now see that the balance or equilibrium of supply and demand comes at point C, where the supply and demand curves intersect. At point C, where the price is $3 per box and the quantity is 12 units, the quantities demanded and supplied are equal: there are no shortages or surpluses; there is no tendency for price to rise or fall. At point C and only at point C, the forces of supply and demand are in balance and the price has settled at a sustainable level.

The equilibrium price and quantity come where the amount willingly supplied equals the amount willingly demanded. In a competitive market, this equilibrium is found at the intersection of the supply and demand curves. There are no shortages or surpluses at the equilibrium price.

Effect of a Shift in Supply or Demand

The analysis of the supply-and-demand apparatus can do much more than tell us about the equilibrium price and quantity. It can also be used to predict the impact of changes in economic conditions on prices and quantities. Let's change our example to the staff of life, bread. Suppose that a spell of bad weather raises the price of wheat, a key ingredient of bread. That shifts the supply curve for bread to the left. This is illustrated in Figure 3-8 (*a*), where the bread supply curve has shifted from SS to S'S'. In contrast, the demand curve has not shifted because people's sandwich demand is largely unaffected by farming weather.

What happens in the bread market? The bad harvest causes bakers to produce less bread at the old price, so quantity demanded exceeds quantity supplied. The price of bread therefore rises, encouraging production and thereby raising quantity

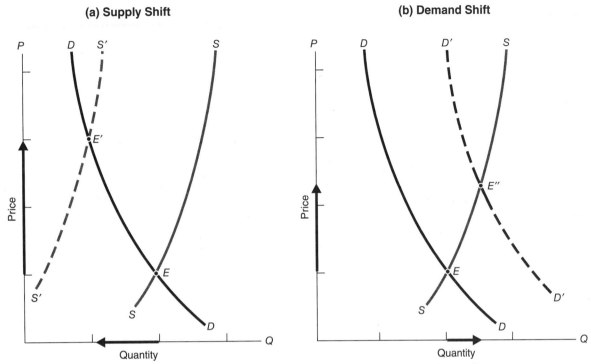

FIGURE 3-8. Shifts in Supply or Demand Change Equilibrium Price and Quantity

(a) If supply shifts leftward, a shortage will develop at the original price. Price will be bid up until quantities willingly bought and sold are equal, at new equilibrium E'. **(b)** A shift in the demand curve leads to excess demand. Price will be bid up as equilibrium price and quantity move upward to E''.

supplied, while simultaneously discouraging consumption and lowering quantity demanded. The price continues to rise until, at the new equilibrium price, the amounts demanded and supplied are once again equal.

As Figure 3-8 (*a*) shows, the new equilibrium is found at E', the intersection of the new supply curve $S'S'$ and the original demand curve. Thus a bad harvest (or any leftward shift of the supply curve) raises prices and, by the law of downward-sloping demand, lowers quantity demanded.

Suppose that new baking technologies lower costs and therefore increase supply. That means the supply curve shifts down and to the right. Draw in a new $S''S''$ curve, along with the new equilibrium E'''. Why is the equilibrium price lower? Why is the equilibrium quantity higher?

We can also use our supply-and-demand apparatus to examine how changes in demand affect the market equilibrium. Suppose that there is a sharp in-

crease in family incomes, so everyone wants to eat more bread. This is represented in Figure 3-8 (*b*) as a "demand shift" in which, at every price, consumers demand a higher quantity of bread. The demand curve thus shifts *rightward* from DD to $D'D'$.

The demand shift produces a shortage of bread at the old price. A scramble for bread ensues, with long lines in the bakeries. Prices are bid upward until supply and demand come back into balance at a higher price. Graphically, the increase in demand has changed the market equilibrium from E to E'' in Figure 3-8 (*b*).

For both examples of shifts—a shift in supply and a shift in demand—a variable underlying the demand or supply curve has changed. In the case of supply, there might have been a change in technology or input prices. For the demand shift, one of the influences affecting consumer demand—incomes, population, the prices of related goods, or tastes—changed and thereby shifted the demand schedule (see Table 3-6).

	Demand and supply shifts	Effect on price and quantity
If demand rises . . .	The demand curve shifts to the right, and . . .	Price ↑ Quantity ↑
If demand falls . . .	The demand curve shifts to the left, and . . .	Price ↓ Quantity ↓
If supply rises . . .	The supply curve shifts to the right, and . . .	Price ↓ Quantity ↑
If supply falls . . .	The supply curve shifts to the left, and . . .	Price ↑ Quantity ↓

TABLE 3-6. The Effect on Price and Quantity of Different Demand and Supply Shifts

When the elements underlying demand or supply change, this leads to shifts in demand or supply and to changes in the market equilibrium of price and quantity.

Interpreting Changes in Price and Quantity

Let's go back to our bread example. Suppose that you go to the store and see that the price of bread has doubled. Does the increase in price mean that the demand for bread has risen, or does it mean that bread has become more expensive to produce? The correct answer is that without more information, you don't know—it could be either one, or even both. Let's look at another example. If fewer airline tickets are sold, is the cause that airline fares have gone up or that demand for air travel has gone down? Airlines will be most interested in the answer to this question.

Economists deal with these sorts of questions all the time: When prices or quantities change in a market, does the situation reflect a change on the supply side or the demand side? Sometimes, in simple situations, looking at price and quantity simultaneously gives you a clue about whether it's the supply curve that's shifted or the demand curve. For example, a rise in the price of bread accompanied by a *decrease* in quantity suggests that the supply curve has shifted to the left (a decrease in supply). A rise in price accompanied by an *increase* in quantity indicates that the demand curve for bread has probably shifted to the right (an increase in demand).

This point is illustrated in Figure 3-9. In both panel (*a*) and panel (*b*), quantity goes up. But in (*a*) the price rises, and in (*b*) the price falls. Figure 3-9

(*a*) shows the case of an increase in demand, or a shift in the demand curve. As a result of the shift, the equilibrium quantity demanded increases from 10 to 15 units. The case of a movement along the demand curve is shown in Figure 3-9 (*b*). In this case, a supply shift changes the market equilibrium from point *E* to point *E″*. As a result, the quantity demanded changes from 10 to 15 units. But demand does not change in this case; rather, quantity demanded increases as consumers move along their demand curve from *E* to *E″* in response to a price change.

The elusive concept of equilibrium

The notion of equilibrium is one of the most elusive concepts of economics. We are familiar with equilibrium in our everyday lives from seeing, for example, an orange sitting at the bottom of a bowl or a pendulum at rest. In economics, equilibrium means that the different forces operating on a market are in balance, so the resulting price and quantity reconcile the desires of purchasers and suppliers. Too low a price means that the forces are not in balance, that the forces attracting demand are greater than the forces attracting supply, so there is excess demand, or a shortage. We also know that a competitive market is a mechanism for producing equilibrium. If the price is too low, demanders will bid up the price to the equilibrium level.

The notion of equilibrium is tricky, however, as is seen by the statement of a leading pundit: "Don't lecture me about supply and demand equilibrium. The supply of oil is always equal to the demand for oil. You simply can't tell the difference." The pundit is right in an accounting sense.

Clearly the oil sales recorded by the oil producers should be exactly equal to the oil purchases recorded by the oil consumers. But this bit of arithmetic cannot repeal the laws of supply and demand. More important, if we fail to understand the nature of economic equilibrium, we cannot hope to understand the way that different forces affect the marketplace.

In economics, we are interested in knowing the quantity of sales that will clear the market, that is, the equilibrium quantity. We also want to know the price at which consumers willingly buy what producers willingly sell. Only at this price will both buyers and sellers be satisfied with their decisions. Only at this price and quantity will there be no tendency for price and quantity to change. Only by looking at the equilibrium of supply and demand can we hope to understand such paradoxes as the fact that im-

migration may not lower wages in the affected cities, that land taxes do not raise rents, and that bad harvests raise (yes, raise!) the incomes of farmers.

Supply, Demand, and Immigration

A fascinating and important example of supply and demand, full of complexities, is the role of immigration in determining wages. If you ask people, they are likely to tell you that immigration into California or Florida surely lowers the wages of people in those regions. It's just supply and demand. They might point to Figure 3-10 (a), which shows a supply-and-demand analysis of immigration. According to this analysis, immigration into a region shifts the supply curve for labor to the right and pushes down wages.

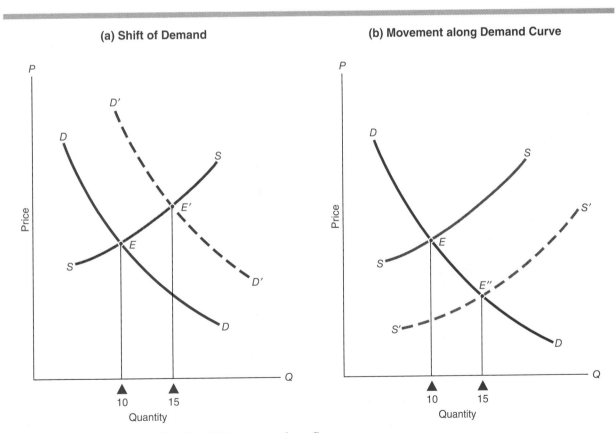

FIGURE 3-9. Shifts of and Movements along Curves

Start out with initial equilibrium at E and a quantity of 10 units. In **(a)**, an increase in demand (i.e., a shift of the demand curve) produces a new equilibrium of 15 units at E'. In **(b)**, a shift in supply results in a movement along the demand curve from E to E''.

(a) Immigration Alone

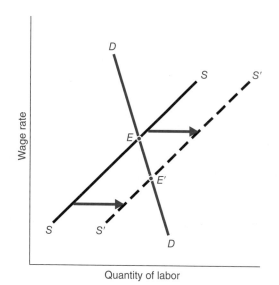

(b) Immigration to Growing Cities

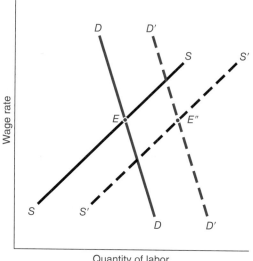

FIGURE 3-10. Impact of Immigration on Wages

In (**a**), new immigrants cause the supply curve for labor to shift from *SS* to *S'S'*, lowering equilibrium wages. But more often, immigrants go to cities with growing labor markets. Then, as shown in (**b**), the wage changes are small if the supply increase comes in labor markets with growing demand.

Careful economic studies cast doubt on this simple reasoning. A recent survey of the evidence concludes:

> [The] effect of immigration on the labor market outcomes of natives is small. There is no evidence of economically significant reductions in native employment. Most empirical analysis . . . finds that a 10 percent increase in the fraction of immigrants in the population reduces native wages by at most 1 percent.[2]

How can we explain the small impact of immigration on wages? Labor economists emphasize the high geographic mobility of the American population. This means that new immigrants will quickly spread around the entire country. Once they arrive, immigrants may move to cities where they can get jobs—workers tend to move to those cities where the demand for labor is already rising because of a strong local economy.

This point is illustrated in Figure 3-10 (*b*), where a shift in labor supply to *S'* is associated with a higher demand curve, *D'*. The new equilibrium wage at *E″* is the same as the original wage at *E*. Another factor is that native-born residents may move out when immigrants move in, so the total supply of labor is unchanged. This would leave the supply curve for labor in its original position and leave the wage unchanged.

Immigration is a good example for demonstrating the power of the simple tools of supply and demand.

RATIONING BY PRICES

Let us now take stock of what the market mechanism accomplishes. By determining the equilibrium prices and quantities, the market allocates or rations out the scarce goods of the society among the possible uses. Who does the rationing? A planning board? Congress? The President? No. The marketplace, through the interaction of supply and demand, does the rationing. This is *rationing by the purse.*

────────────

[2] Rachel M. Friedberg and Jennifer Hunt, "The Impact of Immigrants on Host Country Wages, Employment, and Growth," *Journal of Economic Perspectives*, Spring 1995, pp. 23–44.

What goods are produced? This is answered by the signals of the market prices. High oil prices stimulate oil production, whereas low food prices drive productive resources out of agriculture. Those who have the most dollar votes have the greatest influence on what goods are produced.

For whom are goods produced? The power of the purse dictates the distribution of income and consumption. Those with higher incomes end up with larger houses, more clothing, and longer vacations. When backed up by cash, the most urgently felt needs get fulfilled through the demand curve.

Even the *how* question is decided by supply and demand. When corn prices are low, it is not prof-itable for farmers to use expensive tractors and irrigation systems. When oil prices are high, oil companies drill in deep offshore waters and employ novel seismic techniques to find oil.

With this introduction to supply and demand, we begin to see how desires for goods, as expressed through demands, interact with costs of goods, as reflected in supplies. Further study will deepen our understanding of these concepts and will show how these tools can be applied to other important areas. But even this first survey will serve as an indispensable tool for interpreting the economic world in which we live.

SUMMARY

1. The analysis of supply and demand shows how a market mechanism solves the three problems of *what, how,* and *for whom.* A market blends together demands and supplies. Demand comes from consumers who are spreading their dollar votes among available goods and services while businesses supply the goods and services with the goal of maximizing their profits.

A. The Demand Schedule

2. A demand schedule shows the relationship between the quantity demanded and the price of a commodity, other things held constant. Such a demand schedule, depicted graphically by a demand curve, holds constant other things like family incomes, tastes, and the prices of other goods. Almost all commodities obey the *law of downward-sloping demand,* which holds that quantity demanded falls as a good's price rises. This law is represented by a downward-sloping demand curve.

3. Many influences lie behind the demand schedule for the market as a whole: average family incomes, population, the prices of related goods, tastes, and special influences. When these influences change, the demand curve will shift.

B. The Supply Schedule

4. The supply schedule (or supply curve) gives the relationship between the quantity of a good that producers desire to sell—other things constant—and that good's price. Quantity supplied generally responds positively to price, so the supply curve is upward-sloping.

5. Elements other than the good's price affect its supply. The most important influence is the commodity's production cost, determined by the state of technology and by input prices. Other elements in supply include the prices of related goods, government policies, and special influences.

C. Equilibrium of Supply and Demand

6. The equilibrium of supply and demand in a competitive market occurs when the forces of supply and demand are in balance. The equilibrium price is the price at which the quantity demanded just equals the quantity supplied. Graphically, we find the equilibrium at the intersection of the supply and demand curves. At a price above the equilibrium, producers want to supply more than consumers want to buy, which results in a surplus of goods and exerts downward pressure on price. Similarly, too low a price generates a shortage, and buyers will therefore tend to bid price upward to the equilibrium.

7. Shifts in the supply and demand curves change the equilibrium price and quantity. An increase in demand, which shifts the demand curve to the right, will increase both equilibrium price and quantity. An increase in supply, which shifts the supply curve to the right, will decrease price and increase quantity demanded.

8. To use supply-and-demand analysis correctly, we must (*a*) distinguish a change in demand or supply (which produces a shift in a curve) from a change in the quantity demanded or supplied (which represents a movement along a curve); (*b*) hold other things constant, which requires distinguishing the impact of a change in a commodity's price from the impact of changes in other influences; and (*c*) look always for the supply-and-demand equilibrium, which comes at the point where forces acting on price and quantity are in balance.

9. Competitively determined prices ration the limited supply of goods among those who demand them.

CONCEPTS FOR REVIEW

supply-and-demand analysis
demand schedule or curve, *DD*
law of downward-sloping demand
influences affecting demand curve

supply schedule or curve, *SS*
influences affecting supply curve
equilibrium price and quantity

shifts in supply and demand curves
all other things held constant
rationing by prices

FURTHER READING AND INTERNET WEBSITES

Further Reading

Supply and demand analysis is the single most important and useful tool in microeconomics. Supply and demand analysis was developed by the great British economist, Alfred Marshall, in *Principles of Economics* (9th edition, New York, Macmillan, [1890] 1961). To reinforce your understanding, you might look in textbooks on intermediate microeconomics. Two good references are Hal Varian, *Intermediate Microeconomics* (Norton, New York, 5th edition, 1999) and Walter Nicholson, *Intermediate Microeconomics* (7th edition, 1997, Dryden).

A recent survey of the economic issues in immigration is in George Borjas, *Heaven's Door: Immigration Policy and the American Economy* (Princeton University Press, Princeton, NJ, 1999).

Websites

You can examine a recent study of the impact of immigration on American society from the National Academy of Sciences, *The New Americans* (1997), at www.nap.edu. This site provides free access to over 1000 studies from economics and the other social and natural sciences.

An entertaining site is called "The Dismal Economist" at www.dismal.com. You can look here to see if there are any recent stories on "supply and demand." Another site with much entertaining and useful information is www.economics.miningco.com/finance/economics/.

QUESTIONS FOR DISCUSSION

1. **a.** Define carefully what is meant by a demand schedule or curve. State the law of downward-sloping demand. Illustrate the law of downward-sloping demand with two cases from your own experience.

   b. Define the concept of a supply schedule or curve. Show that an increase in supply means a rightward and downward shift of the supply curve. Contrast this with the rightward and upward shift in the demand curve implied by an increase in demand.

2. What might increase the demand for hamburgers? What would increase the supply? What would inexpensive frozen pizzas do to the market equilibrium for hamburgers? To the wages of teenagers who work at McDonald's?

3. Explain why the price in competitive markets settles down at the equilibrium intersection of supply and demand. Explain what happens if the market price starts out too high or too low.

4. Explain why each of the following is *false:*

   a. A freeze in Brazil's coffee-growing region will lower the price of coffee.

   b. "Protecting" American textile manufacturers from Chinese clothing imports will lower clothing prices in the United States.

   c. The rapid increase in college tuitions will lower the demand for college.

   d. The war against drugs, with increased interdiction of imported cocaine, will lower the price of domestically produced marijuana.

5. The following are four laws of supply and demand. Fill in the blanks. Demonstrate each law with a supply-and-demand diagram.

   a. An increase in demand generally raises price and raises quantity demanded.

   b. A decrease in demand generally _____ price and _____ quantity demanded.

   c. An increase in supply generally lowers price and raises quantity demanded.

ꜜ

d. A decrease in supply generally _____ price and _____ quantity demanded.

6. For each of the following, explain whether quantity demanded changes because of a demand shift or a price change, and draw a diagram to illustrate your answer:
   a. As a result of decreased military spending, the price of Army boots falls.
   b. Fish prices fall after the pope allows Catholics to eat meat on Friday.
   c. An increase in gasoline taxes lowers the consumption of gasoline.
   d. After the Black Death struck Europe in the fourteenth century, wages rose.

7. Examine the graph for the price of gasoline in Figure 3-1, page 47. Then, using a supply-and-demand diagram, illustrate the impact of each of the following on price and quantity demanded:
   a. Improvements in transportation lower the costs of importing oil into the United States in the 1960s.
   b. After the 1973 war, oil producers cut oil production sharply.
   c. After 1980, smaller automobiles get more miles per gallon.
   d. A record-breaking cold winter in 1995–1996 unexpectedly raises the demand for heating oil.
   e. A global economic recovery in 1999–2000 led to a sharp upturn in oil prices.

8. Examine Figure 3-3 on page 50. Does the price-quantity relationship look more like a supply curve or a de-

mand curve. Assuming that the demand curve was unchanged over this period, trace supply curves for 1972 and 2000 that would have generated the (P, Q) pairs for those years. Explain what forces might have led to the shift in the supply curve.

9. From the following data, plot the supply and demand curves and determine the equilibrium price and quantity:

	Supply and Demand for Pizzas	
Price ($ per pizza)	Quantity demanded (pizzas per semester)	Quantity supplied (pizzas per semester)
10	0	40
8	10	30
6	20	20
4	30	10
2	40	0
0	125	0

What would happen if the demand for pizzas tripled at each price? What would occur if the price were initially set at $4 per pizza?

PART TWO

Macroeconomics: The Study of Economic Growth and Business Cycles

CHAPTER

4

Overview of Macroeconomics

The whole purpose of the economy is production of goods or services for consumption now or in the future. I think the burden of proof should always be on those who would produce less rather than more, on those who would leave idle people or machines or land that could be used. It is amazing how many reasons can be found to justify such waste: fear of inflation, balance-of-payments deficits, unbalanced budgets, excessive national debt, loss of confidence in the dollar.

James Tobin,
National Economic Policy

Are jobs easy to find or few and hard to land? Are real wages and living standards growing rapidly, or is the economy stagnating or even depressed? Is the central bank raising interest rates to keep price increases in check, or loosening money to pull the economy out of a recession, or keeping a neutral stance of watchful waiting? How are the forces of globalization and foreign trade affecting domestic employment and output? These questions are central to macroeconomics, which is the subject of the following chapters.

Before we launch into our survey, recall that **macroeconomics** is the study of the behavior of the economy as a whole. It examines the forces that affect many firms, consumers, and workers at the same time. It contrasts with **microeconomics,** which studies individual prices, quantities, and markets.

Two central themes will run through our survey of macroeconomics: (1) the short-term fluctuations in output, employment, and prices that we call the *business cycle* and (2) the longer-term trends in output and living standards known as *economic growth.*

The development of macroeconomics has been one of the major breakthroughs of twentieth-century economics, leading to a much better understanding of how to combat periodic economic crises and how to stimulate long-term economic growth. In response to the Great Depression, John Maynard Keynes developed his revolutionary theory, which helped explain the forces producing economic fluctuations and suggested how governments can control the worst excesses of the business cycle. At the same time, economists have endeavored to understand the mechanics of long-term economic growth. Thanks to Keynes, his critics, and his modern successors, we know that in its choice of macroeconomic policies—those affecting the money supply, taxes, and government spending—a nation can speed or slow its economic growth, trim the excesses of price inflation or unemployment from business cycles, or take measures to deal with imbalances that arise in foreign trade or international finance.

Macroeconomic issues have dominated the U.S. political and economic agenda for much of the twentieth century. In the 1930s, when production, employment, and prices collapsed in the United States and across much of the industrial world, economists and political leaders wrestled with the calamity of the Great Depression. During World War II, and again during the Vietnam war in the 1960s, the problem was one of managing a sustained boom and containing high inflation. In the 1970s the burning issue was "stagflation," a combination of slow growth and rising prices that left Americans feeling miserable.

The 1990s witnessed a period of rapid growth, falling unemployment, and stable prices—a period so unusual that it was called the "new era" economics.

Sometimes, macroeconomic failures raise life-and-death questions for countries and even for ideologies. The communist leaders of the former Soviet Union proclaimed that they would overtake the West economically. History proved that to be a hollow promise, as Russia, a country teeming with natural resources and military might, was unable to produce adequate butter for its citizens along with the guns for its imperial armies. Eventually, macroeconomic failures brought down the communist regimes of the Soviet Union and Eastern Europe and convinced people of the economic superiority of private markets as the best approach to encouraging rapid economic growth.

This chapter will serve as an introduction to macroeconomics. It presents the major concepts and shows how they apply to key historical and policy questions of recent years. But this introduction is only a first course to whet the appetite. Not until you have mastered all the chapters in Parts Five and Six can you fully enjoy the rich macroeconomic banquet that has been a source of both inspiration for economic policy and continued controversy among macroeconomists.

✳
A. KEY CONCEPTS OF MACROECONOMICS

THE BIRTH OF MACROECONOMICS

The 1930s marked the first stirrings of the science of macroeconomics, founded by John Maynard Keynes as he tried to understand the economic mechanism that produced the Great Depression. After World War II, reflecting both the increasing influence of Keynesian views and the fear of another depression, the U.S. Congress formally proclaimed federal responsibility for macroeconomic performance. It enacted the landmark Employment Act of 1946, which stated:

> The Congress hereby declares that it is the continuing policy and responsibility of the federal government to use all practicable means consistent with its

needs and obligations...to promote maximum employment, production, and purchasing power.

For the first time, Congress affirmed the government's role in promoting output growth, fostering employment, and maintaining price stability.

Since the 1946 Employment Act, the nation's priorities among these three goals have shifted; but in the United States, as in all market economies, these goals still frame the central macroeconomic questions:

1. *Why do output and employment sometimes fall, and how can unemployment be reduced?* All market economies show patterns of expansion and contraction known as *business cycles.* The last major business-cycle downturn in the United States came in 1990–1991, when production of goods and services fell and millions of people lost their jobs. For much of the postwar period, one key goal of macroeconomic policy has been to use monetary and fiscal policy to reduce the severity of business-cycle downturns and unemployment.

   From time to time countries experience high unemployment that persists for long periods, sometimes as long as a decade. Such a period occurred in the United States during the Great Depression, which began in 1929. In the next few years, unemployment rose to almost one-quarter of the workforce, while industrial production fell by one-half. European countries in the 1990s had a mild depression, with persistent unemployment of over 10 percent in many countries.

   Macroeconomics examines the sources of persistent unemployment. Having considered the possible diagnoses, macroeconomics also suggests possible remedies, such as increasing aggregate demand or reforming labor market institutions. The lives and fortunes of millions of people depend upon whether macroeconomists can find the right answers to these questions.

2. *What are the sources of price inflation, and how can it be kept under control?* A market economy uses prices as a yardstick to measure economic values and conduct business. During periods of rapidly rising prices, called *price inflation,* the price yardstick loses its value. People become confused, make mistakes, and spend much of their time worrying about inflation eating away at their incomes. Rapid price changes lead to economic inefficiency.

Macroeconomic policy has increasingly emphasized price stability as a key goal. In the United States the overall rate of inflation has fallen from more than 10 percent per year in the late 1970s to around 3 percent per year in the 1990s. Some countries today have not succeeded in containing inflation, however. Formerly socialist countries like Russia and many Latin American and developing countries experienced inflation rates of 50, 100, or 1000 percent per year in the 1980s and early 1990s. Why was the United States able to keep the inflationary tiger in the cage, while Russia failed to do so? Macroeconomics can suggest the proper role of monetary and fiscal policies, of exchange-rate systems, and of an independent central bank in containing inflation.

3. *How can a nation increase its rate of economic growth?* Above all, macroeconomics is concerned with economic growth, which refers to the growth in the productive potential of an economy. An economy's productive potential is the central factor in determining the growth in its real wages and living standards. After World War II, rapid economic growth in Asian countries such as Japan, South Korea, and Taiwan produced dramatic gains in living standards for their peoples. A few countries, particularly those of sub-Saharan Africa, have suffered declining per capita output and living standards over the last two decades. Nations want to know the ingredients in a successful growth recipe. Among the key factors in rapid economic growth are the predominance of free markets, high rates of saving and investment, an outwardly oriented trade policy, and an honest government with strong property rights.

All economies face inevitable trade-offs among these goals. Increasing the rate of growth of output over the long run may require greater investment in education and capital, but higher investment requires lower current consumption of items like food, clothing, and recreation. Additionally, policymakers are sometimes forced to rein in the economy through macroeconomic policies when it grows too fast, or when unemployment falls too low, in order to prevent rising inflation.

There are no simple formulas for resolving these dilemmas, and macroeconomists often differ on the proper approach to take when confronted with high inflation, rising unemployment, or slow growth. But with sound macroeconomic understanding, the inevitable pain that comes from choosing the best route can be minimized.

The patron saint of macroeconomics

Every discussion of macroeconomic policy must begin with John Maynard Keynes. Keynes (1883–1946) was a many-sided genius who won eminence in the fields of mathematics, philosophy, and literature. In addition, he found time to run a large insurance company, advise the British treasury, help govern the Bank of England, edit a world-famous economics journal, collect modern art and rare books, start a repertory theater, and marry a leading Russian ballerina. He was also an investor who knew how to make money by shrewd speculation, both for himself and for his college, King's College, Cambridge.

His principal contribution, however, was his invention of a new way of looking at macroeconomics and macroeconomic policy. Before Keynes, most economists and policymakers accepted the highs and lows of business cycles as being as inevitable as the tides. These long-held views left them helpless in the face of the Great Depression of the 1930s. But Keynes took an enormous intellectual leap in his 1936 book, *The General Theory of Employment, Interest, and Money.* He made a twofold argument: First, he argued that it is possible for high unemployment and underutilized capacity to persist in market economies. In addition, he argued that government fiscal and monetary policies can affect output and thereby reduce unemployment and shorten economic downturns.

These propositions had an explosive impact when Keynes first introduced them, engendering much controversy and dispute. In the postwar period, Keynesian economics came to dominate macroeconomics and government policy. During the 1960s, virtually every analysis of macroeconomic policy was grounded in the Keynesian view of the world. Since then, new developments incorporating supply factors, expectations, and alternative views of wage and price dynamics have undermined the earlier Keynesian consensus. While few economists now believe that government action can eliminate business cycles, as Keynesian economics once seemed to promise, neither economics nor economic policy has been the same since Keynes's great discovery.

OBJECTIVES AND INSTRUMENTS OF MACROECONOMICS

Having surveyed the principal issues of macroeconomics, we now turn to a discussion of the major goals and instruments of macroeconomic policy. How do economists evaluate the success of an economy's overall performance? What are the tools that governments can use to pursue their economic goals? Table 4-1 lists the major objectives and instruments of macroeconomic policy.

Measuring Economic Success

The major macroeconomic goals are a high level and rapid growth of output, low unemployment, and stable prices. We will use this section both to define the major macroeconomic terms and to discuss their importance. A more detailed treatment of the data of macroeconomics is postponed to the next chapter. Some key data are provided in the appendix to this chapter.

Output. The ultimate objective of economic activity is to provide the goods and services that the population desires. What could be more important for an economy than to produce ample shelter, food, education, and recreation for its people?

The most comprehensive measure of the total output in an economy is the **gross domestic product** (GDP). GDP is the measure of the market value of all final goods and services—beer, cars, rock concerts, donkey rides, health care, and so on—produced in a country during a year. There are two ways to measure GDP. *Nominal GDP* is measured in actual market prices. *Real GDP* is calculated in constant or invariant prices (where we measure the number of cars times the prices of cars in a given year such as 1996).

Real GDP is the most closely watched measure of output; it serves as the carefully monitored pulse of a nation's economy. Figure 4-1 shows the history of real GDP in the United States since 1929. Note the economic decline during the Great Depression of the 1930s, the boom during World War II, the recessions in 1975 and 1982, and the steady growth in the long expansion from 1992 to 2000.

Despite the short-term fluctuations seen in business cycles, advanced economies generally exhibit a steady long-term growth in real GDP and an improvement in living standards; this process is known as *economic growth*. The American economy has proved itself a powerful engine of progress over a period of more than a century, as shown by the growth in potential output.

Potential GDP represents the maximum amount the economy can produce while maintaining price stability. Potential output is also sometimes called the *high-employment level of output*. When an economy is operating at its potential, unemployment is low and production is high.

Potential output is determined by the economy's productive capacity, which depends upon the inputs available (capital, labor, land, etc.) and the economy's technological efficiency. Potential GDP tends to grow slowly and steadily because inputs like labor

Objectives	Instruments
Output: High level and rapid growth of output	**Monetary policy:** Controlling the money supply to determine interest rates
Employment: High level of employment with low involuntary unemployment	**Fiscal policy:** Government expenditure Taxation
Price-level stability	

TABLE 4-1. Goals and Instruments of Macroeconomic Policy

The left-hand column displays the major goals of macroeconomic policy. The right-hand column contains the major instruments or policy measures available to modern economies. These are the ways that policymakers can affect the pace and direction of economic activity.

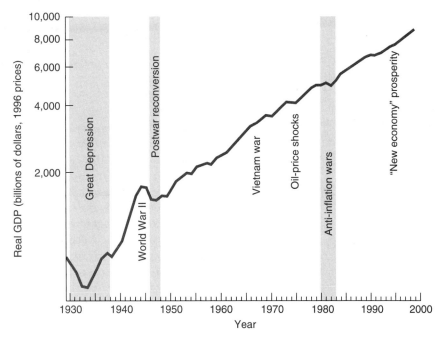

FIGURE 4-1. U.S. Real Gross Domestic Product, 1929–1999

Real GDP is the most comprehensive measure of an economy's output. Note how sharply output fell in the Great Depression of the 1930s. Except for the turmoil of the oil-price shocks of the 1970s and the anti-inflation policies of the early 1980s, economic growth has been steadier after World War II. (Source: U.S. Department of Commerce. Shaded regions are major economic downturns)

and capital and the level of technology change quite slowly over time. By contrast, actual GDP is subject to large business-cycle swings if spending patterns change sharply. Economic policies (like monetary and fiscal policy) can affect actual output quickly, but the impact of policies on potential output trends operates slowly over a number of years.

During business downturns, actual GDP is below its potential and unemployment rises. In 1982, for example, the U.S. economy produced more than $400 billion less than potential output. This represented $6000 lost per family during a single year. Economic downturns are called *recessions* when real output declines for a year or two. A severe and protracted downturn is called a *depression.* Output can be temporarily above potential output during booms and wartime as capacity limits are strained, but the high utilization rates bring rising inflation and are usually brought to an end by monetary or fiscal policy.

Figure 4-2 shows the estimated potential and actual output for the period 1930–1999. Note how large the gap between actual and potential output was during the Great Depression of the 1930s.

High Employment, Low Unemployment. Of all the macroeconomic indicators, employment and unemployment are most directly felt by individuals. People want to be able to get high-paying jobs without searching or waiting too long, and they want to have job security and good benefits. In macroeconomic terms, these are the objectives of *high employment,* which is the counterpart of *low unemployment.* Figure 4-3 shows trends in unemployment over the last six decades. The **unemployment rate** on the vertical axis is the percentage of the labor force that is unemployed. The labor force includes all employed persons and those unemployed individuals who are seeking jobs. It excludes those without work who are not looking for jobs.

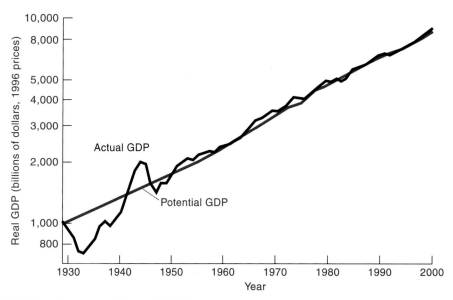

FIGURE 4-2. Actual and Potential GDP

Business cycles occur when actual output departs from its potential. The smooth blue line shows potential or trend output over the period 1929–1999. Potential output has grown about 3 percent annually. Note the large gap between actual and potential output during the Great Depression of the 1930s. (Source: U.S. Department of Commerce and authors' estimates. Note that actual GDP is directly estimated from underlying data while potential output is an analytical concept derived from actual GDP and unemployment data.)

The unemployment rate tends to reflect the state of the business cycle: when output is falling, the demand for labor falls and the unemployment rate rises. Unemployment reached epidemic proportions in the Great Depression of the 1930s, when as much as one-quarter of the workforce was idled. Since World War II, unemployment in the United States has fluctuated but has avoided the high rates associated with depressions and the low levels that would trigger great inflations.

Stable Prices. The third macroeconomic objective is to maintain *stable prices.* What exactly do economists look at when they talk about "the overall price level?" The most common price measure is the **consumer price index,** known as the CPI. The CPI measures the cost of a basket of goods (including items such as food, shelter, clothing, and medical care) bought by the average urban consumer. The overall price level is often denoted by the letter *P.*

The **rate of inflation** denotes the rate of growth or decline of the price level from one year to the next.[1] Figure 4-4 on page 74 illustrates the rate of inflation for the CPI from 1930 to 1999. Over this entire period, inflation averaged 3.3 percent per year. Note that price changes fluctuated greatly over the years, varying from minus 10 percent in 1932 to 14 percent in 1947.

A *deflation* occurs when prices decline (which means that the rate of inflation is negative). At the

---

[1] More precisely, the rate of inflation of the CPI is

$$\text{Rate of inflation of consumer prices (in percent)} = \frac{\text{CPI (this year)} - \text{CPI (last year)}}{\text{CPI (last year)}} \times 100$$

For example, if *P* in 1998 was 200 while *P* in 1999 was 206, the rate of inflation in 1999 would be calculated as

$$\text{Rate of inflation of consumer prices, 1999 (in percent)} = \frac{206 - 200}{200} \times 100 = 3\%$$

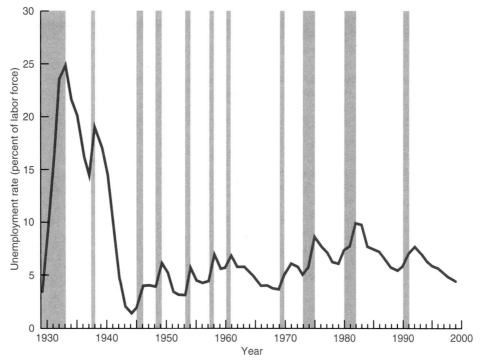

FIGURE 4-3. Unemployment Rises in Recessions, Falls during Expansions

The unemployment rate measures the fraction of the labor force that is looking for work but cannot find work. Unemployment reached tragic proportions during the 1930s, peaking at 25 percent in 1933. Unemployment rises in business-cycle downturns and falls during expansions. Shaded regions are NBER recessions. (Source: U.S. Department of Labor.)

other extreme is a *hyperinflation,* a rise in the price level of a thousand or a million percent a year. In such situations, as in Weimar Germany in the 1920s, Brazil in the 1980s, or Russia in the 1990s, prices are virtually meaningless and the price system breaks down.

Price stability is important because a smoothly functioning market system requires that prices accurately and easily convey information about relative scarcities. History has shown that high inflation imposes many costs—some visible and some hidden—on an economy. With high inflation, taxes become highly variable, the real values of people's pensions are eroded, and people spend real resources to avoid depreciating rubles or pesos. But declining prices or deflation is also costly. Hence, most nations seek the golden mean of stable or slowly rising prices as the best way of encouraging the price system to function efficiently.

To summarize:

The goals of macroeconomic policy are:

1. A high and growing level of national output
2. High employment with low unemployment
3. A stable or gently rising price level

The Tools of Macroeconomic Policy

Put yourself in the shoes of the chief economist advising the government. Unemployment is rising and GDP is falling. Or perhaps productivity growth has declined, and you wish to increase potential output growth. Or your country has a balance-of-payments crisis, with a large trade deficit and an attack on the currency. What policies will help reduce inflation or unemployment, speed economic growth, or correct a trade imbalance?

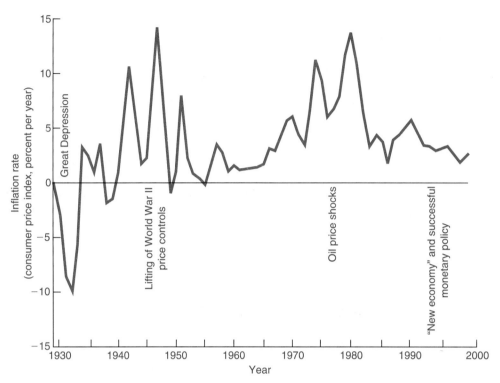

FIGURE 4-4. Consumer Price Inflation, 1929–1999

The rate of inflation measures the rate of change of prices from one year to the next; here we see the rate of inflation as measured by the consumer price index (CPI). Since World War II, prices have mainly moved upward, particularly after the oil shocks of 1973 and 1979. Since 1984, the United States has enjoyed low inflation. (Source: U.S. Department of Labor.)

Governments have certain instruments that they can use to affect macroeconomic activity. A *policy instrument* is an economic variable under the control of government that can affect one or more of the macroeconomic goals. By changing monetary, fiscal, and other policies, governments can avoid the worst excesses of the business cycle or increase the growth rate of potential output. The two major instruments of macroeconomic policy are listed on the right side of Table 4-1.

Fiscal Policy. **Fiscal policy** denotes the use of taxes and government expenditures. *Government expenditures* come in two distinct forms. First there are government purchases. These comprise spending on goods and services—purchases of tanks, construction of roads, salaries for judges, and so forth. In addition, there are government transfer payments, which boost the incomes of targeted groups such as the elderly or the unemployed. Government spending determines the relative size of the public and private sectors, that is, how much of our GDP is consumed collectively rather than privately. From a macroeconomic perspective, government expenditures also affect the overall level of spending in the economy and thereby influence the level of GDP.

The other part of fiscal policy, *taxation,* affects the overall economy in two ways. To begin with, taxes affect people's incomes. By leaving households with more or less disposable or spendable income, taxes tend to affect the amount people spend on goods and services as well as the amount of private saving. Private consumption and saving have important effects on investment and output in the short and long run.

In addition, taxes affect the prices of goods and factors of production and thereby affect incentives and behavior. For example, from 1962 until 1986, the United States employed an investment tax credit, which was a rebate to businesses that bought capital goods, as a way of stimulating investment and boosting economic growth. Many provisions of the tax code have an important impact on economic activity through their effect on the incentives to work and to save.

Monetary Policy. The second major instrument of macroeconomic policy is **monetary policy,** which the government conducts through managing the nation's money, credit, and banking system. You may have read how our central bank, the Federal Reserve System, operates to regulate the money supply. But what exactly is the money supply? **Money** consists of the means of exchange or method of payment. Today, people use currency and checking accounts to pay their bills. By engaging in central-bank operations, the Federal Reserve can regulate the amount of money available to the economy.

How does such a minor thing as the money supply have such a large impact on macroeconomic activity? By changing the money supply, the Federal Reserve can influence many financial and economic variables, such as interest rates, stock prices, housing prices, and foreign exchange rates. Restricting the money supply leads to higher interest rates and reduced investment, which, in turn, causes a decline in GDP and lower inflation. If the central bank is faced with a business downturn, it can increase the money supply and lower interest rates to stimulate economic activity.

The exact nature of monetary policy is one of the most important areas of macroeconomics. A policy of "tight money" in the United States raised interest rates, slowed economic growth, and raised unemployment in the period 1979–1982. Then, from 1982 until 2000, careful monetary management by the Federal Reserve supported the longest economic expansion in American history. Over the last decade, monetary policy has become the major weapon used by the U.S. government to fight the business cycle. Exactly how a central bank can control economic activity will be thoroughly analyzed in the chapters on monetary policy.

Other times, other policies

Countries often seek new ways to solve old economic problems. One problem that has produced many innovative ideas is controlling inflation. The standard approach to slowing inflation, as we will see, has been for governments to take monetary and fiscal steps to reduce output and raise unemployment. Because this is such unpleasant medicine, governments have often searched for other methods of controlling inflation. One experimental approach is called *incomes policies* and involves direct control over prices and wages. This approach is widely applied during wartime and sometimes in peacetime emergencies. Incomes policies have ranged from wage and price controls, used primarily in wartime, to less drastic measures like voluntary wage and price guidelines used in peacetime. A generation ago, many economists thought incomes policies might be an inexpensive way to reduce inflation. For example, the Nixon administration in 1971 imposed a draconian set of mandatory wage and price controls in the hope that they would slow inflation without producing a recession.

A review of incomes policies during the Nixon regime and similar periods generally finds that they had little durable impact in reducing inflation. Those experiences, along with a more conservative attitude toward government intervention, have led to a general disenchantment with direct wage-price policies. Many economists now believe that incomes policies are simply ineffective. Others think they are pernicious—interfering with free markets, gumming up relative price movements, and failing to reduce inflation. Most high-income countries no longer use incomes policies, but they are often employed by developing countries and countries making the transition to a market economy.

A nation has a wide variety of policy instruments that can be used to pursue its macroeconomic goals. The major ones are these:

1. Fiscal policy consists of government expenditure and taxation. Government expenditure influences the relative size of collective as opposed to private consumption. Taxation subtracts from incomes, reduces private spending, and affects private saving. In addition, it affects investment and potential output. Fiscal policy is primarily employed today to affect long-term economic

growth through its impact on national saving and on incentives to work and save.

2. Monetary policy, conducted by the central bank, determines the money supply. Changes in the money supply move interest rates up or down and affect spending in sectors such as business investment, housing, and net exports. Monetary policy has an important effect on both actual GDP and potential GDP.

INTERNATIONAL LINKAGES

No nation is an island unto itself. All nations participate in the world economy and are linked together through trade and finance. The trade linkages of imports and exports of goods and services are seen when the United States imports cars from Japan or exports computers to Mexico. Financial linkages come when the United States lends funds to Mexico to stabilize the Mexican peso or when British pension funds diversify their portfolios by investing in the booming U.S. stock market.

Nations keep a close watch on their foreign-trade flows. One particularly important index is **net exports,** which is the numerical difference between the value of exports and the value of imports. When exports exceed imports, the difference is a surplus, while a negative net-export balance is a deficit. Hence when its exports totaled $998 billion in 1999 while imports were $1252 billion, the United States had a foreign-trade deficit of $254 billion, or 2.7 percent of GDP.

As the costs of transportation and communication have declined, international linkages have become tighter than they were a generation ago. International trade has replaced empire building and military conquest as the surest road to national wealth and influence. Some economies today trade over half their output.

One of the major developments of the 1980s was the changing pattern of U.S. international trade. For most of this century, the United States had a surplus in its foreign trade, exporting more than it imported. But trading patterns changed dramatically in the 1980s. Because of changes in national saving and investment patterns, the U.S. net export position turned sharply toward deficit, reaching a peak of 3 percent of GDP in the late 1980s. As the deficits piled up, the United States by 1999 owed more than $1¹/₂ trillion to foreigners. Many people worry about the costs of paying back or servicing this debt.

As economies become more closely linked, policymakers devote increasing attention to international economic policy. International trade is not an end in itself. Rather, nations are properly concerned about international trade because trade serves the ultimate goal of improving living standards. The major areas of concern are trade policies and international financial management.

Trade policies consist of tariffs, quotas, and other regulations that restrict or encourage imports and exports. Most trade policies have little effect on macroeconomic performance, but from time to time, as was the case in the 1930s, restrictions on international trade are so severe that they cause major economic dislocations, inflations, or recessions.

A second set of policies is *international financial management.* A country's international trade is influenced by its foreign exchange rate, which represents the price of its own currency in terms of the currencies of other nations. As part of their monetary policies, nations adopt different systems to regulate their foreign exchange markets. Particularly in small open economies, managing the exchange rate is the single most important macroeconomic policy.

The international economy is an intricate web of trading and financial connections among countries. When the international economic system runs smoothly, it contributes to rapid economic growth; when trading systems break down, production and incomes suffer throughout the world. Countries therefore consider the impacts of trade policies and international financial policies on their domestic objectives of output, employment, and price stability.

B. AGGREGATE SUPPLY AND DEMAND

The economic history of nations can be seen in their macroeconomic performance. Economists have developed aggregate supply-and-demand analysis to help explain the major trends in output and prices. We begin by explaining this important tool of macroeconomics and then use it to understand some important historical events.

INSIDE THE MACROECONOMY: AGGREGATE SUPPLY AND DEMAND

Definitions of Aggregate Supply and Demand

How do different forces interact to determine overall economic activity? Figure 4-5 shows the relationships among the different variables inside the macroeconomy. It separates variables into two categories: those affecting aggregate supply and those affecting aggregate demand. Dividing variables into these two categories helps us understand what determines the levels of output, prices, and unemployment.

The lower part of Figure 4-5 shows the forces affecting aggregate supply. **Aggregate supply** refers to the total quantity of goods and services that the nation's businesses willingly produce and sell in a given period. Aggregate supply (often written *AS*) depends

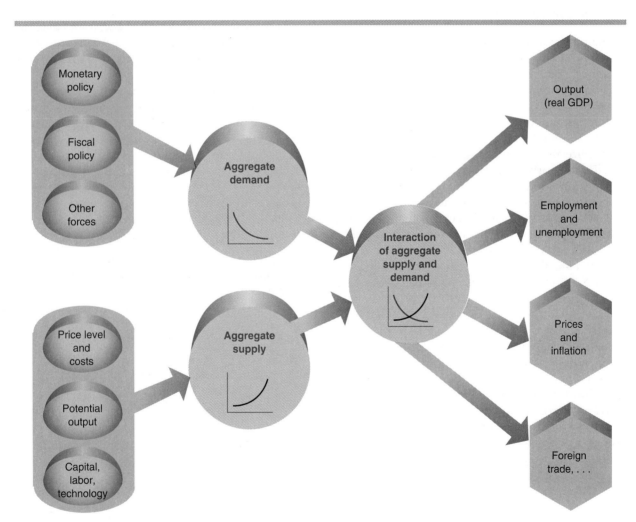

FIGURE 4-5. Aggregate Supply and Demand Determine the Major Macroeconomic Variables

This key diagram shows the major factors affecting overall economic activity. On the left are the major variables determining aggregate supply and demand; these include policy variables, like monetary and fiscal policies, along with stocks of capital and labor. In the center, aggregate supply and demand interact as the level of demand beats upon the available resources. The chief outcomes are shown on the right in hexagons: output, employment, the price level, and international trade.

upon the price level, the productive capacity of the economy, and the level of costs.

In general, businesses would like to sell everything they can produce at high prices. Under some circumstances, prices and spending levels may be depressed, so businesses might find they have excess capacity. Under other conditions, such as during a wartime boom, factories may be operating at capacity as businesses scramble to produce enough to meet all their orders.

We see, then, that aggregate supply depends on the price level that businesses can charge as well as on the economy's capacity or potential output. Potential output in turn is determined by the availability of productive inputs (labor and capital being the most important) and the managerial and technical efficiency with which those inputs are combined.

National output and the overall price level are determined by the twin blades of the scissors of aggregate supply and demand. The second blade is **aggregate demand,** which refers to the total amount that different sectors in the economy willingly spend in a given period. Aggregate demand (often written *AD*) is the sum of spending by consumers, businesses, and governments, and it depends on the level of prices, as well as on monetary policy, fiscal policy, and other factors.

The components of aggregate demand include the cars, food, and other consumption goods bought by consumers; the factories and equipment bought by businesses; the missiles and computers bought by government; and net exports. The total purchases are affected by the prices at which the goods are offered, by exogenous forces like wars and weather, and by government policies.

Using both blades of the scissors of aggregate supply and demand, we achieve the resulting equilibrium, as is shown in the right-hand circle of Figure 4-5. National output and the price level settle at that level where demanders willingly buy what businesses willingly sell. The resulting output and price level determine employment, unemployment, and international trade.

Aggregate Supply and Demand Curves

Aggregate supply and demand curves are often used to help analyze macroeconomic conditions. Recall that in Chapter 3 we used market supply and demand curves to analyze the prices and quantities of individual products. An analogous graphical apparatus

can also help us understand how monetary policy or technological change acts through aggregate supply and demand to determine national output and the price level.

Figure 4-6 shows the aggregate supply and demand schedules for the output of an entire economy. On the horizontal, or quantity, axis is the total output (real GDP) of the economy. On the vertical axis is the overall price level (say, as measured by the consumer price index). We use the symbol *Q* for real output and *P* for the price level.

The downward-sloping curve is the **aggregate demand schedule,** or *AD* curve. It represents what everyone in the economy—consumers, businesses, foreigners, and governments—would buy at different aggregate price levels (with other factors affecting aggregate demand held constant). From the curve, we see that at an overall price level of 150, total spending would be $3000 billion (per year). If the

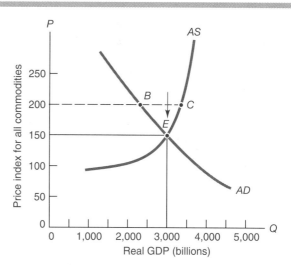

FIGURE 4-6. Aggregate Price and Output Are Determined by the Interaction of Aggregate Supply and Demand

The *AD* curve represents the quantity of total spending at different price levels, with other factors held constant. The *AS* curve shows what firms will produce and sell at different price levels, other things equal.

National output and the overall price level are determined at the intersection of the aggregate demand and supply curves, at point *E*. This equilibrium occurs at an overall price level where firms willingly produce and sell what consumers and other demanders willingly buy.

price level rises to 200, total spending would fall to $2300 billion.

The upward-sloping curve is the **aggregate supply schedule,** or *AS* curve. This curve represents the quantity of goods and services that businesses are willing to produce and sell at each price level (with other determinants of aggregate supply held constant). According to the curve, businesses will want to sell $3000 billion at a price level of 150; they will want to sell a higher quantity, $3300 billion, if prices rise to 200. As the level of total output demanded rises, businesses will want to sell more goods and services at a higher price level.

Warning on AS and AD curves

Before proceeding, here is one important word of caution: Do not confuse the macroeconomic *AD* and *AS* curves with the microeconomic *DD* and *SS* curves. The microeconomic supply and demand curves show the quantities and prices of individual commodities, with such things as national income and other goods' prices held as given. By contrast, the aggregate supply and demand curves show the determination of total output and the overall price level, with such things as the money supply, fiscal policy, and the capital stock held constant. Aggregate supply and demand explain how taxes affect national output and the movement of all prices; microeconomic supply and demand might consider the way increases in gasoline taxes affect purchases of automobiles. The two sets of curves have a superficial resemblance, but they explain very different phenomena.

Macroeconomic Equilibrium. We now see how aggregate output and the price level adjust or equilibrate to bring aggregate supply and aggregate demand into balance. That is, we use the *AS* and *AD* concepts to see how *equilibrium values of price and quantity* are determined or to find the *P* and *Q* that satisfy the buyers and sellers all taken together. For the *AS* and *AD* curves shown in Figure 4-6, the overall economy is in equilibrium at point *E*. Only at that point, where the level of output is *Q* = 3000 and *P* = 150, are spenders and sellers satisfied. Only at point *E* are demanders willing to buy exactly the amount that businesses are willing to produce and sell.

How does the economy reach its equilibrium? Indeed, what do we mean by equilibrium? A **macroeconomic equilibrium** is a combination of overall price and quantity at which all buyers and sellers are satisfied with their purchases, sales, and prices. Figure 4-6 illustrates the concept. If the price level were higher than equilibrium, say, at *P* = 200, businesses would want to sell more than purchasers would want to buy; businesses would desire to sell quantity *C*, while buyers would want to purchase only amount *B*. Goods would pile up on the shelves as firms produced more than consumers bought. Eventually, firms would cut production and begin to shave their prices. As the price level declined from its original too high level of 200, the gap between desired spending and desired sales would narrow until the equilibrium at *P* = 150 and *Q* = 3000 was reached. Once the equilibrium is reached, neither buyers nor sellers wish to change their quantities demanded or supplied, and there is no pressure on the price level to change.

MACROECONOMIC HISTORY: 1900–1999

We can use the aggregate supply-and-demand apparatus to analyze some of the major macroeconomic events of twentieth-century American history. We focus on the economic expansion during the Vietnam war, the stagflation caused by the supply shocks of the 1970s, the deep recession caused by the monetary contraction of the early 1980s, and the phenomenal record of economic growth for that century. For recent data on major macroeconomic variables, see this chapter's appendix.

Wartime Boom. The American economy entered the 1960s having experienced numerous recessions. John Kennedy took over the presidency hoping to resuscitate the economy. This was the era when the "New Economics," as the Keynesian approach was called, came to Washington. Economic advisers to Presidents Kennedy and Johnson recommended expansionary policies, and Congress enacted measures to stimulate the economy, including sharp cuts in personal and corporate taxes in 1963 and 1964. GDP grew 4 percent annually during the early 1960s, unemployment declined, and prices were stable. By 1965, the economy was at its potential output.

Unfortunately, the government underestimated the magnitude of the buildup for the Vietnam war; defense spending grew by 55 percent from 1965 to 1968. Even when it became clear that a major inflationary boom was under way, President Johnson postponed painful fiscal steps to slow the economy. Tax increases and civilian expenditure cuts came only in 1968, which was too late to prevent inflationary pressures from overheating the economy. The Federal Reserve accommodated the expansion with rapid money growth and low interest rates. As a result, the economy grew very rapidly over the period 1966–1970. Under the pressure of low unemployment and high factory utilization, inflation began to rise, inaugurating the "age of inflation" that lasted from 1966 through 1981.

Figure 4-7 illustrates the events of this period. The tax cuts and defense expenditures increased aggregate demand, shifting the aggregate demand curve to the right from *AD* to *AD′*, with the equilibrium shifting from *E* to *E′*. Output and employment rose sharply, and prices began to accelerate as output exceeded capacity limits. Economists learned that it was easier to stimulate the economy than to persuade policymakers to raise taxes to slow the economy when inflation threatened. This lesson led many to question the wisdom of using fiscal policies to stabilize the economy.

Supply Shocks and Stagflation. During the 1970s, the industrial world was struck by a new macroeconomic malady, supply shocks. A **supply shock** is a sudden change in input costs or productivity which shifts aggregate supply sharply. Supply shocks occurred with particular virulence in 1973. Called the "year of the seven plagues," 1973 was marked by crop failures, shifting ocean currents, massive speculation on world commodity markets, turmoil in foreign exchange markets, and a Mideast war that led to quadrupling of the world price of crude oil.

This jolt to crude-material and fuel supplies raised wholesale prices dramatically. The prices of crude materials and fuels rose more from 1972 to 1973 than they had in the entire period from the end of World War II to 1972. Shortly after the supply shock, inflation mounted sharply, and real output fell as the United States experienced a period of stagflation.

How can we understand the combination of falling output and rising prices? This large, unexpected rise in the cost of raw materials constituted a supply shock, which we portray as an upward shift in the aggregate supply curve. An upward shift in *AS* indicates that businesses will supply the same level of output only at substantially higher prices. Figure 4-8 illustrates such a supply shift.

Supply shocks produce higher prices, followed by a decline in output and an increase in unemployment. Supply shocks thus lead to a deterioration of all the major goals of macroeconomic policy.

Tight Money, 1979–1982. By 1979 the economy had recovered from the 1973 supply shock. Output had returned to its potential. But unrest in the Middle East led to another oil shock as the Iranian revolution produced a jump in oil prices from $14 per barrel in early 1978 to $34 per barrel in 1979. Inflation increased dramatically—averaging 12 percent per year from 1978 to 1980.

Double-digit inflation was unacceptable. In response, the Federal Reserve, under the leadership of

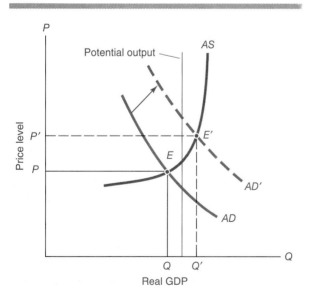

FIGURE 4-7. Wartime Boom Is Propelled by Increasing Aggregate Demand

During wartime, increased military spending increases aggregate spending, moving aggregate demand from *AD* to *AD′*, with equilibrium output increasing from *E* to *E′*. When output rises far above potential output, the price level moves up sharply from *P* to *P′*, and wartime inflation ensues.

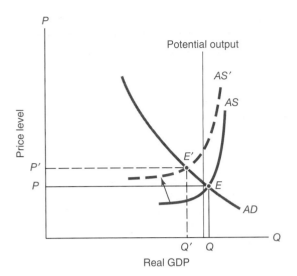

FIGURE 4-8. Effects of Supply Shocks

Sharply higher oil, commodity, or labor costs increase the costs of doing business. This leads to stagflation—stagnation combined with inflation. In the *AS-AD* framework, the higher costs shift the *AS* curve up from *AS* to *AS'*, and the equilibrium shifts from *E* to *E'*. Output declines from *Q* to *Q'*, while prices rise. The economy thus suffers a double whammy— lower output and higher prices. The opposite, favorable supply shocks, led to the "new era" economy of the 1990s.

economist Paul Volcker, prescribed the strong medicine of tight money to slow the inflation. Interest rates rose sharply in 1979 and 1980, the stock market fell, and credit was hard to find. The Fed's tight-money policy slowed spending by consumers and businesses. Particularly hard-hit were interest-sensitive components of aggregate demand. After 1979, housing construction, automobile purchases, business investment, and net exports declined sharply.

We can picture how tight money raised interest rates and reduced aggregate demand in Figure 4-7 simply by reversing the arrow. That is, tight monetary policy reduced spending and produced a leftward and downward shift of the aggregate demand curve—exactly the opposite of the effect of the defense buildup during the 1960s. The decrease in aggregate demand reduced output almost 10 percent below its potential by the end of 1982, and the unemployment rate rose from below 6 percent in 1979 to more than 10 percent at the end of 1982.

The reward for these austere measures was a dramatic decline in inflation, from an average of 12 per-

cent per year in the 1978–1980 period to 4 percent during the period from 1983 to 1988. Tight monetary policies succeeded in bringing to an end the age of inflation, but the nation paid for this achievement through higher unemployment and lower output during the period of tight money.

The tough monetary policies of the 1980s set the stage for the long economic expansion from 1982 through 2000. This period, marked by a single mild recession in 1990–1991, proved to be the period of the greatest macroeconomic stability in American history. Real GDP grew at an average rate of 3 percent annually, with price inflation averaging slightly above $3\frac{1}{2}$ percent. By the late 1990s, many of those in the workforce had never experienced a severe business cycle or inflationary episode, and some were proclaiming naively that the business cycle was abolished in this "new era" economy.

The Growth Century. The final act in our macroeconomic drama concerns the growth of output and prices over the entire period since 1900. Output has grown by a factor of almost 20 since the turn of the century. How can we explain this phenomenal increase?

A careful look at American economic growth reveals that the growth rate during this century has averaged $3\frac{1}{2}$ percent per year. Part of this growth was due to growth in the scale of production as inputs of capital, labor, and even land grew sharply over this period. Just as important were improvements in efficiency due to new products (such as automobiles) and new processes (such as electronic computing). Other, less visible factors also contributed to economic growth, such as improved management techniques and improved services (including such innovations as the assembly line and overnight delivery). Many economists believe that the measured growth understates true growth because our official statistics tend to miss the contribution to living standards from new products and improvements in product quality. For example, with the introduction of the indoor toilet, millions of people no longer had to struggle through the winter snows to relieve themselves in outhouses, yet this increased comfort never showed up in measured gross domestic product.

How can we picture the tremendous rise in output in our *AS - AD* apparatus? Figure 4-9 shows the

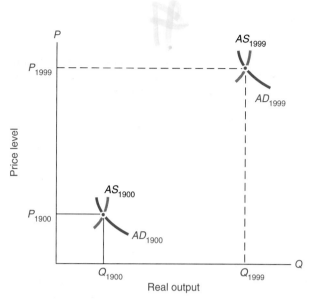

FIGURE 4-9. Growth in Potential Output Determines Long-Run Economic Performance

Over this century, increases in labor, capital, and efficiency have led to a vast increase in the economy's productive potential, shifting aggregate supply far to the right. In the long run, aggregate supply is the primary determinant of output growth.

way. The increase in inputs and improvements in efficiency led to a massive rightward shift of the *AS* curve from AS_{1900} to AS_{1999}. There was also a sharp increase in the cost of production, as average hourly

earnings rose from $0.10 per hour to $13.20 per hour, so the *AS* curve also shifted upward. The overall effect, then, was the increase in both output and prices shown in Figure 4-9.

The Role of Economic Policy

How does macroeconomic policy fit into the picture? Even though the economic environment in the United States was favorable in the 1990s, there were still heated debates about macroeconomic policies. A major debate in the United States surrounded the large projected budget surplus. Democrats wanted to devote the funds to social security and health care, in effect keeping the funds for federal programs. Republicans favored cutting taxes and expenditures and reducing the size of the federal government.

How can macroeconomics contribute to resolving this debate? Economists can provide no scientific answer on the correct use of the budget surplus because it involves *normative* issues of social and political values. But macroeconomists can analyze *positive* questions of macroeconomic impacts. Macroeconomists estimate the impact of cutting tax rates on tax revenues and the budget deficit; they attempt to determine the extent to which setting aside funds for future retirement programs will affect national saving and investment; and they help weigh the relative advantages of investing in people versus building new factories. While answers to these macroeconomic questions cannot resolve all the issues, the study of macroeconomics arms us for the great debate.

SUMMARY

A. Key Concepts of Macroeconomics

1. Macroeconomics is the study of the behavior of the entire economy: it analyzes long-run growth as well as the cyclical movements in total output, unemployment and inflation, the money supply and the budget deficit, and international trade and finance. This contrasts with microeconomics, which studies the behavior of individual markets, prices, and outputs.

2. The United States proclaimed its macroeconomic goals in the Employment Act of 1946, which declared that federal policy was "to promote maximum employment, production, and purchasing power." Since then, the nation's priorities among these three goals have shifted. But all market economies still face three central macro-

economic questions: (*a*) Why do output and employment sometimes fall, and how can unemployment be reduced? (*b*) What are the sources of price inflation, and how can it be kept under control? (*c*) How can a nation increase its rate of economic growth?

3. In addition to these perplexing questions is the hard fact that there are inevitable conflicts or trade-offs among these goals: rapid growth in future living standards may mean reducing consumption today, and curbing inflation may involve a temporary period of high unemployment.

4. Economists evaluate the success of an economy's overall performance by how well it attains these objectives: (*a*) high levels and rapid growth of output and con-

sumption [output is usually measured by the gross domestic product (GDP), which is the total value of all final goods and services produced in a given year; also, GDP should be close to potential GDP, the maximum sustainable or high-employment level of output]; (*b*) low unemployment rate and high employment, with an ample supply of good jobs; (*c*) price-level stability (or low inflation).

5. Before the science of macroeconomics was developed, countries tended to drift around in the shifting macroeconomic currents without a rudder. Today, there are numerous instruments with which governments can steer the economy: (*a*) Fiscal policy (government spending and taxation) helps determine the allocation of resources between private and collective goods, affects people's incomes and consumption, and provides incentives for investment and other economic decisions. (*b*) Monetary policy (particularly central-bank regulation of the money supply to influence interest rates and credit conditions) affects sectors in the economy that are interest-sensitive. The most affected sectors are housing, business investment, and net exports.

6. The nation is but a small part of an increasingly integrated global economy in which countries are linked together through trade of goods and services and through financial flows. A smoothly running international economic system contributes to rapid economic growth, but the international economy can throw sand in the engine of growth when trade flows are interrupted or the international financial mechanism breaks down. Dealing with international trade and finance is high on the agenda of all countries.

B. Aggregate Supply and Demand

7. The central concepts for understanding the determination of national output and the price level are aggregate supply (*AS*) and aggregate demand (*AD*). Aggregate demand consists of the total spending in an economy by households, businesses, governments, and foreigners. It represents the total output that would be willingly bought at each price level, given the monetary and fiscal policies and other factors affecting demand. Aggregate supply describes how much output businesses would willingly produce and sell given prices, costs, and market conditions.

8. *AS* and *AD* curves have the same shapes as the familiar supply and demand curves analyzed in microeconomics. The downward-sloping *AD* curve shows the amount that consumers, firms, and other purchasers would buy at each level of prices, with other factors held constant. The *AS* curve depicts the amount that businesses would willingly produce and sell at each price level, other things held constant. (But beware of potential confusions of microeconomic and aggregate supply and demand.)

9. The overall macroeconomic equilibrium, determining both aggregate price and output, comes where the *AS* and *AD* curves intersect. At the equilibrium price level, purchasers willingly buy what businesses willingly sell. Equilibrium output can depart from full employment or potential output.

10. Recent American history shows an irregular cycle of aggregate demand and supply shocks and policy reactions. In the mid-1960s, war-bloated deficits plus easy money led to a rapid increase in aggregate demand. The result was a sharp upturn in prices and inflation. In 1973 and again in 1979, adverse supply shocks led to an upward shift in aggregate supply. This led to stagflation, with a simultaneous rise in unemployment and inflation. At the end of the 1970s, economic policymakers reacted to the rising inflation by tightening monetary policy and raising interest rates. The result lowered spending on interest-sensitive demands such as housing, investment, and net exports. The period of austerity in the early 1980s ushered in a long period of macroeconomic stability.

11. Over the long run of the twentieth century, the growth of potential output has increased aggregate supply enormously and led to continual growth in output and living standards.

CONCEPTS FOR REVIEW

Major Macroeconomic Concepts

macroeconomics vs. microeconomics
gross domestic product (GDP),
   actual and potential
employment, unemployment, unemployment rate

inflation, deflation
consumer price index (CPI)
net exports
fiscal policy (government expenditures, taxation)
money, monetary policy

Aggregate Supply and Demand

aggregate supply, aggregate demand
AS curve, *AD* curve
equilibrium of *AS* and *AD*
sources of long-run economic growth
three macroeconomic shocks

FURTHER READING AND INTERNET WEBSITES

Further Reading

The great classic of macroeconomics is John Maynard Keynes, *The General Theory of Employment, Interest, and Money* (Harcourt, New York, first published in 1935). Keynes was one of the most graceful writers among economists.

For an advanced treatment of macroeconomic issues, consult a specialized intermediate textbook such as Rudiger Dornbusch, Stanley Fischer, and Richard Startz, *Macroeconomics*, 7th ed. (McGraw-Hill, New York, 1997), or Robert E. Hall and John B. Taylor, *Macroeconomics*, 5th ed. (Norton, New York, 1997).

A textbook presenting a classical point of view is Robert J. Barro, *Macroeconomics*, 5th ed. (MIT Press, Cambridge, Mass., 1997), and many of Barro's columns presenting a conservative viewpoint are reprinted in Robert J. Barro, *Getting It Right* (MIT Press, Cambridge, Mass., 1996).

Websites

Macroeconomic issues are a central theme of analysis in *Economic Report of the President* at w3.access.gpo. gov/eop.

QUESTIONS FOR DISCUSSION

1. What are the major objectives of macroeconomics? Write a brief definition of each of these objectives. Explain carefully why each objective is important.
2. Using the data from the appendix to this chapter, calculate the following:
   a. The inflation rate in 1981 and 1999
   b. The growth rate of real GDP in 1982 and 1984
   c. The average inflation rate from 1970 to 1980 and from 1990 to 1999
   d. The average growth rate of real GDP from 1970 to 1999
3. What would be the effect of each of the following on aggregate demand or on aggregate supply, as indicated (always holding other things constant)?
   a. A large oil-price increase (on *AS*)
   b. An arms-reduction agreement reducing defense spending (on *AD*)
   c. An increase in potential output (on *AS*)
   d. A monetary loosening that lowers interest rates (on *AD*)
4. For each of the events listed in question 3, use the *AS-AD* apparatus to show the effect on output and on the overall price level.
5. Put yourself in the shoes of an economic policymaker. The economy is in equilibrium with $P = 100$ and $Q = 3000 =$ potential GDP. You refuse to "accommodate" inflation; that is, you want to keep prices absolutely stable at $P = 100$, no matter what happens to output. You can use monetary and fiscal policies to affect aggre-

gate demand, but you cannot affect aggregate supply in the short run. How would you respond to:
   a. A surprise increase in investment spending
   b. A sharp food-price increase following catastrophic floods of the Mississippi River
   c. A productivity decline that reduces potential output
   d. A sharp decrease in net exports that followed a deep depression in East Asia
6. In 1981–1983, the Reagan administration implemented a fiscal policy that reduced taxes and increased government spending.
   a. Explain why this policy would tend to increase aggregate demand. Show the impact on output and prices assuming only an *AD* shift.
   b. The supply-side school holds that tax cuts would affect aggregate supply mainly by increasing potential output. Assuming that the Reagan fiscal measures affected *AS* as well as *AD*, show the impact on output and the price level. Explain why the impact of the Reagan fiscal policies on output is unambiguous while the impact on prices is unclear.
7. The Clinton economic package as passed by Congress in 1993 had the effect of tightening fiscal policy by raising taxes and lowering spending. Show the effect of this policy (*a*) assuming that there is no counteracting monetary policy and (*b*) assuming that monetary policy completely neutralized the impact on GDP and that the lower deficit leads to higher investment and higher growth of potential output.

8. The last major business downturn in the United States occurred in the early 1980s. Consider the data on real GDP and the price level in Table 4-2.
   a. For the years 1981 to 1985, calculate the rate of growth of real GDP and the rate of inflation. Can you determine in which year there was a steep business downturn or recession?
   b. In an *AS-AD* diagram like Figure 4-6 (page 78), draw a set of *AS* and *AD* curves that trace out the price and output equilibria shown in the table. How would you explain the recession that you have identified?

Year	Real GDP ($, billion, 1996 prices)	Price level* (1996 = 100)
1980	4,872	57.4
1981	4,994	62.7
1982	4,900	66.5
1983	5,106	69.2
1984	5,477	71.8
1985	5,690	74.0

*Note that the price index shown is the price index for GDP, which measures the price trend for all components of GDP. (Source: *Economic Report of the President*, 2000.)

TABLE 4-2.

Appendix 4

MACROECONOMIC DATA

Table 4A-1 contains some of the major macroeconomic data discussed in this chapter. Major data can be obtained through government websites at www. fedstats.gov or www.whitehouse.gov/fsbr/ esbr.html.

Year	Gross Domestic Product		Unemploy-ment rate %	CPI 1982–84 = 100	Inflation rate (CPI) (% per year)	Federal surplus (+) or deficit (−) ($, billion)	Net exports ($, billion)
	1996 prices ($, billion)	Current prices ($, billion)					
1929	822.2	103.7	3.2	17.1	na	na	0.3
1933	603.3	56.4	24.9	12.9	−5.1	na	0.1
1939	903.5	92.0	17.2	13.9	−1.4	na	0.8
1945	1693.3	223.0	1.9	18.0	2.3	na	−0.8
1948	1560.0	269.6	3.8	24.0	7.8	4.3	5.4
1960	2376.7	527.4	5.5	29.6	1.5	7.4	2.5
1961	2432.0	545.7	6.7	29.9	1.1	2.9	3.3
1962	2578.9	586.5	5.6	30.3	1.2	2.8	2.4
1963	2690.4	618.7	5.6	30.6	1.3	5.4	3.3
1964	2846.5	664.4	5.2	31.0	1.3	0.9	5.5
1965	3028.5	720.1	4.5	31.5	1.6	3.4	3.9
1966	3227.5	789.3	3.8	32.5	3.0	2.6	1.8
1967	3308.3	834.1	3.8	33.4	2.8	−8.3	1.5
1968	3466.1	911.5	3.6	34.8	4.2	−2.8	−1.3
1969	3571.4	985.3	3.5	36.7	5.4	8.7	−1.2
1970	3578.0	1039.7	5.0	38.8	5.9	−14.1	1.2
1971	3697.7	1128.6	6.0	40.5	4.2	−25.3	−3.0
1972	3898.4	1240.4	5.6	41.8	3.3	−20.6	−8.0
1973	4123.4	1385.5	4.9	44.4	6.3	−11.2	0.6
1974	4099.0	1501.0	5.6	49.3	11.0	−16.9	−3.2
1975	4084.4	1635.2	8.5	53.8	9.1	−73.9	13.6
1976	4311.7	1823.9	7.7	56.9	5.8	−57.2	−2.2
1977	4511.8	2031.4	7.1	60.6	6.5	−46.3	−23.6
1978	4760.6	2295.9	6.1	65.2	7.6	−31.7	−26.2
1979	4912.1	2566.4	5.9	72.6	11.3	−18.5	−24.0
1980	4900.9	2795.6	7.2	82.4	13.5	−61.0	−14.9
1981	5021.0	3131.3	7.6	90.9	10.4	−57.8	−15.0
1982	4919.3	3259.2	9.7	96.5	6.2	−134.7	−20.6
1983	5132.3	3534.9	9.6	99.6	3.2	−174.4	−51.6
1984	5505.2	3932.7	7.5	103.9	4.4	−156.0	−102.0
1985	5717.1	4213.0	7.2	107.6	3.5	−162.9	−114.2
1986	5912.4	4452.9	7.0	109.7	1.9	−177.5	−131.9
1987	6113.3	4742.5	6.2	113.7	3.7	−128.9	−142.3
1988	6368.4	5108.3	5.5	118.4	4.1	−121.3	−106.3
1989	6591.8	5489.1	5.3	124.0	4.8	−113.4	−80.7

Year	Gross Domestic Product		Unemploy-ment rate %	CPI 1982–84 = 100	Inflation rate (CPI) (% per year)	Federal surplus (+) or deficit (−) ($, billion)	Net exports ($, billion)
	1996 prices ($, billion)	Current prices ($, billion)					
1990	6707.9	5803.2	5.6	130.8	5.4	−154.6	−71.4
1991	6676.4	5986.2	6.9	136.3	4.2	−196.0	−20.7
1992	6880.0	6318.9	7.5	140.4	3.0	−280.9	−27.8
1993	7062.6	6642.3	6.9	144.6	3.0	−250.7	−60.5
1994	7347.7	7054.3	6.1	148.3	2.6	−186.7	−87.0
1995	7543.8	7400.5	5.6	152.5	2.8	−174.4	−84.2
1996	7813.2	7813.2	5.4	157.0	2.9	−110.3	−88.9
1997	8144.8	8300.8	5.0	160.6	2.3	−21.0	−88.3
1998	8495.7	8759.9	4.5	163.0	1.5	65.7	−149.6
1999	8848.2	9256.1	4.2	166.6	2.2	145.0	−253.9

TABLE 4A-1.

Source: U.S. Department of Commerce and Department of Labor.

Of all the concepts in macroeconomics, the single most important measure is the gross domestic product (GDP), which measures the total value of goods and services produced in a country. GDP is part of the *national income and product accounts* (or *national accounts*), which are a body of statistics that enable policymakers to determine whether the economy is contracting or expanding and whether a severe recession or inflation threatens. When economists want to determine the level of economic development of a country, they look at its GDP per capita.

While the GDP and the rest of the national accounts may seem to be arcane concepts, they are truly among the great inventions of the twentieth century. Much as a satellite in space can survey the weather across an entire continent, so can the GDP give an overall picture of the state of the economy. In this chapter, we explain how economists measure GDP and other major macroeconomic concepts.

CHAPTER

5

Measuring Economic Activity

When you can measure what you are speaking about, and express it in numbers, you know something about it; when you cannot measure it, when you cannot express it in numbers, your knowledge is of a meager and unsatisfactory kind; it may be the beginning of knowledge, but you have scarcely, in your thoughts, advanced to the stage of science.

Lord Kelvin

GROSS DOMESTIC PRODUCT: THE YARDSTICK OF AN ECONOMY'S PERFORMANCE

What is the *gross domestic product*? GDP is the name we give to the total market value of the final goods and services produced within a nation during a given year. It is the figure you get when you apply the measuring rod of money to the diverse goods and services—from apples to zithers—that a country produces with its land, labor, and capital resources. GDP equals the total production of consumption and investment goods, government purchases, and net exports to other lands.

The gross domestic product (GDP) is the most comprehensive measure of a nation's total output of goods and services. It is the sum of the dollar values of consumption (C), gross investment (I), government purchases of goods and services (G), and net exports (X) produced within a nation during a given year.

In symbols:

$$GDP = C + I + G + X$$

GDP is used for many purposes, but the most important one is to measure the overall performance of an economy. If you were to ask an economic historian what happened during the Great Depression, the best short answer would be:

Between 1929 and 1933, GDP fell from $104 billion to $56 billion. This sharp decline in the dollar value of goods and services produced by the American economy caused high unemployment, hardship, a steep stock market decline, bankruptcies, bank failures, riots, and political turmoil.

88

Similarly, if you were to ask what was unusual about the 1990s, a macroeconomist might reply:

> The 1990s were the longest economic expansion in the nation's history. From 1992 to 2000, real GDP grew steadily, increasing by 37 percent with falling unemployment, stable inflation, and rising stock-market prices.

We now discuss the elements of the national income and product accounts. We start by showing different ways of measuring GDP and distinguishing real from nominal GDP. We then analyze the major components of GDP. We conclude with a discussion of the measurement of the general price level and the rate of inflation.

Two Measures of National Product: Goods Flow and Earnings Flow

How do economists actually measure GDP? One of the major surprises is that we can measure GDP in two entirely independent ways. As Figure 5-1 shows, GDP can be measured either as a flow of products or as a sum of earnings.

To demonstrate the different ways of measuring GDP, we begin by considering an oversimplified

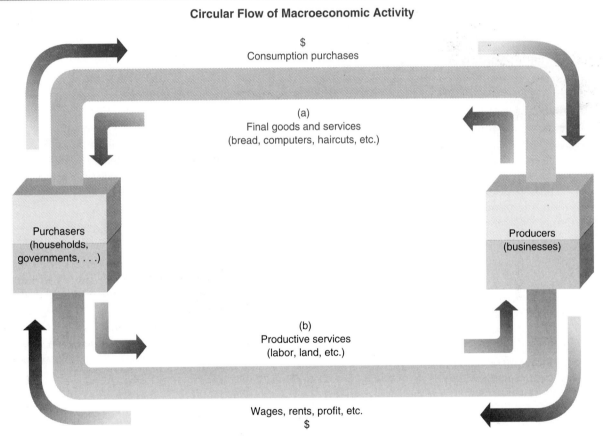

FIGURE 5-1. Gross Domestic Product Can Be Measured Either as (a) a Flow of Final Products or, Equivalently, as (b) a Flow of Costs

In the upper loop, purchasers buy final goods and services. The total dollar flow of their spending each year is one measure of gross domestic product. The lower loop measures the annual flow of costs of output: the earnings that businesses pay out in wages, rent, interest, dividends, and profits.

The two measures of GDP must always be identical. Note that this figure is the macroeconomic counterpart of Fig. 2-1, which presented the circular flow of supply and demand.

world in which there is no government, foreign trade, or investment. For the moment, our little economy produces only *consumption goods,* which are items that are purchased by households to satisfy their wants. (Important note: Our first example is oversimplified to show the basic ideas. In the realistic examples that follow, we will add investment, government, and the foreign sector.)

Flow-of-Product Approach. Each year the public consumes a wide variety of final goods and services: goods such as apples, computer software, and blue jeans; services such as health care and haircuts. We include only *final goods*—goods ultimately bought and used by consumers. Households spend their incomes for these consumer goods, as is shown in the upper loop of Figure 5-1. Add together all the consumption dollars spent on these final goods, and you will arrive at this simplified economy's total GDP.

Thus, in our simple economy, you can easily calculate national income or product as the sum of the annual flow of *final* goods and services: (price of blue jeans × number of blue jeans) plus (price of apples × number of apples) and so forth for all other final goods. The gross domestic product is defined as the total money value of the flow of final products produced by the nation.

National accountants use market prices as weights in valuing different commodities because market prices reflect the relative economic value of diverse goods and services. That is, the relative prices of different goods reflect how much consumers value their last (or marginal) units of consumption of these goods.

Earnings or Cost Approach. The second and equivalent way to calculate GDP is the earnings or cost approach. Go to the lower loop in Figure 5-1. Through it flow all the costs of doing business; these costs include the wages paid to labor, the rents paid to land, the profits paid to capital, and so forth. But these business costs are also the earnings that households receive from firms. By measuring the annual flow of these earnings or incomes, statisticians will again arrive at the GDP.

Hence, a second way to calculate GDP is as the total of factor earnings (wages, interest, rents, and profits) that are the costs of producing society's final products.

Equivalence of the Two Approaches. Now we have calculated GDP by the upper-loop flow-of-product

approach and by the lower-loop earnings-flow approach. Which is the better approach? The surprise is that *they are exactly the same.*

We can see why the product and earnings approaches are identical by examining a simple barbershop economy. Say the barbers have no expenses other than labor. If they sell 10 haircuts at $8 each, GDP is $80. But the barbers' earnings (in wages and profits) are also exactly $80. Hence, the GDP here is identical whether measured as flow of products ($80 of haircuts) or as cost and income ($80 of wages and profits).

In fact, the two approaches are identical because we have included "profit" in the lower loop along with other incomes. What exactly is profit? Profit is what remains from the sale of a product after you have paid the other factor costs—wages, interest, and rents. It is the residual that adjusts automatically to make the lower loop's costs or earnings exactly match the upper loop's value of goods.

To sum up:

GDP, or gross domestic product, can be measured in two different ways: (1) as the flow of final products, or (2) as the total costs or earnings of inputs producing output. Because profit is a residual, both approaches will yield exactly the same total GDP.

National Accounts Derived from Business Accounts

You might wonder where on earth economists find all the data for the national accounts. In practice, government economists draw on a wide array of sources, including surveys, income-tax returns, retail-sales statistics, and employment data.

The most important source of data is business accounts. An *account* for a firm or nation is a numerical record of all flows (outputs, costs, etc.) during a given period. We can show the relationship between business accounts and national accounts by constructing the accounts for an economy made up only of farms. The top half of Table 5-1 shows the results of a year's farming operations for a single, typical farm. We put sales of final products on the left-hand side and the various costs of production on the right. The bottom half of Table 5-1 shows how to construct the GDP accounts for our simple agrarian economy in which all final products are produced on 10 million identical farms. The national accounts simply add together or *aggregate* the outputs and costs of the

(a) Income Statement of Typical Farm

Output in Farming		Earnings	
Sales of goods (corn, apples, etc.)	**$1,000**	Costs of production:	
		Wages	$ 800
		Rents	100
		Interest	25
		Profit (residual)	75
Total	$1,000	Total	$1,000

(b) National Product Account (millions of dollars)

Upper-Loop Flow of Product		Lower-Loop Flow of Earnings	
Final output (10 × 1,000)	**$10,000**	Costs or earnings:	
		Wages (10 × 800)	$ 8,000
		Rents (10 × 100)	1,000
		Interest (10 × 25)	250
		Profit (10 × 75)	750
GDP Total	$10,000	GDP Total	$10,000

TABLE 5-1. Construction of National Product Accounts from Business Accounts

Part (**a**) shows the income statement of a typical farm. The left side shows the value of production, while the right side shows the farm's costs. Part (**b**) then adds up or aggregates the 10 million identical farms to obtain total GDP. Note that GDP from the product side exactly equals GDP from the earnings side.

10 million identical farms to get the two different measures of GDP.

The Problem of "Double Counting"

We defined GDP as the total production of final goods and services. A *final product* is one that is produced and sold for consumption or investment. GDP excludes *intermediate goods*—goods that are used up to produce other goods. GDP therefore includes bread but not wheat, and home computers but not computer chips.

For the flow-of-product calculation of GDP, excluding intermediate products poses no major complications. We simply include the bread and computers in GDP but avoid including the wheat and dough that went into the bread or the chips and plastic that went into the computers. If you look again at the upper loop in Figure 5-1, you will see that bread and computers appear in the flow of products, but you will not find any flour or computer chips.

What has happened to products like flour and computer chips? They are intermediate products and are simply cycling around inside the block marked "Producers." If they are not bought by consumers, they never show up as final products in GDP.

"Value Added" in the Lower Loop. A new statistician who is being trained to make GDP measurements might be puzzled, saying:

I can see that, if you are careful, your upper-loop product approach to GDP will avoid including intermediate products. But aren't you in some trouble when you use the lower-loop cost or earnings approach?

After all, when we gather income statements from the accounts of firms, won't we pick up what grain merchants pay to wheat farmers, what bakers pay to grain merchants, and what grocers pay to bakers? Won't this result in double counting or even triple counting of items going through several productive stages?

These are good questions, but there is an ingenious answer that resolves the problem. In making lower-loop earnings measurements, statisticians are very careful to include in GDP only a firm's value added. **Value added** is the difference between a firm's sales and its purchases of materials and services from other firms.

In other words, in calculating the GDP earnings or value added by a firm, the statistician includes all costs except for payments made to other businesses. Hence business costs in the form of wages, salaries, interest payments, and dividends are included in value added, but purchases of wheat or steel or electricity are excluded from value added. Why are all the purchases from other firms excluded from value added to obtain GDP? Because those purchases will get properly counted in GDP in the values added by other firms.

Table 5-2 uses the stages of bread production to illustrate how careful adherence to the value-added approach enables us to subtract purchases of intermediate goods that show up in the income statements of farmers, millers, bakers, and grocers. The final calculation shows the desired equality between (1) final sales of bread and (2) total earnings, calculated as the sum of all values added in all the different stages of bread production.

Value-added approach: To avoid double counting, we take care to include only final goods in GDP and to exclude the intermediate goods that are used up in making the final goods. By measuring the value added at each stage, taking care to subtract expenditures on the intermediate goods bought from other firms, the lower-loop earnings approach properly avoids all double counting and records wages, interest, rent, and profit exactly one time.

DETAILS OF THE NATIONAL ACCOUNTS

Now that we have an overview of the national income and product accounts, we will proceed, in the rest of this chapter, on a whirlwind tour of the various sectors. Before we start on the journey, look at Table 5-3 to get an idea of where we are going. This table shows a summary set of accounts for both the product and the income sides. If you know the structure

	Bread Receipts, Costs, and Value Added (cents per loaf)				
Stage of production	**(1)** **Sales receipts**	**(2)** *Less:* **Cost of intermediate products**			**(3)** **Value added (wages, profit, etc.)** **(3) = (1) − (2)**
Wheat	23	0	=		23
Flour	53	23	=		30
Baked dough	110	53	=		57
Final product: bread	190	110	=		80
Total	376	186			190 (sum of value added)

TABLE 5-2. GDP Sums Up Value Added at Each Production Stage

To avoid double counting of intermediate products, we calculate value added at each stage of production. This involves subtracting all the costs of materials and intermediate products bought from other businesses from total sales. Note that every black intermediate-product item both appears in column (1) and is subtracted in the next stage of production in column (2). (How much would we overestimate GDP if we counted all receipts, not just value added? The overestimate would be 186 cents per loaf.)

Product approach	Earnings approach
Components of gross domestic product:	**Earnings or costs as sources of gross domestic product:**
Consumption (*C*)	Wages, salaries, and other labor income
+ Gross private domestic investment (*I*)	+ Interest, rent, and other property income
+ Government purchases (*G*)	+ Indirect taxes
+ Net exports (*X*)	+ Depreciation
	+ Profits
Equals: Gross domestic product	**Equals: Gross domestic product**

TABLE 5-3. Overview of the National Income and Product Accounts

This table presents the major components of the two sides of the national accounts. The left side shows the components of the product approach (or upper loop); the symbols *C, I, G,* and *X* are often used to represent these four items of GDP. The right side shows the components of the earnings or cost approach (or lower loop). Each approach will ultimately add up to exactly the same GDP.

of the table and the definitions of the terms in it, you will be well on your way to understanding GDP and its family of components.

Real vs. Nominal GDP: "Deflating" GDP by a Price Index

We define GDP as the dollar value of goods and services. In measuring the dollar value, we use the measuring rod of *market prices* for the different goods and services. But prices change over time, as inflation generally sends prices upward year after year. Who would want to measure things with a rubber yardstick—one that stretches in your hands from day to day—rather than a rigid and invariant yardstick?

The problem of changing prices is one of the problems economists have to solve when they use money as their measuring rod. Clearly, we want a measure of the nation's output and income that uses an invariant yardstick. Economists can replace the elastic yardstick with a reliable one by removing the price-increase component so as to create a real or quantity index of national output.

Here is the basic idea: We can measure the GDP for a particular year using the actual market prices of that year; this gives us the **nominal GDP,** or GDP at current prices. But we are usually more interested in determining what has happened to the **real GDP,** which is an index of the volume or quantity of goods and services produced. We measure real GDP by mul-

tiplying the quantities of goods by an invariant or fixed set of prices. Hence, nominal GDP is calculated using changing prices while real GDP is calculated using constant prices.

When we divide nominal GDP by real GDP, we obtain the **GDP deflator,** which serves as a measure of the overall price level. We can calculate real GDP by dividing nominal GDP by the GDP deflator.

A simple example will illustrate the general idea. Say that a country produces 1000 bushels of corn in year 1 and 1010 bushels in year 2. The price of a bushel is $1 in year 1 and $2 in year 2. We can calculate nominal GDP (PQ) as $1 × 1000 = $1000 in year 1 and $2 × 1010 = $2020 in year 2. Nominal GDP therefore grew by 102 percent between the two years.

But the actual amount of output did not grow anywhere near that rapidly. To find real output, we need to consider what happened to prices. We use year 1 as the base year, or the year in which we measure prices. We set the price index, the GDP deflator, as $P_1 = 1$ in the first, or base, year. From the data in the previous paragraph, we see that the GDP deflator is $P_2 = \$2/\$1 = 2$ in year 2. Real GDP (Q) is equal to nominal GDP (PQ) divided by the GDP deflator (P). Hence real GDP was equal to $1000/1 = $1000 in year 1 and $2020/2 = $1010 in year 2. Thus the growth in real GDP, which corrects for the change in prices, is 1 percent and equals the growth in the output of corn, as it should.

Date	(1) Nominal GDP (current $, billion)	(2) Index number of prices (GDP deflator, 1929 = 1)	(3) Real GDP ($, billion, 1929 prices) $(3) = \dfrac{(1)}{(2)}$
1929	104	1.00	$\dfrac{104}{1.00} = 104$
1933	56	0.77	$\dfrac{56}{0.77} = 73$

TABLE 5-4. Real (or Inflation-Corrected) GDP Is Obtained by Dividing Nominal GDP by the GDP Deflator

Using the price index of column (2), we deflate column (1) to get real GDP, column (3). (Riddle: Can you show that 1929's real GDP was $80 billion in terms of 1933 prices? *Hint*: With 1933 as a base of 1, 1929's price index is 1.30.)

A 1929–1933 comparison will illustrate the deflation process for an actual historical episode. Table 5-4 gives nominal GDP figures of $104 billion for 1929 and $56 billion for 1933. This represents a 46 percent drop in nominal GDP from 1929 to 1933. But the government estimates that prices on average dropped about 23 percent over this period. If we choose 1929 as our base year, with the GDP deflator of 1 in that year, this means that the 1933 price index was about 0.77. So our $56 billion 1933 GDP was really worth much more than half the $104 billion GDP of 1929. Table 5-4 shows that real GDP fell to only seven-tenths of the 1929 level: in terms of 1929 prices, or dollars of 1929 purchasing power, real GDP fell to $73 billion. Hence, part of the near-halving shown by the nominal GDP was due to the rapidly declining price level, or deflation, during the Great Depression.

The black line in Figure 5-2 shows the growth of nominal GDP since 1929, expressed in the actual dollars and prices that were current in each historical year. Then, for comparison, the real GDP, expressed in 1996 dollars, is shown in blue. Clearly, much of the increase in nominal GDP over the last half-century is due to inflation in the price units of our money yardstick.

Table 5-4 shows the simplest way of calculating real GDP and the GDP deflator. Sometimes these calculations give misleading results, particularly when

the prices and quantities of important goods are changing rapidly. For example, over the last two decades, computer prices have been falling very sharply while the quantity of computers produced has risen rapidly (we return to this issue in our discussion of price indexes below).

When relative prices are changing sharply, using prices of a given year will give a misleading estimate of real GDP growth. To correct for this bias, statisticians use *chain weights*. Instead of keeping the relative weights on each good fixed (say, by using prices for a given year, like 1990), chain weights change each year to reflect the evolving spending patterns in the economy. Today, the official U.S. government measures of GDP and GDP price index rely upon chain weights. The technical names for these constructs are "real GDP in chained dollars" and the "chain-type price index for GDP."[1] For simplicity, we

---

[1] The process of chain weighting involves linking the output or price series together by multiplying the growth rates from one period to another. An example for a haircut economy will show how this works. Say that the value of the haircuts was $300 in 1998. Further suppose that the quantity of haircuts increased by 1 percent from 1998 to 1999 and by 2 percent from 1999 to 2000. Then the value of real GDP in 1998 prices would be $300 in 1998, $300 × 1.01 = $303 in 1999, and $303 × 1.02 = $309.06 in 2000. The same procedure would be used to construct the chain price index. With multiple outputs, we simply add together the outputs of the different components of apples, bananas, catamarans, etc.

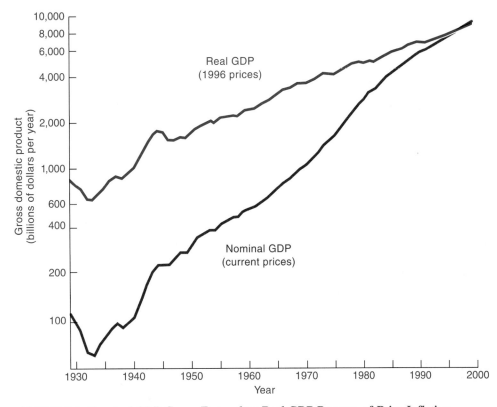

FIGURE 5-2. Nominal GDP Grows Faster than Real GDP Because of Price Inflation

The rise in nominal GDP exaggerates the rise in output. Why? Because growth in nominal GDP includes increases in prices as well as growth in output. To obtain an accurate measure of real output, we must correct GDP for price changes. (Source: U.S. Department of Commerce.)

generally refer to real GDP and the GDP deflator, whose movements track the chain indexes very closely.

To summarize:

Nominal GDP (PQ) represents the total money value of final goods and services produced in a given year, where the values are expressed in terms of the market prices of each year. Real GDP (Q) removes price changes from nominal GDP and calculates GDP in constant prices. The traditional GDP deflator (P) is the "price of GDP" and is defined as follows:

$$Q = \text{real GDP} = \frac{\text{nominal GDP}}{\text{GDP deflator}} = \frac{PQ}{P}$$

To correct for rapidly changing relative prices, the U.S. national accounts use chain weights to construct real GDP and price indexes.

Consumption

The first important part of GDP is consumption, or "personal consumption expenditures." Consumption is by far the largest component of GDP, equaling about two-thirds of the total in recent years. Figure 5-3 shows the fraction of GDP devoted to consumption over the last six decades. Consumption expenditures are divided into three categories: durable goods such as automobiles, nondurable goods such as food, and services such as medical care. The most rapidly growing sector is services.

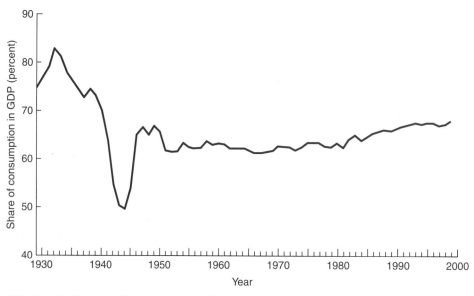

FIGURE 5-3. Share of Consumption in National Output Has Risen Recently

The share of consumption in total GDP rose during the Great Depression as investment prospects soured, then shrank sharply during World War II when the war effort displaced civilian needs. In the last two decades, consumption has grown more rapidly than total output as the national savings rate and government purchases have declined. (Source: U.S. Department of Commerce.)

Investment and Capital Formation

So far, our analysis has banished all capital. In real life, however, nations devote part of their output to production of capital—durable goods that increase future production. Increasing capital requires the sacrifice of current consumption to increase future consumption. Instead of eating more pizza now, people build new pizza ovens to make it possible to produce more pizza for future consumption.

In the accounts, **investment** consists of the additions to the nation's capital stock of buildings, equipment, software, and inventories during a year. The national accounts include mainly tangible capital (such as buildings and computers) but omit most intangible capital (such as research and development or educational expenses).

> **Real investment versus financial investment**
>
> Economists define "investment" (or sometimes *real investment*) as production of durable capital goods. In common usage, "investment" often denotes using money to buy General Motors stock or to open a savings account. For clarity, economists call this *financial investment.* Try not to confuse these two different uses of the word "investment."
>
> If I take $1000 from my safe and buy some Internet stocks, this is not what macroeconomists call investment. I have simply exchanged one financial asset for another. Investment takes place when a physical capital good is produced.

How does investment fit into the national accounts? If people are using part of society's production possibilities for capital formation rather than for consumption, economic statisticians recognize that such outputs must be included in the upper-loop flow of GDP. Investments represent additions to the stock of durable capital goods that increase production possibilities in the future. So we must modify our original definition to read:

Gross domestic product is the sum of all final products. Along with consumption goods and services, we must also include gross investment.

Net vs. Gross Investment. Our revised definition includes "gross investment" along with consumption. What does the word "gross" mean in this context? It indicates that investment includes all investment goods produced. Gross investment is not adjusted for **depreciation,** which measures the amount of capital that has been used up in a year. Thus gross investment includes all the machines, factories, and houses built during a year—even though some were produced simply to replace some old capital goods that burned down or were thrown on the scrap heap.

If you want to get a measure of the increase in society's capital, gross investment is not a sensible measure. Because it excludes a necessary allowance for depreciation, it is too large—too gross.

An analogy to population will make clear the importance of considering depreciation. If you want to measure the increase in the size of the population, you cannot simply count the number of births, for this would clearly exaggerate the net change in population. To get population growth, you must also subtract the number of deaths.

The same point holds for capital. To find the net increase in capital, you must start with gross investment and subtract the deaths of capital in the form of depreciation, or the amount of capital used up.

Thus to estimate capital formation we measure *net investment.* Net investment is always births of capital (gross investment) less deaths of capital (capital depreciation):

Net investment equals gross investment minus depreciation.

Government

Up to now we have talked about consumers but ignored the biggest buyers of all—federal, state, and local governments. Somehow GDP must take into account the billions of dollars of product a nation *collectively* consumes or invests. How do we do this?

Measuring government's contribution to national output is complicated because most government services are not sold on the marketplace. Rather, government purchases both consumption-type goods (like food for the military) and investment-type items (such as computers or roads). In measuring government's contribution to GDP, we simply add all these government purchases to the flow of consumption, investment, and, as we will see later, net exports.

Hence, all the government payroll expenditures on its employees plus the costs of goods it buys from private industry (lasers, roads, and airplanes) are included in this third category of flow of products, called "government consumption expenditures and gross investment." This category equals the contribution of federal, state, and local governments to GDP.

Exclusion of Transfer Payments. Does this mean that every dollar of government expenditure is included in GDP? Definitely not. GDP includes only government purchases of goods and services; it excludes spending on transfer payments.

Government **transfer payments** are government payments to individuals that are not made in exchange for goods or services supplied. Examples of government transfers include unemployment insurance, veterans' benefits, and old-age or disability payments. These payments meet important social purposes, but, since they are not purchases of current goods or services, they are omitted from GDP.

Thus if you receive a wage from the government because you are a teacher, your wage is a factor payment and would be included in GDP. If you receive a welfare payment because you are poor, that payment is not in return for a service but is a transfer payment and would be excluded from GDP.

One peculiar government transfer payment is the interest on the government debt. Interest is treated as a payment for debt incurred to pay for past wars or government programs and is not considered to be a purchase of a current good or service. Government interest payments are considered transfers and are therefore omitted from GDP.

Finally, do not confuse the way the national accounts measure government spending on goods and services (G) with the official government budget. When the Treasury measures its expenditures, it includes expenditures on goods and services (G) *plus* transfers.

Taxes. In using the flow-of-product approach to compute GDP, we need not worry about how the government finances its spending. It does not matter whether the government pays for its goods and services by taxing, by printing money, or by borrowing. Wherever the dollars come from, the statistician computes the governmental component of GDP as the actual cost to the government of the goods and services.

But while it is fine to ignore taxes in the flow-of-product approach, we must account for taxes in the earnings or cost approach to GDP. Consider wages, for example. Part of my wage is turned over to the government through personal income taxes. These direct taxes definitely do get included in the wage component of business expenses, and the same holds for direct taxes (personal or corporate) on interest, rent, and profit.

Or consider the sales tax and other indirect taxes that manufacturers and retailers have to pay on a loaf of bread (or on the wheat, flour, and dough stages). Suppose these indirect taxes total 10 cents per loaf, and suppose wages, profit, and other value-added items cost the bread industry 90 cents. What will the bread sell for in the product approach? For 90 cents? Surely not. The bread will sell for $1, equal to 90 cents of factor costs plus 10 cents of indirect taxes.

Thus the cost approach to GDP includes both indirect and direct taxes as elements of the cost of producing final output.

Net Exports

The United States is an open economy engaged in importing and exporting goods and services. The last component of GDP—and an increasingly important one in recent years—is **net exports,** the difference between exports and imports of goods and services.

How do we draw the line between our GDP and other countries' GDPs? The U.S. GDP represents all goods and services produced within the boundaries of the United States. Production differs from sales in the United States in two respects. First, some of our production (Iowa wheat and Boeing aircraft) is bought by foreigners and shipped abroad, and these items constitute our *exports*. Second, some of what we consume (Mexican oil and Japanese cars) is produced abroad and shipped to the United States, and such items are American *imports*.

A Numerical Example. We can use a simple farming economy to understand how the national accounts work. Suppose that Agrovia produces 100 bushels of corn and 7 bushels are imported. Of these, 87 bushels are consumed (in C), 10 go for government purchases to feed the army (as G), and 6 go into domestic investment as increases in inventories (I). In addition, 4 bushels are exported, so net exports (X) are $4 - 7$, or minus 3.

What, then, is the composition of the GDP of Agrovia? It is the following:

$$\text{GDP} = 87 \text{ of } C + 10 \text{ of } G + 6 \text{ of } I - 3 \text{ of } X$$
$$= 100 \text{ bushels}$$

Gross Domestic Product, Net Domestic Product, and Gross National Product

Although GDP is the most widely used measure of national output in the United States, two other concepts are frequently cited: net domestic product and gross national product.

Recall that GDP includes *gross* investment, which is net investment plus depreciation. A little thought

---

1. **GDP from the product side is the sum of four major components**:
   - Personal consumption expenditure on goods and services (C)
   - Gross private domestic investment (I)
   - Government consumption expenditures and gross investment (G)
   - Net exports of goods and services (X), or exports minus imports
2. **GDP from the cost side is the sum of the following major components**:
   - Wages and salaries, interest, rents, and profit (always with the careful exclusion, by the value-added technique, of double counting of intermediate goods bought from other firms)
   - Indirect business taxes that show up as an expense of producing the flow of products
   - Depreciation
3. **The product and cost measures of GDP are identical** (by adherence to the rules of value-added bookkeeping and the definition of profit as a residual).
4. **Net domestic product (NDP) equals GDP minus depreciation.**

TABLE 5-5. Key Concepts of the National Income and Product Accounts

suggests that including depreciation is rather like including wheat as well as bread. A better measure would include only *net* investment in total output. By subtracting depreciation from GDP we obtain **net domestic product** (NDP). If NDP is a sounder measure of a nation's output than GDP, why do national accountants focus on GDP? They do so because depreciation is somewhat difficult to estimate, whereas gross investment can be estimated fairly accurately.

An alternative measure of national output, widely used until recently, is **gross national product** (GNP). What is the difference between GNP and GDP? GNP is the total output produced with labor or capital *owned* by U.S. residents, while GDP is the output produced with labor and capital *located inside* the United States. For example, some of the U.S. GDP is produced in Honda plants that are owned by Japanese corporations. The profits from these plants are included in U.S. GDP but not in U.S. GNP because Honda is a Japanese company. Similarly, when an American economist flies to Japan to give a paid lecture on baseball economics, payment for that lecture would be included in Japanese GDP and in American GNP. For the United States, GDP is very close to GNP, but these may differ substantially for very open economies.

To summarize:

Net domestic product (NDP) equals the total final output produced within a nation during a year, where output includes net investment, or gross investment less depreciation:

$$NDP = GDP - depreciation$$

Gross national product (GNP) is the total final output produced with inputs owned by the residents of a country during a year.

Table 5-5 provides a comprehensive definition of important components of GDP.

GDP and NDP: A Look at Numbers

Armed with an understanding of the concepts, we can turn to a look at the actual data in the important Table 5-6.

Flow-of-Product Approach. Look first at the left side of the table. It gives the upper-loop, flow-of-product approach to GDP. Each of the four major components appears there, along with the production in each component for 1999. Of these, *C* and *G* and their obvious subclassifications require little discussion.

Gross Domestic Product, 1999
(billions of current dollars)

Product Approach			Earnings or Cost Approach		
1. Personal consumption expenditure		$6,257	1. Wages, salaries, and supplements		$5,332
Durable goods	759		2. Net interest		468
Nondurable goods	1,843		3. Rental income of persons		146
Services	3,656		4. Indirect business taxes, adjustments,		
2. Gross private domestic investment		1,623	and statistical discrepancy		815
Residential fixed	411		5. Depreciation		945
Business fixed	1,167		6. Income of unincorporated enterprises		658
Change in inventories	45		7. Corporate profits before taxes (adjusted)		893
3. Government consumption and			Corporate profit taxes	259	
investment purchases		1,630	Dividends	365	
4. Net exports		−254	Undistributed profits	269	
Exports	998				
Imports	1,252				
Gross domestic product		**$9,256**	**Gross domestic product**		**$9,256**

TABLE 5-6. The Two Ways of Looking at the GDP Accounts, in Actual Numbers

The left side measures flow of products (at market prices). The right side measures flow of costs (factor earnings and depreciation plus indirect taxes). (Source: U.S. Department of Commerce.)

Gross private domestic investment does require one comment. Its total ($1623 billion) includes all new business fixed investment, residential construction, and increase in inventory of goods. This gross total excludes subtraction for depreciation of capital. After subtracting $945 billion of depreciation from gross investment, we obtain $678 billion of net investment.

Finally, note the large negative entry for net exports, −$254 billion. This negative entry represents the fact that in 1999 the United States imported $254 billion more in goods and services than it exported.

Adding up the four components on the left gives the total GDP of $9256 billion. This is the harvest we have been working for: the money measure of the American economy's overall performance for 1999.

Flow-of-Cost Approach. Now turn to the right-hand side of the table, which gives the lower-loop, flow-of-cost approach. Here we have all *net costs of production* plus *taxes* and *depreciation*.

Wages and other employee supplements include all take-home pay, fringe benefits, and taxes on wages. Net interest is a similar item. Remember that interest on government debt is not included as part of *G* or of GDP but is treated as a transfer.

Rent income of persons includes rents received by landlords. In addition, if you own your own home, you are treated as *paying rent to yourself*. This is one of many "imputations" (or derived data) in the national accounts. It makes sense if we really want to measure the housing services the American people are enjoying and do not want the estimate to change when people decide to own a home rather than rent one.

Indirect business taxes are included as a separate item along with some small adjustments, including the inevitable "statistical discrepancy," which reflects the fact that the officials never have every bit of needed data.[2]

Depreciation on capital goods that were used up must appear as an expense in GDP, just like other expenses.

Profit comes last because it is the residual—what is left over after all other costs have been subtracted from total sales. There are two kinds of profits: profit of corporations and net earnings of unincorporated enterprises.

Income of unincorporated enterprises consists of earnings of partnerships and single-ownership businesses. This includes much farm and professional income.

Finally, corporate profits before taxes are shown. This entry's $893 billion in Table 5-6 includes corporate profit *taxes* of $259 billion. The remainder then goes to dividends or to undistributed corporate profits; the latter amount of $269 billion is what corporations leave or "plow back" into the business and is called *net corporate saving*.

On the right side, the flow-of-cost approach gives us the same $9256 billion of GDP as does the flow-of-product approach. The right and left sides do agree.

From GDP to Disposable Income

The basic GDP accounts are of interest not only for themselves but also because of their importance for understanding how consumers and businesses behave. Some further distinctions will help illuminate the way the nation's books are kept.

National Income. To help us understand the division of total income among the different factors of production, we construct data on *national income (NI)*. *NI* represents the total incomes received by labor, capital, and land. It is constructed by subtracting depreciation and indirect taxes from GDP. National income equals total compensation of labor, rental income, net interest, income of proprietors, and corporate profits.

The relationship between GDP and national income is shown in the first two bars of Figure 5-4. The left-hand bar shows GDP, while the second bar shows the subtractions required to obtain *NI*.

Disposable Income. A second important concept asks, How many dollars per year do households actually have available to spend? The concept of disposable personal income (usually called **disposable**

---

[2] Statisticians work with incomplete reports and fill in data gaps by estimation. Just as measurements in a chemistry lab differ from the ideal, so do errors creep into both upper- and lower-loop GDP estimates. These are balanced by an item called the "statistical discrepancy." Along with the civil servants who are heads of units called "Wages," "Interest," and so forth, there actually used to be someone with the title "Head of Statistical Discrepancy." If data were perfect, that individual would have been out of a job. In fact, during the late 1990s, income-side GDP grew substantially faster than product-side GDP, and in 1999 the statistical discrepancy was $125 billion. Economists are scratching their heads and trying to determine where all that income was hidden.

income, or *DI*) answers this question. To get disposable income, you calculate the market and transfer incomes received by households and subtract personal taxes.

Figure 5-4 shows the calculation of *DI*. We begin with national income in the second bar. We then subtract all direct taxes on households and corporations and further subtract net business saving. (Business saving is depreciation plus profits minus dividends. Net business saving is this total minus depreciation.) Finally, we add back the transfer payments that households receive from governments. This constitutes *DI*, shown as the right-hand bar in Figure 5-4.

Disposable income is what actually gets into the public's hands for consumers to dispose of as they please.

As we will see in the next chapters, *DI* is what people divide between (1) consumption spending and (2) personal saving.

Saving and Investment

As we have seen, output can be either consumed or invested. Investment is an essential economic activity because it increases the capital stock available for future production. One of the most important points about national accounting is the identity between saving and investment. We will show that, under the ac-

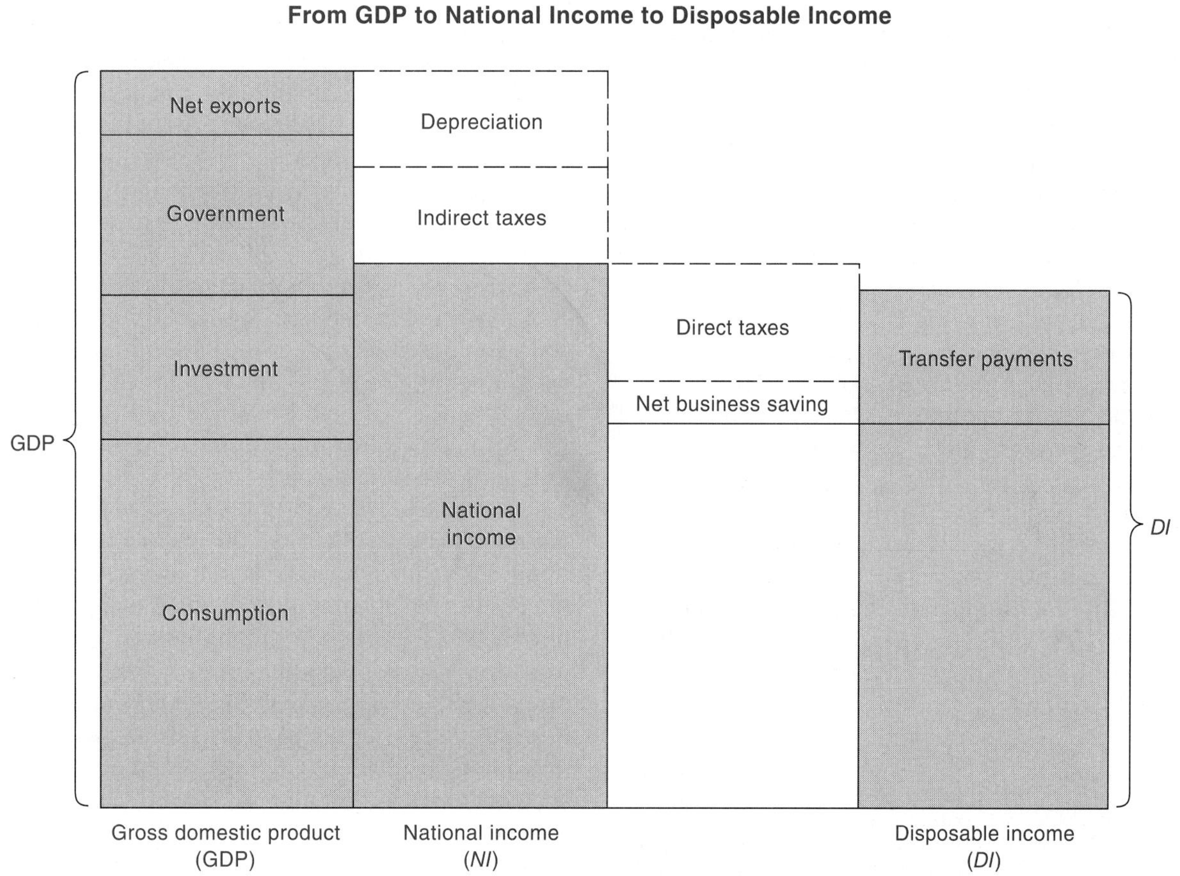

From GDP to National Income to Disposable Income

FIGURE 5-4. Starting with GDP, We Can Calculate National Income (*NI*) and Disposable Personal Income (*DI*)

Important income concepts are (1) GDP, which is total gross income to all factors; (2) national income, which is the sum of factor incomes and is obtained by subtracting depreciation and indirect taxes from GDP; and (3) disposable personal income, which measures the total incomes, including transfer payments, but minus taxes, of the household sector.

counting rules described above, *measured saving is exactly equal to measured investment*. This equality is an *identity*, which means that it must hold by definition.

In the simplest case, assume for the moment that there is no government or foreign sector. Investment is that part of national output which is not consumed. Saving is that part of national income which is not consumed. But since national income and output are equal, this means that saving equals investment. In symbols:

$$I = \text{product-approach GDP minus } C$$
$$S = \text{earnings-approach GDP minus } C$$

But the measures always give the same measure of GDP, so

$$I = S: \text{the identity between measured saving and investment}$$

That is the simplest case. We also need to consider the complete case which brings businesses, government, and net exports into the picture. On the saving side, total or *national saving* (S^T) is composed of *private saving* by households and businesses (S^P) along with *government saving* (S^G). Government saving equals the government's budget surplus or the difference between tax revenues and expenditures.

On the investment side, total or *national investment* (I^T) starts with *gross private domestic investment* (I) but also adds *net foreign investment*, which is approximately the same as net exports (X). Hence, the complete saving-investment identity is given by[3]

$$\begin{array}{l} \frac{\text{National}}{\text{Investment}} = \frac{\text{private}}{\text{investment}} + \frac{\text{net}}{\text{exports}} = \end{array}$$

or

$$\frac{\text{private}}{\text{saving}} + \frac{\text{government}}{\text{saving}} = \frac{\text{national}}{\text{saving}}$$

$$I^T = I + X = S^P + S^G = S^T$$

National saving equals national investment by definition. The components of investment are private domestic investment and foreign investment (or net exports). The sources of saving are private saving (by households and businesses) and government saving (the government budget surplus). Private investment plus net exports equals private saving plus the budget surplus. These identities must hold always, whatever the state of the business cycle.

BEYOND THE NATIONAL ACCOUNTS

Advocates of the existing economic and social system often argue that market economies have produced a growth in real output never before seen in human history. "Look how GDP has grown because of the genius of free markets," say the admirers of capitalism.

But critics point out the deficiencies of GDP. GDP includes many questionable entries and omits many valuable economic activities. As one dissenter said, "Don't speak to me of all your production and your dollars, your gross domestic product. To me, GDP stands for gross domestic pollution!"

What are we to think? Isn't it true that GDP includes government production of bombs and missiles along with salaries paid to prison guards? Doesn't an increase in crime boost sales of home alarms, which adds to the GDP? Doesn't cutting our irreplaceable redwoods show up as a positive output in our national accounts? Doesn't GDP fail to account for environmental degradation such as acid rain and global warming?

In recent years, economists have begun developing new measures to correct the major defects of the standard GDP numbers and better reflect the true satisfaction-producing outputs of our economy. The new approaches attempt to extend the boundaries of the traditional accounts by including important nonmarket activities as well as correcting for harmful activities that are included as part of national output. Let's consider some of the omitted pluses and minuses.

Omitted Nonmarket Activities. Recall that the standard accounts include primarily market activities. Much useful economic activity takes place outside the market. For example, college students are investing in human capital. The national accounts record the tuition, but they omit the opportunity costs of earnings forgone. Studies indicate that inclusion of non-

---

[3] For this discussion, we consider only private investment and therefore treat all government purchases as consumption. In most national accounts today, government purchases are divided between consumption and tangible investments. If we include government investment, then this amount will add to both national investment and the government surplus.

market investments in education and other areas would more than double the national saving rate.

Similarly, many household activities produce valuable "near-market" goods and services such as meals, laundering, and child-care services. Recent estimates of the value of unpaid household work indicate that it might be almost 50 percent as large as total market consumption. Perhaps the largest omission from the market accounts is the value of leisure time. On average, Americans spend as much of their time on utility-producing leisure activities as they do on money-producing work activities. Yet the value of leisure time is excluded from our official national statistics.

You might wonder about the many activities in the underground economy, which covers a wide variety of market activities that are not reported to the government. These include activities like gambling, prostitution, drug dealing, work done by illegal immigrants, bartering of services, and smuggling. Actually, much underground activity is intentionally excluded because national output excludes illegal activities—these are by social consensus "bads" and not "goods." A swelling cocaine trade will not enter into GDP. For other, legal but unreported activities, like unreported tips, the Commerce Department makes estimates on the basis of surveys and audits by the Internal Revenue Service.

Omitted Environmental Damage. In addition to omitting activities, sometimes GDP omits some of the harmful side effects of economic activity. An important example is the omission of environmental damages. For example, suppose the residents of Suburbia buy 10 million kilowatt-hours of electricity to cool their houses, paying Utility Co. 10 cents per kilowatt-hour. That $1 million covers the labor costs, plant costs, and fuel costs. But suppose the company damages the neighborhood with pollution in the process of producing electricity. It incurs no monetary costs for this externality. Our measure of output should not only add in the value of the electricity (which GDP does) but also subtract the environmental damage caused by the pollution (which GDP does not).

Suppose that in addition to paying 10 cents of direct costs, the surrounding neighborhood suffers 1 cent per kilowatt-hour of environmental damage. This is the cost of pollution (to trees, trout, streams, and people) not paid by Utility Co. Then the total

"external" cost is $100,000. To correct for this hidden cost in a set of augmented accounts, we must subtract $100,000 of "pollution bads" from the $1,000,000 flow of "electricity goods."

Augmented national accounts

Considerable progress has been made in recent years in developing *augmented national accounts*, which are accounts designed to include both nonmarket and market activities. The general principle of augmented accounting is to include as much of economic activity as is feasible, whether or not that activity takes place in the market. Examples of augmented accounts include estimates of the value of nonmarket investments in human capital, the value of unpaid home production, the value of forests, and the value of leisure time.

In 1994, the U.S. Commerce Department unveiled its augmented national accounts with the introduction of *environmental accounts* (sometimes called "green accounts") designed to estimate the contribution of natural and environmental resources to the nation's income. The first step was the development of accounts to measure the contribution of subsoil assets like oil, gas, and coal.

Environmental critics have argued that America's wasteful ways are squandering our precious natural capital. Many were surprised by the results of this first assay into green accounting. The estimates take into account that discovery adds to our proven reserves while extraction subtracts from or depletes these reserves. In fact, these two activities just about canceled each other out: the net effect of both discoveries and depletion from 1958 to 1991 was between minus $2 billion and plus $1 billion, depending on the method, as compared to an average GDP over this period of $4200 billion (all these in 1992 prices).

There is much further work needed in this area before we have a full picture of nonmarket economic activity. Economists and environmentalists are watching this exciting new development carefully.

PRICE INDEXES AND INFLATION

We have concentrated in this chapter on the measurement of output. But people are also concerned with price trends, with movements in the overall price level, with inflation. What do these terms mean?

Let us begin with a careful definition:

A *price index* is a measure of the average level of prices. *Inflation* denotes a rise in the general level of prices. The *rate of inflation* is the rate of change of the general price level and is measured as follows:

Rate of inflation (year t)

$$= \frac{\begin{array}{c}\text{price level} \\ \text{(year } t\text{)}\end{array} - \begin{array}{c}\text{price level} \\ \text{(year } t - 1\text{)}\end{array}}{\text{price level (year } t - 1\text{)}} \times 100$$

But how do we measure the "price level" that is involved in the definition of inflation? The price level is a weighted average of the prices of the different goods and services in an economy. The government calculates the price level by constructing **price indexes,** which are averages of prices of goods and services.

As an example, take the year 1999. In that year, the prices of most major categories rose modestly— food prices rose 2 percent and medical-care prices rose 3.5 percent, for example. Apparel prices declined, however, primarily because of sharp declines in the prices of imported clothing. Overall, when weighted by total expenditures in different areas, the consumer price index (CPI) rose 2.1 percent in 1999. In other words, the inflation rate was 2.1 percent.

The opposite of inflation is **deflation,** which occurs when the general level of prices is falling. Deflations have been rare in the late twentieth century. In the United States, the last time consumer prices actually fell from one year to the next was 1955. Sustained deflations, in which prices fall steadily over a period of several years, are associated with depressions, such as those that occurred in the United States in the 1930s and the 1890s. More recently, Japan experienced a deflation in the late 1990s as its economy suffered a prolonged recession.

Price Indexes

When newspapers tell us "Inflation is rising," they are really reporting the movement of a price index. A price index is a weighted average of the prices of a number of goods and services. In constructing price indexes, economists weight individual prices by the economic importance of each good. The most im-

portant price indexes are the consumer price index, the GDP deflator, and the producer price index.

The Consumer Price Index (CPI). The most widely used measure of inflation is the consumer price index, also known as the CPI, calculated by the Bureau of Labor Statistics (BLS). The CPI measures the cost of buying a standard basket of goods at different times. The market basket includes the prices of food, clothing, shelter, fuel, transportation, medical care, college tuition, and other goods and services purchased for day-to-day living. Prices on 364 separate classes of goods and services are collected from 23,000 establishments in 87 areas of the country.

How are the different prices weighted in constructing price indexes? It would clearly be silly merely to add up the different prices or to weight them by their mass or volume. Rather, a price index is constructed by *weighting each price according to the economic importance of the commodity in question.*

In the case of the traditional CPI, each item is assigned a fixed weight proportional to its relative importance in consumer expenditure budgets; the weights for each item are proportional to the total spending by consumers on that item as determined by a survey of consumer expenditures in the 1993– 1995 period. As of December 1999, housing-related costs were the single biggest category in the CPI, taking up more than 40 percent of consumer spending budgets. By comparison, the cost of new cars and other motor vehicles accounts for only 5 percent of the CPI's consumer expenditure budgets. (We are discussing the "traditional CPI" because the government is currently in the process of undertaking a fundamental redesign of the methods for calculating the CPI.)

We can use a numerical example to illustrate how inflation is measured. Assume that consumers buy three commodities: food, shelter, and medical care. A hypothetical budget survey finds that consumers spend 20 percent of their budgets on food, 50 percent on shelter, and 30 percent on medical care.

Using 1998 as the *base year*, we reset the price of each commodity at 100 so that differences in the units of commodities will not affect the price index. This implies that the CPI is also 100 in the base year $[= (0.20 \times 100) + (0.50 \times 100) + (0.30 \times 100)]$. Next, we calculate the consumer price index and the rate of inflation for 1999. Suppose that in 1999 food prices rise 2 percent to 102, shelter prices rise 6 percent to 106, and medical-care prices are up 10 percent to 110. We recalculate the CPI for 1999 as follows:

CPI (1999)
  = $(0.20 \times 102) + (0.50 \times 106) + (0.30 \times 110)$
  = 106.4

In other words, if 1998 is the base year in which the CPI is 100, then in 1999 the CPI is 106.4. The rate of inflation in 1999 is then $[(106.4 - 100)/100] \times 100 = 6.4$ percent per year. Note that in a fixed-weight index like the CPI, the *prices* change from year to year but the weights remain the same.

This example captures the essence of how the traditional CPI measures inflation. The only difference between this simplified calculation and the actual one is that the CPI in fact contains many more commodities and regions. Otherwise, the procedure is exactly the same.

GDP Deflator. Another widely used price index is the *GDP deflator*, which we met earlier in this chapter. The GDP deflator is the price of all goods and services produced in the country (consumption, investment, government purchases, and net exports) rather than of a single component (such as consumption). This index also differs from the traditional CPI because it is a variable-weight index that takes into account the changing shares of different goods. In addition, there are deflators for components of GDP, such as for investment goods, computers, personal consumption, and so forth, and these are sometimes used to supplement the CPI.

In recent years, the U.S. government has introduced chain-weighted price indexes that change the weights on each good each period to reflect changes in expenditure shares (see the discussion of chain weights in note 1 on page 94).

The Producer Price Index (PPI). This index, dating from 1890, is the oldest continuous statistical series published by the BLS. It measures the level of prices at the wholesale or producer stage. It is based on approximately 3400 commodity prices, including prices of foods, manufactured products, and mining products. The fixed weights used to calculate the PPI are the net sales of each commodity. Because of its great detail, this index is widely used by businesses.

Getting the prices right

Measuring prices accurately is one of the central issues of empirical economics. Price indexes affect not only obvious things like the inflation rate. They also are embedded in measures of real output and productivity. And through government policies, they affect monetary policy, taxes, government transfer programs like social security, and many private contracts.

The purpose of the consumer price index is to measure the cost of living. You might be surprised to learn that this is a difficult task. Some problems are intrinsic to price indexes. One issue is the *index-number problem*, which involves how the different prices are weighted or averaged. Recall that the traditional CPI uses a fixed weight for each good. As a result, the cost of living is overestimated compared to the situation where consumers substitute relatively inexpensive for relatively expensive goods.

The case of energy prices can illustrate the problem. When gasoline prices rose sharply in the 1970s, people tended to cut back on their purchases and buy smaller cars or travel less. Yet the CPI assumed that they bought the same quantity of gasoline even though gasoline prices tripled. The overall rise in the cost of living was thereby exaggerated. Statisticians have devised ways of minimizing such index-number problems by using different weighting approaches, such as chain weighting, discussed above, but government statisticians are just beginning to experiment with these newer approaches for the CPI.

A more important problem arises because of the difficulty of adjusting price indexes to capture the contribution of *new and improved goods and services*. An example will illustrate this problem. In recent years, consumers have benefited from compact fluorescent lightbulbs; these lightbulbs deliver light at approximately one-fourth the cost of the older, incandescent bulbs. Yet none of the price indexes incorporate the quality improvement. Similarly, as CDs replaced long-playing records, as cable TV with hundreds of channels replaced the older technology with a few fuzzy channels, as air travel replaced rail or road travel, and in thousands of other improved goods and services, the price indexes did not reflect the improved quality.

Recent studies indicate that if quality change had been properly incorporated into price indexes, the CPI would have risen less rapidly in recent years. This problem is especially acute for medical care. In this sector, reported prices have risen sharply in the last two decades. Yet we have no adequate measure of the quality of medical care, and the CPI completely ignores the introduction of new products, such as pharmaceuticals which replace intrusive and expensive surgery.

A panel of distinguished economists led by Stanford's Michael Boskin (chief economist to President George Bush) recently estimated that the upward bias in the CPI was slightly more than 1 percent per year. This is a small number with large implications. It indicates that our real output numbers may have been *overdeflated* by the same amount. If the CPI bias carries through to the GDP deflator, then output per worker-hour in the United States has grown at 2 percent per year over the last two decades rather than the 1 percent per year as measured in the official national accounts.

This finding also implies that cost-of-living adjustments (which are used for social security benefits and in many labor agreements) have overcompensated people for movements in the cost of living. The Boskin panel estimated that if the government were to index transfer programs according to their bias estimate rather than using the current CPI, this would by 2008 reduce the government deficit by $180 billion and lower the U.S. national debt by more than $1 trillion over a decade. These findings indicate that the economics of accounting and of index numbers are no longer just abstruse concepts of interest only to a handful of technicians. Proper construction of price and output indexes affects our government budgets, our retirement programs, and even the way we assess our national economic performance.

In response to its own research and to its critics, the BLS has undertaken a major overhaul of the CPI. The most important planned change is to fix the index-number problem by replacing the fixed-weight price index with a system (like the chain weights used in the GDP accounts) that accounts for consumer substitution. Measuring quality change accurately is a much tougher nut and is unlikely to be cracked soon.[4]

ACCOUNTING ASSESSMENT

This chapter has examined the way economists measure national output and the overall price level. Having reviewed the measurement of national output and analyzed the shortcomings of the GDP, what should we conclude about the adequacy of our measures? Do they capture the major trends? Are they adequate measures of overall social welfare? The answer was aptly stated in a review by Arthur Okun:

> It should be no surprise that national prosperity does not guarantee a happy society, any more than personal prosperity ensures a happy family. No growth of GDP can counter the tensions arising from an unpopular and unsuccessful war, a long overdue self-confrontation with conscience on racial injustice, a volcanic eruption of sexual mores, and an unprecedented assertion of independence by the young. Still, prosperity . . . is a precondition for success in achieving many of our aspirations.[5]

---

[4] See this chapter's Further Reading section for a symposium on CPI design.

[5] *The Political Economy of Prosperity* (Norton, New York, 1970), p. 124.

SUMMARY

1. The national income and product accounts contain the major measures of income and product for a country. The gross domestic product (GDP) is the most comprehensive measure of a nation's production of goods and services. It comprises the dollar value of consumption (C), gross private domestic investment (I), government purchases (G), and net exports (X) produced within a nation during a given year. Recall the formula:

$$\text{GDP} = C + I + G + X$$

This will sometimes be simplified by combining private domestic investment and net exports into total gross national investment ($I^T = I + X$):

$$\text{GDP} = C + I^T + G$$

2. Because of the way we define residual profit, we can match the upper-loop, flow-of-product measurement of GDP with the lower-loop, flow-of-cost measurement, as shown in Figure 5–1. The flow-of-cost approach uses factor earnings and carefully computes value added to

eliminate double counting of intermediate products. And after summing up all (before-tax) wage, interest, rent, depreciation, and profit income, it adds to this total all indirect tax costs of business. GDP does not include transfer items such as interest on government bonds or welfare payments.

3. By use of a price index, we can "deflate" nominal GDP (GDP in current dollars) to arrive at a more accurate measure of real GDP (GDP expressed in dollars of some base year's purchasing power). Use of such a price index corrects for the "rubber yardstick" implied by changing levels of prices.

4. Net investment is positive when the nation is producing more capital goods than are currently being used up in the form of depreciation. Since depreciation is hard to estimate accurately, statisticians have more confidence in their measures of gross investment than in those of net investment.

5. National income and disposable income are two additional official measurements. Disposable income (*DI*) is what people actually have left—after all tax payments, corporate saving of undistributed profits, and transfer adjustments have been made—to spend on consumption or to save.

6. Using the rules of the national accounts, measured saving must exactly equal measured investment. This is easily seen in a hypothetical economy with nothing but households. In a complete economy, *private saving and government surplus equal domestic investment plus net foreign investment.* The identity between saving and investment is just that: saving must equal investment no matter whether the economy is in boom or recession, war or peace. It is a consequence of the definitions of national income accounting.

7. Gross domestic product and even net domestic product are imperfect measures of genuine economic welfare. In recent years, statisticians have started correcting for nonmarket measures such as unpaid work at home and environmental externalities.

8. Inflation occurs when the general level of prices is rising (and deflation occurs when it is falling). We measure the overall price level and rate of inflation using price indexes—weighted averages of the prices of thousands of individual products. The most important price index is the consumer price index (CPI), which traditionally measured the cost of a fixed market basket of consumer goods and services relative to the cost of that bundle during a particular base year. Recent studies indicate that the CPI trend has a major upward bias because of index-number problems and omission of new and improved goods, and the government has undertaken steps to correct some of this bias.

CONCEPTS FOR REVIEW

national income and product
    accounts (national accounts)
real and nominal GDP
GDP deflator
GDP = $C + I + G + X$
net investment =
    gross investment − depreciation

GDP in two equivalent views:
    product (upper loop)
    earnings (lower loop)
intermediate goods, value added
NDP = GDP − depreciation
government transfers
disposable income (*DI*)

investment-saving identity
    $I = S$
    $I^T = I + X = S^P + S^G = S^T$
inflation, deflation
price index:
    CPI
    GDP deflator
    PPI

FURTHER READING AND INTERNET WEBSITES

Further Reading

A magnificent compilation of historical data on the United States is contained in *Historical Statistics of the United States* (Washington, D.C., Government Printing Office, 1975, two volumes). A review of the issues involving measuring the consumer price index is contained in "Symposium on the CPI," *Journal of Economic Perspectives*, Winter 1998.

Websites

The premium site for the U.S. National Income and Product Accounts is from the Bureau of Economic Analysis (BEA) at www.bea.doc.gov. This site also contains recent issues of *The Survey of Current Business*, which discusses recent economic trends.

A comprehensive launching pad for government data in many sectors can be found at www.lib.umich.edu/libhome/Documents.center/stats.html. The best single statistical source for data on the United States is *The Statistical Abstract of the United States*, published annually. It is available online at www.census.gov/statab/www.

A recent review of alternative approaches to augmented and environmental accounting is contained in a report by the National Academy of Sciences in William Nordhaus and Edward Kokkelenberg, eds., *Nature's Numbers: Expanding the National Accounts to Include the Environment* (Washington, D.C., National Academy Press, 1999) available at www.nap.edu.

✳ QUESTIONS FOR DISCUSSION

1. Define carefully the following and give an example of each:
   a. Consumption
   b. Gross private domestic investment
   c. Government consumption and investment purchase (in GDP)
   d. Government transfer payment (not in GDP)
   e. Exports

2. You sometimes hear, "You can't add apples and oranges." Show that we can and do add apples and oranges in the national accounts. Explain how.

3. Examine the data in the appendix to Chapter 4. Locate the figures for nominal and real GDP for 1999 and 1998. Calculate the GDP deflator. What were the rates of growth of nominal GDP and real GDP for 1999? What was the rate of inflation (as measured by the GDP deflator) for 1999?

4. Robinson Crusoe produces upper-loop product of $1000. He pays $750 in wages, $125 in interest, and $75 in rent. What must his profit be? If three-fourths of Crusoe's output is consumed and the rest invested, calculate Crusoeland's GDP with both the product and the income approaches and show that they must agree exactly.

5. Here are some brain teasers. Can you see why the following are not counted in U.S. GDP?
   a. The gourmet meals produced by a fine chef
   b. The purchase of a plot of land
   c. The purchase of an original Rembrandt painting
   d. The value I get in 2000 from playing a 1997 compact disc

   e. Damage to houses and crops from pollution emitted by electric utilities
   f. Profits earned by IBM on production in a British factory

6. Consider the country of Agrovia, whose GDP is discussed in "A Numerical Example" on page 98. Construct a set of national accounts like that in Table 5–6 assuming that wheat costs $5 per bushel, there is no depreciation, wages are three-fourths of national output, indirect business taxes are used to finance 100 percent of government spending, and the balance of income goes as rent income to farmers.

7. Review the discussion of bias in the CPI. Explain why failure to consider the quality improvement of a new good leads to an upward bias in the trend of the CPI. Pick a good you are familiar with. Explain how its quality has changed and why it might be difficult for a price index to capture the increase in quality.

8. In recent decades, women have worked more hours in paid jobs and fewer hours in unpaid housework.
   a. How would this increase in work hours affect GDP?
   b. Explain why this increase in measured GDP will overstate the true increase in output. Also explain how a set of augmented national accounts which includes home production would treat this change from nonmarket work to market work.
   c. Explain the paradox, "When a person marries his or her gardener, GDP goes down."

Consumption, saving, and investment play a central role in a nation's economic performance. Nations that save and invest large fractions of their incomes tend to have rapid growth of output, income, and wages; this pattern characterized the United States in the nineteenth century, Japan in the twentieth century, and the "miracle" economies of East Asia in the last three decades. By contrast, nations which consume most of their incomes, like many poor countries in Africa and Latin America, invest little in new plant and equipment and show low rates of growth of productivity and wages. High consumption relative to income spells low investment and slow growth; high saving leads to high investment and rapid growth.

The interaction between spending and income plays quite a different role during business-cycle expansions and contractions. When economic conditions give rise to rapidly growing consumption and investment, this increases total spending or aggregate demand, raising output and employment in the short run. America's economic boom of the late 1990s was largely fueled by rapid growth in consumer spending. And when consumption falls because of higher taxes or loss of consumer confidence, as happened in Japan in the 1990s, this tends to reduce total spending and may produce a recession.

Because consumption and investment are so central to macroeconomics, we devote this chapter to them. Figure 6-1 shows how this chapter's analysis fits into the overall structure of the economy.

Annual income twenty pounds, annual expenditure nineteen nineteen six, result happiness. Annual income twenty pounds, annual expenditure twenty pounds ought and six, result misery.

Charles Dickens, *David Copperfield*

A. CONSUMPTION AND SAVING

This section considers consumption and saving behavior, beginning with individual spending patterns and then looking at aggregate consumption behavior. Recall from Chapter 5 that *consumption* (or, more precisely, personal consumption expenditures) is expenditures by households on final goods and services. *Saving* is that part of personal disposable income that is not consumed.

Consumption is the largest single component of GDP, constituting 66 percent of total spending over the last decade. What are the major elements of consumption? Among the most important categories are housing, motor vehicles, food, and medical care. Table 6-1 displays the major elements, broken down into the three categories of durable goods, nondurable goods, and services. The items themselves are familiar, but their relative importance, particularly the increasing importance of services, is worth a moment's study.

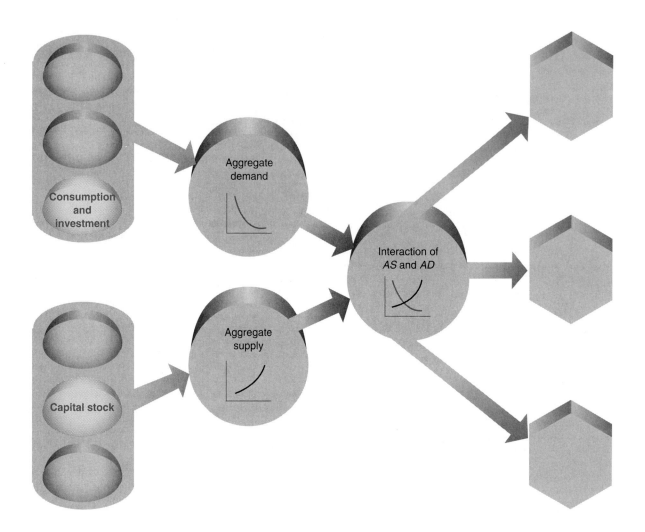

FIGURE 6-1. What Are the Major Forces Affecting Consumption and Investment?

This chapter analyzes two major components of GDP: consumption and investment. In later chapters, we will see that they affect both aggregate supply and aggregate demand.

Budgetary Expenditure Patterns

How do the patterns of consumption spending differ across different households in the United States? No two families spend their disposable incomes in exactly the same way. Yet statistics show that there is a predictable regularity in the way people allocate their expenditures among food, clothing, and other major items. The thousands of budgetary investigations of household spending patterns show remarkable agreement on the general, qualitative patterns of behavior.[1] Figure 6-2 on page 111 tells the story. Poor families must spend their incomes largely on the necessities of life: food and shelter. As income increases, expenditure on many food items goes up.

---

[1] The spending patterns shown in Fig. 6-2 are called "Engel's Laws," after the nineteenth-century Prussian statistician Ernst Engel. The average behavior of consumption expenditure does change fairly regularly with income. But averages do not tell the whole story. Within each income class, there is a considerable spread of consumption around the average.

Category of consumption	Value of category, 1999 ($ billion)		Percent of total
Durable goods		759	12.1
Motor vehicles and parts	316		
Furniture and household equipment	291		
Other	152		
Nondurable goods		1,843	29.5
Food	904		
Clothing and shoes	306		
Energy goods	139		
Other	494		
Services		3,655	58.4
Housing	903		
Household operation	362		
Transportation	255		
Medical care	941		
Recreation	246		
Other	948		
Total personal consumption expenditures		6,257	100.0

TABLE 6-1. The Major Components of Consumption

We divide consumption into three categories: durable goods, nondurable goods, and services. The service sector is growing in importance as basic needs for food are met and as health, recreation, and education claim a larger part of family budgets. (Source: U.S. Department of Commerce.)

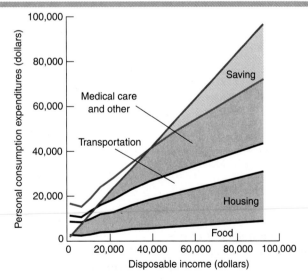

FIGURE 6-2. Family Budget Expenditures Show Regular Patterns

Surveys verify the importance of disposable income as a determinant of consumption expenditures. Notice the drop in food as a percentage of income as incomes rise. Note also that saving is negative at low incomes but rises substantially at high incomes. (Source: U.S. Department of Labor, *Consumer Expenditure Surveys, 1998*, available on the Internet at www.bls.gov/csxstnd.htm.)

People eat more and eat better. There are, however, limits to the extra money people will spend on food when their incomes rise. Consequently, the proportion of total spending devoted to food declines as income increases.

Expenditure on clothing, recreation, and automobiles increases more than proportionately to after-tax income, until high incomes are reached. Spending on luxury items increases in greater proportion than income. Finally, as we look across families, note that saving rises very rapidly as income increases. Saving is the greatest luxury of all.

The evolution of consumption in the twentieth century

Continual changes in technology, incomes, and social forces have led to dramatic changes in U.S. consumption patterns over time. In 1918, American households on average spent 41 percent of their incomes on food and drink. By comparison, households now spend only about 19 percent on these items. What lies behind this striking decline? The major factor is that spending on food tends to grow more slowly than incomes. Similarly, spending on apparel has fallen from 18 percent of household income at the beginning of the twentieth century to only 6 percent today.

What are the "luxury goods" that Americans are spending more on? One big item is transportation. In 1918, Americans spent only 1 percent of their incomes on vehicles—but of course Henry Ford didn't sell his first Model T until 1908. Today, there are 1.3 cars for every household, so it is not surprising that 23 percent of spending goes for vehicle-related transportation expenses. What about recreation and entertainment? Households now lay out large sums for televisions, cellular phones, and VCRs, items that didn't exist 75 years ago. These new inventions have lifted entertainment expenses to 6 percent of household budgets, up from 3 percent. Housing services, too, take a bigger share of income—20 percent compared to 14 percent in the earlier period. That reflects, in part, the success of the American Dream: owning a big house in the suburbs is more expensive than renting a small apartment in the city.

Over the last decade, the biggest increase in consumption spending has been for health care, as both consumer payments for medical care and employer and government contributions for health care have soared. Surprisingly, consumers' out-of-pocket expenses for health care take about the same share of the *household* budget as they did in the early part of the twentieth century. The major increase has come as governments have taken over ever-larger fractions of health-care spending, contributing to the growth in government spending in the United States and other high-income countries.

CONSUMPTION, INCOME, AND SAVING

Income, consumption, and saving are all closely linked. More precisely, **personal saving** is that part of disposable income that is not consumed; saving equals income minus consumption. The relationship between income, consumption, and saving for the United States in 1999 is shown in Table 6-2. Begin

Item	Amount, 1999 ($, billion)
Personal income	**7,792**
Less: Personal taxes	1,152
Equals: Disposable personal income	**6,640**
Less: Personal outlays (consumption and interest)	6,483
Equals: Personal saving	**156**
Memo: Personal saving as percent of disposable personal income	2.4

TABLE 6-2. Saving Equals Disposable Income less Consumption

Source: U.S. Department of Commerce.

with personal income (composed, as Chapter 5 showed, of wages, interest, rents, dividends, transfer payments, and so forth). In 1999, some $1,152 billion of personal income, or 14.8 percent, went to personal taxes. This left $6,640 billion of personal disposable income. Household outlays for consumption (including interest) amounted to 97.6 percent of disposable income, or $6,483 billion, leaving $156 billion as personal saving. The last item in the table shows the important **personal saving rate.** This is equal to personal saving as a percent of disposable income (2.4 percent in 1999).

Economic studies have shown that income is the primary determinant of consumption and saving. Rich people save more than poor people, both absolutely and as a percent of income. The very poor are unable to save at all. Instead, as long as they can borrow or draw down their wealth, they tend to dissave. That is, they tend to spend more than they earn, reducing their accumulated saving or going deeper into debt.

Table 6-3 contains illustrative data on disposable income, saving, and consumption drawn from budget studies on American households. The first column shows seven different levels of disposable income. Column (2) indicates saving at each level of income, and the third column indicates consumption spending at each level of income.

The *break-even point*—where the representative household neither saves nor dissaves but consumes all its income—comes at around $25,000. Below the break-even point, say, at $24,000, the household actually consumes more than its income; it dissaves (see the −$110 item). Above $25,000 it begins to show positive saving [see the +$150 and other positive items in column (2)].

Column (3) shows the consumption spending for each income level. Since each dollar of income is divided between the part consumed and the remaining part saved, columns (3) and (2) are not independent; they must always exactly add up to column (1).

To understand the way consumption affects national output, we need to introduce some new tools. We need to understand how many extra dollars of consumption and saving are induced by each extra dollar of income. This relationship is shown by

- The consumption function, relating consumption and income
- Its twin, the saving function, relating saving and income

The Consumption Function

One of the most important relationships in all macroeconomics is the **consumption function.** The consumption function shows the relationship between

	(1) Disposable income ($)	(2) Net saving (+) or dissaving (−) ($)	(3) Consumption ($)
A	24,000	−110	24,110
B	25,000	0	25,000
C	26,000	+150	25,850
D	27,000	+400	26,600
E	28,000	+760	27,240
F	29,000	+1,170	27,830
G	30,000	+1,640	28,360

TABLE 6-3. Consumption and Saving Are Primarily Determined by Income

Consumption and saving rise with disposable income. The break-even point at which people have zero saving is shown here at $25,000. How much of each extra dollar do people devote to extra consumption at this income level? How much to extra saving? (Answer: About 85 cents and 15 cents, respectively, when we compare row B and row C.)

the level of consumption expenditures and the level of disposable personal income. This concept, introduced by Keynes, is based on the hypothesis that there is a stable empirical relationship between consumption and income.

We can see the consumption function most vividly in the form of a graph. Figure 6-3 below plots the seven levels of income listed in Table 6-3. Disposable income [column (1) of Table 6-3] is placed on the horizontal axis, and consumption [column (3)] is on the vertical axis. Each of the income-consumption combinations is represented by a single point, and the points are then connected by a smooth curve.

The relation between consumption and income shown in Figure 6-3 is called the consumption function.

The "Break-Even" Point. To understand the figure, it is helpful to look at the 45° line drawn northeast from the origin. Because the vertical and horizontal axes have exactly the same scale, the 45° line has a very special property. At any point on the 45° line, the distance up from the horizontal axis (consumption) exactly equals the distance across from the vertical axis (disposable income). You can use your eyes or a ruler to verify this fact.

The 45° line tells us immediately whether consumption spending is equal to, greater than, or less than the level of disposable income. The **break-even point** on the consumption schedule that intersects the 45° line represents the level of disposable income at which households just break even.

This break-even point is at *B* in Figure 6-3. Here, consumption expenditure is exactly equal to disposable income: the household is neither a borrower

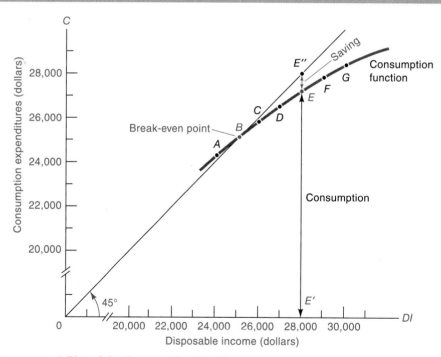

FIGURE 6-3. A Plot of the Consumption Function

The curve through A, B, C, . . . , *G* is the consumption function. The horizontal axis depicts the level of disposable income (*DI*). For each level of *DI*, the consumption function shows the dollar level of consumption (*C*) for the household. Note that consumption rises with increases in *DI*. The 45° line helps locate the break-even point and helps our eye measure net saving. (Source: Table 6-3.)

nor a saver. To the right of point *B*, the consumption function lies below the 45° line. The relationship between income and consumption can be seen by examining the thin black line from *E'* to *E* in Figure 6-3. At an income of $28,000 the level of consumption is $27,240 (see Table 6-3). We can see that consumption is less than income by the fact that the consumption function lies below the 45° line at point *E*.

What a household is not spending, it must be saving. The 45° line enables us to find how much the household is saving. Net saving is measured by the vertical distance from the consumption function up to the 45° line, as shown by the *EE″* saving arrow in blue.

The 45° line tells us that to the left of point *B* the household is spending more than its income. The excess of consumption over income is "dissaving" and is measured by the vertical distance between the consumption function and the 45° line.

To review:

At any point on the 45° line, consumption exactly equals income and the household has zero saving. When the consumption function lies above the 45° line, the household is dissaving. When the consumption function lies below the 45° line, the household has positive saving. The amount of dissaving or saving is always measured by the vertical distance between the consumption function and the 45° line.

The Saving Function

The saving function shows the relationship between the level of saving and income. This is shown graphically in Figure 6-4. Again we show disposable income on the horizontal axis; but now saving, whether negative or positive in amount, is on the vertical axis.

This saving function comes directly from Figure 6-3. It is the vertical distance between the 45° line and the consumption function. For example, at point *A* in Figure 6-3, we see that the household's saving is negative because the consumption function lies above the 45° line. Figure 6-4 shows this dissaving directly—the saving function is below the zero-saving line at point *A*. Similarly, positive saving occurs to the right of point *B* because the saving function is above the zero-saving line.

The Marginal Propensity to Consume

Modern macroeconomics attaches much importance to the response of consumption to changes in income. This concept is called the marginal propensity to consume, or *MPC*.

The *marginal propensity to consume* is the extra amount that people consume when they receive an extra dollar of disposable income.

The word "marginal" is used throughout economics to mean extra or additional. For example, "marginal cost" means the additional cost of

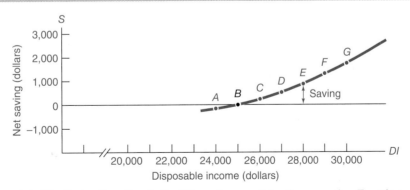

FIGURE 6-4. The Saving Function Is the Mirror Image of the Consumption Function

This saving schedule is derived by subtracting consumption from income. Graphically, the saving function is obtained by subtracting vertically the consumption function from the 45° line in Fig. 6-3. Note that the break-even point *B* is at the same $25,000 income level as in Fig. 6-3.

	(1) Disposable income (after taxes) $	(2) Consumption expenditure $	(3) Marginal propensity to consume (MPC)	(4) Net saving ($) (4) = (1) − (2)	(5) Marginal propensity to save (MPS)
A	24,000	24,110		−110	
			890/1,000 = 0.89		110/1,000 = 0.11
B	25,000	25,000		0	
			850/1,000 = 0.85		150/1,000 = 0.15
C	26,000	25,850		+150	
			750/1,000 = 0.75		250/1,000 = 0.25
D	27,000	26,600		+400	
			640/1,000 = 0.64		360/1,000 = 0.36
E	28,000	27,240		+760	
			590/1,000 = 0.59		410/1,000 = 0.41
F	29,000	27,830		+1,170	
			530/1,000 = 0.53		470/1,000 = 0.47
G	30,000	28,360		+1,640	

TABLE 6-4. The Marginal Propensities to Consume and to Save

Each dollar of disposable income not consumed is saved. Each extra dollar of disposable income goes either into extra consumption or into extra saving. Combining these facts allows us to calculate the marginal propensity to consume (*MPC*) and the marginal propensity to save (*MPS*).

producing an extra unit of output. "Propensity to consume" designates the desired level of consumption. The *MPC* is therefore the additional or extra consumption that results from an extra dollar of disposable income.

Table 6-4 above rearranges Table 6-3's data in a more convenient form. First, verify its similarity to Table 6-3. Then, look at columns (1) and (2) to see how consumption expenditure goes up with higher levels of income.

Column (3) shows how we compute the marginal propensity to consume. From B to C, income rises by $1000, going from $25,000 to $26,000. How much does consumption rise? Consumption grows from $25,000 to $25,850, an increase of $850. The extra consumption is therefore 0.85 of the extra income. Out of each extra dollar of income, 85 cents goes to consumption and 15 cents goes to saving. As we move from B to C, we see that the marginal propensity to consume, or *MPC*, is 0.85.

You can compute *MPC* between other income levels. In Table 6-4, *MPC* begins at 0.89 for the poor and finally falls to 0.53 at higher incomes.

Marginal Propensity to Consume as Geometrical Slope. We now know how to calculate the *MPC* from data on income and consumption. Figure 6-5 shows how we can calculate the *MPC* graphically. Near points *B* and *C* a little right triangle is drawn. As income increases by $1000 from point *B* to point *C*, the amount of consumption rises by $850. The *MPC* in this range is therefore $850/$1000 = 0.85. But, as the appendix to Chapter 1 showed, the numerical slope of a line is "the rise over the run."[2] We can therefore see that the slope of the consumption function is the same as the marginal propensity to consume.

The slope of the consumption function, which measures the change in consumption per dollar change in disposable income, is the marginal propensity to consume.

---

[2] For curved lines, we calculate the slope as the slope of the tangent line at a point.

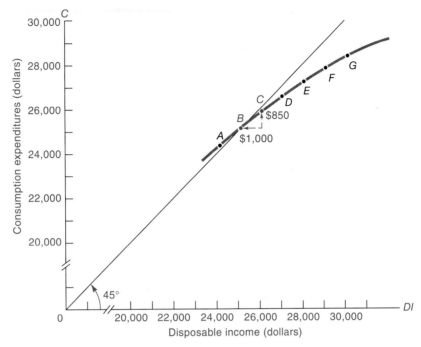

FIGURE 6-5. The Slope of the Consumption Function Is Its *MPC*

To calculate the marginal propensity to consume (*MPC*), we measure the slope of the consumption function by forming a right triangle and relating height to base. From point *B* to point *C*, the increase in consumption is $850 while the change in disposable income is $1000. The slope, equal to the change in *C* divided by the change in *DI*, gives the *MPC*. If the consumption function is everywhere upward-sloping, what does this imply about the *MPC*?

The Marginal Propensity to Save

Along with the marginal propensity to consume goes its mirror image, the marginal propensity to save, or *MPS*. The **marginal propensity to save** is defined as the fraction of an extra dollar of disposable income that goes to extra saving.

Why are *MPC* and *MPS* related like mirror images? Recall that disposable income equals consumption plus saving. This implies that each extra dollar of disposable income must be divided between extra consumption and extra saving. Thus if *MPC* is 0.85, then *MPS* must be 0.15. (What would *MPS* be if *MPC* were 0.6? Or 0.99?) Comparing columns (3) and (5) of Table 6-4 confirms that at any income level, *MPC* and *MPS* must always add up to exactly 1, no more and no less. *Everywhere and always, MPS ≡ 1 − MPC.*

Brief Review of Definitions

Let's review briefly the main definitions we have learned:

1. The consumption function relates the level of consumption to the level of disposable income.
2. The saving function relates saving to disposable income. Because what is saved equals what is not consumed, saving and consumption schedules are mirror images.
3. The marginal propensity to consume (*MPC*) is the amount of extra consumption generated by an extra dollar of disposable income. Graphically, it is given by the slope of the consumption function.

4. The marginal propensity to save (*MPS*) is the extra saving generated by an extra dollar of disposable income. Graphically, this is the slope of the saving schedule.

5. Because the part of each dollar of disposable income that is not consumed is necessarily saved, $MPS \equiv 1 - MPC$.

NATIONAL CONSUMPTION BEHAVIOR

Up to now we have examined the budget patterns and consumption behavior of typical families at different incomes. Let's now consider consumption for the entire nation. This transition from household behavior to national trends exemplifies the methodology of macroeconomics: We begin by examining economic activity on the individual level and then add up or aggregate the totality of individuals to study the way the overall economy operates.

Why are we interested in national consumption trends? Consumption behavior is crucial for under-

standing both short-term business cycles and long-term economic growth. In the short run, consumption is a major component of aggregate spending. When consumption changes sharply, the change is likely to affect output and employment through its impact on aggregate demand. This mechanism will be described in the chapters on Keynesian macroeconomics.

Additionally, consumption behavior is crucial because what is not consumed—that is, what is saved—is available to the nation for investment in new capital goods; capital serves as a driving force behind long-term economic growth. *Consumption and saving behavior are key to understanding economic growth and business cycles.*

Determinants of Consumption

We begin by analyzing the major forces that affect consumer spending. What factors in a nation's life and livelihood set the pace of its consumption outlays?

Current Disposable Income. Figure 6-6 shows how closely consumption followed current disposable in-

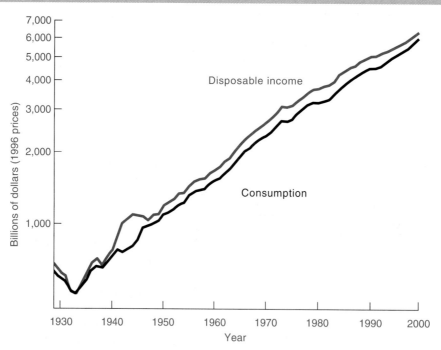

FIGURE 6-6. Consumption and Disposable Income, 1929–1999

U.S. consumption spending has closely tracked the level of personal disposable income over the last seven decades. Macroeconomists can forecast consumption accurately based on the historical consumption function. (Source: U.S. Department of Commerce. Real disposable income is calculated using the deflator for personal consumption expenditures.)

come over the period 1929–1999. The only period when income and consumption did not move in tandem was during World War II, when goods were scarce and rationed and people were urged to save to help the war effort.

Both observation and statistical studies show that the current level of disposable income is the central factor determining a nation's consumption.

Permanent Income and the Life-Cycle Model of Consumption.

The simplest theory of consumption uses only the current year's income to predict consumption expenditures. Consider the following examples, which suggest otherwise:

> If bad weather destroys a crop, farmers will draw upon their previous saving.

> Similarly, law-school students borrow for consumption purposes while in school because they believe that their postgraduate incomes will be much higher than their meager student earnings.

In both these circumstances, people are in effect asking, "Given my current and future income, how much can I consume today without incurring excessive debts?"

Careful studies show that consumers generally choose their consumption levels with an eye to both current income and long-run income prospects. In order to understand how consumption depends on long-term income trends, economists have developed the permanent-income theory and the life-cycle hypothesis.[3]

Permanent income is the trend level of income—that is, income after removing temporary or transient influences due to the weather or windfall gains or losses. According to the permanent-income theory, consumption responds primarily to permanent income. This approach implies that consumers do not respond equally to all income shocks. If a change in income appears permanent (such as being promoted to a secure and high-paying job), people are likely to consume a large fraction of the increase in income. On the other hand, if the income change is clearly transitory (for example, if it arises from a one-time bonus or a good harvest), a significant fraction of the additional income may be saved.

The *life-cycle hypothesis* assumes that people save in order to smooth their consumption over their lifetime. One important objective is to have an adequate retirement income. Hence, people tend to save while working so as to build up a nest egg for retirement and then spend out of their accumulated saving in their twilight years. One implication of the life-cycle hypothesis is that a program like social security, which provides a generous income supplement for retirement, will reduce saving by middle-aged workers since they no longer need to save as much for retirement.

Wealth and Other Influences.

A further important determinant of the amount of consumption is wealth. Consider two consumers, both earning $50,000 per year. One has $200,000 in the bank, while the other has no savings at all. The first person may consume part of wealth, while the second has no wealth to draw down. The fact that higher wealth leads to higher consumption is called the *wealth effect.*

Wealth usually changes slowly from year to year. However, when wealth grows or declines rapidly, this can cause sharp movements in consumption. One important historical case was the stock market crash after 1929, when fortunes collapsed and paper-rich capitalists became paupers overnight. Economic historians believe that the sharp decline in wealth after the 1929 stock market crash reduced consumption spending and contributed to the depth of the Great Depression.

The opposite case occurred during the great stock market boom of the 1990s. Because of the sharp increase in asset prices, household net worth increased from $24 trillion to $40 trillion from 1995 to 1999. This increased consumption and lowered measured saving. Many macroeconomists worry about the impact on consumption and the economy if the stock market fell sharply from its exalted level of 2000. (We discuss this question in the next section.)

---

[3] The pathbreaking studies on longer-term influences were by Milton Friedman (on the permanent-income hypothesis) and Franco Modigliani (for the life-cycle model). Both received the Nobel Prize in economics for their accomplishments in these and other areas.

The National Consumption Function

Having reviewed the determinants of consumption, we may conclude that the level of disposable income is the primary determinant of the level of national consumption. Armed with this result, we can plot recent annual data on consumption and disposable income in Figure 6-7. The scatter diagram shows data for the period 1970–1999, with each point representing the level of consumption and disposable income for a given year.

In addition, you might draw a line in Figure 6-7 through the scatter points and label it "Fitted consumption function." This fitted consumption function shows how closely consumption has followed disposable income over the last quarter-century. In fact, economic historians have found that a close relationship between disposable income and consumption holds back to the nineteenth century.

The declining saving rate

Although consumption behavior tends to be stable over time, the personal saving rate dropped sharply in the United States over the last two decades. The personal saving rate as measured in the national accounts averaged around 8 percent of personal disposable income over most of the twentieth century. Starting about 1980, however, it began to decline and by the end of the 1990s the personal saving rate was just barely positive.

This drop alarmed many economists because, over the long run, the growth in a nation's capital stock is largely determined by its national saving rate. National saving is composed of private and government saving. A high-saving nation has a rapidly growing capital stock and enjoys a rapid growth in its potential output. When a nation's saving rate is low, its equipment and factories become obsolete and its infrastructure begins to rot away.

What were the reasons for the sharp decline in the personal saving rate? This is a highly controversial question today, but economists point to the following potential causes:

- *Social security system.* Some economists argued that the social security system has removed some of the need for private saving. In earlier times, as the life-cycle model of consumption suggests, a household would save during working years to build up a nest egg for retirement. When the government collects social security taxes and pays out social security benefits, people have less need to save for retirement. Other income-support systems have a similar effect, reducing the need to save for a rainy day: crop insurance for farmers, unemployment insurance for workers, and medical care for the poor and elderly all alleviate the precautionary motive for people to save.

- *Capital markets.* Until recently, capital markets had numerous imperfections. People found it hard to borrow funds for worthwhile purposes, whether for buying a house, financing an education, or starting a business. As capital markets developed, often with the help of government, new loan instruments allowed people to borrow more easily. One example is the proliferation of credit cards, which encourage people to borrow (even though the interest rates are quite high). A generation ago, it would be difficult to borrow more than $1000 unless a person had substantial assets. Today, credit-card solicitations arrive daily in the mail. It is not unusual to receive multiple promotions offering credit lines of $10,000 or more in a single week! Some believe that the availability of easy credit reduces saving among those who have little in liquid assets.

- *The rapid growth in wealth.* Many economists believe that personal saving in the 1990s was reduced by the rapid growth in personal wealth, primarily due to the exploding stock market. From 1995 to 1999, for example, the value of stocks rose by about $6 trillion. If households spent 3 percent of this gain each year (a figure consistent with past experience), the "wealth effect" would lower the personal saving rate by about 3 percentage points.

Alternative Measures of Saving

You might at this point ask, "If people are saving so little, why are there so many rich people?" This question raises an important point about measuring personal saving. Saving looks different to the household than to the nation as a whole. This is so because saving as measured in the national income and product accounts is not the same as that measured by accountants or in individual balance sheets. The *national-accounts* measure of saving excludes capital

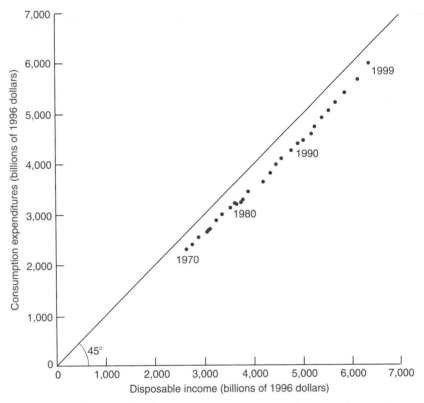

FIGURE 6-7. A Consumption Function for the United States, 1970–1999

Draw a straight line through the scatter of data points. Can you verify that the *MPC* slope of the fitted line is close to 0.95? How can you see that the average saving rate has declined (or that the *APC* has risen) in the last two decades? (Source: U.S. Department of Commerce.)

gains (increases in asset values), while *balance-sheet* measures include capital gains.

The different perspectives of the national accounts and household balance sheets are shown in Figure 6-8 on page 122. When the major increase in the value of assets (particularly stocks) is included, the saving rate in the 1990s was a healthy 17 percent as compared to the 3 percent measured in the national acounts. Many economists believe that the wealth effect can go a long way to explaining the decline in saving as measured in the national income accounts.

Does this alternative view mean that we can breathe a sigh of relief? Probably not. The reason is that the high saving during the 1990s was largely in

"paper wealth." But a rise in stock-market valuations on existing assets may not reflect the productivity or "real wealth" of the economy. Although people feel richer when asset prices rise in a speculative bubble, the economy cannot produce more cars, computers, food, or housing. Moreover, if everyone decided to cash in their stocks, they would find that prices would fall and they could not convert their paper wealth into consumption.

Hence, economists are justified in worrying about the decline in the national-accounts saving rate. While consumers may *feel* richer because of the booming stock market, the nation is *actually* richer only when its productive tangible and intangible assets increase.

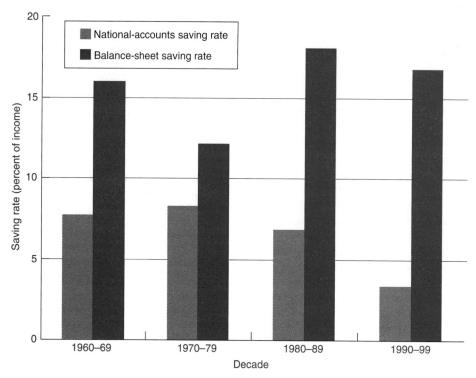

FIGURE 6-8. Two Measures of the Personal Saving Rate

According to the national accounts, the saving rate has fallen sharply in the last two decades. This measure is different from saving as seen in household balance sheets, which is the change in real net worth (including capital gains on assets) divided by income. Because of the sharp increase in stock prices in the 1990s, the balance sheet personal saving rate was high even as the national-accounts personal saving rate dropped sharply. (Source: William G. Gale and John Sabelhaus, "Perspectives on the Household Saving Rate," *Brookings Papers on Economic Activity,* no. 1, 1999; and U.S. Department of Commerce. These estimates exclude the 1999 revisions in the national accounts.)

B. INVESTMENT

The second major component of private spending is investment. Investment plays two roles in macroeconomics. First, because it is a large and volatile component of spending, investment often leads to changes in aggregate demand and affects the business cycle. In addition, investment leads to capital accumulation. Adding to the stock of buildings and equipment increases the nation's potential output and promotes economic growth in the long run.

Thus investment plays a dual role, affecting short-run output through its impact on aggregate demand and influencing long-run output growth through the impact of capital formation on potential output and aggregate supply.

The meaning of "investment" in economics

Remember that macroeconomists use the term "investment" or "real investment" to mean additions to the stock of productive assets or capital goods like computers or trucks. When Amazon.com builds a new warehouse or when the Smiths build a new house, these activities represent investment.

Many people speak of "investing" when buying a piece of land, an old security, or any title to property. In economics, these purchases are really financial transactions or "financial investments," because what one person is buying, someone else is selling. There is investment only when real capital is produced.

DETERMINANTS OF INVESTMENT

In this discussion, we focus on *gross private domestic investment,* or *I.* This is the domestic component of national investment. Recall, however, that *I* is but one component of total social investment, which also includes foreign investment, government investment, and intangible investments in human capital and improved knowledge.

The major types of gross private domestic investment are the building of residential structures; investment in business fixed equipment, software, and structures; and additions to inventory. Of the total, about one-quarter is residential housing, one-twentieth is normally change in inventories, and the rest—averaging 70 percent of total investment in recent years—is investment in business plant, equipment, and software.

Why do businesses invest? Ultimately, businesses buy capital goods when they expect that this action will earn them a profit—that is, will bring them revenues greater than the costs of the investment. This simple statement contains the three elements essential to understanding investment: revenues, costs, and expectations.

Revenues

An investment will bring the firm additional revenue if it helps the firm sell more product. This suggests that the overall level of output (or GDP) will be an important determinant of investment. When factories are lying idle, firms have relatively little need for new factories, so investment is low. More generally, investment depends upon the revenues that will be generated by the state of overall economic activity. Most studies find that investment is very sensitive to the business cycle. A recent example of a large output effect was seen during the business downturn of 1979–1982, when output fell sharply and investment declined by 15 percent.

Costs

A second important determinant of the level of investment is the costs of investing. Because investment goods last many years, reckoning the costs of investment is somewhat more complicated than doing so for other commodities like coal or wheat. For durable goods, the cost of capital includes not only the price of the capital good but also the interest rate that borrowers pay to finance the capital as well as the taxes that firms pay on their incomes.

To understand this point, note that investors often raise the funds for buying capital goods by borrowing (say, through a mortgage or in the bond market). What is the cost of borrowing? It is the *interest rate* on borrowed funds. Recall that the interest rate is the price paid for borrowing money for a period of time; for example, you might have to pay 8 percent to borrow $1000 for a year. In the case of a family buying a house, the interest rate is the mortgage interest rate.

Additionally, taxes can have a major effect on investment. One important tax is the federal corporation income tax. This tax takes up to 34 cents of the last dollar of corporate profits, thereby discouraging investment in the corporate sector. Sometimes, the government gives tax breaks to particular activities or sectors. For example, the government encourages home ownership by allowing homeowners to deduct real-estate taxes and mortgage interest from their taxable income.

Expectations

The third element in the determination of investment is profit expectations and business confidence. Investment is, above all, a gamble on the future, a bet that the revenue from an investment will exceed its costs. If businesses are concerned that political conditions in Russia are unstable, they will be reluctant to invest there. Conversely, because businesses believe (rightly or wrongly) that Internet commerce will be an important feature of the distribution network, they are investing heavily in that sector.

Thus investment decisions hang by a thread on expectations and forecasts. But, as one wit said, forecasting is hazardous, especially about the future. Businesses spend much energy analyzing investments and trying to narrow the uncertainties about their investments.

We can sum up our review of the forces lying behind investment decisions as follows:

Businesses invest to earn profits. Because capital goods last many years, investment decisions depend on (1) the demand for the output produced by the new investment, (2) the interest rates and taxes that influence the costs of the investment, and (3) business expectations about the state of the economy.

THE INVESTMENT DEMAND CURVE

In analyzing the determinants of investment, we focus particularly on the relationship between interest rates and investment. This linkage is crucial because interest rates (influenced by central banks) are the major instrument by which governments influence investment. To show the relationship between interest rates and investment, economists use a schedule called the *investment demand curve.*

Consider a simplified economy where firms can invest in different projects: A, B, C, and so forth, up to H. These investments are so durable (like power plants or buildings) that we can ignore the need for replacement. Further, they yield a constant stream of net income each year, and there is no inflation. Table 6-5 shows the financial data on each of the investment projects.

Consider project A. This project costs $1 million. It has a very high return—$1500 per year of revenues per $1000 invested (this is a rate of return of 150 percent per year). Columns (4) and (5) show the cost of investment. For simplicity, assume that the investment is financed purely by borrowing at the market interest rate, here taken alternatively as 10 percent per year in column (4) and 5 percent in column (5).

Thus at a 10 percent annual interest rate, the cost of borrowing $1000 is $100 a year, as is shown in all entries of column (4); at a 5 percent interest rate, the borrowing cost is $50 per $1000 borrowed per year.

Finally, the last two columns show the *annual net profit* from each investment. For lucrative project A, the net annual profit is $1400 a year per $1000 invested at a 10 percent interest rate. Project H loses money.

(1)	(2)	(3)	(4)	(5)	(6)	(7)
			Cost per $1,000 of Project at Annual Interest Rate of		Annual Net Profit per $1,000 Invested at Annual Interest Rate of	
Project	Total investment in project ($, million)	Annual revenues per $1,000 invested ($)	10% ($)	5% ($)	10% ($) (6) = (3) − (4)	5% ($) (7) = (3) − (5)
A	1	1,500	100	50	1,400	1,450
B	4	220	100	50	120	170
C	10	160	100	50	60	110
D	10	130	100	50	30	80
E	5	110	100	50	10	60
F	15	90	100	50	−10	40
G	10	60	100	50	−40	10
H	20	40	100	50	−60	−10

TABLE 6-5. The Profitability of Investment Depends on the Interest Rate

The economy has eight investment projects, ranked in order of return. Column (2) shows the investment in each project. Column (3) calculates the perpetual return each year per $1000 invested. Columns (4) and (5) then show the cost of the project, assuming all funds are borrowed, at interest rates of 10 and 5 percent; this is shown per $1000 of the project.

The last two columns calculate the annual net profit per $1000 invested in the project. If net profit is positive, profit-maximizing firms will undertake the investment; if negative, the investment project will be rejected.

Note how the cutoff between profitable and unprofitable investments moves as the interest rate rises. (Where would the cutoff be if the interest rate rose to 15 percent per year?)

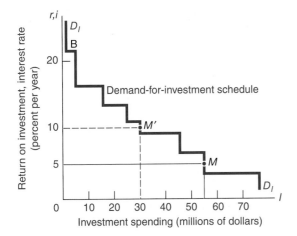

FIGURE 6-9. Investment Depends upon Interest Rate

The downward-stepping demand-for-investment schedule plots the amount that businesses would invest at each interest rate, as calculated from the data in Table 6-5. Each step represents a lump of investment: project A has such a high rate that it is off the figure; the highest visible step is project B, shown at the upper left. At each interest rate, all investments that have positive net profit will be undertaken.

To review our findings: In choosing among investment projects, firms compare the annual revenues from an investment with the annual cost of capital, which depends upon the interest rate. The difference between annual revenue and annual cost is the annual net profit. When annual net profit is positive, the investment makes money, while a negative net profit denotes that the investment loses money.[4]

Look again at Table 6-5 and examine the last column, showing annual net profit at a 5 percent interest rate. Note that at this interest rate, investment projects A through G would be profitable. We would thus expect profit-maximizing firms to invest in all seven projects, which [from column (2)] total up to $55 million in investment. Thus at a 5 percent interest rate, investment demand would be $55 million.

However, suppose that the interest rate rises to 10 percent. Then the cost of financing these investments would double. We see from column (6) that investment projects F and G become unprofitable at an interest rate of 10 percent; investment demand would fall to $30 million.

We show the results of this analysis in Figure 6-9. This figure shows the *demand-for-investment schedule* which is here a downward-sloping step function of the interest rate. This schedule shows the amount of investment that would be undertaken at each interest rate; it is obtained by adding up all the investments that would be profitable at each level of the interest rate.

Hence, if the market interest rate is 5 percent, the desired level of investment will occur at point *M*, which shows investment of $55 million. At this interest rate, projects A through G are undertaken. If interest rates were to rise to 10 percent, projects F and G would be squeezed out; in this situation, investment demand would lie at point *M'* in Figure 6-9, with total investment of $30 million.[5]

Shifts in the Investment Demand Curve

We have seen how interest rates affect the level of investment. Investment is affected by other forces as well. For example, an increase in the GDP will shift the investment demand curve out, as shown in Figure 6-10(*a*) on the next page.

An increase in business taxation would depress investment. Say that the government taxes away half the net yield in column (3) of Table 6-5, with interest costs in columns (4) and (5) not being deductible. The net profits in columns (6) and (7) would therefore decline. [Verify that at a 10 percent interest rate, a 50 percent tax on column (3) would raise the cutoff to between projects B and C, and the demand for investment would decline to $5 million.] The case of a tax increase on investment income is shown in Figure 6-10(*b*).

Finally, note the importance of expectations. What if investors become optimistic about e-commerce? They might project rapid growth rates for companies like AOL–Time Warner or Yahoo! and set aside tra-

---

[4] This example greatly simplifies the calculations businesses must make in actual investment decisions. Usually, investments involve an uneven stream of returns, depreciation of capital, inflation, taxes, and multiple interest rates on borrowed funds. Discussion of the economics of discounting and present values is found in books on money and finance. See the Further Reading section at the end of this chapter.

[5] We will later see that when prices are changing, it is appropriate to use a real interest rate, which represents the nominal or money interest rate corrected for inflation.

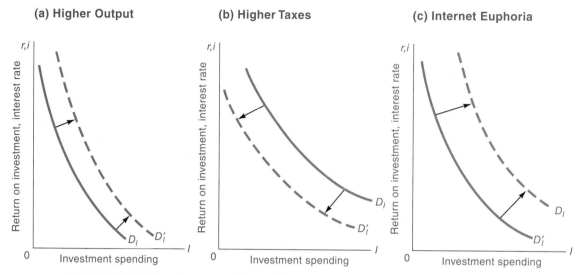

FIGURE 6-10. Shifts in Investment Demand Function

In the demand-for-investment (*DI*) schedule, the arrows show the impact of (**a**) a higher level of GDP, (**b**) higher taxes on capital income, and (**c**) a burst of business euphoria induced by enthusiasm about prospects for the Internet.

ditional precepts that business schools teach about investment. As a result, the demand for investment in software and factories for Internet companies might temporarily increase sharply. Figure 6-10(*c*) displays how a bout of business optimism would shift out the investment demand schedule. The opposite case, of pessimism about profits in corrupt Russia, would explain why Western firms have invested warily in that economy. These are but two examples of how expectations can have powerful effects on investment.

After learning about the factors affecting investment, you will not be surprised to discover that investment is the most volatile component of spending. Investment behaves unpredictably because it depends on such uncertain factors as the success or failure of new and untried products, changes in tax rates and interest rates, political attitudes and approaches to stabilizing the economy, and similar changeable events of economic life. *In virtually every business cycle, investment fluctuations have been the driving force behind boom or bust.*

ON TO THE THEORY OF AGGREGATE DEMAND

We have now completed our introduction to the basic concepts of macroeconomics. We have examined the determinants of consumption and investment and seen how they can fluctuate from year to year, sometimes quite sharply.

At this point, macroeconomics branches into one of two major themes—business cycles and economic growth. In the chapters that follow, we begin our survey of business cycles, or the behavior of the economy in the short run. This approach, known as Keynesian economics, shows how changes in investment, government spending and taxation, foreign trade, and the money supply can be transmitted to the rest of the economy. We will see that actual GDP can diverge from its full-employment potential. We will also see how government fiscal and monetary policies can combat recessions and booms. At the heart of the analysis is the movement of consumption and investment that we explored in this chapter.

SUMMARY

A. Consumption and Saving

1. Disposable income is an important determinant of consumption and saving. The consumption function is the schedule relating total consumption to total disposable income. Because each dollar of disposable income is either saved or consumed, the saving function is the other side or mirror image of the consumption function.

2. Recall the major features of consumption and saving functions:

   a. The consumption (or saving) function relates the level of consumption (or saving) to the level of disposable income.

   b. The marginal propensity to consume (*MPC*) is the amount of extra consumption generated by an extra dollar of disposable income.

   c. The marginal propensity to save (*MPS*) is the extra saving generated by an extra dollar of disposable income.

   d. Graphically, the *MPC* and the *MPS* are the slopes of the consumption and saving schedules, respectively.

   e. $MPS \equiv 1 - MPC$.

3. Adding together individual consumption functions gives us the national consumption function. In simplest form, it shows total consumption expenditures as a function of disposable income. Other variables, such as permanent income or the life-cycle effect, wealth, and age also have a significant impact on consumption patterns.

4. The personal saving rate has declined sharply in the last two decades. To explain this decline, economists point to social security and government health programs, changes in capital markets, and the rapid rise in personal wealth due to the stock market boom of the 1990s. Declining saving hurts the economy because personal saving is a major component of national saving and investment. While people feel richer because of the booming stock market, the nation's true wealth increases only when its productive tangible and intangible assets increase.

B. Investment

5. The second major component of spending is gross private domestic investment in housing, plant, software, and equipment. Firms invest to earn profits. The major economic forces that determine investment are therefore the revenues produced by investment (primarily influenced by the state of the business cycle), the cost of investment (determined by interest rates and tax policy), and the state of expecatations about the future. Because the determinants of investment depend on highly unpredictable future events, investment is the most volatile component of aggregate spending.

6. An important relationship is the investment demand schedule, which connects the level of investment spending to the interest rate. Because the profitability of investment varies inversely with the interest rate, which affects the cost of capital, we can derive a downward-sloping investment demand curve. As the interest rate declines, more investment projects become profitable, showing why the investment demand schedule slopes downward.

CONCEPTS FOR REVIEW

Consumption and Saving

disposable income, consumption, saving
consumption and saving functions
personal saving rates
marginal propensity to consume (*MPC*)
marginal propensity to save (*MPS*)

$MPC + MPS \equiv 1$
break-even point
45° line
determinants of consumption:
  current disposable income
  permanent income
  wealth
  life-cycle effect

Investment

determinants of investment:
  revenues
  costs
  expectations
role of interest rates in I
investment demand function

FURTHER READING AND INTERNET WEBSITES

Further Reading

Economists have studied consumer expenditure patterns in order to improve predictions and help improve economic policy. One of the most influential studies is Milton Friedman, *The Theory of the Consumption Function* (University of Chicago Press, 1957). A historical overview by an economic historian is Stanley Lebergott, *Pursuing Happiness: American Consumers in the Twentieth Century* (Princeton University Press, Princeton, N.J., 1993).

Firms devote much management time to deciding about investment strategies. A good survey can be found in Richard A. Brealey and Stewart C. Myers, *Principles of Corporate Finance*, 5th ed. (McGraw-Hill, New York, 1996).

Websites

Data on total personal consumption expenditures for the United States are provided at the website of the Bureau of Economic Analysis, www.bea.doc.gov. Data on family budgets is contained in Bureau of Labor Statistics, *Consumer Expenditures*, available at www.bls.gov.

Data and analysis of investment for the U.S. economy are provided by the Bureau of Economic Analysis at www.bea.doc.gov.

Milton Friedman and Franco Modigliani made major contributions to our understanding of the consumption function. Visit the Nobel website at www.nobel.se/laureates to read about the importance of their contributions for macroeconomics.

QUESTIONS FOR DISCUSSION

1. Summarize the budget patterns for food, clothing, luxuries, saving.
2. In working with the consumption function and the investment demand schedule, we need to distinguish between shifts of and movements along these schedules.
   a. Define carefully for both curves changes that would lead to shifts of and those that would produce movements along the schedules.
   b. For the following, explain verbally and show in a diagram whether they are shifts of or movements along the consumption function: increase in disposable income, decrease in wealth, fall in stock prices.
   c. For the following, explain in words and show in a diagram whether they are shifts of or movements along the investment demand curve: expectation of a decline in output next year, rise of interest rates, increase in taxes on profits.
3. Exactly how were the *MPC* and *MPS* in Table 6-4 computed? Illustrate by calculating *MPC* and *MPS* between points *A* and *B*. Explain why it must always be true that *MPC* + *MPS* ≡ 1.
4. I consume all my income at every level of income. Draw my consumption and saving functions. What are my *MPC* and *MPS*?
5. Estimate your income, consumption, and saving for last year. If you dissaved (consumed more than your income), how did you finance your dissaving? Estimate the composition of your consumption in terms of each of the major categories listed in Table 6-1.
6. "Along the consumption function, income changes more than consumption." What does this imply for the *MPC* and *MPS*?
7. "Changes in disposable income lead to movements along the consumption function; changes in wealth or other factors lead to a shift of the consumption function." Explain this statement with an illustration of each case.
8. What would be the effects of the following on the investment demand function illustrated in Table 6-5 and Figure 6-9?
   a. A doubling of the annual revenues per $1000 invested shown in column (3).
   b. A rise in interest rates to 15 percent per year.
   c. The addition of a ninth project with data in the first three columns of (J, 10, 70).
   d. A 50 percent tax on net profits shown in columns (6) and (7).
9. Using the augmented investment demand schedule from question 8(c) and assuming that the interest rate is 10 percent, calculate the level of investment for cases **a** through **d** in question 8.
10. **Advanced problem:** According to the life-cycle model, people consume each year an amount that depends upon their *lifetime* income rather than upon their cur-

(1)	(2)	(3)	(4)	(5)
Year	Income ($)	Consumption ($)	Saving ($)	Cumulative saving (end of year) ($)
1	30,000	————	————	————
2	30,000	————	————	————
3	25,000	————	————	————
4	15,000	————	————	————
5*	0	————	————	0
*Retired.				

TABLE 6-6.

rent income. Assume that you expect to receive future income (in constant dollars) according to the schedule in Table 6-6.

Assume that there is no interest paid on saving. You have no initial saving. Further assume that you want to "smooth" your consumption (enjoying equal consumption each year) because of diminishing extra satisfaction from extra consumption. Derive your best consumption trajectory for the 5 years, and write the figures in column (3). Then calculate your saving and enter the amounts in column (4); put your end-of-period wealth, or cumulative saving, for each year into column (5). What is your average saving rate in the first 4 years?

Next, assume that a government social security program taxes you $2000 in each of your working years and provides you with an $8000 pension in year 5. If you still desire to smooth consumption, calculate your revised saving plan. How has the social security program affected your consumption? What is the effect on your average saving rate in the first 4 years? Can you see why some economists claim that social security can lower saving?

The history of American capitalism is one of recurrent periods of boom and bust, of recessions and expansions. Sometimes, jobs are hard to find, factories are idle, and profits are low. These downturns are usually short and mild, as was the case in 1990–1991. Infrequently, as during the 1930s in the Great Depression, the contraction may persist for a decade and cause widespread economic hardships.

At other times, business conditions are healthy, with plenty of job vacancies, factories working overtime, and robust profits. The long expansion of the 1990s was a prosperous period for American consumers—but a perplexing one for economists. The economy grew rapidly; labor and product markets were exceptionally tight; unemployment was low and capacity utilization was high. Yet, unlike earlier long expansions, inflation remained low throughout the expansion. The stock market rose to levels never seen before anywhere. Was this a "new era" of American capitalism fueled by globalization and the information economy? Or was this the same old capitalism accompanied by "special circumstances" that led to rapid growth and low inflation?

The short-term variations in economic activity are known as business cycles, or business fluctuations, and are covered in the first part of this chapter. Understanding business cycles has proved one of the most durable problems in all of macroeconomics. What causes business fluctuations? How can government policies reduce their virulence? Economists were largely unable to answer these questions until the 1930s. At that point, the revolutionary macroeconomic theories of John Maynard Keynes pointed to the importance of the forces of aggregate demand in determining business cycles. The lesson of Keynesian economics is that *changes in aggregate demand can have a powerful impact on the overall level of output, employment, and prices in the short run.*

There have been many challenges, modifications, and elaborations to the basic Keynesian framework since its earliest days. Still, the theory of aggregate demand remains the best way to understand the business cycle. In the second part of this chapter, therefore, we describe the foundations of aggregate demand analysis and show the basic Keynesian approach to business cycles. This discussion paves the way for the next chapter's examination of the Keynesian multiplier model, which describes the simplest income-determination theory. Figure 7-1 provides a road map for the analysis.

CHAPTER

7

Business Fluctuations and the Theory of Aggregate Demand

The fault, dear Brutus, is not in our stars—but in ourselves.

William Shakespeare, *Julius Caesar*

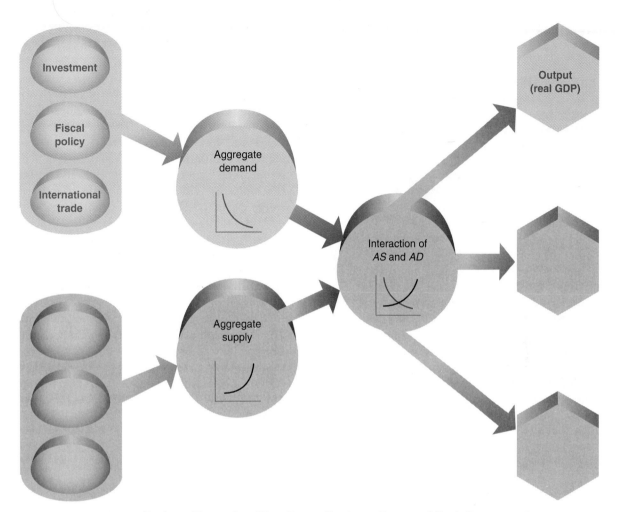

FIGURE 7-1. Business Fluctuations Have Been a Persistent Feature of Capitalism

The chapter begins with an analysis of the business cycle. It then develops the theory of aggregate demand to explain how demand shifts produce business fluctuations.

A. BUSINESS FLUCTUATIONS

Economic history shows that the economy never grows in a smooth and even pattern. A country may enjoy several years of exhilarating economic expansion and prosperity, as the United States did in the 1990s. This might be followed by a recession or even a financial crisis or, on rare occasions, a prolonged depression. Then national output falls, profits and real incomes decline, and the unemployment rate jumps to uncomfortably high levels as legions of workers lose their jobs.

Eventually the bottom is reached, and recovery begins. The recovery may be slow or fast. It may be incomplete, or it may be so strong as to lead to a new boom. Prosperity may mean a long, sustained period of brisk demand, plentiful jobs, and rising living standards. Or it may be marked by a quick, inflationary flaring up of prices and speculation, to be followed by another slump.

Upward and downward movements in output, inflation, interest rates, and employment form the business cycle that characterizes all market economies.

FEATURES OF THE BUSINESS CYCLE

What exactly do we mean by "business cycles"?

Business cycles are economywide fluctuations in total national output, income, and employment, usually lasting for a period of 2 to 10 years, marked by widespread expansion or contraction in most sectors of the economy.

Typically economists divide business cycles into two main phases, *recession* and *expansion.* Peaks and troughs mark the turning points of the cycles. Figure 7-2 shows the successive phases of the business cycle. The downturn of a business cycle is called a recession. A **recession** is a recurring period of decline in total output, income, and employment, usually lasting from 6 months to a year and marked by widespread contractions in many sectors of the economy. A **depression** is a recession that is major in both scale and duration.

According to the organization which dates the beginning and end of business cycles, the National Bureau of Economic Research, the last U.S. recession occurred in 1990–1991. The economy hit the trough in March 1991 and then entered the expansion. When the expansion continued unbroken through February 2000, it became the longest business expansion in recorded U.S. history. (See "Websites" at the end of this chapter for further information.)

Although we call short-term fluctuations "cycles," the actual pattern is irregular. No two business cycles are quite the same. No exact formula, such as might apply to the revolutions of the planets or of a pendulum, can be used to predict the duration and timing of business cycles. Rather, in their irregularities, business cycles more closely resemble the fluctuations of the weather. Figure 7-3 shows the American business cycles throughout recent history. You can see that cycles are like mountain ranges, with different levels of hills and valleys. Some valleys are very deep and broad, as in the Great Depression; others are shallow and narrow, as in the recession of 1991.

While business cycles are not identical twins, they often have a familial similarity. If a reliable economic forecaster announces that a recession is about to arrive, are there any typical phenomena that you should expect to accompany the recession? The following are a few of the *customary characteristics* of a recession:

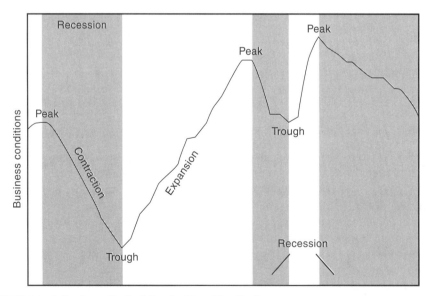

FIGURE 7-2. A Business Cycle, Like the Year, Has Its Seasons

Business cycles are the irregular expansions and contractions in economic activity. (These are the actual monthly data on industrial production for a recent business-cycle period.)

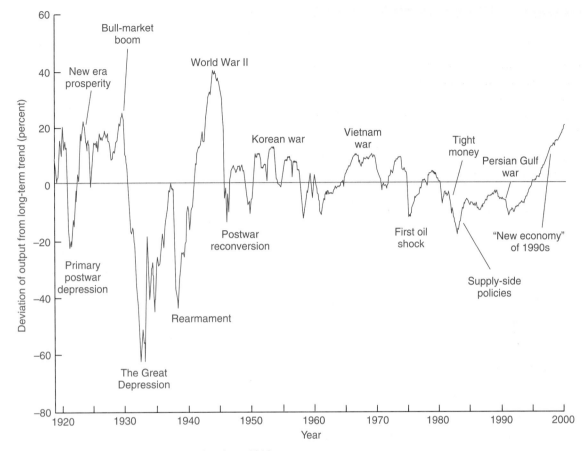

FIGURE 7-3. Business Activity since 1919

Industrial production has fluctuated irregularly around its long-run trend. Note how the long boom and information revolution of the 1990s has given a pronounced upward tilt to the business cycle. Can you detect a more stable economy in recent years? (Source: Federal Reserve Board, detrended by authors.)

- Often, consumer purchases decline sharply, while business inventories of automobiles and other durable goods increase unexpectedly. As businesses react by curbing production, real GDP falls. Shortly afterward, business investment in plant and equipment also falls sharply.
- The demand for labor falls—first seen in a drop in the average workweek, followed by layoffs and higher unemployment.
- As output falls, inflation slows. As demand for crude materials declines, their prices tumble. Wages and prices of services are unlikely to decline, but they tend to rise less rapidly in economic downturns.
- Business profits fall sharply in recessions. In anticipation of this, common-stock prices usually fall as investors sniff the scent of a business downturn. However, because the demand for credit falls, interest rates generally also fall in recessions.

Expansions are the mirror images of recessions, with each of the above factors operating in the opposite direction.

BUSINESS-CYCLE THEORIES

Exogenous vs. Internal Mechanisms. Over the years macroeconomics has been energized by vigorous debates about the sources of business fluctuations. What causes aggregate demand to shift suddenly? Why should market economies blow hot and cold? There is certainly no end of possible explanations, but it is useful to classify the different sources into two categories, exogenous and primarily internal. Economists use the term "exogenous" to refer to forces operating from outside the system. The *exogenous* theories find the root of the business cycle in the fluctuations of factors outside the economic system—in wars, revolutions, and elections; in oil prices, gold discoveries, and migrations; in discoveries of new lands and resources; in scientific breakthroughs and technological innovations; even in sunspots or the weather. The long economic boom of the 1990s was fueled by an investment boom radiating out of the information technologies sector and largely based on fundamental scientific and engineering developments in microprocessors.

By contrast, the *internal* theories look for mechanisms within the economic system itself that give rise to self-generating business cycles. In this approach, every expansion breeds recession and contraction, and every contraction breeds revival and expansion—in a quasi-regular, repeating chain. One important case is the *multiplier-accelerator theory*. According to the accelerator principle, rapid output growth stimulates investment. High investment in turn stimulates more output growth, and the process continues until the capacity of the economy is reached, at which point the economic growth rate slows. The slower growth in turn reduces investment spending and inventory accumulation, which tends to send the economy into a recession. The process then works in reverse until the trough is reached, and the economy then stabilizes and turns up again. This internal theory of the business cycle shows a mechanism, like the motion of a pendulum, in which an exogenous shock tends to propagate itself throughout the economy in a cyclical fashion.

Demand-Induced Cycles. One important source of business fluctuations is shocks to aggregate demand.

A typical case is illustrated in Figure 7-4, which shows how a decline in aggregate demand lowers output. Say that the economy begins in short-run equilibrium at point *B*. Then, perhaps because of a decline in defense spending or tight money, the aggregate demand curve shifts leftward to *AD'*. If there is no change in aggregate supply, the economy will reach a new equilibrium at point *C*. Note that output declines from *Q* to *Q'*. In addition, prices are lower than they were at the previous equilibrium, and the rate of inflation falls.

The case of a boom is, naturally, just the opposite. Here, the *AD* curve shifts to the right, output approaches potential GDP or perhaps even overshoots it, and prices and inflation rise.

Business-cycle fluctuations in output, employment, and prices are often caused by shifts in aggregate demand. These occur as consumers, businesses, or governments change total spending relative to the economy's productive capacity. When these shifts in aggregate demand lead to sharp business downturns, the economy suffers recessions or even depressions. A sharp upturn in economic activity can lead to inflation.

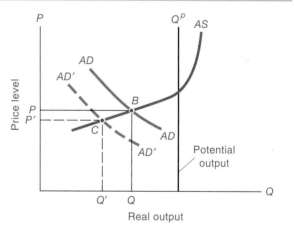

FIGURE 7-4. A Decline in Aggregate Demand Leads to an Economic Downturn

A downward shift in the *AD* curve along a relatively flat and unchanging *AS* curve leads to lower levels of output. Note that as a result of the downward shift in the *AD* curve, actual output declines relative to potential output in a recession.

Thinking about business cycles

Economists have observed business cycles for almost two centuries. Here are some of the different approaches that have been proposed, along with their proponents:

1. *Monetary* theories attribute business fluctuations to the expansion and contraction of money and credit (M. Friedman). Under this approach, monetary factors are the primary source of fluctuations in aggregate demand. For example, the recession of 1981–1982 was triggered when the Federal Reserve raised nominal interest rates to 18 percent to fight inflation.

2. The *multiplier-accelerator model*, described above, proposes that exogenous shocks are propagated by the multiplier mechanism, which we examine in the next chapter, along with a theory of investment called the accelerator principle (P. Samuelson). This theory shows how the interaction of multiplier and accelerator can lead to regular cycles in aggregate demand; it is one of the few models that generates internal cycles.

3. *Political* theories of business cycles attribute fluctuations to politicians who manipulate economic policies in order to be reelected (W. Nordhaus, E. Tufte). Historically, presidential elections are sensitive to economic conditions in the year preceding the election. As a result, if they have a choice, most presidents would prefer to follow President Ronald Reagan's example. Although the U.S. economy went through a deep recession early in his term, by the time he was running for reelection in 1984, the economy was growing rapidly, which contributed to a reelection landslide.

4. *Equilibrium-business-cycle* theories claim that misperceptions about price and wage movements lead people to supply too much or too little labor, which leads to fluctuations of output and employment (R. Lucas, R. Barro, T. Sargent). In one version of these theories, unemployment rises in recessions because workers are holding out for wages that are too high.

5. *Real-business-cycle* proponents hold that innovations or productivity shocks in one sector can spread to the rest of the economy and cause recessions and booms (J. Schumpeter early in the twentieth century and E. Prescott, P. Long, C. Plosser in recent years). In this classical approach, cycles are caused primarily by shocks to aggregate supply, and not by changes in aggregate demand. Such an approach looks particularly attractive for explaining situations like the one in Rus-

sia, which made the transition from central planning to the market in the 1990s. That nation had rapid output declines largely due to disruption and confusion.

6. *Supply shocks* occur when business fluctuations are caused by shifts in aggregate supply (R. J. Gordon). The classic examples came during the oil crises of the 1970s, when sharp increases in oil prices contracted aggregate supply, increased inflation, and lowered output and employment. Many economists think that the low inflation and rapid growth of the American economy in the 1994–1999 period may be explained by favorable supply shocks. During this period, costs grew slowly because of declining oil and commodity prices, declining import prices, rapid productivity growth, and below-par increases in medical-care prices.

These theories will be explored in greater depth in the chapters that follow—keep a mental list of the major approaches as we proceed.

Which of these theories best explains the facts of business cycles? Actually, each of the competing theories contains elements of truth, but none is universally valid in all times and places. *The key to macroeconomic wisdom is to combine understanding of the different theories with knowledge of where and when to apply them.*

FORECASTING BUSINESS CYCLES

Economists have developed forecasting tools to help them foresee changes in the economy. Like bright headlights on a car, a good forecast illuminates the economic terrain ahead and helps decision makers adapt their actions to economic conditions.

Econometric Modeling and Forecasting

In an earlier era, economists tried to peer into the future by looking at easily available data on items like money, boxcar loadings, and steel production. For example, a drop in steel production was a sign that businesses had reduced purchases and that the economy would soon slow down. Eventually this process was formalized by combining several different statistics into an "index of leading indicators." While it is not infallible, the index does give an early and mechanical warning on whether the economy is heading up or down.

For a more detailed look into the future, economists turn to computerized econometric forecasting models. An *econometric model* is a set of equations, representing the behavior of the economy, that has been estimated using historical data. Early pioneers in this area were Jan Tinbergen of the Netherlands and Lawrence Klein of the University of Pennsylvania—both winners of the Nobel Prize for their development of empirical macroeconomic models. Today, there is an entire industry of econometricians estimating macroeconomic models and forecasting the future of the economy.

How are computer models of the economy constructed? Generally modelers start with an analytical framework containing equations representing both aggregate demand and aggregate supply. Using the techniques of modern econometrics, each equation is "fitted" to the historical data to obtain parameter estimates (such as the *MPC*, the slope of the investment demand function, etc.). In addition, at each stage modelers use their own experience and judg-

ment to assess whether the results are reasonable.

Finally, the whole model is put together and run as a system of equations. In small models there are one or two dozen equations. Today, large systems forecast from a few hundred to 10,000 variables. Once the exogenous and policy variables are specified (population, government spending and tax rates, monetary policy, etc.), the system of equations can project important economic variables into the future.

Under ordinary circumstances, the forecasts do a fairly good job of illuminating the road ahead. At other times, particularly when there are major policy changes, forecasting is a hazardous profession. Figure 7-5 shows the results of a recent survey of forecasts of real GDP (or, earlier, real GNP) by the major forecasting groups in the United States. For comparison purposes, the study used as a benchmark a "naive forecast" in which the next year's forecasted output growth was simply equal to the current year's growth rate.

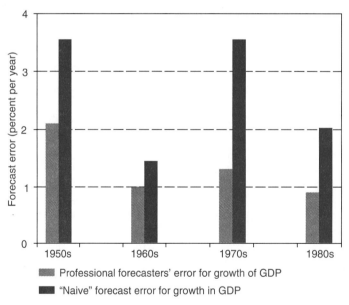

FIGURE 7-5. **How Have Professional Forecasts Performed?**

The record of professional forecasters is compared with that of "naive" forecasts. In every decade since systematic forecasting began, macroeconomic forecasts have improved upon guesswork, and the margin of improvement has grown slightly over time. (Source: Stephen McNees, *New England Economic Review*, July 1992. Figures are averages for each year of the decade.)

As the figure shows, professional forecasters systematically beat naive forecasts. In the first two decades, the average forecast error among professionals was more than half the error of naive forecasts, while in the 1970s and 1980s, professionals' errors dropped to less than half those of the naive approach. Another interesting feature shown in Figure 7-5 is that instability varies from period to period, with the 1950s and 1970s being relatively volatile while the 1960s and 1980s were tranquil periods. Clearly, forecasting is as much art as science in our uncertain world. Still, the strength of economic forecasting is that, year in and year out, professional forecasters provide more accurate forecasts than do those who use unsystematic or unscientific approaches.

B. FOUNDATIONS OF AGGREGATE DEMAND

The first half of this chapter described the short-term changes in output, employment, and prices that characterize business fluctuations in market economies. We showed how cyclical movements can occur when there are shifts in aggregate demand.

The time has come to explore in depth the foundations of aggregate demand. What are the major components of aggregate demand? How do they interact with aggregate supply to determine output and prices? What is the Keynesian theory of output determination, and how does it explain short-run fluctuations in GDP? We began to explore these questions in Chapter 4's introduction to macroeconomics. We now look at aggregate demand in more detail in order to get a better understanding of the forces which drive the economy. In the next chapter, we derive the simplest model of aggregate demand—the multiplier model.

Aggregate demand (or *AD*) is the total or aggregate quantity of output that is willingly bought at a given level of prices, other things held constant. *AD* is the desired spending in all product sectors: consumption, private domestic investment, government purchases of goods and services, and net exports. It has four components:

1. *Consumption.* As we saw in the last chapter, consumption (C) is primarily determined by disposable income, which is personal income less taxes. Other factors affecting consumption are longer-term trends in income, household wealth, and the aggregate price level. Aggregate demand analysis focuses on the determinants of *real* consumption (that is, nominal or dollar consumption divided by the price index for consumption).

2. *Investment.* Investment (I) spending includes purchases of buildings, software, and equipment and accumulation of inventories. Our analysis in Chapter 6 showed that the major determinants of investment are the level of output, the cost of capital (as determined by tax policies along with interest rates and other financial conditions), and expectations about the future. The major channel by which economic policy can affect investment is monetary policy.

3. *Government purchases.* A third component of aggregate demand is government purchases of goods and services (G): purchases of goods like tanks or road-building equipment as well as the services of judges and public-school teachers. Unlike private consumption and investment, this component of aggregate demand is determined directly by the government's spending decisions; when the Pentagon buys a new fighter aircraft, this output directly adds to the GDP.

4. *Net exports.* A final component of aggregate demand is net exports (X), which equal the value of exports minus the value of imports. Imports are determined by domestic income and output, by the ratio of domestic to foreign prices, and by the foreign exchange rate of the dollar. Exports (which are imports of other countries) are the mirror image of imports, determined by foreign incomes and outputs, by relative prices, and by foreign exchange rates. Net exports, then, will be determined by domestic and foreign incomes, relative prices, and exchange rates.

Figure 7-6 on page 138 shows the *AD* curve and its four major components. At price level *P*, we can read the levels of consumption, investment, government purchases, and net exports, which sum to GDP, or *Q*. The sum of the four spending streams at this price level is aggregate spending, or aggregate demand, at that price level.

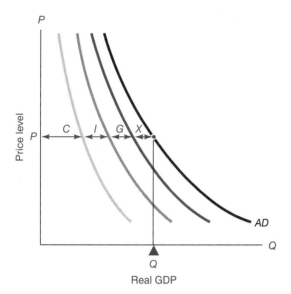

FIGURE 7-6. Components of Aggregate Demand

Aggregate demand (*AD*) consists of four components—consumption (*C*), domestic private investment (*I*), government spending on goods and services (*G*), and net exports (*X*).

Aggregate demand shifts when there are changes in macroeconomic policies (such as monetary-policy changes or changes in government expenditures or tax rates) or when exogenous events change spending (as would be the case with changes in foreign output, affecting *X*, or in business confidence, affecting *I*).

THE DOWNWARD-SLOPING AGGREGATE DEMAND CURVE

You will first notice that the aggregate demand curve in Figure 7-6 slopes downward. This means that, holding other things constant, the level of real spending declines as the overall price level in the economy rises.

The aggregate demand curve slopes downward primarily because of the *money-supply effect*. Remember that when we draw an *AD* curve, we hold other things constant. One important variable held constant is nominal money supply (i.e., the dollar value of the money supply). So when prices rise, the *real money supply* (defined as the nominal money supply divided by the price level) must fall. For example,

suppose the nation's money supply is constant at $600 billion. Then, if the consumer price index doubles, the real money supply falls from $600 billion to $300 billion.

As the real money supply contracts, money becomes scarce or "tight." Interest rates and mortgage payments rise, and credit becomes harder to obtain; tight money causes a decline in investment and consumption. In short, a rise in prices with a fixed money supply, holding other things constant, leads to tight money and produces a decline in total real spending.[1] The net effect is a movement up and to the left along the downward-sloping *AD* curve.

We illustrate the money-supply effect in Figure 7-7(*a*). Say that the economy is in equilibrium at point *B*, with a price level of 100 (in constant prices), a real GDP of $3000 billion, and a money supply of $600 billion. Next assume that price inflation increases prices by 50 percent, so the price index *P* rises from 100 to 150. With a fixed nominal money supply, the real money supply declines from $600 billion to $400 billion. Tight money raises interest rates and lowers spending in interest-sensitive sectors like housing, plant and equipment, and automobiles. The net effect is that total real spending declines to $2000 billion, shown as point *C*. The decline in the real money supply will affect aggregate demand through the important monetary mechanism, which is discussed in detail in later chapters.

Other factors also contribute to the relationship between real spending and the price level, although they are today quantitatively less significant than the money-supply effect.

To summarize:

The *AD* curve slopes downward. This implies that real spending declines as the price level rises, other things held constant. The primary reason for the downward-sloping *AD* curve is the money-supply effect, whereby higher prices operating on a fixed nominal money supply produce tight money and lower aggregate spending.

---

[1] We explore the monetary transmission mechanism in more detail in following chapters.

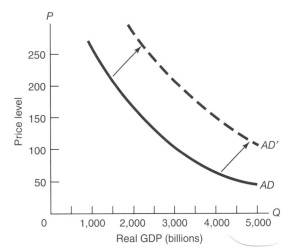

FIGURE 7-7. Movement along vs. Shifts of Aggregate Demand

In (**a**), a higher price level with a fixed nominal money supply leads to tight money, higher interest rates, and declining spending on interest-sensitive investment and consumption. This illustrates a *movement along* the *AD* curve from *B* to *C* when other things are held constant.

In (**b**), other things are no longer constant. Changes in variables underlying *AD*—such as the money supply, tax policy, or military spending—lead to changes in total spending at a given price level. This leads to a *shift of* the *AD* curve.

Microeconomic versus macroeconomic demand

We pause for an important reminder about the difference between macroeconomic and microeconomic demand curves. Recall from our study of supply and demand that the microeconomic demand curve has the price of an individual commodity on the vertical axis and production of that commodity on the horizontal axis, with all other prices and total consumer incomes held constant.

In the aggregate demand curve, the general price level varies along the vertical axis, while total output and incomes vary along the horizontal axis. By contrast, incomes and output are held constant for the microeconomic demand curve.

Finally, the negative slope of the microeconomic demand curve occurs because consumers substitute other goods for the good in question. If the meat price rises, the quantity demanded falls because consumers substitute bread and potatoes for meat, using more of the relatively inexpensive commodities and less of the relatively expensive one. The aggregate demand curve is downward-sloping for quite a different reason: Total spending falls when the overall price level rises primarily because a fixed dollar money supply must be rationed among those who need money by raising interest rates, tightening credit, and reducing total spending.

Macroeconomic *AD* curves differ from their microeconomic cousins because aggregate demand relates prices and output for the entire economy while the micro curve analyzes the price and quantity for a single commodity. The *AD* curve slopes downward primarily because of the money-supply effect, while the micro demand curve slopes downward because consumers substitute other goods for the good whose price has risen.

Shifts in Aggregate Demand

We have seen that total spending in the economy tends to decline as the price level rises, holding other things constant. But those other things tend to change, and their influences produce changes in aggregate demand. What are the key variables that lead to shifts in aggregate demand?

We can separate the determinants of *AD* into two categories, as shown in Table 7-1 below. One set includes the macroeconomic *policy variables* under government control. These are monetary policy (steps by which the central bank can affect the supply of money and other financial conditions) and fiscal policy (taxes and government expenditures). Table 7-1 illustrates how these government policies can affect different components of aggregate demand.

The second category is *exogenous variables,* or variables that are determined outside the *AS-AD* framework. As Table 7-1 shows, some of these variables (such as wars or revolutions) are outside the scope of macroeconomic analysis proper, some (such as foreign economic activity) are outside the control of domestic policy, and others (such as the stock market) have significant independent movement.

What would be the effect of changes in the variables lying behind the *AD* curve? Suppose, for example, that the government increased its purchases of missiles and fuel to fight an air war in the Balkans. The effect of these purchases would be an increase of spending in *G*. Unless some other component of spending offset the increase in *G*, the total *AD* curve would shift out and to the right as *G* increased. Similarly, an increase in the money supply, a radical new innovation that increased the profitability of new investment, or an increase in the value of consumer wealth because of a stock-price increase would lead to an increase in aggregate demand and an outward shift of the *AD* curve.

Figure 7-7(*b*) on page 139 shows how the changes in the variables listed in Table 7-1 would affect the *AD* curve. To test your understanding, construct a similar table showing forces that would tend to decrease aggregate demand (see question 4 at the chapter's end).

Variable	Impact on aggregate demand
Policy variables	
Monetary policy	Increase in money supply lowers interest rates and relaxes credit conditions, inducing higher levels of investment and consumption of durable goods. In an open economy, monetary policy affects the exchange rate and net exports.
Fiscal policy	Increases in government purchases of goods and services directly increase spending; tax reductions or increases in transfers raise disposable income and induce higher consumption. Tax incentives like an investment tax credit can induce higher spending in a particular sector.
Exogenous variables	
Foreign output	Output growth abroad leads to an increase in net exports.
Asset values	Rise in stock market increases household wealth and thereby increases consumption; also, this leads to lower cost of capital and increases business investment.
Advances in technology	Technological advances can open up new opportunities for business investment. Important examples have been the railroad, the automobile, and the Internet.
Other	Political events, free-trade agreements, and the end of the cold war promote business and consumer confidence and increase spending on investment and consumer durables.

TABLE 7-1. Many Factors Can Increase Aggregate Demand and Shift Out the *AD* Curve

The aggregate demand curve relates total spending to the price level. But numerous other influences affect aggregate demand—some policy variables, others exogenous factors. The table lists changes that would tend to increase aggregate demand and shift out the *AD* curve.

RELATIVE IMPORTANCE OF FACTORS INFLUENCING DEMAND

While economists generally agree on the factors influencing demand, they differ in the emphasis they place on different forces. Some economists concentrate primarily on monetary forces in analyzing movements in aggregate demand, especially stressing the role of the money supply. According to these economists, who are often called *monetarists,* the supply of money is the primary determinant of the total dollar value of spending.

Other economists focus on exogenous factors instead. For example, some have argued that technological progress is one of the key determinants of booms and busts. For instance, railroads first became commercially practical in the 1850s. That innovation opened up two decades of massive investment in railroads all over the world and helped the industrial economies enjoy a sustained economic expansion. Economists looking at the 1990s have concluded that the fundamental technological changes in computer hardware, software, and communications have triggered rapid declines in prices in that sector and in the economy; have led to a significant increase in the overall potential growth of the economy; and have produced a remarkable increase in investment. Some believe that the potential growth of the Internet may spawn yet another investment boom as companies spend hundreds of billions of dollars developing communications and software to prepare for e-commerce.

The mainstream of macroeconomic thinking today is an eclectic approach, which has its roots in the Keynesian tradition but incorporates modern developments as well. This approach, called *Keynesian macroeconomics,* accepts that different policy and exogenous forces move the economy during different periods. For example, fiscal policy would be seen as the leading determinant of aggregate demand during World War II, when military spending was absorbing almost half of GDP and monetary policy was passive. In recent years, however, as the federal budget was limited by Congressional rules and the Federal Reserve became more active in combating inflation and unemployment, monetary policy exercised the dominant influence over fluctuations in economic activity.

We now have seen the major elements of the theory of aggregate demand. The next chapter explores the theory in greater depth by analyzing the simplest approach, the multiplier model.

Is the Business Cycle Avoidable?

The history of business cycles in the United States shows a remarkable trend toward greater stability over the last 150 years (look back at Figure 7-3). The period through 1940 witnessed numerous crises and depressions—prolonged, cumulative slumps like those of the 1870s, 1890s, and 1930s. Since 1945, business cycles have become less frequent and milder, and many Americans enter the millennium never having witnessed a major business downturn.

What has changed? Some believe that capitalism is inherently more stable now than it was in earlier times. Some of the stability comes from a larger and more predictable government sector. More important, in our view, is that a better understanding of macroeconomics now permits the government to conduct its monetary and fiscal policies to prevent shocks from turning into recessions and to keep recessions from snowballing into depressions.

During the 1990s, the American economy enjoyed the most stable period of its macroeconomic history. Some people wondered whether the business cycle was dead. Perhaps with wise management and free markets, they wrote, we have banished major recessions and inflations from the land. Is such a prognosis warranted? We believe that such pronouncements are premature. Business cycles may have been absent from North America, but they were actually *more prevalent* in other economies during the 1990s than in earlier decades. We take heed of the following prophetic words of one of the leading analysts of business cycles, Arthur Okun, written toward the end of the second-longest expansion in American history:

> Recessions are now generally considered to be fundamentally preventable, like airplane crashes and unlike hurricanes. But we have not banished air crashes from the land, and it is not clear that we have the wisdom or the ability to eliminate recessions. The danger has not disappeared. The forces that produce recurrent recessions are still in the wings, merely waiting for their cue.[2]

Shortly after Okun wrote these words, the United States entered the stormiest period of the postwar era.

---

[2] Arthur M. Okun, *The Political Economy of Prosperity* (Norton, New York, 1970), pp. 33 ff.

SUMMARY

A. Business Fluctuations

1. Business cycles or fluctuations are swings in total national output, income, and employment, marked by widespread expansion or contraction in many sectors of the economy. They occur in all advanced market economies. We distinguish the phases of expansion, peak, recession, and trough.

2. Many business cycles occur when shifts in aggregate demand cause sharp changes in output, employment, and prices. Aggregate demand shifts when changes in spending by consumers, businesses, or governments change total spending relative to the economy's productive capacity. A decline in aggregate demand leads to recessions or depressions. An upturn in economic activity can lead to inflation.

3. Business-cycle theories differ in their emphasis on exogenous and internal factors. Importance is often attached to fluctuations in such exogenous factors as technology, elections, wars, exchange-rate movements, or oil-price shocks. Most theories emphasize that these exogenous shocks interact with internal mechanisms, such as the multiplier and investment-demand shifts, to produce cyclical behavior. Just as people suffer from different diseases, so do business-cycle ailments vary in different times and countries.

B. Foundations of Aggregate Demand

4. Ancient societies suffered when harvest failures produced famines. The modern market economy can suffer from poverty amidst plenty when insufficient aggregate demand leads to deteriorating business conditions and soaring unemployment. At other times, excessive reliance on the monetary printing press leads to runaway inflation. Understanding the forces that affect aggregate demand, including government fiscal and monetary policies, can help economists and policymakers design steps to smooth out the cycle of boom and bust.

5. Aggregate demand represents the total quantity of output willingly bought at a given price level, other things held constant. Components of spending include (a) consumption, which depends primarily upon disposable income; (b) investment, which depends upon present and expected future output and upon interest rates and taxes; (c) government purchases of goods and services; and (d) net exports, which depend upon foreign and domestic outputs and prices and upon foreign exchange rates.

6. Aggregate demand curves differ from demand curves used in microeconomic analysis. The *AD* curves relate overall spending on all components of output to the overall price level, with policy and exogenous variables held constant. The aggregate demand curve is downward-sloping primarily because of the money-supply effect, which occurs when a rise in the price level, with the nominal money supply constant, reduces the real money supply. A lower real money supply raises interest rates, tightens credit, and reduces total real spending. This represents a movement along an unchanged *AD* curve.

7. Factors that change aggregate demand include (a) macroeconomic policies, such as monetary and fiscal policies, and (b) exogenous variables, such as foreign economic activity, technological advances, and shifts in asset markets. When these variables change, they shift the *AD* curve.

CONCEPTS FOR REVIEW

Business Fluctuations or Cycles

business cycle or business fluctuation
business-cycle phases:
   peak
   trough
   expansion
   contraction
recession

aggregate demand shifts and business
   fluctuations
exogenous and internal cycle
   theories
macroeconomic models

Aggregate Demand

real variable = nominal
   variable/price level

aggregate demand, *AD* curve
major components of aggregate
   demand: *C, I, G, X*
downward-sloping *AD* curve through
   money-supply effect
factors underlying and shifting the
   AD curve

FURTHER READING AND INTERNET WEBSITES

Further Reading

The classic study of business cycles by leading scholars at the National Bureau of Economic Research (NBER) is Arthur F. Burns and Wesley Clair Mitchell, *Measuring Business Cycles* (Columbia University Press, New York, 1946). A discussion of the NBER approach is contained in Geoffrey H. Moore, *Business Cycles, Inflation and Forecasting*, 2d ed. (Ballinger 2, Cambridge, Mass., 1983).

One of the major critics of Keynesian business cycle theory is Robert E. Lucas. See his *Studies in Business-Cycle Theory* (MIT Press, Cambridge, Mass., 1981).

Websites

A consortium of macroeconomists participate in the NBER program on economic fluctuations and growth. You can sample the writings and data at www.nber.org/programs/efg/efg.html. The NBER also dates business cycles for the United States. You can see the recessions and expansions at www.nber.org/cycles.html.

Business-cycle data and discussion can be found at the site of the Bureau of Economic Analysis (www.bea.doc.gov). The first few pages of the *Survey of Current Business* (available at www.bea.doc.gov/bea/pubs.html) has a discussion of recent business cycle developments.

Other business-cycle links can be found at www.cris.com/~netlink/bci/bci.html.

QUESTIONS FOR DISCUSSION

1. Define carefully the difference between movements along the *AD* curve and shifts of the *AD* curve. Explain why a change in production costs would shift the *AS* curve and lead to a movement along the *AD* curve. Explain why a tax cut would shift the *AD* curve outward (increase aggregate demand). What would be the effect of a decrease in the money supply (a monetary tightening) on aggregate demand?

2. Describe the different phases of the business cycle. In which phase is the U.S. economy now?

3. Some changes in aggregate output originate from the demand side, while others arise from supply shocks.
   a. Give examples of each. Using the *AS-AD* apparatus, explain how you can distinguish between a business downturn originating from the supply side and one from the demand side. (*Hint*: What happens to *P* in each case?)
   b. State whether each of the following would lead to a supply-side business cycle or a demand-side cycle, and illustrate the impact using an *AS-AD* diagram like Figure 7-4: a wartime increase in defense spending; devastation from wartime bombing of factories and power plants; a decrease in net exports from a deep recession in Europe; a sharp increase in innovation and productivity growth caused by increased computer use.

4. Construct a table parallel to Table 7-1, listing events that would lead to a *decrease* in aggregate demand. (Your table should provide different examples rather than simply changing the direction of the factors mentioned in Table 7-1.)

5. In recent years, a new theory of real business cycles (or RBCs) has been proposed (this approach is further analyzed in Chapter 17). RBC theory suggests that business fluctuations are caused by shocks to productivity which then propagate through the economy.
   a. Show the RBC theory in the *AS-AD* framework.
   b. Discuss whether the RBC theory can explain the customary characteristics of business fluctuations described on page 133.

6. **Advanced problem:** Find two dice and use the following technique to see if you can generate something that looks like a business cycle: Record the numbers from 20 or more rolls of the dice. Take five-period moving averages of the successive numbers. Then plot these. They will look very much like movements in GDP, unemployment, or inflation.

   One sequence thus obtained was 7, 4, 10, 3, 7, 11, 7, 2, 9, 10. . . . The averages were $(7 + 4 + 10 + 3 + 7)/5 = 6.2$, $(4 + 10 + 3 + 7 + 11)/5 = 7$, and so forth.

   Why does this look like a business cycle? [*Hint*: The random numbers generated by the dice are like exogenous shocks of investment or wars. The moving average is like the economic system's (or a rocking chair's) internal multiplier or smoothing mechanism. Taken together, they produce what looks like a cycle.]

7. **Advanced problem:** An eminent macroeconomist, George Perry of Brookings, wrote the following after the Persian Gulf war of 1990–1991:

> Wars have usually been good for the U.S. economy. Traditionally they bring with them rising output, low unemployment, and full use of industrial capacity as military demands add to normal economic activity. This time, for the first time, war and recession occurred together. What does this anomaly tell us about the recession? (*Brookings Review*, Spring 1991)

Use the Internet or go to the library and find data on the major determinants of aggregate demand during the 1990–1991 period as well as during earlier wars (World War II, Korean war, Vietnam war). Examine particularly government spending on goods and services (especially defense spending), taxes, investment, and interest rates. Can you explain the anomaly that Perry describes? (Locations of macroeconomic data on the Internet are listed in the Introduction and under "Websites" in Chapter 5's Further Reading section).

0. **Data problem:** Find data on real GDP for the United States for the period 1948–2000 (see the website of the Bureau Economic Analysis, www.bea.doc.gov).

   a. Define "recessions" as years in which real GDP declined. Which years were recessions?

   b. Calculate the average growth rate of real GDP for 1948–1973, 1973–1988, 1988–2000. What was the trend in the average growth rate over this period?

   [Hint: you can calculate the average growth rate by solving the equation
   $(1 + g) = (\text{GDP}_{1973}/ \text{GDP}_{1948})^{1/(1973-1948)}$,
   where g is the average growth rate per year.]

   c. Some macroeconomists prefer to identify growth recessions, which are periods when GDP growth was significantly slower than trend growth. For example, define a "growth recession" as one where real GDP growth was at least 2 percentage points below the average. Which years were growth recessions during this period?

The United States and other market-oriented economies are subject to frequent and unpredictable fluctuations in output, prices, and unemployment. In the past, these fluctuations, known as business cycles, generally occurred because of changes in spending on investment, consumer durables, or defense. As economists, we want to understand the *mechanism* by which changes in spending get translated into changes in output and employment. This chapter develops the simplest approach to understanding business cycles, the *Keynesian multiplier model*.

We will see in the first part of this chapter how an increase in investment raises the incomes of consumers and thereby leads to a cascading but ever-decreasing chain of further spending increases. Investment changes are therefore *multiplied* into larger output increases. The multiplier mechanism actually applies much more broadly than to investment alone, as we will see in the second half of this chapter. In fact, changes in government purchases, exports, or other exogenous spending streams will also be amplified into larger output changes. We show below how government purchases have a multiplied effect upon output in much the same way as does investment; this point led many macroeconomists to recommend using fiscal policy as a tool for stabilizing the economy.

The multiplier model is the first complete model of short-run output determination that we will develop. It is an oversimplified description of the economy, however, because it omits important elements such as financial markets and monetary policy, interactions with the rest of the world, and price and wage behavior. These further elaborations will come onto the stage in due time. For now, we focus primarily on the leading role of changes in investment and government spending in determining movements in national output.

CHAPTER

8

The Multiplier Model

The outstanding faults of the economic society in which we live are its failure to provide for full employment and its arbitrary and inequitable distribution of wealth and incomes.

John Maynard Keynes, *The General Theory of Employment, Interest and Money* (1936)

A. THE BASIC MULTIPLIER MODEL

When economists attempt to understand why major increases in wartime military spending led to rapid increases in GDP, or why the tax cuts of the 1960s or 1980s ushered in long periods of business-cycle expansions, or why the investment boom of the late 1990s produced America's longest expansion, they often turn to the multiplier model for the simplest explanation.

What exactly is the **multiplier model?** It is a macroeconomic theory used to explain how output is determined in the short run. The name "multiplier" comes from the finding that each dollar change in exogenous expenditures (such as investment) leads to more than a dollar change (or a multiplied change) in GDP. The multiplier model explains how shocks to investment, foreign trade, and government tax and spending policies can affect output and employment in an economy. The key assumptions underlying the multiplier model are that wages and prices are fixed and that there are unemployed resources. In addition, we are suppressing the role of monetary policy and assuming that there are no financial market reactions to changes in the economy.

OUTPUT DETERMINATION WITH SAVING AND INVESTMENT

We first show how investment and saving are equilibrated in the multiplier model for a highly simplified economy. Recall Chapter 6's picture of the national consumption and saving functions; these are redrawn in Figure 8-1.[1] Each point on the consumption function shows desired or planned consumption at that level of disposable income. Each point on the saving schedule shows desired or planned saving at that income level. The two schedules are closely related: Since $C + S$ always equals disposable income, the consumption and saving curves are mirror twins that will always add up to the 45° line. We also carry over the SS schedule into Figure 8-2 on page 147.

We have seen that saving and investment are dependent on quite different factors: saving depends primarily on disposable income, while investment depends on factors such as output, interest rates, tax policy, and business confidence. For simplicity here, we treat investment as an *exogenous* variable, one whose level is determined outside the model.

Say that investment opportunities are such that investment would be exactly $200 billion per year regardless of the level of GDP. This means that if we draw a schedule of investment against GDP, it will

---

[1] Here we shall initially simplify the picture by leaving out taxes, undistributed corporate profits, foreign trade, depreciation, and government fiscal policy. For the time being, we will assume that disposable income equals GDP.

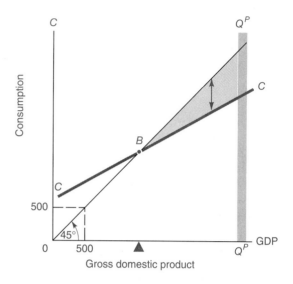

(a) Consumption Function

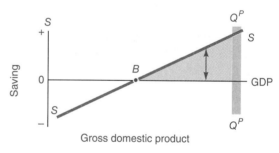

(b) Saving Function

FIGURE 8-1. National Output Determines the Levels of Consumption and Saving

Recall from Chapter 6 the consumption and saving functions, CC and SS. These are mirror-image curves, so the break-even point at B on the upper diagram is the zero-saving point on the lower diagram where SS intersects the horizontal axis. The two points in **(a)** marked "500" emphasize the important property of the 45° line: Any point on it depicts a vertical distance exactly equal to the horizontal distance. The gray band marked $Q^P Q^P$ shows the level of potential GDP.

have to be a horizontal line. The case of exogenous investment is shown in Figure 8-2, where the investment schedule is labeled II to distinguish it from the SS saving schedule. (Note that II does not mean Roman numeral 2.)

The saving and investment schedules intersect at point E in Figure 8-2. This point corresponds to a level of GDP given at point *M* and represents the equilibrium level of output in the multiplier model.

This intersection of the saving and investment schedules is the equilibrium level of GDP toward which national output will gravitate.

Reminder on the meaning of equilibrium

We often look for a macroeconomic "equilibrium" when analyzing business cycles or economic growth. What exactly does this term mean here? An **equilibrium** is a situation where the different forces at work are in balance. For example, if you see a ball rolling down a hill, the ball is not in equilibrium because the forces at work are pushing the ball down (this is therefore a **disequilibrium**). When the ball comes to rest in a hole at the bottom of the hill, the forces operating on the ball are in balance and the ball is in equilibrium.

Similarly, in macroeconomics, an equilibrium level of output is one where the different forces of spending and saving are in balance; in equilibrium, the level of output tends to persist until there are changes in the forces affecting the economy.

Looking now at Figure 8-2, we see that point *E* is an equilibrium. The reason is that at this level of output, the desired saving of households equals the desired investment of firms. When desired saving and desired investment are not equal, output will tend to adjust up or down.

The saving and investment schedules shown in Figure 8-2 represent *desired* (or *planned*) levels. Thus at output level *M*, businesses will want to invest an amount equal to the vertical distance *ME*. Also, at that income level, households desire to save the amount *ME*. But there is no logical necessity for actual saving to equal planned saving (or for actual investment to equal planned investment). People can make mistakes. Or they may forecast events incorrectly. When mistakes happen, saving or investment might deviate from planned levels.

To see how output adjusts until desired saving and desired investment are equated, we consider three cases. In the first case, the system is at *E*, where the schedule of what business firms want to invest intersects the saving schedule of what households want

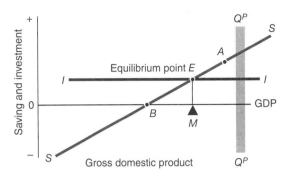

FIGURE 8-2. The Equilibrium Level of National Output Is Determined by Intersection of Saving and Investment Schedules

The horizontal *II* line indicates constant investment. *E* marks the spot where the investment and saving curves intersect. Equilibrium GDP comes at the intersection of the *SS* and *II* curves because this is the only level of GDP at which the desired saving of households exactly matches the desired investment of business.

to save. When everyone's plans are satisfied, everyone will be content to go on doing just what he or she has been doing.

At equilibrium, firms will not find inventories piling up on their shelves, nor will their sales be so brisk as to force them to produce more goods. So production, employment, income, and spending will remain the same. In this case GDP stays at point *E*, and we can rightly call it an *equilibrium*.

The second case—of a disequilibrium—begins with a GDP higher than at *E*. Consider point *A*, where GDP is to the right of *M* at an income level where the saving schedule is higher than the investment schedule. This is not an equilibrium because at this income level households are saving more than business firms want to invest. Firms will have too few customers and larger inventories of unsold goods than they want. What can businesses do to correct this situation? They can cut back production and lay off workers. This response reduces GDP, moving output leftward in Figure 8-2. The economy returns to equilibrium when it gets back to *E* and has no further tendency to change.

At this point, you should be able to analyze the third case. Show that if GDP were *below* its equilibrium level, strong forces would be set up to move it eastward back to *E*.

All three cases lead to the same conclusion:

The only equilibrium level of GDP occurs at E, where planned saving and investment are equal. At any other output, the desired saving of households does not coincide with the desired investment of businesses. This discrepancy will cause businesses to change their production and employment levels, thereby returning the system to the equilibrium GDP.

OUTPUT DETERMINATION BY CONSUMPTION AND INVESTMENT

In addition to the saving-investment balance, there is a second way of showing how output is determined. The equilibrium is exactly the same, but many people find this second approach easier to understand.

This method is called the consumption-plus-investment (or $C + I$) approach. It is illustrated in Figure 8-3, which shows a curve of total spending graphed against total output or income. The black CC line is the consumption function, showing the level of desired consumption corresponding to each level of income. We then add desired investment (which is at fixed level I) to the consumption function. This yields the level of total desired spending, or $C + I$, represented by the blue $C + I$ curve in Figure 8-3.

We next put in a 45° line to help us identify the equilibrium. At any point on the 45° line, the total level of consumption plus investment spending (measured vertically) exactly equals the total level of output (measured horizontally).

We can now calculate the equilibrium level of output in Figure 8-3. Where the desired amount of spending, represented by the $C + I$ curve, equals total output, the economy is in equilibrium.

The total spending (or $C + I$) curve shows the level of desired expenditure by consumers and businesses corresponding to each level of output. The economy is in equilibrium at the point where the $C + I$ curve crosses the 45° line—at point E in Figure 8-3. At point E the economy is in equilibrium because at that level desired spending on consumption and investment exactly equals the level of total output.

The Adjustment Mechanism

We will pause to emphasize why point E is an equilibrium. *An economy is in equilibrium when planned spending* (on C and I) *equals planned output.* What

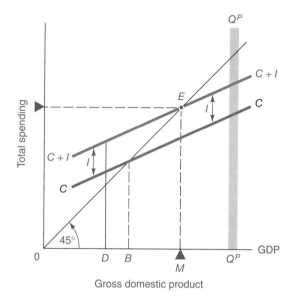

FIGURE 8-3. In the Expenditure Approach, Equilibrium GDP Level Is Found at the Intersection of the $C + I$ Schedule with the 45° Line

Adding II to CC gives the $C + I$ curve of total desired spending. At E, where this curve intersects the 45° line, we get the same equilibrium as in the saving-and-investment diagram. (Note the similarities between this figure and Fig. 8-2: the investment added to CC is the same as II of Fig. 8-2, and so must be the E intersection.)

would happen if the system were to deviate from equilibrium, say, at output level D in Figure 8-3? At this level of output, the $C + I$ spending line is above the 45° line, so planned $C + I$ spending would be greater than planned output. This means that consumers would be buying more goods than businesses were producing. Auto dealers would find their lots emptying, and the backlog for ordering computers would be getting longer and longer.

In this disequilibrium situation, auto dealers and computer manufacturers would respond by increasing their orders. Automakers would recall workers from layoff and gear up their production lines, while computer makers would add additional shifts. Thus, *a discrepancy between planned output and planned spending leads to a change in output.*

By following this chain of reasoning, we see that only when firms are producing what households and firms plan to spend on C and I, precisely at point E, will the economy be in equilibrium. (You should also work through what happens when output is above equilibrium.)

Planned versus actual amounts

In this section, we repeatedly discuss "planned" or "desired" spending and output. These words call attention to the difference between (1) the amount of planned or desired consumption or investment given by the consumption function or by the investment demand schedule and (2) the actual amount of consumption or investment measured after the fact.

The following dialogue will help you remember this distinction:

Confusio: I thought you said that saving always equals investment.

Clario: That is correct. As measured in the national accounts, saving and investment will always be exactly equal, in recession or boom.

Confusio: But why do I have to worry about desires and plans if *S* and *I* are always equal?

Clario: The reason is that the economy is in equilibrium only when firms and consumers are spending and producing their desired amounts.

Confusio: What happens when planned and actual amounts are different?

Clario: In fact, actual investment often differs from planned investment. For example, General Motors may sell fewer cars than what it had planned. When this happens, GM finds its inventories of cars increasing. This *involuntary* increase in inventory investment would not be an equilibrium, so GM would reduce its production.

Confusio: Aha! I see the point: Only when the level of output is such that planned spending on *C + I* equals planned output will there be no tendency for output, income, or spending to change.

Clario: Exactly.

An Arithmetic Analysis

An arithmetic example may help show why the equilibrium level of output occurs where planned spending and planned output are equal.

Table 8-1 on p. 150 shows a simple example of consumption and saving functions. The break-even level of income, where the nation is too poor to do

any net saving on balance, is assumed to be $3000 billion ($3 trillion). Each change of income of $300 billion is assumed to lead to a $100 billion change in saving and a $200 billion change in consumption; in other words, for simplicity *MPC* is assumed to be constant and exactly equal to $\frac{2}{3}$. Therefore, $MPS = \frac{1}{3}$.

Again, we assume that investment is exogenous. Suppose that the only level of investment that will be sustained indefinitely is exactly $200 billion, as shown in column (4) of Table 8-1. That is, at each level of GDP, businesses desire to purchase $200 billion of investment goods, no more and no less.

Columns (5) and (6) are the crucial ones. Column (5) shows the total GDP—this is simply column (1) copied once again into column (5). The figures in column (6) represent what business firms would actually be selling year in and year out; this is the planned consumption spending plus planned investment. It is the *C + I* schedule from Figure 8-3 in numbers.

When businesses as a whole are producing too high a level of total product (higher than the sum of what consumers and businesses want to purchase), they will be involuntarily piling up inventories of unsalable goods.

Reading the top row of Table 8-1, we see that if firms are temporarily producing $4200 billion of GDP, planned or desired spending [shown in column (6)] is only $4000 billion. In this situation, excess inventories will be accumulating. Firms will respond by contracting their operations, and GDP will fall. In the opposite case, represented by the bottom row of Table 8-1, total spending is $3000 billion and output is $2700 billion. Inventories are being depleted and firms will expand operations, raising output.

We see, then, that when business firms as a whole are temporarily producing more than they can profitably sell, they will contract their operations, and GDP will fall. When they are selling more than their current production, they will increase their output, and GDP will rise.

Only when the level of actual output in column (5) exactly equals planned spending in column (6) will business firms be in equilibrium. Their sales will then be just enough to justify continuing their current level of aggregate output. GDP will neither expand nor contract.

GDP Determination Where Output Equals Planned Spending
(billions of dollars)

(1) Levels of GDP and DI	(2) Planned consumption	(3) Planned saving (3) = (1) − (2)	(4) Planned investment	(5) Level of GDP (5) = (1)	(6) Total planned consumption and investment (6) = (2) + (4)	(7) Resulting tendency of output
4,200	3,800	400	200	4,200 >	4,000	Contraction
3,900	3,600	300	200	3,900 >	3,800	Contraction
3,600	**3,400**	**200**	**200**	**3,600 =**	**3,600**	**Equilibrium**
3,300	3,200	100	200	3,300 <	3,400	Expansion
3,000	3,000	0	200	3,000 <	3,200	Expansion
2,700	2,800	−100	200	2,700 <	3,000	Expansion

TABLE 8-1. Equilibrium Output Can Be Found Arithmetically at the Level Where Planned Spending Equals GDP

The darker blue row depicts the equilibrium GDP level, where the $3600 that is being produced is just matched by the $3600 that households plan to consume and that firms plan to invest. In upper rows, firms will be forced into unintended inventory investment and will respond by cutting back production until equilibrium GDP is reached. Interpret the lower rows' tendency toward expansion of GDP toward equilibrium.

THE MULTIPLIER

Where is the multiplier in all this? To answer this question, we need to examine how a change in exogenous investment spending affects GDP. It is logical that an increase in investment will raise the level of output and employment. But by how much? The multiplier model shows that an increase in investment will increase GDP by an amplified or multiplied amount—by an amount greater than itself.

The **multiplier** is the number by which the change in investment must be multiplied in order to determine the resulting change in total output.

For example, suppose investment increases by $100 billion. If this causes an increase in output of $300 billion, the multiplier is 3. If, instead, the resulting increase in output is $400 billion, the multiplier is 4.

Woodsheds and Carpenters. Why is it that the multiplier is greater than 1? Let's suppose that I hire unemployed resources to build a $1000 woodshed. My carpenters and lumber producers will get an extra $1000 of income. But that is not the end of the story. If they all have a marginal propensity to consume of $\frac{2}{3}$, they will now spend $666.67 on new consumption goods. The producers of these goods will now have

extra incomes of $666.67. If their *MPC* is also $\frac{2}{3}$, they in turn will spend $444.44, or $\frac{2}{3}$ of $666.67 (or $\frac{2}{3}$ of $\frac{2}{3}$ of $1000). The process will go on, with each new round of spending being $\frac{2}{3}$ of the previous round.

Thus an endless chain of *secondary consumption spending* is set in motion by my *primary* investment of $1000. But, although an endless chain, it is an ever-diminishing one. Eventually it adds up to a finite amount.

Using straightforward arithmetic, we can find the total increase in spending in the following manner:

$$
\left.
\begin{array}{c}
\$1000.00 \\
+ \\
666.67 \\
+ \\
444.44 \\
+ \\
296.30 \\
+ \\
197.53 \\
+ \\
\vdots \\
\hline
\$3000
\end{array}
\right\}
=
\left\{
\begin{array}{c}
1 \times \$1000 \\
+ \\
\frac{2}{3} \times \$1000 \\
+ \\
(\frac{2}{3})^2 \times \$1000 \\
+ \\
(\frac{2}{3})^3 \times \$1000 \\
+ \\
(\frac{2}{3})^4 \times \$1000 \\
+ \\
\vdots \\
\hline
\frac{1}{1 - \frac{2}{3}} \times \$1000, \text{ or } 3 \times \$1000
\end{array}
\right.
$$

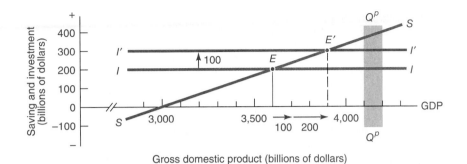

FIGURE 8-4. Each Dollar of Investment Is "Multiplied" into 3 Dollars of Output

New investment shifts II up to $I'I'$. E' gives the new equilibrium output, with output increasing by 3 for each 1 increase in investment. (*Note:* The broken horizontal blue arrow is 3 times the length of the vertical blue arrow of the investment shift and is broken to show 2 units of secondary consumption spending for each 1 unit of primary investment.)

This shows that, with an *MPC* of $\frac{2}{3}$, the multiplier is 3; it consists of the 1 of primary investment plus 2 extra of secondary consumption responding.

The same arithmetic would give a multiplier of 4 for an *MPC* of $\frac{3}{4}$, because $1 + \frac{3}{4} + (\frac{3}{4})^2 + (\frac{3}{4})^3 + \cdots$ eventually adds up to 4. For an *MPC* of $\frac{1}{2}$, the multiplier would be 2.[2]

The size of the multiplier thus depends upon how large the *MPC* is. It can also be expressed in terms of the twin concept, the *MPS*. For an *MPS* of $\frac{1}{4}$, the *MPC* is $\frac{3}{4}$ and the multiplier is 4. For an *MPS* of $\frac{1}{3}$, the multiplier is 3. If the *MPS* were $1/x$, the multiplier would be x.

By this time it should be clear that the simple multiplier is always the inverse, or reciprocal, of the marginal propensity to save. It is thus equal to $1/(1 - MPC)$. Our simple multiplier formula is

$$
\begin{aligned}
\text{Change} \atop \text{in output} &= \frac{1}{MPS} \times \text{change in investment} \\
&= \frac{1}{1 - MPC} \times \text{change in investment}
\end{aligned}
$$

In other words, the greater the extra consumption spending, the greater the multiplier.

---

[2] The formula for an infinite geometric progression is

$$1 + r + r^2 + r^3 + \cdots + r^n + \cdots = \frac{1}{1 - r}$$

as long as *MPC* (r) is less than 1 in absolute value.

Up to now, we have discussed the multiplier as relating to the extra consumption and saving. This is only part of the picture. In the next chapter, we will see that the multiplier applies to changes in total spending and changes in total leakages from spending.

Graphical Picture of the Multiplier

Our discussion of the multiplier has relied up to now largely on common sense and arithmetic. Can we get the same result using our graphical analysis of saving and investment? The answer is yes.

Suppose, as in Table 8-1, that the *MPS* is $\frac{1}{3}$ and a burst of inventions gives rise to an extra $100 billion of continuing investment. What will be the new equilibrium GDP? If the multiplier is indeed 3, the answer is $3900 billion.

A look at Figure 8-4 can confirm this result. Our old investment schedule II is shifted upward by $100 billion to the new level $I'I'$. The new intersection point is E'; the increase in income is exactly 3 times the increase in investment. As the blue arrows show, the horizontal output distance is 3 times as great as the upward shift in the investment schedule. We know that desired saving must rise to equal the new and higher level of investment. The only way that saving can rise is for national income to rise. With an *MPS* of $\frac{1}{3}$ and an increase in investment of $100 billion, income must rise by $300 billion to bring forth $100 billion of additional saving to match the new investment. Hence, at equilibrium, $100 billion of additional investment induces $300 billion of additional income, verifying our multiplier arithmetic.[3]

THE MULTIPLIER MODEL IN PERSPECTIVE

The simplest multiplier model has been enormously influential in business-cycle theory over the last half-century. But it gives an oversimplified picture of the economy. One of the most important omissions is the impact of financial markets and monetary policy on the economy. Changes in output tend to affect interest rates, which in turn come back and affect the economy. Additionally, the simplest multiplier model omits the interactions between the domestic economy and the rest of the world. Finally, the model omits the supply side of the economy as represented by the interaction of spending with aggregate supply and prices. All these shortcomings will be remedied in later chapters, and it is useful to keep in mind that this first model is really a stepping stone on the path to understanding the economy in all its fascinating complexity.

It will be useful to put all this in perspective and to see how the multiplier model fits into a broader view of the macroeconomy. We are trying to understand what determines the level of national output in a country. In the long run, a country's production and living standards are largely determined by its potential output. But in the short run, business conditions will push the economy above or below its long-term trend. It is this deviation of output and employment from trend that is addressed by the simplest multiplier model and by its more complex and complete cousins.

While the relationships presented here have been simplified, their essence will remain valid even when extended to situations involving government fiscal policy, monetary policy, and foreign trade. The main point to retain is that the multiplier analysis holds when there are unemployed resources. With excess capacity, an increase in aggregate demand can raise output levels. By contrast, if an economy is producing at capacity, there is no room for expansion when aggregate demand increases. In conditions of full employment, then, demand increases lead to higher prices rather than to output increases.

When investment or other spending increases in an economy with excess capacity and unemployed workers, much of the extra spending will end up in extra real output, with only small increases in the price level. However, as the economy reaches its capacity, it is not possible to coax out more production at the going price level. Hence, at full employment, higher spending will result in higher price levels rather than higher real output or employment.

The Multiplier Model Compared with the AS-AD Model

As you read about the multiplier model, you may have asked yourself how this approach fits with the *AS-AD* model of Chapter 4. There is no contradiction—they are in no way different theories. Rather, *the multiplier model explains the workings of aggregate demand by showing how consumption, investment, and other variables interact to determine aggregate demand—it is a special case of the aggregate demand-and-supply model.*

The key assumption in the multiplier analysis is that prices and wages are fixed in the short run; because they are fixed, all the adjustments in the economy come through output and employment. In other words, we assume the *AS* curve is horizontal. This assumption of fixed wages and prices is an oversimplification because these variables definitely do react to short-run business conditions. In later chapters we will consider the price and wage reactions that occur as markets respond to supply and demand shocks.

The relationship between the multiplier analysis and the *AS-AD* approach is shown in Figure 8-5. Part (*b*) displays an upward-sloping *AS* curve that becomes relatively steep as output exceeds potential output. In the region where there are unemployed resources, to the left of potential output, output is determined primarily by the strength of aggregate demand. As investment increases, this increases *AD*, and equilibrium output rises.

The same economy can be described by the multiplier diagram in the top panel of Figure 8-5. The multiplier equilibrium gives the same level of output

---

[3] Alter Table 8-1, on page 150, to verify this answer. In column (4), we now put $300 billion instead of $200 billion of investment. Show that the new equilibrium output shifts one row up from the old blue equilibrium row. Can you also show that the multiplier works downward?

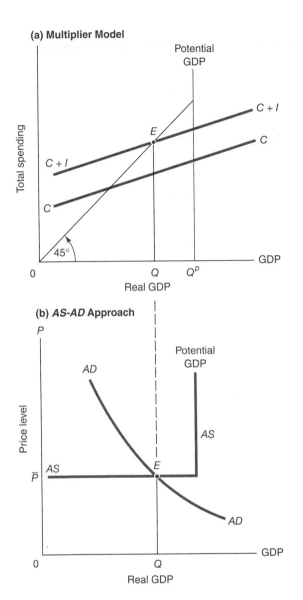

(a) Multiplier Model

(b) AS-AD Approach

FIGURE 8-5. How the Multiplier Model Fits the AS-AD Approach

The multiplier model is a way of understanding the workings of the AS-AD equilibrium.

(**a**) The top panel shows the output-expenditure equilibrium in the multiplier model. At point E, the spending line just cuts the 45° line, leading to equilibrium output of Q.

(**b**) The equilibrium can also be seen in the bottom panel, where the AD curve cuts the AS curve at point E. In the simplest multiplier model, wages and prices are assumed to be fixed, so the AS curve is horizontal until full employment is reached. Both approaches lead to exactly the same equilibrium output, Q.

as the AS-AD equilibrium—both lead to a real GDP of Q. They simply stress different features of output determination.

This discussion again points to a crucial feature of the multiplier model. While it may be a highly useful approach to describe depressions or even recessions, it cannot apply to periods of full employment. Once factories are operating at full capacity and all workers are employed, the economy simply cannot produce more output.

We have now completed our presentation of the simple multiplier model. We next move on to extend the analysis of aggregate demand by showing how government fiscal policy enters the picture.

B. FISCAL POLICY IN THE MULTIPLIER MODEL

For centuries, economists have understood the *allocational* role of fiscal policy (government tax and spending programs). It has long been known that fiscal programs are instrumental in deciding how the nation's output should be divided between collective and private consumption and how the burden of payment for collective goods should be divided among the population.

Only with the development of modern macroeconomic theory has a further surprising fact been uncovered: Government fiscal powers also have a major *macroeconomic* impact upon the short-run movements of output, employment, and prices. The knowledge that fiscal policy has powerful effects upon economic activity led to the *Keynesian approach to macroeconomic policy,* which is the active use of government action to moderate business cycles. The approach was described by the Nobel-prize winning macroeconomist, James Tobin, as follows:

> Keynesian policies are, first, the explicit dedication of macroeconomic policy instruments to real economic goals, in particular full employment and real growth of national income. Second, Keynesian demand management is activist. Third, Keynesians have wished to put both fiscal and monetary policies in consistent and coordinated harness in the pursuit of macroeconomic objectives.

In this section we use the multiplier model to show how government purchases affect output.

HOW GOVERNMENT FISCAL POLICIES AFFECT OUTPUT

To understand the role of government in economic activity, we need to look at government purchases and taxation, along with the effects of those activities on private-sector spending. As you might guess, we now add G to get a $C + I + G$ spending schedule for charting macroeconomic equilibrium when government, with its spending and taxing, is in the picture.

It will simplify our task in the beginning if we analyze the effects of government purchases with total taxes collected held constant (taxes that do not change with income or other economic variables are called *lump-sum taxes*). But even with a fixed dollar value of taxes, we can no longer ignore the distinction between disposable income and gross domestic product. Under simplified conditions (including no foreign trade, transfers, or depreciation), we know from Chapter 5 that GDP equals disposable income plus taxes. But with tax revenues held constant, GDP and DI will always differ by the same amount; thus, after taking account of such taxes, we can still plot the CC consumption schedule against GDP rather than against DI.

An example will clarify how we can depict our consumption function when taxes are present. In Figure 8-6, we have drawn our original consumption function with zero taxes as the black CC line. In this case, GDP = DI. Here, consumption is 3000 at a DI of 3000; consumption is 3400 at a GDP of 3600.

Now introduce taxes of 300. At a DI of 3600, GDP must be equal to 3600 + 300 = 3900. Consumption is thus 3400 at a DI of 3600 or at a GDP of 3900. So we can write consumption as a function of GDP by shifting the consumption function to the right to the blue $C'C'$ curve; the amount of the rightward shift is exactly equal to the amount of taxes, 300.

Alternatively, we can plot the new consumption function as a parallel *downward* shift by 200. As Fig-

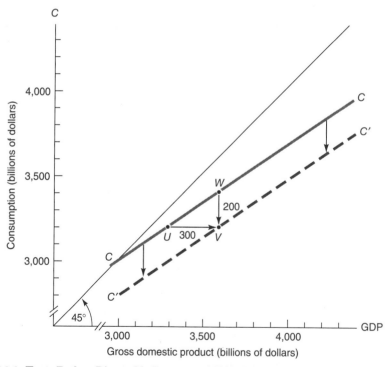

FIGURE 8-6. Taxes Reduce Disposable Income and Shift CC Schedule to the Right and Down

Each dollar of tax shifts the CC schedule to the right by the amount of the tax. A rightward CC shift also means a downward CC shift, but the downward CC shift is less than the rightward shift. Why? Because the downward shift is equal to the rightward shift times the *MPC*. Thus, if the *MPC* is $2/3$, the downward shift is $2/3$ times \$300 billion = \$200 billion. Verify that $WV = 2/3 UV$.

ure 8-6 shows, 200 is the result of multiplying a decrease in income of 300 times the *MPC* of ⅔.

Turning next to the different components of aggregate demand, recall from Chapter 5 that GDP consists of four elements:

GDP = consumption expenditure
       + gross private domestic investment
       + government purchases of goods and
         services
       + net exports
    = $C + I + G + X$

For now, we consider a closed economy with no foreign trade, so our GDP consists of the first three components, $C + I + G$. (We add the final component of net exports when we consider open-economy macroeconomics.)

Figure 8-7 shows the effect of G. This diagram is almost the same as the one used earlier in this chap-

ter (see Figure 8-3). In this diagram, however, we have added one new variable, G (government purchases of goods and services), on top of the consumption function and the fixed amount of investment. That is, the vertical distance between the $C + I$ line and the $C + I + G$ line is the amount of government purchases of goods and services (police, tanks, roads, etc.).

Why do we simply add G on the top? Because spending on government buildings (G) has the same macroeconomic impact as spending on private buildings (I); the collective expenditure involved in buying a government vehicle (G) has the same effect on jobs as private consumption expenditures on automobiles (C).

We end up with the three-layer cake of $C + I + G$, calculating the amount of total spending forthcoming at each level of GDP. We now must go to its point of intersection with the 45° line to find the equilib-

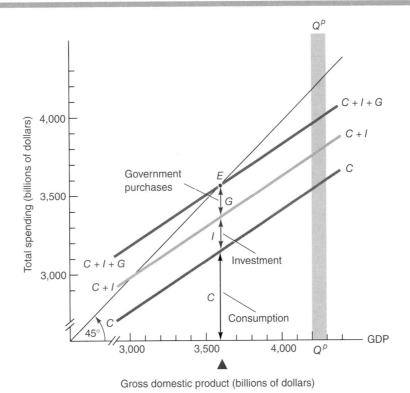

FIGURE 8-7. Government Purchases Add On Just like Investment to Determine Equilibrium GDP

We now add government purchases on top of consumption and investment spending. This gives us the $C + I + G$ schedule. At E, where this schedule intersects the 45° line, we find the equilibrium level of GDP.

rium level of GDP. At this equilibrium GDP level, denoted by point E in Figure 8-7, total planned spending exactly equals total planned output. Point E is thus the equilibrium level of output when we add government purchases to the multiplier model.

Impact of Taxation on Aggregate Demand

How does government taxation tend to reduce aggregate demand and the level of GDP? Extra taxes lower our disposable incomes, and lower disposable incomes tend to reduce our consumption spending. Clearly, if investment and government purchases remain the same, a reduction in consumption spending will then reduce GDP and employment. Thus, in the multiplier model, higher taxes without increases in government purchases will tend to reduce real GDP.[4]

A look back at Figure 8-6 confirms this reasoning. In this figure, the upper CC curve represents the level of the consumption function with no taxes. But the upper curve cannot be the consumption function because consumers definitely pay taxes on their incomes. Suppose that consumers pay $300 billion in taxes at every level of income; thus, DI is exactly

---

[4] Strictly speaking, by "taxes" in this chapter we mean net taxes, or taxes minus transfer payments.

$300 billion less than GDP at every level of output. As shown in Figure 8-6, this level of taxes can be represented by a rightward shift in the consumption function of $300 billion. This rightward shift will also appear as a downward shift; if the MPC is $\frac{2}{3}$, the rightward shift of $300 billion will be seen as a downward shift of $200 billion.

Without a doubt, taxes lower output in our multiplier model, and Figure 8-7 shows why. When taxes rise, $I + G$ does not change, but the increase in taxes will lower disposable income, thereby shifting the CC consumption schedule downward. Hence, the $C + I + G$ schedule shifts downward. You can pencil in a new, lower $C' + I + G$ schedule in Figure 8-7. Confirm that its new intersection with the 45° line must be at a lower equilibrium level of GDP.

Keep in mind that G is government purchases of goods and services. It excludes spending on transfers such as unemployment insurance or social security payments. These transfers are treated as negative taxes, so the taxes (T) considered here can best be thought of as taxes less transfers. Therefore, if direct and indirect taxes total $400 billion, while all transfer payments are $100 billion, then net taxes, T, are $400 − $100 = $300 billion. (Can you see why an increase in social security benefits lowers T, raises DI, shifts the $C + I + G$ curve upward, and raises equilibrium GDP?)

			Output Determination with Government (billions of dollars)				
(1) Initial level of GDP	(2) Taxes (T)	(3) Disposable income (DI)	(4) Planned consumption (C)	(5) Planned investment (I)	(6) Government expenditure (G)	(7) Total planned purchases (C + I + G)	(8) Resulting tendency of economy
4,200	300	3,900	3,600	200	200	4,000 ↓	Contraction
3,900	300	3,600	3,400	200	200	3,800 ↓	Contraction
3,600	**300**	**3,300**	**3,200**	**200**	**200**	**3,600**	**Equilibrium**
3,300	300	3,000	3,000	200	200	3,400 ↑	Expansion
3,000	300	2,700	2,800	200	200	3,200 ↑	Expansion

TABLE 8-2. Government Purchases, Taxes, and Investment Determine Equilibrium GDP

This table shows how output is determined when government purchases of goods and services are added to the multiplier model. In this example, taxes are "lump-sum" or independent of the level of income. Disposable income is thus GDP minus $300 billion. Total spending is $I + G +$ the consumption determined by the consumption function.

At levels of output less than $3600 billion, planned spending is greater than output, so output expands. Levels of output greater than $3600 are unsustainable and lead to contraction. Only at output of $3600 is output in equilibrium—that is, planned spending equals output.

A Numerical Example

The points made up to now are illustrated in Table 8-2. This table is very similar to Table 8-1, which illustrated output determination in the simplest multiplier model. The first column shows a reference level of GDP, while the second shows a fixed level of taxes, $300 billion. Disposable income in column (3) is GDP less taxes. Planned consumption, taken as a function of *DI*, is shown in column (4). Column (5) shows the fixed level of planned investment, while column (6) exhibits the level of government purchases. To find total planned spending in column (7), we add together the *C*, *I*, and *G* in columns (4) through (6).

Finally, we compare total desired spending in column (7) with the initial level of GDP in column (1). If desired spending is above GDP, firms raise production to meet the level of spending, and output consequently rises; if desired spending is below GDP, output falls.

This tendency, shown in the last column, assures us that output will tend toward equilibrium at $3600 billion.

FISCAL-POLICY MULTIPLIERS

The multiplier analysis shows that government fiscal policy is high-powered spending much like investment. The parallel suggests that fiscal policy should also have multiplier effects upon output. And this is exactly right.

The **government expenditure multiplier** is the increase in GDP resulting from an increase of $1 in government purchases of goods and services. An initial government purchase of a good or service will set in motion a chain of spending: if the government builds a road, the road-builders will spend some of their incomes on consumption goods, which in turn will generate additional incomes, some of which will

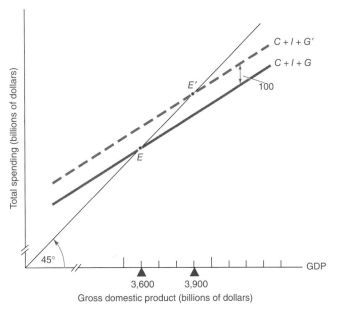

FIGURE 8-8. The Effect of Higher *G* on Output

Suppose that the government raises defense purchases by $100 billion in response to a threat to Mideast oil fields. This shifts upward the $C + I + G$ line by $100 billion to $C + I + G'$.

The new equilibrium level of GDP is thus read off the 45° line at E' rather than at E. Because the *MPC* is $\frac{2}{3}$, the new level of output is $300 billion higher. That is, the government expenditure multiplier is

$$3 = \frac{1}{1 - \frac{2}{3}}$$

(What would the government expenditure multiplier be if the *MPC* were $\frac{3}{4}$? $\frac{9}{10}$?)

be spent. In the simple model examined here, the ultimate effect on GDP of an extra dollar of G will be the same as the effect of an extra dollar of I: the multipliers are equal to $1/(1 - MPC)$. Figure 8-8 shows how a change in G will result in a higher level of GDP, with the increase being a multiple of the increase in government purchases.

To show the effects of an extra $100 billion of G, the $C + I + G$ curve in Figure 8-8 has been shifted up by $100 billion. The ultimate increase in GDP is equal to the $100 billion of primary spending times the expenditure multiplier. In this case, because the MPC is $\frac{2}{3}$, the multiplier is 3, so the equilibrium level of GDP rises by $300 billion.

This example, as well as common sense, tells us that the government expenditure multiplier is exactly the same number as the investment multiplier. They are both called **expenditure multipliers.**

Also, note that the multiplier horse can be ridden in both directions. If government purchases were to fall, with taxes and other influences held constant, GDP would decline by the change in G times the multiplier.

The effect of G on output can be seen as well in the numerical example of Table 8-2. You can pencil in a different level of G—say, $300 billion—and find the equilibrium level of GDP. It should give the same answer as Figure 8-8.

We can sum up:

> Government purchases of goods and services (G) are an important force in determining output and employment. In the multiplier model, if G increases, output will rise by the increase in G times the expenditure multiplier. Government purchases therefore have the potential to stabilize or destabilize output over the business cycle.

Defense spending and the economy

One of the principal features of the twentieth-century U.S. economy is that major wars have always been associated with rapid growth and low unemployment. Figure 8-9 shows how rapidly output grew during the three last major wars. This is the government expenditure multiplier at work: wars have rapidly growing G, while taxes are generally not raised sufficiently to reduce C and I enough to offset the rising G.

In reverse fashion, postwar demobilizations often led to recessions and rising unemployment. The last example came in the late 1980s and early 1990s. As the cold war gradually wound down, defense spending started declining as a share of GDP. The cuts in defense spending accelerated in 1990, when it became clear that Soviet communism was no longer a military danger. Real defense spending declined by $40 billion from 1990 to 1993.

As defense spending was cut, the multiplier worked in reverse and defense spending became a drag on the economy. To take one example, from 1990 to 1993 the aircraft manufacturing industry lost 170,000 jobs, mainly because of defense cuts. And southern California, which had benefitted from the rapid growth in defense spending a decade earlier, ended up being stuck in recession much longer than the rest of the country as defense layoffs slowed growth in that region.

Impact of Taxes

Taxes also have an impact upon equilibrium GDP, although the size of tax multipliers is smaller than that of expenditure multipliers. Consider the following example: Suppose the economy is at its potential GDP and the nation raises defense spending by $200 billion. Such sudden increases have occurred at many points in the history of the United States—in the early 1940s for World War II, in 1951 for the Korean war, in the mid-1960s for the Vietnam war, and in the early 1980s during the Reagan administration's military buildup. Furthermore, say that economic planners wish to raise taxes just enough to offset the effect on GDP of the $200 billion increase in G. How much would taxes have to be raised?

We are in for a surprise. To offset the $200 billion increase in G, we need to increase tax collections by more than $200 billion. In our numerical example, we can find the exact size of the tax, or T, increase from Figure 8-6. That figure shows that a $300 billion increase in T reduces disposable income by just enough to produce a consumption decline of $200 billion when the MPC is $\frac{2}{3}$. Put differently, a tax increase of $300 billion will shift the CC curve down by $200 billion. Hence, while a $1 billion increase in defense spending shifts up the $C + I + G$ line by $1 billion, a $1 billion tax increase shifts down the $C + I + G$ line by only $\frac{2}{3}$ billion (when the MPC is $\frac{2}{3}$). Thus offsetting an increase in government purchases requires an increase in T larger than the increase in G.

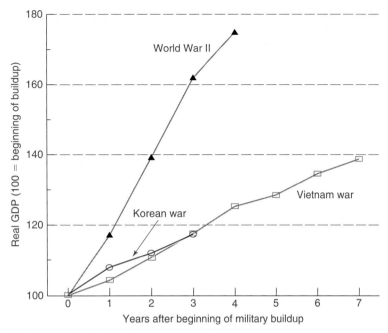

FIGURE 8-9. Output during Wartime

Note how U.S. output grew rapidly during each of the major wars of the mid- and late twentieth century. Growth was especially rapid in World War II, when the economy was pulled out of the Great Depression and half of GDP was eventually devoted to the war effort. (Source: U.S. Department of Commerce. Note that the output level is indexed so that GDP = 100 in the first year of the war or the buildup.)

Tax changes are a powerful weapon in affecting output. But the tax multiplier is smaller than the expenditure multiplier by a factor equal to the *MPC*:

Tax multiplier = *MPC* × expenditure multiplier

The reason the tax multiplier is smaller than the expenditure multiplier is straightforward. When government spends $1 on *G*, that $1 gets spent directly on GDP. On the other hand, when government cuts taxes by a dollar, only part of that dollar is spent on *C*, while a fraction of that $1 tax cut is saved. The difference in the responses to a dollar of *G* and to a dollar of *T* is enough to lower the tax multiplier below the expenditure multiplier.[5]

Fiscal Policy in Practice

President John F. Kennedy adopted the principles of Keynesian economics in 1961, and fiscal policy became one of the nation's main weapons for fighting recession or inflation. He proposed substantial tax cuts to lift the economy out of a slump; after these were enacted, the economy grew rapidly. However, when the fiscal expansion from the Vietnam war buildup during 1965–1966 was added to the tax cuts, output rose above potential GDP and inflation began to heat up. To fight the rising inflation and offset the increased Vietnam war expenditures, Congress passed a temporary surtax on incomes in 1968.

---

[5] For simplicity, we take the absolute value of the tax multiplier (since the multiplier is actually negative). The different multipliers can be seen using the device of the "expenditure rounds" shown on pages 150–151. Let the *MPC* be *r*. Then if *G* goes up by 1 unit, the total increase in spending is the sum of secondary respending rounds:

$$1 + r + r^2 + r^3 + \cdots = \frac{1}{1 - r}$$

Now, if taxes are reduced by $1, consumers save $(1 - r)$ of the increased disposable income and spend *r* dollars on the first round. With the further rounds, the total spending is thus

$$r + r^2 + r^3 + \cdots = \frac{r}{1 - r}$$

Thus the tax multiplier is *r* times the expenditure multiplier, where *r* is the *MPC*.

The 1980s provided another dramatic demonstration of how fiscal policy works. In 1981, Congress passed President Ronald Reagan's "supply-side tax cuts" along with a large increase in defense spending. The fiscal expansion helped pull the American economy out of the deep recession of 1981–1982.

The mid-1980s ushered in a new fiscal era. The Reagan fiscal policy led to a sharp increase in the government's budget deficit (equal to the difference between spending and revenues). The government deficit and government debt rose sharply during the 1980s. The era of budget deficits put tight reins on the introduction of new government programs as Congress struggled to reduce the budget deficit.

Upon entering office in 1993, President William Clinton faced a painful dilemma. The deficit remained stubbornly high, yet the economy was stagnating and the rate of joblessness was unacceptably high. Should the president tackle the deficit, increasing the level of *public saving* by raising taxes and lowering spending, so that the higher public saving might lead to an increase in *national saving and investment?* Or should the president worry that higher taxes and lower G might lower output as the fiscal contraction reduced $C + I + G$ and choked off investment? In the end, the president decided that deficit reduction was the chief priority. The Budget Act of 1993 enacted fiscal measures that lowered the deficit by about $150 billion (or 2 percent of GDP) over the next 5 years. The combination of tight spending, rising tax revenues, and a booming economy surprised all the experts by producing a budget surplus in 1998.

The twenty-first century ushered in a period of budget surpluses for the United States. With the new fiscal position, and deficit reduction no longer a priority, political candidates debated fiercely about the best fiscal course to steer. Some argued for using the surplus to reduce the government debt; others wanted to reduce taxes; still others advocated increasing spending programs, particularly on health care. These debates were focused primarily on the allocational role of fiscal policy, and the stabilization impacts were largely ignored.

The Other Partner in Stabilization Policy

Our multiplier analysis has focused primarily on fiscal policy as a tool for stabilizing the economy. But Keynesian economists emphasize that fiscal policy is only one of the tools that can be used in business-cycle management. The government has another equally powerful weapon in monetary policy. Although monetary policy works quite differently, as we will see in the next two chapters, it has many advantages as a policy for combating unemployment and inflation.

Like two locomotives on a train—sometimes pulling in one direction and sometimes in different directions—monetary and fiscal policies are powerful engines for affecting output, employment, and prices in the short run.

MULTIPLIERS IN ACTION

A realistic understanding of the size of multipliers is a crucial part of diagnosis and prescription in economic policy. Just as a physician prescribing a painkiller must know the effect of different dosages, so an economist must know the quantitative magnitude of expenditure and tax multipliers. When the economy is growing too rapidly and a dose of fiscal austerity is prescribed, the economic doctor needs to know the actual size of multipliers before deciding how large a dose of tax increases or expenditure reductions to order.

Textbook models give a highly simplified picture of the structure of the macroeconomy. For a more realistic picture of the response of output to changes in government purchases, economists estimate large-scale econometric models (see the discussion of this in Chapter 7) and then perform numerical experiments on their models by calculating the impact of a change in government purchases on the economy. Such models can serve as the basis for policy recommendations. These large-scale models include not only the bare-bones factors that we have sketched up to now but also factors that we consider later such as a more realistic treatment of taxes, a complete monetary sector, and the behavior of wages and prices. Including these additional factors tends to reduce the numerical size of multipliers.

A recent comprehensive survey of econometric models of the United States provides a representative sample of multiplier estimates. The models surveyed include equations to predict the behavior of

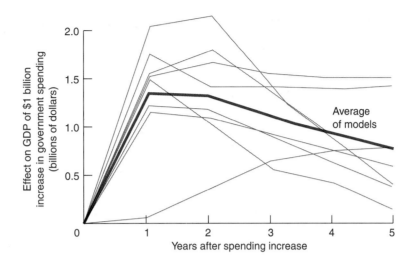

FIGURE 8-10. Expenditure Multipliers in Macroeconomic Models

A careful survey shows the estimated government expenditure multipliers in different macroeconomic models. These experiments show the estimated impact of a permanent $1 billion increase in the real value of government purchases of goods and services on real GDP at different intervals following the spending increase. That is, they show the impact of a $1 billion change in G on Q. The heavy blue line shows the average multiplier for the different models, while the gray lines represent the multipliers for each individual model. [Source: Ralph C. Bryant, Gerald Holtham, and Peter Hooper, "Consensus and Diversity in Model Simulations," in *Empirical Macroeconomics for Interdependent Economies* (Brookings Institution, Washington, D.C., 1988).]

all major sectors of the economy (including both monetary and financial sectors, along with investment demand schedules and consumption functions), and they incorporate a full set of links with the rest of the world. In the estimates, the level of real government purchases of goods and services is permanently increased by $1 billion. The models then calculate the impact on real GDP. The change in real GDP resulting from the increase in government purchases provides an estimate of the size of the government expenditure multiplier.

Figure 8-10 presents the results of this survey. The heavy blue line shows the average government expenditure multiplier estimated by eight models, while the light gray lines show the range of estimates of the individual models. The average multiplier for the first and second years is around 1.4, but after the second year the multiplier tends to decline slightly as monetary forces and international impacts come

into play. (The monetary forces represent the impact of higher GDP on interest rates, which leads to a crowding out of investment, as we will explain in later chapters.)

One interesting feature of these estimates is that the different models (represented by the light gray lines in Figure 8-10) show considerable disagreement about the size of multipliers. Why do the estimates differ? To begin with, there is inherent uncertainty about the nature of economic relationships. Uncertainty about the structure of nature or society is of course what makes science so exciting; if everything were perfectly understood, scientists would be out of business. But understanding economic systems poses even greater challenges because economists cannot conduct controlled experiments in a laboratory. Even more vexing is the fact that the economy itself evolves over time, so the "correct" model for 1960 is different from the "correct" model for 2000.

In addition, economists have fundamental disagreements about the underlying nature of the macroeconomy. Some economists believe that a Keynesian approach best explains macroeconomic behavior, while others are convinced that a classical or real-business-cycle approach yields better insights. With all these uncertainties and differences in points of view, we can hardly be surprised that economists will provide different estimates of multipliers.

Beyond the Multiplier Model

We have completed our survey of the most important applications of the Keynesian multiplier model. This analysis is an indispensable aid in understanding business fluctuations and the linkage between fiscal policy and national output.

But it would be a mistake to believe you can turn a parrot into a macroeconomist by simply teaching it to say "$C + I + G$" or "Polly has a multiplier." Behind such concepts are important assumptions and qualifications.

Recall that the multiplier model assumes that investment is fixed and ignores the impact of money and credit. Remember that we have not yet considered the interaction between the United States and the rest of the world. Recall that aggregate supply is left out of the story, so we have no way of analyzing how increases in spending are divided between prices and output. And these are not trifling concerns—rather, they are essential to understanding modern macroeconomics. But before we can incorporate these further realistic elements, we must master monetary theory and policy, as well as the essentials of economic growth and inflation theory. Once we have incorporated the influence of money and interest rates, along with the behavior of wages and prices, we will see that the impact of fiscal policy on the economy may be quite different from the simplest multiplier model.

We turn next to an analysis of one of the most fascinating parts of all economics: the study of money. Once we understand how the central bank determines the money supply, we will have a fuller appreciation of how governments can tame the business cycles that have run wild through much of the history of capitalism.

SUMMARY

A. The Basic Multiplier Model

1. The multiplier model provides a simple way to understand the impact of aggregate demand on the level of output. In the simplest approach, household consumption is a function of disposable income while investment is fixed. People's desire to consume and the willingness of businesses to invest are brought into balance by adjustments in output. The equilibrium level of national output must be at the intersection of the saving and investment schedules, *SS* and *II*. We can also see this using the expenditure-output approach, in which equilibrium output comes at the intersection of the consumption-plus-investment schedule, $C + I$, with the 45° line.

2. If output is temporarily above its equilibrium level, businesses find output higher than sales, with inventories piling up involuntarily and profits plummeting. Firms therefore cut production and employment back toward the equilibrium level. The only sustainable level of output comes when buyers voluntarily purchase exactly as much as businesses desire to produce.

3. Thus, for the simplified Keynesian multiplier model, investment calls the tune and consumption dances to the music. Investment determines output, while saving responds passively to income changes. Output rises or falls until planned saving has adjusted to the level of planned investment.

4. Investment has a *multiplied effect* on output. When investment changes, output will at first rise by an equal amount. But as the income receivers in the capital-goods industries get more income, they set in motion a whole chain of additional secondary consumption spending and employment.

   If people always spend r of each extra dollar of income on consumption, the total of the multiplier chain will be

$$1 + r + r^2 + \cdots = \frac{1}{1 - r} = \frac{1}{1 - MPC} = \frac{1}{MPS}$$

   The simplest multiplier is numerically equal to the reciprocal of the *MPS* or, equivalently, to $1/(1 - MPC)$.

The multiplier works in either direction, amplifying either increases or decreases in investment. This result occurs because it always takes more than a dollar of increased income to increase saving by a dollar.

5. Key points to remember are (*a*) the basic multiplier model emphasizes the importance of shifts in aggregate demand in affecting output and income and (*b*) it is primarily applicable for situations with unemployed resources.

B. Fiscal Policy in the Multiplier Model

6. The analysis of fiscal policy elaborates the Keynesian multiplier model. It shows that an increase in government purchases—taken by itself, with taxes and investment unchanged—has an expansionary effect on national output much like that of investment. The schedule of $C + I + G$ shifts upward to a higher equilibrium intersection with the 45° line.

7. A decrease in taxes—taken by itself, with investment and government purchases unchanged—raises the equilibrium level of national output. The CC schedule of consumption plotted against GDP is shifted upward and leftward by a tax cut. But since extra dollars of disposable income go partly into saving, the dollar increase in consumption will not be quite so great as the dollars of new disposable income. Therefore, the tax multiplier is smaller than the government expenditure multiplier

8. Using statistical techniques and macroeconomic theory, economists have developed realistic models to estimate expenditure multipliers. For mainstream approaches, these tend to show multipliers of between 1 and $1\frac{1}{2}$ for periods of up to 4 years.

CONCEPTS FOR REVIEW

The Basic Multiplier Model

$C + I$ schedule
two ways of viewing GDP
    determination:
    planned saving = planned
      investment
    planned C + planned I = planned
      GDP

investment equals saving: planned vs.
    actual levels
multiplier effect of investment
multiplier
$$= 1 + MPC + (MPC)^2 + \cdots$$
$$= \frac{1}{1 - MPC} = \frac{1}{MPS}$$

Government Purchases and Taxation

fiscal policy:
    G effect on equilibrium GDP
    T effect on CC and on GDP
multiplier effects of government
    purchases (G) and taxes (T)
$C + I + G$ curve
estimated multipliers in practice

FURTHER READING AND INTERNET WEBSITES

Further Reading

The multiplier model was developed by John Maynard Keynes in *The General Theory of Employment, Interest and Money* (Harcourt, New York, first published in 1935).

Advanced treatments can be found in the intermediate textbooks listed in the Further Reading section in Chapter 4.

Websites

Brad DeLong of the University of California at Berkeley has created a web page devoted to Keynes at www.econ161. berkeley.edu/Economists/keynes.html. One of Keynes's most influential books, *The Economic Consequences of the Peace* (1919), predicted with uncanny accuracy that the Treaty of Versailles would lead to disastrous consequences for Europe—it is available at socserv2.socsci.mcmaster.ca/ ~econ/ugcm/3ll3/keynes/peace. A controversial article on Keynes by one of today's most accomplished economist-essayists, Paul Krugman, is at www.web.mit.edu/krugman/www/keynes.html.

QUESTIONS FOR DISCUSSION

1. In the simple multiplier model, assume that investment is always zero. Show that equilibrium output in this special case would come at the break-even point of the consumption function. Why would equilibrium output come *above* the break-even point when investment is positive?

2. Define carefully what is meant by equilibrium in the multiplier model. For each of the following, state why the situation is *not* an equilibrium. Also describe how the economy would react to each of the situations to restore equilibrium.
   a. In Table 8-1, GDP is $3300 billion.
   b. In Figure 8-2, actual investment is zero.
   c. Car dealers find that their inventories of new cars are rising unexpectedly.
   d. In the simplest model of Section A, consumers plan to save $600 while businesses plan to invest $700.

3. Reconstruct Table 8-1 assuming that planned investment is equal to (*a*) $300 billion, (*b*) $400 billion. What is the resulting difference in GDP? Is this difference greater or smaller than the change in *I*? Why? When *I* drops from $200 billion to $100 billion, how much must GDP drop?

4. Give (*a*) the common sense, (*b*) the arithmetic, and (*c*) the geometry of the multiplier. What are the multipliers for *MPC* = 0.9? 0.8? 0.5? For *MPS* = 0.1? 0.8?

5. We have seen that investment responds to output through the accelerator principle (see Chapter 6). We might then define the *marginal propensity to invest*, or *MPI*, as the change in investment per unit change in output. Suppose that investment is $I = \bar{I} + 1.2Q$ (which has an *MPI* of 1.2), while the *MPC* is 0.8. What is the marginal propensity to spend = *MPC* + *MPI*? Work out the explosive (!) chain of spending and respending when the marginal propensity to spend = 2. Try to explain the economics of the divergent infinite geometric series.

6. Explain in words and using the notion of expenditure rounds why the tax multiplier is smaller than the expenditure multiplier.

7. Explain why governments might use fiscal policy to stabilize the economy. Why would fiscal policy be effective in raising output in a Keynesian economy but not in an economy where aggregate supply is vertical?

8. "Even if the government spends billions on wasteful military armaments, this action can create jobs in a recession." Discuss.

9. The saving-and-investment diagram and the 45° line *C* + *I* diagram are two different ways of showing how national output is determined in the multiplier model. Describe each. Show their equivalence.

10. **Advanced problem:** The growth of nations depends crucially on saving and investment. And from youth we are taught that thrift is important and that "a penny saved is a penny earned." But will higher saving necessarily benefit the economy? In a striking argument called *the paradox of thrift*, Keynes pointed out that when people attempt to save more, this will not necessarily result in more saving for the nation as a whole.

    To see this point, assume that people decide to save more. Illustrate how this shifts up the *SS* curve in the multiplier model of Figure 8-4. Explain why this will *decrease output with no increase in saving*! Provide the intuition here that if people try to increase their saving and lower their consumption for a given level of business investment, sales will fall and businesses will cut back on production. Explain how far output will fall. Here then is the paradox of thrift: When the community desires to save more, the effect may actually be a lowering of income and output with no increase of saving.

    Explain why this is a good example of the fallacy of composition. Further explain why the paradox might hold in an economy experiencing unemployment, whereas in a "classical" economy with full employment higher saving would indeed raise investment without a decline in output.

If you think about it for a moment, you will see that money is a strange thing. We study for years so that we can earn a good living, yet each dollar bill is just paper, with no intrinsic value. Money is useless until we get rid of it.

But money is anything but useless from a macroeconomic point of view. In this and the following chapter, we will see that monetary policy is today the most important tool that the government has to stabilize the business cycle. The central bank uses its control over the supply of money to stimulate the economy when unemployment begins to rise or to brake the economy when prices rise too quickly. When money is well managed, as was the case for the United States in the 1990s, output grows smoothly with stable prices. But an unreliable monetary system, such as that seen in unstable Russia over the last decade, can lead to inflation or depression. Many of the world's most devastating macroeconomic problems of the twentieth century can be traced to malfunctioning monetary systems.

We now begin our study of money, banking, and financial markets. Using our thematic diagram, Figure 9-1 shows the topics covered in this chapter. We start by looking at the essence of money and then analyze interest rates. In the second section of this chapter, we examine the banking system and the supply of money. This will serve as an introduction to the next chapter's analysis of central banking and of the impact of money on overall economic activity. We conclude this chapter by analyzing a crucial part of our financial system—the stock market.

A. MONEY AND INTEREST RATES

THE EVOLUTION OF MONEY

The History of Money

What is money? *Money is anything that serves as a commonly accepted medium of exchange.* Because money has a long and fascinating history, we will begin with a description of money's evolution.

Barter. In an early textbook on money, when Stanley Jevons wanted to illustrate the tremendous leap forward that occurred as societies introduced money, he used the following experience:

Some years since, Mademoiselle Zélie, a singer of the Théâtre Lyrique at Paris, . . . gave a concert in the Society Islands. In exchange for an air from *Norma* and a few other songs, she was to receive a third part of the receipts.

CHAPTER

9

Money, Banking, and Financial Markets

Over all history, money has oppressed people in one of two ways: either it has been abundant and very unreliable, or reliable and very scarce.

John Kenneth Galbraith, *The Age of Uncertainty* (1977)

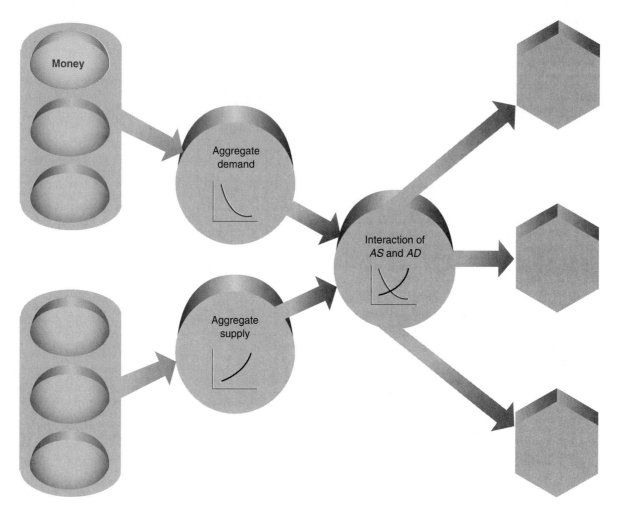

FIGURE 9-1. We Now Turn to Money: Its Demand and the Role of Banks in Its Supply

When counted, her share was found to consist of three pigs, twenty-three turkeys, forty-four chickens, five thousand cocoa-nuts, besides considerable quantities of bananas, lemons, and oranges. . . . [I]n Paris . . . this amount of live stock and vegetables might have brought four thousand francs, which would have been good remuneration for five songs. In the Society Islands, however, pieces of money were scarce; and as Mademoiselle could not consume any considerable portion of the receipts herself, it became necessary in the mean time to feed the pigs and poultry with the fruit.

This example describes **barter,** which consists of the exchange of goods for other goods. Exchange

through barter contrasts with exchange through money because pigs, turkeys, and lemons are not generally acceptable monies that we or Mademoiselle Zélie can use for buying things. Although barter is better than no trade at all, it operates under grave disadvantages because an elaborate division of labor would be unthinkable without the introduction of the great social invention of money.

As economies develop, people no longer barter one good for another. Instead, they sell goods for money and then use money to buy other goods they wish to have. At first glance this seems to complicate rather than simplify matters, as it replaces one transaction with two. If you have apples and want nuts, would it not be simpler to trade one for the other rather than to sell the apples for money and then use the money to buy nuts?

Actually, the reverse is true: two monetary transactions are simpler than one barter transaction. For example, some people may want to buy apples, and some may want to sell nuts. But it would be a most unusual circumstance to find a person whose desires exactly complement your own—eager to sell nuts and buy apples. To use a classical economic phrase, instead of there being a "double coincidence of wants," there is likely to be a "want of coincidence." So, unless a hungry tailor happens to find an undraped farmer who has both food and a desire for a pair of pants, under barter neither can make a direct trade.

Societies that traded extensively simply could not overcome the overwhelming handicaps of barter. The use of a commonly accepted medium of exchange, money, permits the farmer to buy pants from the tailor, who buys shoes from the cobbler, who buys leather from the farmer.

Commodity Money. Money as a medium of exchange first came into human history in the form of commodities. A great variety of items have served as money at one time or another: cattle, olive oil, beer or wine, copper, iron, gold, silver, rings, diamonds, and cigarettes.

Each of the above has advantages and disadvantages. Cattle are not divisible into small change. Beer does not improve with keeping, although wine may. Olive oil provides a nice liquid currency that is as minutely divisible as one wishes, but it is a bit messy to handle. And so forth.

By the nineteenth century, commodity money was almost exclusively limited to metals like silver and gold. These forms of money had *intrinsic value*, meaning that they had use value in themselves. Because money had intrinsic value, there was no need for the government to guarantee its value, and the quantity of money was regulated by the market through the supply and demand for gold or silver. But metallic money has shortcomings because scarce resources are required to dig it out of the ground; moreover, it might become abundant simply because of accidental discoveries of ore deposits.

The advent of monetary control by central banks has led to a much more stable currency system. The intrinsic value of money is now the least important thing about it.

Modern Money. The age of commodity money gave way to the age of *paper money*. The essence of money is now laid bare. Money is wanted not for its own sake but for the things it will buy. We do not wish to consume money directly; rather, we use it by getting rid of it. Even when we choose to keep money, it is valuable only because we can spend it later on.

The use of paper currency has become widespread because it is a convenient medium of exchange. Currency is easily carried and stored. The value of money can be protected from counterfeiting by careful engraving. The fact that private individuals cannot legally create money keeps it scarce. Given this limitation on supply, currency has value. It can buy things. As long as people can pay their bills with currency, as long as it is accepted as a means of payment, it serves the function of money.

Most money today is *bank money*—checking deposits in a bank or other financial institution. Checks are accepted in place of cash payment for many goods and services. In fact, if we calculate the total dollar amount of transactions, nine-tenths take place by bank money, the rest by currency.

Today there is rapid innovation in developing different forms of money. For example, some financial institutions will now link a checking account to a savings account or even to a stock portfolio, allowing customers to write checks on the value of their stock. Firms are working on ways for people to use the Internet to pay all their bills electronically.

Components of the Money Supply

Let us now look more carefully at the different kinds of money that Americans use. The major *monetary aggregates* are the quantitative measures of the supply of money. They are known today as M_1 and M_2, and you can read about their week-to-week movements in the newspaper, along with sage commentaries on the significance of the latest wiggle. Here we will provide the exact definitions as of 2000.

Narrow (Transactions) Money. One important and closely watched measure of money is narrow or transactions money, denoted by M_1, which consists of items that are actually used for transactions. The following are the components of M_1:

- *Coins.* M_1 includes coins not held by banks.
- *Paper currency.* More significant is paper currency. Most of us know little more about a $1 or $5 bill than that it is inscribed with the picture of an American statesman, that it bears some official signatures, and that each has a numeral showing its face value. Examine a $10 bill or some other paper bill. You will find that it says "Federal Reserve Note." But what "backs" our paper currency? Many years ago, paper money was backed by gold or silver. There is no such pretense today. Today, all U.S. coins and paper currency are *fiat money.* This term signifies something determined to be money by the government even if it has no value.

Paper currency and coins are *legal tender,* which must be accepted for all debts, public and private. Coins and paper currency (the sum known as *currency*) add up to almost one-half of total narrow money, M_1.

- *Checking accounts.* There is a third component of narrow money—checking deposits or bank money. These are funds, deposited in banks and other financial institutions, on which you can write checks. They are technically known as "demand deposits and other checkable deposits." If I have $1000 in my checking account at the Albuquerque National Bank, that deposit can be regarded as money. Why? For the simple reason that I can pay for purchases with checks drawn on it. The deposit is like any other medium of exchange.[1] Possessing the essential properties of money, bank checking-account deposits are counted as narrow money, as part of M_1.

Table 9-1 shows the dollar values of the different components of narrow money, M_1.

Broad Money. Although M_1 is, strictly speaking, the most appropriate measure of money as a means of payment, a second closely watched aggregate is *broad money,* or M_2. Sometimes called *near-money,* M_2 includes M_1 as well as savings accounts in banks and

similar assets that are very close substitutes for narrow money.

Examples of such near-monies in M_2 include deposits in a savings account in your bank, a money market mutual fund account operated by your stockbroker, a deposit in a money market deposit account run by a commercial bank, and so on.

Why are these not narrow money? Because they cannot be used as means of exchange for all purchases; they are forms of near-money, however, because you can convert them into cash very quickly with no loss of value.

There are many other technical definitions of money that are used by specialists in monetary economics. But for our purposes, we need master only the two major definitions of money.

Money is anything that serves as a commonly accepted medium of exchange. The most important concept is **narrow money,** or M_1, which is the sum of coins and paper currency in circulation outside the banks, plus checkable deposits. Another important monetary aggregate is **broad money** (called M_2), which includes assets such as savings accounts in addition to coins, paper currency, and checkable deposits.

INTEREST RATES: THE PRICE OF MONEY

When we later examine how money affects economic activity, we will focus on the interest rate, which is often called "the price of money."

Interest is the payment made for the use of money. The **interest rate** is the amount of interest paid per unit of time expressed as a percentage of the amount borrowed. In other words, people must pay for the opportunity to borrow money. The cost of borrowing money, measured in dollars per year per dollar borrowed, is the interest rate.

Some examples will illustrate how interest works:

- When you graduate from college, you have $500 to your name. You decide to keep it in currency. If you spend none of your funds, at the end of a year you still have $500 because currency has a zero interest rate.
- You place $2000 in a savings account in your local bank, where the interest rate on savings accounts is 4 percent per year. At the end of 1 year,

---

[1] Students are often surprised to learn that credit cards are not money. The reason is that a credit card is actually an easy (but not cheap!) way to *borrow* money. When paying with a credit card, you are actually promising to pay the credit-card company—with money—at a later date.

Kinds of money	Billions of Dollars		
	1959	**1973**	**2000**
Currency (outside of financial institutions)	28.8	61.7	518.1
Demand deposits (excludes government deposits and certain foreign deposits)	110.8	209.7	338.2
Other checkable deposits	0.4	0	248.7
Total narrow (or transactions) money (M_1)	140.0	271.4	1,105.0
Savings accounts, small time deposits, and other	158.8	300.2	3,578.0
Total broad money (M_2)	298.8	571.6	4,683.0

TABLE 9-1. Components of the Money Supply of the United States

Two widely used definitions of the money supply are narrow money (M_1) and broad money (M_2). M_1 consists of currency and checking accounts. M_2 adds to these certain "near-monies" such as savings accounts and time deposits. (Source: Federal Reserve Board.)

the bank will have paid $80 in interest into your account, so the account is now worth $2080.

- You start your first job and decide to buy a small house that costs $100,000. You go to your local bank and find that 30-year, fixed-interest-rate mortgages have an interest rate of 10 percent per year. Each month you make a mortgage payment of $877.58. Note that this payment is a little bit more than the pro-rated monthly interest charge of $^{10}/_{12}$ percent per month. Why? Because it includes not only interest but also *amortization*. This is repayment of *principal*, the amount borrowed. By the time you have made your 360 monthly payments, you will have completely paid off the loan.

From these examples we see that interest rates are measured in percent per year. Interest is the price paid to borrow money, which allows the borrower to obtain real resources over the time of the loan.

Higher interest rates tend to lower asset prices

One important fact in financial markets is the inverse relationship between interest rates and asset prices. We can understand this using the concept of present value.

Suppose you own a mineral-water spring and decide to sell it. The market price will depend upon both the stream of future income and the interest rate. Putting these together yields the present value of the asset.

The **present value** of an asset is the dollar value today of a stream of income over time. It is determined by calculating how much money invested today would be needed, at the going interest rate, to generate the asset's future stream of receipts. Here are some examples:

- Begin with a 1-year bond. The bond returns $50 of interest plus the original principal of $1050 exactly 1 year from now. Furthermore, suppose the interest rate is 10 percent per year. How much should you pay for the bond today? Pay exactly $1000, because $1000 invested today at the market interest rate of 10 percent will be worth $1100 in 1 year. So the present value of the bond is $1000.

- A perpetual asset has a constant yield forever. Suppose your mineral spring is expected to yield $N of water forever. What is the present value (V) if the interest rate is i percent per year? The present value is simply $V = \$N/i$.

- Say there is a variable stream of income in the future. The general formula for present value evaluates the present value of each part of the stream of future receipts and then adds together all these separate present values. The summation in the following formula will give you the asset's present value:

$$V = \frac{N_1}{1 + i} + \frac{N_2}{(1 + i)^2} + \cdots + \frac{N_t}{(1 + i)^t} + \cdots$$

In this equation, i is the one-period market interest rate assumed to be constant. Further, N_1 is the net receipts (positive or negative) in period 1, N_2 the net receipts in period 2, N_t the net receipts in period t, and so forth.

We can now see that asset prices tend to move inversely with interest rates because the present value is reduced as the interest rate rises. For example, in the perpetuity case, a doubling of i in the denominator will halve the value of V. You can work through with a calculator the impact of a higher interest rate on the 1-year bond example. Generally, when interest rates rise, the value of stocks, bonds, real estate, and many other long-lived assets will decline.

An Array of Interest Rates

Textbooks often speak of "*the* interest rate," but in fact today's complex financial system has a vast array of interest rates. Interest rates differ mainly in terms of the characteristics of the loan or of the borrower. Let us review the major differences.

Loans differ in their *term* or *maturity*—the length of time until they must be paid off. The shortest loans are overnight. Short-term securities are for periods up to a year. Companies often issue bonds that have maturities of 10 to 30 years, and mortgages are often up to 30 years in maturity. Longer-term securities generally command a higher interest rate than do short-term issues because lenders are willing to sacrifice quick access to their funds only if they can increase their yield.

Loans also vary in terms of *risk*. Some loans are virtually riskless, while others are highly speculative. Investors require that a premium be paid when they invest in risky ventures. The safest assets in the world are the securities of the U.S. government. These bonds and bills are backed by the full faith, credit, and taxing powers of the government. Intermediate in risk are borrowings of creditworthy corporations, states, and localities. Risky investments, which bear a significant chance of default or nonpayment, include those of companies close to bankruptcy, cities with shrinking tax bases, or countries like Russia with large overseas debts and unstable political systems. The U.S. government pays what is called the "riskless" interest rate; over the last two decades this has

ranged from 3 to 15 percent per year for short-term loans. Riskier securities might pay 1, 2, or 5 percent per year more than the riskless rate; this premium reflects the amount necessary to compensate the lender for losses in case of default.

Assets vary in their liquidity. An asset is said to be *liquid* if it can be converted into cash quickly and with little loss in value. Most marketable securities, including common stocks and corporate and government bonds, can be turned into cash quickly for close to their current value. Illiquid assets include unique assets for which no well-established market exists. For example, if you own the only Victorian mansion in a small town, you might find it difficult to sell the house quickly or at a price near its realistic market value—your house is an illiquid asset. Because of the higher risk and the difficulty of realizing the asset values quickly, illiquid assets or loans usually require higher interest rates than do liquid, riskless ones.

When these three factors (along with other considerations such as tax status and administrative costs) are considered, it is not surprising that we see so many different financial instruments and so many different interest rates. Figure 9-2 and Table 9-2 show the behavior of a few important interest rates over the last three decades. In the discussion that follows, when we speak of "the interest rate," we are generally referring to the interest rate on short-term government securities, such as the 90-day Treasury-bill rate. As Figure 9-2 shows, most other interest rates rise and fall in step with the 3-month Treasury-bill rate.

Real vs. Nominal Interest Rates

Interest is measured in dollar terms, not in terms of houses or cars or goods in general. The *nominal interest rate* measures the yield in dollars per year per dollar invested. But dollars can become distorted yardsticks. The prices of houses, cars, and goods in general change from year to year—these days prices generally rise due to inflation. Put differently, the interest rate on dollars does not measure what a lender really earns in terms of goods and services. Let us say that you lend $100 today at 5 percent–per–year interest. You would get back $105 at the end of a year. But because prices changed over the year, you would not be able to obtain the same quantity of goods that you could have bought at the beginning of the year if you had $105.

FIGURE 9-2. Most Interest Rates Move Together

This graph shows the major interest rates in the U.S. economy. (Source: Federal Reserve System.)

Asset class	Period	Real rate of return (% per year)
United States		
Short-term U.S. government securities (Treasury bills)	1926–1996	0.6
Corporate bonds:		
Safe (Aaa)	1926–1983	0.5
Risky (<Baa)	1926–1983	2.0
Corporate equities	1925–1998	7.5
Consumer loans:		
Mortgages	1975–1988	4.8
Credit cards	1975–1988	6.8
New-car loans	1975–1988	11.2
High-income industrial countries		
Bonds	1960–1984	1.6
Equities	1960–1984	5.4

TABLE 9-2. Real Interest Rates on Major Investments

The real cost of funds depends upon the type of instrument. High-grade corporate bonds have the lowest yield, while consumers pay the highest interest rates. All interest rates are corrected for inflation. [Source: Roger G. Ibbotson and Gary P. Brinson, *Investment Markets* (McGraw-Hill, New York, 1987); *Stocks, Bonds, Bills, and Inflation—1997 Yearbook* (Ibbotson Associates, Chicago, IL, 1997); Federal Reserve Board; United Nations Development Program; U.S. Bureau of Economic Affairs; data updated by authors.]

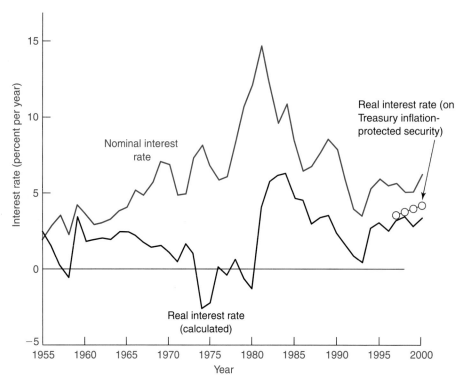

FIGURE 9-3. Real vs. Nominal Interest Rates

The blue line shows the nominal interest rate on safe short-term securities (1-year Treasury notes). The black curve shows the real interest rate, equal to the nominal or money rate less the realized inflation rate over the prior year. Note that real interest rates drifted downward until 1980. After 1980, however, real interest rates moved up sharply. The short line since 1997 shows the real interest rate on inflation-indexed securities. (Source: Federal Reserve Board, U.S. Department of Labor.)

Clearly, we need another concept of interest that measures the return on investments in terms of real goods and services rather than the return in terms of dollars. This alternative concept is the *real interest rate*, which measures the quantity of goods we get tomorrow for goods forgone today. The real interest rate is obtained by correcting nominal or dollar interest rates for the rate of inflation.

The **nominal interest rate** (sometimes also called the *money interest rate*) is the interest rate on money in terms of money. When you read about interest rates in the newspaper, or examine the interest rates

in Figure 9-2, you are looking at nominal interest rates; they give the dollar return per dollar of investment.

In contrast, the **real interest rate** is corrected for inflation and is calculated as the nominal interest rate minus the rate of inflation. As an example, suppose the nominal interest rate is 8 percent per year and the inflation rate is 3 percent per year; we can calculate the real interest rate as 8 − 3 = 5 percent per year. In other words, if you lend out 100 market baskets of goods today, next year you will get back only 105 (and not 108) market baskets of goods as principal and real interest payments.[2]

During inflationary periods, we must use real interest rates, not nominal or money interest rates, to calculate the yield on investments in terms of goods earned per year on goods invested. The real interest rate is approximately equal to the nominal interest rate minus the rate of inflation.

The difference between nominal and real interest rates is illustrated in Figure 9-3. It shows that most of the rise in nominal interest rates from 1960 to 1980 was purely illusory, for nominal interest rates were just keeping up with inflation during those years. After 1980, however, real interest rates rose sharply and remained high for a decade.

Inflation-indexed bonds

In 1997, the U.S. government introduced *inflation-indexed bonds*, which are a new financial asset in the United States. These bonds are indexed to the general price level and pay a constant real interest rate over their lifetime. The basic idea is simple. When the bonds were auctioned in January 1997, they had a real interest rate of $3\frac{1}{2}$ percent. This means that the bonds would pay interest of $3\frac{1}{2}$ percent plus the rate of inflation during the prior year. Suppose, for example, that the inflation rate in 2000 is 3 percent (as measured by the consumer price index). Then the interest during that year would be $3\frac{1}{2} + 3 = 6\frac{1}{2}$ percent. In addition, when the principal is returned at the end of the 10-year loan, it includes any rise in the price level over that period. If inflation were to heat up, people who hold indexed bonds would be protected against loss of income and principal.

Economists have been enthusiasts of indexed bonds for many years. Such bonds can be bought by pensioners who wish to guarantee that their retirement incomes will not be eroded by inflation. Similarly, parents who wish to save for their children's education can sock away some of their investment knowing that it will keep up with the general price level. Even monetary-policy makers find value in indexed bonds, for the difference between conventional bonds and indexed bonds gives an indication of what is happening to expected inflation. The main puzzle to many economists is why it took so long to introduce this important innovation.

THE DEMAND FOR MONEY

The demand for money is different from the demand for ice cream or movies. Money is not desired for its own sake; you cannot eat nickels, and we seldom hang $100 bills on the wall for the artistic quality of their engraving. Rather, we demand money because it serves us indirectly, as a lubricant to trade and exchange.

Money's Functions

Before we analyze the demand for money, let's note money's functions:

- By far the most important function of money is to serve as a *medium of exchange*. Without money we would be constantly roving around looking for someone to barter with. We are often reminded of money's utility when it does not work properly. Think about the case of Russia in the early 1990s, when people spent hours in line waiting for goods and tried to get dollars or other foreign currencies because the ruble had ceased to function as an acceptable means of exchange.
- Money is also used as the *unit of account,* the unit by which we measure the value of things. Just as we measure weight in kilograms, we measure value in money. The use of a common unit of account simplifies economic life enormously.
- Money is sometimes used as a *store of value;* it allows value to be held over time. In comparison with risky assets like stocks or real estate or gold, money is relatively riskless. In earlier days, people held currency as a safe form of wealth. Today, when people seek a safe haven for their wealth, they put some of their assets in cash and checking deposits (M_1). However, the vast preponderance of wealth is held in other assets, such as savings accounts, stocks, bonds, and real estate.

---

[2] The exact algebra of real interest rates is as follows: Let π be the inflation rate, i the nominal interest rate, and r the real interest rate. If you invest $1 today, you get $$(1 + i)$ back in 1 year. However, prices have risen, so that you need $$(1 + \pi)$ in 1 year to buy the same amount of goods that you could buy with $1 today. Instead of buying 1 unit of goods today, you can therefore buy $(1 + r)$ units tomorrow, where $(1 + r) = (1 + i)/(1 + \pi)$. For small values of i and π, $r = i - \pi$.

The Costs of Holding Money

These three functions of money are extremely important to people, so important that individuals are willing to incur a cost to hold currency or low-yielding checking accounts. What is the *opportunity cost of holding money?* It is the sacrifice in interest that you must incur by holding money rather than a riskier, less liquid asset or investment.

Say that you put $1000 in a savings account at the beginning of 2000; you would earn about 5 percent interest and would have $1050 at the end of 2000. This represents a 5 percent nominal interest rate. By contrast, suppose that you had left your $1000 in currency rather than in the savings account. You would end up with only $1000, for currency pays no interest. The opportunity cost of holding money as currency in this case would be $50.

Money allows easy and quick transactions, unambiguous determination of price, plus easy storage of value over time. These benefits are not free, however. If wealth were held in interest-paying assets rather than money, it would yield a higher interest rate.

Two Sources of Money Demand

Transactions Demand for Money. Why do people need money? The primary reason is that people's incomes and expenditures do not come at the same time. For example, I might be paid on the last day of the month, but I buy food, newspapers, gasoline, and clothing throughout the month. If I made all my purchases the very instant that I got paid, then I would have no need to hold money for the rest of the time. The need to have money to pay for purchases, or transactions, of goods, services, and other items constitutes the *transactions demand for money.*

Figure 9-4 illustrates the mechanics of the transactions demand for money. This figure shows the average money holdings of a family that earns $3000 per month, keeps it in money, and spends it during the month. Calculation will show that the family holds $1500 on average in money balances.

This example can help us see how the demand for money responds to different economic influences. If all prices and incomes double, the vertical axis in Figure 9-4 is simply relabeled by doubling all the dollar values. Clearly the nominal demand for M doubles. Thus the transactions demand for money

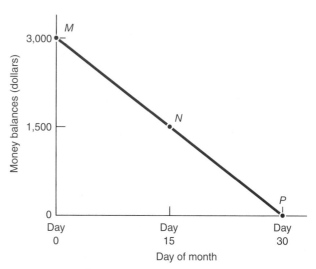

FIGURE 9-4. The Transactions Demand for Money

Assume that the family is paid $3000 at the beginning of the month and spends the whole amount over the course of the month at a constant rate of $100 per day. Moreover, the family does not put any of its money in another asset during the month. Thus the family has $3000 on day 0, $1500 on day 15, and nothing at the end of the month. This is illustrated by the line *MNP*.

How much money does the family hold on average? Answer: ½ of $3000 = $1500.

To understand the way the demand for money behaves, consider how this figure would change if all prices and incomes doubled, or if real incomes doubled, or if interest rates on savings accounts went to 20 percent.

doubles if nominal GDP doubles with no change in real GDP or other real variables.

But how does the demand for money vary with interest rates? Recall that our family is paying an opportunity cost for its checking account—the interest rate on M is less than that on other assets. As interest rates rise, the family might say, "Let's put only half of our money in the checking account at the beginning of the month and put the other half in a savings account earning 8 percent per annum. Then on day 15, we'll take that $1500 out of the savings account and put it in our checking account to pay the next 2 weeks' bills."

This means that as interest rates rose and the family decided to put half its earnings in a savings account, the average money balance of our family fell from $1500 to $750. This shows how money holdings (or the demand for money) may be sensitive to interest rates: *other things equal, as interest rates rise, the quantity of money demanded declines.*

You might think that the economic gain from a constant reshuffling of portfolios is so trivial that money holdings are not likely to be affected by interest-rate fluctuations. For the household sector, you would be correct: average bank balances change very little when people find they can earn 2 or 4 percent more on their money funds.

In the business sector, however, interest rates have a major impact on the demand for money. Large companies can easily find themselves with bank balances of $100 million one day, $250 million the next day, and so forth. If they do nothing, they could easily lose $20 to $50 million a year in interest payments. Today, large companies engage in "cash management," whereby their funds are constantly invested in high-yield assets rather than lying fallow in zero-yield checking accounts. And with higher interest rates, corporations work a little harder to keep their cash balances at a minimum.

Asset Demand. In addition to its use for transactions needs, what is money's role as a store of value? This crucial question is addressed by **financial economics,** which analyzes how investors should invest their funds to attain their objectives in the best possible manner. We discuss the fundamentals of finance in the last section of this chapter and will summarize here only the major point concerning money.

In general, a well-constructed portfolio (or combination of assets) will contain low-risk investments as well as riskier ventures. But it is not generally advisable to hold M_1 (currency or checking deposits) as one of these nest eggs. The reason is that other assets (such as government securities) are just as safe as M_1 and have higher interest rates. In the language of finance, narrow money is a "dominated" asset because other assets are equally safe but have higher yields. However, it might be sensible to hold your assets in M_2 (say, in savings accounts) because these are high-yielding safe assets.[3]

---

[3] Today, a substantial fraction of U.S. currency is held abroad because dollars are a safe and stable asset compared to local assets, particularly in countries that have unstable currencies. These holdings are largely asset demands rather than for transactions purposes.

We summarize our findings on the demand for money as follows:

The major reason we own narrow money (M_1) is the transactions demand—that is, because we need a generally acceptable medium of exchange to buy goods and pay our bills. As our incomes rise the dollar value of the goods we buy goes up, and we therefore need more money for transactions, raising our demand for money.

The transactions demand for M will be sensitive to the cost of holding money. When interest rates on alternative assets rise relative to the interest rate on money, people and businesses tend to reduce their money holdings.

In addition, people sometimes hold money as an asset or store of value. But modern finance theory shows that narrow money (M_1) should generally not be part of a well-designed portfolio.

B. BANKING AND THE SUPPLY OF MONEY

We have now reviewed the nature of money and the reasons that people hold money. The other side of the money market is the supply of money. In most countries, currency is issued by central banks, while commercial banks generate the rest of money as checking deposits. Surprisingly, however, the central bank actually controls the total supply of money. This section explains the process of money creation.

BANKING AS A BUSINESS

Bank money and many other financial services are today provided by **financial intermediaries,** which are institutions like commercial banks that take deposits of funds from one group and lend these funds to other groups. For example, financial intermediaries accept checking deposits from households and firms and then lend these funds out to other households and businesses for a variety of purposes. Financial institutions differ from other businesses because their assets are largely financial rather than real assets like plant and equipment.

The largest class of financial intermediaries comprises commercial banks, institutions which contain most of the nation's checking accounts or "checkable deposits." Other important categories are savings banks, life-insurance companies, pension funds, and money market mutual funds. Altogether, in the middle of 1998, all such intermediaries had a total of $288 trillion of assets and liabilities.

In what follows, we will focus on commercial banks, or "banks" for short. We do so because these institutions are the main source of checking accounts, or the bank-money component of M_1.

Financial institutions transfer funds from lenders to borrowers. In doing this, they create financial assets (like checking and savings accounts). But from a macroeconomic vantage point the most important asset is bank money (or checking accounts), primarily provided by commercial banks.

A Business Venture

Banks and other financial intermediaries are much like other businesses. They are organized to earn profits for their owners. A commercial bank is a relatively simple business concern. It provides certain services for customers and in return receives payments from them.

Table 9-3 shows the consolidated balance sheet of all U.S. commercial banks. A *balance sheet* is a statement of a firm's financial position at a point in time. It lists *assets* (items that a firm owns) and *liabilities* (items the firm owes). The difference between assets and liabilities is called *net worth*. Each entry in a bal-

ance sheet is valued at its actual market value or its historical cost.[4]

Except for minor rearrangements, a bank's balance sheet looks much like the balance sheet of any business. The unique feature of the bank balance sheet is an item called **reserves,** which appears on the asset side; these are assets banks hold in the form of cash on hand or of funds deposited by the bank with the central bank. Some reserves are held for day-to-day business needs, but most serve to meet legal reserve requirements.

How Banks Developed from Goldsmith Establishments

Commercial banking began in England with the goldsmiths, who developed the practice of storing people's gold and valuables for safekeeping. At first, such establishments were simply like baggage checkrooms or warehouses. Depositors left gold for safekeeping and were given a receipt. Later they presented their receipt, paid a small fee for the safekeeping, and got back their gold.

The goldsmiths soon found it more convenient not to worry about returning exactly the same piece of gold that each customer had left. Customers were quite willing to accept any gold as long as it was equivalent in value to what they had deposited. This

---

[4] Balance sheets, assets, and liabilities are extensively discussed in Chapter 7 of the *Microeconomics* chapters.

Balance Sheet of All Commercial Banking Institutions, 1998 (billions of dollars)			
Assets		**Liabilities**	
Reserves	$ 42	Checking deposits	$ 621
Loans	3,558	Savings and time deposits	2,952
Investments and securities	1,256	Other liabilities and net worth	2,111
Other assets	828		
Total	$5,684	Total	$5,684

TABLE 9-3. Reserves and Checking Deposits Are Major Balance Sheet Entries of Commercial Banks

Reserves and checking deposits are key to bank creation of money. Checking accounts are payable on demand and thus can be used quickly when customers write checks. Reserves are held primarily to meet legal requirements, not to provide against possible unexpected withdrawals. (Source: Federal Reserve Board.)

"anonymity" was important for it freed goldsmiths to relend the gold.

What would balance sheets of a typical goldsmith establishment look like? Perhaps like Table 9-4. We assume that First Goldsmith Bank no longer hammers gold bars but is occupied solely with storing people's money for safekeeping. A total of $1 million has been deposited in its vaults, and this whole sum is held as a cash asset (this is the item "Reserves" in the balance sheet). To balance this asset, there is a demand deposit of the same amount. Cash reserves are therefore 100 percent of deposits.

If the Goldsmith Bank were here today, its demand deposits would be part of the money supply; they would be "bank money." However, the bank money just offsets the amount of ordinary money (gold or currency) placed in the bank's safe and withdrawn from active circulation. No money creation has taken place. The process would be of no more interest than if the public decided to convert nickels into dimes. *A 100 percent reserve banking system has a neutral effect on money and the macroeconomy because it has no effect on the money supply.*

Modern Fractional-Reserve Banking

Profit-maximizing goldsmith-bankers soon recognized that although deposits are payable on demand, they are not all withdrawn together. Reserves equal to total deposits would be necessary if all depositors suddenly had to be paid off in full at the same time, but this almost never occurred. On a given day, some people make withdrawals while others make deposits. The two kinds of transactions generally balanced out.

The bankers did not need to keep 100 percent of deposits as sterile reserves; reserves earn no interest when they are sitting in a vault. So early banks hit upon the idea of using the money entrusted to them to make investments. By putting most of the money deposited with them in earning assets and keeping only fractional cash reserves against deposits, banks maximize their profits.

The transformation into *fractional-reserve banks*—holding fractional rather than 100 percent reserves against deposits—was revolutionary. It enabled banks to create money. That is, banks could turn each dollar of reserves into several dollars of deposits. Later in this section we will see how this process works.

Legal Reserve Requirements

In modern banking, bank reserves are held either as cash on hand or as deposits with the central bank. A prudent banker, concerned only with assuring customers that the bank has enough cash for daily transactions, might choose to keep only 5 percent of the bank's checking deposits in reserves. In fact, banks today set aside about 10 percent of their checking deposits in reserves. These are held in cash or in deposits with our central bank, the Federal Reserve System, often called "the Fed."

Reserves are so high because all financial institutions are required by law and Federal Reserve regulations to keep a fraction of their deposits as reserves. Reserve requirements apply to all types of checking and savings deposits, independent of the actual need for cash on hand. (We describe the regulatory system in the next chapter.)

Bank reserves are kept above the prudent commercial level because of legal reserve requirements.

Goldsmith Balance Sheet			
Assets		**Liabilities**	
Reserves	+$1,000,000	Demand deposits	+$1,000,000
Total	+$1,000,000	Total	+$1,000,000

TABLE 9-4. First Goldsmith Bank Held 100 Percent Cash Reserves against Demand Deposits

In a primitive banking system, with 100 percent backing of deposits, no creation of money out of reserves is possible.

The main function of legal reserve requirements is to enable the Federal Reserve to control the amount of checking deposits that banks can create. By imposing high fixed legal reserve requirements, the Fed can better control the money supply.

THE PROCESS OF DEPOSIT CREATION

In our simplified discussion of goldsmith banks, we suggested that banks turn reserves into bank money. There are, in fact, two steps in the process:

- The central bank determines the quantity of reserves of the banking system. The detailed process by which the central bank does this is discussed in the next chapter.
- Using those reserves as an input, the banking system transforms them into a much larger amount of bank money. The currency plus this bank money is the money supply, M_1. This process is called the *multiple expansion of bank deposits*.

How Deposits Are Created: First-Generation Banks

Let us consider what happens when new reserves are injected into the banking system. Assume that the Federal Reserve buys a $1000 government bond from Ms. Bondholder, and she deposits the $1000 in her checking account at Bank 1.

The change in the balance sheet of Bank 1, as far as the new demand deposit is concerned, is shown in Table 9-5(*a*).[5] When Ms. Bondholder made the

---

[5] For simplicity, our tables will show only the *changes* in balance sheet items, and we use reserve ratios of 10 percent. Note that when bankers refer to their loans and investments, by "investments" they mean their holdings of bonds and other financial assets. They don't mean what economists mean by "investment," which is capital formation.

deposit, $1000 of bank money, or checking deposits, was created. Now, if the bank were to keep 100 percent of deposits in reserves, as did the old goldsmiths, no extra money would be created from the new deposit of $1000. The depositor's $1000 checking deposit would just match the $1000 of reserves. But modern banks do not keep 100 percent reserves for their deposits. Because banks are assumed to keep a reserve requirement of 10 percent, Bank 1 must set aside as reserves $100 of the $1000 deposit.

But Bank 1 now has $900 more in reserves than it needs to meet the reserve requirement. Because reserves earn no interest, our profit-minded bank will lend or invest the excess $900. The loan might be for a car, or the investment might be a purchase of a Treasury bond. Let's say the bank makes a loan. The person who borrows the money takes the $900 (in cash or check) and deposits it in her account in another bank. Very quickly, then, the $900 will be paid out by Bank 1.

After it has lent or invested $900, Bank 1's legal reserves are just enough to meet its legal reserve requirement. The balance sheet of Bank 1, after it has made all possible loans or investments (but still meets its reserve requirement), is shown in Table 9-5(*b*).

But if we calculate the amount of money, we are in for a big surprise. In addition to the original $1000 of deposits shown on the right of Table 9-5(*b*), there is $900 of demand deposits in another account (i.e., in the checking account of the person who got the $900). Hence, the total amount of *M* is now $1900. *Bank 1's activity has created $900 of new money.*

Chain Repercussions on Other Banks

After the $900 created by Bank 1 leaves the bank, it will soon be deposited in another bank, and at that point it starts up a chain of expansion whereby still more bank money is created.

Assets		Liabilities	
Reserves	+$1,000	Deposits	+$1,000
Total	+$1,000	Total	+$1,000

TABLE 9-5(a). Bank 1 in Initial Position

Multiple-bank deposit creation is a story with many successive stages. At the start, $1000 of newly created reserves are deposited in the original, first-generation bank.

Assets		Liabilities	
Reserves	+$ 100	Deposits	+$1,000
Loans and investments	+ 900		
Total	+$1,000	Total	+$1,000

TABLE 9-5(b). Bank 1 in Final Position

A profit-maximizing bank will lend or invest any excess reserves. Thus Bank 1 has kept only $100 of the original cash deposit (as required reserves) and has lent or invested the other $900.

Assets		Liabilities	
Reserves	+$900	Deposits	+$900
Total	+$900	Total	+$900

TABLE 9-5(c). Second-Generation Banks in Initial Position

Assets		Liabilities	
Reserves	+$ 90	Deposits	+$900
Loans and investments	+ 810		
Total	+$900	Total	+$900

TABLE 9-5(d). Final Position of Second-Generation Banks

Next, the money lent out by Bank 1 soon goes to second-generation banks, which in turn lend out nine-tenths of it.

To see what happens to the $900, let's call all the banks that receive the $900 *second-generation banks* (or Bank 2). Their combined balance sheets now appear as shown in Table 9-5(*c*). To these banks, the dollars deposited function just like our original $1000 deposit. These banks do not care that they are second in a chain of deposits. Their only concern is that they are holding too much non-earning cash, or excess reserves. Only one-tenth of $900, or $90, is legally needed against the $900 deposit. They will use the other nine-tenths to acquire $810 worth of loans and investments. Their balance sheets will soon reach the equilibrium in Table 9-5(*d*).

At this point, the original $1000 taken out of hand-to-hand circulation has produced a total of

$2710 (=$1900 + 810) of money. The total of *M* has increased, and the process continues.

The $810 spent by the second-generation banks in acquiring loans and investments will go to a new set of banks called third-generation banks. You can create the balance sheets (initial and final) for *third-generation banks*. Eventually, the third-generation banks will lend out their excess reserves and will thereby create $729 of new money. A fourth generation of banks will clearly end up with nine-tenths of $810 in deposits, or $729, and so on.

Final System Equilibrium

Now let's sum up all the money creation: $1000 + $900 + $810 + $729 + ⋯ ? Table 9-6 shows that

Position of bank	New deposits ($)	New loans and investments ($)	New reserves ($)
Original banks	1,000.00	900.00	100.00
2d-generation banks	900.00	810.00	90.00
3d-generation banks	810.00	729.00	81.00
4th-generation banks	729.00	656.10	72.90
5th-generation banks	656.10	590.49	65.61
6th-generation banks	590.49	531.44	59.05
7th-generation banks	531.44	478.30	53.14
8th-generation banks	478.30	430.47	47.83
9th-generation banks	430.47	387.42	43.05
10th-generation banks	387.42	348.68	38.74
Sum of first 10 generations of banks	6,513.22	5,861.90	651.32
⋮	⋮	⋮	⋮
Sum of remaining generations of banks	3,486.78	3,138.10	348.68
Total for banking system as a whole	10,000.00	9,000.00	1,000.00

TABLE 9-6. Finally, through This Long Chain, All Banks Create New Deposits of 10 Times New Reserves

The actions of all banks together produce the multiple expansion of reserves into *M*. The final equilibrium is reached when every dollar of original new reserves supports $10 of demand deposits. Note that in every generation each bank has "created" new money in the following sense: It ends up with a final bank deposit 10 times the reserve it finally retains. (Make sure you understand why the number is 10 times.)

the complete effect of the chain of money creation is $10,000. We can get the answer by arithmetic, by common sense, and by elementary algebra.

Common sense tells us that the process of deposit creation must come to an end only when every bank in the system has reserves equal to 10 percent of deposits. In all our examples, no cash reserves ever leaked out of the banking system; the money simply went from one set of banks to another set of banks. The banking system will reach equilibrium when the $1000 of new reserves is all used up as required reserves on new deposits. In other words, the final equilibrium of the banking system will be the point at which 10 percent of new deposits (*D*) equals the new reserves of $1000. What level of *D* satisfies this condition? The answer is *D* = $10,000.

We can also see the answer intuitively by looking at a consolidated balance sheet for all the generations of banks together. This is shown in Table 9-7. If total new deposits were less than $10,000, the 10

percent reserve ratio would not yet have been reached, and full equilibrium would not yet have been attained.[6]

Figure 9-5 gives a schematic overview of the process. It shows how $1 of new deposits or reserves, at the upper left, is transformed into $10 of total deposits, or bank money, on the right. Inside the rectangle, which represents the banking system as a whole, Bank 1 receives the initial new deposit. The blue arrows circulating around show how reserves are redistributed, while the black lines show new deposits. Though the chain has many links, each is a dwindling fraction and the whole effect does add up to the 10-to-1 total.

---

[6] The algebraic solution can be shown as follows:

$$\$1000 + \$900 + \$810 + \cdots$$

$$= \$1000 \times [1 + \tfrac{9}{10} + (\tfrac{9}{10})^2 + (\tfrac{9}{10})^3 + \cdots]$$

$$= \$1000 \left(\frac{1}{1 - \tfrac{9}{10}} \right) = \$1000 \times \frac{1}{0.1} = \$10,000$$

Assets		Liabilities	
Reserves	+$ 1,000	Deposits	+$10,000
Loans and investments	+ 9,000		
Total	+$10,000	Total	+$10,000

TABLE 9-7. Consolidated Balance Sheet Showing Final Position of All Banks

All banks together ultimately increase deposits and M by a multiple of the original injection of reserves.

The Money-Supply Multiplier. We see that there is a new kind of multiplier operating on reserves. For every additional dollar in reserves provided to the banking system, banks eventually create $10 of additional deposits or bank money.

We described the expenditure multiplier as the ratio of the change in output to new investment or other spending. The money multiplier is the ratio of the new money created to the change in reserves. Note that the arithmetic of M expansion is similar to that of the expenditure multiplier, *but don't confuse the two because they multiply different things.* The amplification here is from the stock of reserves to the stock of total M; it has nothing to do with the extra output induced by investment or money.

The ratio of new checking deposits to the increase in reserves is called the money-supply multi-plier. In the simple case analyzed here, the **money-supply multiplier** is defined as follows:

Money-supply multiplier

$$= \frac{\text{change of money}}{\text{change of reserves}}$$

$$= 10 = \frac{1}{0.1} = \frac{1}{\text{required reserve ratio}}$$

The money-supply multiplier summarizes the logic of how banks create money. The entire banking system can transform an initial increase in reserves into a multiplied amount of new deposits or bank money.

The process of deposit creation can also work in reverse when a drain in reserves reduces bank money. It is useful to reinforce your understanding of money creation by tracing in detail what happens when the Fed permanently destroys $2000 of reserves by selling a government bond to someone who withdraws cash from his checking account to pay for it. In the end, the withdrawal of $2000 of reserves from the banking system kills off $20,000 worth of deposits throughout the whole system.

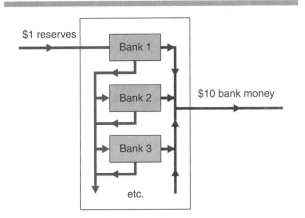

FIGURE 9-5. Multiple-Bank Expansion of Money

For each dollar of new reserves deposited in a bank, the system as a whole creates about $10 of bank money. The blue arrows in the box show that Bank 1 cannot do it alone. The money supply increases as reserves spread through the banking system.

The contagion of bank panics

Fractional-reserve banking has great risks as well as great advantages. The fact that banks cover only a fraction of their deposits opens up the possibility of "bank panics" or "a run on the banks." Remember that under fractional-reserve banking, a bank has on hand only a small portion of the money that it owes to its depositors. Ordinarily, that is no problem, since only a small number of people will want to withdraw their money at any one time.

But what if too many people want their money at once? Then we can have the feeding frenzy known as a *bank run*. As soon as one depositor has trouble getting his or her money immediately, the other depositors get scared that their money is also gone. Driven by fear, depositors descend on the bank like a horde of hungry animals, demanding all of their money right away. Not even healthy banks can withstand this sort of mass demand for deposits. The United States was hit with major bank panics in 1893, 1895, and then in 1907. The bank panics of the 1930s, during the Great Depression, pushed more than 9000 banks into failure.

In the modern financial system, bank runs are rare and less dangerous, for two reasons. One reason is that the federal government ensures that all but the largest depositors will get their money back no matter what happens to the bank. Depositors therefore need not rush down to their bank at the first sign of trouble. In addition, the Federal Reserve takes an active role as the "lender of last resort," providing funds to healthy banks with temporary liquidity problems and making sure sick banks get liquidated in an orderly way.

Still, despite these precautions, bank runs do occasionally happen. In 1985, there were runs at state-chartered banks in Ohio which were not covered by federal deposit insurance. And in 1991, the Bank of New England, one of the largest banks in the country, was hit by a wave of panicky withdrawals which drained perhaps $1 billion from the bank's accounts in only 2 days. The run, which was threatening to spread to other banks in the area, was quickly stopped when the federal government stepped in to take over the bank.

Two Qualifications to Deposit Creation

The actual financial system is more complicated than our simple banking example. We have shown that $1000 of new reserves put into a bank will ultimately result in an increase of $10,000 of bank deposits. This example assumed that all the new money remained as checking accounts in the banking system and that no bank would have excess reserves. Let us see what would happen if some money leaked into circulation or if some banks had excess reserves.

Leakage into Hand-to-Hand Circulation. It is possible that, somewhere along the chain of deposit expansion, an individual who receives a check will not leave the proceeds in a bank checking account. He might put some cash in a cookie jar. Or some of the $1000 might be sent to a cousin in Argentina and used there instead of in the United States.

The effects of such withdrawals on our analysis are simple. When $1000 stayed in the banking system, $10,000 of new deposits was created. If $100 were to leak into circulation outside the banks and only $900 of new reserves were to remain in the banking system, the new checking deposits created would be $9000 ($900 × 10). Therefore, the 10-to-1 amplification would occur only if no reserves leaked from banks.

Possible Excess Reserves. Our analysis proceeded on the assumption that the commercial banks follow their legal reserve requirements to the letter. What would happen if the bank decided to keep rather than lend the new reserves? Then the whole process of multiple deposit creation would stop dead, with no expansion of deposits at all.

This decision would of course make no sense for the bank. Because the bank earns no interest on reserves, it would lose interest payments on the $900. So as long as the interest rate on investments is above the interest rate on reserves (set at zero), banks have a strong incentive to avoid holding any excess reserves.

In certain situations, it might be reasonable to have excess reserves. During the Great Depression, interest rates fell to 0.1 percent per year, so banks during this period often held significant excess reserves. In 1999, short-term interest rates were essentially zero in Japan, and banks had significant quantities of excess reserves. In such pathological situations, central-bank control of the money supply becomes much more difficult.

With a required reserve ratio of 10 percent, reserves will be multiplied tenfold into new deposits. However, when some of the increased deposits spill into currency or nonmonetary assets, or when banks hold excess reserves, the deposit creation will depart from the ratio of 1/(legal reserve ratio).

We have now surveyed the essentials of the demand for money along with the behavior of commercial banks. We conclude this chapter with an analysis of a fascinating part of our financial system— the stock market. Then in the next chapter we will see how our central bank, the Federal Reserve, can control bank reserves and thereby increase or decrease the total money supply. Armed with our analysis of the supply and demand for money, we can then show how the money supply helps influence output, inflation, and employment.

C. FINANCIAL ECONOMICS

Greed run amok has been an essential feature of every spectacular boom in history.

Burton Malkiel, *A Random Walk down Wall Street* **(1998)**

This chapter has concentrated on money markets because they are central to understanding the functioning of the macroeconomy. But money is just a small part of the enormous variety of financial markets. The world of finance comes much closer to home when we borrow for a mortgage, invest for our retirement, or engage in online trading of Internet companies. In this final section, therefore, we take a

tour through the fascinating world of *financial economics*, which studies how rational investors should allocate their funds to attain their objectives in the best possible manner. It is an exciting field of economics—and a crucial one for people who want to invest their funds wisely.

A Menu of Financial Assets

Table 9-8 shows the major financial assets of households. **Financial assets** are monetary claims by one party against another party. These consist primarily of *dollar-denominated assets* (whose payments are fixed in dollar terms) and *equities* (whose values are set by the market). Here are the major kinds of assets:

- *Money* was defined earlier in this chapter.
- *Savings accounts* are deposits with banks, usually guaranteed by governments, that have a fixed-dollar principal value and interest rates determined by short-term market interest rates.
- *Government securities* are bills and bonds of the federal, state, and local governments. They guarantee repayment of principal on maturity and pay interest along the way. Federal securities are considered the safest of all investments.
- *Equities* are ownership rights to companies. They yield dividends, which are payments drawn from

Financial Assets of Households			
	Percentage of Total Assets		
Class of asset	1963	1988	1998
Dollar denominated:			
Currency and checking deposits (M_1)	4.6	4.2	1.5
Savings accounts	14.3	21.0	9.5
Government securities	6.4	8.5	2.0
Other	3.3	2.2	2.5
Equity in businesses:			
Corporate (including mutual funds)	31.3	18.4	29.7
Noncorporate	25.7	19.8	19.8
Pension-fund and life-insurance reserves	13.4	23.9	32.2
Other	1.0	1.9	4.3
Total	100.0	100.0	100.0
Total assets of households ($, billion)	1,641	12,139	30,711

TABLE 9-8. Financial Assets of Households

Households own a wide variety of financial assets ranging from money to pension funds. (Source: Federal Reserve Board.)

the companies' net profits. Publicly traded equities (or common stocks) are priced on stock markets, where the prices are determined by the market valuation of future earnings and dividends. Noncorporate equities are the values of partnerships, farms, and other entities, usually owned by only a few people.

- *Financial derivatives* are new forms of financial instruments whose values are based on or derived from the values of other assets. One important example is stock options, which are instruments whose value depends upon the value of the stock to which they are benchmarked.
- *Pension funds* represent ownership in the assets that are held by companies or pension plans. Workers and companies contribute to these funds during working years, and the funds are then drawn down to pay pensions during retirement.

Note that these financial assets exclude the single most important assets owned by most people—their houses, which are tangible as opposed to financial assets. In addition, people have implicit assets in their future social security payments and government-provided medical care, but these have no ready market value.

Risk and Return on Different Assets

Recall from our discussion in Section A of this chapter that assets have different characteristics. The most important characteristics are the rate of return (or interest rate) and the risk.

The *rate of return* is the total dollar gain from a security (measured as a percent of the price at the beginning of the period). For savings accounts and short-term bonds, the return would be the interest rate. For example, the return on 1-year Treasury bonds in 1999 was a certain 5.5 percent. For most other assets, the return combines an income (like dividends) with a *capital gain* or *loss*, which represents the increase or decrease in the value of the asset.

We can illustrate the rate of return on stocks using data on stocks. (For this example, we ignore taxes and commissions.) Say that you bought a representative portfolio of $10,000 worth of stocks in U.S. companies in December 1997. During 1998, your fund paid dividends of $256. Moreover, because 1998 was an unusually good year for stocks, your fund rose

in value to $13,500 at the end of the year, for a capital gain of 35 percent. Your total return was therefore (256 + 3500)/10,000 = 37.6 percent for 1998.

But before you get too excited about these fantastic gains, be warned that you could easily have a big loss. If you had bought your stocks in July 1987, you would have had a *minus 12 percent* return over the next year. Or if you had bought German bonds in 1922 or Cuban bonds in 1958 or Russian bonds in 1990, you would have lost almost everything to confiscation or inflation.

The fact that some assets have predictable rates of return while others are quite risky leads to the next important characteristic of investments: **Risk** refers to the variability of the returns on an investment. If I buy a 1-year Treasury bond with a 6 percent return, the bond is a riskless investment because I am sure to get my return. On the other hand, if I buy $10,000 of stocks, I am uncertain about their year-end value.

Economists often measure risk in terms of the standard deviation of returns; this is a measure of dispersion whose range encompasses about two-thirds of the variation.[7] For example, from 1926 to 1999, common stocks had an annual standard deviation of return of 22 percent and an average annual return of 11 percent. This normally implies that the return was between −10 percent and +33 percent two-thirds of the time. The largest return was 54 percent in 1933, and the largest loss was −43 percent in 1931.

Looking at both return and risk, individuals generally prefer higher return, but they also prefer lower risk because they are *risk-averse*. This means that they must be rewarded by higher returns to induce them to hold investments with higher risks. We would not be surprised, therefore, to learn that over the long run safe investments like bonds have lower returns than risky investments like stocks.

Table 9-2 on page 171 showed the historical returns or interest rates on a number of important investments. We show the most important assets in the *risk-return diagram* in Figure 9-6 on the next page. This diagram shows the average real (or inflation-

---

[7] The standard deviation is a measure of variability that can be found in any elementary statistics text. As an example, if a variable takes the values of 1, 3, 1, 3, the mean or expected value is 2 while the standard deviation is 1.

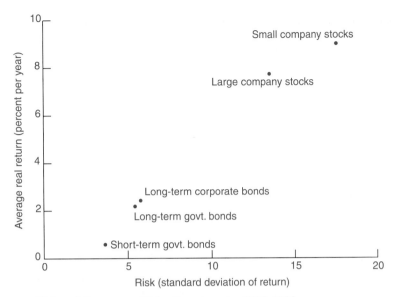

FIGURE 9-6. Risk and Return on Major Investments, 1926–1998

Investments vary in their average returns and riskiness. Bonds tend to be safe, while stocks have much higher returns but face higher risks. This diagram shows the *historical* risk and return on different financial assets. Depending upon market sentiments, the *expected* risk and return may differ markedly from the historical experience. Many economists believed that the prospective return on stocks for the next decade would be much lower than the high returns garnered during the 1990s. [Source: Ibbotson Associates, *Stocks, Bonds, Bills, and Inflation: 1999 Yearbook* (Ibbotson Associates, Inc., Chicago, IL, 1999).]

corrected) return on the vertical axis and the historical risk (measured as a standard deviation) on the horizontal axis. Note the strong relationship between risk and return.

THE STOCK MARKET

A **stock market** is a place where the shares in publicly owned companies, the titles to business firms, are bought and sold. In 2000, the value of these titles was estimated at $15 trillion in the United States. Sales in a single year might total more than $10 trillion. The stock market is the hub of our corporate economy.

The New York Stock Exchange is America's main stock market, listing more than a thousand securities, although recently the NASDAQ, with many companies traded "over the counter," or outside organized exchanges, has had a meteoric rise in values. Every large financial center has a stock exchange. Major ones are located in Tokyo, London, Frankfurt, Hong Kong, Toronto, Zurich, and, of course, New York. A stock exchange is a critical part of modern market economies. When the countries of Eastern Europe decided to scrap their centrally planned systems and become market economies, one of their first acts was to introduce a stock market to buy and sell ownership rights in companies.

Bubbles and Crashes

The history of finance is one of the most exciting, and sobering, parts of economics, as is illustrated by the quote from Burton Malkiel that leads off this section.

Investors are sometimes divided into those who invest on firm foundations and those who try to outguess the market psychology. The firm-foundation approach holds that assets should be valued on the basis of their intrinsic value. For common stocks, the intrinsic value is the expected present value of the dividends. If a stock has a constant dividend of $2 per year and the appropriate interest rate with which to discount dividends is 5 percent per year, the intrinsic value would be $2/.05 = $40 per share. The firm-foundation approach is the slow but safe way of getting rich.

Impatient souls might echo Keynes, who argued that investors are more likely to worry about market psychology and to speculate on the future value of assets rather than wait patiently for stocks to prove their intrinsic value. He argued, "It is not sensible to pay 25 for an investment which is worth 30, if you also believe that the market will value it at 20 three months hence." The market psychologist tries to guess what the average investor thinks, which requires considering what the average investor thinks about the average investor, and so on, ad infinitum.

When a psychological frenzy seizes the market, it can result in speculative bubbles and crashes. A *speculative bubble* occurs when prices rise because people think they are going to rise in the future—it is the reverse of Keynes's just-cited dictum. A piece of land may be worth only $1000, but if you see a land-price boom driving prices up 50 percent each year, you might buy it for $2000 hoping you can sell it to someone else next year for $3000. A speculative bubble fulfills its own promises. If people buy because they think stocks will rise, their act of buying sends up the price of stocks. This causes people to buy even more and sends the dizzy dance off on another round. But, unlike people who play cards or dice, no one apparently loses what the winners gain. Of course, the prizes are all on paper and would disappear if everyone tried to cash them in. But why should anyone want to sell such lucrative securities? Prices rise because of hopes and dreams, not because the profits and dividends of companies are soaring.

History is marked by bubbles in which speculative prices were driven up far beyond the intrinsic value of the asset. In seventeenth-century Holland, a tulip mania drove tulip prices to levels higher than the price of a house. In the eighteenth century, the stock of the South Sea Company rose to fantastic levels on empty promises that the firm would enrich its stockholders. In more recent times, similar bubbles have been found in biotechnology, Japanese land, "emerging markets," and a vacuum-cleaning company called ZZZZ Best, which turned out to have profited from laundering money for the Mafia.

The most famous bubble of them all occurred in the American stock market in the 1920s. The "roaring twenties" saw a fabulous stock market boom, when everyone bought and sold stocks. Most pur-

chases in this wild bull market were on margin. This means a buyer of $10,000 worth of stocks put up only part of the price in cash and borrowed the difference, pledging the newly bought stocks as collateral for the purchase. What did it matter that you had to pay the broker 6, 10, or 15 percent per year on the borrowing when Auburn Motors or Bethlehem Steel might jump 10 percent in value overnight?

The Great Crash. Speculative bubbles always produce crashes and sometimes lead to economic panics. One traumatic event has cast a shadow over stock markets for decades—the 1929 panic and crash. This event ushered in the long and painful Great Depression of the 1930s.

The crash came in "black October" of 1929. Everyone was caught off-guard, the big-league professionals as well as the piddling amateurs—Andrew Mellon, John D. Rockefeller, engineer-turned-president Herbert Hoover in the White House, and America's greatest economist, Irving Fisher.

When the bottom fell out of the market in 1929, investors, big and small, who had bought on margin could not put up funds to cover their holdings, and the market fell still further. The bull market (rising) turned into a bear (or declining) market. By the trough of the Depression in 1933, the market had declined 85 percent.

Trends in the stock market are tracked using *stock-price indexes*, which are weighted averages of the prices of a basket of company stocks. Commonly followed averages include the Dow-Jones Industrial Average (DJIA) of 30 large companies and Standard and Poor's index of 500 companies (the "S&P 500"), which is a weighted average of the stock prices of the 500 largest American corporations.

Figure 9-7 on page 187 shows the history since 1920 of the Standard and Poor's 500. The lower curve shows the nominal stock-price average, which records the actual average during a particular year. The upper line shows the real price of stocks; this equals the nominal price divided by an index of consumer prices that equaled 1 in 2000.

Note the experience of the 1980s, which illustrates both the perils and rewards of "playing the market." Beginning in 1982, the stock market surged steadily upward for 5 years, gaining almost 140 percent. Those who had the luck or vision to put all their assets into stocks made a lot of money. The market

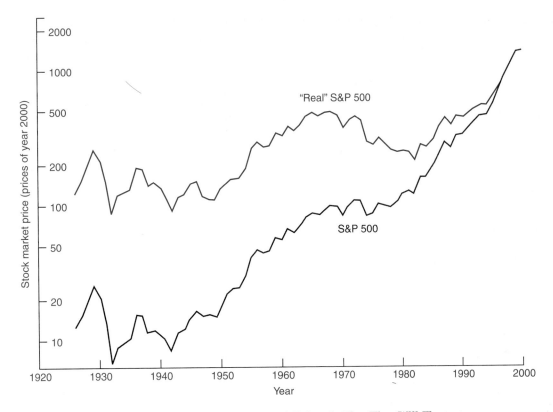

FIGURE 9-7. The Only Guarantee about Stock Prices Is That They Will Fluctuate

Stock prices in nominal terms, shown in the bottom line, tend to rise with inflation. The Standard and Poor's index (the S&P 500) shown here tracks the value-weighted average of the stock prices of the 500 largest American companies.

The top line shows the "real" S&P 500, which is the S&P 500 corrected for movements in the consumer price index.

peaked in the summer of 1987. On October 19, 1987—"black Monday"—the stock market lost 22 percent of its value in 6 hours. The shock to securities markets was a vivid reminder of the risks you take when you buy stocks.

The 1990s were yet another period of buoyant economic performance and booming stock prices. The major stock-price indexes rose by more than 300 percent over this period. Internet stocks became the darling of investors and sold at price-earnings ratios of more than 100 while traditional stocks sold for price-earnings ratios of 20 or 30. Federal Reserve chairman Alan Greenspan cautioned against "irrational exuberance"; graybeards noted the parallel between the infatuation with the Internet and earlier disastrous investments in tulips or Florida real estate; Yale economist Robert Shiller published a best-seller warning of an overvalued market pushed ever higher by unrealistic herd-like behavior. But investors ignored these financial Cassandras and plunged ahead.

Where will it all end? Is there a crystal ball that will foretell the movement of stock prices? This is the subject of modern finance theory.

Efficient Markets and the Random Walk

Economists and finance professors have long studied prices in speculative markets, like the stock market, and markets for commodities such as corn. Their findings have stirred great controversy and have even angered many financial analysts. Yet this is an area in which the facts have largely corroborated the theories.

Modern economic theories of stock prices are grouped under the heading of **efficient-market theory.**[8] One way of expressing the fundamental theory is: *You can't beat the market.*

We'll see in a minute why this proposition is plausible. First, let's consider its factual basis. There have been numerous studies over the years about rules or formulas for making money. Typical rules are "Buy after 2 days of increases" or "Buy on the bad news and sell on the good news." An early study by Alfred Cowles investigated the recommendations of stockbrokers. He examined how well different brokers performed by looking at the return (in dollars of total income per year per dollar invested) on the stocks they selected. He found that, on average, a stockbroker's choices did no better than a random portfolio (or combination) of stocks.

This observation led to the *dartboard theory* of stock selection: you can throw a dart at the *Wall Street Journal* as a way of selecting stocks. Better still, buy a little of everything in the market so that you hold a diversified "index" portfolio of the stock market. This would probably leave you better off than your cousins who follow a broker's advice. Why? Because they would have to pay brokers' commissions while their stocks, on average, would not outperform yours.

This paradoxical view has been generally confirmed in hundreds of studies over the last four decades. Their lesson is not that you will never become rich by following a rule or formula but that, on average, such rules cannot outperform a diversified portfolio of stocks.

Rationale for the Efficient-Market View. Finance theorists have spent many years analyzing stock and bond markets in order to understand why the dartboard theory might hold. Why do well-functioning financial markets rule out persistent excess profits? The theory of efficient markets explains this.

An **efficient financial market** is one where all new information is quickly understood by market partic-

ipants and becomes immediately incorporated into market prices. For example, say that Lazy-T Oil Company has just struck oil in the Gulf of Alaska. This event is announced at 11:30 A.M. on Tuesday. When will the price of Lazy-T's shares rise? The efficient-market theory holds that the news will be incorporated into prices immediately. The market participants will react at once, bidding the price of Lazy-T up by the correct amount. In short, at every point in time, markets have already digested and included in stock prices or corn prices or other speculative prices all the latest available information.

This means that if you read about a heavy frost in Florida over breakfast, you can't enrich yourself by buying frozen-orange-juice futures during your lunch break: the orange-juice price went up the minute the news was reported, or even earlier.

The theory of efficient markets holds that market prices contain all available information. It is not possible to make profits by looking at old information or at patterns of past price changes. Returns on stocks will be primarily determined by their riskiness relative to the market.

A Random Walk. The efficient-market view provides an important way of analyzing price movements in organized markets. Under this approach, the price movements of stocks should look highly erratic, like a random walk, when charted over a period of time.

A price follows a *random walk* when its movements over time are completely unpredictable. For example, toss a coin for heads or tails. Call a head "plus 1" and a tail "minus 1." Then keep track of the running score of 100 coin tosses. Draw it on graph paper. This curve is a random walk. Now, for comparison, also graph 100 days' movement of Microsoft stock or of Standard and Poor's 500 index. Note how similar all three figures appear.

Why do speculative prices resemble a random walk? Economists, on reflection, have arrived at the following truths: In an efficient market all predictable things have already been built into the price. It is the arrival of *new* information—a surprisingly large increase in the CPI, a revolution in Saudi Arabia, a report that the Federal Reserve has unexpectedly raised interest rates—that affects stock or commodity prices. Moreover, the news must be random and unpredictable (or else it would be predictable and therefore not truly news).

---

[8] "Efficiency" is used differently in finance theory than in other parts of economics. Here, "efficiency" means that information is quickly absorbed, not that resources produce the maximal outputs.

To summarize:

The efficient-market theory explains why movements in stock prices look so erratic. Prices respond to news, to surprises. But surprises are unpredictable events—like the flip of a coin or next month's rainstorm—that may move in any direction. Because stock prices move in response to erratic events, stock prices themselves move erratically, like a random walk.

Qualifications to the Efficient-Market View. Although the efficient-market view has been the canon of finance in economics and business, many believe that it is oversimplified and misleading. Here are some of the reservations:

1. Some people are quicker and smarter than others. Some have much money to spend on information that reduces uncertainty about the future. Doesn't it stand to reason that they will make higher profits? There are many such people competing against each other. The Rockefellers can buy the best financial counsel there is. But so can pension funds, university endowments, and large banks. Competition provides the checks and balances of efficiency and ensures minimal excess profits. Studies show that few outstanding investors outperform the market year in and year out, although some poorly managed funds with high turnover can show perennial poor yields for investors.

2. Economists who look at the historical record ask whether it is plausible that sharp movements in stock prices could actually reflect new information. Consider the sharp drop in the stock market from October 15 to October 19, 1987. The efficient-market view would hold that this drop was caused by economic events that depressed the expected value of future corporate earnings. What were those events? James Tobin, Yale's Nobel Prize–winning economist, commented, "There are no visible factors that could make a 30 percent difference in the value of stock [prices over these four days]." Efficient-market theorists fall silent before this criticism.

3. Finally, the efficient-market view applies to individual stocks but not necessarily to the market as a whole. Some economists have found evidence of long, self-reversing swings in stock market prices. Others believe that these swings reflect changes in the general mood of the financial community. These long-term swings may lie behind the boom psychology of the 1920s and 1990s or the depression mentality of the 1930s. Let us say that we believed that the whole stock market in 1999 showed an "irrational exuberance" and was overvalued. What could we do? We could not individually buy or sell enough stocks to overcome the entire national mood. So, from a macroeconomic perspective, speculative markets can exhibit waves of pessimism or optimism without powerful economic forces moving in to correct these swings of mood.

PERSONAL FINANCIAL STRATEGIES

While taking a course in economics is no guarantee of great wealth, the principles of modern finance can definitely help you invest your nest egg wisely and avoid the worst financial blunders. What lessons does economics teach about personal investment decisions? We have culled the following five rules from the wisdom of the best brains on the street:

Lesson 1: Know thy investments. The absolute bedrock of a sound investment strategy is to be realistic and prudent in your investment decisions. For important investments, study the materials and get expert advice. Be skeptical of approaches that claim to have found the quick route to success. You can't get rich by listening to your barber or consulting the stars (although, unbelievably, some financial advisers push astrology to their clients). Hunches work out to nothing in the long run. Moreover, the best brains on Wall Street do not, on average, beat the averages (Dow-Jones, Standard and Poor's, etc.). This is not surprising. Although the big money managers have plenty of money for research, they are all competing with one another.

Lesson 2: Diversify, diversify, that is the law of the prophets of finance. One of the major lessons of finance is the advantage of diversifying your investments. "Don't put all your eggs in one basket" is one way of expressing this rule. By putting funds in a number of different investments, you can continue to average a high yield while reducing the risk. For example, suppose that stocks and real estate each have average returns of 10 percent while their risk index (standard deviation) is 30 percent. A portfolio that contains equal shares of each investment would also have an average return of 10 percent. But because a bad year for one of them may be balanced by a good year for the other, the risk of the overall portfolio can be reduced. Under simplified conditions (independence of risk and a normal probability distribution), the risk index for the diversified portfolio is only 21.2 percent. Calculations show that by diversifying their wealth among a broad array of investments—different common stocks, conventional and inflation-indexed bonds, real estate, domestic and foreign securities—people can attain a good return while minimizing the downside risk on their investments.

Lesson 3: Consider common-stock index funds. Investors who want to invest in the stock market can achieve a good return with the least possible risk by holding a broadly diversified portfolio of common stocks. A good vehicle for diversifying is an *index fund.* This is a portfolio of the stocks of many companies, weighting each company in proportion to its market value, and often tracking a major stock index like the S&P 500. One major advantage of index funds is that they have minimal expenses and turnover-induced taxes.

Lesson 4: Minimize unnecessary expenses and taxes. People often find that a substantial amount of their investment earnings is nibbled away by taxes or expenses. For example, some mutual funds charge a high initial fee when you purchase the fund. Others might charge a management fee of 1 or even 2 percent of assets each year. Additionally, heavily "managed" funds have high turnover and may lead to large taxes on capital gains. Day traders may find great enjoyment in lightning movements in and out, and they may strike it rich, but they *definitely* will pay heavy brokerage and investment charges. By choosing your investments carefully, you can avoid these unnecessary drains on your investment income.

Lesson 5: Match your investments with your risk preference. You can increase your expected return by picking riskier investments (see Figure 9-6). But always consider how much risk you can afford—financially *and psychologically.* As one adviser said, investments are a trade-off between eating well and sleeping well. If you get insomnia worrying about the ups and downs of the market, you can maximize your sleep by keeping your assets in inflation-indexed U.S. Treasury bonds. But in the long run, you might be snoozing soundly on a cot! If you want to eat well and can tolerate disappointments, you might invest more heavily in stocks, including those in foreign countries and emerging markets, and incorporate more volatile small companies into your portfolio—rather than concentrating on short-term bonds and bank deposits.

Such are the lessons of history and economics. But no one can guarantee that the next decade will be as buoyant as the 1990s. Many economists believe that the stock market was significantly overvalued in 2000 and look for a major stock-price decline in the future. So take care that you don't repeat the mistake of 1929 investors who bought at the peak of a speculative frenzy and didn't recover their losses for three decades.

If, after reading all this, you still want to try your hand in the stock market, do not be daunted. But take to heart the caution of one of America's great financiers, Bernard Baruch:

> If you are ready to give up everything else—to study the whole history and background of the market and all the principal companies whose stocks are on the board as carefully as a medical student studies anatomy—if you can do all that, and, in addition, you have the cool nerves of a great gambler, the sixth sense of a kind of clairvoyant, and the courage of a lion, you have a ghost of a chance.

SUMMARY

A. Money and Interest Rates

1. Money is anything that serves as a commonly accepted medium of exchange or means of payment. Money also functions as a unit of account and a store of value. Before money came into use, people exchanged goods for goods in a process called barter. Money arose to facilitate trade. Early money consisted of commodities, which were superseded by paper money and then bank money. Unlike other economic goods, money is valued because of social convention. We value money indirectly for what it buys, not for its direct utility.

2. Two definitions of money are commonly used today. The first is narrow (or transactions) money (M_1)—made up of currency and checking deposits. The second important concept is broad money (M_2), which includes M_1 plus highly liquid near-monies like savings accounts. The definitions of the M's have changed over the last two decades as a result of rapid innovation in financial markets.

3. Interest rates are the prices paid for borrowing money; they are measured in dollars per year paid back per dollar borrowed or in percent per year. People willingly pay interest because borrowed funds allow them to buy goods and services to satisfy consumption needs or make profitable investments.

4. We observe a wide variety of interest rates. These rates vary because of many factors such as the term or maturity of loans, the risk and liquidity of investments, and the tax treatment of the interest.

5. Nominal or money interest rates generally rise during inflationary periods, reflecting the fact that the purchasing power of money declines as prices rise. To calculate the interest yield in terms of real goods and services, we use the real interest rate, which equals the nominal or money interest rate minus the rate of inflation. The U.S. government recently issued inflation-indexed bonds, which guarantee a fixed real return on investments.

6. The demand for money differs from that for other commodities. Money is held for its indirect rather than its direct value. But money holdings are limited because keeping funds in money rather than in other assets has an opportunity cost: we sacrifice interest earnings when we hold money.

7. People hold money primarily because they need it to pay bills or buy goods. Such transactions needs are met by M_1 and are chiefly related to the value of transactions or to nominal GDP. Economic theory predicts, and empirical studies confirm, that the demand for money is sensitive to interest rates; higher interest rates lead to a lower demand for M.

B. Banking and the Supply of Money

8. Banks are commercial enterprises that seek to earn profits for their owners. One major function of banks is to provide checking accounts to customers. Modern banks gradually evolved from the old goldsmith establishments in which money and valuables were stored. Eventually it became general practice for goldsmiths to hold less than 100 percent reserves against deposits; this was the beginning of fractional-reserve banking.

9. If banks kept 100 percent cash reserves against all deposits, there would be no creation of money when new reserves were injected by the central bank into the system. There would be only a 1-to-1 exchange of one kind of money for another kind of money.

10. Today, banks are legally required to keep reserves on their checking deposits. These can be in the form of cash on hand or of non-interest-bearing deposits at the Federal Reserve. For illustrative purposes, we examined a required reserve ratio of 10 percent. In this case, the banking system as a whole—together with public or private borrowers and the depositing public—creates bank money 10 to 1 for each new dollar of reserves created by the Fed and deposited somewhere in the banking system.

11. Each small bank is limited in its ability to expand its loans and investments. It cannot lend or invest more than it has received from depositors; it can lend only about nine-tenths as much. Although no bank alone can expand its reserves 10 to 1, the banking system as a whole can. Each bank receiving $1000 of new deposits lends nine-tenths of its newly acquired cash on loans and investments. If we follow through the successive groups of banks in the dwindling, never-ending chain, we find for the system as a whole new deposits of

$$\$1000 + \$900 + \$810 + \$729 + \cdots$$
$$= \$1000 \times [1 + \tfrac{9}{10} + (\tfrac{9}{10})^2 + (\tfrac{9}{10})^3 + \cdots]$$
$$= \$1000 \left(\frac{1}{1 - \tfrac{9}{10}} \right) = \$1000 \left(\frac{1}{0.1} \right)$$
$$= \$10,000$$

More generally:

$$\text{Money-supply multiplier} = \frac{\text{change of money}}{\text{change of reserves}}$$
$$= \frac{1}{\text{required reserve ratio}}$$

12. There may be some leakage of new cash reserves of the banking system into circulation outside the banks and into assets other than checking accounts. When some of the new reserves leak into assets other than checking deposits, the relationship of money creation to new reserves may depart from the 10-to-1 formula given by the money-supply multiplier.

C. Financial Economics

13. Households own a variety of financial assets. The most important are money, savings accounts, government securities, equities, and pension funds.

14. Assets have different characteristics, the most important being the rate of return and the risk. The rate of return is the total dollar gain from a security. Risk refers to the variability of the returns on an investment. Because people are risk-averse, they require higher returns to induce them to buy riskier assets.

15. Stock markets, of which the New York Stock Exchange is the most important, are places where titles of ownership to the largest companies are bought and sold. The history of stock prices is filled with violent gyra-

tions, such as the Great Crash of 1929. Trends are tracked by the use of stock-price indexes, such as the Standard and Poor's 500 and the familiar Dow-Jones Industrial Average.

16. Modern economic theories of stock prices generally focus on the role of efficient markets. An efficient market is one in which all information is quickly absorbed by speculators and is immediately built into market prices. In efficient markets, there are no easy profits; looking at yesterday's news or past patterns of prices or elections or business cycles will not help predict future price movements. Thus, in efficient markets, prices respond to surprises. Because surprises are inherently random, stock prices and other speculative prices move erratically, as in a random walk.

17. Implant the five rules of personal finance firmly in your long-term memory: (*a*) Know thy investments. (*b*) Diversify, diversify, that is the rule of the prophets of finance. (*c*) Consider common-stock index funds. (*d*) Minimize unnecessary expenses and taxes. (*e*) Match your investments with your risk preference.

CONCEPTS FOR REVIEW

Money and Interest Rates

money, narrow money (M_1), broad money (M_2)
commodity M, paper M, bank M
interest rate, real and nominal
interest-rate premiums due to:
   maturity
   risk
   illiquidity
motives for money demand:
   transactions demand
   asset demand

interest as opportunity cost of holding money
inflation-indexed bonds

Banking and Money Supply

banks, financial intermediaries
bank reserves (vault cash and deposits with the Fed)
required reserve ratio
fractional-reserve banking
money-supply multiplier

The Stock Market

common stocks (corporate equities)
Standard and Poor's 500
efficient market, random walk of stock prices
index fund
new news, old information, and speculative prices
five rules for personal investing

FURTHER READING AND INTERNET WEBSITES

Further Reading

There are many entertaining histories of money. A good one is John Kenneth Galbraith, *Money, Whence It Came, Where It Went* (Houghton, Boston, Mass., 1975). You can pursue advanced topics in monetary theory in an intermediate textbook, such as Lawrence S. Ritter, William L. Silber, and Gregory F. Udell, *Principles of Money, Banking,*

and Financial Markets, 9th ed. (Addison Wesley Longman, New York, 1997). The standard reference on U.S. monetary history is Milton Friedman and Anna Jacobson Schwartz, *Monetary History of the United States 1867–1960* (Princeton University Press, Princeton, N.J., 1963).

Modern capital and finance theory are very popular subjects, often covered in the macroeconomics part of an introductory course or in special courses. Good books on the subject are Burton Malkiel, *A Random Walk down Wall Street* (Norton, New York, 1999). A recent book surveying financial history and theory and arguing that the stock market has become extraordinarily overvalued in the bull market of 1981–2000 is Robert Schiller, *Irrational Exuberance* (Princeton University Press, Princeton, N.J., 2000).

Websites

Basic data on money, interest rates, and monetary policy can be found at the website of the Federal Reserve,

www.federalreserve.gov. Interesting articles on monetary policy can be found in the *Federal Reserve Bulletin* at www.bog.frb.fed.us/pubs/bulletin/. The Federal Reserve also collects survey data on wealth, available in the January 2000 issue of *Federal Reserve Bulletin* at the same site.

A good source for data on financial markets is www.finance.yahoo.com/. If you are interested in the latest buzz on Internet stocks and hot topics in technology, go to www.techstocks.com or the Motley Fool at www.fool.com.

QUESTIONS FOR DISCUSSION

1. Define M_1 and M_2. What is included in M_1? What is in M_2 but not M_1? Relate each of the components of M_2 to the factors behind the demand for money.

2. Suppose that all banks kept 100 percent reserves. Construct new versions of Tables 9-5(*a*) and 9-6 to reflect $1000 of reserves added to a banking system that keeps 100 percent reserves. What is the net effect of a reserve addition to the money supply in this case? Do banks "create" money?

3. Suppose that banks hold 20 percent of deposits as reserves and that $200 of reserves is subtracted from the banking system. Redo Tables 9-5(*a*) through 9-7. What is the money-supply multiplier in this case? Calculate the money-supply multiplier in a second way by using the technique shown in footnote 6.

4. What would be the effect on the demand for money (M_1) of each of the following (with other things held equal)?
   a. An increase in real GDP
   b. An increase in the price level
   c. A rise in the interest rate on savings accounts and Treasury securities
   d. A doubling of all prices, wages, and incomes (Can you calculate exactly the effect on the demand for money?)

5. The opportunity cost of holding money is equal to the yield on safe short-term assets (such as Treasury bills) minus the interest rate on money. What is the impact of the following on the opportunity cost of holding money in checking deposits?
   a. Before 1980 (when checking deposits had zero yield) market interest rates increased from 8 to 9 percent.
   b. In 1984 (when checking accounts had a maximum yield of 5 percent) interest rates increased from (1) 3 to 4 percent and (2) 8 to 9 percent.

   c. In 1991 (when the interest rates on certain checking accounts were deregulated), market interest rates increased from (1) 3 to 4 percent and (2) 8 to 9 percent.

      How would you expect the demand for money to respond to the change in market interest rates in each of the above cases if the elasticity of demand for money with respect to the opportunity cost of money is 0.2?

6. Interest-rate problems (which may require a calculator):
   a. You invest $2000 at 13.5 percent per year. What is your total balance after 6 months?
   b. Interest is said to be "compounded" when you earn interest on whatever interest has already been paid; most interest rates quoted today are compounded. If you invest $10,000 for 3 years at a compound annual interest rate of 10 percent, what is the total investment at the end of each year?
   c. Consider the following data: The consumer price index in 1977 was 60.6, and in 1981 it was 90.9. Interest rates on government securities in 1978 through 1981 (in percent per year) were 7.2, 10.0, 11.5, and 14.0. Calculate the average nominal and real interest rates for the 4-year period 1978–1981.
   d. Treasury bills (T-bills) are usually sold on a discounted basis; that is, a 90-day T-bill for $10,000 would sell today at a price such that collecting $10,000 at maturity would produce the market interest rate. If the market interest rate is 6.6 percent per year, what would be the price on a $10,000 90-day T-bill?

7. Present value questions:
   a. Consider the 1-year bond in the discussion of present value. Calculate the present value of the bond if the interest rate is 1, 5, and 20 percent.

b. What is the value of a perpetuity yielding $16 per year at interest rates of 1, 5, 10, and 20 percent per year?

c. Compare the answers to **a** and **b**. Which asset is more sensitive to interest-rate changes? Quantify the difference.

8. Explain whether you think that each of the following should be counted as part of the narrow money supply (M_1) for the United States: traveler's checks, savings accounts, subway tokens, postage stamps, credit cards, and $20 bills used by Russians in Moscow.

9. According to the efficient-market theory, what effect would the following events have on the price of GM's stock?

a. A surprise announcement that the government is going to lower business taxes next July 1

b. A decrease in business taxes on July 1, which is 6 months after Congress passed the enabling legislation

c. An announcement, unexpected by experts, that the United States is imposing quotas on imports of Japanese cars for the coming year

d. Implementation of **c** by issuing regulations on December 31

10. Suppose reserve requirements were abolished. What would determine the level of reserves in the banking system? What would happen to the money-supply multiplier in this situation?

11. Suppose that one giant bank, the Humongous Bank of America, held all the checking deposits of all the people, subject to a 10 percent legal reserve requirement. If there were an injection of reserves into the economy, could the Humongous Bank lend out more than 90 percent of the deposit addition, knowing that the new deposit must come back to it? Would this change the ultimate money-supply multiplier?

12. **Advanced problem:** An option is the right to buy or sell a stock or other security for a specified price on or before a specific date. A "call option" is the right to buy the stock, while a "put option" is the right to sell the stock. Suppose you have a call option to buy 100 shares in a highly volatile stock, Fantasia.com, any time in the next 3 months at $10 per share. Fantasia currently sells at $9 per share.

a. Can you see why the value of the option is more than $1 per share?

b. Suppose the option were to expire tomorrow and had an even chance of rising $5 or falling $5 before then. What would be the value of the option?

13. Flip a coin 100 times. Count a head as "plus 1 " and a tail as "minus 1." Keep a running score of the total. Plot it on graph paper. This is a random walk. (Those with access to a computer can do this using a computer program, a random-number generator, and a plotter.)

Next, keep track of the closing price of the stock of your favorite company for a few weeks (or get it from past issues of the newspaper). Plot the price against time. Can you see any difference in the pattern of changes? Do both look like random walks?

Where would you look to find the most important macroeconomic policymakers today? In the White House? Or in the Congress? Perhaps in the United Nations or the World Bank? Surprisingly, the answer is that you would look in an obscure marble building in Washington that houses the Federal Reserve System. It is here that the Federal Reserve (or "Fed") sets the level of short-term interest rates, thereby profoundly affecting financial markets, wealth, output, employment, and prices. Indeed, the Fed's influence spreads not only throughout the 50 states but even, through financial and trade linkages, to virtually every corner of the world.

CHAPTER
10

Central Banking and Monetary Policy

There have been three great inventions since the beginning of time: fire, the wheel, and central banking.

Will Rogers

The Federal Reserve's central goal is low and stable inflation. It also seeks to promote steady growth in national output, low unemployment, and orderly financial markets. If output is growing rapidly and inflation is rising, the Federal Reserve Board is likely to raise interest rates, as this puts a brake on the economy and reduces price pressures. If the economy is sluggish and business is languishing, the Fed may consider lowering interest rates, a move which will give a boost to aggregate demand, increase output, and reduce unemployment. Every major country has a central bank that is responsible for managing its monetary affairs. This chapter will help you understand the Federal Reserve's central role in the U.S. economy.

Figure 10-1 shows the role of central banking in the economy and depicts its relationship to the banks, financial markets, and interest rates. Section A surveys how the Fed uses its instruments—bank reserves, the discount rate, and other tools—to determine the money supply and affect interest rates. Section B then analyzes the impact of monetary policy on the macroeconomy.

A. CENTRAL BANKING AND THE FEDERAL RESERVE SYSTEM

THE FEDERAL RESERVE SYSTEM
Structure of the Federal Reserve

History and Purpose. During the nineteenth century, the United States was plagued by banking panics. These occurred when people suddenly attempted to turn their bank deposits into currency (review the example on bank panics in the last chapter). When they arrived at the banks, they found that the banks had an inadequate supply of currency because the supply of currency

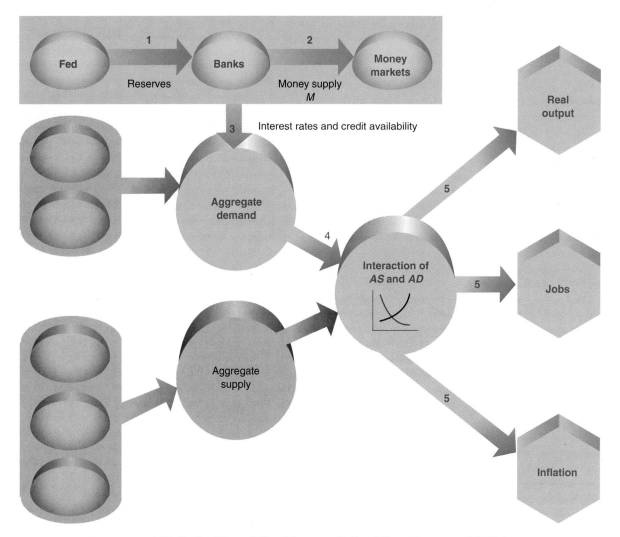

FIGURE 10-1. A Bird's-Eye View of How Monetary Policy Affects Output and Inflation

This diagram shows graphically the steps by which Fed policy affects economic activity. (1) is a change in reserves; leading to a change in M in (2); leading to (3), changes in interest rates and credit conditions. In (4), AD is changed by a response of investment and other interest-sensitive spending. In (5), changes in output, employment, and inflation follow.
    Remember that fiscal policy also feeds into the aggregate demand circle.

was fixed and smaller than the amount of bank deposits. Bank failures and economic downturns ensued. After the severe panic of 1907, agitation and discussion led to the Federal Reserve Act of 1913 which was to "provide for the establishment of Federal reserve banks [and] to furnish an elastic currency."

As currently constituted, the Federal Reserve System consists of 12 regional Federal Reserve Banks, located in New York, Chicago, Richmond, Dallas, San Francisco, and other major cities. The regional structure was originally designed in the populist age to ensure that different areas would have a voice in banking matters and to avoid too great a concentration of central-banking powers in Washington or in the hands of the eastern bankers.

Each Federal Reserve Bank today distributes coins and currency, supervises and regulates banks in its districts, and is part of a nationwide payments system.

The major purposes of the Federal Reserve are as follows:

> Today the Federal Reserve's duties fall into four general areas: (1) conducting the nation's monetary policy; (2) supervising and regulating banking institutions; (3) maintaining the stability of the financial system; and (4) providing certain financial services to the government and the public.

Who's in Charge? The core of the Federal Reserve is the *Board of Governors* of the Federal Reserve System, which consists of seven members nominated by the president and confirmed by the Senate to serve overlapping terms of 14 years. Members of the board are generally bankers or economists who work full time at the job.

The key decision-making body in the Federal Reserve System is the *Federal Open Market Committee* (FOMC). The 12 voting members of the FOMC include the seven governors plus five of the presidents of the regional Federal Reserve Banks. This key group controls the single most important and frequently used tool of modern monetary policy—the supply of bank reserves.

At the pinnacle of the entire system is the *Chairman of the Board of Governors*, currently an economist, Alan Greenspan. He chairs the Board of Governors and the FOMC, acts as public spokesman for the Fed, and exercises enormous power over monetary policy. Because of his long tenure (first appointed as Fed chairman in 1987) and successful management of the economy, Greenspan is often called the "second most powerful individual in America," reflecting the extent to which he can influence the entire economy through his impact on monetary policy.

In spite of the formally dispersed structure of the Fed, close observers think that power is quite centralized. The Federal Reserve Board, joined at meetings by the presidents of the 12 regional Federal Reserve Banks, operates under the Fed Chairman to formulate and carry out monetary policy. The structure of the Federal Reserve System is shown in Figure 10-2.

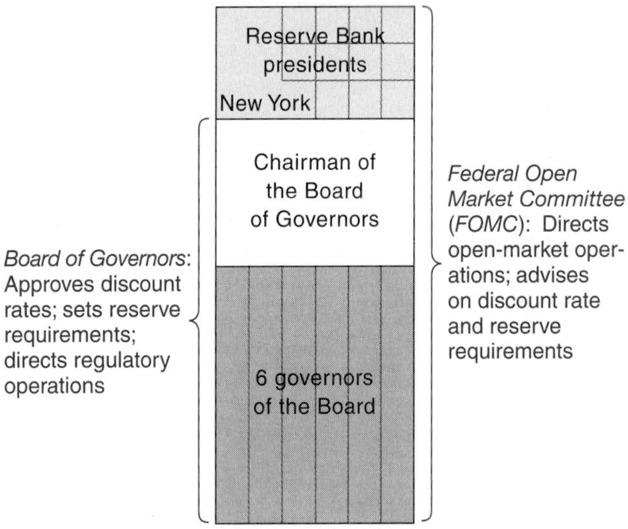

FIGURE 10-2. The Major Players in Monetary Policy

Two important committees are at the center of monetary policy. The seven-member Board of Governors approves changes in discount rates and sets reserve requirements. The FOMC directs the setting of bank reserves. The Chairman of the Board of Governors heads both committees. The size of each box indicates that person's or group's relative power; note the size of the Chairman's box.

Is the Fed too independent?

On examining the structure of the Fed, one might ask, "In which of the three branches of government does the Fed lie?" The answer is, "None. Legally, the 12 regional banks are private.

In reality, the Fed as a whole behaves as an independent government agency."

Although nominally a corporation owned by the commercial banks that are members of the Federal Reserve System, the Federal Reserve is in practice a public agency. It is directly responsible to Congress; it listens carefully to the advice of the president; and whenever any conflict arises between its making a profit and promoting the public interest, it acts unswervingly in the public interest. The Fed prints the nation's currency, in return for which it holds interest-bearing government securities. Through this activity, it earns billions of dollars of profits each year. But, to reflect its public mission, all of its profits go to the U.S. government.

Above all, the Federal Reserve is an *independent* agency. While it listens carefully to Congress and the president, and even to the election returns, in the end the Fed decides monetary policy according to its views about the nation's economic interests. As a result, the Fed sometimes comes into conflict with the executive branch. Almost every president has advice on Fed policy. When Fed policies clash with administration goals, presidents occasionally use harsh words. The Fed listens politely but generally chooses the path it thinks best for the country, for its decisions do not have to be approved by anybody.

From time to time, critics argue that the Fed is too independent—that it is undemocratic for a small group of unelected people to govern the nation's financial markets. This is a sobering thought, for unelected bodies sometimes lose touch with social and economic realities. Defenders of independence respond that an independent central bank is the guardian of a nation's currency and the best protector against rampant inflation. Moreover, independence ensures that monetary policy is not subverted for partisan political objectives, as sometimes happens in countries where the executive branch controls the central bank. Historical studies show that countries with independent central banks have generally been more successful in keeping down inflation than those whose central banks are under the thumbs of elected officials.

Policy Objectives. What are the goals of the Federal Reserve System? This is how the Fed sees its role:

> The [Federal Reserve's] objectives include economic growth in line with the economy's potential to expand; a high level of employment; stable prices (that is, stability in the purchasing power of the dollar); and moderate long-term interest rates.[1]

While it is not always easy to understand the exact reasoning that led to a particular monetary-policy step, historians who sift through the decisions usually find that the Fed is ultimately concerned with preserving the integrity of our financial institutions, combating inflation, defending the exchange rate of the dollar, and preventing excessive unemployment.

---

[1] See *The Federal Reserve System: Purposes and Functions*, p. 2, under "Websites" in this chapter's Further Reading section.

To summarize:

The Federal Reserve Board in Washington, together with the 12 Federal Reserve Banks, constitutes our American central bank. Every modern country has a central bank. Its primary mission is to control the nation's money supply and credit conditions.

Overview of the Fed's Operations

Figure 10-3 shows the various stages of Federal Reserve operations as seen by the Fed. The Federal Reserve has at its disposal a number of policy instruments. These can affect certain intermediate targets (such as reserves, the money supply, and interest rates). These instruments are intended to help achieve the ultimate objectives of a healthy economy—low inflation, rapid growth in output, and low unemployment. It is important to keep these different groups (policy instruments, intermediate targets, and ultimate objectives) clearly distinct in our analysis.

The three major instruments of monetary policy are:

- *Open-market operations*—buying or selling of U.S. government securities in the open market to influence the level of reserves
- *Discount-rate policy*—setting the interest rate, called the *discount rate*, at which commercial banks and other depository institutions can borrow reserves from a regional Federal Reserve Bank
- *Reserve-requirements policy*—setting and changing the legal reserve-ratio requirements on deposits with banks and other financial institutions

In managing money, the Federal Reserve must keep its eye on a set of variables known as *intermediate targets*. These are economic variables that are intermediate in the transmission mechanism between Fed instruments and ultimate policy goals. When the Fed wants to affect its ultimate objectives, it first changes one of its instruments, such as the discount rate. This change affects an intermediate variable like interest rates, credit conditions, or the money supply. Much as a doctor interested in the health of a patient will monitor pulse and blood pressure, so the Federal Reserve keeps a careful watch on its intermediate targets.

The World as Seen from the Fed

| Instruments | Intermediate targets | Ultimate objectives |

FIGURE 10-3. While the Fed Ultimately Pursues Objectives like Stable Prices, Its Short-Term Operations Focus on the Intermediate Targets

In determining monetary policy, the Fed directly manipulates the instruments or policy variables under its control—open-market operations, the discount rate, and reserve requirements. These help determine bank reserves, the money supply, and interest rates—the intermediate targets of monetary policy. Ultimately, monetary and fiscal policies are partners in pursuing the major objectives of rapid growth, low unemployment, and stable prices.

Balance Sheet of the Federal Reserve Banks

In analyzing central banking, we need to describe the consolidated balance sheet of the Federal Reserve System, shown in Table 10-1 on page 200. U.S. government securities (e.g., bonds) make up most of the Fed's assets. The small items, loans and acceptances, are primarily loans or advances to commercial banks. The interest rate the Fed charges banks for such loans, or "discounts," is called the discount rate, which is another of the Fed's tools.

There are two unique items among its liabilities: currency and reserves. Federal Reserve *currency* is the Fed's principal liability. These represent the coins and paper bills we use every day. The other major liability is *bank reserves,* which are balances kept on deposit by commercial banks with the Federal Reserve Banks. Taken along with the banks' vault cash, these are the reserves we have been talking about. They provide the basis for multiple deposit creation by the nation's banking system.

By altering its holding of government securities, the Fed can change bank reserves and thereby trigger the sequence of events that ultimately determines the total supply of money.

THE NUTS AND BOLTS OF MONETARY POLICY

Open-Market Operations

The Fed's most useful tool is "open-market operations."

By selling or buying government securities in the open market, the Fed can lower or raise bank reserves. These so-called **open-market operations** are a central bank's most important monetary-policy instrument.

In setting policy, the FOMC decides whether to pump more reserves into the banking system by buying Treasury bills (i.e., short-term bonds) and longer-term government bonds or whether to tighten monetary policy by selling government securities.

To see how an open-market operation changes reserves, let us suppose that the Fed thinks the economic winds are blowing up a little inflation. The FOMC holds its meeting in Washington and hears presentations and projections from its staff of talented economists. The committee decides to tighten money and credit by selling bonds. To whom are the bonds sold? *To the open market.* This includes dealers

Combined Balance Sheet of 12 Federal Reserve Banks, February 2000 (billions of dollars)			
Assets		**Liabilities and Net Worth**	
U.S. government securities	$500.5	Federal Reserve currency	$539.0
Loans and acceptances	0.1	Deposits:	
Miscellaneous other assets	80.9	Bank deposits	10.8
		U.S. Treasury	4.9
		Miscellaneous liabilities	26.8
Total	$581.5	Total	$581.5

TABLE 10-1. Federal Reserve Notes and Deposits Underlie Our Money Supply

By controlling its earning assets (government securities and loans), the Fed controls its liabilities (bank deposits and Federal Reserve notes). Bank deposits with the Fed plus vault cash of banks are total reserves and can be used to meet reserve requirements. Through changing reserves, the Fed determines the economy's money supply (currency and demand deposits, M_1), and thereby affects GDP, unemployment, and inflation. (Source: *Federal Reserve Bulletin;* www.bog.frb.fed.us/releases/H41.)

in government bonds, who then resell them to commercial banks, big corporations, other financial institutions, and individuals.

The purchasers usually buy the bonds by writing checks to the Fed, drawn from an account in a commercial bank. For example, if the Fed sells $10,000 worth of bonds to Ms. Smith, she writes a check on the Coyote Bank of Santa Fe. The Fed presents the check at the Coyote Bank. When the Coyote Bank pays the check, it will reduce its balance with the Fed by $10,000. At the end of the day, the Coyote Bank, and the entire commercial banking system, will lose $10,000 in reserves at the Federal Reserve System.

Table 10-2(*a*) shows the effect of a $1 billion open-market sale on the Federal Reserve balance sheet. The open-market sale changes the Federal Reserve balance sheet by reducing both assets and liabilities by $1 billion: the Fed has sold $1 billion of government bonds, and its liabilities have declined by exactly the same amount, $1 billion of bank reserves.

Effects on Money Supply. To understand the effect of the reserve change on the money supply, we must consider the banks' response. In this chapter, we continue the algebraic convenience of assuming that banks hold 10 percent of their deposits as reserves with the central bank; the legal reason for this

practice is discussed in greater detail later in this chapter.

What happens to the money supply? Reserves go down by $1 billion, and that tends to set off a contraction of deposits. The last chapter showed how a change in bank reserves would lead to a multiplied change in total bank deposits. If the legal reserve requirement is 10 percent, the $1 billion sale of government bonds will result in a $10 billion cut in the community's money supply. Table 10-2(*b*) shows the banks' ultimate position after $1 billion of reserves have been extinguished by the open-market operation. In the end, the Fed's open-market sale has caused a $10 billion contraction in the money supply.

Operating Procedures

The FOMC meets eight times a year to decide upon monetary policy and give operating instructions to the front-line troops at the Federal Reserve Bank of New York, which conducts open-market operations on a day-to-day basis. The operating procedures have changed over time. Sometimes they were vague instructions to "loosen credit a little." Then in the 1970s, the Fed altered its operating procedures to pay closer attention to movements in the money supply. The most dramatic shift in policy came in 1979, when the Fed undertook its "monetarist experiment"

Changes in Federal Reserve Balance Sheet (billions of dollars)			
Assets		**Liabilities**	
U.S. securities	−$1	Bank reserves	−$1
Total	**−$1**	**Total**	**−$1**

TABLE 10-2(a). Open-Market Sale by Fed Cuts Reserves Initially

Changes in Commercial Banks' Balance Sheet (billions of dollars)			
Assets		**Liabilities**	
Reserves	− $1	Checking deposits	−$10
Loans and investments	− 9		
Total	**−$10**	**Total**	**−$10**

TABLE 10-2(b). . . . and Ultimately Cuts Deposits 10 to 1

This crucial set of tables shows how open-market operations affect the Fed's balance sheet and the balance sheet of banks.

In (**a**), the Fed has sold $1 billion of securities. The funds used to pay for the securities are deposited in the Fed, reducing bank reserves by $1 billion. Bank reserves thus decline by $1 billion as a result of the open-market operation.

Then, in (**b**), we see the effect on the balance sheet of banks. With a required reserve ratio of 10 percent of deposits, the reserve contraction cascades through the banking system. Thus, deposits must fall by $10 billion for the banking system to be back in equilibrium.

to slow the rapid inflation. This involved targeting reserves and the money supply in a fashion recommended by monetarists. (We will review the monetarist experiment later in this chapter and in our discussion of monetarism in Chapter 17.)

Today, the Fed primarily operates by setting a short-term target for the **federal funds rate,** which is the interest rate that banks pay each other for the overnight use of bank reserves. Figure 10-4 on the next page shows the federal funds rate, which is under the control of the Fed, along with one of the important long-term interest rates, the 30-year interest rate on Treasury bonds. While the Fed charts the general level and trend in interest rates, there are clearly many other factors at work in determining interest rates and financial conditions.

What is the objective of Fed policy today? Like many central banks around the world, the Fed is principally concerned with ensuring low and stable inflation while attempting to moderate swings in output and unemployment. There is no single variable that triggers monetary tightening or loosening. Rather, the Fed tends to look at a wide variety of indicators as well as at economic forecasts. It will track actual movements in wages and consumer and wholesale prices as well as movements in fiscal policy, exchange rates, and a multitude of economic indicators.

Discount-Rate Policy: A Second Instrument

When commercial banks are short of reserves, they are allowed to borrow from the Federal Reserve Banks. Their loans were included under the asset heading "Loans and acceptances" in the Fed balance sheet in Table 10-1. These loans are called *borrowed reserves.* When borrowed reserves are growing, the banks are borrowing from the Fed, thereby increasing total bank reserves (borrowed plus unborrowed reserves). Conversely, a drop in borrowed reserves promotes a contraction in total bank reserves.

In the early years, the discount window was the primary vehicle for providing reserves to the banking system. As financial markets developed and the role of monetary policy was better understood, the Fed has turned to open-market operations as the primary tool for adjusting the overall level of reserves. Today, the discount window is used primarily to buffer the day-to-day fluctuations in member-bank reserves. Because banks can go to the discount window when there are unanticipated fluctuations in required reserves, the extent of short-term volatility in interest rates is reduced.

Sometimes, the Fed may raise or lower the **discount rate,** which is the interest rate charged on bank borrowings from the 12 regional Federal Reserve Banks. For many years, the discount rate was the

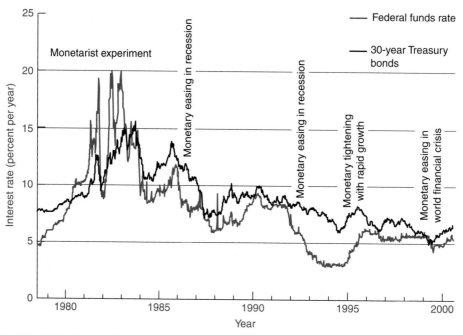

FIGURE 10-4. Federal Reserve Determines Federal Funds Rate

The Fed sets a target for the federal funds rate, which is the interest rate charged by banks on overnight loans. This rate then affects all other interest rates, although the linkage is variable and is affected by expectations of future interest rates as well as overall financial conditions. Note the period from 1979 to 1982, when the Fed experimented with monetary targeting and produced much more volatile interest rates. (Source: Federal Reserve Board.)

bellwether of monetary policy. For example, in 1965 when the Fed wanted to send a signal to markets that the Vietnam war boom threatened to become inflationary, it raised the discount rate. So powerful was this signal that Fed Chairman Martin was called to the LBJ ranch for a dressing-down by President Johnson, who was afraid the higher discount rate would slow the economy.

Today, the discount rate is a relatively minor instrument of monetary policy. Sometimes, a change in the discount rate is used to signal markets of a major policy change. But mostly, the discount rate simply follows market interest rates to prevent banks from making windfall profits by borrowing at a low discount rate and lending at a higher rate on the open market.

Changing Reserve Requirements

If there were no government rules, banks would probably keep only a small fraction of their deposits in the form of reserves. In fact, American banks are today required to keep substantially more reserves than are necessary for meeting customers' needs. These legal reserve requirements are a crucial part of the mechanism by which the Fed controls the supply of bank money. This subsection describes the nature of legal reserve requirements and shows how they affect the money supply.

Legal Reserve Requirements. We have mentioned that banks are required to hold a minimum amount as non-interest-bearing reserves. Table 10-3 shows current reserve requirements along with the Fed's discretionary power to change reserve requirements. The key concept is the level of *required reserve ratios*. They range from 10 percent against checkable deposits down to zero for personal savings accounts. For convenience in our numerical examples, we use 10 percent reserve ratios, with the understanding that the actual ratio may differ from 10 percent from time to time.

Type of deposit	Reserve ratio (%)	Range in which Fed can vary (%)
Checking (transactions) accounts:		
First $47 million	3	No change allowed
Above $47 million	10	8–14
Time and savings deposits:		
Personal	0	
Nonpersonal:		
Up to $1\frac{1}{2}$ years' maturity	0	0–9
More than $1\frac{1}{2}$ years' maturity	0	0–9

TABLE 10-3. Required Reserves for Financial Institutions

Reserve requirements are governed by law and regulation. The reserve-ratio column shows the percent of deposits in each category that must be held in non-interest-bearing deposits at the Fed or in cash on hand. Checking-type accounts in large banks face required reserves of 10 percent, while other major deposits have no reserve requirements. The Fed has power to alter the reserve ratio within a given range but does so only on the rare occasion when economic conditions warrant a sharp change in monetary policy. (Source: *Federal Reserve Bulletin*, February 2000.)

Legal reserve requirements are set high in order to allow the central bank to control the money supply. Reserve requirements help the Fed conduct its open-market operations by ensuring a stable demand for reserves. By setting reserve requirements above the level that banks desire, the central bank can determine the level of reserves and can thereby control the money supply more precisely. The net effect is an increase in the Federal Reserve's control over short-term interest rates.

Put differently, high reserve requirements ensure that banks will want to hold just that legal minimum. The supply of bank money will then be determined by the supply of bank reserves (determined by the Fed through open-market operations) and by the money-supply multiplier (determined by the required reserve ratio). Because the Fed controls both bank reserves and the required reserve ratio, it has (within a small margin of error) control over the money supply.

Changes in Required Reserves. The Fed can change reserve requirements if it wants to change the money supply quickly. For instance, if the Fed wants to tighten money overnight, it can raise the required reserve ratio on checking accounts for the big banks to the 14 percent statutory limit. It might even raise reserve requirements on time deposits.

Exactly how does an increase in required ratios operate to tighten credit? Suppose the required reserve ratio is 10 percent and banks had built up their reserves to meet this requirement. Now suppose the Fed decides to tighten credit, and Congress allows it to raise the required reserve ratio to 20 percent. (This fantastic figure is for algebraic simplicity. The Fed cannot and would not take such a drastic step today.)

Even if the Fed does nothing by way of open-market operations or discount policy to change bank reserves, banks now have to contract their loans and investment greatly—and their deposits as well. As the last chapter showed, bank deposits can now be only 5 times reserves, not 10 times reserves. So there must be a drop by one-half in all deposits!

This painful cut will start to take place quickly. As soon as the new rule raising the requirement to 20 percent goes into effect, banks will find that they have insufficient reserves. They will have to sell some bonds and call in some loans. The bond buyers and borrowers will drain their checking accounts. The process ends only after banks have brought down their deposits to 5 rather than 10 times their reserves.

Such an enormous change in so short a time would lead to very high interest rates, credit rationing, large declines in investment, and massive reductions in GDP and employment. So this extreme example warns that this powerful tool of changing reserve requirements has to be used with great caution. *Changes in reserve requirements are made extremely sparingly because they cause too large and abrupt a change in policy. Open-market operations can achieve the same results in a less disruptive way.*

Trends in financial regulation

The financial sector has historically been the source of economic disturbances and crises, and these led to pervasive regulation during the first half of the twentieth century. Widespread banking crises during the Great Depression led to controls on mergers and interest rates. Until the 1980s, interest rates paid by commercial banks were tightly controlled. Banks were not allowed to pay interest on checking accounts, and there were ceilings on interest rates on savings accounts and time deposits. As financial markets became more competitive, however, regulated interest rates could not long survive. Financial institutions devised new types of instruments which lured funds from low-yield deposits, and this trend accelerated in the high-interest-rate environment of the late 1970s and early 1980s. Eventually the regulatory edifice constructed during the Great Depression began to crumble.

Congress reacted with the Banking Acts of 1980 and 1982, which largely deregulated interest rates. The basis of the new approach was to separate transactions accounts from nontransactions accounts. The primary purpose of a *transactions account*, such as a checking account, is to serve as a means of payment. A *nontransactions account* contains assets whose primary purpose is for investment, not payment of bills (a savings account is an example of a nontransactions account).

Once this distinction had been made, the 1980 and 1982 acts effectively deregulated nontransactions accounts. Today, nontransactions accounts earn market interest rates and are effectively outside the regulatory structure of the Federal Reserve. Transactions assets like checking accounts have with one major exception also been deregulated. The remaining and critical regulation is, as we see in Table 10-3, that these accounts are subject to substantial reserve requirements.

Although most interest-rate controls have been removed, the government continues its "fiduciary" regulation of banks. To instill confidence in the banking system and prevent "bank runs," the government inspects the books of banks and takes over insolvent banks. Additionally, the government guarantees up to $100,000 per deposit at banks that are members of the Federal Deposit Insurance Corporation (FDIC). The Fed and other regulatory agencies also inspect banking practices to ensure that the fraud and abuse of the 1980s savings and loan scandal does not recur.

The latest chapter came in 1999 when Congress repealed the 1933 Glass-Steagall Act. Glass-Steagall prohibited banks from selling other financial services, such as brokerage services or insurance, in order to reduce the riskiness of banks. The repeal removed the barriers among different financial institutions. Banks, insurance companies, and investment houses are now allowed to compete with one another and to offer one-stop financial shopping. Some economists worry that integrating heavily regulated banks, which enjoy the protection of deposit insurance, with competitive financial sectors may increase the overall riskiness of the financial sector in turbulent times.

Monetary Policy in the Open Economy

Central banks are particularly important in open economies, where they manage reserve flows and the exchange rate and monitor international financial developments.

Reserve Flows. The dollar is today used extensively both as a store of value and as a medium of international exchange by those who are involved in international trade and finance. Foreigners own hundreds of billions of dollars in U.S. dollar–denominated assets. Because narrow money has a zero or low interest rate, foreigners prefer to hold interest-bearing assets (bonds, stocks, etc.). However, foreigners do hold narrow money in U.S. dollar checking accounts because they need to buy and sell goods and assets. Additionally, many people in unstable or inflation-prone countries hold U.S. currency.

Why are we concerned about international money holdings at this point? The reason is that deposits by foreigners in the banking system increase the total amount of bank reserves in the same way that deposits by domestic residents do. Thus, changes in foreigners' dollar money holdings can set off a chain of expansion or contraction of the U.S. money supply.

For example, say the Japanese decide to deposit $1000 of U.S. currency in U.S. banks. What happens? There is a $1000 increase in reserves in the domestic banking system, as illustrated in Table 9-5(*a*) in the previous chapter. As a result, the banking system can expand deposits tenfold, in this case to $10,000.

Thus, the Fed's control of the nations's *M* is modified by international disturbances to bank reserves. But the Fed has the power to offset any change in reserves coming from abroad. It affects this by engaging in what is called sterilization. *Sterilization* refers to actions by a central bank that insulate the domestic money supply from international reserve flows. Sterilization usually is accomplished when the central bank implements an open-market operation that reverses the international reserve movement. In practice, the Fed routinely sterilizes international disturbances to reserves.

To summarize:

The central bank's control over bank reserves is subject to disturbances from abroad. These disturbances can, however, be offset if the central bank sterilizes the international flows.

The Role of the Exchange-Rate System.[2] One important element in a country's financial market is its exchange-rate system. As we will see in later chapters, international trade and finance involve the use of different national currencies, which are linked by relative prices called foreign exchange rates.

One important exchange-rate system is floating exchange rates, in which a country's foreign exchange rate is determined by market forces of supply and demand. The United States, Europe, and Japan today operate floating-exchange-rate systems. These three regions can pursue their monetary policies independently of other countries. This chapter's

analysis concerns mainly the operation of monetary policy under floating exchange rates.

Some economies, such as Hong Kong or Argentina (as well as virtually all countries in earlier periods), maintain fixed exchange rates and "peg" their currencies to one or more external currencies. We will see shortly that *when a country has a fixed exchange rate, it must align its monetary policy with the country to which its currency is pegged*. For example, if Argentina has open capital markets and a fixed exchange rate with the U.S. dollar, then Argentina must have the same interest rates as those in the United States.

We return to issues of open economies later. They are particularly crucial for understanding monetary policy outside the United States.

The Foreign Desk. The Federal Reserve acts as the government's operating arm in the international financial system. The Fed buys and sells different currencies on foreign exchange markets on behalf of the Treasury. While this task is generally routine, from time to time foreign exchange markets become disorderly, and the Fed, in cooperation with the Treasury, steps in. Sometimes, the Treasury decides that foreign-exchange-rate *intervention* is necessary—because the exchange rate of the dollar is either significantly higher or considerably lower than seems warranted by underlying fundamentals. The Fed is the agent of the Treasury in such intervention activities.

In addition, the Federal Reserve often takes the lead in working with foreign countries and with international agencies when international financial crises erupt. The Fed played an important role in the Mexican loan package from the United States after the peso crisis in 1994–1995 and worked with other countries to help calm markets during the East Asian crisis and global liquidity crisis in 1997 and 1998.

We have completed our analysis of the money supply. It can be summarized as follows:

The money supply is ultimately determined by the policies of the Fed. By setting reserve requirements and the discount rate, and especially by undertaking open-market operations, the Fed determines the level of reserves, the money supply, and short-term interest rates. Banks and the public are cooperating partners in this process. Banks create money by multiple expansion of reserves; the public agrees to hold money in depository institutions.

---

[2] This section contains materials that will be covered more extensively in Chapters 13 and 14 and should be reread after those chapters.

B. THE EFFECTS OF MONEY ON OUTPUT AND PRICES

THE MONETARY TRANSMISSION MECHANISM

Having examined the building blocks of monetary theory, we now describe the **monetary transmission mechanism,** the route by which changes in the supply of money are translated into changes in output, employment, prices, and inflation. For concreteness, assume that the Federal Reserve is concerned about inflation and has decided to slow down the economy. There are five steps in the process:

1. *To start the process, the Fed takes steps to reduce bank reserves.* As we saw in Section A of this chapter, the Fed reduces bank reserves primarily by selling government securities in the open market. This open-market operation changes the balance sheet of the banking system by reducing total bank reserves.

2. *Each dollar reduction in bank reserves produces a multiple contraction in checking deposits, thereby reducing the money supply.* This step was described in Chapter 9, where we saw that changes in reserves lead to a multiplied change in deposits. Since the money supply equals currency plus checking deposits, the reduction in checking deposits reduces the money supply.

3. *The reduction in the money supply increases interest rates and tightens credit conditions.* With an unchanged demand for money, a reduced supply of money will raise interest rates. In addition, the amount of credit (loans and borrowing) available to people will decline. Interest rates will rise for mortgage borrowers and for businesses that want to build factories, buy new equipment, or add to inventories. Higher interest rates tend to reduce asset prices (such as those of stocks, bonds, and houses) and therefore depress the values of people's assets.[3]

4. *With higher interest rates and lower wealth, interest-sensitive spending—especially investment—tends to fall.* The combination of higher interest rates, tighter credit, and lower wealth tends to reduce investment and consumption spending. Businesses will scale down their investment plans, as will state and local governments. For example, higher interest rates may lead airlines to stretch out their purchases of new aircraft. Similarly, consumers may decide to buy a smaller house, or to renovate their existing one, when rising mortgage interest rates increase monthly payments relative to monthly income. And in an economy increasingly open to international trade, higher interest rates may raise the foreign exchange rate of the dollar, depressing net exports. Hence, tight money will raise interest rates and reduce spending on interest-sensitive components of aggregate demand.

5. *Finally, the pressures of tight money, by reducing aggregate demand, will reduce income, output, jobs, and inflation.* The aggregate supply-and-demand (or, equivalently, the multiplier) analysis showed how such a drop in investment and other autonomous spending may depress output and employment sharply. Furthermore, as output and employment fall below the levels that would otherwise occur, prices tend to rise less rapidly or even to fall. Inflationary forces subside. If the Fed's diagnosis of inflationary conditions was correct, the drop in output and the rise in unemployment will help relieve inflationary forces.

We can summarize the steps as follows:

R down → M down → i up → I, C, X down →
AD down → real GDP down and inflation down

This five-step sequence—from the Fed's changes in commercial-bank reserves, to a multiple change in total M, to changes in interest rates and credit availability, to changes in investment spending that shift aggregate demand, and finally to the response of output, employment, and inflation—is vital to the determination of output and prices. If you look back at Figure 10-1, you will see how each of the five steps fits into our thematic flowchart. We have already explained the first two steps; the balance of this chapter is devoted to analyzing steps 3 through 5.

---

[3] To refresh your memory on the relationship between interest rates and asset prices, see the box "Higher interest rates tend to lower asset prices" on page 169 in Chapter 9.

THE MONEY MARKET

Step 3 in the transmission mechanism is the response of interest rates and credit conditions to changes in the supply of money. Recall from Chapter 9 that the *demand for money* depends primarily on the need to undertake transactions. Households, businesses, and governments hold money so that they may buy goods, services, and other items. In addition, some part of the demand for M derives from the need for a supersafe and highly liquid asset.

The *supply of money* is jointly determined by the private banking system and the nation's central bank. The central bank, through open-market operations and other instruments, provides reserves to the banking system. Commercial banks then create deposits out of the central-bank reserves. By manipulating reserves, the central bank can determine the money supply within a narrow margin of error.

Supply of and Demand for Money

The supply of and demand for money jointly determine the market interest rates. Figure 10-5 shows the total quantity of money (M) on the horizontal axis and the nominal interest rate (i) on the vertical axis. The supply curve is drawn as a vertical line on the assumption that the Federal Reserve keeps the money supply constant at M^* in Figure 10-5.

In addition, we show the money demand schedule as a downward-sloping curve because the holdings of money decline as interest rates rise. At higher interest rates, people and businesses shift more of their funds to higher-yield assets and away from low-yield or zero-yield money, as described in the previous chapter.

The intersection of the supply and demand schedules in Figure 10-5 determines the market interest rate. Recall that interest rates are the prices paid for the use of money. Interest rates are determined in **money markets,** which are the markets where short-term funds are lent and borrowed. Important interest rates include short-term rates such as the rates on 3-month Treasury bills and on short-term commercial paper (notes issued by large corporations). As noted above, the Federal Reserve operates primarily in the market for federal funds and affects the federal funds rate. Longer-term interest rates include 10-year or 20-year government and corporate bonds and mortgages on real estate.

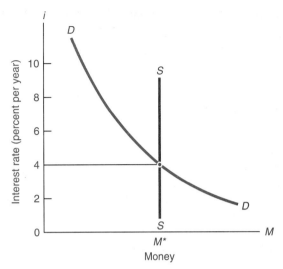

FIGURE 10-5. The Money Market

The interaction of the demand for and supply of money determines the interest rate. The Fed has a money target at M^*. The public has a downward-sloping money demand schedule. Here the money market is in equilibrium with a nominal interest rate of 4 percent per year.

(See Figure 9-2 for a graph of recent trends in interest rates.)

In Figure 10-5, the equilibrium interest rate is 4 percent per year. Only at 4 percent is the level of the money supply that the Fed has targeted consistent with the desired money holdings of the public. At a higher interest rate, there would be excessive money balances. People would get rid of their excessive money holdings by buying bonds and other financial instruments, thereby lowering market interest rates toward the equilibrium 4 percent rate. (What would happen at an interest rate of 2 percent?)

Money Market Shifts. To understand the monetary transmission mechanism, we need to see how changes in the money market affect interest rates. Suppose that the Federal Reserve becomes worried about inflation and tightens monetary policy by selling securities and reducing the money supply.

The impact of a monetary tightening is shown in Figure 10-6(*a*) on page 208. The leftward shift of the money supply schedule means that market interest rates must rise to induce people to swap their money

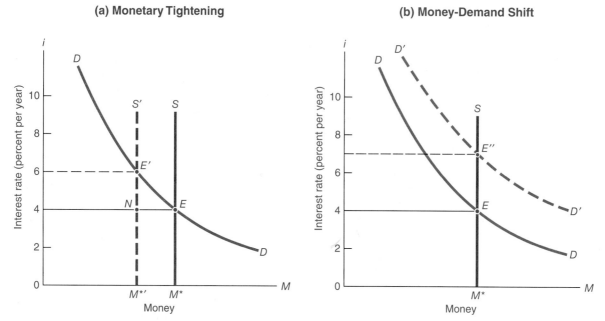

FIGURE 10-6. Changes in Monetary Policy or Prices Affect Interest Rates

In (**a**), the Federal Reserve contracts the money supply in response to fears of rising prices. The lower money supply produces an excess demand for money, shown by the gap *NE*. As the public adjusts its portfolio, interest rates rise to the new equilibrium at *E'*.

In (**b**), the demand for money increases as prices rise, other things held constant. The higher demand for money drives up market interest rates until the quantity of money demanded equals the money supply.

for bonds and other nonmonetary assets. The gap between *E* and *N* shows the extent of excess demand for money at the old interest rate. Interest rates rise until the new equilibrium is attained, shown in Figure 10-6(*a*) at point *E'*, with a new and higher interest rate of 6 percent per year.

There are also frequent shocks to money demand. For example, suppose that an increase in oil or commodity prices raised the overall price level. With higher prices, the demand for money would increase, shifting the money demand curve to the right from *DD* to *D'D'*, as shown in Figure 10-6(*b*), and leading to an increase in equilibrium interest rates. (To check your understanding, make sure you can answer question 1 at the end of the chapter.)

To summarize our findings about the money market:

The money market is affected by a combination of (1) the public's desire to hold money (represented by the demand-for-money *DD* curve) and (2) the Fed's monetary policy (which is shown as a fixed money supply, *SS*). Their interaction determines the market interest rate, *i*. A restrictive monetary policy shifts the *SS* curve to the left, raising market interest rates. An increase in the nation's output or price level shifts the *DD* curve to the right and raises interest rates. An expansion of the money supply or a decline in money demand has the opposite effects.

The press and monetary policy
Financial markets are one of the most heavily covered sectors of the economy. Every day, the media feature reports on the impact of monetary policy on interest rates, foreign exchange rates, the trade and budget deficits, output, employment, inflation, and virtually every sector of the economy. Newspaper accounts of money markets often contain stories like the following:

Alan Greenspan has launched yet another monetary missile. Last week, for the fourth time in three months, the central bank hiked short-term interest rates in an effort to blast inflation off his radar screen. But his target, growing price pressure, is barely a blip. (*U.S. News and World Report*)

Federal Reserve Chairman Greenspan and Senate Banking Committee Democrats clashed today as Senators accused the Fed of putting the skids on economic growth. (*National Journal Congress Daily*)

A [1999] survey in Great Britain asked respondents to name the most important person in their life. Topping the list: Alan Greenspan. (*The International Economy*)

Or consider the following pronouncement on the stock market by Chairman Greenspan, which sent financial markets temporarily into a tailspin:

But how do we know when irrational exuberance has unduly escalated asset values, which then become subject to unexpected and prolonged contractions as they have in Japan over the past decade? And how do we factor that assessment into monetary policy? [W]e should not underestimate or become complacent about the complexity of the interactions of asset markets and the economy. Thus, evaluating shifts in balance sheets generally, and in asset prices particularly, must be an integral part of the development of monetary policy. (Alan Greenspan in a famous speech in December 1996)

You should study the press to see how the principles developed here play out in daily events.

THE MONETARY MECHANISM

The newspaper excerpts above give the flavor of the debate about monetary policy. We turn now to examine how monetary policy affects the economy.

Graphical Analysis of Monetary Policy

Figure 10-7 on the next page illustrates the effects of a monetary expansion upon economic activity. Part (a), in the lower left, shows the money market; (b), in the lower right, shows the determination of investment; and (c), in the upper right, shows the determination of aggregate demand and GDP by the multiplier mechanism. We can think of the causality as moving counterclockwise from the money market through investment to the determination of aggregate demand and GDP as a whole.

Starting at the lower left, in Figure 10-7 (a), we see the demand for and supply of money that were depicted in Figures 10-5 and 10-6. For purposes of the present discussion, assume that the money supply schedule was initially S_A and that the interest rate was 8 percent per year. If the Fed were concerned about a looming recession, it might increase the money supply by making open-market purchases, shifting the curve to S_B. In the case shown in Figure 10-7(a), market interest rates would thereby fall to 4 percent per year.

Figure 10-7(b) picks up the story to show how lower interest rates increase spending on interest-sensitive components of aggregate demand. We saw in Chapter 6 that a decline in interest rates would induce businesses to increase their spending on plant, equipment, and inventories. The effects of eased monetary policy are quickly seen in the housing market, where lower interest rates mean lower monthly mortgage payments on the typical house, encouraging households to increase housing purchases.

Additionally, asset prices tend to rise with lower interest rates. Consumption spending increases, both because lower interest rates generally increase the value of wealth—as stock, bond, and housing prices tend to rise—and because consumers tend to spend more on automobiles and other big-ticket consumer durables when interest rates are low and credit is plentiful. Moreover, as we will explore in a moment, lower interest rates tend to reduce the foreign exchange rate on the dollar, thereby increasing the level of net exports. We see, then, how lower interest rates lead to increased spending in many different areas of the economy.

These consequences are evident in Figure 10-7(b), where the drop in interest rates (caused by the increase in the money supply) leads to a rise in invest-

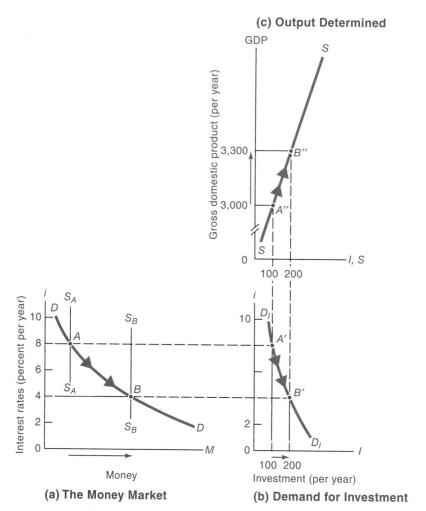

FIGURE 10-7. Central Bank Determines the Money Supply, Changing Interest Rates and Investment, Thereby Affecting GDP

When the Fed raises the money supply, from S_A to S_B, interest rates fall as people increase their money balances, moving down the money demand schedule in (**a**).

Lower interest rates reduce the cost of investment, thus encouraging business purchases of plant and equipment and consumer purchases of houses. The economy moves down the demand-for-investment schedule from A' to B' in (**b**).

By the multiplier mechanism in (**c**), the higher investment raises aggregate demand and GDP from A'' to B''.

ment from A' to B'. In this case, we should construe "investment" in the very broad sense sketched a moment ago: it includes not only business investment but also consumer durables and residences, as well as net foreign investment in the form of net exports.

Finally, Figure 10-7(c) shows the impact of changes in investment in the multiplier model. This

diagram is really Figure 8-2 turned on its side. Recall from Chapter 8 that, in the simplest multiplier model, equilibrium output is attained when desired saving equals desired investment. In Figure 10-7(c), we have shown this relationship by drawing the saving schedule as the SS schedule; this line represents the desired level of saving (measured along the horizontal axis) as a function of GDP on the vertical axis. Equilibrium GDP is attained at that level where the investment demand from panel (*b*) equals the desired saving from the *SS* schedule.

The initial level of investment was 100, as read off at *A′* in panel (*b*), producing a level of GDP of 3000. After easier money has lowered the interest rate from 8 to 4 percent, investment rises to 200 at point *B′*. This higher level of investment raises aggregate spending to the new equilibrium at *B″* in panel (*c*) with a new equilibrium GDP of 3300.

What has occurred? The rise in the money supply from S_A to S_B lowered the interest rate from *A* to *B*; this caused investment to rise from *A′* to *B′*; and this in turn, acting through the multiplier, led to a rise in GDP from *A″* to *B″*.

Such is the route by which monetary policy acts through intermediate targets like the money supply and interest rates to affect its ultimate targets.

Economic policy in the recession of 1982

One of the most dramatic economic policies in the United States occurred when the Fed decided to reduce inflation in the 1979–1982 period. As a result of low unemployment and a major increase in oil prices, annual inflation in 1979 surged to 13 percent. The Federal Reserve in 1979 responded with its "monetarist experiment," concentrating on the growth of reserves and the money supply rather than on interest rates. It hoped that a clear and decisive strategy of targeting the monetary aggregates would help slow the unacceptable inflation.

The shift to targeting monetary aggregates in 1979 was highly controversial. The immediate result was a sharp reduction in the growth of the money supply and a consequent tightening of monetary policy. This led to an increase of market interest rates to levels not seen since the Civil War. As interest rates rose, investment and other interest-sensitive spending fell sharply, which led to the deepest recession since the 1930s. The policy was definitely successful in reducing inflation to 4 percent by 1982.

As the recession deepened, the Fed worried that its tight monetary policies had gone too far. Unemployment was over 10 percent, and Congress was up in arms. We can use this incident to see how the Fed conducts its monetary policies—tuning in as the Fed decided to relax its monetary policy.

Let's begin with the August 1982 directive. In the midst of the deepest recession of the postwar period, the FOMC began with its review of the economy:[4]

> The information reviewed at this meeting suggests only a little further advance in real GDP in the current quarter, following a relatively small increase in the second quarter, while prices on the average are continuing to rise more slowly than in 1981.

What objectives did the Fed establish for monetary policy? It stated:

> The Federal Open Market Committee seeks to foster monetary and financial conditions that will help to reduce inflation, promote a resumption of growth in output on a sustainable basis, and contribute to a sustainable pattern of international transactions.

The FOMC then gave the following operational directive to the New York Federal Reserve Bank in August 1982:

> In the short run, the Committee continues to seek behavior of reserve aggregates consistent with growth of M_1 and M_2 from June to September [1982] at annual rates of about 5 percent and about 9 percent respectively.

How should we interpret these words? They are saying that, in light of the sharp recession of 1982, the Fed concluded that its monetary policy had become overly restrictive. Also, the definitions of the monetary aggregates became confused at this time because of the addition of a number of new assets (such as interest-bearing checking accounts) to M_1 and M_2. The ambiguity about the meaning of the *M*'s meant that basing policy only on *M* movement was unwise.

The Fed therefore abandoned its strict monetary targeting in the fall of 1982. Interest rates fell sharply, with the 3-month Treasury-bill rate falling from 15 percent in the middle of 1981 to 8 percent at the end of 1982. As a result, real spending on housing almost doubled from 1982 to 1984, and the economy began to recover sharply in 1983.

Although the monetary policies of this period were extremely unpopular, in retrospect many economists believe that they were a good "investment in stable prices."

---

[4] The FOMC quotations are from the *Federal Reserve Bulletin*, which contains monthly reports on Federal Reserve activities and other important financial developments.

Monetary Policy in an Open Economy

The monetary transmission mechanism in the United States has evolved over the last two decades as the economy became more open and changes occurred in the exchange-rate system. The relationship between monetary policy and foreign trade has always been a major concern for smaller and more open economies like Canada and Britain. However, after the introduction of flexible exchange rates in 1973 and in the presence of increasing cross-border linkages, international trade and finance have come to play a new and central role in U.S. macroeconomic policy.

Let's review briefly the new route using the historical episode just analyzed. When the Federal Reserve tightened money in the 1979–1982 period, this process drove up interest rates on assets denominated in U.S. dollars. Attracted by higher dollar interest rates, investors bought dollar securities, driving up the foreign exchange rate on the dollar. The higher exchange rate on the dollar encouraged imports into the United States and hurt U.S. exports. Net exports fell, reducing aggregate demand. This had the impact of both lowering real GDP and lowering the rate of inflation.

We will study the international aspects of macroeconomics in Chapters 13 and 14. For now, the main point to grasp is that foreign trade opens up another link in the monetary transmission mechanism. Monetary policy has the same impact on international trade as it has on domestic investment—tight money lowers foreign and domestic investment, thereby depressing output and prices. *The international-trade impact of monetary policy reinforces the domestic-economy impact.*

Monetary Policy in the AD-AS Framework

The three-part diagram in Figure 10-7 illustrates how an increase in the money supply would lead to an increase in aggregate demand. We can now show the effect on the overall macroeconomic equilibrium by using aggregate supply and demand curves.

The increase in aggregate demand produced by an increase in the supply of money causes a rightward shift of the *AD* curve as drawn in Figure 10-8 in the next column. This shift illustrates a monetary expansion in the presence of unemployed resources, with a relatively flat *AS* curve. The monetary expan-

Expansionary Monetary Policy

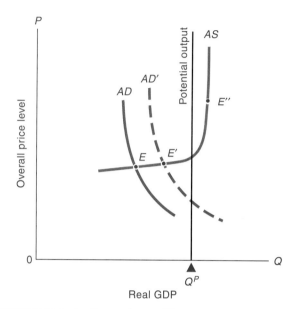

FIGURE 10-8. An Expansionary Monetary Policy Shifts *AD* Curve to the Right, Raising Output and Prices

Earlier discussion and Fig. 10-7 showed how an increase in the money supply would lead to an increase in investment and net exports and thereby to a multiplied increase in aggregate demand. This results in a rightward shift of the *AD* curve.

In the Keynesian region where the *AS* curve is relatively flat, a monetary expansion has its primary effect on real output, with only a small effect on prices. In a fully employed economy, the *AS* curve is near-vertical (shown at point *E″*), and a monetary expansion will primarily raise prices and nominal GDP with little effect on real GDP. Can you see why in the long run money may have little impact on real output?

sion shifts aggregate demand from *AD* to *AD′*, shifting the equilibrium from *E* to *E′*. This example demonstrates how monetary expansion can increase aggregate demand and have a powerful impact on real output.

The sequence therefore runs as follows:

Monetary expansion bids down market interest rates. This stimulates interest-sensitive spending on business investment, housing, net exports, and the like. Aggregate demand increases via the multiplier mechanism, raising output and prices above the levels they would otherwise attain. Therefore, the basic sequence is

$$M \text{ up} \rightarrow i \text{ down} \rightarrow I,\ C,\ X \text{ up} \rightarrow AD \text{ up} \rightarrow$$
$$\text{GDP up and } P \text{ up}$$

But never forget the role of unemployed resources. The effect of an AD shift in a fully employed economy can be illustrated in Figure 10-8. Pencil in an AD'' curve going through E'' on the steep segment of the AS curve; then pencil in a monetary expansion as a higher AD'''. Note how the monetary expansion would have little impact on real output. In a fully employed economy, the higher money stock would be chasing the same amount of output and would therefore mainly end up raising prices.

To clinch your understanding of this vital sequence, work through the opposite case of a monetary contraction. Say that the Federal Reserve decides, as it did in 1979–1982, to raise interest rates, slow the economy, and reduce inflation. You can trace this sequence in Figure 10-7 by reversing the direction of the monetary policy, thereby seeing how money, interest rates, investment, and aggregate demand interact when monetary policy is tightened. Then see how a leftward shift of the AD curve in Figure 10-8 would reduce both output and prices.

Monetary Effects in the Long Run

Many economists believe that changes in the supply of money in the long run will mainly affect the price level with little or no impact upon real output. We can understand this point by analyzing the effects of monetary changes in economies with different conditions of aggregate supply. As shown in Figure 10-8, monetary changes will affect aggregate demand and will tend to change real GDP in the short run when there are unemployed resources and the AS curve is relatively flat.

In our analysis of aggregate supply in the following chapters, we will see that the AS curve tends to be vertical or near-vertical in the long run as wages and prices adjust. Because of the price-wage adjustments and near-vertical AS curve, the output effects of AD shifts will diminish, and the price effects will tend to dominate in the long run. *This means that as prices and wages become more flexible in the long run, money-supply changes tend to have a larger impact on prices and a smaller impact on output.*

What is the intuition behind this difference between the short run and the long run? We can construct a highly simplified example to see the difference. Suppose we start out as in Figure 10-7, with a nominal GDP of 3000 and stable prices; then a monetary expansion that increases the money supply by 10 percent might increase nominal GDP by 10 percent to 3300. Studies by Robert J. Gordon and others indicate that, in the short run, "nominal GDP changes have been divided consistently, with two-thirds taking the form of output change and the remaining one-third the form of price change." Consequently, in the first year, the money-supply expansion might increase real GDP around 7 percent and increase prices around 3 percent. (Or, as is illustrated in Figure 10-8, with a gently sloping AS curve we see a large Q response and a small P response to the AD shift.)

As time passes, however, wages and prices begin to adjust more completely to the higher price and output levels. Higher demand in both labor and product markets raises wages and prices; wages are adjusted to reflect the higher cost of living; cost-of-living provisions in contracts raise wages and prices even further. After a second year, prices might rise another 1 or 2 percent, with output then being only 5 or 6 percent above its original level. In the third year, prices might rise again while output falls somewhat. Where would it end? This process might continue until prices rise by fully 10 percent and output is back to the original level. Thus, the monetary policy would raise prices and wages by about 10 percent and real output would be unchanged.

If all adjustments eventually come in prices, all nominal variables are increased by 10 percent while all real variables are unchanged. In other words, nominal variables like the GDP deflator, the CPI, nominal GDP, wages, the money supply, dollar consumption, dollar imports, the dollar value of wealth, and so forth, are 10 percent higher. But real GDP, real consumption, real wages, real incomes, and the real value of wealth are all unchanged by the monetary policy. In such a case, then, we say that *money is neutral*, meaning that changes in the money supply have no effect on real variables.

A word of caution is in order: The scenario that money changes lead to proportionate changes in all nominal variables but no changes in real variables is intuitively plausible and supported by certain empirical evidence. But it is not a universal law. The long run may be a period of many decades; intervening events may throw the economy off the idealized long-run trajectory; and interest-rate changes along the path might have irreversible impacts upon the economy because of bankruptcies, trade changes, and other impacts. The long-run neutrality of money is therefore only a tendency and not a universal law.

This discussion of monetary policy has taken place without reference to fiscal policy. In reality, whatever the philosophical predilections of the government, every advanced economy simultaneously conducts both fiscal and monetary policies. Each policy has strengths and weaknesses. In the chapters that follow, we return to an integrated consideration of the roles of monetary and fiscal policies both in combating the business cycle and in promoting economic growth.

From Aggregate Demand to Aggregate Supply

We have completed our introductory analysis of the determinants of aggregate demand. We examined the foundations of aggregate demand and saw that *AD* is determined by exogenous factors, such as investment and net exports, along with government policies, such as monetary and fiscal policies. In the short run, changes in these factors lead to changes in spending and to changes in both output and prices.

In today's volatile world, economies are exposed to shocks from both inside and outside their borders. Wars, revolutions, financial and currency crises, oil shocks, defaults, and government miscalculations have led to periods of high inflation or high unemployment or both. No market mechanism provides an automatic pilot that can quickly eliminate macroeconomic fluctuations, and governments therefore take responsibility for moderating the swings of the business cycle. The United States was fortunate in the 1990s to have avoided serious business cycles, but other countries were not so lucky, with prolonged slumps in Japan and much of Europe and periodic financial crises in Latin America and East Asian countries. These events are a reminder that there is no universal cure to unemployment and inflation in the face of all the shocks to which an economy is exposed.

We now turn to issues of economic growth, the open economy, and economic policy. We begin with an analysis of the process of long-run economic growth, which will deepen our understanding of the determinants of potential output and aggregate supply. We next broaden our horizon to include the macroeconomics of international trade and finance. We then tackle the interrelated topics of inflation and unemployment and see how modern market economies are severely constrained by the need to maintain stable prices. Finally, we return to the pressing dilemmas of macroeconomic policy today: fiscal policy and the government debt, the interrelation between fiscal policy and monetary policy, and the need to promote long-term economic growth.

✳

SUMMARY

A. Central Banking and the Federal Reserve System

1. The Federal Reserve System is a central bank, a bank for bankers. Its objectives are to allow sustainable economic growth, maintain a high level of employment, ensure orderly financial markets, and above all preserve reasonable price stability.

2. The Federal Reserve System (or "Fed") was created in 1913 to control the nation's money and credit and to act as the "lender of last resort." It is run by the Board of Governors and the Federal Open Market Committee (FOMC). The Fed acts as an independent government agency and has great discretion in determining monetary policy.

3. The Fed has three major policy instruments: (*a*) open-market operations, (*b*) the discount rate on bank borrowing, and (*c*) legal reserve requirements on depository institutions. Using these instruments, the Fed affects intermediate targets, such as the level of bank reserves, market interest rates, and the money supply. All these operations aim to improve the economy's performance with respect to the ultimate objectives of monetary policy: achieving the best combination of low inflation, low unemployment, rapid GDP growth, and orderly financial markets. In addition, the Fed along with other federal agencies must backstop the domestic and international financial system in times of crisis.

4. The most important instrument of monetary policy is the Fed's open-market operations. Sales by the Fed of government securities in the open market reduce the Fed's assets and liabilities and thereby reduce the reserves of banks. The effect is a decrease in banks' reserve base for deposits. People end up with less M and more government bonds. Open-market purchases do the opposite, ultimately expanding M by increasing bank reserves.

5. Outflows of international reserves can reduce reserves and M unless offset by sterilization through open-market purchases of bonds. Inflows have the opposite effects unless offset. In recent years, the Fed has routinely sterilized international reserve movements. In open economies with fixed exchange rates, monetary policies must be closely aligned with those in other countries.

B. The Effects of Money on Output and Prices

6. If the Fed desires to slow the growth of output, the five-step sequence goes thus:
   a. The Fed reduces bank reserves through open-market operations.
   b. Each dollar reduction of bank reserves produces a multiple contraction of bank money and the money supply.
   c. In the money market, a reduction in the money supply moves along an unchanged money demand schedule, raising interest rates, restricting the amount and terms of credit, and tightening money.
   d. Tight money reduces investment and other interest-sensitive items of spending like consumer durables or net exports.
   e. The reduction in investment and other spending reduces aggregate demand by the familiar multiplier mechanism. The lower level of aggregate demand lowers output and the price level or inflation.

The sequence is summarized by

$$R \text{ down} \rightarrow M \text{ down} \rightarrow i \text{ up} \rightarrow I, C, X \text{ down} \rightarrow$$
$$AD \text{ down} \rightarrow \text{real GDP down and inflation down}$$

7. Although the monetary mechanism is often explained in terms of money affecting "investment," in fact the monetary mechanism is an extremely rich and complex process whereby changes in interest rates and asset prices influence a wide variety of elements of spending. These sectors include housing, affected by changing mortgage interest rates and housing prices; business investment, affected by changing interest rates and stock prices; spending on consumer durables, influenced by interest rates and credit availability; state and local capital spending, affected by interest rates; and net exports, determined by the effects of interest rates upon foreign exchange rates.

8. In an open economy, the international-trade linkage reinforces the domestic impacts of monetary policy. In a regime of flexible exchange rates, changes in monetary policy affect the exchange rate and net exports, adding yet another facet to the monetary mechanism. The trade link tends to reinforce the impact of monetary policy, operating in the same direction on net exports as it does on domestic investment.

9. Monetary policy may have different effects in the short run and the long run. In the short run, with a relatively flat AS curve, most of the change in AD will affect output and only a small part will affect prices. In the longer run, as the AS curve becomes more nearly vertical, monetary shifts lead predominantly to changes in the price level and much less to output changes. In the polar case where money-supply changes affect only nominal variables and have no effects on real variables, we say money is neutral. Most real-world monetary shifts have left real economic effects in their wake.

CONCEPTS FOR REVIEW

Central Banking
bank reserves
Federal Reserve balance sheet
open-market purchases and sales
discount rate, borrowings from Fed
legal reserve requirements
FOMC, Board of Governors
policy instruments, intermediate targets, ultimate objectives

The Monetary Transmission Mechanism
demand for and supply of money
five-step monetary transmission mechanism:
   reserve change
   reserves to money
   money to interest rates
   interest rates to investment
   investment to GDP

interest-sensitive components of spending
monetary policy in the AS-AD framework
R down $\rightarrow M$ down $\rightarrow i$ up $\rightarrow I$ down $\rightarrow AD$ down $\rightarrow$ GDP down and P down
monetary policy in the short run and the long run
"neutrality" of money

FURTHER READING AND INTERNET WEBSITES

Further Reading

The *Federal Reserve Bulletin* contains monthly reports on Federal Reserve activities and other important financial developments. (The *Bulletin* is available on the Internet at www.bog.frb.fed.us/pubs/bulletin.)

Websites

The Federal Reserve System: Purposes and Functions (Board of Governors of the Federal Reserve System, Washington, DC, 1994), available on the Internet at www.bog.frb.fed.us/pf/pf.htm, provides a useful description of the operations of the Fed. Also see the **Further Reading and**

Websites section in Chapter 9 for a more detailed list of sites on monetary policy.

If you want to see which Reserve Bank region you live in, see www.bog.frb.fed.us/otherfrb.htm. Why are the eastern regions so small?

There is usually a website devoted to the thinking of the Fed Chairman. You can find it through most search engines, such as www.yahoo.com. Biographies of the members of the Board of Governors can be found at www.bog.frb.fed.us/BIOS. Particularly interesting are the transcripts and minutes of Fed meetings, www.bog.frb.fed.us/fomc.

QUESTIONS FOR DISCUSSION

1. Using Figure 10-6, work through each of the following:
   a. The Federal Reserve has decided that unemployment is rising too sharply and wants to reverse this trend by expanding the money supply. What steps must the Fed take to expand money? What will be the impact on the money supply curve? What is the reaction in money markets?
   b. As a result of a rapid economic expansion abroad, exports rise and real GDP increases. What happens to the demand for money? What is the impact upon the market interest rate?
   c. With the spread of automated teller machines (ATMs), people find they need lower "precautionary" balances of currency. The amount of money demanded at each level of interest rate and GDP falls. The Fed is uncertain about the significance of this behavior and therefore keeps the money supply constant. What will be the impact of the asset switch on money supply and demand? On market interest rates?
2. Suppose you are the Chairperson of the Fed's Board of Governors at a time when the economy is beginning to overheat and you are called to testify before a congressional committee. Write an explanation for an interrogating senator outlining how you would proceed to maintain stable prices.
3. Consider the balance sheet of the Fed in Table 10-1. Construct a corresponding balance sheet for banks

(like the one in Table 9-3 in the previous chapter) assuming that reserve requirements are 10 percent on checking accounts and zero on everything else.
   a. Construct a new set of balance sheets, assuming the Fed sells $1 billion in government securities by open-market operations.
   b. Construct another set of balance sheets to show what happens when the Fed increases reserve requirements to 20 percent.
   c. Assume banks borrow $1 billion of reserves from the Fed. How will this action change the balance sheets?
4. Study the three newspaper excerpts on page 209. Using the theories developed in the last few chapters, explain the reasoning behind each statement.
5. Using Figure 10-7, explain how the tight-money policies after 1979 lowered GDP. Also, explain each of the steps in words.
6. "A government deficit is bad because it leads to rapid monetary growth." Explain why this statement is wrong.
7. In Japan in 1998 and 1999, prices were falling at 2 percent per year while the short-term interest rate was 0.1 percent per year.
   a. What was the real interest rate?
   b. "In 1998 and 1999, Japan was caught in a *liquidity trap*, where the central bank could not lower real interest rates and was therefore unable to stimulate the economy." Explain this statement.

8. After the reunification of Germany in 1990, payments to rebuild the east led to a major expansion of aggregate demand in Germany. The German central bank responded by slowing money growth and driving German real interest rates extremely high. Trace through why this German monetary tightening would be expected to lead to a depreciation of the dollar. Explain why the depreciation would stimulate economic activity in the United States. Also, explain why European countries that had pegged their currencies to the German mark would find themselves plunged into deep recessions as German interest rates rose and pulled other European rates up with them.

PART THREE

Economic Growth and the Open Economy

Two issues have dominated macroeconomics since its birth: the need to reduce the instability of a market economy caught between the twin evils of high inflation and high unemployment and the desire to increase a nation's rate of growth of output and consumption. Earlier chapters surveyed how shifts in spending patterns could lead to business cycles and the role of monetary and fiscal policy in taming business cycles. We now turn to the longer-term issues raised by the growth of aggregate supply and potential output—to the theory and policy of economic growth.

The daily press is dominated by business-cycle developments. However important, these concerns are but small ripples on the larger wave of economic growth, in which advanced economies such as the United States accumulate larger quantities of capital equipment, push out the frontiers of technological knowledge, and become steadily more productive. Over the long run of decades and generations, living standards as measured by output per capita or consumption per household are primarily determined by aggregate supply and the level of productivity of a country.

This chapter begins with a survey of the theory of economic growth and then reviews the historical trends in economic activity with particular application to wealthy countries like the United States. The next chapter looks at the other end of the income spectrum by examining the plight of the developing countries, struggling to reach the level of affluence enjoyed in the West. The two chapters that follow examine the role of international trade and finance in macroeconomics. Figure 11-1 presents an overview of the growth chapters, using our familiar flowchart.

CHAPTER

11

The Process of Economic Growth

The Industrial Revolution was not an episode with a beginning and an end.... It is still going on.

E. J. Hobsbawm, *The Age of Revolution* **(1962)**

The Long-Term Significance of Growth

Look at the inside front cover of this book, where you will see the advance of real output over the twentieth century. You can see that real GDP has grown *by a factor of almost 18 since 1900.* This is perhaps the central economic fact of the century. Continuing rapid economic growth enabled advanced industrial countries to provide more of everything to their citizens—better food and bigger homes, more resources for medical care and pollution control, universal education for children, and public pensions for retirees.

Nations continue to view economic growth as a central objective of policy. Countries which succeed in the economic growth race, such as Britain in the nineteenth century or the United States in the twentieth century, rise in the pecking order of nations and serve as role models for other countries

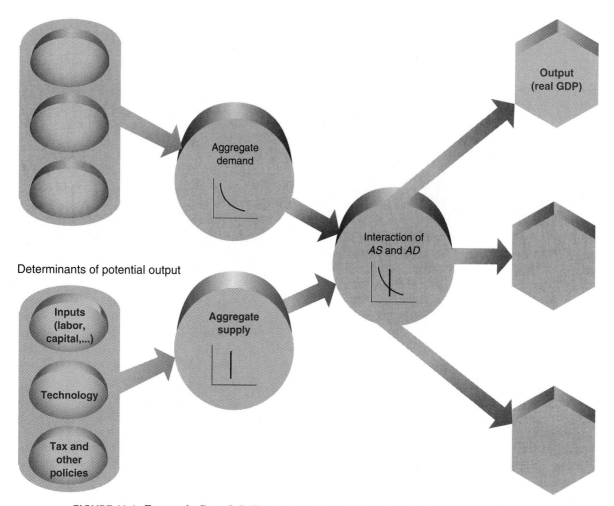

FIGURE 11-1. Economic Growth Is Key to Long-Term Living Standards

In the long run, a nation's economic fortunes depend upon the growth of its potential output. This chapter examines the long-term growth trends along with the theories that explain the basic trends.

seeking the path to affluence. At the other extreme, countries in economic decline often experience political and social turmoil. The revolutions in Eastern Europe and the Soviet Union in 1989–1991 were sparked by economic stagnation and low economic growth as compared to that of their Western neighbors. Economic growth is the single most important factor in the success of nations in the long run.

⊕
A. THEORIES OF ECONOMIC GROWTH

Let's begin with a careful definition of exactly what we mean by economic growth: **Economic growth** represents the expansion of a country's potential GDP or national output. Put differently, economic growth occurs when a nation's production-possibility frontier (*PPF*) shifts outward.

A closely related concept is the growth rate of *output per person*. This determines the rate at which the country's living standards are rising. Countries are primarily concerned with the growth in per capita output because this leads to rising average incomes.

What are the long-term patterns of economic growth in high-income countries? Table 11-1 shows the history of economic growth since 1870 for 16 high-income countries including the major countries of North America and Western Europe, Japan, and Australia. We see the steady growth of output over this period. Even more important for living standards is the growth in output per hour worked, which moves closely with the increase in living standards. Over the entire period, output per worker grew by an average rate of 2.4 percent annually, which compounds to a growth factor of 16 over the 120-year period.

What were the major forces behind this growth? What can nations do to speed up their economic growth rate? And what are the prospects for the twenty-first century, given the slowdown in productivity growth of the last three decades along with the possibility of tighter environmental constraints? These are the issues that must be confronted by economic-growth analysis.

Economic growth involves the growth of potential output over the long run. The growth in output per capita is an important objective of government because it is associated with rising average real incomes and living standards.

THE FOUR WHEELS OF GROWTH

What is the recipe for economic growth? To begin with, many roads lead to Rome. There are many successful strategies on the road to self-sustained economic growth. Britain, for example, became the world economic leader in the 1800s by pioneering the Industrial Revolution, inventing steam engines and railroads, and emphasizing free trade. Japan, by contrast, came to the economic-growth race later. It made its mark by first imitating foreign technologies and protecting domestic industries from imports and then developing tremendous expertise in manufacturing and electronics.

Even though their individual paths may differ, all rapidly growing countries share certain common traits. The same fundamental process of economic growth and development that helped shape Britain and Japan is at work today in developing countries like China and India. Indeed, economists who have studied growth have found that the engine of economic progress must ride on the same four wheels, no matter how rich or poor the country.

| Period | GDP | Average Annual Growth Rate in: | | |
		GDP per hour worked	Total hours worked	Labor force
1870–1913	2.5	1.6	0.9	1.2
1913–1950	1.9	1.8	0.1	0.8
1950–1973	4.8	4.5	0.3	1.0
1973–1996	2.6	2.1	0.5	1.1

TABLE 11-1. Patterns of Growth in 16 Industrial Countries

Over the last century, major high-income countries like the United States, Germany, France, and Japan have grown rapidly. Output has grown faster than inputs of labor, reflecting increases in capital and technological advance. [Source: Angus Maddison, *Phases of Capitalist Development* (Oxford, 1982), updated by authors from data from Maddison, the World Bank, and other publications.]

These four wheels, or factors of growth, are:

- Human resources (labor supply, education, discipline, motivation)
- Natural resources (land, minerals, fuels, environmental quality)
- Capital formation (machines, factories, roads)
- Technology (science, engineering, management, entrepreneurship)

Often, economists write the relationship in terms of an *aggregate production function* (or *APF*), which relates total national output to the inputs and technology. Algebraically, the *APF* is

$$Q = AF(K, L, R)$$

where Q = output, K = productive services of capital, L = labor inputs, R = natural-resource inputs, A represents the level of technology in the economy, and F is the production function. As the inputs of capital, labor, or resources rise, we would expect that output would increase, although output will probably show diminishing returns to additional inputs of production factors. We can think of the role of technology as augmenting the productivity of inputs. **Productivity** denotes the ratio of output to a weighted average of inputs. As technology (A) improves through new inventions or the adoption of technologies from abroad, this advance allows a country to produce more output with the same level of inputs.

Let's now see how each of the four factors contributes to growth.

Human Resources

Labor inputs consist of quantities of workers and of the skills of the workforce. Many economists believe that the quality of labor inputs—the skills, knowledge, and discipline of the labor force—is the single most important element in economic growth. A country might buy fast computers, modern telecommunications devices, sophisticated electricity-generating equipment, and hypersonic fighter aircraft. However, these capital goods can be effectively used and maintained only by skilled and trained workers. Improvements in literacy, health, and discipline, and most recently the ability to use computers, add greatly to the productivity of labor.

Natural Resources

The second classical factor of production is natural resources. The important resources here are arable land, oil and gas, forests, water, and mineral resources. Some high-income countries like Canada and Norway have grown primarily on the basis of their ample resource base, with large output in agriculture, fisheries, and forestry. Similarly, the United States, with its fertile farmlands, is the world's largest producer and exporter of grains.

But the possession of natural resources is not necessary for economic success in the modern world. New York City prospers primarily on its high-density service industries. Many countries, such as Japan, had virtually no natural resources but thrived by concentrating on sectors that depend more on labor and capital than on indigenous resources. Indeed, tiny Hong Kong, with but a minute fraction of the land area of resource-rich Russia, actually has a larger volume of international trade than does that giant country.

Capital Formation

Recall that tangible capital includes structures like roads and power plants, equipment like trucks and computers, and stocks of inventories. The most dramatic stories in economic history often involve the accumulation of capital. In the nineteenth century, the transcontinental railroads of North America brought commerce to the American heartland, which had been living in isolation. In the last century, waves of investment in automobiles, roads, and power plants increased productivity and provided the infrastructure which created entire new industries. Many believe that computers and the information superhighway will do for the twenty-first century what railroads and highways did in earlier times.

Accumulating capital, as we have seen, requires a sacrifice of current consumption over many years. Countries that grow rapidly tend to invest heavily in new capital goods; in the most rapidly growing countries, 10 to 20 percent of output may go into net capital formation. By contrast, many economists believe that the low national saving rate in the United States—only 2 percent of output in 1999—poses a major economic problem for the country.

When we think of capital, we must not concentrate only on computers and factories. Many investments will only be undertaken by governments and lay the framework for a thriving private sector. These investments are called **social overhead capital** and consist of the large-scale projects that precede trade and commerce. Roads, irrigation and water projects, and public-health measures are important examples. All these involve large investments that tend to be "indivisible," or lumpy, and sometimes have increasing returns to scale. These projects generally involve external economies, or spillovers that private firms cannot capture, so the government must step in to ensure that these social overhead or infrastructure investments are effectively undertaken. Some investments, such as transportation and communication systems, involve "network" externalities in which productivity depends upon the density of the using population.

Technological Change and Innovation

In addition to the three classical factors discussed above, technological advance has been a vital fourth ingredient in the rapid growth of living standards. Historically, growth has definitely not been a process of simple replication, adding rows of steel mills or power plants next to each other. Rather, a never-ending stream of inventions and technologi-

cal advances led to a vast improvement in the production possibilities of Europe, North America, and Japan.

We are today witnessing an explosion of new technologies, particularly in information, computation, communication, and the life sciences. But this is not the first time that American society has been shaken by fundamental inventions. Electricity, radio, the automobile, and television also diffused rapidly through the American economy in an earlier age. Figure 11-2 shows the diffusion of major inventions of the twentieth century. This S-shaped pattern is typical of the diffusion of new technologies.

Technological change denotes changes in the processes of production or introduction of new products or services. Process inventions that have greatly increased productivity were the steam engine, the generation of electricity, antibiotics, the internal-combustion engine, the wide-body jet, and the fax machine. Fundamental product inventions include the telephone, the radio, the airplane, the phono-

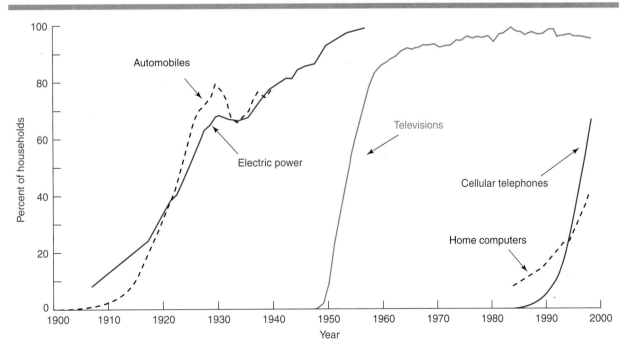

FIGURE 11-2. Diffusion of Major Technologies during the Twentieth Century

Today's information technologies such as cellular telephones and computers are spreading rapidly through American society. Similar diffusion patterns were seen with other fundamental inventions in the past. (Source: *Economic Report of the President, 2000.*)

graph, the television, the microprocessor, and the VCR. The most dramatic technological developments of the modern era are occurring in electronics and computers, where today's tiny notebook computers can outperform the fastest computer of the 1960s. These inventions provide the most spectacular examples of technological change. Nonetheless, technological advance is in fact a continuous process of small and large improvements, as witnessed by the fact that the United States issues over 100,000 new patents annually and that millions of other small refinements are routine progress in a modern economy.

Because of its importance in raising living standards, economists have long pondered how to encourage technological progress. Increasingly, it is becoming clear that technological change is not a mechanical procedure of simply finding better products and processes. Instead, rapid innovation requires the fostering of an entrepreneurial spirit. Consider the thriving Internet industry today—an industry that is reshaping the face of commerce and retailing. Why did the entrepreneurial spirit thrive in America? One key reason is the combination of an open spirit of inquiry, the lack of regulation, and the lure of free-market profits in Silicon Valley.

Table 11-2 summarizes the four wheels of economic growth.

Institutions, incentives, and innovation

In the very long run, the growth in the world's output and wealth has come primarily because of improvements in knowledge. Yet institutions to promote the creation and spread of knowledge, along with incentives to devote our human effort to that task, were developed late in human history—slowly in Western Europe over the last 500 years. This point was eloquently argued by William Baumol:

> The museum at Alexandria was the center of technological innovation in the Roman Empire. By the first century B.C., that city knew of virtually every form of machine gearing that is used today, including a working steam engine. But these seemed to be used only to make what amounted to elaborate toys. The steam engine was used to open and close the doors of a temple.[1]

Baumol and economic historian Joel Mokyr argue that innovation depends crucially on the development of incentives and institutions. They particularly point to the role of private ownership, the patent system, and a rule-based system of adjudicating disputes as devices for fostering innovation.

---

[1] See Baumol in the Further Reading section at the end of this chapter.

Factor in economic growth	Examples
Human resources	Size of labor force Quality of workers (education, skills, discipline)
Natural resources	Oil and gas Soils and climate
Capital formation	Equipment and factories Social overhead capital
Technology and entrepreneurship	Quality of scientific and engineering knowledge Managerial know-how Rewards for innovation

TABLE 11-2. The Four Wheels of Progress

Economic growth inevitably rides on the four wheels of labor, natural resources, capital, and technology. But the wheels may differ greatly among countries, and some countries combine them more effectively than others.

THEORIES OF ECONOMIC GROWTH

Virtually everyone is in favor of economic growth. But there are strong disagreements about the best way to accomplish this goal. Some economists and policymakers stress the need to increase capital investment. Others advocate measures to stimulate research and development and technological change. Still a third group emphasizes the role of a better-educated workforce. Some believe that economic protectionism is useful.

Economists have long studied the question of the relative importance of different factors in determining growth. In the discussion below, we look at the theories of economic growth, which offer some clues about the driving forces behind growth. Then, in the final part of this section, we see what can be learned about growth from its historical patterns over the last century.

The Classical Dynamics of Smith and Malthus

Early economists like Adam Smith and T. R. Malthus stressed the critical role of land in economic growth. In *The Wealth of Nations* (1776), Adam Smith provided a handbook of economic development. He began with a hypothetical idyllic age: "that original state of things, which precedes both the appropriation of land and the accumulation of [capital] stock." This was a time when land was freely available to all, and before capital accumulation had begun to matter.

What would be the dynamics of economic growth in such a "golden-age"? Because land is freely available, people would simply spread out onto more acres as the population increases, just as the settlers did in the American west. Because there is no capital, national output would exactly double as population doubles. What about real wages? The entire national income would go to wages because there is no subtraction for land rent or interest on capital. Output expands in step with population, so the real wage rate per worker would be constant over time.

But this golden age cannot continue forever. Eventually, as population growth continues, all the land will be occupied. Once the frontier disappears, balanced growth of land, labor, and output is no longer possible. New laborers begin to crowd onto already-worked soils. Land becomes scarce, and rents rise to ration it among different uses.

Population still grows, and so does the national product. But output must grow more slowly than does population. Why? With new laborers added to fixed land, each worker now has less land to work with, and the law of diminishing returns comes into operation. The increasing labor-land ratio leads to a declining marginal product of labor and hence to declining real wage rates.[2]

How bad could things get? The dour Reverend T. R. Malthus thought that population pressures would drive the economy to a point where workers were at the minimum level of subsistence. Malthus reasoned that whenever wages were above the subsistence level, population would expand; below-subsistence wages would lead to high mortality and population decline. Only at subsistence wages could there be a stable equilibrium of population. He believed the working classes were destined to a life that is brutish, nasty, and short. This gloomy picture led Thomas Carlyle to criticize economics as "the dismal science."

Figure 11-3(*a*) shows the process of economic growth in Smith's golden age. Here, as population doubles, the production-possibility frontier (*PPF*) shifts out by a factor of 2 in each direction, showing that there are no constraints on growth from land or resources. Figure 11-3(*b*) shows the pessimistic Malthusian case, where a doubling of population leads to a less-than-doubling of food and clothing, lowering per capita output, as more people crowd onto limited land and diminishing returns drive down output per person.

---

[2] The theory in this chapter relies on an important finding from microeconomics. In analysis of the determination of wages under simplified conditions, including perfect competition, it is shown that the wage rate of labor will be equal to the extra or marginal product of the last worker hired. For example, if the last worker contributes goods worth $12.50 per hour to the firm's output, then under competitive conditions the firm will be willing to pay up to $12.50 per hour in wages to that worker. Similarly, the rent on land is the marginal product of the last unit of land, and the real interest rate will be determined by the marginal product of the least productive piece of capital.

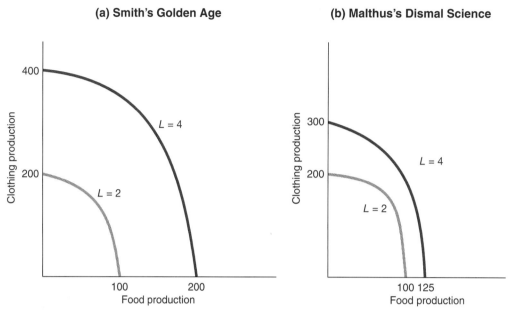

(a) Smith's Golden Age

(b) Malthus's Dismal Science

FIGURE 11-3. The Classical Dynamics of Smith and Malthus

In **(a)**, unlimited land on the frontier means that when population doubles, labor can simply spread out and produce twice the quantity of any food and clothing combination. In **(b)**, limited land means that increasing population from 2 million to 4 million triggers diminishing returns. Note that potential food production rises by only 25 percent with a doubling of labor inputs.

Are there limits to growth?

Often, earlier ideas reemerge in light of new social trends or scientific findings. In the last two decades, Malthusian ideas have surfaced as many antigrowth advocates and environmentalists have argued that economic growth is limited due to the finiteness of our natural resources and because of environmental constraints.

Economic growth involves a rapid increase in the use of land and mineral resources and (if not controlled) in the emissions of air and water pollution. For example, U.S. energy consumption from fuels totaled 220 trillion Btu (British thermal units) in 1850. By 1900, the total reached 7600 trillion Btu, and in 1995 energy use was 66,000 trillion Btu. At the same time, the emissions of sulfur dioxide grew from around 0.2 million tons annually in 1850, peaked at 31 million tons in 1970, and declined to 20 million tons in 1997. This important example shows why people are concerned that rapid economic growth may lead to resource exhaustion and environmental degradation.

Worries about the viability of growth surfaced prominently with a series of studies in the early 1970s by an ominous-sounding group called the "Club of Rome." Growth critics found a receptive audience because of mounting alarm about rapid population growth in developing countries and, after 1973, the upward spiral in oil prices and the sharp decline in the growth of productivity and living standards in the major industrial countries. This first wave of anxiety subsided with declines in natural-resource prices after 1980 and slowing population growth in developing countries.

A second wave of growth pessimism emerged over the last decade. It involves not the depletion of mineral resources like oil and gas but the presence of environmental constraints on long-term economic growth. The possibility of global environmental problems arises because of mounting scientific evidence that industrial activity is significantly changing the earth's climate and ecosystems. Among today's concerns are global warming, in which use of fossil fuels is warming the climate;

widespread evidence of acid rain; the appearance of the Antarctic "ozone hole" along with ozone depletion in temperate regions; deforestation, especially of the tropical rain forests, which may upset the global ecological balance; soil erosion, which threatens the long-term viability of agriculture; and species extinction, which threatens to limit potential future medical and other technologies.

Global environmental constraints are closely linked to the Malthusian constraints of an earlier age. Whereas Malthus held that production would be limited by finite land, today's growth pessimists argue that growth will be limited by the finite absorptive capacity of our environment. We can, some say, burn only a limited amount of fossil fuel before we face the threat of dangerous climate change. The need to reduce the use of fossil fuels might well slow our long-term economic growth.

The dilemma is illustrated in Figure 11-4. An economy begins in period 1 with the illustrated *PPF* between environmental quality and output labeled as *AA*. Economic growth without technological change moves the *PPF* to *BB*. In this new situation, society might experience higher output at the expense of deteriorating environmental quality. A happier state occurs when technological change—introducing equipment to mine and burn low-sulfur coal, requiring pollution-control devices on automobiles, or developing economical solar power—pushes out the *PPF* to *CC* so that society can have both more output and a cleaner environment.

What is the empirical evidence on the effect of resource exhaustion and environmental limits on economic growth? There is evidence that the quality of land and mineral resources has deteriorated over the last century and that we are required to drill deeper for oil, use more marginal lands, and mine lower-grade mineral ores. But until now technological advance has largely outweighed these trends, so the prices of oil, gas, most minerals, and land have actually declined relative to the price of labor. Moreover, new environmentally friendly technologies have become increasingly important, and many of the worst environmental abuses have been alleviated in the last two decades. Nonetheless, environmental constraints have become more costly, and some economists believe that the United States has experienced a significant slowdown in measured productivity growth because of the costs of environmental regulations.

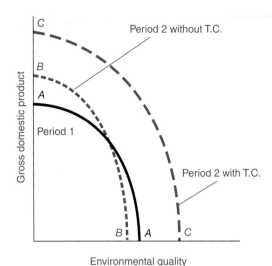

FIGURE 11-4. Environmental Constraints Can Be Overcome with New Technologies

Economic growth with resource and environmental constraints can increase GDP from period 1 to period 2. This may result in a deterioration in environmental quality when old, polluting technologies continue to be employed and there are no environmental regulations. The pessimistic case is shown by the *BB* curve labeled "Period 2 without T.C." (i.e., without technological change). However, application of prudent environmental policies along with development of environmentally sound new technologies may push the *PPF* outward to *CC* so that a society can have its environmental cake and eat a full measure of GDP as well.

Economic Growth with Capital Accumulation: The Neoclassical Growth Model

Malthus's forecast was dramatically wide of the mark because he did not recognize that technological innovation and capital investment could overcome the law of diminishing returns. Land did not become the limiting factor in production. Instead, the first Industrial Revolution brought forth power-driven machinery that increased production, factories that gathered teams of workers into giant firms, railroads and steamships that linked together the far points of the world, and iron and steel that made possible stronger machines and faster locomotives. As market economies entered the twentieth century, a second Industrial Revolution grew up around the telephone, automobile, and electricity industries. Capital accumulation and new technologies became the dominant force affecting economic development. Moreover, if the growth pessimists of today prove wrong, it will be largely because new environmentally friendly and resource-saving capital replaces today's resource-intensive, polluting technologies.

To understand how capital accumulation and technological change affect the economy, we must understand the **neoclassical model of economic growth.** This approach was pioneered by Robert Solow of MIT, who was awarded the 1987 Nobel Prize for this and other contributions to economic-growth theory. The neoclassical growth model serves as the basic tool for understanding the growth process in advanced countries and has been applied in empirical studies of the sources of economic growth.

Apostle of economic growth

Robert M. Solow was born in Brooklyn and educated at Harvard and then moved to the MIT Economics Department in 1950. Over the next few years he developed the neoclassical growth model and applied it in the growth-accounting framework discussed later in this chapter. One of Solow's major studies was "A Contribution to the Theory of Economic Growth" in 1956. This was a mathematical version of the neoclassical growth model surveyed in this chapter. The importance of this study was highlighted as follows in Solow's Nobel Prize citation:

> Solow's theoretical model had an enormous impact on economic analysis. From simply being a tool for the analysis of the growth process, the model has been generalized in several different directions. It has been extended by the introduction of other types of production factors and it has been reformulated to include stochastic features. The design of dynamic links in certain "numerical" models employed in general equilibrium analysis has also been based on Solow's model. But, above all, Solow's growth model constitutes a framework within which modern macroeconomic theory can be structured.
>
> The increased interest of government to expand education and research and development was inspired by these studies. Every long-term report ... for any country has used a Solow-type analysis.[3]

Solow has also contributed to empirical studies of economic growth, to natural-resource economics, and to the development of capital theory. In addition, Solow served as a macroeconomic adviser for the Kennedy administration.

Solow is known for his enthusiasm for economics as well as for his humor. He worries that the hunger for publicity has led some economists to exaggerate their knowledge. He criticized economists for "an apparently irresistible urge to push their science further than it will go, to answer questions more delicate than our limited understanding of a complicated question will allow. Nobody likes to say 'I don't know.'"

A lively writer, Solow worries that economics is terrifically difficult to explain to the public. At his news conference after winning the Nobel Prize, Solow quipped, "The attention span of the people you write for is shorter than the length of one true sentence." Nonetheless, Solow continues to labor for his brand of economics, and the world increasingly listens to the apostle of economic growth from MIT.

Basic Assumptions. The neoclassical growth model describes an economy in which a single homogeneous output is produced by two types of inputs—capital and labor. In contrast to the Malthusian analysis, labor growth is assumed to be a given. In addition, we assume that the economy is competitive and always operates at full employment, so we can analyze the growth of potential output.

The major new ingredients in the neoclassical growth model are capital and technological change. For the moment, assume that technology remains constant. Capital consists of durable produced goods that are used to make other goods. Capital goods include structures like factories and houses, equipment like computers and machine tools, and inventories of finished goods and goods in process.

For convenience, we will assume that there is a single kind of capital good (call it K). We then measure the aggregate stock of capital as the total quantity of capital goods. In our real-world calculations, we approximate the universal capital good as the total dollar value of capital goods (i.e., the constant-dollar value of equipment, structures, and inventories). If L is the number of workers, then (K/L) is equal to the quantity of capital per worker, or the

---

[3] The citations of the committees for the Nobel Prizes in economics can be found on the Internet at www.nobel.se/laureates.

capital-labor ratio. We can write our aggregate production function for the neoclassical growth model without technological change as $Q = F(K, L)$.

Turning now to the economic-growth process, economists stress the need for **capital deepening,** which is the process by which the quantity of capital per worker increases over time. Examples of capital deepening include the multiplication of farm machinery and irrigation systems in farming, of railroads and highways in transportation, and of the increasing use of computers in banking. These are all examples of how the economy invests in capital goods, increasing the amount of capital per worker. As a result, the output per worker has grown enormously in farming, transportation, and banking.

What happens to the return on capital in the process of capital deepening? For a given state of technology, a rapid rate of investment in plant and equipment tends to depress the rate of return on capital.[4] This occurs because the most worthwhile investment projects get undertaken first, after which later investments become less and less valuable. Once a full railroad network or telephone system has been constructed, new investments will branch into more sparsely populated regions or duplicate existing lines. The rates of return on these later investments will be lower than the high returns on the first lines between densely populated regions.

In addition, the wage rate paid to workers will tend to rise as capital deepening takes place. Why? Each worker has more capital to work with and his or her marginal product therefore rises. As a result, the competitive wage rate rises along with the marginal product of labor.

We can summarize the impact of capital deepening in the neoclassical growth model as follows:

Capital deepening occurs when the stock of capital grows more rapidly than the labor force. In the absence of technological change, capital deepening will produce a growth of output per worker, of the marginal product of labor, and of real wages; it also will lead to diminishing returns on capital and therefore to a decline in the rate of return on capital.

---

[4] Under perfect competition and without risk, taxes, or inflation, the rate of return on capital is equal to the real interest rate on bonds and other financial assets.

Geometrical Analysis of the Neoclassical Model

We can analyze the effects of capital accumulation by using Figure 11-5. This figure shows the aggregate production function graphically by depicting output per worker on the vertical axis and capital per worker on the horizontal axis. In the background, *and held constant for the moment,* are all the other variables that were discussed at the start of this section—the amount of land, the endowment of natural resources, and, most important of all, the technology used by the economy.

What happens as the society accumulates capital? As each worker has more and more capital to work with, the economy moves up and to the right on the aggregate production function. Say that the capital-labor ratio increases, from $(K/L)_0$ to $(K/L)_1$. Then the amount of output per worker increases, from $(Q/L)_0$ to $(Q/L)_1$.

What happens to the factor prices of labor and capital? As capital deepens, diminishing returns to capital set in, so the rate of return on capital and the real interest rate fall. (The slope of the curve

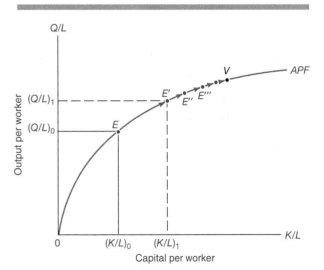

FIGURE 11-5. Economic Growth through Capital Deepening

As the amount of capital per worker increases, output per worker also increases. This graph shows the importance of "capital deepening," or increasing the amount of capital each worker has on hand. Remember, however, that other factors are held constant, such as technology, quality of the labor force, and natural resources.

in Figure 11-5 is the marginal product of capital, which is seen to fall as capital deepening occurs.) Also, because each worker can work with more capital, workers' marginal productivities rise and the real wage rate consequently also rises. The reverse would happen if the amount of capital per workers were to fall for some reason. For example, wars tend to reduce much of a nation's capital to rubble and lower the capital-labor ratio; after wars, therefore, we see a scarcity of capital and high returns on capital. Hence, our earlier verbal summary of the impact of capital deepening is verified by the analysis in Figure 11-5.

Long-Run Steady State. What is the long-run equilibrium in the neoclassical growth model without technological change? Eventually, the capital-labor ratio will stop rising. *In the long-run, the economy will enter a steady state in which capital deepening ceases, real wages stop growing, and capital returns and real interest rates are constant.*

We can show how the economy moves toward the steady state in Figure 11-5 on the last page. As capital continues to accumulate, the capital-labor ratio increases as shown by the arrows from E' to E'' to E''' until finally the capital-labor ratio stops growing at V. At that point, output per worker (Q/L) is constant, and real wages stop growing.

Without technological change, output per worker and the wage rate stagnate. This is certainly a far better outcome than the world of subsistence wages predicted by Malthus. But the long-run equilibrium of the neoclassical growth model makes it clear that if economic growth consists only of accumulating capital through replicating factories with existing methods of production, then the standard of living will eventually stop rising.

The Importance of Technological Change

While the capital-accumulation model is a good first step down the road to understanding economic growth, it leaves some major questions unanswered. To begin with, the model with an unchanging technology predicts that real wages will gradually stagnate. But real wages have certainly not stagnated in the twentieth century. Additionally, it cannot explain the tremendous growth in productivity over time, nor does it account for the tremendous differences in per capita income among countries.

What is missing is technological change. We can depict technological change in our growth diagram as an upward shift in the aggregate production function, as illustrated in Figure 11-6. In this diagram, we show the aggregate production function for both 1950 and 2000. Because of technological change, the aggregate production function has shifted upward from APF_{1950} to APF_{2000}. This upward shift shows the advances in productivity that are generated by the vast array of new processes and products like electronics, computers, advances in metallurgy, improved service technologies, and so forth.

Therefore, in addition to considering the capital deepening described above, we must also take into account advances in technology. The sum of capital deepening and technological change is the arrow in Figure 11-6, which produces an increase in output per worker from $(Q/L)_{1950}$ to $(Q/L)_{2000}$. Instead of settling into a steady state, the economy enjoys rising output per worker, rising wages, and increasing living standards.

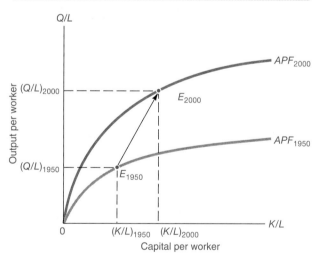

FIGURE 11-6. Technological Advance Shifts Up the Production Function

As a result of improvements in technology, the aggregate production function shifts *upward over time*. Hence improvements in technology combine with capital deepening to raise output per worker and real wages.

Of particular interest is the impact of changing technologies on rates of profits and real interest rates. As a result of technological progress, the real interest rate need not fall. Invention increases the productivity of capital and offsets the tendency for a falling rate of profit.

Technological Change as an Economic Output

Up to now we have treated technological change as something that floats mysteriously down from scientists and inventors like manna from heaven. Recent research on economic growth has begun to focus on the *sources of technological change*. This research, sometimes called *new growth theory* or the "theory of endogenous technological change," seeks to uncover the processes by which private market forces, public-policy decisions, and alternative institutions lead to different patterns of technological change.

One important point is that technological change is an output of the economic system. Edison's lightbulb was the result of years of research into different lightbulb designs; the transistor resulted from the efforts of scientists in Bell Labs to find a process that would improve telephone switching devices; pharmaceutical companies spend hundreds of millions of dollars doing research on and testing new drugs. Those who are talented and lucky may earn supernormal profits, or even become billionaires like Bill Gates of Microsoft, but many are the disappointed inventors or companies who end up with empty pockets.

The other unusual feature of technologies is that they are public goods, or "nonrival" goods in technical language. This means that they can be used by many people at the same time without being used up. A new piece of software, a new miracle drug, a design for a new steelmaking process—I can use each of these without reducing its productivity for you and the British and the Japanese and everyone else. In addition, inventions are expensive to produce but inexpensive to reproduce. These features of technological change can produce severe market failures—they mean that inventors sometimes have great difficulty profiting from their inventions because other people can copy them. The market failures are largest for the most basic and fundamental forms of research. Therefore, governments must be careful to ensure that inventors have adequate incentives to engage in research and development. Governments increasingly pay attention to *intellectual property rights*, such as patents and copyrights, to provide adequate market rewards for creative activities.

What is the major contribution of new growth theory? It has changed the way we think about the growth process and public policies. If technological differences are the major reason for differences in living standards among nations, and if technology is a produced factor, then economic-growth policy will have to focus much more sharply on how nations can improve their technological performance. This is just the lesson drawn by Stanford's Paul Romer, one of the leaders of new growth theory:

> Economists can once again make progress toward a complete understanding of the determinants of long-run economic success. Ultimately, this will put us in position to offer policymakers something more insightful than the standard neoclassical prescription —more saving and more schooling. We will be able to rejoin the ongoing policy debates about tax subsidies for private research, antitrust exemptions for research joint ventures, the activities of multinational firms, the effects of government procurement, the feedback between trade policy and innovation, the scope of protection for intellectual property rights, the links between private firms and universities, the mechanisms for selecting the research areas that receive public support, and the costs and benefits of an explicit government-led technology policy.[5]

To summarize:

Technological change—which increases output produced for a given bundle of inputs—is a crucial ingredient in the growth of nations. The new growth theory seeks to uncover the processes which generate technological change. This approach emphasizes that technological change is an output that is subject to severe market failures because technology is a public good that is expensive to produce but cheap to reproduce. Governments increasingly seek to provide strong intellectual property rights for those who develop new technologies.

---

[5] See Paul Romer in this chapter's Further Reading section.

✳

B. THE PATTERNS OF GROWTH IN THE UNITED STATES

The Facts of Economic Growth

The first part of this chapter described the basic theories of economic growth. But economists have not been content to rest with theory. A major research area all around the world has been measuring the different components of the economic-growth process and applying them to the important theories. An understanding of the patterns of economic growth will help sort out the reasons that some nations prosper while others decline.

Figure 11-7 depicts the key trends of economic development for the United States in the twentieth century. Similar patterns have been found in most of the major industrial countries.

Figure 11-7(a) shows the trends in real GDP, the capital stock, and population. Population and employment have more than tripled since 1900. At the same time, the stock of physical capital has risen more than tenfold. Thus the amount of capital per worker (the K/L ratio) has increased by a factor of almost 3. Clearly, capital deepening has been an important feature of twentieth-century American capitalism.

What about the growth in output? Has output grown less rapidly than capital, as would occur in a model that ignored technological change? No. The fact that the output curve in Figure 11-7(a) is not in between the two factor curves, but actually lies above the capital curve, demonstrates that technological progress must have increased the productivity of capital and labor. Indeed, the capital-output ratio—shown in Figure 11-7(b)—has fallen over time, rather than rising as would be expected in the capital-accumulation model without technological progress.

For most people, an economy's performance is measured by earnings, shown in Figure 11-7(c) in terms of real average hourly earnings (or money earnings corrected for inflation). Hourly earnings have grown impressively for most of this century, as we would expect from the growth in the capital-labor ratio and from steady technological advance.

The real interest rate (i.e., the money interest rate minus the rate of inflation) is shown in Figure 11-7(d). Interest rates and profit rates fluctuate greatly in business cycles and wars but display no strong trend upward or downward for the whole period. Either by coincidence or because of an economic mechanism inducing this pattern, technological change has largely offset diminishing returns to capital.

Output per worker-hour is the solid black curve in Figure 11-7(c). As could be expected from the deepening of capital and from technological advance, output per worker has risen steadily.

The fact that wages rise at the same rate as output per worker does not mean that labor has captured all the fruits of productivity advance. Rather, it means that labor has kept about the same share of total product, with capital also earning about the same relative share throughout the period. Actually, a close look at Figure 11-7(c) shows that real wages grew slightly faster than output per worker in the first three quarters of the twentieth century, but then grew more slowly recently. Over the entire century, real wages grew by a factor of nine, which is almost exactly the growth in output per hour worked. This implies that labor's share of national income (and therefore also property's share) changed very little over the course of the twentieth century.

💡 **Seven basic trends of economic growth**

Economists studying the economic history of the advanced nations have found that the following trends apply in most countries:

1. The capital stock has grown more rapidly than population and employment, resulting in capital deepening.
2. For most of the twentieth century, there has been a strong upward trend in real average hourly earnings.
3. The share of labor compensation in national income has been remarkably stable over the last century.
4. There have been major oscillations in real interest rates and the rate of profit, particularly during business cycles, but there was no strong upward or downward trend in the twentieth century.
5. Instead of steadily rising, which would be predicted by the law of diminishing returns with unchanging technology, the capital-output ratio has actually declined since 1900.
6. For most of the twentieth century, the ratios of national saving and of investment to GDP were stable.

(a) Output, Labor, Capital

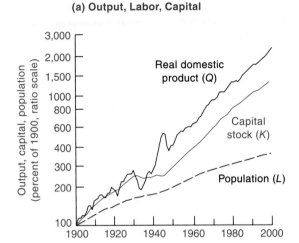

(b) Capital-Output Ratio

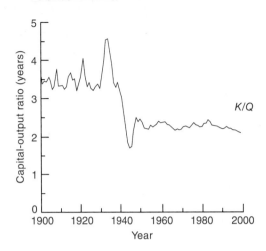

(c) Real Compensation and Output per Worker-Hour

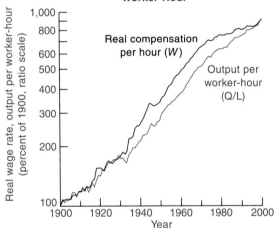

(d) Real Interest Rate

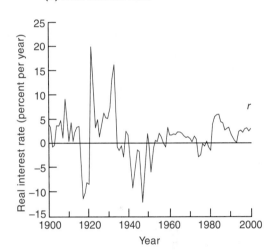

FIGURE 11-7. Economic Growth Displays Striking Regularities

(a) The capital stock has grown faster than population and labor supply. Nonetheless, total output has grown even more rapidly than capital. **(b)** The capital-output ratio declined sharply during the first half of the twentieth century, but it has remained steady over the last five decades. **(c)** Real average hourly earnings have grown steadily and at the same rate as average product per worker-hour over the entire century. Note the slowdown of growth in output, real wages, and productivity since 1973. **(d)** The real interest rate has been trendless over the twentieth century, suggesting that technological change has offset diminishing returns to capital accumulation. (Source: U.S. Departments of Commerce and Labor, Federal Reserve Board, U.S. Bureau of the Census, and historical studies by John Kendrick.)

Since 1980, the national saving rate has declined sharply in the United States.

7. After effects of the business cycle are removed, national product has grown at an average rate of close to 3 percent per year. Output growth has been much higher than a weighted average of the growth of capital, labor, and resource inputs, suggesting that technological innovation must have played a key role in economic growth.

Relationship of the Seven Trends to Economic-Growth Theories

While the seven trends of economic history are not like the immutable laws of physics, they do portray fundamental facts about growth in the modern era. How do they fit into our economic-growth theories?

Trends 2 and 1—higher wage rates when capital deepens—fit nicely into our neoclassical growth model shown in Figure 11-5. Trend 3—that the wage share has been remarkably stable—is an interesting coincidence that is consistent with a wide variety of production functions relating Q to L and K.

Trends 4 and 5, however, warn us that technological change must be playing a role here, so Figure 11-6, with its picture of advancing technology, is more realistic than the steady state depicted in Figure 11-5. A steady profit rate and a declining, or steady, capital-output ratio cannot hold if the K/L ratio rises in a world with unchanging technology; taken together, they contradict the basic law of diminishing returns under deepening of capital. We must therefore recognize the key role of technological progress in explaining the seven trends of modern economic growth. Our models confirm what our intuition suggests.

The Sources of Economic Growth

We have seen that advanced market economies grow through increases in labor and capital and by technological change as well. But what are the relative contributions of labor, capital, and technology? To answer this question, we turn to an analysis of the quantitative aspects of growth and of the useful approach known as growth accounting. This approach is the first step in the quantitative analysis of economic growth for any country.

The Growth-Accounting Approach. Detailed studies of economic growth rely on what is called **growth accounting.** This technique is not a balance sheet or national product account of the kind we met in earlier chapters. Rather, it is a way of separating out the contributions of the different ingredients driving observed growth trends.

Growth accounting usually begins with the aggregate production function we met earlier in this chapter, $Q = AF(K, L, R)$. Often resources are omitted because land is constant. Using elementary calculus and some simplifying assumptions, we can express the growth of output in terms of the growth of the inputs plus the contribution of technological change. Growth in output (Q) can be decomposed into three separate terms: growth in labor (L) times its weight, growth in capital (K) times its weight, and technological innovation itself (T.C.).

Momentarily ignoring technological change, an assumption of constant returns to scale means that a 1 percent growth in L together with a 1 percent growth in K will lead to a 1 percent growth in output. But suppose L grows at 1 percent and K at 5 percent. It is tempting, but wrong, to guess that Q will then grow at 3 percent, the simple average of 1 and 5. Why wrong? Because the two factors do not necessarily contribute equally to output. Rather, the fact that three-fourths of national income goes to labor while only one-fourth goes to capital suggests that labor growth will contribute more to output than will capital growth.

If labor's growth rate gets 3 times the weight of K's, we can calculate the answer as follows: Q will grow at 2 percent per year (= $\frac{3}{4}$ of 1 percent + $\frac{1}{4}$ of 5 percent). To growth of inputs, we add technological change and thereby obtain all the sources of growth.

Hence, output growth per year follows the *fundamental equation of growth accounting*:

$$\% \ Q \text{ growth} \tag{1}$$
$$= \tfrac{3}{4}(\% \ L \text{ growth}) + \tfrac{1}{4}(\% \ K \text{ growth}) + \text{T.C.}$$

where "T.C." represents technological change (or total factor productivity) that raises productivity and where $\frac{3}{4}$ and $\frac{1}{4}$ are the relative contributions of each input to economic growth. Under conditions of perfect competition, these fractions are equal to the shares of national income of the two factors;

naturally, these fractions would be replaced by new fractions if the relative shares of the factors were to change or if other factors were added.

To explain per capita growth, we can eliminate L as a separate growth source. Now, using the fact that capital gets one-fourth of output, we have from equation (1)

$$\% \frac{Q}{L} \text{ growth} = \% \ Q \text{ growth} - \% \ L \text{ growth}$$
$$= \frac{1}{4} \left(\% \frac{K}{L} \text{ growth} \right) + \text{T.C.} \tag{2}$$

This relation shows clearly how capital deepening would affect per capita output if technological advance were zero. Output per worker would grow only one-fourth as fast as capital per worker, reflecting diminishing returns.

One final point remains: We can measure Q growth, K growth, and L growth, as well as the shares of K and L. But how can we measure T.C. (technological change)? We cannot. Rather, we must *infer* T.C. as the residual or leftover after the other components of output and inputs are calculated. Thus if we examine the equation above, T.C. is calculated by subtraction from equation (1) as

$$\text{T.C.} = \% \ Q \text{ growth} - \frac{3}{4} (\% \ L \text{ growth})$$
$$- \frac{1}{4} (\% \ K \text{ growth}) \tag{3}$$

This equation allows us to answer critically important questions about economic growth. What part of per capita output growth is due to capital deepening, and what part is due to technological advance? Does society progress chiefly by dint of thrift and the forgoing of current consumption? Or is our rising living standard the reward for the ingenuity of inventors and the daring of innovator-entrepreneurs?

Numerical Example. To determine the contributions of labor, capital, and other factors in output growth, we substitute representative numbers for the period 1900–1999 into equation (2) for the growth of Q/L. Since 1900, worker-hours have grown 1.3 percent per year, and K has grown 2.5 percent per year, while Q has grown 3.1 percent per year. Thus, by arithmetic, we find that

$$\% \frac{Q}{L} \text{ growth} = \frac{1}{4} (\% \frac{K}{L} \text{ growth}) + \text{T.C.}$$

becomes

$$1.8 = \frac{1}{4} (1.2) + \text{T.C.} = 0.3 + 1.5$$

Thus of the 1.8 percent–per-year increase in output per worker, about 0.3 percentage point is due to capital deepening, while the largest portion, 1.5 percent per year, stems from T.C. (technological change).

Detailed Studies. More thorough studies refine the simple calculation but show quite similar conclusions. Table 11-3 on page 238 presents the results of studies by the Department of Labor for the 1948–1997 period. During this time, output (measured as gross output of the private business sector) grew at an average rate of 3.5 percent per year, while input growth (of capital, labor, and land) contributed 2.2 percentage points per year. Hence **total factor productivity**—the growth of output less the growth of the weighted sum of all inputs, or what we have called T.C—averaged 1.3 percent annually.

Somewhat less than two-thirds of the growth in output in the United States can be accounted for by the growth in labor and capital. The remaining third is a residual factor that can be attributed to education, research and development, innovation, economies of scale, advances in knowledge, and other factors.

Other countries show different patterns of growth. For example, scholars have used growth accounting to study the Soviet Union, which grew rapidly during the period from 1930 until the mid-1960s. It appears, however, that the high growth rate came primarily from forced-draft increases in capital and labor inputs. For the last few years of the U.S.S.R.'s existence, productivity actually *declined* as the central-planning apparatus became more dysfunctional, as corruption deepened, and as incentives worsened. On the whole, the estimated pace of growth in total factor productivity for the Soviet Union over the half-century before its collapse was slower than that for the United States and other major market economies. Only the ability of the central government forcibly to divert output into investment (and away from consumption) offset the system's inefficiency.

Contribution of Different Elements to Growth in Real GDP, United States, 1948–1997	In percent per year	As percent of total
Real GDP growth (private business sector)	3.52	100
Contribution of inputs	2.22	63
Capital	0.66	19
Labor	1.56	44
Total factor productivity growth (research and development, education, advances in knowledge, and other sources)	1.30	37

TABLE 11-3. Advances in Knowledge Outweigh Capital in Contributing to Economic Growth

Studies using the techniques of growth accounting break down the growth of GDP in the private business sector into contributing factors. Recent comprehensive studies find that capital growth accounted for 19 percent of output growth. Education, research and development, and other advances in knowledge made up 37 percent of total output growth and about half of the growth of output per worker. (Source: U.S. Department of Labor.)

THE PRODUCTIVITY SLOWDOWN

Given the importance of productivity to living standards, economists viewed with alarm the decline in U.S. productivity growth. This break in the trend, which is called the **productivity slowdown,** can be seen in Figure 11-8. This graph shows the growth in labor productivity in the private business economy. (Growth in multifactor productivity has been somewhat lower but shows similar trends.) Labor productivity growth began to slow in the early 1970s. A careful look at the data indicates that labor productivity slowed in virtually all sectors of the economy. Among the areas with the biggest deterioration in productivity were mining, construction, and services. Similar patterns, with a slowdown of productivity growth in the aggregate and in most sectors after 1970, characterize all major industrial countries.

Productivity is particularly important because of its association with growth in living standards. Table 11-4 shows the effect of the productivity decline on real wages. Some elementary arithmetic shows that if labor's share of national income is constant, this implies that real wages will grow at the rate of growth of labor productivity.[6] The slowdown in productivity in the last two decades is therefore largely responsible for the stagnation in living standards over that period. Those who entered the labor force after World War II experienced healthy growth in real wages, while the average worker over the last three decades experienced very slow growth in living standards.

Explaining the Slowdown. Studies of productivity point to a number of unfavorable factors converging on the American economy at about the same time, including the following:

- Beginning in the 1970s, environmental regulations required that firms spend substantial sums on plant and operations to reduce pollution and

---

[6] To see this relationship, write labor's share as $W \times L = s \times P \times Q$, where s = labor's share, W = money wage rate, L = hours of work, P = price index, and Q = output. Dividing both sides by L and P yields $(W/P) = s \times (Q/L)$, which signifies that the real wage equals labor's share times labor productivity. Hence, if the share of labor of national income is constant, real wages will grow at the same rate as labor productivity.

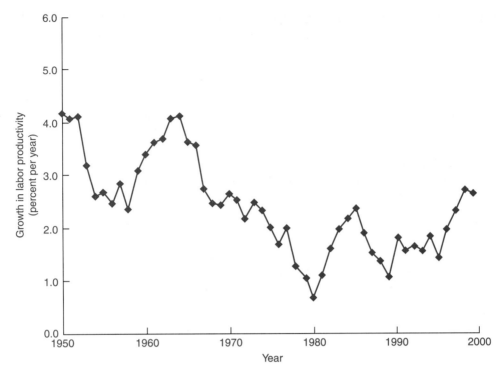

FIGURE 11-8. Productivity Growth Slowed in 1970s but Recovered in Late 1990s

The growth in labor productivity, or output per hour worked in the private business sector, is the most important factor in growing living standards. Productivity growth slowed from an average rate of 3.2 percent per year in the 1948–1973 period to 1.7 percent per year from 1973 to 1999. Spurred by tremendous gains in computers and electronics, productivity growth has moved up in recent years. (Source: U.S. Department of Labor; figures are 5-year averages.)

Productivity and Real Wages		
	Average Annual Percentage Growth in:	
Period	**Labor productivity**	**Real wages**
1959–1973	3.4	2.9
1973–1999	1.7	0.9

TABLE 11-4. Real Wages Mirror Productivity Growth

Over the long run, real wages tend to move with trends in labor productivity. After the productivity slowdown in 1973, real wages stagnated. (Source: U.S. Department of Labor. Productivity is for the U.S. business sector; nominal compensation is deflated using the consumer price index.)

improve worker and consumer safety, yet these improvements did not show up as measured output increases. One of the most dramatic cases was productivity in nuclear-power plants, in which regulations increased costs so sharply that they became uneconomical to build and sometimes even to run.

- The increase in energy prices in the 1970s led firms to substitute other inputs (labor and capital) for energy. As a result, the productivity of labor and capital declined relative to earlier periods.
- Labor economists believe that a deterioration in labor quality (or perhaps a slowdown in the increase in quality) was a contributor to the

productivity-growth slowdown. The important indicators here include a deterioration in test scores of American students and a sharp increase in the share of low-skilled immigrants in the workforce.

A brave new world for productivity?

Economists have been waiting for an upturn in productivity growth, hoping that the revolution in information technology would spur rapid growth throughout the economy. Indeed, innovations in information technology (computer hardware, software, and communications) have produced astonishing improvements in every corner of the economy. The prices of computers have fallen more than a thousand-fold in the last three decades. Electronic mail and the Internet are changing the face of retailing. Computers are the nerve system of business—running airline pricing and reservation systems, scanning price and quantity data in stores, dispatching electricity, clearing checks, dunning taxpayers, and sending students their tuition bills. Some economists think that computers are like a new fourth factor of production.

Until recently, experts were puzzled, in the words of Robert Solow, that "[c]omputers can be found everywhere except in the productivity statistics." Even as computers invaded every aspect of economic life, productivity growth showed little response. But this changed in about 1995, when productivity began growing rapidly and regained a substantial part of the ground lost after 1973. Having grown at 3.2 percent per year from 1948 to 1973, productivity growth slowed to 1.4 percent in the 1973–1995 period; productivity then surged ahead at 2.9 percent per year from 1995 to 1999 (see the first set of bars in Figure 11-9).

Enthusiasts spoke of a "new era" and a "brave new world of American capitalism." Even Fed Chairman Alan Greenspan, known primarily for his understatement, joined technological enthusiasts, arguing, "A perceptible quickening in the pace at which technological innovations are applied argues for the hypothesis that the recent acceleration in labor productivity is not just a cyclical phenomenon or a statistical aberration, but reflects, at least in part, a more deep-seated, still developing, shift in our economic landscape."

Economists who have looked at the numbers under a microscope have uncovered some interesting facts about productivity in the late 1990s. Among the important factors in the productivity acceleration were the following:

- *Productivity explosion in computers.* The productivity explosion (and consequent price decline) in computers is extraordinary. From 1972 to 1995, the relative price of computers fell at about 18 percent per year, and in the 1995–1999 period the decline amounted to 29 percent per year. Computer productivity alone added 0.23 percent per year to the productivity acceleration after 1995.
- *Capital deepening because of investment in computers.* Companies have invested heavily in computers and software over the 1990s. According to the Council of Economic Advisers, this investment has added almost 0.5 percent per year to labor productivity.
- *Pro-cyclical productivity.* The final factor leading to strong productivity growth in the 1995–1999 period was the robust economy and strong output growth.

Putting all these factors together, the Council of Economic Advisers estimated that one-half of the upturn in labor productivity in the late 1990s—about 0.70 percent per year—was due to production and use of computers. The balance was a combination of cyclical productivity and productivity increases in other sectors.

Some economists believe that outside of computers and measurement, there has been little or no improvement in productivity growth. Figure 11-9 shows the trends in different parts of the economy using estimates by Robert Gordon. Productivity growth in the nonfarm business economy has definitely increased in the last 4 years. According to Gordon, however, the entire upturn in manufacturing productivity growth is due to computers while the improvement in nonmanufacturing is due to the business cycle and to measurement improvements.

Many are skeptical about this controversial finding. They point to the fact that overall productivity growth in the late 1990s was actually above the long-term trend. They also argue that much of the benefit of the information revolution is not captured in the official numbers. Some economists have found that productivity is significantly underestimated for software and communications equipment (see the discussion of price measurement in Chapter 5). Or consider the time that consumers save by shopping on the Internet, the saving of time and postage from the switch from snail-mail to e-mail, or the convenience of cellular telephones—none of these show up in measured productivity. Others think the true gains from

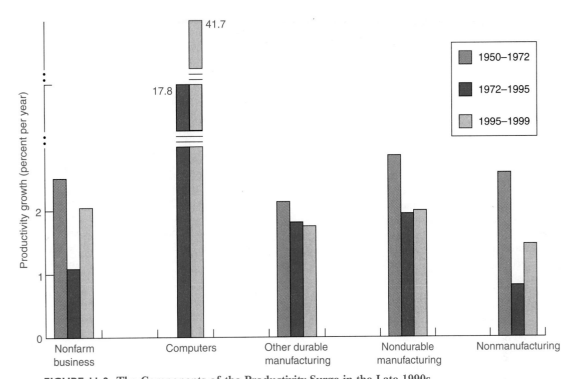

FIGURE 11-9. The Components of the Productivity Surge in the Late 1990s

Productivity growth turned up sharply in the late 1990s. Analysis points to the tremendous increase in productivity in computers, to capital deepening, and to the long economic expansion as the key factors behind the upturn. (Source: Robert J. Gordon and the Bureau of Labor Statistics.)

computers lie in the future. Stanford economic historian Paul David, who has studied past inventions like the electric motor, believes that it takes decades for the economy to reap the full benefits of fundamental inventions.

Whether or not productivity made a permanent upward turn, it is clear that computers are shaping our economy and our lives in surprising ways.[7]

---

[7] See "Websites" in this chapter's Further Reading section for references to the *Economic Report of the President, 2000,* and to the Gordon article.

This concludes our introduction to the principles of economic growth. The next chapter applies these principles to the struggle of poor countries to improve their living standards. In the remaining chapters in this part, we open our inquiry to international trade and finance.

SUMMARY

A. Theories of Economic Growth

1. The analysis of economic growth examines the factors that lead to the growth of potential output over the long run. The growth in output per capita is an important objective of government because it is associated with rising average real incomes and living standards.

2. Reviewing the experience of nations over space and time, we see that the economy rides on the four wheels of economic growth: (*a*) the quantity and quality of its labor force; (*b*) the abundance of its land and other natural resources; (*c*) the stock of accumulated capital; and, perhaps most important, (*d*) the technological change and innovation that allow greater output to be produced with the same inputs. There is no unique combination of these four ingredients, however; the United States, Europe, and Asian countries have followed different paths to economic success.

3. The classical models of Smith and Malthus describe economic development in terms of land and population. In the absence of technological change, increasing population ultimately exhausts the supply of free land. The resulting increase in population density triggers the law of diminishing returns, so growth produces higher land rents with lower competitive wages. The Malthusian equilibrium is attained when the wage rate has fallen to the subsistence level, below which population cannot sustain itself. In reality, however, technological change has kept economic development progressing in industrial countries by continually shifting the productivity curve of labor upward.

4. Concerns about limitations of natural resources and increasing environmental spillovers from economic activity have led many to question whether economic growth at present rates can long continue. One set of worries based on limited supplies of land, energy, and mineral resources has receded with continuing new discoveries and resource-saving technological change. Global environmental constraints may lead to costly environmental damages or the need for expensive preventive measures.

5. Capital accumulation with complementary labor forms the core of modern growth theory in the neoclassical growth model. This approach uses a tool known as the aggregate production function, which relates inputs and technology to total potential GDP. In the absence of technological change and innovation, an increase in capital per worker (capital deepening) would not be matched by a proportional increase in output per worker because of diminishing returns to capital. Hence, capital deepening would lower the rate of return on capital (equal to the real interest rate under risk-free competition) while raising real wages.

6. Technological change increases the output producible with a given bundle of inputs. This pushes upward the aggregate production function, making more output available with the same inputs of labor and capital. Recent analysis in the "new growth theory" seeks to uncover the processes which generate technological change. This approach emphasizes (*a*) that technological change is an output of the economic system, (*b*) that technology is a public or nonrival good that can be used simultaneously by many people, and (*c*) that new inventions are expensive to produce but inexpensive to reproduce. These features mean that governments must pay careful attention to ensuring that inventors have adequate incentives, through strong intellectual property rights, to engage in research and development.

B. The Patterns of Growth in the United States

7. Numerous trends of economic growth are seen in data for the twentieth century. Among the key findings are that real wages and output per hour worked have risen steadily, although there has been a marked slowdown since the 1970s; that the real interest rate has shown no major trend; and that the capital-output ratio has declined. The major trends are consistent with the neoclassical growth model augmented by technological advance. Thus economic theory confirms what economic history tells us—that technological advance increases the productivity of inputs and improves wages and living standards.

8. The last trend, continual growth in potential output over the twentieth century, raises the important question of the sources of economic growth. Applying quantitative techniques, economists have used growth accounting to determine that "residual" sources—such as technological change and education—outweigh capital deepening in their impact on GDP growth or labor productivity.

9. After 1970, productivity growth slowed under the weight of energy-price increases, increasing environmental regulation, and other structural changes. In the late 1990s, however, the explosion of productivity and investment in computers along with improved measurement have led to a sharp upturn in measured productivity growth.

CONCEPTS FOR REVIEW

four wheels of growth:
   labor
   resources
   capital
   technology
aggregate production function
Smith's golden age
capital-labor ratio
Malthus's limited land

modern Malthusianism: limited
   resources and environmental
   constraints
neoclassical growth model
K/L rise as capital deepens
new growth theory
technology as a produced good
seven trends of economic growth

growth accounting:
   % Q growth = $3/4$ (% L growth)
   + 1/4 (% K growth)
   + T.C.
   % Q/L growth = $1/4$ (% K/L
   growth) + T.C.
recent productivity trends: slowdown
   and computer-led upturn

FURTHER READING AND INTERNET WEBSITES

Further Reading

One of the best surveys of economic growth is Robert Solow, *Economic Growth* (Oxford University Press, Oxford, U.K., 1970). See his pathbreaking article, "A Contribution to the Theory of Economic Growth," *Quarterly Journal of Economics*, 1956. The text reference is William Baumol, "Entreprenuership: Productive, Unproductive, and Destructive," *Journal of Political Economy*, October 1990, pp. 893–921.

Two excellent recent books on growth economics are Charles Jones, *Introduction to Economic Growth* (Norton, New York, 1977) and the more technical monograph by Robert Barro and Xavier Sala-i-Martin, *Economic Growth* (McGraw-Hill, New York, 1995). A good survey of the role of technological change in growth theory is Paul Romer, "The Origins of Endogenous Growth," *Journal of Economic Perspectives*, Winter 1994, pp. 3–22.

Websites

A website devoted to economic growth is maintained by Jonathan Temple of Oxford at www.nuff.ox.ac.uk/

Economics/Growth and contains many references and links. The articles by Solow and Baumol are available at www.jstor.org. One of the most entertaining web pages among economists is maintained by growth theorist Xavier Sala-i-Martin at www.columbia.edu/~xs23.

Data sets on economic growth can be found at www.nuff. ox.ac.uk/Economics/Growth/datasets.htm. Technological change is often associated with particular inventions. The lives and patents of great inventors can be found at www. invent.org/book/index.html.

For those who wish to pursue the issue of productivity in the new economy, see *The Economic Report of the President 2000* at w3.access.gpo.gov/eop, Chapter 3. Also see Robert J. Gordon, "Has the 'New Economy' Rendered the Productivity Explosion Obsolete?" June 1999, available at Gordon's home page, www.econ.nwu.edu/faculty-frame. html. A convenient discussion is contained in *The Economist*, July 24–30, 1999, available at that magazine's archives at www.economist.com.

QUESTIONS FOR DISCUSSION

1. According to economic data, the living standards of a family in 1999 were about 6 times those of a family in 1900. What does this mean in terms of actual consumption patterns? Discuss with your parents or older relatives how your living standards today compare with those of their parents; make a comparison of the difference.

2. "If the government strengthens intellectual property rights, subsidizes basic science, and controls business cycles, we will see economic growth that would astound the classical economists." Explain what the writer meant by this statement.

3. "With zero population growth and no technological change, persistent capital accumulation would ulti-

mately destroy the capitalist class." Explain why such a scenario might lead to a zero real interest rate and to a disappearance of profits.

4. Recall the growth-accounting equation [equation (1) on page 236]. Calculate the growth of output if labor grows at 1 percent per year, capital grows at 4 percent per year, and technological change is $1\frac{1}{2}$ percent per year.

   How would your answer change if:
   a. Labor growth slowed to 0 percent per year?
   b. Capital growth increased to 5 percent per year?
   c. Labor and capital had equal shares in GDP?

   Also, calculate for each of these conditions the rate of growth of output per worker.

5. Reinterpret Figure 11-4 to explain why Malthus's predictions were faulty.

6. A brooding pessimist might argue that 1973 marked the end of the great expansion that began with the Industrial Revolution. Assume that all the features of the earlier era were still present today except that technological change and innovation were to cease. What would the new seven trends look like for coming decades? What would happen to the important real wage? What steps could be taken to counteract the new trends and put the economy back on the earlier path?

7. **Advanced problem:** Many fear that computers will do to humans what tractors and cars did to horses—the horse population declined precipitously early in this century after technological change made horses obsolete. If we treat computers as a particularly productive kind of K, what would their introduction do to the capital-labor ratio in Figure 11-5? Can total output go down with a fixed labor force? Under what conditions would the real wage decline? Can you see why the horse analogy might not apply?

Of the 6 billion people on this planet, perhaps 1 billion live in absolute poverty—barely able to survive from day to day. By contrast, the richest 1 percent, living in the affluent North, garner about 20 percent of world income. What causes the great differences in the wealth of nations? Can the world peacefully survive with poverty in the midst of plenty, with much conspicuous consumption and agricultural surpluses in America alongside starvation and environmental degradation in Africa? What steps can poorer nations take to improve their living standards? What are the responsibilities of affluent countries? These questions, concerning the obstacles facing developing countries, are among the greatest challenges facing modern economics. It is here that the tools of economics can make the greatest difference to people's daily lives. It is here that economics can literally make the difference between life and death. We begin by describing the characteristics of developing countries and reviewing some of the key ingredients in the process of economic development. The second part of this chapter examines alternative approaches to economic growth in developing countries, particularly the more successful models in Asia along with the failed communist experiment in Russia.

CHAPTER 12

The Challenge of Economic Development

I believe in materialism. I believe in all the proceeds of a healthy materialism— good cooking, dry houses, dry feet, sewers, drain pipes, hot water, baths, electric lights, automobiles, good roads, bright streets, long vacations away from the village pump, new ideas, fast horses, swift conversation, theaters, operas, orchestras, bands—I believe in them all for everybody. The man who dies without knowing these things may be as exquisite as a saint, and as rich as a poet; but it is in spite of, not because of, his deprivation.

Francis Hackett

A. ECONOMIC GROWTH IN POOR COUNTRIES

ASPECTS OF A DEVELOPING COUNTRY

What is meant by a developing country? The most important characteristic of a **developing country** is that it has low per capita income. In addition, people in developing countries usually have poor health and short life expectancy, have low levels of literacy, and suffer from malnutrition.

Table 12-1 is a key source of data for understanding the major players in the world economy, as well as important indicators of underdevelopment. Countries are grouped into the categories of low-income, lower-middle-income, upper-middle-income, and high-income economies.

A number of interesting features emerge from the table. Clearly, low-income countries are much poorer than advanced countries like the United States. People in countries with the lowest average incomes earn only about one-twentieth as much as people in high-income countries. For the table's data, *purchasing-power parity* calculations were used to measure relative incomes. Market exchange rates tend to understate the incomes of low-wage

245

| Country group | Population, 1998 (million) | Gross National Product (at purchasing-power parity exchange rates) | | | Adult illiteracy, 1998 (%) | Life expectancy at birth (years) |
| | | Total, 1998 ($, billion) | Per Capita GNP | | | |
			Level, 1998 ($)	Growth, 1990–1998 (% per year)		
Low-income economies	3,515	7,475.1	2,130	7.3	32	63
Excluding China and India	1,296	1,821.3	1,400	3.6	39	56
Lower-middle-income economies (e.g., Peru, Philippines, Thailand)	908	3,709.4	4,080	−1.3	15	68
Upper-middle-income economies (e.g., Brazil, Malaysia, Mexico)	588	4,606.3	7,830	3.9	11	68
High-income economies (e.g., United States, Japan, France)	885	20,766.0	23,440	2.1	<5	78

TABLE 12-1. Important Indicators for Different Country Groups

Countries are grouped by the World Bank into four major categories depending upon their per capita incomes. In each, a number of important indicators of economic development are shown. Note that low-income countries tend to have high illiteracy and low life expectancy. (Source: World Bank, *World Development Report*, www.worldbank.org.)

countries. (The use of purchasing-power parity exchange rates to evaluate living standards is discussed in Chapter 13.)

In addition, many social and health indicators show the effects of poverty in low-income nations. Life expectancy is low, and educational attainment and literacy are modest, reflecting low levels of investment in human capital.

There is a great diversity among developing countries. Some remain at the ragged edge of starvation—these are the poorest countries like Chad, Bangladesh, or Somalia. Other countries that were in that category two or three decades ago have graduated to the rank of middle-income countries. The more successful ones—Hong Kong, South Korea, and Taiwan—have graduated from the developing group, and the most successful of these have per capita incomes that have reached the ranks of high-income countries. Yesterday's successful developing countries will be tomorrow's high-income countries.

Life in low-income countries

To bring out the contrasts between advanced and developing economies, imagine that you are a typical 21-year-old in a low-income country such as Mali, India, or Bangladesh. You are poor. Even after making allowance for the goods that you produce and consume, your annual income barely averages $1000. Your counterpart in North America might have more than $30,000 in average earnings. Perhaps you can find cold comfort in the thought that only 1 person in 4 in the world averages more than $3000 in annual income.

For each of your fellow citizens who can read, there is one like you who is illiterate. Your life expectancy is four-fifths that of the average person in an advanced country; already two of your brothers and sisters have died before reaching adulthood. Birth rates are high, particularly for families where women receive no education, but mortality rates are also much higher here than in countries with good health-care systems.

Most people in your country work on farms. Few can be spared from food production to work in factories. You work with but one-sixtieth the horsepower of a prosperous North American worker. You know little about science, but much about your village traditions.

You and your fellow citizens in the 40 poorest countries constitute 55 percent of the world population but must divide among yourselves only 4 percent of world income. You are often hungry, and the food you eat is mainly roughage or rice. While you were among those who got some primary schooling, like most of your friends you did not go on to high school, and only the wealthiest go to a university. You work long hours in the fields without the benefit of machinery. At night you sleep on a mat. You have little household furniture, perhaps a table and a radio. Your only mode of transportation is an old pair of boots.

Human Development

This review of life in the poorest countries of the world reminds us of the importance of adequate incomes in meeting basic needs as well as the fact that life involves more than market incomes. An interesting new approach that combines economic indicators with social indicators is the *Human Development Index,* or HDI, developed by the United Nations Development Program with the assistance of economists Amartya Sen and Gustav Ranis. The HDI includes four different indexes: per capita real GDP, life expectancy at birth, school enrollment, and adult literacy. The idea is that economic growth should enrich people's health and education as well as their purses.

Figure 12-1 on page 248 shows a plot of the HDI and per capita output. The correlation is strong, but there are exceptions to the general positive relationship. Some countries, such as Algeria, Gabon, and Singapore, score poorly on the HDI scale for their income levels. Others—Costa Rica, Canada, and Sri Lanka—emphasize human development and score high relative to other countries with their income levels. This interesting new approach is a reminder that we should not neglect the human dimensions of economic growth.

THE FOUR ELEMENTS IN DEVELOPMENT

Having seen what it means to be a developing country, we now turn to an analysis of the process by which low-income countries improve their living standards. We saw in Chapter 11 that economic growth in the United States—growth in its potential output—rides on four wheels. These are (1) human resources, (2) natural resources, (3) capital formation, and (4) technology. These four wheels operate in rich and poor countries, although the mix and strategy for combining them will differ depending on the state of development. Let's see how each of the four wheels operates in developing countries and consider how public policy can steer the growth process in favorable directions.

Human Resources

Population Explosion: The Legacy of Malthus. Many poor countries are forever running hard just to stay in place. Even as a poor nation's GDP rises, so does its population. Recall our discussion in Chapter 11 of the Malthusian population trap, where population grows so rapidly that incomes remain at subsistence levels. While the high-income countries left Malthus behind long ago, Africa is still caught in the Malthusian bind of high birth rates and stagnant incomes. And the population expansion has not stopped—demographers project that the poor countries will add about 1 billion people over the next 25 years.

It's hard for poor countries to overcome poverty with birth rates so high. But there are escape routes from overpopulation. One strategy is to take an active role in curbing population growth, even when such actions run against prevailing religious norms. Many countries have introduced educational campaigns and subsidized birth control. China has been particularly forceful in curbing population growth among its more than 1 billion inhabitants, putting tight quotas on the number of births and imposing economic penalties and mandatory sterilization on those who violate their "baby quota."

And for countries which manage to boost their per capita incomes, there is the prospect of making the *demographic transition,* which occurs when a population stabilizes with low birth rates and low death rates. Once countries get rich enough, and infant

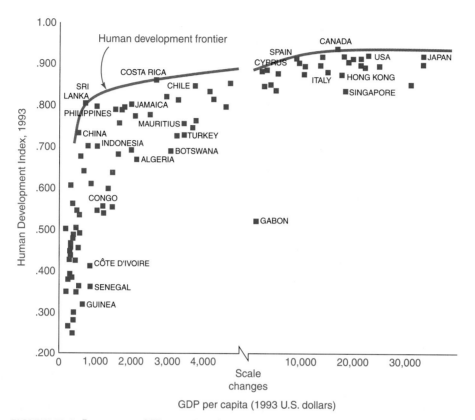

FIGURE 12-1. Incomes and Human Development Are Linked, but Some Countries Do Better for Their Income Levels

The Human Development Index (HDI) includes schooling, literacy, and life expectancy along with income. Most poor countries fare poorly on the HDI, but an emphasis on the human side of economic growth can reduce inequality and improve the quality of life. [Source: United Nations Development Program, *Human Development Report 1996* (Oxford, New York, 1996), p. 67.]

mortality drops, people voluntarily reduce their birth rates. When women are educated and emerge from subservience, they usually decide to spend less of their lives in childbearing. Families substitute quality for quantity—devoting time and incomes to a better education for fewer children. Mexico, Korea, and Taiwan have all seen their birth rates drop sharply as their incomes have risen and their populations have received more education.

Slowly the results of economic development and birth control are being felt. The birth rate in poor countries has declined from 42 per 1000 in 1965 to 30 per 1000 in 1990, but that's still far higher than

the birth rate of 13 per 1000 in the high-income countries. The struggle against poverty induced by excessive population growth continues.

But the demographic transition has not been reached everywhere. Fertility continues at a rapid pace in much of tropical Africa even as an AIDS epidemic rages through the population and lowers life expectancies in a way not experienced since the great plagues of earlier centuries. The specter of Malthus hangs over much of central Africa.

Human Capital. In addition to dealing with excessive population growth, developing countries must also be concerned with the quality of their human resources. Economic planners in developing countries emphasize the following specific programs: (1) *Control disease and improve health and nutrition.* Raising the population's health standards not only makes people happier but also makes them more productive workers. Health-care clinics and provision of safe drinking water are vitally useful social capital. (2) *Improve education, reduce illiteracy, and train workers.* Educated people are more productive workers because they can use capital more effectively, adopt new technologies, and learn from their mistakes. For advanced learning in science, engineering, medicine, and management, countries will benefit by sending their best minds abroad to bring back the newest advances. But countries must beware of the brain drain, in which the most able people get drawn off to high-wage countries. (3) *Above all, do not underestimate the importance of human resources.* Most other factors can be bought in the international marketplace. Most labor is home-grown, although labor can sometimes be augmented through immigration. The crucial role of skilled labor has been shown again and again when sophisticated mining, defense, or manufacturing machinery fell into disrepair and disuse because the labor force of developing countries had not acquired the necessary skills for its operation and maintenance.

Natural Resources

Some poor countries of Africa and Asia have meager endowments of natural resources, and such land and minerals as they do possess must be divided among dense populations. Perhaps the most valuable natural resource of developing countries is arable land. Much of the labor force in developing countries is employed in farming. Hence, the productive use of land—with appropriate conservation, fertilizers, and tillage—will go far in increasing a poor nation's output.

Moreover, land ownership patterns are a key to providing farmers with strong incentives to invest in capital and technologies that will increase their land's yield. When farmers own their own land, they have better incentives to make improvements, such as in irrigation systems, and undertake appropriate conservation practices.

Some economists believe that natural wealth from oil or minerals is not an unalloyed blessing.

Countries like the United States, Canada, and Norway have used their natural wealth to form the solid base of industrial expansion. In other countries, the wealth has been subject to plunder and *rent seeking* by corrupt leaders and military cliques. Countries like Nigeria and Congo (formerly Zaire), which are fabulously wealthy in terms of mineral resources, failed to convert their underground assets into productive human or tangible capital because of venal rulers who drained that wealth into their own bank accounts and conspicuous consumption.

Capital Formation

A modern economy requires a vast array of capital goods. Countries must abstain from current consumption to engage in fruitful roundabout production. But there's the rub, for the poorest countries are near a subsistence standard of living. When you are poor to begin with, reducing current consumption to provide for future consumption seems impossible.

The leaders in the growth race invest at least 20 percent of output in capital formation. By contrast, the poorest agrarian countries are often able to save only 5 percent of national income. Moreover, much of the low level of saving goes to provide the growing population with housing and simple tools. Little is left over for development.

But let's say a country has succeeded in hiking up its rate of saving. Even so, it takes many decades to accumulate the highways, telecommunications systems, computers, electricity-generating plants, and other capital goods that underpin a productive economic structure.

Even before acquiring the most sophisticated computers, however, developing countries must first build up their *infrastructure*, or social overhead capital, which consists of the large-scale projects upon which a market economy depends. For example, a regional agricultural adviser helps farmers in an area learn of new seeds or crops; a road system links up the different markets; a public-health program inoculates people against typhoid or diphtheria and protects the population beyond those inoculated. In each of these cases it would be impossible for an enterprising firm to capture the social benefits involved, because the firm cannot collect fees from the thousands or even millions of beneficiaries. Because of the large indivisibilities and external effects of infrastructure, the government must step in to make or ensure the necessary investments.

In many developing countries, the single most pressing problem is too little saving. Particularly in the poorest regions, urgent current consumption competes with investment for scarce resources. The result is too little investment in the productive capital so indispensable for rapid economic progress.

Foreign borrowing and emerging-market crisis

If there are so many obstacles to finding domestic saving for capital formation, why not borrow abroad? Economic theory tells us that a rich country, which has tapped its own high-yield investment projects, can benefit both itself and the recipient by investing in high-yield projects abroad.

The trend in financial flows to developing countries is shown in Figure 12-2. This illustrates how both portfolio and direct investment in developing countries have grown in recent years and shows one of the major indicators of globalization of financial markets.

But risks are the necessary companion of reward in foreign lending. The history of lending from rich to poor regions shows a cycle of opportunity, lending, profits, over-expansion, speculation, crisis, and drying-up of funds, followed by a new round of lending by yet another group of starry-eyed investors. No sooner has one crisis been forgotten than another erupts.

The latest crisis arose in 1997–1998 following the rapid growth of investments in *emerging markets*, which is the name often given to rapidly growing low- and middle-income countries that are promising areas for foreign investment. In the 1990s, investors in wealthy countries sent their funds abroad in search of higher returns; poor countries, hungry for funds, welcomed this flow of foreign funds. From Thailand to South Africa, both loans and equity investments grew rapidly during the 1990s.

As long as the growth in emerging markets continued, all seemed well. But a slowdown in growth combined with a series of banking crises led to massive outflows of short-term funds from Thailand, Indonesia, and South Korea. Bankers who had invested heavily called in their loans. This led to a sharp increase in the supply of the currencies of these countries. Most were on fixed exchange systems, and the selling overwhelmed the countries' reserves. One after

another, the East Asian countries found their currencies depreciating sharply. Many called upon the IMF to provide short-term funds, but the IMF required contractionary monetary and fiscal policies. All these together produced sharp business recessions throughout East Asia.

By 2000, most of these countries had recovered from the crisis after a period of *adjustment*—slow output growth, declining real wages, debt reschedulings, and trade surpluses. Economic growth had resumed. The world had survived another financial crisis. But the international-financial virus is always lying dormant, waiting to infect the next herd of exuberant speculators.

Technological Change and Innovations

The final and most important wheel is technological advance. Here developing countries have one major advantage: They can hope to benefit by relying on the technological progress of more advanced nations.

Imitating Technology. Poor countries need not find modern Newtons to discover the law of gravity; they can read about it in any physics book. They don't have to repeat the slow, meandering route to the Industrial Revolution; they can buy tractors, computers, and power looms undreamed of by the great merchants of the past.

Japan and the United States clearly illustrate this in their historical developments. The United States provides a hopeful example to the rest of the world. The key inventions involved in the automobile originated almost exclusively abroad. Nevertheless, Ford and General Motors applied foreign inventions and rapidly became the world leaders in the automotive industry.

Japan joined the industrial race late, and only at the end of the nineteenth century did it send students abroad to study Western technology. The Japanese government took an active role in stimulating the pace of development and in building railroads and utilities. By adopting productive foreign technologies, Japan moved into its position today as the world's second-largest industrial economy. The examples of the United States and Japan show how countries can thrive by adapting foreign science and technology to local market conditions.

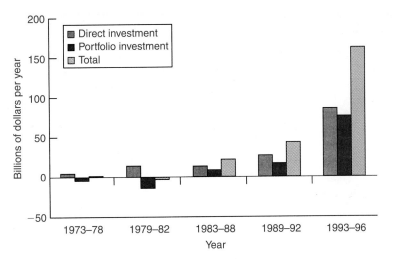

FIGURE 12-2. Investment in Developing Countries

Investments in developing countries have grown rapidly. These include both direct investment (which involves purchasing tangible assets) and portfolio investment (which involves purchasing stocks, bonds, and other financial instruments). This trend shows one of the leading indicators of "globalization." (Source: Council of Economic Advisers.)

Entrepreneurship and Innovation. From the histories of the United States and Japan, it might appear that adaptation of foreign technology is an easy recipe for development. You might say: "Just go abroad; copy more efficient methods; put them into effect at home; then sit back and wait for the extra output to roll in."

Alas, implementing technological change is not that simple. You can send a textbook on chemical engineering to Poorovia, but without skilled scientists, engineers, entrepreneurs, and adequate capital, Poorovia couldn't even think about building a working petrochemical plant. The advanced technology was itself developed to meet the special conditions of the advanced countries—including ample skilled engineers and workers, reliable electrical service, and quickly available spare parts and repair services. These conditions do not prevail in poor countries.

One of the key tasks of economic development is promoting an entrepreneurial spirit. A country cannot thrive without a group of owners or managers willing to undertake risks, open new businesses, adopt new technologies, and import new ways of doing business. At the most fundamental level, innovation and entrepreneurship thrives when property

rights are clear and complete, and taxes and other drains on profits (such as corruption) are low and predictable. Government can also foster entrepreneurship through specific investments: by setting up extension services for farmers, by educating and training the workforce, and by establishing management schools.

Vicious Cycles to Virtuous Circles

We have emphasized that poor countries face great obstacles in combining the four elements of progress—labor, capital, resources, and innovation. In addition, countries find that the difficulties reinforce each other in a *vicious cycle of poverty.*

Figure 12-3 illustrates how one hurdle raises yet other hurdles. Low incomes lead to low saving; low saving retards the growth of capital; inadequate capital prevents introduction of new machinery and rapid growth in productivity; low productivity leads to low incomes. Other elements in poverty are also self-reinforcing. Poverty is accompanied by low levels of education, literacy, and skill; these in turn prevent the adoption of new and improved technologies and lead to rapid population growth, which eats away at improvements in output and food production.

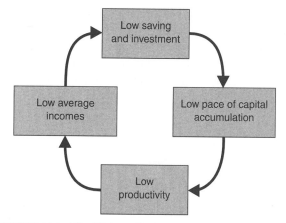

FIGURE 12-3. The Vicious Cycle of Poverty

Many obstacles to development are self-reinforcing. Low levels of income prevent saving, retard capital growth, hinder productivity growth, and keep income low. Successful development may require taking steps to break the chain at many points.

Overcoming the barriers of poverty often requires a concerted effort on many fronts, and some development economists recommend a "big push" forward to break the vicious cycle. If a country is fortunate, simultaneous steps to invest more, improve health and education, develop skills, and curb population growth can break the vicious cycle of poverty and stimulate a virtuous circle of rapid economic development.

STRATEGIES OF ECONOMIC DEVELOPMENT

We see how countries must combine labor, resources, capital, and technology in order to grow rapidly. But this is no real formula; it is the equivalent of saying that an Olympic sprinter must run like the wind. Why do some countries succeed in running faster than others? How do poor countries ever get started down the road of economic development?

Historians and social scientists have long been fascinated by the differences in the pace of economic growth among nations. Some early theories stressed climate, noting that all advanced countries lie in the earth's temperate zone. Others have pointed to custom, culture, or religion as a key factor. Max Weber

emphasized the "Protestant ethic" as a driving force behind capitalism. More recently, Mancur Olson has argued that nations begin to decline when their decision structure becomes brittle and interest groups or oligarchies prevent social and economic change.

No doubt each of these theories has some validity for a particular time and place. But they do not hold up as universal explanations of economic development. Weber's theory leaves unexplained why the cradle of civilization appeared in the Near East and Greece while the later-dominant Europeans lived in caves, worshiped trolls, and wore bearskins. Where do we find the Protestant ethic in bustling Hong Kong? How can we explain that a country like Japan, with a rigid social structure and powerful lobbies, has become one of the world's most productive economies?

Even in the modern era, people become attached to simple, holistic explanations of economic development. Two decades ago, people considered import substitution (the replacement of imports with domestically produced goods) to be the most secure development strategy. Then, in the 1970s, reliance on labor-intensive techniques was thought advantageous. Today, as we will see, economists tend to emphasize reliance on market forces with an outward orientation. This history should serve as a warning to be wary of oversimplified approaches to complex processes.

Nonetheless, historians and development economists have learned much from the study of the varieties of economic growth. What are some of the lessons? The following account represents a montage of important ideas developed in recent years. Each approach describes how countries might break out of the vicious cycle of poverty and begin to mobilize the four wheels of economic development.

The Backwardness Hypothesis

One view emphasizes the international context of development. We saw above that poorer countries have important advantages that the first pioneers along the path of industrialization did not. Developing nations can now draw upon the capital, skills, and technology of more advanced countries. A hypothesis advanced by Alexander Gerschenkron of Harvard suggests that *relative backwardness* itself may aid development. Countries can buy modern textile machinery, efficient pumps, miracle seeds, chemical fertilizers, and medical supplies. Because they can lean on the technologies of advanced countries, today's developing countries can grow more rapidly than did Britain or Western Europe in the period 1780–1850. As low-income countries draw upon the more productive technologies of the leaders, we would expect to see *convergence* of countries toward the technological frontier. Convergence occurs when those countries or regions that have initially low incomes tend to grow more rapidly than ones with high incomes.

Industrialization vs. Agriculture

In most countries, incomes in urban areas are almost double those in agriculture. And in affluent nations, much of the economy is in industry and services. Hence, many nations jump to the conclusion that industrialization is the cause rather than the effect of affluence.

We must be wary of such inferences, which confuse the association of two characteristics with causality. Some people say, "Rich people drive BMWs, but driving a BMW will not make you a rich person." Similarly, there is no economic justification for a poor country to insist upon having its own national airline and large steel mill. These are not the fundamental necessities of economic growth.

The lesson of decades of attempts to accelerate industrialization at the expense of agriculture has led many analysts to rethink the role of farming. Industrialization is capital-intensive, attracts workers into crowded cities, and often produces high levels of unemployment. Raising productivity on farms may require less capital, while providing productive employment for surplus labor. Indeed, if Bangladesh could increase the productivity of its farming by 20 percent, that advance would do more to release resources for the production of comforts than would trying to construct a domestic steel industry to displace imports.

State vs. Market

The cultures of many developing countries are hostile to the operation of markets. Often, competition among firms or profit-seeking behavior is contrary to traditional practices, religious beliefs, or vested interests. Yet decades of experience suggest that extensive reliance on markets provides the most effective way of managing an economy and promoting rapid economic growth.

What are the important elements of a market-oriented policy? The important elements include the predominance of private property and ownership, an outward orientation in trade policy, low tariffs and few quantitative trade restrictions, the promotion of small business, and the fostering of competition. Moreover, markets work best in a stable macroeconomic environment—one in which taxes are predictable and inflation is low.

Growth and Openness

A fundamental issue of economic development concerns a country's stance toward international trade. Should developing countries attempt to be self-sufficient, replacing most imports with domestic production? (This is known as a strategy of *import substitution*.) Or should a country strive to pay for the imports it needs by improving efficiency and competitiveness, developing foreign markets, and keeping trade barriers low? (This is called a strategy of *openness* or *outward orientation*.)

Policies of import substitution were often popular in Latin America until the 1980s. The policy most frequently used toward this end was to build high tariff walls around manufacturing industries so that local firms could produce and sell goods that would otherwise be imported.

A policy of openness keeps trade barriers as low as practical, relying primarily on tariffs rather than quotas and other nontariff barriers. It minimizes the interference with financial flows and allows supply and demand to operate in financial markets. It avoids a state monopoly on exports and imports. It keeps government regulation to the minimum necessary for an orderly market economy. Above all, it relies primarily on a private market system of profits and losses to guide production, rather than depending on public ownership and control or the commands of a government planning system.

The success of outward-expansion policies is best illustrated by the successful East Asian countries. A generation ago, countries like Taiwan, South Korea, and Singapore had per capita incomes one-quarter to one-third of those in the wealthiest Latin American countries. Yet, by saving large fractions of their national incomes and channeling these to high-return export industries, the East Asian countries overtook every Latin American country by the late 1980s. The secret to success was not a doctrinaire laissez-faire policy, for the governments in fact engaged in selective planning and intervention. Rather, the openness and outward orientation allowed the countries to reap economies of scale and the benefits of international specialization and thus to increase employment, use domestic resources effectively, enjoy rapid productivity growth, and provide enormous gains in living standards.

While openness provides many benefits, excessive openness, particularly to short-term financial flows, is an invitation to speculative attack. What investors lendeth, investors can taketh back. This syndrome can cause financial and banking crises, as we noted for the East Asian economies in our discussion earlier in this chapter.

The fruits of openness were demonstrated in a recent study by Jeffrey Sachs and Andrew Warner.[1] They examined the relationship between openness and economic growth. An *open economy* is defined as one characterized by low trade barriers, open financial markets, and private markets. A *closed economy* is the opposite.

They find that openness is strongly associated with rapid economic growth. The basic story is shown in Figure 12-4. The left panel shows the performance of closed economies. The closed economies had an average growth rate of per capita income of only 0.9 percent annually over the 1970–1989 period. There

---

[1] See this chapter's Further Reading section.

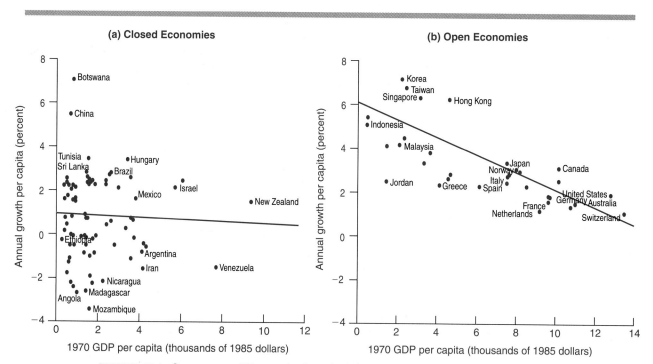

FIGURE 12-4. Openness and Economic Growth, 1970–1989

What is the impact of openness on economic growth? Panel **(a)** shows that closed economies grow slowly and do not converge to high-income countries. Panel **(b)** shows the open economies—nonsocialist economies with relatively low barriers to trade and financial flows. They grow much more rapidly and tend to converge to the highest-income regions. (Source: Jeffrey Sachs and Andrew Warner, "Economic Reform and the Process of Global Integration," *Brookings Papers on Economic Activity*, no. 1, 1995, pp. 42–43.)

was no convergence of these countries—many with low incomes—toward the high-income countries. Figure 12-4(*b*) shows the growth of open economies. These grew at an average rate of 4.5 percent annually over the same period; moreover, low-income open economies showed strong convergence toward rich countries. The importance of openness could hardly be more emphatically shown than by these trends.

Summary Judgment

Decades of experience in dozens of countries have led many development economists to the following summary view of the way government can best promote rapid economic development:

The government has a vital role in establishing and maintaining a healthy economic environment. It must ensure respect for the rule of law, enforce contracts, and orient its regulations toward competition and innovation. Government often plays a leading role in investment in human capital through education, health, and transportation, but it should look to the private sector where it has no comparative advantage. Government should focus its efforts on areas where there are clear signs of market failures and should dismantle regulatory impediments to the private sector in areas where government has comparative disadvantage.

B. ALTERNATIVE MODELS FOR DEVELOPMENT

People continually look for ways to improve their living standards. Economic betterment is particularly compelling for poor countries seeking a path to the riches they see around them. This textbook has surveyed in depth the mixed market economy of the United States, which combines fundamentally free markets with a sizable government sector. What other alternatives are available?

A BOUQUET OF "ISMS"

At one extreme is *free-market absolutism*, which holds that the best government is the least government. At the other extreme is complete communism, with the government operating a collectivized economic order in which the first-person singular hardly exists. Between the extremes of laissez-faire and communism lie mixed capitalism, managed markets, socialism, and many combinations of these models. In this section, we describe briefly some of the influential alternative strategies for growth and development:

1. *The Asian managed-market approach.* South Korea, Taiwan, Singapore, and other countries of East Asia have devised their own brands of economics that combine strong government oversight with powerful market forces.
2. *Socialism.* Socialist thinking encompasses a wide variety of different approaches. In Western Europe after World War II, socialist governments operating in a democratic framework, expanded the welfare state, nationalized industries, and planned their economies. In recent years, however, these countries moved back toward a free-market framework with extensive deregulation and privatization.
3. *Soviet-style communism.* For many years, the clearest alternative to the market economy existed in the Soviet Union. Under the Soviet model, the state owned all the land and most of the capital, set wages and most prices, and directed the microeconomic operation of the economy.

The Central Dilemma: Market vs. Command

A survey of alternative economic systems may seem like a bewildering array of economic "isms." And indeed, there is a great variety in the way countries organize their economies.

These are the issues that run through all the debates about alternative economic systems: Should economic decisions be taken primarily in the private market or by government command? Should private ownership and decisions guide the economy, or should government take the commanding heights?

At one end of the spectrum is the *market economy*. In a market system, people act voluntarily and primarily for financial gain or personal satisfaction. Firms buy factors and produce outputs, selecting inputs and outputs in a way that will maximize their profits. Consumers supply factors and buy consumer goods to maximize their satisfactions. Agreements on production and consumption are made voluntarily and with the use of money, at prices determined in free markets, and on the basis of arrangements between buyers and sellers. Although individuals differ greatly in terms of economic power, the relations between individuals and firms are horizontal in nature, essentially voluntary, and nonhierarchical.

At the other end of the spectrum is the *command economy*, where decisions are made by government bureaucracy. In this approach, people are linked by a vertical relationship, and control is exercised by a multilevel hierarchy. The planning bureaucracy determines *what* goods are produced, *how* they are produced, and *for whom* output is produced. The highest level of the pyramid makes the major decisions and develops the elements of the plan for the economy. The plan is subdivided and transmitted down the bureaucratic ladder, with the lower levels of the hierarchy executing the plan with increasing attention to detail. Individuals are motivated by coercion and legal sanctions; organizations compel individuals to accept orders from above. Transactions and commands may or may not use money; trades may or may not take place at established prices.

In between are the socialist and the managed-market economies. In both cases government plays an important role in guiding and directing the economy, though much less so than in a command economy. The tension between markets and command runs through all discussions about alternative economic systems. Let us look in more detail at some of the alternatives to the mixed market economies.

THE ASIAN MODELS

Dragons and Laggards

The East Asian *crisis* has captured most of the headlines over the last few years, but the really impressive fact of that region is the East Asian *miracle* of rapid economic growth over the last half-century in South Korea, Singapore, Hong Kong, and Taiwan. Table 12-2 compares the performance of the "Asian dragons" to that of the "Latin laggards" and the stagnant economies of sub-Saharan Africa. Even with the crisis of the late 1990s, the East Asian countries show an outstanding growth record.

A recent World Bank study analyzed the economic policies of different regions to see whether any patterns emerged.[2] The results confirmed common views but also found a few surprises. Here are the high points:

- *Investment rates.* The Asian dragons followed the classical recipe of high investment rates to ensure that their economies benefitted from the latest technology and could build up the necessary infrastructure. As Table 12-2 shows, investment rates among the Asian dragons were almost 20 percentage points higher than those of other regions.

- *Macroeconomic fundamentals.* Successful countries had a steady hand on macroeconomic policies, keeping inflation low and saving rates high. They invested heavily in human capital as well as in physical capital and did more to promote

---

[2] See this chapter's Further Reading section for the World Bank study on the East Asian miracle.

Regions	Average growth of per capita GDP, 1965–1998	Investment as percent of GDP, 1990
East Asia & Pacific	5.7	35
South Asia	2.7	19
Latin America & Caribbean	1.3	17
Sub-Saharan Africa	−0.3	9

TABLE 12-2. Attention to Fundamentals Spurred Growth for the Asian Dragons

Sources: World Bank, *The East Asia Miracle: Economic Growth and Government Policies* (1993) and *World Development Indicators* (2000).

education than any other developing region. The financial systems were managed to ensure monetary stability and a sound currency.

- *Outward orientation.* The Asian dragons were outward-oriented, often keeping their exchange rates undervalued to promote exports, encouraging exports with fiscal incentives, and pursuing technological advance by adopting best-practice techniques of high-income countries.

The crisis of the late 1990s revealed certain flaws in the development strategies of some of these countries—reminding us of J. K. Galbraith's remark that depression reveals what the auditors missed. The strategy of "managed" capitalism, involving subsidies and directed loans, has significant potential for corruption, sometimes called "crony capitalism." This can lead to overinvestment in privileged sectors and to low returns to capital. This syndrome was particularly prominent in Indonesia and South Korea, while other countries such as Singapore managed to avoid the misallocations associated with rampant corruption.

The perils of corruption

What is corruption, and why is it so debilitating? The following discussion by economic development specialist Robert Klitgaard explains how corruption influences the economy:

At the broadest level, corruption is the misuse of office for unofficial ends. The catalogue of corrupt acts includes bribery, extortion, influence-peddling, nepotism, fraud, speed money, embezzlement, and more. Although we tend to think of corruption as a sin of government, of course it also exists in the private sector. Indeed, the private sector is involved in most government corruption.

Different varieties of corruption are not equally harmful. Corruption that undercuts the rules of the game—for example, the justice system or property rights or banking and credit—devastates economic and political development. Corruption that allows polluters to foul rivers or hospitals to extort patients can be environmentally and socially corrosive. In comparison, some speed money for public services and mild corruption in campaign financing are less damaging. Of course the extent of corruption matters, too. Most systems can stand some corruption, and it is possible that some truly awful systems can be improved by it. But when corruption becomes the norm, its effects are crippling. So, although every country has corruption, the varieties and extent differ. The killer is systematic corruption that destroys the rules of the game. It is one of the principal reasons why the most underdeveloped parts of our planet stay that way.[3]

Battling corruption is particularly difficult because the state, which is the instrument of justice, is often itself corrupt.

The Chinese Giant: Market Leninism

One of the major surprises in economic development during the last decade was the rapid growth in the Chinese economy. After the Chinese revolution of 1949, China initially adopted a Soviet-style central-planning system. The high-water mark of centralization came with the Cultural Revolution of 1966–1969, which led to an economic slowdown in China. After the death of the revolutionary leader Mao Tse-tung, a new generation concluded that economic reform was necessary if the Communist party was to survive. Under Deng Xiaoping (1977–1997), China decentralized a great deal of economic power and allowed competition. Economic reform was, however, not accompanied by political reform; the democracy movement was ruthlessly repressed in Tiananmen Square in 1989, and the Communist party has continued to monopolize the political process.

To spur economic growth, the Chinese leadership has taken dramatic steps such as setting up "special economic zones" and allowing alternative forms of ownership. The most rapidly growing parts of China have been the coastal regions, such as the southern region near Hong Kong. This area has become closely integrated with countries outside China and has attracted considerable foreign investment. In addition, China has allowed collective, private, and foreign firms, free from central planning or control, to operate alongside state-owned firms. These more innovative forms of ownership have grown rapidly and by the late 1990s were producing more than half of China's GDP.

---

[3] See the reference under "Websites" in the Further Reading section at the end of the chapter.

dustrialized countries like the United States or Britain. World War I brought great hardship to Russia and allowed the communists to seize power. From 1917 to 1933, the Soviet Union experimented with different socialist models before settling on central planning. But dissatisfaction with the pace of industrialization led Stalin to undertake a radical new venture around 1928—collectivization of agriculture, forced-draft industrialization, and central planning of the economy.[4]

Under the collectivization of Soviet agriculture between 1929 and 1935, 94 percent of Soviet peasants were forced to join collective farms. In the process, many wealthy peasants were deported, and conditions deteriorated so much that millions perished. The other part of the Soviet "great leap forward" came through the introduction of economic planning for rapid industrialization. The planners created the first 5-year plan to cover the period 1928–1933. The first plan established the priorities of Soviet planning: heavy industry was to be favored over light industry, and consumer goods were to be the residual sector after all the other priorities had been met. Although there were many reforms and changes in emphasis, the Stalinist model of a command economy applied in the Soviet Union, and after World War II in Eastern Europe, until the fall of Soviet communism at the end of the 1980s.

How the Command Economy Functioned. In the Soviet-style command economy, the broad categories of output were determined by political decisions. Military spending in the Soviet Union was always allocated a substantial part of output and scientific resources, while the other major priority was investment. Consumption claimed the residual output after the quotas of higher-priority sectors were filled.

In large part, decisions about how goods were to be produced were made by the planning authorities. Planners first decided on the quantities of final outputs (the *what*). Then they worked backward from outputs to the required inputs and the flows among different firms. Investment decisions were specified in great detail by the planners, while firms had considerable flexibility in deciding upon their mix of labor inputs.

Clearly no planning system could specify all the activities of all the firms—this would have required trillions of commands every year. Many details were left to the managers of individual factories. It was here, in what is called the *principal-agent problem*, that the command economy ran into its deepest difficulties.

The principal-agent problem arises because the person at the top of a hierarchy (the "principal") wants to provide appropriate incentives for the people making the decisions down the hierarchy (the "agents") to behave according to the principal's wishes. In a market economy, profits and prices serve as the mechanism for coordinating consumers and producers. A command economy is plagued by an inability to find an efficient substitute for profits and prices as a way of motivating the agents.

A useful example of the failure to solve the principal-agent problem is found in Soviet book publication. In a market economy, commercial decisions about books are made primarily on the basis of profit and loss. In the Soviet Union, because profits were taboo, planners instead used quantitative targets. A first approach was to reward firms according to the number of books produced, so publishers printed thousands of thin unread volumes. Faced with a clear incentive problem, the center (principal) changed the system so that the producers (agents) were rewarded on the basis of the number of pages printed, and the result was fat books with onion-skin paper and large type. The planners then changed the criterion to the number of words—to which the publishers responded by printing huge volumes with tiny type. None of these mechanisms was capable of signaling consumer wants effectively.

The principal-agent problem crops up in organizations in all countries, but the Soviet model had few mechanisms (like bankruptcy in markets and elections for public goods) to provide an ultimate check on waste.

Comparative Economic Performance. From World War II until the mid-1980s, the United States and the Soviet Union engaged in a superpower competition for public opinion, military superiority, and economic dominance. How well did the command economies perform in the economic growth race? Any attempt at answering this question is bedeviled by the absence of reliable statistics. Most economists

---

[4] See this chapter's Further Reading section for studies of Soviet economic history.

believed until recently that the Soviet Union grew rapidly from 1928 until the mid-1960s, with growth rates perhaps surpassing those in North America and Western Europe. After the mid-1960s, growth in the Soviet Union stagnated and output actually began to decline. Estimates of living standards today are treacherous, but per capita income in Russia in the early 1990s appears to be less than one-quarter of that in the United States.

A revealing comparison of the performance of market and command economies can be made by contrasting the experiences of East Germany and West Germany. These countries started out with roughly equal levels of productivity and similar industrial structures at the end of World War II. After four decades of capitalism in the West and Soviet-style socialism in the East, productivity in East Germany had fallen to a level estimated between one-fourth and one-third of that in West Germany. Moreover, the East German growth tended to emphasize production of intermediate goods and commodities of little value to consumers. Quantity, not quality, was the goal.

Finally, what of the scourges of capitalism—unemployment and inflation? Unemployment was traditionally low in Soviet-style economies because labor was generally in short supply as a result of the ambitious economic plans. Furthermore, controlled prices tended to be quite stable, so measured inflation was absent. In the late 1980s and early 1990s, however, open inflation erupted. In addition, prices were well below market-clearing levels, and acute shortages arose in what is called *repressed inflation.*

Balance Sheet. Is there a final balance sheet on the experience with Soviet central planning? The Soviet model demonstrated that a command economy can work—it is capable of mobilizing capital and labor and producing both guns and butter. But the Soviet economy, with borders closed to trade, technologies, and people, became increasingly obsolete over time. Innovation withered because of poor incentives. In competition with the open-market economies, particularly as the world turned to increasingly high-quality goods and services, Russia could export virtually nothing except raw materials.

Growth slowed, and per capita income declined in the latest period of central planning. Its leaders finally abandoned Soviet central planning as it was seen to be morally, politically, and economically bankrupt.

From Marx to Market

Beginning in 1989, the countries of Eastern Europe and the former Soviet Union rejected the communist experiment and introduced market economies. A cruel joke heard in Eastern Europe is "Question: What is communism? Answer: The longest road from capitalism to capitalism." Having decided to take the road back to a market economy, a command economy has an arduous path to follow. Among the major obstacles on the road to reform are the following:

- *Price reform and free-market pricing.* Prices of both inputs and outputs were often far below market-clearing levels. Food, housing, and energy were generally heavily subsidized, while automobiles and consumer durables sold at levels far above the world price levels. The first step in most countries was to allow supply and demand to set prices.

- *Hard budget constraints.* Enterprises in command economies operated with "soft budget constraints." This term means that operating losses are covered by subsidies and do not lead to bankruptcy. In a market economy, firms must be fiscally responsible—enterprises know that unprofitability ultimately means economic bankruptcy for the firm and economic ruin for the managers.

- *Privatization.* In market economies, output is primarily produced in private firms; in the United States, for example, only 3 percent of GDP is produced by the federal government. In Soviet-style communist countries, by contrast, between 80 and 90 percent of output was produced by the state. Moving to the market required that the actual decisions about buying, selling, pricing, producing, borrowing, and lending be made by private agents.

- *Other reforms.* Transition to the market required setting up the legal framework for a market, establishing a modern banking system, breaking up the pervasive monopolies, tightening monetary and fiscal policy in order to prevent runaway inflation, and opening up the economy to international competition.

- *Sequencing of the transition.* The most difficult issue in moving to the market was where to begin. The reform debate divided between a radical (or "shock-therapy") approach and a gradual (or "step-by-step") approach. One influential advisor was Harvard's Jeffrey Sachs, a brilliant young economist who has nursed many ailing countries back to health. He persuaded the Polish government to adopt the shock-therapy approach in January 1990. This was the model that Russia followed in 1991–1992 under President Yeltsin and a government led by economist Yegor Gaidar. The radical Russian reformers freed prices and international trade, dismantled the planning apparatus, and attempted to keep money tight. The next few years saw pitched battle between the reformers, bureaucrats from the old regime, and wistful romantics who yearned for the "good old days" under communism. "Two steps forward and one step backward" has characterized the reform movement in Russia and many formerly socialist countries.

This checklist of reforms applies also to other countries that have traveled some distance down the road to a centrally planned economy and want a more market-oriented economy.

Reform's progress

Reforms in centrally planned countries have been through a decade of transition, and the initial returns are sobering. First, virtually all countries suffered deep depressions as they shucked off their socialist structures. The sources of the decline in output are varied, but a major reason is undoubtedly that the delicate web of buyer-seller relationships was completely disrupted by the transition. Second, many countries experienced rapid inflation, and some (like Ukraine) suffered from hyperinflation. The major impetus of the rapid price rises came when the freeing of prices and wages triggered an initial inflation, and this was followed by a classic wage-price spiral. An additional shock to inflation came in those countries where a weak government was unable to contain the budget deficit and government consequently relied upon the monetary printing press to finance its expenditures.

Figure 12-5 shows the growth trajectories of the major transition economies over the 1990s. What were the characteristics of countries with the most successful transitions? These countries had relatively short histories

of central planning, had deeper traditions of civil society and greater "social capital," made more rapid transitions to the market, were closer to the rich core countries of Western Europe, and moved more quickly to integrate themselves into the larger world economy. Poland and Slovenia exemplified successful transitions. The greatest difficulties came in the remnants of the former Soviet Union, particularly in those countries like Ukraine and Russia where the transition was slow and reluctant. Russia was torn by corruption, great inequality, budget deficits, inflation, civil war, and political instability during much of the 1990s. With President Boris Yeltsin's resignation and the transition to the little-known leader Alexander Putin in 2000, Russia's rocky transition to a market democracy took another turn into the unknown.

A CAUTIONARY FINAL NOTE

This chapter has described the problems and prospects of poor countries struggling to be rich and free—to provide the dry houses, education, electric lights, fast horses, automobiles, and long vacations of the excerpt that opened this chapter. What are the prospects of attaining these goals? We close with a hopeful note and sober warning from Sachs and Warner:

> The world economy at the end of the twentieth century looks much like the world economy at the end of the nineteenth century. A global capitalist system is taking shape, drawing almost all regions of the world into arrangements of open trade and harmonized economic institutions. As in the nineteenth century, this new round of globalization promises to lead to economic convergence for the countries that join the system. . . .
>
> And yet there are also profound risks for the consolidation of market reforms in Russia, China, and Africa, as well as for the maintenance of international agreements among the leading countries. . . . The spread of capitalism in the [last] twenty-five years is an historic event of great promise and significance, but whether we will be celebrating the consolidation of a democratic and market-based world system [twenty-five years hence] will depend on our own foresight and good judgments in the years to come.[5]

---

[5] See the reference in the Further Reading section at the end of the chapter.

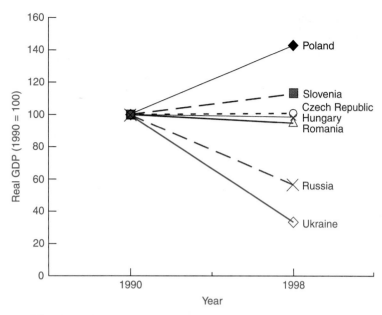

FIGURE 12-5. The Transition to the Market Has Been a Mixed Success

Those countries like Poland and Slovenia with strong market traditions, decisive economic reforms, and close links to Western Europe have grown relatively rapidly over the transitional decade of the 1990s. Others, like Russia and Ukraine, introduced reforms in a more halting way, had weaker market-economy traditions, and had inconsistent macroeconomic policies with high inflation—they consequently experienced sharp economic declines when making the transition. [Source: World Bank, *World Development Report, 1999* (World Bank, Washington, D.C., 1999).]

SUMMARY

A. Economic Growth in Poor Countries

1. Most of the world's population live in developing countries, which have relatively low per capita incomes. Such countries often exhibit rapid population growth, a low level of literacy, poor health, and a high proportion of their population living and working on farms.

2. The key to development lies in four fundamental factors: human resources, natural resources, capital formation, and technology. Explosive population causes problems as the Malthusian prediction of diminishing returns haunts the poorest countries. On the constructive agenda, improving the population's health, education, and technical training has high priority.

3. Investment and saving rates in poor countries are low because incomes are so depressed that little can be saved for the future. International financing of investment in poor countries has witnessed many crises over the last two centuries. The most recent cycle came in 1997–1998 when many East Asian countries borrowed heavily and were unable to repay their loans.

4. Technological change is often associated with investment and new machinery. It offers much hope to the developing nations because they can adopt the more productive technologies of advanced nations. This requires entrepreneurship. One task of development is to spur internal growth of the scarce entrepreneurial spirit.

5. Numerous theories of economic development help explain why the four fundamental factors are present or absent at a particular time. Geography and climate, custom, religious and business attitudes, class conflicts and political systems—each affects economic devel-

opment. But none does so in a simple and invariable way. Development economists today emphasize the growth advantage of relative backwardness, the need to respect the role of agriculture, and the art of finding the proper boundary between state and market. The most recent consensus is on the advantages of openness.

B. Alternative Models for Development

6. Other approaches have competed with the mixed market economy as models for economic development. Alternative strategies include the managed-market approach of the East Asian countries, socialism, and the Soviet-style command economy.

7. The managed-market approach of Japan and the Asian dragons, such as South Korea, Hong Kong, Taiwan, and Singapore, has proved remarkably successful over the last quarter-century. Among the key ingredients are macroeconomic stability, high investment rates, a sound financial system, rapid improvements in education, and an outward orientation in trade and technology policies.

8. Socialism is a middle ground between capitalism and communism, stressing government ownership of the means of production, planning by the state, income redistribution, and peaceful transition to a more egalitarian world.

9. Historically, Marxism took its deepest roots in semifeudal Russia. A study of resource allocation in the Soviet-style command economy shows great central planning of broad elements of resource allocation, particularly the emphasis on heavy industry. The Soviet economy grew rapidly in its early decades, but stagnation and collapse have today put Russia and other formerly communist countries at income levels far below those of North America, Japan, and Western Europe.

10. Faced with slowing economic growth and the desire for economic reform, Russia and other formerly communist countries are making the difficult transition to market economies. Transition raises many obstacles, such as soft budget constraints, frozen and distorted prices, and an inadequate legal framework. Two major transition strategies are the shock-therapy approach of multiple simultaneous measures and the more cautious step-by-step approach, in which reforms are sequenced to prevent disruption. The lessons of the transition are broadly applicable to countries hoping to cast off government controls for a market-oriented system.

CONCEPTS FOR REVIEW

Economic Development

developing country
indicators of development
Human Development Index
four elements in development
vicious cycles, virtuous circles

backwardness hypothesis
openness and convergence

Alternative Models for Development

the central dilemma of markets vs. command

socialism, communism
the principal-agent problem
Soviet-style command economy
transition to the market

FURTHER READING AND INTERNET WEBSITES

Further Reading

The influential study on the East-Asian miracle is contained in World Bank, *The East Asia Miracle: Economic Growth and Government Policies* (World Bank, Washington, D.C., 1993). The data in Figure 12-4 are from the fascinating paper by Jeffrey Sachs and Andrew Warner, "Economic Reform and the Process of Global Integration," *Brookings Papers on Economic Activity*, no. 1, 1995, pp. 42–43, while the quote at the end of the chapter is at pp. 63–64.

A highly readable account of developments in Soviet economic history is contained in Alec Nove, *An Economic His-*

tory of the U.S.S.R., third ed. (Penguin, Baltimore, 1986). A careful study of the Soviet economic system is provided by Paul R. Gregory and Robert C. Stuart, *Russian and Soviet Economic Performance and Structure*, sixth ed. (Harper & Row, New York, 1997).

Websites

The World Bank (www.worldbank.org) has information on its programs and publications at its site, as does the International Monetary Fund, or IMF at www.imf.org. The United Nations website has links to most international institutions and their databases at www.unsystem.org. Another good source of information about high-income countries is the Organisation for Economic Cooperation and Development, or OECD, www.oecd.org. U.S. trade data are available at www.census.gov. You can find information on many countries through their statistical offices. A compendium of national agencies is available at www.census.gov/main/ www/stat_int.html.

One of the best sources for studies of developing countries is the World Bank, especially the annual *World Development Review* at www.worldbank.org. A gateway to other organizations interested in economic development is at www.worldbank.org/html/extdr/institutions/index.htm.

The quote from Klitgaard was published in *Finance and Development*, March 1998, and can be found at www.gwdg.de/~uwww/icr.htm. A number of papers on economic development by Harvard's Jeffrey Sachs and his collaborators can be found at www.ksg.harvard.edu/cid/cid_public_data.htm.

QUESTIONS FOR DISCUSSION

1. Do you agree with the celebration of material well-being expressed in the chapter's opening quotation? What would you add to the list of the benefits of economic development?

2. Delineate each of the four important factors driving economic development. With respect to these, how was it that the high-income oil-exporting countries became rich? What hope is there for a country like Mali, which has very low per capita resources of capital, land, and technology?

3. Some fear the "vicious cycle of underdevelopment." In a poor country, rapid population growth eats into whatever improvements in technology occur and lowers living standards. With a low per capita income, the country cannot save and invest and mainly engages in subsistence farming. With most of the population on the farm, there is little hope for education, decline in fertility, or industrialization. If you were to advise such a country, how would you break through the vicious cycle?

4. Compare the situation a developing country faces today with the one it might have faced (at an equivalent level of per capita income) 200 years ago. Considering the four wheels of economic development, explain the advantages and disadvantages that today's developing country might experience.

5. Some economists today question whether it is wise to allow complete openness on both financial and current accounts. They argue that allowing free flow of short-term financial movements increases vulnerability to speculative attacks. Give the pros and cons of limiting short-term financial movements. Might you want to use a tax on short-term flows rather than quantitative restrictions?

6. Analyze the way that *what, how,* and *for whom* are solved in a Soviet-style command economy, and compare your analysis with the solution of the three central questions in a market economy.

7. **Advanced problem** (relying upon the growth accounting of Chapter 11): We can extend our growth-accounting equation to include three factors and write the following equation:

$$g_Q = s_L g_L + s_K g_K + s_R g_R + \text{T.C.}$$

where g_Q = the growth rate of output, g_i = the growth rate of inputs (i = inputs to production: L for labor, K for capital, and R for land and other natural resources), and s_i = the contribution of each input to output growth as measured by its share of national income ($0 \leq s_i \leq 1$ and $s_L + s_K + s_R = 1$). T.C. measures technological change.

   a. In the poorest developing countries, the share of capital is close to zero, the main resource is agricultural land (which is constant), and there is little technological change. Can you use this to explain the Malthusian hypothesis in which per capita output is likely to be stagnant or even to decline (i.e., $g_Q < g_L$)?

   b. In advanced industrial economies, the share of land resources drops to virtually zero. Why does this lead to the growth-accounting equation studied in the last chapter? Can you use this to explain how countries can avoid the Malthusian trap of stagnant incomes?

   c. According to economists who are pessimistic about future prospects (including a group of *neo-Malthusians* from the Club of Rome, which was discussed in the previous chapter), T.C. is close to zero, the available supply of natural resources is declining, and the share of resources is large and rising. Does this explain why the future of industrial societies might be bleak? What assumptions of the neo-Malthusians might you question?

CHAPTER 13

Exchange Rates and the International Financial System

The benefit of international trade—a more efficient employment of the productive forces of the world.

John Stuart Mill

INTERNATIONAL LINKAGES

The twentieth century divides into two distinct periods. The period from 1914 to 1945 was characterized by destructive competition, shrinking international trade, growing financial isolation, hot and cold military and trade wars, despotism, and depression. After World War II, most of the world enjoyed growing economic cooperation, widening trade linkages, increasingly integrated financial markets, an expansion of democracy, and rapid economic growth.

The stark contrast between the first and second halves of this century is a reminder of the high stakes in the wise management of our national and global economies. Economically, no nation is an island unto itself. When the bell tolls depression or financial crisis, the sounds reverberate around the world. What are the economic links among nations? The important economic concepts involve international trade and finance. International trade in goods and services allows nations to raise their standards of living by specializing in areas of comparative advantage in production, exporting goods and services in which they are relatively efficient and importing those in which they are relatively inefficient. In a modern economy, trade takes place using different currencies. The international financial system plays an important role for it is the lubricant that facilitates exchange through the buying and selling of commodities for dollars, Euros, and other currencies and of exchanging one currency for another.

International trade often seems a zero-sum Darwinian conflict for market shares, profits, and vital resources. A closer look reveals, however, that nations in the second half of the twentieth century evolved beyond the red-in-tooth-and-claw struggle—they built institutions that serve the common cause of growth and fairness in the international arena. But economic integration is not without its perils. The 1990s saw a rapid succession of financial crises—a crisis of confidence in the exchange-rate regime in Europe in 1991–1992, a collapse of the currency in Mexico in 1994–1995, a series of banking and currency crises in East Asia in 1997, and a default on Russian debt and a global liquidity crisis in 1998. Each of these required that policymakers consider the need for intervention and policy adjustments, but in the end none led to widespread economic collapse.

The next two chapters survey international macroeconomics. This topic includes the principles governing the international monetary system, which is the major focus of the present chapter, as well as the impact of foreign trade on output, employment, and prices, which is covered in the next chapter.

International macroeconomics involves many of the most controversial questions of the day: Does foreign trade raise or lower our output and employment? What is the link between domestic saving, domestic investment, and the trade balance? What are the causes of the occasional financial crises that spread contagiously from country to country? What will be the effect of the European Monetary Union on Europe's macroeconomic performance? And why has the United States become the world's largest debtor country in the last decade? The economic stakes are high in finding wise answers to these questions.

TRENDS IN FOREIGN TRADE

An economy that engages in international trade is called an **open economy.** A useful measure of open-

ness is the ratio of a country's exports or imports to its GDP. Figure 13-1 shows the trend in the shares of imports and exports for the United States over the last half-century. It shows the large export surplus in the early years after World War II as America financed the reconstruction of Europe. But the share of imports and exports was low in the 1950s and 1960s. With growth abroad and a lowering of trade barriers, the share of trade grew steadily and reached an average of 13 percent of GDP by the turn of the century.

You might be surprised to learn that the United States is a relatively self-sufficient economy. Figure 13-2 on the next page shows the trade proportions of selected countries. Small countries and those in highly integrated regions like Western Europe are more open than the United States. Moreover, the degree of openness is much higher in many U.S. industries than in

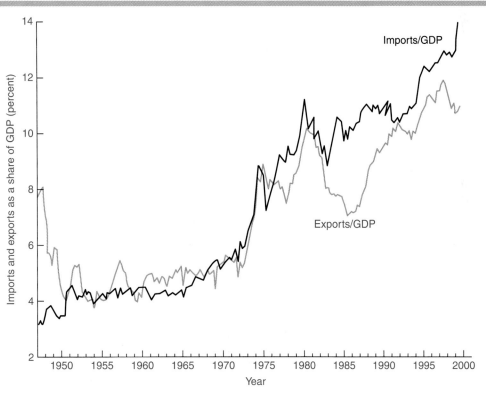

FIGURE 13-1. Growing U.S. Openness

Like all major market economies, the United States has increasingly opened its borders to foreign trade over the last half-century. The result is a growing share of output and consumption involved in international trade. Since the 1980s, imports have far outdistanced exports, causing the United States to become the world's largest debtor nation. (Source: U.S. Department of Commerce.)

the overall economy, particularly in manufacturing industries like steel, textiles, consumer electronics, and autos. Some industries, such as education and health care, are largely insulated from foreign trade.

A. THE BALANCE OF INTERNATIONAL PAYMENTS

BALANCE-OF-PAYMENTS ACCOUNTS

We begin this chapter with a review of the way nations keep their international accounts. Economists keep score by looking at income statements and balance sheets. In the area of international economics, the key accounts are a nation's balance of payments. A country's **balance of international payments** is a systematic statement of all economic transactions between that country and the rest of the world. Its major components are the current account and the financial account. The basic structure of the balance of payments is shown in Table 13-1, and each element is discussed below.

Debits and Credits

Like other accounts, the balance of payments records each transaction as either a plus or a minus. The general rule in balance-of-payments accounting is the following:

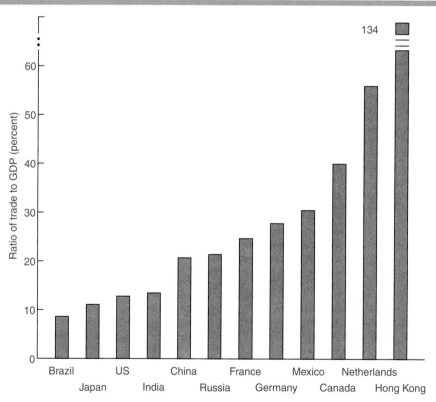

FIGURE 13-2. Openness of Different Economies, 1997

Large countries like the United States and Brazil have small trade shares, while city-states are entrepots which trade more than their net output. (Source: World Bank, www.world-bank.org/data/wdi. Shares are the average of imports and exports of goods and services divided by GDP.)

If a transaction earns foreign currency for the nation, it is called a *credit* and is recorded as a plus item. If a transaction involves spending foreign currency, it is a *debit* and is recorded as a negative item. In general, exports are credits and imports are debits.

Exports earn foreign currency, so they are credits. Imports require spending foreign currency, so they are debits. How is the U.S. import of a Japanese camera recorded? Since we ultimately pay for it in Japanese yen, it is clearly a debit. How shall we treat interest and dividend income on investments received by Americans from abroad? Clearly, they are credit items like exports because they provide us with foreign currencies.

Details of the Balance of Payments

Balance on Current Account. The totality of items under section I in Table 13-1 is the **balance on current account.** This includes all items of income and outlay—imports and exports of goods and services, investment income, and transfer payments. The current-account balance is akin to the net income of a nation. It is conceptually similar to net exports in the national output accounts.

I. **Current account**
    Merchandise (or "trade balance")
    Services
    Investment income
    Unilateral transfers

II. **Financial account**
    Private
    Government
        Official reserve changes
        Other

TABLE 13-1. Basic Elements of the Balance of Payments

The balance of payments has two fundamental parts. The *current account* represents the spending and receipts on goods and services along with transfers. The *financial account* includes purchases and sales of financial assets and liabilities. An important principle is that the two must always sum to zero:

Current account + financial account = I + II = 0

In the past, many writers concentrated on the **trade balance,** which consists of merchandise imports or exports. The composition of merchandise imports and exports consists mainly of primary commodities (like food and fuels) and manufactured goods. In an earlier era, the mercantilists strove for a trade surplus (an excess of exports over imports), calling this a "favorable balance of trade." They hoped to avoid an "unfavorable trade balance," by which they meant a trade deficit (an excess of imports over exports). Even today, we find traces of mercantilism when many nations seek to maintain trade surpluses.

Today, economists avoid this language because a trade deficit is not necessarily harmful. As we will see, the trade deficit is really a reflection of the imbalance between domestic investment and domestic saving. Often, a nation has a trade deficit because its domestic capital is highly profitable and it is beneficial to borrow abroad to invest at home and raise domestic incomes.

In addition, *services* are increasingly important in international trade. Services consist of such items as shipping, financial services, and foreign travel. A third item in the current account is *investment income,* which includes the earnings on foreign investments (such as earnings on U.S. assets abroad). One of the major developments of the last two decades has been the growth in services and investment income. A final element is transfers, which represent payments not in return for goods and services.

Table 13-2 presents a summary of the U.S. balance of international payments for 1999. Note its two main divisions: current account and financial account. Each item is listed by name in column (a). Credits are listed in column (b), while column (c) shows the debits. Column (d) then lists the net credits or debits; it shows a credit if on balance the item added to our stock of foreign currencies or a debit if the total subtracted from our foreign-currency supply.

In 1999 our merchandise exports gave us credits of $683 billion. But our merchandise imports gave us debits of $1030 billion. The *net* difference between credits and debits was a debit of $347 billion. This trade deficit is listed in column (d), in the second row. (Be sure you know why the algebraic sign is shown as − rather than as +.) From the table we see that services provided a surplus, while net investment income was slightly negative. Our current-account deficit was thus $339 billion for 1999.

U.S. Balance of Payments, 1999 (billions of dollars)			
(a) Items	**(b)** Credits (+)	**(c)** Debits (−)	**(d)** Net credits (+) or debits (−)
I. Current account			−339
a. Merchandise trade balance	683	−1030	−347
b. Services	277	−197	80
c. Investment income	274	−299	−25
d. Unilateral transfers			−46
II. Financial account [lending (−) or borrowing (+)]			339
a. Private borrowing or lending	706	−381	325
b. Government			
Official U.S. reserve assets, changes			8
Foreign official assets in the U.S., changes			45
c. Statistical discrepancy			−39
III. Sum of Current and Financial Account			0

TABLE 13-2. Basic Elements of Balance of Payments, 1999

Source: U.S. Department of Commerce, website, April 2000.

Financial Account.[1] We have now completed analysis of the current account. But how did the United States "finance" its $339 billion current-account deficit in 1999? It must have either borrowed or reduced its foreign assets, for by definition, when you buy something, you must either pay for it or borrow for it. This identity means that *the balance of international payments as a whole must by definition show a final zero balance.*

Financial-account transactions are asset transactions between Americans and foreigners. They occur, for example, when a Japanese pension fund buys U.S. government securities or when an American buys stock in a German firm.

Credits and debits are somewhat more complicated in the financial accounts. The general rule, which is drawn from double-entry business accounting, is this: Increases in a country's assets and decreases in its liabilities are entered as debits; conversely, decreases in a country's assets and increases in its liabilities are entered as credits. A debit entry is represented by a negative (−) sign and a credit entry by a positive (+) sign.

You can usually get the right answer more easily if you remember this simplified rule: think of the United States as exporting and importing stocks, bonds, or other securities—that is, exporting and importing IOUs in return for foreign currencies. Then you can treat these exports and imports of securities like other exports and imports. When we borrow abroad to finance a current-account deficit, we are sending IOUs (in the form of Treasury bills) abroad and getting foreign currencies. Is this a credit or a debit? Clearly this is a credit because it brought foreign currencies into the United States.

Similarly, if U.S. banks lend abroad to finance a computer assembly plant in Mexico, the U.S. banks are importing IOUs from the Mexicans and the United States is losing foreign currencies; this is clearly a debit item in the U.S. balance of payments.

[1] In 1999, the United States revised its international accounts to conform to new guidelines. What was formerly called the "capital account" became the "financial account." A newly defined capital account consists of capital transfers and the acquisition and disposal of nonproduced nonfinancial assets. This new terminology is helpful because it emphasizes that the financial account involves flows of financial assets and liabilities rather than aircraft and factories. The newly defined capital account is extremely small and has been omitted from the discussion in this chapter.

Line II shows that in 1999 the United States was a net *borrower*: we borrowed abroad more than we lent to foreigners. The United States was a net exporter of IOUs (a net borrower) in the amount of $339 billion.[2]

Official Reserves. One item of the financial account—official-reserve changes—plays a very important role in international finance. These are the funds that governments and central banks use to manage their exchange rates. We will see later in this chapter that when a country maintains a fixed exchange rate, it does so by buying and selling foreign currencies (or by "intervening" in foreign exchange markets). Such transactions show up in the balance of payments as changes in *official reserves*.

By contrast, when countries have market-determined (or flexible) exchange rates, there is little intervention, and changes in official reserves are relatively small. In today's increasingly integrated global financial markets, financial flows are dominated by private asset transactions.

The life cycle of the balance of payments
The balance of payments of industrial countries often have similar life cycles as the nations grow from young debtors to mature creditors. This sequence is found, with variations related to their particular histories, in the advanced economies of North America, Europe, and Southeast Asia. We can illustrate the stages by recounting briefly the history of the balance of payments of the United States:

1. *Young and growing debtor nation.* From the Revolutionary War until the Civil War, the United States imported on current account more than it exported. Europe lent the difference, which allowed the country to build up its capital stock. The United States was a typical young and growing debtor nation.

2. *Mature debtor nation.* From about 1873 to 1914, the U.S. balance of trade moved into surplus. But growth of the dividends and interest that were owed abroad on past borrowing kept the current account more or less in balance. Financial flows were also nearly in balance as lending just offset borrowing.

3. *New creditor nation.* During World War I, the United States expanded its exports tremendously. America lent money to allies England and France for war equipment and postwar relief needs. The United States emerged from the war a creditor nation.

4. *Mature creditor nation.* In the fourth stage, earnings on foreign investments provided a large surplus that was matched by a deficit on merchandise trade. This pattern was followed by the United States until the early 1980s. Countries like Japan today play the role of mature creditor nation as they enjoy large current-account surpluses which they in turn invest abroad.

The United States has entered an interesting new position over the last two decades. Surprisingly, the nation borrowed heavily from abroad to finance its domestic investment. In part, the foreign borrowing was caused by low U.S. domestic saving relative to its investment. While Americans were saving relatively little, financial flows came to the United States because of the country's political stability, low inflation, booming stock market, and robust technological innovation. The counterpart of American dissaving was that other countries, particularly Japan, were saving more than they were investing and were running a current-account surplus.

Is this new stage of the U.S. balance of payments a temporary aberration? Or does it mark the beginning of a long period of "structural" current-account deficits? Many economists worry about the large deficit and wonder whether it will lead to a major decline in the exchange rate of the dollar. Even if the U.S. current account swings back toward balance, however, the country will still have a large foreign debt to service. When balance occurs, the United States will once again be a mature debtor nation, going back to stage 2, above.

---

[2] As with all economic statistics, the balance-of-payments accounts necessarily contain statistical errors (called the "statistical discrepancy"). These reflect the fact that many flows of goods and finance (from small currency transactions to the drug trade) are not recorded. We include the statistical discrepancy in the private financial account in line II(c) of Table 13-2.

B. THE DETERMINATION OF FOREIGN EXCHANGE RATES

FOREIGN EXCHANGE RATES

We are all familiar with domestic trade. When I buy Florida oranges or California computers, I naturally want to pay in dollars. Luckily, the orange grower and the computer manufacturer want payment in U.S. currency, so all trade can be carried out in dollars. Economic transactions within a country are relatively simple.

But suppose I am in the business of selling Japanese bicycles. Here, the transaction becomes more complicated. The bicycle manufacturer wants to be paid in Japanese currency rather than in U.S. dollars. Therefore, in order to import the Japanese bicycles, I must first buy Japanese yen (¥) and use those yen to pay the Japanese manufacturer. Similarly, if the Japanese want to buy U.S. merchandise, they must first obtain U.S. dollars. This new complication involves foreign exchange.

Foreign trade involves the use of different national currencies. The *foreign exchange rate* is the price of one currency in terms of another currency. The foreign exchange rate is determined in the foreign exchange market, which is the market where different currencies are traded.

That little paragraph contains much information that will be explained in this section. We begin with the fact that most major countries have their own currencies—the U.S. dollar, the Japanese yen, the Mexican peso, and so forth. (European countries are an exception in that they have a common currency, the Euro.) *We follow the convention of measuring exchange rates as the amount of foreign currency that can be bought with 1 unit of the domestic currency.* For example, the foreign exchange rate of the dollar might be 100 yen per U.S. dollar (¥100/$).

When we want to exchange one national money for another, we do so at a foreign exchange rate. For example, if you traveled to Canada in 2000, you would get about 1.4 Canadian dollars for 1 U.S. dollar. There is a foreign exchange rate between U.S. dollars and the currency of each and every other country. In fall 2000, the foreign exchange rate per U.S. dollar was 0.90 Euro, 0.62 British pound, 1.96 German marks, 95 Japanese yen, and 9.2 Mexican pesos.

With foreign exchange, it is possible for me to buy a Japanese bicycle. Suppose its quoted price is 20,000 yen. I can look in the newspaper for the foreign exchange rate for yen. Suppose the rate is ¥100/$. I could go to the bank to convert my $200 into ¥20,000. With my Japanese money, I then can pay the exporter for my bicycle in the currency it wants.

You should be able to show what Japanese importers of American trucks have to do if they want to buy, say, a $36,000 truck from an American exporter. Here yen must be converted into dollars. You will see that, when the foreign exchange rate is 100 yen per dollar, the truck shipment costs them ¥3,600,000.[3]

Businesses and tourists do not have to know anything more than this for their import or export transactions. But the economics of foreign exchange rates cannot be grasped until we analyze the forces underlying the supply and demand for foreign currencies and the functioning of the foreign exchange market.

THE FOREIGN EXCHANGE MARKET

Like most other prices, foreign exchange rates vary from week to week and month to month according to the forces of supply and demand. The **foreign exchange market** is the market in which currencies of different countries are traded and foreign exchange rates are determined. Foreign currencies are traded at the retail level in many banks and firms specializing in that business. Organized markets in New York, Tokyo, London, and Zurich trade hundreds of billions of dollars worth of currencies each day.

We can use our familiar supply and demand curves to illustrate how markets determine the price of foreign currencies. Figure 13-3 shows the supply and demand for U.S. dollars that arise in dealings

---

[3] These examples ignore transactions costs and the spread between buying price and selling price (the "bid-ask spread"). These costs can be substantial, particularly for small transactions. One of the advantages of a common currency among regions with substantial trade is that it reduces transactions costs and thereby improves efficiency.

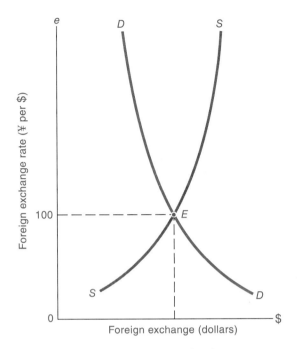

FIGURE 13-3. Exchange-Rate Determination

Behind the supplies and demands for foreign exchange lie purchases of goods, services, and financial assets. Behind the demand for dollars is the Japanese desire for American goods and investments. The supply of dollars comes from Americans desiring Japanese goods and assets. Equilibrium comes at *E*. If the foreign exchange rate were above *E*, there would be an excess supply of dollars. Unless the government bought this excess supply with official reserves, market forces would push the foreign exchange rate back down to balance supply and demand at *E*.

with Japan.[4] The *supply* of U.S. dollars comes from people in the United States who need yen to purchase Japanese goods, services, or financial assets. The *demand* for dollars comes from people in Japan who buy U.S. goods, services, or investments and who, accordingly, need dollars to pay for these items. The price of foreign exchange—the foreign exchange rate—settles at that price where supply and demand are in balance.

Let us first consider the supply side. The supply of U.S. dollars to the foreign exchange market orig-

inates when Americans need yen to buy Japanese automobiles, cameras, and other commodities, to vacation in Tokyo, and so forth. In addition, foreign exchange is required if Americans want to purchase Japanese assets, such as shares in Japanese companies. In short, *Americans supply dollars when they purchase foreign goods, services, and assets.*

In Figure 13-3, the vertical axis is the crucial foreign exchange rate (*e*), measured in units of foreign currency per unit of domestic currency—that is, in yen per dollar, in Mexican pesos per dollar, and so forth. Make sure you understand the units here. The horizontal axis shows the quantity of dollars bought and sold in the foreign exchange market.

The supply of U.S. dollars is represented by the upward-sloping *SS* curve. The upward slope indicates that as the foreign exchange rate rises, the number of yen that can be bought per dollar increases. This means, with other things held constant, that the prices of Japanese goods fall relative to those of American goods. Hence, Americans will tend to buy more Japanese goods, and the supply of U.S. dollars therefore increases. This shows why the supply curve slopes upward. Let's take the example of bicycles. If the foreign exchange rate were to rise from ¥100/$ to ¥200/$, the bicycle which cost ¥20,000 would fall in price from $200 to $100. If other things are constant, Japanese bicycles would be more attractive, and Americans would sell more dollars in the foreign exchange market to buy more bicycles. Hence, the quantity supplied of dollars would be higher at a higher exchange rate.

What lies behind the demand for dollars (represented in Figure 13-3 by the *DD* demand curve for dollar foreign exchange)? Foreigners demand U.S. dollars when they buy American goods, services, and assets. For example, suppose a Japanese student buys an American economics textbook or takes a trip to the United States. She will require U.S. dollars to pay for these items. Or when Japan Airlines buys a Boeing 767 for its fleet, this transaction increases the demand for U.S. dollars. If Japanese pension funds invest in U.S. Internet stocks, this would require a purchase of dollars. *Foreigners demand U.S. dollars to pay for their purchases of American goods, services, and assets.*

The demand curve in Figure 13-3 slopes downward to indicate that as the dollar's value falls (and the yen therefore becomes more expensive),

---

[4] This is a simplified example in which we consider only the bilateral trade between Japan and the United States.

Japanese residents will want to buy more foreign goods, services, and investments. They will therefore demand more U.S. dollars in the foreign exchange market. Consider what happens when the foreign exchange rate on the dollar falls from ¥100/$ to ¥50/$. American computers, which had sold at $2000 × (¥100/$) = ¥200,000 now sell for only $2000 × (¥50/$) = ¥100,000. Japanese purchasers will therefore tend to buy more American computers, and the quantity demanded of U.S. foreign exchange will increase.

Market forces move the foreign exchange rate up or down to balance the supply and demand. The price will settle at the *equilibrium foreign exchange rate*, which is the rate at which the dollars willingly bought just equal the dollars willingly sold.

The balance of supply and demand for foreign exchange determines the foreign exchange rate of a currency. At the market exchange rate of 100 yen per dollar shown at point *E* in Figure 13-3, the exchange rate is in equilibrium and has no tendency to rise or fall.

We have discussed the foreign exchange market in terms of the supply and demand for dollars. But in this market, there are two currencies involved, so we could just as easily analyze the supply and demand for Japanese yen. To see this, you should sketch a supply-and-demand diagram with yen foreign exchange on the horizontal axis and the yen rate ($ per ¥) on the vertical axis. If ¥100/$ is the equilibrium looking from the point of view of the dollar, then $0.01/¥ is the *reciprocal exchange rate*. As an exercise, go through the analysis in this section for the reciprocal market. You will see that in this simple bilateral world, for every dollar statement there is an exact yen counterpart: supply of dollars is demand for yen; demand for dollars is supply of yen.

There is just one further extension necessary to get to actual foreign exchange markets. In reality, there are many different currencies. We therefore need to find the supplies and demands for each and every currency. And in a world of many nations, it is the many-sided exchange and trade, with demands and supplies coming from all parts of the globe, that determines the entire array of foreign exchange rates.

Terminology for exchange-rate changes
Foreign exchange markets have a special vocabulary. By definition, a fall in the price of one currency in terms of one or all others is called a *depreciation*. A rise in the price of a currency in terms of another currency is called an *appreciation*. In our example above, when the price of the dollar rose from ¥100/$ to ¥200/$, the dollar appreciated. We also know that the yen depreciated.

In the supply-and-demand diagram for U.S. dollars, a fall in the foreign exchange rate (*e*) is a depreciation of the U.S. dollar, and a rise in e represents an appreciation.

The term "devaluation" is often confused with the term "depreciation." Devaluation is confined to situations in which a country has officially fixed or "pegged" its exchange rate relative to one or more other currencies. In this case, a *devaluation* occurs when the pegged or fixed exchange rate is changed by lowering the price of the currency. A *revaluation* occurs when the official price is raised.

For example, in December 1994 Mexico devalued its currency when it lowered the official price at which it was defending the peso from 3.5 pesos per dollar to 3.8 pesos per dollar. Mexico soon found it could not defend the new parity and "floated" its exchange rate. At that point, the peso fell, or depreciated, even further.

When a country's currency falls in value relative to that of another country, we say that the domestic currency has undergone a **depreciation** while the foreign currency has undergone an **appreciation**.

When a country's official foreign exchange rate is lowered, we say that the currency has undergone a **devaluation**. An increase in the official foreign exchange rate is called a **revaluation**.

Effects of Changes in Trade

What would happen if there were changes in demand? For example, if Japan has a recession, its demand for imports declines. As a result, the demand for American dollars would decrease. The result is shown in Figure 13-4. The decline in purchases of American goods, services, and investments decreases the demand for dollars in the market. This change is represented by a leftward shift in the demand curve. The result will be a lower foreign exchange

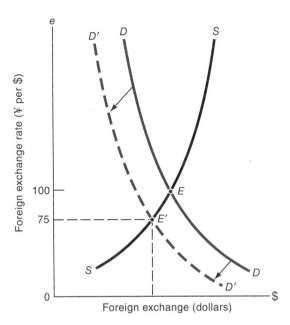

FIGURE 13-4. A Decrease in Demand for Dollars Leads to Dollar Depreciation

Suppose that a recession or deflation in Japan reduces the Japanese demand for dollars. This would shift the demand for dollars to the left from DD to $D'D'$. The exchange rate of the dollar depreciates, while the yen appreciates. Why would the new exchange rate discourage American purchases of Japanese goods?

rate—that is, the dollar will depreciate and the yen will appreciate. At the lower exchange rate, the quantity of dollars supplied by Americans to the market will decrease because Japanese goods are now more expensive. Moreover, the quantity of dollars demanded by the Japanese will decline because of the recession. How much will exchange rates change? Just enough so that the supply and demand are again in balance. In the example shown in Figure 13-4, the dollar has depreciated from ¥100/$ to ¥75/$.

Let's take a case involving the financial account. Suppose, as happened in 2000, that the Federal Reserve tightens U.S. monetary policy because inflationary pressures have been increasing. This would make U.S. dollar assets more attractive than foreign assets as dollar interest rates rise relative to interest rates on Japanese or European securities. As a result, the demand for dollars increases and the dollar appreciates. This sequence is shown in Figure 13-5.

Exchange Rates and the Balance of Payments

What is the connection between exchange rates and adjustments in the balance of payments? In the simplest case, assume that exchange rates are determined by private supply and demand with no government intervention. Consider what happened in 1990 after German unification when the German central bank decided to raise interest rates to curb inflation. After the monetary tightening, foreigners moved some of their assets into German

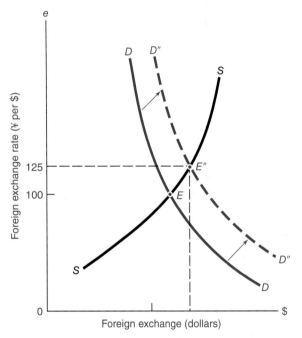

FIGURE 13-5. Monetary Tightening Increases Demand for Dollars and Produces Dollar Appreciation

Monetary policy can affect the exchange rate through the financial account. If the central bank raises dollar interest rates, this induces investors into dollar securities and raises the demand for dollar foreign exchange. The result is an appreciation of the dollar. (Explain why this leads to depreciation of the Japanese yen or the Euro.)

marks to benefit from high German interest rates. This produced an excess demand for the German mark at the old exchange rate. In other words, at the old foreign exchange rate, people were, on balance, buying German marks and selling other currencies. (You can redraw Figure 13-5 to show this situation.)

Here is where the exchange rate plays its role as equilibrator. As the demand for German marks increased, it led to an appreciation of the German mark and a depreciation of other currencies, such as the U.S. dollar. The movement in the exchange rate continued until the financial and current accounts were back in balance. The equilibration for the current account is easiest to understand. Here, the appreciation of the mark made German goods more expensive and led to a decline in German exports and an increase in German imports. Both of these factors tended to reduce the German current-account surplus.

Exchange-rate movements serve as a balance wheel to remove disequilibria in the balance of payments.

Purchasing-Power Parity and Exchange Rates

In the short run, market-determined exchange rates are highly volatile in response to monetary policy, political events, and changes in expectations. But over the longer run, exchange rates are determined primarily by the relative prices of goods in different countries. An important implication is the *purchasing-power parity (PPP) theory of exchange rates.* Under this theory, a nation's exchange rate will tend to equalize the cost of buying traded goods at home with the cost of buying those goods abroad.

The PPP theory can then be illustrated with a simple example. Suppose the price of a market basket of goods (automobiles, jewelry, oil, foods, and so forth) costs $1000 in the United States and 10,000 pesos in Mexico. At an exchange rate of 100 pesos to a dollar, this bundle would cost $100 in Mexico. Given these relative prices and the free trade between the two countries, we would expect to see American firms and consumers streaming across the border to buy at the lower Mexican prices. The result would be higher imports from Mexico and an increased demand for Mexican pesos. That would cause the exchange rate of the Mexican peso to appreciate relative to the U.S. dollar, so you would need more dollars to buy the same number of pesos. As a result, the prices of the Mexican goods *in dollar terms* would rise even though the prices in pesos have not changed.

Where would this process end? With unchanged domestic prices in the two countries, the peso's exchange rate must fall to 10 pesos to the dollar. Only at this exchange rate would the price of the market basket of goods be equal in the two markets. At 10 pesos to the dollar, we say that the currencies have equal purchasing power in terms of the traded goods. (You can firm up your understanding of this discussion by calculating the price of the market basket in both Mexican pesos and U.S. dollars before and after the appreciation of the peso.)

The PPP doctrine also holds that countries with high inflation rates will tend to have depreciating currencies. For example, if Country A's inflation rate is 10 percent while inflation in Country B is 2 percent, the currency of Country A will tend to depreciate relative to that of Country B by the difference in the inflation rates, that is, 8 percent annually. Alternatively, let's say that runaway inflation leads to a 100-fold rise of prices in Russia over the course of a year, while prices in the United States are unchanged. According to the PPP theory, the Russian ruble should depreciate by 99 percent in order to bring the prices of American and Russian goods back into equilibrium.

We should caution that the PPP theory is only an approximation and cannot predict the precise movement of exchange rates. The leeway in the PPP theory is seen in the relationship between the U.S. dollar and the Japanese yen over the last decade; this exchange rate has been as high as 168 yen to a dollar and as low as 85 yen to a dollar, even though most economists calculate the PPP level as being around 120 yen to a dollar. Trade barriers, transportation costs, and the presence of nontraded services allow prices to diverge significantly across countries. In addition, financial flows can overwhelm trade flows in the short run. So while the PPP theory is a useful guide to exchange rates in the long run, exchange rates can diverge from their PPP level for many years.

PPP and the size of nations

By any measure, the United States still has the largest economy in the world. But which country has the second largest? Is it Japan, Germany, Russia, or some other country? You would think this would be an easy question to answer, like measuring height or weight. The problem, however, is that Japan totes up its national output in yen, while Russia's national output is given in rubles, and America's is in dollars. To be compared, they all need to be converted into the same currency.

The customary approach is to use the market exchange rate to convert each currency into dollars, and by that yardstick Japan has the second-largest economy. However, there are two difficulties with using the market rate. First, because market rates can rise and fall sharply, the "size" of countries might change by 10 or 20 percent overnight.

Moreover, using market exchange rates, many poor countries appear to have a very small national output.

Today, economists generally prefer to use PPP exchange rates to compare the living standards in different countries. The difference can be dramatic, as Figure 13-6 shows. When market exchange rates are used, the outputs of low-income countries like China and India tend to be understated. This understatement occurs because a substantial part of their output comes in labor-intensive services, which are usually extremely inexpensive in low-wage countries. Hence, when we calculate PPP exchange rates including the prices of non-traded goods, the GDPs of low-income countries rise relative to those of high-wage countries. For example, when PPP exchange rates are used, China's GDP is 5 times the level calculated with market exchange rates. Furthermore, on the basis of PPP exchange rates, China leaps ahead of Japan to become the second-largest economy in the world.

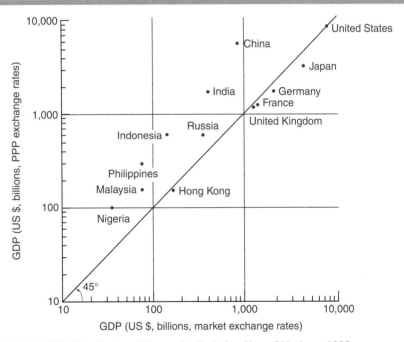

FIGURE 13-6. PPP Calculations Change the Relative Size of Nations, 1998

Using PPP exchange rates changes the economic ranking of nations. After correcting for the purchasing power of incomes, China moves from a middle-ranking country to an economic superpower. Note that points along the 45° line are ones for which GDPs using the two exchange rates are equal. Points above the line, such as China, are ones for which the PPP estimate of GDP is above the standard calculation. Japan is below the line because relative prices in Japan are high due to high rents and trade barriers. (Source: World Bank. Note that outputs are shown on a ratio scale.)

C. THE INTERNATIONAL MONETARY SYSTEM

While the simple supply-and-demand diagrams for the foreign exchange market explain the major determinants, they do not capture the drama and central importance of the international monetary system. The 1990s witnessed crisis after crisis in international finance—in Europe in 1991–1992, in Mexico and Latin America in 1994–1995, and in East Asia and Russia in 1997–1998. Although the United States avoided most of the fallout from these crises, this period underlined the importance of a well-functioning international monetary system.

What is the **international monetary system**? This term denotes the institutions under which payments are made for transactions that cross national boundaries. In particular, the international monetary system determines how foreign exchange rates are set and how governments can affect exchange rates.

The importance of the international monetary system was well described by economist Robert Solomon:

> Like the traffic lights in a city, the international monetary system is taken for granted until it begins to malfunction and to disrupt people's lives. . . . A well-functioning monetary system will facilitate international trade and investment and smooth adaptation to change. A monetary system that functions poorly may not only discourage the development of trade and investment among nations but subject their economies to disruptive shocks when necessary adjustments to change are prevented or delayed.[5]

The central element of the international monetary system involves the arrangements by which exchange rates are set. In recent years, nations have used one of three major exchange-rate systems:

- A system of fixed exchange rates
- A system of flexible or floating exchange rates, where exchange rates are determined by market forces
- Managed exchange rates, in which nations intervene to smooth exchange-rate fluctuations or to move their currency toward a target zone.

---

[5] See this chapter's Further Reading section for the citation.

FIXED EXCHANGE RATES: THE CLASSICAL GOLD STANDARD

At one extreme is a system of **fixed exchange rates,** where governments specify the exact rate at which dollars will be converted into pesos, yen, and other currencies. Historically, the most important fixed-exchange-rate system was the **gold standard,** which was used off and on from 1717 until 1933. In this system, each country defined the value of its currency in terms of a fixed amount of gold, thereby establishing fixed exchange rates among the countries on the gold standard.[6]

The functioning of the gold standard can be seen easily in a simplified example. Suppose people everywhere insisted on being paid in bits of pure gold metal. Then buying a bicycle in Britain would merely require payment in gold at a price expressed in ounces of gold. By definition there would be no foreign-exchange-rate problem. Gold would be the common world currency.

This example captures the essence of the gold standard. Once gold became the medium of exchange or money, foreign trade was no different from domestic trade; everything could be paid for in gold. The only difference between countries was that they could choose different *units* for their gold coins. Thus, Queen Victoria chose to make British coins about $\frac{1}{4}$ ounce of gold (the pound) and President McKinley chose to make the U.S. unit $\frac{1}{20}$ ounce of gold (the dollar). In that case, the British pound, being 5 times as heavy as the dollar, had an exchange rate of $5/£1.

This was the essence of the gold standard. In practice, countries tended to use their own coins. But anyone was free to melt down coins and sell them at the going price of gold. So exchange rates were fixed for all countries on the gold standard. The exchange rates (also called "par values" or "parities") for different currencies were determined by the gold content of their monetary units.

---

[6] Why was gold used as the standard of exchange and means of payment, rather than some other commodity? Certainly other materials could have been used, but gold had the advantages of being in limited supply, being relatively indestructible, and having few industrial uses. Can you see why wine, wheat, or cattle would not be a useful means of payment among countries?

Hume's Adjustment Mechanism

The purpose of an exchange-rate system is to promote international trade and finance while facilitating adjustment to shocks. How exactly does the *international adjustment mechanism* function? What happens if a country's wages and prices rise so sharply that its goods are no longer competitive in the world market? Under flexible exchange rates, the country's exchange rate could depreciate to offset the domestic inflation. But under fixed exchange rates, equilibrium must be restored by deflation at home or inflation abroad.

Let's examine the international adjustment mechanism under a fixed-exchange-rate system with two countries, America and Britain. Suppose that American inflation has made American goods uncompetitive. Consequently, America's imports rise and its exports fall. It therefore runs a trade deficit with Britain. To pay for its deficit, America would have to ship gold to Britain. Eventually—if there were no adjustments in either America or Britain—America would run out of gold.

In fact, an automatic adjustment mechanism does exist, as was demonstrated by the British philosopher David Hume in 1752. He showed that the outflow of gold was part of a mechanism that tended to keep international payments in balance. His argument, though nearly 250 years old, offers important insights for understanding how trade flows get balanced in today's economy.

Hume's explanation rested in part upon the quantity theory of prices, which is a theory of the overall price level that is analyzed in macroeconomics. This doctrine holds that the overall price level in an economy is proportional to the supply of money. Under the gold standard, gold was an important part of the money supply—either directly, in the form of gold coins, or indirectly, when governments used gold as backing for paper money.

What would be the impact of a country's losing gold? First, the country's money supply would decline either because gold coins would be exported or because some of the gold backing for the currency would leave the country. Putting both these consequences together, a loss of gold leads to a reduction in the money supply. According to the quantity theory, the next step is that prices and costs would change proportionally to the change in the money supply. If the United States loses 10 percent of its gold to pay for a trade deficit, the quantity theory predicts that U.S. prices, costs, and incomes would fall 10 percent. In other words, the economy would experience a deflation. If gold discoveries in California increase America's gold supplies, we would expect to see a major increase in the price level in the United States.

The Four-Pronged Mechanism. Now consider Hume's theory of international payments equilibrium. Suppose that America runs a large trade deficit and begins to lose gold. According to the quantity theory of prices, this loss of gold reduces America's money supply, driving down America's prices and costs. As a result, (1) America decreases its imports of British and other foreign goods, which have become relatively expensive; and (2) because America's domestically produced goods have become relatively inexpensive on world markets, America's exports increase.

The opposite effect occurs in Britain and other foreign countries. Because Britain's exports are growing rapidly, it receives gold in return. Britain's money supply therefore increases, driving up British prices and costs according to the quantity theory. At this point, two more prongs of the Hume mechanism come into play: (3) British and other foreign exports have become more expensive, so the volume of goods exported to America and elsewhere declines; and (4) British citizens, faced with a higher domestic price level, now import more of America's low-priced goods.

Figure 13-7 illustrates the logic in Hume's mechanism. Make sure you can follow the logical chain from the original deficit at the top through the adjustment to the new equilibrium at the bottom.

The result of Hume's four-pronged gold-flow mechanism is an improvement in the balance of payments of the country losing gold and a worsening in that of the country gaining the gold. In the end, an equilibrium of international trade and finance is reestablished at new relative prices, which keep trade and international lending in balance with no net gold flow. This equilibrium is a stable one and requires no tariffs or other government intervention.

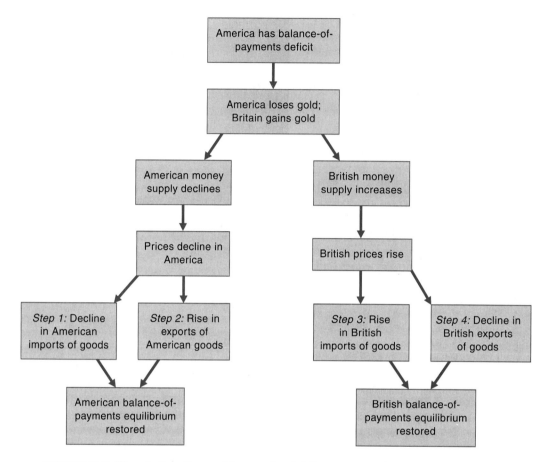

FIGURE 13-7. Hume's Four-Pronged International Adjustment Mechanism

Hume explained how a balance-of-payments disequilibrium would automatically produce equilibrating adjustments under a gold standard. Trace the lines from the original disequilibrium at the top through the changes in prices to the restored equilibrium at the bottom. This mechanism works in modified form under any fixed-exchange-rate system. Modern economics augments the mechanism in the fourth row of boxes by replacing the fourth row with "Prices, output, and employment decline in America" and "Prices, output, and employment rise in Britain."

Adjustment with Fixed Exchange Rates. Understanding the gold standard is important not only because of its historical role but also because it is a pure example of a fixed-exchange-rate system. The same analysis applies to all fixed-exchange-rate systems: If exchange rates are not free to move when the prices or incomes among countries get out of line, *domestic* prices and incomes must adjust to restore equilibrium. Now that Europe has adopted a common currency, any imbalance in output or employment among the European nations must be made through changes in domestic price levels rather than changes in exchange rates.

In Hume's mechanism, it is gold flows that move prices and wages and ensure equilibrium. In modern macroeconomic thinking, prices and wages adjust through movements in output and employment. *The necessity of having real output and employment adjust to ensure relative-price equilibrium among countries on a fixed exchange rate is a crucial dilemma faced by countries considering a fixed exchange rate.*

INTERNATIONAL MONETARY INSTITUTIONS AFTER WORLD WAR II

In the early part of the twentieth century, even nations which were ostensibly at peace engaged in debilitating trade wars and competitive devaluations. After World War II, international institutions were developed to foster economic cooperation among nations. These institutions continue to be the means by which nations coordinate their policies and seek solutions to common problems.

The United States emerged from World War II with its economy intact—able and willing to help rebuild the countries of friends and foes alike. The postwar international political system responded to the needs of war-torn nations by establishing durable institutions that facilitated the quick recovery of the international economy. The major international economic institutions of the postwar period were the General Agreement on Tariffs and Trade (rechartered as the World Trade Organization in 1995), the Bretton Woods exchange-rate system, the International Monetary Fund, and the World Bank. These four institutions helped the industrial democracies rebuild themselves and grow rapidly after the devastation of World War II, and they continue to be the major international institutions today.

The International Monetary Fund

An integral part of the Bretton Woods system was the establishment of the International Monetary Fund (or IMF), which still administers the international monetary system and operates as a central bank for central banks. Member nations subscribe by lending their currencies to the IMF; the IMF then relends these funds to help countries in balance-of-payments difficulties. The main function of the IMF is to make temporary loans to countries which have balance-of-payments problems or are under speculative attack in financial markets.

The World Bank

Another international financial institution created after World War II was the World Bank. The Bank is capitalized by high-income nations that subscribe in proportion to their economic importance in terms of GDP and other factors. The Bank makes long-term low-interest loans to countries for projects which are economically sound but which cannot get private-

sector financing. As a result of such long-term loans, goods and services flow from advanced nations to developing countries. In 1999, the World Bank group had outstanding loans in developing countries of $119 billion and made new loan commitments of $22 billion.

The Bretton Woods System of Fixed but Adjustable Exchange Rates

Economists of the 1930s and 1940s, particularly John Maynard Keynes, were greatly influenced by the economic crisis of the prewar period. They were determined to avoid the economic chaos and competitive devaluations that had occurred during the Great Depression. They believed that the gold standard was too inflexible and served to deepen and lengthen business cycles.

Under the intellectual leadership of Keynes and American Harry Dexter White, nations gathered in 1944 at Bretton Woods, New Hampshire, and hammered out an agreement that led to the formation of the major economic institutions. For the first time, nations agreed upon a system for regulating international financial transactions. Even though some of the rules have changed since 1944, the institutions established at Bretton Woods continue to play a vital role today.

To replace the gold standard, the **Bretton Woods system** established a parity for each currency in terms of both the U.S. dollar and gold. Currencies were defined in terms of both gold and the dollar, and exchange rates among currencies were determined in much the same way as they had been under the gold standard. For example, the parity of the British pound was set at £12.5 per ounce of gold. Given that the gold price of the dollar was $35 per ounce, this implied an official exchange rate between the dollar and the pound of $35/£12.5 = $2.80 per £1, which was thereby set as the official parity on the pound.

The revolutionary innovation of the Bretton Woods system was that exchange rates were *fixed but adjustable*. When one currency got too far out of line with its appropriate or "fundamental" value, the parity could be adjusted. The ability to adjust exchange rates when fundamental disequilibrium arose was the central distinction between the Bretton Woods system and the gold standard. Ideally, exchange-rate changes would be worked out among countries in a cooperative way.

By creating a fixed but adjustable system, the designers of Bretton Woods hoped to have the best of two worlds. They could maintain the *stability* of the gold standard, a world in which exchange rates would be predictable from one month to the next, thereby encouraging trade and financial flows. At the same time, the system would allow the *adjustment* provided by flexible exchange rates. Exchange-rate changes could occasionally offset persistent relative-price differences among countries instead of relying on the painful deflation and unemployment necessary under the gold standard.

Demise of the Bretton Woods System

For the first three decades after World War II, under the Bretton Woods arrangements, the U.S. dollar was the key currency. Most international trade and finance were carried out in dollars, and payments were most often made in dollars. During this period of rapid economic growth, the world was on a dollar standard.

But recovery contained the seeds of its own destruction. U.S. trade deficits were fueled by an overvalued currency, budget deficits to finance the Vietnam war, and growing overseas investment by American firms. By 1971, the stock of liquid dollar balances had become so large that governments had difficulty defending the official parities. And the lower barriers to financial flows meant that billions of dollars could cross the Atlantic in minutes and threaten to overwhelm existing parities.

On August 15, 1971, President Nixon formally severed the link between the dollar and gold, bringing the Bretton Woods era to an end. No longer would the United States automatically convert dollars into other currencies or into gold at $35 per ounce. No longer would the United States set an official parity of the dollar and then defend this exchange rate at all costs. As the United States abandoned the Bretton Woods system, the world moved into the modern era.

How to ensure a credibly fixed exchange rate through the "hard fix"

Although the demise of the Bretton Woods system marked the end of a predominantly fixed exchange-rate system among major countries, many countries continue to opt for fixed exchange rates. A recurrent problem arises when countries adopt adjustable or "soft" fixed-exchange-rate systems like the Bretton Woods system: They are prey to speculative attacks. (We will return to this problem in the next chapter.) How can countries improve the credibility of their fixed-exchange-rate systems? Are there "hard" fixed-exchange-rate systems that will better withstand speculative attacks?

Economists who study this type of situation emphasize the importance of establishing credibility. In this instance, credibility may be enhanced by creating a system that would actually make it *hard* for the country to change its exchange rate. This approach is similar to a military strategy of burning the bridges behind the army so that there is no retreat and the soldiers will have to fight to the death. Indeed, Argentina's leader said that his new system would have "death before devaluation."

One solution is to create **currency boards.** A currency board is a monetary institution that issues only currency that is fully backed by foreign assets in a key foreign currency, usually the U.S. dollar. A currency board defends an exchange rate that is fixed by law rather than just by policy, and the currency board is usually independent, and sometimes even private. Under currency boards, a payments deficit will generally trigger Hume's automatic adjustment mechanism. That is, balance-of-payments deficit will reduce the money supply, leading to an economic contraction and eventually reducing domestic prices and restoring adjustment. Important examples of currency boards today are found in Hong Kong and Argentina.

An even harder fixed exchange rate is established when countries adopt a **common currency** through monetary union. The United States has had a common currency since 1776. The most important recent example of a monetary union occurred when eleven European countries adopted the "Euro" as their common currency in 1999. This is the hardest fix of all because the currencies of the different countries are defined to be the same. (We will return to a further analysis of the Euro in the next chapter.) A variant of the common currency comes when a country adopts a key currency for its own money. This approach was followed when Ecuador adopted the U.S. dollar as its currency in 2000.

These novel ways to devise hard fixed exchange rates are being watched carefully to see if they can help prevent the financial disruptions that plagued countries with soft fixed-exchange-rate systems in the 1990s.

Intervention

When a government fixes its exchange rate, it must "intervene" in foreign exchange markets to maintain the rate. Government exchange-rate **intervention** occurs when the government buys or sells foreign exchange to affect exchange rates. For example, the Japanese government on a given day might buy $1 billion worth of Japanese yen with U.S. dollars. This would cause a rise in value, or an appreciation, of the yen.

Figure 13-8 illustrates the operation of a fixed-exchange-rate system. In 1991, Argentina established a currency board which fixed the exchange rate at 1 U.S. dollar per peso. The initial equilibrium is shown as point A in Figure 13-8. At an exchange rate of $1 per peso, the quantities of pesos supplied and demanded are equal.

Suppose that the demand for pesos falls—perhaps because inflation in Argentina is higher than that in the United States or because Brazil, an important trading partner, has a recession or a depreciation. This produces a downward shift in the demand for pesos from D to D'. In a world of flexible exchange rates, the peso would depreciate and reach a new equilibrium, say, at B in Figure 13-8.

Recall that Argentina is committed to maintaining the parity of $1 per peso. What can it do?

- One approach is to intervene by *buying the depreciating currency (pesos) and selling the appreciating currency (dollars)*. In this example, if Argentina's central bank buys the amount shown by the segment *CA*, this will increase the demand for pesos and maintain the official parity.
- An alternative would be to use monetary policy. Argentina could *induce the private sector to increase its demand for pesos* by raising interest rates. Say that Argentinian interest rates rise relative to U.S. rates; this would lead investors to move funds into pesos and increase the private demand for pesos, in effect moving the private demand curve back toward the original D demand curve.

These two operations are not really as different as they sound. In effect, both involve monetary policies in Argentina. In fact, one of the complications of managing the open economy, as we will see shortly, is that the need to use monetary policies to manage the exchange rate can collide with the need to use monetary policy to stabilize the domestic business cycle.

FLEXIBLE EXCHANGE RATES

Fixed exchange rates are one of the cornerstones of today's international monetary system—the other important system is flexible exchange rates. A country has **flexible exchange rates** when exchange rates move purely under the influence of supply and demand. In such a system, the government neither announces an exchange rate nor takes steps to enforce one. Another term often used is **floating exchange rates,** which means the same thing.

Today, flexible exchange rates are used by the three major economic regions—the United States, the countries of Euroland, and Japan. For these three regions, the movements of exchange rates are determined almost entirely by private supply and demand for goods, services, and investments.

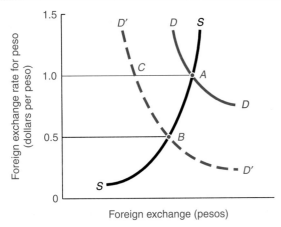

FIGURE 13-8. Governments Intervene to Defend Fixed Exchange Rate

Say that Argentina establishes a currency board with a fixed exchange rate of 1 U.S. dollar per peso. Initial equilibrium is at *A*. Deteriorating economic conditions—perhaps inflation or concerns over recession in Brazil—lead to a decline in the demand for pesos. In a flexible-exchange-rate system, the new equilibrium would be at *B*, with an exchange rate of 0.5 dollars to the peso (or 2 pesos to the dollar). Argentina can reestablish official parity by buying *CA* worth of pesos, in effect shifting the demand back to the original demand curve, *D*. Alternatively, by raising Argentina's interest rates, the government can induce private investors to increase their demand for pesos by *CA*.

Many middle-size countries also rely upon flexible rates. Let us see how exchange rates are determined under flexible rates. In 1994, the peso was under attack in foreign exchange markets, and the Mexicans allowed the peso to float. At the original exchange rate of approximately 4 pesos per U.S. dollar, there was an excess supply of pesos. This meant that at that exchange rate, the supply of pesos by Mexicans who wanted to buy American and other foreign goods and assets outweighed the demand for pesos by Americans and others who wanted to purchase Mexican goods and assets.

What was the outcome? As a result of the excess supply, the peso depreciated relative to the dollar. How far did the exchange rates move? Just far enough so that—at the depreciated exchange rate of about 6 pesos to the dollar—the quantities supplied and demanded were balanced.

What is behind the equilibration of supply and demand? Two main forces are involved: (1) With the dollar more expensive, it costs more for Mexicans to buy American goods, services, and investments, causing the supply of pesos to fall off in the usual fashion. (2) With the depreciation of the peso, Mexican goods and assets become less expensive for foreigners. This increases the demand for pesos in the marketplace. (Note that this simplified discussion assumes that all transactions occur only between the two countries; a more complete discussion would involve the demands and supplies of currencies from all countries.)

Where is the government? In a freely flexible exchange-rate system, the government is on the sidelines. It allows the foreign exchange market to determine the value of the dollar, just as it allows markets to determine the value of lettuce, machinery, GM stock, or copper. Consequently, it is possible to get enormous swings in flexible exchange rates over relatively short periods.

MANAGED EXCHANGE RATES

In between the two extremes of rigidly fixed and completely flexible is the middle ground of **managed exchange rates.** Here, exchange rates are basically determined by market forces but governments buy or sell currencies or change their money supplies to affect their exchange rates. Sometimes governments lean against the winds of private markets. At other times governments have "target zones" which guide their policy actions. This system is becoming less important as countries are increasingly gravitating toward fixed- or flexible-exchange-rate systems.

TODAY'S HYBRID SYSTEM

Unlike the earlier uniform system under either the gold standard or Bretton Woods, today's exchange-rate system fits into no tidy mold. Without anyone's having planned it, the world has moved to a hybrid exchange-rate system. The major features are as follows:

- A few countries allow their currencies to *float freely.* In this approach, a country allows markets to determine its currency's value and it rarely intervenes. The United States has fit this pattern for most of the last two decades. While the Euro is just an infant as a common currency, Europe appears to be leaning toward the freely floating group.

- Some major countries have *managed but flexible* exchange rates. Today, this group includes Canada, Japan, and many developing countries. Under this system, a country will buy or sell its currency to reduce the day-to-day volatility of currency fluctuations. In addition, a country will sometimes engage in systematic intervention to move its currency toward what it believes to be a more appropriate level.

- Many countries, particularly small ones, peg their currencies to a major currency or to a "basket" of currencies in a *fixed exchange rate.* Sometimes, the peg is allowed to glide smoothly upward or downward in a system known as a gliding or crawling peg. A few countries have the hard fix of a currency board.

- In addition, almost all countries tend to intervene either when markets become "disorderly" or when exchange rates seem far out of line with the "fundamentals"—that is, when they are inappropriate for existing price levels and trade flows.

To summarize:

A *freely flexible* exchange rate is one determined purely by supply and demand without any government intervention. A *fixed-exchange-rate* system is one where governments state official exchange rates, which they defend through intervention and monetary policies. A *managed-exchange-rate* system is a hybrid of fixed and flexible rates in which governments attempt to affect their exchange rates *directly* by buying or selling foreign currencies or *indirectly*, through monetary policy, by raising or lowering interest rates.

SUMMARY

A. The Balance of International Payments

1. The balance of international payments is the set of accounts that measures all the economic transactions between a nation and the rest of the world. It includes exports and imports of goods, services, and financial instruments. Exports are credit items, while imports are debits. More generally, a country's credit items are transactions that make foreign currencies available to it; debit items are ones that reduce its holdings of foreign currencies.

2. The major components of the balance of payments are:

   I. Current account (merchandise trade, services, investment income, transfers)

   II. Financial account (private, government, and official-reserve changes)

   The fundamental rule of balance-of-payments accounting is that the sum of all items must equal zero: I + II = 0.

3. Historically, countries tend to go through stages of the balance of payments: from the young debtor borrowing for economic development, through mature debtor and young creditor, to mature creditor nation living off earnings from past investments. In the 1980s, the United States moved to a different stage where low domestic saving and attractive investment opportunities again led it to borrow heavily abroad and become a debtor nation.

B. The Determination of Foreign Exchange Rates

4. International trade involves the new element of different national currencies, which are linked by relative prices called foreign exchange rates. When Americans import Japanese goods, they ultimately need to pay in Japanese yen. In the foreign exchange market, Japanese yen might trade at ¥100/$ (or reciprocally, ¥1 would trade for $0.01). This price is called the foreign exchange rate.

5. In a foreign exchange market involving only two countries, the supply of U.S. dollars comes from Americans who want to purchase goods, services, and investments from Japan; the demand for U.S. dollars comes from Japanese who want to import commodities or financial assets from America. The interaction of these supplies and demands determines the foreign exchange rate. More generally, foreign exchange rates are determined by the complex interplay of many countries buying and selling among themselves. When trade or financial flows change, supply and demand shift and the equilibrium exchange rate changes.

6. A fall in the market price of a currency is a depreciation; a rise in a currency's value is called an appreciation. In a system where governments announce official foreign exchange rates, a decrease in the official exchange rate is called a devaluation, while an increase is a revaluation.

7. According to the purchasing-power parity (PPP) theory of exchange rates, exchange rates tend to move with changes in relative price levels of different countries. The PPP theory applies better to the long run than the short run. When this theory is applied to measure the purchasing power of incomes in different countries, it raises the per capita outputs of low-income countries.

C. The International Monetary System

8. A well-functioning international economy requires a smoothly operating exchange-rate system, which denotes the institutions that govern financial transactions among nations. Three important exchange-rate systems are (*a*) flexible exchange rates, in which a country's foreign exchange rate is determined by market forces of supply and demand; (*b*) fixed exchange rates, such as the gold standard or the Bretton Woods system, in which countries set and defend a given structure of exchange rates; and (*c*) managed exchange rates, in which government interventions and market forces interact to determine the level of exchange rates.

9. Classical economists like David Hume explained international adjustments to trade imbalances by the gold-flow mechanism. Under this process, gold move-

ments would change the money supply and the price level. For example, a trade deficit would lead to a gold outflow and a decline in domestic prices that would (*a*) raise exports and (*b*) curb imports of the gold-losing country while (*c*) reducing exports and (*d*) raising imports of the gold-gaining country. This mechanism shows that under fixed exchange rates, countries which have balance-of-payments problems must adjust through changes in domestic price and output levels.

10. After World War II, countries created a group of international economic institutions to organize international trade and finance. Under the Bretton Woods sys-

tem, countries "pegged" their currencies to the dollar and to gold, providing fixed but adjustable exchange rates. When official parities deviated too far from fundamentals, countries could adjust parities and achieve a new equilibrium without incurring the hardships of inflation or recession.

11. When the Bretton Woods system broke down in 1971, it was replaced by today's hybrid system. Today, the major economic regions (the United States, Euroland, and Japan) have currencies that float relative to each other. Most small countries peg their currencies to the dollar or to other currencies.

CONCEPTS FOR REVIEW

Balance of Payments

balance of payments
   I. current account
   II. financial account
balance-of-payments identity:
   I + II = 0
official-reserve changes
debits and credits
stages of balance of payments

Foreign Exchange Rates

foreign exchange rate, foreign
   exchange market
supply of and demand for foreign
   exchange
exchange-rate terminology:
   appreciation and depreciation
   revaluation and devaluation

International Monetary System

exchange-rate systems:
   flexible
   fixed rates (gold standard, Bretton
     Woods, currency board)
   managed
   common currency
international adjustment mechanism
Hume's four-pronged gold-flow
   mechanism

FURTHER READING AND INTERNET WEBSITES

Further Reading

A fascinating collection of essays on international macroeconomics is Paul Krugman, *Pop International* (MIT Press, Cambridge, Mass., 1997). The quotation on the international monetary system is from Robert Solomon, *The International Monetary System, 1945–1981: An Insider's View* (Harper & Row, New York, 1982), pp. 1, 7.

Websites

Data on trade and finance for different countries can be found in the websites listed for Chapter 12. An extensive page on the Euro is maintained by Giancarlo Corsetti at www.econ.yale.edu/~corsetti/euro/Euroit.htm.

Data on exchange rates can be found at finance.yahoo. com/m3?u and www.uta.fi/~ktmatu/rates. html.

Some of the best popular writing on international economics is found in *The Economist*, which is also available at www.economist.com. One of the best sources for policy writing on international economics is www.iie.com/homepage.htm, the website of the Institute for International Economics. One of the leading scholar-journalists of today is Paul Krugman of Princeton. His web page at web.mit.edu/krugman/www contains many interesting readings on international economics.

QUESTIONS FOR DISCUSSION

1. Table 13-3 shows some foreign exchange rates (in units of foreign currency per dollar) as of early 1997. Fill in the last column of the table with the reciprocal price of the dollar in terms of each foreign currency, being especially careful to write down the relevant units in the parentheses.

2. Figure 13-3 shows the demand and supply for U.S. dollars in an example in which Japan and the United States trade only with each other.

   a. Describe and draw the reciprocal supply and demand schedules for Japanese yen. Explain why the supply of yen is equivalent to the demand for dollars. Also explain and draw the schedule that corresponds to the supply of dollars. Find the equilibrium price of yen in this new diagram and relate it to the equilibrium in Figure 13-3.

   b. Assume that Americans develop a taste for Japanese goods. Show what would happen to the supply and demand for yen. Would the yen appreciate or depreciate relative to the dollar? Explain.

3. Draw up a list of items that belong on the credit side of the balance of international payments and another list of items that belong on the debit side. What is meant by a trade surplus? By the balance on current account?

4. Construct hypothetical balance-of-payments accounts for a young debtor country, a mature debtor country, a new creditor country, and a mature creditor country.

5. Consider the situation for Germany described on pages 275–276. Using a figure like Figure 13-3, show the supply and demand for German marks before and after the shock. Identify on your figure the excess demand for marks *before* the appreciation of the mark. Then show how an appreciation of the mark would wipe out the excess demand.

6. A Middle East nation suddenly discovers huge oil resources. Show how its balance of trade and current account suddenly turn to surplus. Show how it can acquire assets in New York as a financial-account offset. Later, when it uses the assets for internal development, show how its current and financial items reverse their roles.

7. Consider the following quotation from the 1984 *Economic Report of the President*:

   > In the long run, the exchange rate tends to follow the differential trend in the domestic and foreign price level. If one country's price level gets too far out of line with prices in other countries, there will eventually be a fall in demand for its goods, which will lead to a real depreciation of its currency.

   Explain how the first sentence relates to the PPP theory of exchange rates. Explain the reasoning behind the PPP theory. In addition, using a supply-and-demand diagram like that of Figure 13-3, explain the sequence of events, described in the second sentence of the quotation, whereby a country whose price level is relatively high will find that its exchange rate depreciates.

Currency	Price	
	Units of foreign currency per dollar	**Dollars per unit of foreign currency**
Zloty (Poland)	4.41	_____ ($/zloty)
Real (Brazil)	1.82	_____ (_____)
Yuan (China)	8.28	_____ (_____)
Peso (Mexico)	9.28	_____ (_____)
Drachma (Greece)	387.	_____ (_____)
Euro	1.15	_____ (_____)

TABLE 13-3.

8. A nation records the following data for 2000: exports of automobiles ($100) and corn ($150); imports of oil ($150) and steel ($75); tourist expenditures abroad ($25); private lending to foreign countries ($50); private borrowing from foreign countries ($40); official-reserve changes ($30 of foreign exchange bought by domestic central bank). Calculate the statistical discrepancy and include it in private lending to foreign countries. Create a balance-of-payments table like Table 13-2.

9. James Tobin has written, "A great teacher of mine, Joseph Schumpeter, used to find puzzling irony in the fact that liberal devotees of the free market were unwilling to let the market determine the prices of foreign currencies." For what reasons might economists allow the foreign exchange market to be an exception to a general inclination toward free markets?

10. Consider the following three exchange-rate systems: the classical gold standard, freely flexible exchange rates, and the Bretton Woods system. Compare and contrast the three systems with respect to the following characteristics:
   a. Role of government vs. that of market in determining exchange rates
   b. Degree of exchange-rate volatility
   c. Method of adjustment of relative prices across countries
   d. Need for international cooperation and consultation in determining exchange rates
   e. Potential for establishment and maintenance of severe exchange-rate misalignment

11. Consider the European monetary union. List the pros and cons. How do you come down on the question of the advisability of monetary union? Would your answer change if the question concerned the United States?

CHAPTER

14

Open-Economy Macroeconomics

Before I built a wall I'd ask to know
What I was walling in or walling out ...

Robert Frost

Today is the era of the global economy. Revolutionary developments in communications, transportation, and trade policy have increasingly linked together the economic fortunes of nations. Trading ties among Japan, Mexico, Canada, and the United States are closer today than were those between New York and California a century ago. The international business cycle exerts a powerful effect on every nation of the globe. American monetary policy can produce depressions, poverty, and revolutions in South America. Political disturbances in the Middle East can set off a spiral in oil prices that sends the world into recessions. Revolution or default in Russia can rock stock markets around the world. To ignore international trade is to miss half the economic ball game.

The last chapter surveyed the major concepts of international macroeconomics—the balance of payments, the determination of exchange rates, and the international monetary system. The present chapter continues the story by showing how macroeconomic shocks in one country have ripple effects on the output and employment of other countries and examining the linkage between domestic saving and investment and the trade balance. The chapter concludes with a review of some of the key international issues of today.

A. FOREIGN TRADE AND ECONOMIC ACTIVITY

Net Exports and Output in the Open Economy

Open-economy macroeconomics is the study of how economies behave when the trade and financial linkages among nations are considered. The previous chapter described the basic concepts of the balance of payments. We can restate those here in terms of the national income and product accounts.

Foreign trade involves imports and exports. Although the United States produces most of what it consumes, it nonetheless has a large quantity of **imports,** which are goods and services produced abroad and consumed domestically. **Exports** are goods and services produced domestically and purchased by foreigners.

Net exports are defined as exports of goods and services minus imports of goods and services. For 1999, net exports for the United States were minus $254 billion, derived from $998 billion of exports minus $1252 billion of imports. When a country has positive net exports, it is accumulating foreign assets. The counterpart of net exports is therefore **net foreign investment,** which denotes net saving or investment abroad and is approximately equal to the value of net exports.

289

In 1999, the United States had negative net exports, which signifies that the U.S. was borrowing from abroad and therefore had negative net foreign investment. In other words, *foreigners were making a significant contribution to U.S. investment.* Why is it that rich America borrowed so much from abroad? This puzzling phenomenon is explained by a relatively low U.S. saving rate and a high domestic investment rate driven by the long economic boom and the technological dynamism of the United States.

In an open economy, a nation's expenditures may differ from its production. Total domestic *expenditures* (sometimes called *domestic demand*) are equal to consumption plus domestic investment plus government purchases. This measure differs from total *domestic product* (or GDP) for two reasons. First, some part of domestic expenditures will be on goods produced abroad, these items being imports (denoted by *Im*) like Mexican oil and Japanese automobiles. In addition, some part of America's domestic production will be sold abroad as exports (denoted by *Ex*)—items like wheat and Boeing aircraft. The difference between national output and domestic expenditures is exports minus imports equals net exports, or $Ex - Im = X$.

To calculate the *total production* of American goods and services, we need to add trade to domestic demand. That is, we need to know the total production for American residents as well as the net production for foreigners. This total includes domestic expenditures $(C + I + G)$ plus sales to foreigners (Ex) less domestic purchases from foreigners (Im). Total output, or GDP, equals consumption plus domestic investment plus government purchases plus net exports:

$$\text{Total domestic output} = \text{GDP}$$
$$= C + I + G + X$$

Determinants of Trade and Net Exports

What determines the levels of exports and imports and therefore of net exports? It is best to think of the import and export components of net exports separately.

Imports into the United States are positively related to U.S. income and output. When U.S. GDP rises, imports into the U.S. increase (1) because some of the increased $C + I + G$ purchases (such as cars and shoes) come from foreign production and also

(2) because America uses foreign-made inputs (like oil or steel) in producing its own goods. The demand for imports depends upon the relative price of foreign and domestic goods. If the price of domestic cars rises relative to the price of Japanese cars, say, because the dollar's exchange rate appreciates, Americans will buy more Japanese cars and fewer American ones. Hence *the volume and value of imports will be affected by domestic output and the relative prices of domestic and foreign goods.*

Exports are the mirror image of imports: U.S. exports are other countries' imports. *American exports therefore depend primarily upon foreign output as well as upon the prices of U.S. exports relative to foreign goods.* As foreign output rises, or as the exchange rate of the dollar depreciates, the volume and value of American exports tend to grow.

Figure 14-1 shows the ratio of net exports to GDP. After World War II, the United States had a large trade surplus as it financed the rebuilding of Europe through the Marshall Plan. For most of the postwar period, the U.S. external accounts were in balance. In the early 1980s, a sharp decline in domestic saving led to a sharp appreciation of the dollar from 1980 to 1985. Also, foreign economies grew less rapidly than the home economy, depressing exports. The ensuing effect was a massive turn toward a deficit in net exports.

After a period of recovery, the United States had another sharp increase in its trade deficit in the late 1990s. During this period, the U.S. economy grew rapidly, while Japan was stuck in a deep recession, Europe experienced slow growth, and many developing economies faced sharp financial restraints. As a result, exports stagnated while imports boomed, and net exports once again turned sharply negative. Many bemoaned the large trade deficit. Was it a good thing or a bad thing? The following discussion in 2000 by the President's Council of Economic Advisers puts the U.S. trade deficit in an economic context:

> By themselves, external trade and current account deficits are neither inherently good nor inherently bad. What matter are the reasons for the deficits. The main reason for the deficits today appears to be the strength of the U.S. economic expansion relative to the slow or negative growth in many other countries.... These deficits are essentially a macroeconomic phenomenon, reflecting a higher rate of

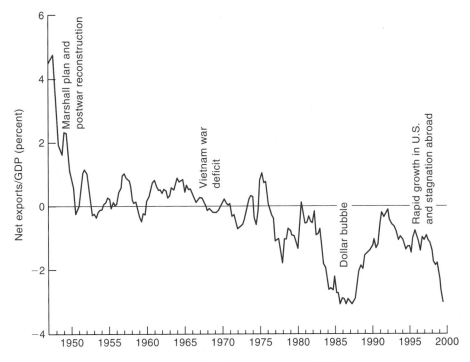

FIGURE 14-1. U.S. Net Exports Turned Sharply Negative in 1980s

The United States had a large surplus after World War II as it helped rebuild Europe. Note how net exports turned sharply negative in the early 1980s as domestic saving declined sharply and the dollar appreciated. In the late 1990s, net exports again turned negative with strong economic growth at home and recessions abroad.

domestic investment than of national saving. The deficit's growth . . . reflects rising investment rather than falling saving.[1]

SHORT-RUN IMPACT OF TRADE ON GDP

How do changes in a nation's trade flows affect its GDP and employment? We first analyze this question in the context of our short-run model of output determination, the multiplier model of Chapter 9. The multiplier model shows how, in the short run when there are unemployed resources, changes in trade will affect aggregate demand, output, and employment.

There are two major new macroeconomic elements in the presence of international trade: First, we have a fourth component of spending, net exports, which adds to aggregate demand. Second, an open economy has different multipliers for private investment and government domestic spending because some spending leaks out to the rest of the world.

Table 14-1 on the next page shows how introducing net exports affects output determination. This table begins with the same components as those for a closed economy. (Look back to Table 9-2 to refresh your memory about the major components and the way they sum to total spending.) Total domestic demand in column (2) is composed of the consumption, investment, and government purchases we analyzed earlier. Column (3) then adds the exports of goods and services. As described above, these depend upon foreign incomes and outputs and upon prices and exchange rates,

---

[1] See *The Economic Report of the President 2000*, pp. 231–235, in this chapter's Further Reading Section.

(1) Initial level of GDP	(2) Domestic demand ($C + I + G$)	(3) Exports (Ex)	(4) Imports (Im)	(5) Net exports ($X = Ex - Im$)	(6) Total spending ($C + I + G + X$)		(7) Resulting tendency of economy
4,100	4,000	250	410	−160	3,840		Contraction
3,800	3,800	250	380	−130	3,670	↓	Contraction
3,500	3,600	250	350	−100	3,500		Equilibrium
3,200	3,400	250	320	−70	3,330	↑	Expansion
2,900	3,200	250	290	−40	3,160		Expansion

Output Determination with Foreign Trade (billions of dollars)

TABLE 14-1. Net Exports Add to Aggregate Demand of Economy

To the domestic demand of $C + I + G$, we must add net exports of $X = Ex - Im$ to get total aggregate demand for a country's output. Higher net exports affect aggregate demand just as do investment and government purchases.

all of which are also taken as given for this analysis. Exports are assumed to be a constant level of $250 billion of foreign spending on domestic goods and services.

The interesting new element arises from imports, shown in column (4). Like exports, imports depend upon exogenous variables such as prices and exchange rates. But, in addition, imports depend upon domestic incomes and output, which clearly change in the different rows of Table 14-1. For simplicity, we assume that the country always imports 10 percent of its total output, so imports in column (4) are 10 percent of column (1).

Subtracting column (4) from column (3) gives net exports in column (5). Net exports are a negative number when imports exceed exports and a positive number when exports are greater than imports. Net exports in column (5) are the net addition to the spending stream contributed by foreign trade. Total spending on domestic output in column (6) equals domestic demand in column (2) plus net exports in column (5). Equilibrium output in an open economy occurs where total net domestic and foreign spending in column (6) exactly equals total domestic output in column (1). In this case, equilibrium comes with net exports of −100, indicating that the country is importing more than it is exporting. At this equilibrium, note as well that domestic demand is greater than output. (Make sure that you

can explain why the economy is not in equilibrium when spending does not equal output.)

Figure 14-2 shows the open-economy equilibrium graphically. The upward-sloping black line marked $C + I + G$ is the same curve used in Figure 9-7. To this line we must add the level of net exports that is forthcoming at each level of GDP. Net exports from column (5) of Table 14-1 are added to get the blue line of total aggregate demand or total spending. When the blue line lies below the black curve, imports exceed exports and net exports are negative. When the blue line is above the black line, the country has a net-export or trade surplus and output is greater than domestic demand.

Equilibrium GDP occurs where the blue line of total spending intersects the 45° line. This intersection comes at exactly the same point, at $3500 billion, that is shown as equilibrium GDP in Table 14-1. Only at $3500 billion does GDP exactly equal what consumers, businesses, governments, and foreigners want to spend on goods and services produced in the United States.

The Marginal Propensity to Import and the Spending Line

Note that the aggregate demand curve, the blue $C + I + G + X$ curve in Figure 14-2, has a slightly smaller slope than the black curve of domestic demand. The explanation of this is that *there is an additional*

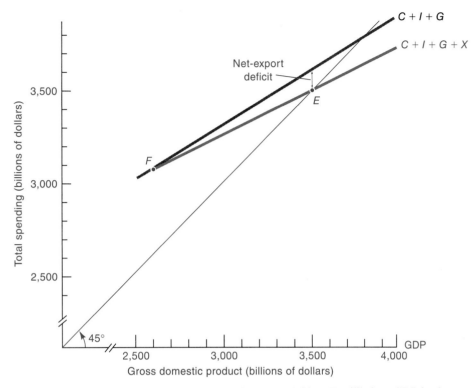

FIGURE 14-2. Adding Net Exports to Domestic Demand Gives Equilibrium GDP in the Open Economy

The black line represents domestic demand ($C + I + G$), purchases by domestic consumers, businesses, and governments. To this must be added net foreign spending. Net exports plus domestic demand give the blue line of total spending. Equilibrium comes at point E, where total GDP equals total spending on goods and services produced in the United States. Note that the slope of the blue total demand curve is less than that of domestic demand to reflect the leakage from spending into imports.

leakage from spending into imports. This new leakage arises from our assumption that 10 cents of every dollar of income is spent on imports. To handle this requires introducing a new term, the **marginal propensity to import.** The marginal propensity to import, which we will denote *MPm*, is the increase in the dollar value of imports for each $1 increase in GDP.

The marginal propensity to import is closely related to the marginal propensity to save (*MPS*). Recall that the *MPS* tells us what fraction of an additional dollar of income is not spent but leaks into saving. The marginal propensity to import tells how much of additional output and income leaks into imports. In our example, the *MPm* is 0.10 because every $300 billion of increased income leads to $30 billion of in-

creased imports. (What is the marginal propensity to import in an economy with no foreign trade? Zero.)

Now examine the slope of the total spending line in Figure 14-2—that line shows total spending on $C + I + G + X$. Note that the slope of the total spending line is less than the slope of the domestic demand line of $C + I + G$. As GDP and total incomes rise by $300, spending on consumption rises by the income change times the *MPC* (assumed to be two-thirds), or by $200. At the same time, spending on imports, or foreign goods, also rises by $30. Hence spending on domestic goods rises by only $170 ($200 − $30), and the slope of the total spending line falls from 0.667 in our closed economy to $170/$300 = 0.567 in our open economy.

The Open-Economy Multiplier

Surprisingly, opening up an economy lowers the multiplier.

One way of understanding the expenditure multiplier in an open economy is to calculate the rounds of spending and respending generated by an additional dollar of government spending, investment, or exports. Suppose that Germany needs to buy American computers to modernize antiquated facilities in what used to be East Germany. Each extra dollar of U.S. computers will generate $1 of income in the United States, of which $2/3 = $0.667 will be spent by Americans on consumption. However, because the marginal propensity to import is 0.10, one-tenth of the extra dollar of income, or $0.10, will be spent on foreign goods and services, leaving only $0.567 of spending on domestically produced goods. That $0.567 of domestic spending will generate $0.567 of U.S. income, from which $0.567 \times $0.567 = 0.321 will be spent on consumption of domestic goods and services in the next round. Hence the total increase in output, or the open-economy multiplier, will be

$$\text{Open-economy multiplier} = 1 + 0.567 + (0.567)^2 + \cdots$$

$$= 1 + (\tfrac{2}{3} - \tfrac{1}{10}) + (\tfrac{2}{3} - \tfrac{1}{10})^2 + \cdots$$

$$= \frac{1}{1 - \tfrac{2}{3} + \tfrac{1}{10}} = \frac{1}{\tfrac{13}{30}} = 2.3$$

This compares with a closed-economy multiplier of $1/(1 - 0.667) = 3$.

Another way of calculating the multiplier is as follows: Recall that the multiplier in our simplest model was $1/MPS$, where MPS is the "leakage" into saving. As we noted above, imports are another leakage. The total leakage is the dollars leaking into saving (the MPS) plus the dollars leaking into imports (the MPm). Hence, the open-economy multiplier should be $1/(MPS + MPm) = 1/(0.333 + 0.1) = 1/0.433 = 2.3$. Note that both the leakage analysis and the rounds analysis provide exactly the same answer.

To summarize:

Because a fraction of any income increase leaks into imports in an open economy, the open-economy multiplier is smaller than that of a closed economy. The exact relationship is

$$\text{Open-economy multiplier} = \frac{1}{MPS + MPm}$$

where MPS = marginal propensity to save and MPm = marginal propensity to import.

MACROECONOMIC POLICY AND THE EXCHANGE-RATE SYSTEM

Our analysis of business cycles and economic growth has generally focused on policies in a closed economy. We analyzed the way that monetary and fiscal policies can help stabilize the business cycle, shaving the peaks off inflation and the troughs off output. How do macroeconomic policies change in an open economy? Surprisingly, the answer to this question depends crucially on whether the country has a fixed or flexible exchange rate.

Our survey here will concentrate on high-income countries whose financial markets are closely linked together—including countries like the United States, Canada, Britain, and Germany. When financial investments can flow easily among countries and the regulatory barriers to financial investments are low, we say that these countries have *high mobility of financial capital.*

Fixed Exchange Rates. The key feature of countries with fixed exchange rates and high capital mobility is that their interest rates must be very closely aligned. Any interest-rate divergence between two such countries will attract speculators who will sell one currency and buy the other until the interest rates are equalized.

Consider a small country which pegs its exchange rate to a larger country. It might be Argentina, which has a currency board pegging its peso to the U.S. dollar. *Because the small country's interest rates are determined by the monetary policy of the large country, the small country no longer has an independent monetary policy.* The small country's monetary policy must be devoted to ensuring that its interest rates are aligned with its partner's. Argentina's interest rates are determined in the United States.

Macroeconomic policy in such a situation is therefore exactly the case described in our multiplier model above. From the small country's point of view, investment is exogenous, because it is determined by world interest rates. Fiscal policy will be highly effective because there will be no monetary reaction to changes in G or T.

Flexible Exchange Rates. One important insight in this area is that macroeconomic policy with flexible exchange rates operates in quite a different way from the fixed-exchange-rate case. Monetary policy becomes highly effective with a flexible exchange rate.

Let's consider the case of the United States. The monetary transmission mechanism in the United States has changed significantly over the last two decades as a result of increased openness and an evolving exchange-rate system. After the introduction of flexible exchange rates in 1973, and in the presence of increasingly linked financial markets, international trade and finance have come to play a new and central role in U.S. macroeconomic policy.

One of the best examples of the operation of macroeconomic policy with flexible exchange rates occurred when the Federal Reserve tightened money in the 1979–1982 period. The monetary tightening raised U.S. interest rates, which attracted funds into dollar securities. This increase in demand for dollars drove up the foreign exchange rate on the dollar. (Review the previous chapter's Figure 13-5.) At this point, the multiplier mechanism swung into action. The high dollar exchange rate decreased net exports and contributed to the deep U.S. recession of 1981–1983 in the way we described earlier. This had the impact of both lowering real GDP and lowering the rate of inflation.

Foreign trade actually opens up another link in the monetary transmission mechanism when a country has flexible exchange rates. Monetary policy operates through exchange rates to affect net exports as well as domestic investment. The interest-rate impact on net exports reinforces the impact on domestic investment: tight money lowers output and prices.

TRADE AND ECONOMIC ACTIVITY, 1980–1999

In a world where nations are increasingly linked by trade and finance, foreign trade can have a major impact on domestic output and employment. Figure 14-3 shows two major troughs in U.S. net exports—in

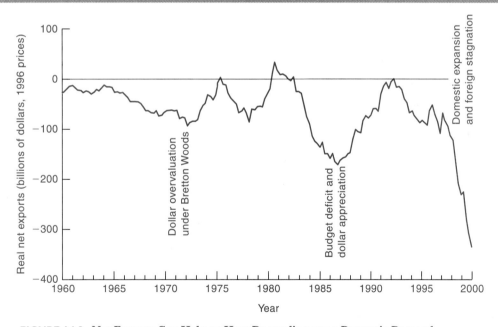

FIGURE 14-3. Net Exports Can Help or Hurt Depending upon Domestic Demand

With a strong rise of the dollar and weak economic growth abroad, U.S. real net exports turned sharply negative in the early 1980s. The shift produced a massive drag on aggregate spending in the $C + I + G + X$ equation and helped produce the deepest recession of the last half-century. The growing trade deficit after 1995 coincided with strong growth in domestic demand, which moderated output and price growth. (Source: U.S. Department of Commerce.)

the early 1980s and in the late 1990s. Describing each of these periods will help us understand the role of international trade in domestic performance.

The Overvalued Dollar of the 1980s. The decade of the 1980s witnessed a dramatic cycle of dollar appreciation and depreciation. The rise of the dollar began in 1980 after tight monetary policy and loose fiscal policy in the United States drove interest rates up sharply. High interest rates at home and economic turmoil abroad attracted funds into the dollar. Figure 14-4 shows that during the period from 1979 to early 1985 the exchange rate on the dollar rose 80 percent.

In 1985, many economists believed the dollar was overvalued—an *overvalued currency* is one whose value is high relative to its long-run or sustainable level.

As the dollar rose, American export prices increased and the prices of goods imported into the United States fell. From 1980 to 1985, the prices of imported goods and services fell by 6 percent, while the prices of our exports in foreign currencies rose over 80 percent. In response, the volume of imports rose 51 percent while export volumes rose only 2 percent.

Figure 14-5 illustrates the dramatic effect of the appreciating dollar on trade flows. From the peak in

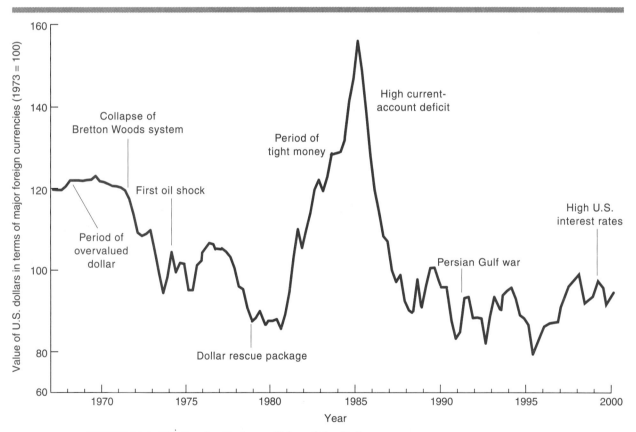

FIGURE 14-4. The Foreign Exchange Value of the Dollar

Before the collapse of the Bretton Woods system, the dollar's value was stable in exchange markets. Then, as the United States pursued its tight-money policies in the early 1980s, the high interest rates pulled up the dollar. In the late 1990s, rising interest rates in the U.S. along with stagnation in Japan and Europe led to appreciation of the dollar and a growing trade deficit. (Source: Federal Reserve System.)

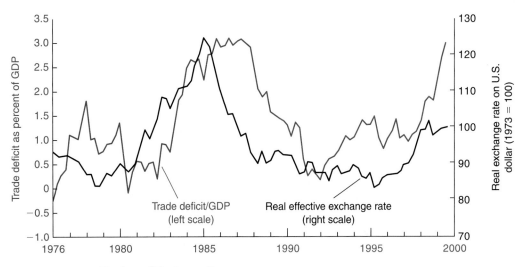

FIGURE 14-5. Trade and Exchange Rates

Trade flows respond to exchange-rate changes, but with a time lag. The real appreciation of the dollar during the early 1980s increased U.S. export prices and reduced prices of goods imported into the United States. As a result, the trade deficit rose sharply. When the dollar depreciated after 1985, the trade deficit began to shrink. The recent increase in the current-account deficit has resulted from dollar appreciation and slow growth outside the United States. (Source: Council of Economic Advisers, *Economic Report of the President, 2000.*)

1980 to the trough in 1986, real net exports declined by $158 billion—this amounted to 3 percent of 1983 GDP.

By itself, this sharp decline in net exports would be contractionary. Unfortunately, the trade impact reinforced a decline in domestic demand induced by tight monetary policy. The result was the deepest recession in 50 years.

Countercyclical Trade in the 1990s. The late 1990s were the opposite—and a happier—story. After 1995, a combination of low real interest rates and a booming stock market led to rapid growth in domestic demand in the United States, particularly private investment. Unemployment fell sharply. Interest rates were relatively high in the United States, and the dollar appreciated. Import prices and net exports consequently declined. Had they not, the American economy would probably have experienced rising inflation and the Fed would have found it necessary to choke off the boom. In this case, a dollar appreciation and declining net exports were just what the macroeconomic doctor ordered.

Global impact, global citizen

Foreign economic relations add an important dimension to economic policy. Domestic policymakers must concern themselves with foreign repercussions of domestic policies. Rising interest rates at home change interest rates, exchange rates, and trade balances abroad, and these changes may be unwelcome. When Mexico teetered on the edge of default in 1994 and 1995, the United States had to proceed cautiously in its monetary policies lest interest-rate increases cause Mexico, and indirectly the United States, greater financial difficulties. When East Asian nations ran into financial difficulties in 1997–1998, the United States reduced dollar interest rates to protect the U.S. economy and at the same time helped prevent the contagion from spreading more widely.

While the United States is primarily concerned with the impacts of its policies on its own economy, as the world's economic superpower it must also move carefully when its policies have a major impact on other countries.

B. INTERDEPENDENCE IN THE GLOBAL ECONOMY

ECONOMIC GROWTH IN THE OPEN ECONOMY

The first section described the short-run impact of international trade and policy changes in the open economy. These issues are crucial for open economies combating unemployment and inflation. But countries must also keep their eye on the implications of their policies for long-run economic growth. Particularly for small countries, the concerns about economic-growth policies are paramount. Sometimes, it is useful to think of an individual region within the United States (such as a state or metropolitan area) as a small open economy with a fixed exchange rate.

Economic growth involves a wide variety of issues, as we saw in Chapter 11. Perhaps the single most important approach for promoting rapid economic growth is to ensure high levels of saving and investment. Figure 14-6 shows the association of national investment rates with rates of growth of per capita GDP. We begin by examining the determinants of saving and investment in the open economy.

But economic growth involves more than just capital. It requires moving toward the technological frontier by adopting the best technological practices. It requires developing institutions that nurture investment and the spirit of enterprise. Other issues—trade policies, intellectual property rights, policies toward direct investment, and the overall macroeconomic climate—are essential ingredients in the growth of open economies.

SAVING AND INVESTMENT IN THE OPEN ECONOMY

In a closed economy, total investment equals domestic saving. For open economies, world financial markets are another source of investment funds and another outlet for domestic saving. Countries that are hungry for funds because of profitable domestic investment opportunities can go to world financial markets to finance their investments. Traditionally,

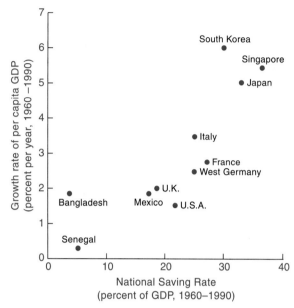

FIGURE 14-6. National Investment and Economic Growth

Countries that have high saving and investment rates also have above-average rates of per capita economic growth. In the long run, promoting high saving and investment is one of the most secure routes to increasing growth. (Source: World Bank.)

middle-income countries in Latin America or Asia have borrowed from abroad to finance domestic capital. Surprisingly, the United States has been a magnet for foreign saving in recent years because of its robust investment and low domestic saving.

The other side of the coin comes in countries that have high saving rates but lack sufficient high-yield domestic investment opportunities. Countries like England in the last century or Japan in recent years have provided substantial funds to capital-short countries. We first review the investment-saving relationship and then examine the mechanisms for allocating saving among countries.

The saving-investment relation in an open economy

Let's pause to recall our saving-investment identities from Chapter 5:

$$I_T = I + X = S + (T - G)$$

This states that total national investment (I_T) consists of investment in domestic capital (I) plus net foreign investment or net exports (X). This must equal total private saving (S) by households and businesses plus total public saving, which is given by the government surplus ($T - G$).

We can rewrite the identity as follows to emphasize the components of net exports:

$$X = S + (T - G) - I$$

or

Net exports =   private saving
                + government saving
                − domestic investment

This important equation shows that net exports are the difference between domestic saving and domestic investment. The components of total U.S. national investment for recent decades are shown in Table 14-2.

Determination of Saving and Investment at Full Employment

We need to go beyond the identities to understand the mechanism by which saving and investment are equalized in the open economy. The equilibration of saving and investment in the short run is just the mirror image of the multiplier mechanism shown in Figure 14-2.

It is useful to consider how saving and investment are allocated in the long run in a "classical" economy with full employment and flexible prices. We consider the simplest case where there is no inflation or uncertainty. We begin with a closed economy and then extend the analysis to an open economy.

Closed Economy. In a closed economy, we know that investment must equal private saving plus the government surplus. We simplify by assuming that taxes, government spending, and private saving are independent of interest rates. Hence, total domestic saving (public and private) is a given amount at full employment.

By contrast, as we learned in Chapter 6, investment is very sensitive to the interest rate. Higher interest rates reduce spending on housing and business plant and equipment. We therefore write our investment schedule as $I(r)$ to indicate that investment depends upon the real interest rate, r.

	Saving and Investment as Percentage of GDP		
	1959–1981	**1982–1997**	**1998–1999**
Net national saving	7.8%	3.7%	5.5%
Net private saving	9.7%	8.1%	5.1%
Net government saving	−1.9%	−4.4%	0.4%
Net national investment	7.8%	3.7%	5.5%
Net private domestic investment	7.4%	5.3%	8.4%
Net foreign investment	0.4%	−1.5%	−2.9%

TABLE 14-2. Trade Balance and Net Foreign Investment Are Part of National Saving and Investment

After large budget deficits began in 1982, national saving and investment were squeezed. About half the squeeze resulted in lower domestic investment, while the rest came through a trade and net export deficit. The budget turnaround in 1998 and 1999 increased national saving, but in this case it was domestic rather than foreign investment that responded. (Source: Bureau of Economic Analysis. Statistical discrepancy is included in investment.)

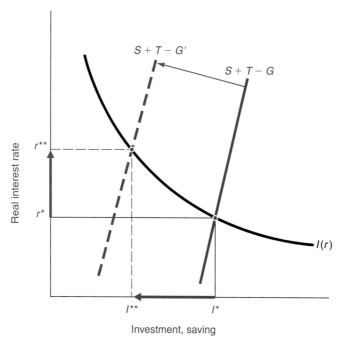

FIGURE 14-7. Saving and Investment in the Closed Economy

Investment is inversely related to the real interest rate, while private saving and public saving are relatively unresponsive to the interest rate. Equilibrium saving and investment comes at r^*. Suppose that government purchases increase. This increases the government deficit and therefore reduces public saving. The result is a shift in the national saving curve to the left to $S + T - G'$, raising the market interest rate to r^{**} and reducing national saving and investment to I^{**}.

Figure 14-7 shows how national saving and investment are equilibrated in a full-employment closed economy. The saving and investment schedules determine an interest rate at r^* with healthy levels of saving and investment.

Now suppose that the government increases its purchases, increasing the government deficit or reducing the surplus. This will shift the saving schedule to the left to $S + T - G'$. As a result, the real interest rate increases to equilibrate saving and investment, and the level of investment falls. The major point is that *a higher government deficit lowers investment in the full-employment closed economy.*

Open-Economy Saving. An open economy has alternative sources of investment and alternative outlets for saving. We show this situation in Figure 14-8 for a small open economy with a high degree of mobility of financial capital. A small open economy must

equate its domestic interest rate with the world real interest rate, r^W. It is too small to affect the world interest rate, and because capital mobility is high, financial capital will move to equilibrate interest rates at home and abroad.

Figure 14-8 helps explain the determination of saving, investment, and net exports in the open economy. At the prevailing world interest rate, domestic investment is shown at point *A*, which is the intersection of the investment schedule and the interest rate. Total national saving is given at point *B* on the total saving schedule, $S + T - G$. The difference between them—given by the line segment *AB*—is net exports. (This equality is shown by the saving-investment identity in the box on page 299.)

Hence net exports are determined by the balance between national saving and investment as determined by domestic factors plus the world interest rate.

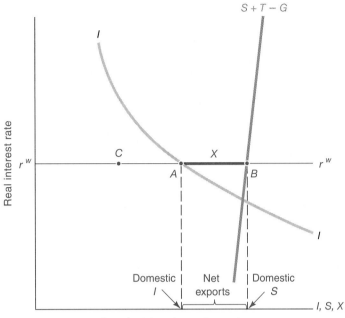

FIGURE 14-8. Saving and Investment in a Small Open Economy

Domestic investment and domestic saving are determined by income, interest rates, and government fiscal policy, as in Fig. 14-7. But the small open economy with mobile financial capital has its real interest rates determined in world financial markets. At the relatively high real interest rate at r^W, domestic saving exceeds domestic investment and the excess saving flows to more lucrative investment opportunities abroad. The difference is net exports and net foreign investment, X, which is the difference between national saving and domestic investment at the prevailing interest rate. A trade surplus such as has been seen in Japan and Germany for most of the last two decades is caused by the interaction of high domestic saving and depleted domestic investment.

This discussion pushes into the background the mechanism by which a country adjusts its trade, saving, and investment. It is here that the exchange rate plays the crucial equilibrating role. *Changes in exchange rates are the mechanism by which saving and investment adjust.* That is, exchange rates move to ensure that the level of net exports balances the difference between domestic saving and investment.[2]

This analysis can help explain the trends in saving, investment, and trade patterns in major countries in recent years. Figure 14-8 describes well the role of Japan in the world economy. Japan has traditionally had a high domestic saving rate. Yet in recent years—because of high production costs at home and competitive conditions in neighboring newly industrialized countries—the return on Japanese capital has been depressed. Japanese saving therefore seeks outlets abroad, with the consequence that Japan has had a large trade surplus and high net exports. Similar trends were seen in high-saving and low-investment Germany until German reunification in 1990.

The United States has seen an interesting twist in its saving and investment position, as was shown

___

[2] More generally, the adjustment occurs through changes in the relative prices of domestic and foreign goods. The relative price of domestic to foreign goods is determined by both the foreign exchange rate and the domestic and foreign price levels. Under a flexible exchange rate, the adjustment would occur quickly through changes in the exchange rate itself. With a fixed exchange rate, the price levels of the two countries would do the adjustment. The required end result—a change in the relative prices—is the same in either case.

in Table 14-2. Until 1980, the United States had a modestly positive net-export position. But in the early 1980s the U.S. government's fiscal position shifted sharply toward deficit. You can depict this by drawing a new $S + T' - G'$ line in Figure 14-8 that intersects the real-interest-rate line at point C. You can see that total national saving would decline with a larger government deficit. Domestic investment would be unchanged. Net exports would turn negative and be given by the line segment CA.

We can also use this analysis to explain the mechanism by which net exports adjust to provide the necessary investment when the government runs a budget deficit. Consider a country with a net-export surplus as shown in Figure 14-8. Suppose that the government suddenly begins to run a large budget deficit. This change will lead to an imbalance in the saving-investment market, which would tend to push up domestic interest rates relative to world interest rates. The rise in domestic interest rates will attract funds from abroad and will lead to an appreciation in the foreign exchange rate of the country running the budget deficit. The appreciation will lead to falling exports and rising imports, or a decrease in net exports. This trend will continue until net exports have fallen sufficiently to close the saving-investment gap.

Other important examples of the open-economy saving-investment theory in the small open economy are the following:

- An increase in private saving or lower government spending in a country will increase national saving as represented by a rightward shift in the national saving schedule in Figure 14-8. This will

lead to a depreciation of the exchange rate until net exports have increased enough to balance the increase in domestic saving.

- An increase in domestic investment, say, because of an improved business climate or a burst of innovations, will lead to a shift in the investment schedule. This will lead to an appreciation of the exchange rate until net exports decline enough to balance saving and investment. In this case, domestic investment crowds out foreign investment.

- An increase in world interest rates will reduce the level of investment. This will lead to an increase in the difference between saving and investment, to a depreciation in the foreign exchange rate, and to an increase in net exports and foreign investment. (This would be a shift along the investment schedule.)

Table 14-3 summarizes the major results for the small open economy. Also make sure you can work through the cases of decreases in the government's fiscal deficit, in private saving, in investment, and in world interest rates. This handy table and its explanation deserve careful study.[3]

---

[3] This discussion covers "small" open economies that cannot affect the world interest rate. For "large" open economies like the United States, the impact would be somewhere between the small-economy and the closed-economy cases. This more complex case is covered in intermediate textbooks (see the Further Reading section in Chapter 4).

Change in policy or exogenous variable	Change in exchange rate	Change in investment	Change in net exports
Increase in G or decrease in T	$e \uparrow$	0	$X \downarrow$
Increase in private S	$e \downarrow$	0	$X \uparrow$
Increase in investment demand	$e \uparrow$	$I \uparrow$	$X \downarrow$
Increase in world interest rates	$e \downarrow$	$I \downarrow$	$X \uparrow$

TABLE 14-3. Major Conclusions of Saving-Investment Model in Small Open Economy
Make sure you understand the mechanism by which each of these occurs.

Integration of a country into the world financial system adds an important new dimension to economic performance and economic policy. The foreign sector provides another source for domestic investment and another outlet for domestic saving. Higher saving at home—whether in the form of private or public saving—will lead to a combination of higher investment at home and higher net exports. A country's trade balance is primarily a reflection of its national saving and investment rather than of its productivity or wealth. Adjustments in a country's trade accounts require a change in domestic saving or investment, and in the long run the adjustments will be brought about by movements in the country's relative prices, often through exchange-rate changes.

PROMOTING GROWTH IN THE OPEN ECONOMY

Increasing the growth of output in open economies involves more than just waving a magic wand that will attract investors or savers. The saving and investing climate involves a wide array of policies, including a stable macroeconomic environment, secure property rights, and, above all, a predictable and attractive climate for investment. We review in this section some of the ways that open economies can improve their growth rates by using the global marketplace to their best advantage.

Over the long run, the single most important way of increasing per capita output and living standards is to ensure that the country *adopts best-practice techniques* in its production processes. It does little good to have a high investment rate if the investments are in the wrong technology. This point was abundantly shown in the last years of Soviet central planning (discussed in Chapter 12), when the investment rate was extremely high but much investment was poorly designed, left unfinished, or put in unproductive sectors. Moreover, individual small countries do not need to start from scratch in designing their own turbines, machinery, computers, and management systems. Often, reaching the technological frontier will involve engaging in joint ventures with foreign firms, which in turn requires that the institutional framework be hospitable to foreign capital.

Another important set of policies is *trade policies.* Evidence suggests that an open trading system promotes competitiveness and adoption of best-practice technologies. By keeping tariffs and other barriers to trade low, countries can ensure that domestic firms feel the spur of competition and that foreign firms are permitted to enter domestic markets when domestic producers sell at inefficiently high prices or monopolize particular sectors.

When countries consider their saving and investment, they must not concentrate entirely on physical capital. *Intangible capital* is just as important. Studies show that countries that invest in human capital through education tend to perform well and be resilient in the face of shocks. Many countries have valuable stocks of natural resources—forests, minerals, oil and gas, fisheries, and arable land—that must be managed carefully to ensure that they provide the highest yield for the country.

One of the most complex factors in a country's growth involves *immigration* and *emigration.* Historically, the United States has attracted large flows of immigrants that not only have increased the size of its labor forces but also have enhanced the quality of its culture and scientific research. More recently, however, the immigrants have possessed less education and lower skills than the domestic labor force. As a result, according to some studies, immigration has depressed the relative wages of low-wage workers in the United States. Countries that "export" workers, such as Mexico, often have a steady stream of earnings that are sent home by citizens to their relatives, and this can provide a nice supplement to export earnings.

One of the most important and subtle influences concerns the *institutions of the market.* The most successful open economies—like the Netherlands and Luxembourg in Europe or Taiwan and Hong Kong in Asia—have provided a secure environment for investment and entrepreneurship. This involved establishing a secure set of property rights, guided by the rule of law. Increasingly important is the development of intellectual property rights so that inventors and creative artists are assured that they will be able to profit from their activities. Countries must fight corruption, which is a kind of private taxation system that preys on the most profitable enterprises, creates uncertainty about property rights, raises costs, and has a chilling effect on investment.

A *stable macroeconomic climate* means that taxes are reasonable and predictable and that inflation is low so that lenders need not worry about inflation confiscating their investments. It is crucial that exchange rates be relatively stable, with a convertibility that allows easy and inexpensive entry into and exit out of the domestic currency. Countries that provide a favorable institutional structure attract large flows of foreign financial capital, while countries that have unstable institutions, like Russia or Iraq, attract relatively little foreign funds and suffer "capital flight," in which local residents move their funds abroad to avoid taxes, expropriation, or loss of value.

Figure 14-9 illustrates the impact of the investment climate on national investment. The left-hand panel depicts a country that has a favorable invest-

ment climate, so the domestic interest rate is equal to the world interest rate. The overall level of investment there is high, and the country can attract foreign funds to finance domestic investment. Panel (*b*) shows a high-risk country—plagued by revolution, high inflation, unpredictable taxes, nationalizations, corruption, an unstable foreign exchange rate, and so on. In the high-risk country, domestic interest rates have a high "risk premium" over world interest rates, so the real cost of capital might be 10 or 20 or 30 percent per year compared to 5 percent in the low-risk country. The risky country will have trouble attracting domestic *and* foreign investment, and the resulting level of investment will be low.

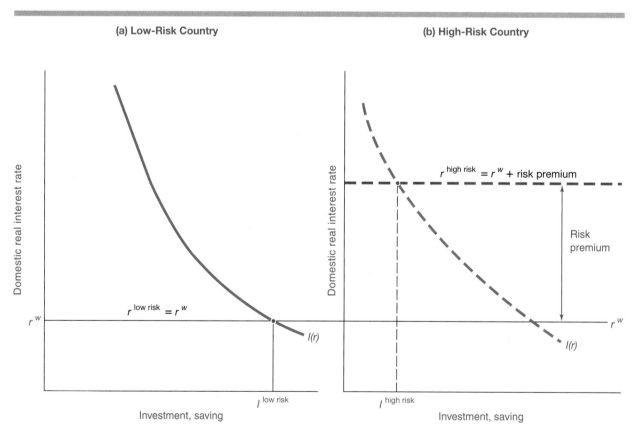

(a) Low-Risk Country

(b) High-Risk Country

FIGURE 14-9. Business Climate Affects Interest Rate and Investment Level

In the low-risk country in **(a)**, a stable economic climate leads to a low domestic interest rate at r^W and a high level of investment at $I^{\text{low risk}}$. In the high-risk country, racked by political turmoil, corruption, and economic uncertainty, investors require a large risk premium on their investments, so the domestic interest rate is far above the world interest rate. The result is a depressed level of investment as foreign investors seek safer terrain.

Promoting economic growth in an open economy involves ensuring that business is attractive for foreign and domestic investors who have a wide array of investment opportunities in the world economy. The ultimate goals of policy are to have high rates of saving and investment in productive channels and to ensure that businesses use the best-practice techniques. Achieving these goals involves setting a stable macroeconomic climate, guaranteeing dependable property rights for both tangible investments and intellectual property, providing exchange-rate convertibility that allows investors to take home their profits, and maintaining confidence in the political and economic stability of the country.

C. INTERNATIONAL ECONOMIC ISSUES AT CENTURY'S END

In this final section, we apply the tools of international economics to examine two of the central issues that have concerned nations in recent years. In the first part, we examine the issue of the difference between competitiveness and productivity. In the final part, we will turn to one of the durable issues of the global economy—the choice between fixed and flexible exchange rates.

COMPETITIVENESS AND PRODUCTIVITY

"The Deindustrialization of America"

Often, when unemployment rises sharply in the presence of trade deficits, people raise alarms about a nation's productivity and competitiveness. Just such a situation occurred in the United States in the 1980s, and a review of this history is a helpful reminder about the determinants of trade flows.

The overvalued dollar in the 1980s produced severe economic hardships in many U.S. sectors exposed to international trade. Industries like automobiles, steel, textiles, and agriculture found the demand for their products shrinking as exchange-rate appreciation led to a rise in their prices relative to the prices of foreign competitors. Unemployment in America's manufacturing heartland increased sharply, factories were closed, and the Midwest became known as the "rust belt."

Many noneconomists interpreted U.S. trade problems as indicative of "America in decline." They fretted that America's technological leadership was eroding because of excessive regulation, declining innovation, and managerial sloth. Some advocated economic protection against Japan and Western Europe, while others argued for "industrial policies" for beleaguered industries to help stem the "deindustrialization of America." America was pictured as a land condemned to serving potato chips while others were manufacturing our computer chips.

Economists saw a different syndrome at work—the classic disease of an overvalued exchange rate. To understand the fundamentals, we must distinguish a nation's competitiveness from its productivity. *Competitiveness* refers to the extent to which a nation's goods can compete in the marketplace; this depends primarily upon the relative prices of domestic and foreign products. Competitiveness must be distinguished from *productivity*, which is measured by the output per unit of input. Productivity is fundamental to the growth in living standards in a nation: to a first approximation, a nation's real income grows in step with its productivity growth.

It is true that U.S. competitiveness fell sharply during the 1980s. But the cause was not a deterioration in productivity growth. Rather, deteriorating competitiveness during the 1980s arose because the appreciation of the dollar raised American prices relative to those of its trading partners. In fact, there was no major change in the overall trend in productivity growth during the 1980s, and if anything productivity probably grew more rapidly during that period than in the prior decade.

Make sure you understand this fundamental point about competitiveness: As the theory of comparative advantage demonstrates, nations are not inherently uncompetitive. Rather, they become uncompetitive when their prices move out of line from those of their trading partners because of an overvalued exchange rate.

Trends in Productivity

The real story about U.S. real income is not about competitiveness but about productivity. Recall that productivity measures the output per worker or per bundle of inputs. Real incomes in the United States stagnated until recently because productivity growth slowed and not because America became uncompetitive in the global marketplace.

Competitiveness is important for trade but has no intrinsic relationship to the level or growth of real incomes. China has enjoyed a massive trade surplus in the 1990s at the same time that the United States ran a large trade deficit. But surely that does not mean that Americans would trade their living standards for those in China. Loss of competitiveness in international markets results from a nation's *prices* being out of line from those of its trading partners; it has no necessary connection with how a nation's *productivity* compares with other countries' productivity.

A particularly revealing study by the McKinsey Global Institute found that in 1990 manufacturing productivity in Japan was 17 percent below that in the United States while German productivity was 21 percent below U.S. levels.[4] Furthermore, the United States maintained a productivity lead in four of the nine manufacturing industries studied: computers, soaps and detergents, beer, and food. Japanese workers had higher productivity than U.S. workers in automobiles, auto parts, metalworking, steel, and consumer electronics production. In none of the industries surveyed were German workers the most productive, and indeed German productivity had declined relative to that in the United States during the 1980s.

The McKinsey study investigated the sources of productivity differences among the major countries in the nine industries studied. What emerged was surprising:

- Economies of scale and manufacturing technologies played a small role in some industries.
- Surprisingly, workers' skill levels and education were of little importance, being essentially the same in all three nations.
- Large differences in productivity exist within firms in the same industry. Managers could significantly improve productivity in *all* industries by adopting best-practice technologies.

One of the most striking findings of the McKinsey study was the importance of *globalization*, which the study defined as exposure to competition with the world leader in a particular industry. The study

found that foreign direct investment by the most productive country (such as the Japanese auto transplants on American soil) has contributed to dramatic productivity improvements both through introducing leading-edge technologies and in stimulating competition.

The surest route to high productivity and therefore to high living standards is to open markets to trade, finance, and ideas from the most advanced countries and to allow vigorous competition with companies that have adopted the most advanced technologies.

EVOLUTION OF MONETARY SYSTEMS IN EUROPE

An ideal exchange-rate system is one that allows high levels of predictability of relative prices while ensuring smooth adjustment to economic shocks. In a well-functioning system, people can trade and invest in other countries without worrying that exchange rates will suddenly change and make their ventures unprofitable. This ideal seemed to be attained during most of the Bretton Woods era, when exchange-rate changes were infrequent yet output and trade grew rapidly.

In the last decade, however, fixed-exchange-rate systems have more often been sources of instability than stability. Fixed-exchange-rate systems were the subject of intense speculative attack that reached global proportions on three occasions during the 1990s: in Europe in 1991–1992, in Mexico in 1994–1995, and in East Asia in 1997–1998. In this subsection, we describe some of the pitfalls of fixed-exchange-rate systems and chart the evolution of the European Monetary Union from a fixed-rate system to a common currency.

European Monetary System: Europe's Bretton Woods System

The first stirs of a common European currency came in Europe with the creation in 1978 of a currency bloc known as the European Monetary System (or EMS). A group of West European countries, primarily Germany and France, designed this system along the lines of the Bretton Woods

[4] See the Further Reading section at the end of this chapter.

regime. As members of the EMS, nations commit to keeping their exchange rates within prescribed and narrow bands. These bands might be periodically realigned, but in between realignments each nation would ensure that member-country exchange rates remain inside the band.

One implication of a fixed-exchange-rate system, as we explained earlier in this chapter, is that countries must give up control over domestic interest rates. If France has an exchange rate that is tightly tied to Germany, free-market French interest rates cannot diverge significantly from those in Germany. A major divergence would lead to an avalanche of financial flows that would either overturn the exchange-rate system or drive interest rates together.

The Crisis of the European Monetary System

The loss of control over monetary policy would not be fatal during normal times. But in times of crisis, the actual and desired monetary policies may diverge too much. That is exactly what happened in 1989–1993, and this divergence almost destroyed the European Monetary System and eventually led to monetary union.

The first key factor in the crisis of the EMS was the reunification of Germany in 1990. Following reunification, Germany's fiscal policy turned sharply expansionary as it poured money into East Germany. The expansion in western Germany led to an uptick in the German inflation rate. The German central bank responded by raising German interest rates to dampen domestic demand. Here monetary policy was being used for domestic macroeconomic management, and the effects of the measures on Germany's trading partners were subordinated to domestic economic concerns.

Faced with rising German interest rates, other nations in the EMS had to raise their interest rates to prevent their currencies from depreciating against the German mark and moving outside the prescribed range. Many countries found themselves with overvalued exchange rates. These interest-rate increases, along with a worldwide recession and a sharp decline in output from the collapsing communist bloc, pushed Europe, outside of Germany, into ever-deeper recession.

The fundamental contradiction of fixed exchange rates

"You can't have it all" is one of the central tenets of economics. This was driven home in macroeconomic affairs on several occasions during the 1990s. As countries on fixed exchange rates liberalized their financial markets, they encountered a *fundamental contradiction of fixed exchange rates: A country cannot simultaneously have (a) a fixed but adjustable exchange rate, (b) free capital and financial movements, and (c) an independent domestic monetary policy.*

This contradiction among the three objectives was explained by Paul Krugman as follows:

> The point is that you can't have it all: A country must pick two out of three. It can fix its exchange rate without emasculating its central bank, but only by maintaining controls on capital flows (like China today); it can leave capital movement free and retain monetary autonomy, but only by letting the exchange rate fluctuate (like Britain—or Canada); or it can choose to leave capital free and stabilize the currency, but only by abandoning any ability to adjust interest rates to fight inflation or recession (like Argentina today, or for that matter most of Europe).[5]

Speculative Attack!

European countries ran into the fundamental contradiction in the early 1990s when their exchange rates were attacked by speculators who believed that countries would not tolerate overvalued exchange rates and too high interest rates indefinitely. One by one, currencies came under attack—the Finnish mark, the Swedish crown, the Italian lira, the British pound, the Spanish peseta. In the end, only the inner sanctum of France and Germany withstood the speculative attacks.

This episode shows a corollary of the fundamental contradiction: A fixed-exchange-rate system is prone to devastating speculative attack if financial capital flows freely among countries. The reason is the following: A fixed but adjustable exchange rate is susceptible to attack whenever speculators believe that changes in the exchange rate are imminent. If a currency is likely to be devalued, speculators will quickly start selling that currency. The supply of the currency increases while demand drops.

At this point, central banks step in to defend the currency (recall the graphical description of inter-

---

[5] See this chapter's Further Reading section.

vention in Figure 13-8 on page 283). But given the private resources available for speculative attacks— easily tens of billions of dollars in a few hours—the defender of a weak currency quickly runs out of reserves. Unless "hard-currency" countries are willing to provide unlimited lines of credit, the defending central bank will sooner or later give up and either devalue or allow the currency to float.

Toward a Common Currency: The Euro

Since World War II, the democratic countries of Western Europe have pursued ever-closer economic integration, primarily to promote political stability after two devastating conflicts. Peace and trade go hand in hand, according to many political scientists. Beginning in 1957 with a free-trade agreement establishing the European Community, Western Europeans gradually removed all barriers to trade in goods, services, and finance.

Many Europeans believe that complete market integration requires monetary union through a common currency—they look at the United States as a model monetary and financial system. This general belief was reinforced by the breakdown of the European Monetary System in the early 1990s, discussed above. Countries recognized that, due to the fundamental contradiction of fixed exchange rates, markets would become increasingly unstable with the growing integration of European financial markets.

After three decades of integration, the countries of the European Union resolved this contradiction by adopting a common currency. Countries were required to satisfy certain *convergence criteria* before they were allowed in the club. These included inflation and interest rates close to the lowest among the countries, along with stringent limitations on government deficits and government debts. Eleven European countries joined the European Monetary Union (EMU) and met the convergence criteria. On January 1, 1999, these countries, sometimes called Euro-land, adopted the "Euro" as the new money of Western Europe.

The monetary structure under a European monetary union resembles that of the United States. Monetary policy is lodged in the European central bank (ECB), which conducts monetary policy for countries in the EMU. The ECB undertakes open-market operations and thereby determine interest rates for the Euro.

One of the major questions for monetary policy involves the objectives of the central bank. The ECB

is directed under its charter to pursue "price stability" as its primary objective, although it can pursue other community-wide goals as long as these do not compromise price stability. The ECB defines price stability as an increase in Euroland consumer prices of below 2 percent over the medium term. As we will see in our discussion of monetary policy in Chapter 18, this emphasis on inflation targeting has been widely adopted by central banks outside the United States.

Costs and Benefits of Monetary Union

What are the costs and benefits of European monetary union? Advocates of monetary union see important *benefits*. Under a common currency, exchange-rate volatility within Europe will be reduced to zero, so trade and finance will no longer have to contend with the uncertainties about prices induced by changing exchange rates. The primary result will be a reduction in transactions costs among countries. To the extent that national financial markets are segmented, moving to a common currency may allow a more efficient allocation of capital across countries. Some believe that firm macroeconomic discipline will be preserved by having an independent European central bank committed to strict inflation targets. Perhaps the most important benefit may be political integration and stability of Western Europe—a continent at peace for half a century after being at war with itself for most of recorded history.

Many economists are skeptical and point to significant *costs* of monetary union. The dominant concern is that the individual countries will lose the use of both monetary policy and exchange rates as tools for macroeconomic adjustment. This question concerns the optimal currency area, a concept first proposed by Columbia's Robert Mundell, who won the 1999 Nobel Prize for his contributions in this area. An **optimal currency area** is one whose regions have high labor mobility or have common and synchronous aggregate supply or demand shocks. In an optimal currency area, significant changes in exchange rates are not necessary to ensure rapid macroeconomic adjustment.

Most economists believe that the United States is an optimal currency area. When the United States is faced with a shock that affects the different regions asymmetrically, labor migration tends to restore balance. For example, workers left the hard-hit northern states and migrated to the oil-rich southwestern states after the oil shocks of the 1970s.

Many economists worry that Western Europe is not an optimal currency area because of the rigidity of its wage structures and the low degree of labor mobility among the different countries. When a shock occurs— for example, after the 1990 reunification of Germany—inflexible wages and prices lead to rising inflation in the regions with a demand increase and rising unemployment in depressed regions. Monetary union may therefore condemn unfortunate regions to persistent low growth and high unemployment.

Notwithstanding these reservations, Europeans resolved to move ahead with monetary union. Although the long-run impacts will not be known for many years, the beginnings were auspicious. The handoff to the new currency in early 1999 proceeded smoothly, and the new market for Euro securities grew rapidly.

European Monetary Union is one of history's great economic experiments. Never before has such a large and powerful group of countries turned its economic fortunes over to a multinational body like the European Central Bank. Never before has a central bank been charged with the macroeconomic fortunes of a large group of nations with 300 million people producing $7 trillion of goods and services. While optimists point to the microeconomic benefits of a larger market and lower transactions costs, skeptics worry that monetary union threatens stagnation and unemployment because of the lack of price and wage flexibility and insufficient labor mobility among countries. All will be watching this important economic innovation.

FINAL ASSESSMENT

This survey of international economics must acknowledge a mixed picture, with some successes and some failures. But if we step back from the individual issues, an impartial jury of historians would surely rate the second half of the twentieth century as one of unparalleled success for the countries of North America and Western Europe:

- *Robust economic performance.* The period has seen the most rapid and sustained economic growth in recorded history. It is the only half-century since the Industrial Revolution that has avoided a deep depression, and none of the major industrial countries have suffered from the cancer of hyperinflation.

- *The emerging monetary system.* The international monetary system continues to be a source of turmoil, with frequent crises as countries encounter balance-of-payments or currency crises. Nonetheless, we can see an emerging system in which the major economic regions of the United States, Europe, and Japan conduct independent monetary policies with flexible exchange rates while smaller countries either float or have "hard" fixed rates tied to one of the major blocks. The major testing ground of the next few years will be the strength of the new European Monetary Union.

- *The reemergence of free markets.* You often hear that imitation is the sincerest form of flattery. In economics, imitation occurs when a nation adopts another nation's economic structure in the hope that it will produce growth and stability. In the last decade, country after country threw off the shackles of communism and stifling central planning—not only because the textbooks convinced them to do so but primarily because they used their own eyes to see how the market-oriented countries of the West prospered while the command economies of the East collapsed. *For the first time, an empire collapsed simply because it could not produce sufficient butter along with its guns.*

Maintaining and strengthening the current international economic system is a worthy challenge for all.

SUMMARY

A. Foreign Trade and Economic Activity

1. An open economy is one that engages in international exchange of goods, services, and investments. Exports are goods and services sold to buyers outside the country, while imports are those purchased from foreigners. The difference between exports and imports of goods and services is called net exports.

2. When foreign trade is introduced, domestic demand can differ from national output. Domestic demand comprises consumption, investment, and government

purchases $(C + I + G)$. To obtain GDP, exports (Ex) must be added and imports (Im) subtracted, so

$$GDP = C + I + G + X$$

where X = net exports = $Ex - Im$. Imports are determined by domestic income and output along with the prices of domestic goods relative to those of foreign goods; exports are the mirror image, determined by foreign income and output along with relative prices. The dollar increase of imports for each dollar increase in GDP is called the marginal propensity to import (MPm).

3. Foreign trade has an effect on GDP similar to that of investment or government purchases. As net exports rise, there is an increase in aggregate demand for domestic output. Net exports hence have a multiplier effect on output. But the expenditure multiplier in an open economy will be smaller than that in a closed economy because of leakages from spending into imports. The multiplier is

$$\text{Open-economy multiplier} \ = \frac{1}{MPS + MPm}$$

Clearly, other things equal, the open-economy multiplier is smaller than the closed-economy multiplier, where $MPm = 0$.

4. The operation of monetary policy has new implications in an open economy. An important example involves the operation of monetary policy in a small open economy that has a high degree of capital mobility. Such a country must align its interest rates with those in the countries to whom it pegs its exchange rate. This means that countries operating on a fixed exchange rate essentially lose monetary policy as an independent instrument of macroeconomic policy. Fiscal policy, by contrast, becomes a powerful instrument because fiscal stimulus is not offset by changes in interest rates.

5. An open economy operating with flexible exchange rates can use monetary policy for macroeconomic stabilization which operates independently of other countries. In this case, the international link adds another powerful channel to the domestic monetary mechanism. A monetary tightening leads to higher interest rates, attracting foreign financial capital and leading to a rise (or appreciation) of the exchange rate. The exchange-rate appreciation tends to depress net exports, so this impact reinforces the contractionary impact of higher interest rates on domestic investment.

6. The international monetary mechanism was an important factor in changing the U.S. investment pattern in the 1980s. Loose fiscal policy and tight money reduced net exports and shifted the composition of GDP away from tradeable goods to nontradeable goods.

B. Interdependence in the Global Economy

7. In the longer run, operating in the global marketplace provides new constraints and opportunities for countries to improve their economic growth. Perhaps the most important element concerns saving and investment, which are highly mobile and respond to incentives and the investment climate in different countries.

8. The foreign sector provides another source for saving and another outlet for investment. Higher domestic saving—whether through private saving or government fiscal surpluses—will increase the sum of domestic investment and net exports. Recall the identity:

$$X = S + (T - G) - I$$

or

$$\begin{aligned}\text{Net exports} = \ &\text{private saving}\\ &+ \text{government saving}\\ &- \text{domestic Investment}\end{aligned}$$

In the long run, a country's trade position primarily reflects its national saving and investment rates. Reducing a trade deficit requires changing domestic saving and investment. One important mechanism for bringing trade flows in line with domestic saving and investment is the exchange rate.

9. Besides promoting high saving and investment, countries increase their growth through a wide array of policies and institutions. Important considerations are a stable macroeconomic climate, strong property rights for both tangible investments and intellectual property, a convertible currency with few restrictions on financial flows, and political and economic stability.

C. International Economic Issues at Century's End

10. Popular analysis looks at large trade deficits and sees "deindustrialization." But this analysis overlooks the important distinction between productivity and competitiveness. Competitiveness refers to how well a nation's goods can compete in the global marketplace and is determined primarily by relative prices. Productivity denotes the level of output per unit of input. Real incomes and living standards depend primarily upon productivity, whereas the trade and current-account positions depend upon competitiveness. There is no close linkage between competitiveness and productivity.

11. Fixed exchange rates are a source of instability in a world of highly mobile financial capital. Recall the fundamental contradiction of fixed exchange rates: A country cannot simultaneously have a fixed but adjustable exchange rate, free capital and financial movements, and an independent domestic monetary policy.

12. European countries chose to move to the "superhard" fixed exchange rates in a common currency and a

unitary central bank. A common currency is appropriate when a region forms an optimal currency area. Advocates of European monetary union point to the improved predictability, lower transactions costs, and potential for better capital allocation. Skeptics worry that a common currency—like any irrevocably fixed exchange-rate system—will require flexible wages and prices to promote adjustment to macroeconomic shocks. In an area with relatively low labor mobility, monetary union may doom major regions or countries to long periods of slow growth and high unemployment.

CONCEPTS FOR REVIEW

$C + I + G + X$ curve for open economy
net exports = $X = Ex - Im$
domestic demand vs. spending on GDP
marginal propensity to import (MPm)

multiplier:
in closed economy = $1/MPS$
in open economy = $1/(MPS + MPm)$
impact of trade flows and exchange rates on GDP

saving-investment identity in open economies:
$X = S + (T - G) - I$
equilibration in saving-investment market in closed and open economies
growth policies in the open economy
competitiveness vs. productivity

FURTHER READING AND INTERNET WEBSITES

Further Reading

The quotation from the *Economic Report of the President 2000* (Washington, D.C., GPO, 2000) can also be found at w3.access.gpo.gov/eop. The McKinsey study is from McKinsey Global Institute, *Manufacturing Productivity* (Washington, D.C., 1993).

Websites

Data on trade and finance for different countries can be found in the websites for Chapter 12.

Robert Mundell won the Nobel Prize in 1999 for his contribution to international macroeconomics. Visit www.nobel.se/laureates to read about his contribution. The quotation from Krugman is from his article in *Slate* at slate.msn.com/Dismal/99-10-18/Dismal.asp describing Mundell's accomplishments.

The website of the European Central Bank at www.ecb.int explains some of the issues involved in the management of the Euro. Also see the sites listed for Chapter 12.

QUESTIONS FOR DISCUSSION

1. Assume that an expansionary monetary policy leads to a decline or depreciation of the U.S. dollar relative to the currencies of America's trading partners in the short run with unemployed resources. Explain the mechanism by which this will produce an economic expansion in the United States. Explain how the trade impact reinforces the impact on domestic investment.

2. Explain the short-run impact upon net exports and GDP of the following in the multiplier model, using Table 14-1 where possible:

   a. An increase in investment (I) of $100 billion
   b. A decrease in government purchases (G) of $50 billion
   c. An increase of foreign output which increased exports by $10 billion
   d. A depreciation of the exchange rate that raised exports by $30 billion and lowered imports by $20 billion at every level of GDP

3. What would the expenditure multiplier be in an economy without government spending or taxes where the *MPC* is 0.8 and the *MPm* is 0? Where the *MPm* is 0.1? Where the *MPm* is 0.9? Explain why the multiplier might even be less than 1.

4. Consider Table 14-3.
   a. Explain each of the entries in the table.
   b. Add another column with the heading "Change in interest rates" to Table 14-3. Then, on the basis of the graph in Figure 14-7, fill in the table for a closed economy.

5. An eminent macroeconomist recently wrote: "Moving toward a monetary union by adopting a common currency is not really about the currency. The most important factor is that countries in the union must agree on a single monetary policy for the entire region." Explain this statement. Why might adopting a single monetary policy cause troubles?

6. Consider the city of New Heaven, which is a very open economy. The city exports reliquaries and has no investment or taxes. The city's residents consume 50 percent of their disposable incomes, and 90 percent of all purchases are imports from the rest of the country. The mayor proposes levying a tax of $100 million to spend on a public-works program. Mayor Cains argues that output and incomes in the city will rise nicely because of something called "the multiplier." Estimate the impact of the public-works program on the incomes and output of New Heaven. Do you agree with the mayor's assessment?

7. Review the bulleted list of the three interactions of saving, investment, and trade on page 302. Make a graph like that of Figure 14-8 to illustrate each of the impacts. Make sure that you can explain the reverse cases mentioned in the sentence that follows the bulleted list.

8. Politicians often decry the large trade deficit of the United States. Economists reply that to reduce the trade deficit would require a tax increase or a cut in government expenditures. Explain the economists' view using the analysis of the saving-investment balance in Figure 14-8. Also, explain the quotation from the *Economic Report 2000* on pages 290–291.

9. Consider a country like Russia, which is trying to make a transition to the market. It has had high inflation, many changes in its tax treatment of foreign investment, political instability (including two civil wars in Chechnya in the 1990s), and highly uncertain and vari-

able property rights. Explain why each of these factors would reduce the attractiveness of investment in Russia, and use your discussion to explain the risk premium on investment in Figure 14-9.

10. Consider the example of small open economies like Belgium and the Netherlands that have highly mobile financial capital and fixed exchange rates but also have high government budget deficits. Suppose that these countries find themselves in a depressed economic condition, with low output and high unemployment. Explain why they cannot use monetary policy to stimulate their economies. Why would fiscal expansion be effective if they could tolerate higher budget deficits? Why would a depreciation of the exchange rate produce both higher output and a lower government deficit?

11. **Advanced problem.** After the reunification of Germany, payments to rebuild the former East Germany led to a major expansion of aggregate demand in Germany. The German central bank responded by slowing money growth and driving up German real interest rates. These actions took place in the context of the European Monetary System, in which most countries had fixed exchange rates and where the German central bank was dominant in monetary policy.
   a. Explain why European countries having fixed exchange rates and following the lead of the German central bank would find their interest rates rising along with German interest rates. Explain why other European countries would thereby be plunged into deep recessions.
   b. Explain why countries would prefer the European Monetary Union to the earlier system.
   c. Trace through why this German monetary tightening would be expected to lead to a depreciation of the dollar. Explain why the depreciation would stimulate economic activity in the United States.

12. **Advanced problem.** Reread the definition of the fundamental contradiction as well as the discussion by Paul Krugman on page 307. Explain why the three elements cannot go together. Use this result to explain the European monetary crisis of 1989–1993. Why is there not a fundamental contradiction for the fixed-exchange-rate system between "California dollars" and "Texas dollars." Explain the arguments for and against each of the three "possible" choices in the contradiction described by Krugman.

PART FOUR

Unemployment, Inflation, and Economic Policy

The United States enjoyed an extraordinary period of rapid economic growth and declining unemployment over the 1990s. From the trough of the last recession in 1992 until midyear 2000, the number of employed workers grew by almost 30 million while unemployment fell by 4 million. Other regions, in Europe and East Asia, were not so fortunate and had persistently high unemployment. Although better understanding of macroeconomics has allowed most countries to avoid the worst depressions, occasional bouts of high unemployment continue to plague many market economies.

In the present chapter, we first review the foundations of aggregate supply and see how unemployment is determined by the interaction of aggregate supply and demand. We then examine the major policy issues surrounding unemployment.

CHAPTER

15

Unemployment and the Foundations of Aggregate Supply

Be nice to people on your way up because you'll meet them on your way down.

Wilson Mizner

A. THE FOUNDATIONS OF AGGREGATE SUPPLY

Earlier chapters focused on aggregate demand and economic growth. This section describes the factors determining aggregate supply, which is critical for understanding the evolution of the economy. In the short run, the nature of the inflationary process and the effectiveness of government countercyclical policies depend on aggregate demand. In the long run of a decade or more, economic growth and rising living standards are closely linked with increases in aggregate supply.

This distinction between short-run and long-run aggregate supply is crucial to modern macroeconomics. In the short run, it is the interaction of aggregate supply and demand that determines business-cycle fluctuations, inflation, unemployment, recessions, and booms. But in the long run, it is the growth of potential output working through aggregate supply which explains the trend in output and living standards.

Let's start with a few definitions. Recall that **aggregate supply** describes the behavior of the production side of the economy. The **aggregate supply curve**, or *AS* curve, is the schedule showing the level of total national output that will be produced at each possible price level, other things being equal.

In analyzing aggregate supply, it is crucial to distinguish *AS* curves according to the period. The short run of up to a few years involves the **short-run aggregate supply schedule**. Aggregate supply in the short run is seen as an *upward-sloping AS* curve—one along which higher prices are associated with increases in the production of goods and services.

For the long run (several years or a decade or more), we look at the **long-run aggregate supply schedule**. This relationship is shown as a *vertical AS* schedule, one in which increases in the price level are not associated with an increase in total output supplied.

This section is devoted to explaining these central points.

DETERMINANTS OF AGGREGATE SUPPLY

Aggregate supply depends fundamentally upon two distinct sets of forces: potential output and input costs. Let us examine each of these influences.

Potential Output

The key concept for understanding aggregate supply is *potential output* or *potential GDP*. Potential output is the maximum sustainable output that can be produced without triggering rising inflationary pressures.

Over the long run, aggregate supply depends primarily upon potential output. Hence, long-run *AS* is

determined by the same factors which influence long-run economic growth: the amount and quality of available labor, the quantity of machines and other capital goods used by workers, and the level of technology. The analysis of long-run growth trends therefore concerns both the growth of potential output and the determination of aggregate supply.

For quantitative purposes, macroeconomists generally use the following definition of potential output:

Potential GDP is the highest sustainable level of national output. We measure potential GDP as the output that would be produced at a benchmark level of the unemployment rate called the *nonaccelerating inflation rate of unemployment* (or the *NAIRU*). Current estimates of the NAIRU for the United States are in the range of 5 to 6 percent of the labor force.

Potential output is a growing target. As the economy grows, potential output increases as well, and the aggregate supply curve shifts to the right. Table 15-1 shows the key determinants of aggregate supply, broken down into factors affecting potential output and production costs. From our analysis of economic

Variable	Impact on aggregate supply
Potential output	
Inputs	Supplies of capital, labor, and land are the important inputs. Potential output comes when unemployment of labor and other resources is at non-inflationary levels. Growth of inputs increases potential output and aggregate supply.
Technology and efficiency	Innovation, technological improvement, and increased efficiency increase the level of potential output and raise aggregate supply.
Production costs	
Wages	Lower wages lead to lower production costs; lower costs mean that quantity supplied will be higher at every price level for a given potential output.
Import prices	A decline in foreign prices or an appreciation in the exchange rate reduces import prices. This leads to lower production costs and raises aggregate supply.
Other input costs	Lower oil prices or less burdensome environmental regulation lowers production costs and thereby raises aggregate supply.

TABLE 15-1. Aggregate Supply Depends upon Potential Output and Production Costs

Aggregate supply relates total output supplied to the price level. Behind the *AS* curve lie fundamental factors of productivity as represented by potential output as well as production costs. Listed factors would increase aggregate supply, shifting the *AS* curve down or to the right.

growth, we know that the prime factors determining the growth in potential output are the growth in inputs and technological progress.

Potential output is not maximum output

We must emphasize a subtle point about potential output: Potential output is the maximum sustainable output but not the absolute maximum output that an economy can produce. The economy can operate with output levels above potential output for a short time, and indeed this was the situation during the long economic expansion of the late 1990s. Factories and workers can work overtime for a while, but production above potential is not indefinitely sustainable. If the economy produces more than its potential output for long, price inflation tends to rise as unemployment falls, factories are worked intensively, and

workers and businesses try to extract higher wages and profits.

A useful analogy is someone running a marathon. Think of potential output as the maximum speed that a marathoner can run without becoming "overheated" and dropping out from exhaustion. Clearly, the runner can run faster than the sustainable pace for a while, just as the U.S. economy grew faster than its potential growth rate during the 1990s. But over the entire course, the economy, like the marathoner, can produce only at a maximum sustainable "speed," and this sustainable output speed is what we call potential output.

Input Costs

The aggregate supply curve is affected not only by potential output but also by changes in the costs of production. As production costs rise, businesses are willing to supply a given level of output only at a

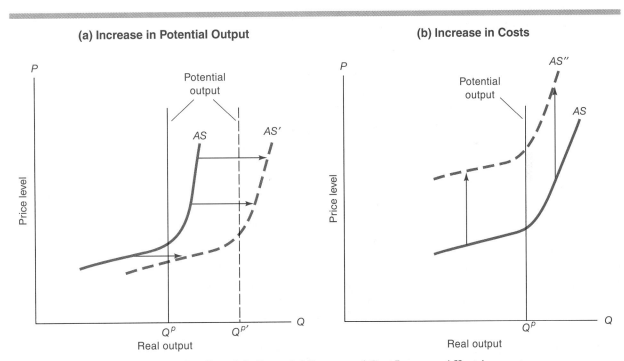

(a) Increase in Potential Output

(b) Increase in Costs

FIGURE 15-1. How Do Growth in Potential Output and Cost Increases Affect Aggregate Supply?

In **(a)**, growth in potential output with unchanged production costs shifts the AS curve rightward from AS to AS'. When production costs increase, say, because of higher wages or import costs, but with unchanged potential output, the AS curve shifts vertically upward, as from AS to AS'' in **(b)**.

higher price. For example, if input costs rose so much that production costs exactly doubled, the price at which businesses would supply each level of output would also double. The *AS* curve would shift upward so that each output *AS* pair (P, Q) would be replaced by $(2P, Q)$.

Table 15-1 on page 316 shows some of the cost factors affecting aggregate supply. By far the most important cost is labor earnings, which constitute about three-quarters of the overall cost of production for a country like the United States. For the small open economies like the Netherlands or Hong Kong, import costs play an even greater role than wages in determining aggregate supply.

How can we graph the relationship between potential output, costs, and aggregate supply? Figure 15-1 on page 317 illustrates the effect of changes in potential output and in costs on aggregate supply. The left-hand panel shows that an increase in potential output with no change in production costs would shift the aggregate supply curve outward from *AS* to *AS'*. If production costs were to increase with no change in potential output, the curve would shift straight up from *AS* to *AS''*, as shown in Figure 15-1(*b*).

The real-world shifting of *AS* is displayed in Figure 15-2. The curves are realistic empirical estimates for two different years, 1982 and 1999. The vertical lines, marked Q^p and $Q^{p'}$, indicate the levels of potential output in the two years. According to studies, real potential output grew about 62 percent over this period.

The figure shows how the *AS* curve shifted outward and upward over the period. The *outward* shift was caused by the increase in potential output that came from growth in the labor force and capital as well as from improvements in technology. The *upward* shift was caused by increases in the cost of production, as wages, import prices, and other production costs rose. Putting together the cost increases and the potential-output growth gives the aggregate supply shift shown in Figure 15-2.

AGGREGATE SUPPLY IN THE SHORT RUN AND LONG RUN

How do shifts in aggregate demand affect output and employment? This question engages one of the major controversies about modern macroeconomics—the determination of aggregate supply.

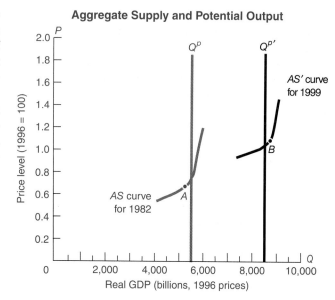

Aggregate Supply and Potential Output

FIGURE 15-2. In Reality, Aggregate Supply Shifts Combine Cost Increases and Increased Potential Output

Between 1982 and 1999, potential output grew due to increases in capital and labor inputs along with technological improvements. At the same time, increases in wages and other costs meant that the price level at which businesses would produce the economy's potential output increased.

The major bone of contention is how aggregate supply responds to changes in demand. Economists of the **Keynesian school** believe that changes in aggregate demand have a significant and lasting effect on output. Hence, if aggregate demand falls because of a monetary tightening or a falloff in consumer spending, Keynesians hold that this will in the short run lead to falling output and employment. In terms of our curves, this means that the *AS* curve is relatively flat in the short run; a decline in *AD* will therefore lead to a small decline in prices but a relatively large decrease in output.

A contrary view is represented by the **classical approach** to macroeconomics. This school emphasizes that the price mechanism contains powerful equilibrating forces that will keep the economy near full employment without any government actions; consequently, there is little involuntary unemployment. In terms of the *AS* function, the classical approach holds that the *AS* curve is very steep or even vertical; changes in aggregate demand therefore have little effect on output.

Which view is correct? Actually, each view has merit in certain circumstances, as is illustrated in Figure 15-3. The key difference is the time period of the analysis. The short-run *AS* curve on the left is upward-sloping or Keynesian. It indicates that firms are willing to increase their output levels in response to changes in aggregate demand, particularly when there is slack in the economy. But the expansion of output cannot go on forever. As output increases, labor shortages appear and factories operate close to capacity. Wages and prices begin to rise more rapidly. A larger fraction of the response to aggregate demand increase comes in the form of price increases and a smaller fraction comes in output increases.

Figure 15-3(*b*) shows what happens in the long run—after wages and prices have had time to react. When all adjustments have taken place, the long-run *AS* curve becomes vertical or classical. In the long-run and classical case, the level of output supplied is independent of aggregate demand.

Why Do Short-Run *AS* and Long-Run *AS* Differ?

Why does aggregate supply behave differently in the long and short runs? Why do firms raise both prices and output in the short run as aggregate demand increases? Why, by contrast, do increases in demand lead to price changes with little output change in the long run?

The key to these puzzles lies in the behavior of wages and prices in a modern market economy. Some elements of business costs are *inflexible* or *sticky* in the short run. As a result of this inflexibility, businesses can profit from higher levels of aggregate demand by producing more output.

Suppose that concerns over national security lead to an increase in defense spending. Firms know that in the short run many of their production costs are fixed in dollar terms—workers are paid $15 per hour, rent is $1500 per month, and so forth. In

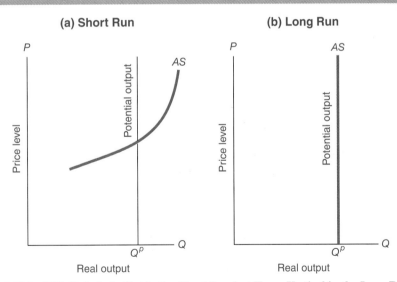

FIGURE 15-3. *AS* **Is Relatively Flat in the Short Run but Turns Vertical in the Long Run**

The short-run *AS* curve in **(a)** slopes upward because many costs are inflexible in the short run. But inflexible prices and wages become unstuck as time passes, so the long-run *AS* curve in **(b)** is vertical and output is determined by potential output. Can you see why a Keynesian economist in **(a)** might desire to stabilize the economy through demand-management policies while a classical economist in **(b)** would concentrate primarily on increasing potential output?

response to the higher demand, firms will generally raise their output prices and increase production. This positive association between prices and output is seen in the upward-sloping *AS* curve in Figure 15-3(*a*).

We have spoken repeatedly of "sticky" or "inflexible" costs. What are some examples? The most significant is wages. For a variety of reasons, wages adjust slowly when economic conditions change. Take unionized workers as an example. They are usually paid according to a long-term union contract which specifies a dollar wage rate. For the life of the labor agreement, the wage rate faced by the firm will be largely fixed in dollar terms. It is quite rare for wages to be raised more than once a year even for nonunion workers. It is even more uncommon for money wages or salaries actually to be cut, except when a company is visibly facing the threat of bankruptcy.[1]

Other prices and costs are similarly sticky in the short run. When a firm rents a building, the lease will often last for a year or more and the rental is generally set in dollar terms. In addition, firms often sign contracts with their suppliers specifying the prices to be paid for materials or components. Some prices are fixed by government regulation, particularly those for utilities like electricity, water, and local telephone service.

Putting all these cases together, you can see how a certain short-run stickiness of wages and prices exists in a modern market economy.

What happens in the long run? Eventually, the inflexible or sticky elements of cost—wage contracts, rent agreements, regulated prices, and so forth—become unstuck and negotiable. Firms cannot take advantage of fixed-money wage rates in their labor agreements forever; labor will soon recognize that prices have risen and insist on compensating increases in wages. Ultimately, all costs will adjust to the higher output prices. If the general price level rises by *x* percent because of the higher demand, then money wages, rents, regulated prices, and other costs will in the end respond by moving up around *x* percent as well.

Once costs have adjusted upward as much as prices, firms will be unable to profit from the higher level of aggregate demand. In the long run, after all elements of cost have fully adjusted, firms will face the same

ratio of price to costs as they did before the change in demand. There will be no incentive for firms to increase their output. The long-run *AS* curve therefore tends to be vertical, which means that output supplied is independent of the level of prices and costs.

The aggregate supply for an economy will differ from potential output in the short run because of inflexible elements of costs. In the short run, firms will respond to higher demand by raising both production and prices. In the longer run, as costs respond to the higher level of prices, most or all of the response to increased demand takes the form of higher prices and little or none the form of higher output. Whereas the short-run *AS* curve is upward-sloping, the long-run *AS* curve is vertical because, given sufficient time, all costs adjust.

✳ B. UNEMPLOYMENT

The United States has had the good fortune to avoid a major business downturn with high and prolonged unemployment for almost two decades; by contrast, Europe and Japan spent most of the 1990s with stagnant economic conditions and massive unemployment. How can millions of people be unemployed when there is so much work to be done? What flaw in a modern mixed economy forces so many who want work to remain idle? To what extent is high unemployment primarily due to flawed unemployment insurance and other government programs that reduce the incentive to work? The balance of this chapter provides a tour of the meaning of unemployment and some answers to these important questions.

MEASURING UNEMPLOYMENT

Changes in the unemployment rate make monthly headlines. Look back to Figure 4-3 on page 73 to refresh your memory about the long-term trend. You can also look forward to Figure 16-11 on page 353 to compare the unemployment rate with the NAIRU. What lies behind the numbers?[2] Statistics on

---

[1] See the study by Bewley in this chapter's Further Reading section for a discussion of why wages are sticky.

[2] For data on and methods for estimating employment and unemployment, see the Website listings in this chapter's Further Reading section.

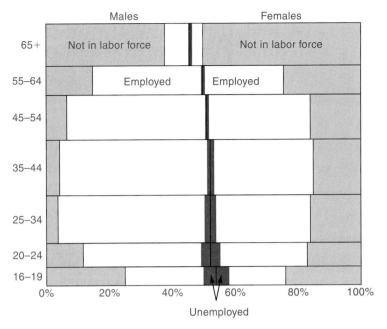

FIGURE 15-4. Labor-Force Status of the Population, 1999

How do Americans spend their time? This figure shows how males and females of different ages are divided among employed, unemployed, and not in the labor force. The size of each block indicates the relative proportion of the population in the designated category. Note the continuing difference in labor-force behavior of men and women. (Source: U.S. Department of Labor, *Employment and Earnings*.)

unemployment and the labor force are among the most carefully designed and comprehensive economic data the nation collects. The data are gathered monthly in a procedure known as *random sampling* of the population.[3] Each month about 50,000 households are interviewed about their recent work history.

The survey divides the population of those 16 years and older into four groups:[4]

- **Employed.** These are people who perform any paid work, as well as those who have jobs but are absent from work because of illness, strikes, or vacations.

- **Unemployed.** This group includes people who are not employed but are actively looking for work or waiting to return to work. To be counted as unemployed, a person must do more than simply think about work. A person must report specific efforts to find a job (such as having a job interview or sending out résumés).

- **Not in the labor force.** This includes the 34 percent of the adult population that is keeping

---

[3] Random sampling is an essential technique for estimating the behavior or characteristics of an entire population. It consists of choosing a subgroup of the population at random (say, by selecting telephone digits through a computer-generated series of random numbers) and then surveying the selected group. Random sampling is used in many social sciences, as well as in market research.

[4] The following classifications from the Bureau of Labor Statistics give the complete definitions for the United States: People are classified as *employed* if they did any work at all as paid employees during the reference week; worked in their own business or profession or on their own farm; or worked without pay at least 15 hours in a family business or farm. People are also counted as employed if they were temporarily absent from their jobs because of illness, bad weather, vacation, labor-management disputes, or personal reasons.

People are classified as *unemployed* if they meet all of the following criteria: They had no employment during the reference week; they were available for work at that time; and they made specific efforts to find employment sometime during the 4-week period ending with the reference week. Persons laid off from a job and expecting recall are counted as unemployed.

	Average unemployment rate (%)	Lost Output	
		GDP loss ($, billion, 1999 prices)	As percentage of GDP during the period
Great Depression (1930–1939)	18.2	2,420	27.6
Oil and inflation crises (1975–1984)	7.7	1,480	3.0
New economy period (1985–1999)	5.7	240	0.3

TABLE 15-2. Economic Costs from Periods of High Unemployment

The two major periods of high unemployment since 1929 occurred during the Great Depression and during the oil shocks and high inflation from 1975 to 1984. The lost output is calculated as the cumulative difference between potential GDP and actual GDP. Note that during the Great Depression losses relative to GDP were 10 times greater than in the 1970s and 1980s. In recent years, the economy has produced close to its potential output. (Source: Authors' estimates on the basis of official GDP and unemployment data.)

house, retired, too ill to work, or simply not looking for work.

● **Labor force.** This includes all those who are either employed or unemployed.

Figure 15-4 shows how the male and female populations in the United States are divided among the categories of employed, unemployed, and not in the labor force. (The status of students is examined in question 6 at the end of this chapter.)

The definition of labor-force status used by the government is the following:

People with jobs are employed; people without jobs but looking for work are unemployed; people without jobs who are not looking for work are outside the labor force. The **unemployment rate** is the number of unemployed divided by the total labor force.

IMPACT OF UNEMPLOYMENT

High unemployment is both an economic and a social problem. Unemployment is an economic problem because it represents waste of a valuable resource. Unemployment is a major social problem because it causes enormous suffering as unemployed workers struggle with reduced incomes. During periods of high unemployment, economic distress spills over to affect people's emotions and family lives.

Economic Impact

When the unemployment rate goes up, the economy is in effect throwing away the goods and services that the unemployed workers could have produced. During recessions, it is as if vast quantities of automobiles, housing, clothing, and other commodities were simply dumped into the ocean.

How much waste results from high unemployment? What is the opportunity cost of recessions? Table 15-2 provides a calculation of how far output fell short of potential GDP during the major periods of high unemployment over the last half-century. The largest economic loss occurred during the Great Depression, but the oil and inflation crises of the 1970s and 1980s also generated more than a trillion dollars of lost output. The last decade has been one of unprecedented stability in the United States, with very small business-cycle losses.

The economic losses during periods of high unemployment are the greatest documented wastes in a modern economy. They are many times larger than the estimated inefficiencies from microeconomic waste due to monopoly or than the waste induced by tariffs and quotas.

Social Impact

The economic cost of unemployment is certainly large, but no dollar figure can adequately convey the human and psychological toll of long periods of persistent involuntary unemployment. The personal tragedy of unemployment has been proved again and again. We can read of the futility of a job search in San Francisco during the Great Depression:

> I'd get up at five in the morning and head for the waterfront. Outside the Spreckles Sugar Refinery, outside the gates, there would be a thousand men. You know dang well there's only three or four jobs. The guy would come out with two little Pinkerton cops: "I need two guys for the bull gang. Two guys to go into the hole." A thousand men would fight like a pack of Alaskan dogs to get through. Only four of us would get through.[5]

Or we can listen to the recollection of an unemployed construction worker:

> I called the roofing outfits and they didn't need me because they already had men that had been working for them five or six years. There wasn't that many openings. You had to have a college education for most of them. And I was looking for anything, from car wash to anything else.
>
> So what do you do all day? You go home and you sit. And you begin to get frustrated sitting home. Everybody in the household starts getting on edge. They start arguing with each other over stupid things 'cause they're all cramped in that space all the time. The whole family kind of got crushed by it.[6]

It would be surprising if such experiences did not leave scars. Psychological studies indicate that being fired from a job is generally as traumatic as the death of a close friend or failure in school. In the late 1980s and early 1990s, many people who lost their jobs were well-paid managers, professionals, and similar white-collar workers who had never expected to be out of work. For them, the shock of being unemployed hit hard. Listen to the story of one middle-aged corporate manager who lost his job in 1988 and was still without permanent work in 1992:

> I have lost the fight to stay ahead in today's economy. . . . I was determined to find work, but as the months and years wore on, depression set in. You can only be rejected so many times; then you start questioning your self-worth.[7]

---

[5] Studs Terkel, *Hard Times: An Oral History of the Great Depression in America* (Pantheon, New York, 1970).

[6] Harry Maurer, *Not Working: An Oral History of the Unemployed* (Holt, New York, 1979).

[7] *Business Week*, Mar. 23, 1992.

Perhaps the most dramatic evidence of the social impact of economic downturns came in Russia after the shock therapy of market reforms (see the discussion in Chapter 12). By 1995, 1 in 5 workers was out of work, and real output had dropped sharply. Health conditions deteriorated and life expectancy fell sharply.

Economist as policymaker

Arthur Okun (1929–1979) was one of the most creative American economic policymakers of the postwar era. Educated at Columbia, he taught at Yale until he joined the staff of President Kennedy's Council of Economic Advisers in 1961. He became a CEA member in 1964 and President Johnson's chairman in 1968. After he left the CEA, Okun stayed in Washington at the Brookings Institution.

Okun was concerned with developing tools that would help the United States track and manage the business cycle. He created the concept of potential output and then showed the relation between output and unemployment that is now known as Okun's Law. Using these tools, he advised Presidents Kennedy and Johnson on the fiscal policies necessary to steer the economy between excessive unemployment and rising inflation. One of Okun's central concerns was to find ways of containing inflation without throwing millions of people out of work. He espoused a novel approach to anti-inflation policies called *tax-based incomes policies* (TIP), which we will discuss in Chapter 16.

In addition, Okun was renowned for his use of simple homilies to illustrate economic points. He compared arguments against a tax increase to his 7-year-old's arguments against taking medicine: "He is perfectly well; he is so sick that nothing can possibly help him; he will take it later in the day if his throat doesn't get better; it isn't fair unless his brothers take it too." Okun proved time and again that a well-told tale is often worth more than 1000 equations.

OKUN'S LAW

The most distressing consequence of any recession is a rise in the unemployment rate. As output falls, firms need fewer labor inputs, so new workers are not hired and current workers are laid off. The impact can be dramatic: By the end of the recession of 1981–1982, about 1 out of every 10 American workers was unemployed. Conditions in Europe were equally depressed in the mid-1990s, when unemployment reached over 10 percent of the workforce.

It turns out that unemployment usually moves in tandem with output over the business cycle. The remarkable co-movement of output and unemployment, along with the numerical relationship, was first identified by Arthur Okun and is known as Okun's Law.

Okun's Law states that for every 2 percent that GDP falls relative to potential GDP, the unemployment rate rises about 1 percentage point.

This means that if GDP begins at 100 percent of its potential and falls to 98 percent of potential, the unemployment rate rises by 1 percentage point, say, from 6 to 7 percent. Figure 15-5 shows how output and unemployment have moved together over time. We can illustrate Okun's Law by examining output and unemployment trends in the 1990s. During the last recession in 1991, the unemployment rate rose to 6.9 percent. At that point, actual GDP was estimated to be 2.5 percent below potential output. Then, over the next 9 years, output grew 5.8 percent faster than potential output, so that in 1999 actual GDP was estimated to be 3.3 percent above potential output. According to Okun's Law, the unemployment rate should have fallen by 2.9 per-

centage points (5.8/2) to 4.0 percent (6.9–2.9). In fact, the unemployment rate for 1999 was 4.2 percent—a remarkably accurate prediction. This shows how Okun's Law can be used to relate changes in the unemployment rate to the growth in output.

One important consequence of Okun's Law is that actual GDP must grow as rapidly as potential GDP just to keep the unemployment rate from rising. In a sense, GDP has to keep running just to keep unemployment in the same place. Moreover, if you want to bring the unemployment rate down, actual GDP must be growing faster than potential GDP.

Okun's Law provides the vital link between the output market and the labor market. It describes the association between short-run movements in real GDP and changes in unemployment.

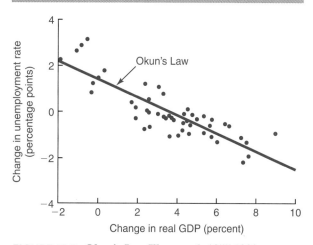

FIGURE 15-5. Okun's Law Illustrated, 1955-1999

According to Okun's Law, whenever output grows 2 percent faster than potential GDP, the unemployment rate declines 1 percentage point. This graph shows that unemployment changes are well predicted by the rate of GDP growth. What output growth would lead to no change in unemployment according to the line? (Source: U.S. Departments of Commerce and Labor.)

Unemployment and politics

Unemployment is one of the most important issues to voters. When unemployment is high during election years, incumbent politicians are often thrown out of office. During depressions and recessions, as in 1932, 1960, 1980, and 1992, incumbent parties lost the White House. By contrast, in boom years with low unemployment (like 1964, 1972, 1984, and 1996), incumbents were reelected.

Suppose you are the economic adviser to President Mary James, who has just been elected. Here is the dialogue:

PRESIDENT JAMES: Unemployment is too high. I would like fiscal and monetary policy to get the unemployment rate down from 7 percent to 5 percent by the time we are running for reelection. How fast must the economy grow over the next 4 years to meet my target?

CHIEF ECONOMIST ECOSTUDENT: We can figure that out from Okun's Law. The economy must grow at the growth rate of potential GDP (about 3 percent annually for the United States today), *plus* enough to reduce the unemployment rate about $1/2$ percentage point each year. The average annual growth rate for GDP must then be 3 percent for trend plus 1 percent to reduce unemployment. Therefore, we must target a growth rate of real GDP of 4 percent per year until the election.

Make sure that you can explain the reasoning of the chief economist.

ECONOMIC INTERPRETATION OF UNEMPLOYMENT

Let's turn now to the economic analysis of unemployment. Some of the important questions we address are: What are the reasons for being unemployed? What is the distinction between "voluntary" and "involuntary" unemployment? What is the relationship between different kinds of unemployment and the business cycle?

Three Kinds of Unemployment

In sorting out the structure of labor markets, economists identify three different kinds of unemployment: frictional, structural, and cyclical.

Frictional unemployment arises because of the incessant movement of people between regions and jobs or through different stages of the life cycle. Even if an economy were at full employment, there would always be some turnover as students search for jobs when they graduate from school or parents reenter the labor force after having children. Because frictionally unemployed workers are often moving between jobs, or looking for better jobs, it is often thought that they are *voluntarily unemployed.*

Structural unemployment signifies a mismatch between the supply of and the demand for workers. Mismatches can occur because the demand for one kind of labor is rising while the demand for another kind is falling, and supplies do not quickly adjust. We often see structural imbalances across occupations or regions as certain sectors grow while others decline. For example, an acute shortage of nurses arose in the mid-1980s as the number of nurses grew slowly while the demand for nursing care grew rapidly because of an aging population and other forces. Not until nurses' salaries rose rapidly and the supply adjusted did the structural shortage of nurses decline. By contrast, the demand for coal miners has been depressed for decades because of the lack of geographic mobility of labor and capital; unemployment rates in coal-mining communities remain high today. In European countries, high real wages, welfare benefits, and taxes have created high levels of structural unemployment for entire economies over the last decade.

Cyclical unemployment exists when the overall demand for labor is low. As total spending and output fall, unemployment rises virtually everywhere. In the recession year 1982, the unemployment rate rose in 48 of the 50 states. This simultaneous rise in unemployment in many markets signaled that the increased unemployment was largely cyclical. Similarly, from the recessions's trough in 1991 to the boom year of 2000, the unemployment rate fell in every state in the United States.

The distinction between cyclical, frictional, and structural unemployment helps economists diagnose the general health of the labor market. High levels of frictional or structural unemployment can occur even though the overall labor market is in balance, for example, when turnover is high or when high minimum wages price certain groups out of the labor force. Cyclical unemployment occurs during recessions, when employment falls as a result of an imbalance between aggregate supply and demand.

Microeconomic Foundations

On the face of it, the cause of unemployment seems clear: too many workers chasing too few jobs. Yet this simple phenomenon has presented a tremendous puzzle for economists for 60 years. Experience shows that prices rise or fall to clear competitive markets. At the market-clearing price, buyers willingly buy what sellers willingly sell. But something is gumming up the workings of the labor market when many hospitals are searching for nurses but cannot find them while thousands of coal miners want to work at the going wage but cannot find a job. Similar symptoms of labor market failures are found in all market economies.

Economists look to the microeconomics of labor markets to help understand the existence of unemployment. Although no universally accepted theory has emerged, many analysts believe that unemployment arises because wages are not flexible enough to clear markets. We explore below why wages are inflexible and why inflexible wages lead to involuntary unemployment.

Voluntary and Involuntary Unemployment

Let us first start by examining the causes of *voluntary unemployment* in a typical labor market. A group of workers has a labor supply schedule shown as *SS* in Figure 15-6 on page 326. The supply curve becomes completely inelastic at labor quantity L^* when wage levels are high. We will call L^* the labor force.

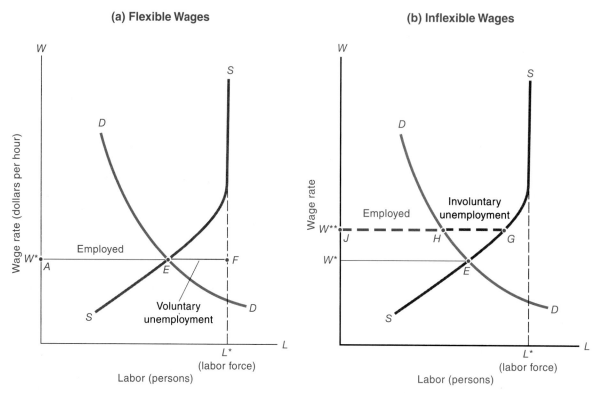

FIGURE 15-6. Inflexible Wages Can Lead to Involuntary Unemployment

We can depict different kinds of unemployment by using the microeconomic supply-and-demand framework. In **(a)**, wages move to W^* to clear the labor market. All unemployment is voluntary. Part **(b)** shows what happens if wages do not adjust to clear the labor market. At the too high wage at W^{**}, JH workers are employed, but HG workers are involuntarily unemployed. Many believe that **(a)** resembles the flexible labor market of the United States while **(b)** shows the impact of high labor taxes, comprehensive minimum wages, and generous social-welfare legislation in Europe.

The left-hand panel of Figure 15-6 shows the usual picture of competitive supply and demand, with a market equilibrium at point E and a wage of W^*. At the competitive, market-clearing equilibrium, firms willingly hire all qualified workers who desire to work at the market wage. The number of employed is represented by the line from A to E. Some members of the labor force would like to work, but only at a higher wage rate. These unemployed workers, represented by the segment EF, are voluntarily unemployed in the sense that they choose not to work at the market wage rate.

The existence of voluntary unemployment implies an often misunderstood point: *Unemployment*

may be an efficient outcome in a situation where heterogeneous workers are searching for and testing different kinds of jobs. The voluntarily unemployed workers might prefer leisure or other activities to jobs at the going wage rate. Or they may be frictionally unemployed, perhaps searching for their first job. Or they might be low-productivity workers who prefer retirement or unemployment insurance to low-paid work. There are countless reasons why people might voluntarily choose not to work at the going wage rate, and yet these people might be counted as unemployed in the official statistics.

But now go back to reread the quotations from unemployed workers on page 323. Who would seriously argue that these workers are voluntarily unemployed? They surely do not sound like people carefully balancing the value of work against the value of leisure. Nor do they resemble people choosing unemployment as they search for a better job. We simply cannot reconcile the experience of many unemployed workers with an elegant classical theory of voluntary unemployment. One of Keynes's great breakthroughs was to let the facts oust this beautiful but irrelevant theory. He explained why we see occasional bouts of involuntary unemployment, periods in which qualified workers are unable to get jobs at the going wage rates.

The key to his approach was to note that wages do not adjust to clear labor markets. Instead, wages tend to respond sluggishly to economic shocks. If wages do not move to clear markets, a mismatch between job seekers and job vacancies can arise. This mismatch may lead to the patterns of unemployment that we see today.

We can understand how inflexible wages lead to involuntary unemployment with an analysis of a *non-clearing labor market*, shown in Figure 15-6(*b*). Here, an economic disturbance leaves the labor market with too high a wage rate. Labor's wage is at W^{**} rather than at the equilibrium or market-clearing wage of W^*.

At the too high wage rate, there are more qualified workers looking for work than there are vacancies looking for workers. The number of workers willing to work at wage W^{**} is at point G on the supply curve, but firms want to hire only H workers, as shown by the demand curve. Because the wage exceeds the market-clearing level, there is a surplus of workers. The unemployed workers represented by the dashed line segment HG are said to be **involuntarily unemployed,** signifying that they are qualified workers who want to work at the prevailing wage but cannot find jobs. When there is a surplus of workers, firms will ration out the jobs by setting more stringent skill requirements and hiring the most qualified or most experienced workers.

The opposite case occurs when the wage is below the market-clearing rate. Here, in a labor-shortage economy, employers cannot find enough workers to fill the existing vacancies. Firms put help-wanted signs in their windows, advertise in newspapers, and even recruit people from other towns.

Sources of Wage Inflexibility

The theory of involuntary unemployment assumes that wages are inflexible. But this raises a further question: Why do wages not move up or down to clear markets? Why are labor markets not like the auction markets for grain, corn, and common stocks?

These questions are among the deepest unsolved mysteries of modern economics. Few economists today would argue that wages move quickly to erase labor shortages and surpluses. Yet no one completely understands the reasons for the sluggish behavior of wages and salaries. We can therefore provide no more than a tentative assessment of the sources of wage inflexibility.

A helpful distinction is that between auction markets and administered markets. An *auction market* is a highly organized and competitive market where the price floats up or down to balance supply and demand. At the Chicago Board of Trade, for example, the price of "number 2 hard red wheat delivered in Kansas City" or "dressed 'A' broiler chickens delivered in New York" changes every minute to reflect market conditions—market conditions that are seen in frantic buy and sell orders of farmers, millers, packers, merchants, and speculators.

Most goods and all labor are sold in administered markets and not in competitive auction markets. Nobody grades labor into "grade B web page developer" or "class AAA assistant professor of economics." No specialist burns the midnight oil trying to make sure that the wages of computer programmers or professors are set at just the market-clearing level where all qualified workers are placed into jobs.

Rather, most firms *administer* their wages and salaries, setting pay scales and hiring people at an entry-level wage or salary. These wage scales are generally fixed for a year or so, and when they are adjusted, the pay goes up for all categories. For example, a bank might have 15 different categories of staff: three grades of secretaries, two grades of tellers, and so forth. Each year, the bank managers will decide how much to increase wages and salaries—say, 3 percent in 1999 on average. Sometimes, the compensation in each category will move up by that percentage; sometimes, the firm might decide to move one category up or down more than the average. Given the procedure by which wages and salaries are determined, there is little room for major adjustments when the firm finds shortages or gluts in a particular area. Except in extreme cases, the firm will tend to adjust the minimum qualifications required for a job rather than its wages when it finds labor market disequilibrium.[8]

For unionized labor markets, the wage patterns are even more rigid. Wage scales are typically set for a 3-year contract period; during that period, wages are not adjusted for excess supply or demand in particular areas. Moreover, unionized workers seldom accept wage cuts even when many of the union's workers are unemployed.

To summarize:

Most wages in America and other market economies are administered by firms or contracts. Wages and salaries are set infrequently and adjust to meet shortages or surpluses only over an extended period of time.

Let's go a step further and ask, What is the economic reason for the sluggishness of wages and salaries? Many economists believe that the inflexibility arises because of the costs of administering compensation (such costs are called "menu costs"). To take the example of union wages, negotiating a contract is a long process that requires much worker and management time and produces no output. It is because collective bargaining is so costly that such agreements are generally negotiated only once every 3 years.

Setting compensation for nonunion workers is less costly, but it nevertheless requires scarce management time and has important effects on worker morale. Every time wages or salaries are set, every time fringe

---

[8] The example of college admissions illustrates the kind of adjustment that takes place when shortages or gluts occur. Many colleges found that applications for places soared in the 1990s. How did they react? Did they raise their tuition enough to choke off the excess demand? No. Instead, they raised their admission standards, requiring better grades in high school and higher average SAT scores. Upgrading the requirements rather than changing wages and prices is exactly what happens in the short run when firms experience excess supply of labor.

Labor market group	Unemployment Rate of Different Groups (% of labor force)		Distribution of Total Unemployment across Different Groups (% of total unemployed)	
	Recession (1982)	Boom (March 2000)	Recession (1982)	Boom (March 2000)
By age:				
16–19	23.2	13.3	18.5	20.2
20 years and older	8.6	3.3	81.5	80.0
By race:				
White	8.6	3.6	77.2	77.6
Black and other	17.3	7.3	22.8	22.4
By sex (adults only):				
Male	8.8	3.8	58.5	50.5
Female	8.3	4.3	41.5	49.5
All workers	9.7	4.1	100.0	100.0

TABLE 15-3. Unemployment by Demographic Group

This table shows how unemployment varies across different demographic groups in boom and recession years. The first set of figures shows the unemployment rate for each group in 1982 and during the boom period of 2000. The last two columns show the percent of the total pool of unemployed that is in each group. (Source: U.S. Department of Labor, *Employment and Earnings.*)

benefits are changed, earlier compensation agreements are changed as well. Some workers will feel the changes are unfair, others will complain about unjust procedures, and grievances may be triggered.

Personnel managers therefore prefer a system in which wages are adjusted infrequently and most workers in a firm get the same pay increase, regardless of the market conditions for different skills or categories. This system may appear inefficient to economists, because it does not allow for a perfect adjustment of wages to reflect market supply and demand. But it does economize on scarce managerial time and helps promote a sense of fair play and equity in the firm. In the end, it may be cheaper to recruit workers more actively or to change the required qualifications than to upset the entire wage structure of a firm simply to hire a few new workers.

The theory of sticky wages and involuntary unemployment holds that the slow adjustment of wages produces surpluses and shortages in individual labor markets. Labor markets are nonclearing markets in the short run. But labor markets do eventually respond to market conditions as wages of high-demand occupations move up relative to those of low-demand occupations. In the long run, major pockets of unemployment and job vacancies tend to disappear as wages and employment adjust to market conditions. But the long run may be many years, and periods of unemployment can therefore persist for many years.

LABOR MARKET ISSUES

Having analyzed the causes of unemployment, we turn next to major labor market issues for today. Which groups are most likely to be unemployed? How long are they unemployed? Why has unemployment in Europe skyrocketed in the last decade?

Who Are the Unemployed?

We can diagnose labor market conditions by comparing years in which output is above its potential (of which 1999–2000 was a recent period) with those of deep recessions (such as was seen in 1982). Differences between these years show how business cycles affect the amount, sources, duration, and distribution of unemployment.

Table 15-3 shows unemployment statistics for boom and recession years. The first two columns of numbers are the unemployment rates by age, race, and sex. These data show that the unemployment rate of every group tends to rise during recession. The last two columns show how the total pool of unemployment is distributed among different groups; observe that the distribution of unemployment across groups changes relatively little throughout the business cycle.

Note also that nonwhite workers tend to experience unemployment rates more than twice those of whites in both recession and boom periods. Until the 1980s, women tended to have higher unemployment rates than men, but in the last two decades unemployment rates differed little by gender. Teenagers, with high frictional unemployment, have generally had unemployment rates much higher than adults.

Duration of Unemployment

Another key question concerns duration. How much of the unemployment experience is long term and of major social concern, and how much is short term as people move quickly between jobs?

Figure 15-7 shows the duration of unemployment in the full-employment year of 1999. A surprising

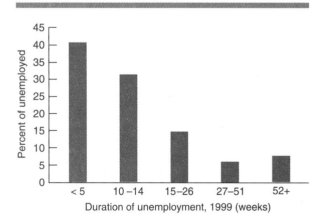

FIGURE 15-7. Most Unemployment in the United States Is Short-Term

How long have workers been unemployed? The duration figures show the distribution of length of unemployment. In the full-employment year 1999, only 14 percent of the unemployed were unemployed for more than 26 weeks, while 41 percent were unemployed for less than 5 weeks. In recessions, the duration of unemployment increases. European countries with stagnant labor markets find that more than half of their unemployed have been without jobs for more than a year. (Source: U.S. Department of Labor, *Employment and Earnings*, January 2000.)

feature of American labor markets is that a very large fraction of unemployment is of short duration. In 1999, two-fifths of unemployed workers were jobless for less than 5 weeks, and long-term unemployment was rare.

In Europe, with lower mobility and greater legal obstacles to economic change, long-term unemployment in the mid-1990s reached 50 percent of the unemployed. Long-term unemployment poses a serious social problem because the resources that families have available—their savings, unemployment insurance, and goodwill toward one another—begin to run out after a few months.

Sources of Joblessness

Why are people unemployed? Figure 15-8 shows how people responded when asked the source of their un-

employment, looking at the recession year of 1982 and the high-employment year of 1999.

There is always some frictional unemployment that results from changes in people's residence or from the life cycle—moving, entering the labor force for the first time, and so forth. The major changes in the unemployment rate over the business cycle arise from the increase in job losers. This source swells enormously in a recession for two reasons: First, the number of people who lose their jobs increases, and then it takes longer to find a new job.

Unemployment by Age

How does unemployment vary over the life cycle? Teenagers generally have the highest unemployment rate of any demographic group, and nonwhite teenagers in recent years have experienced unem-

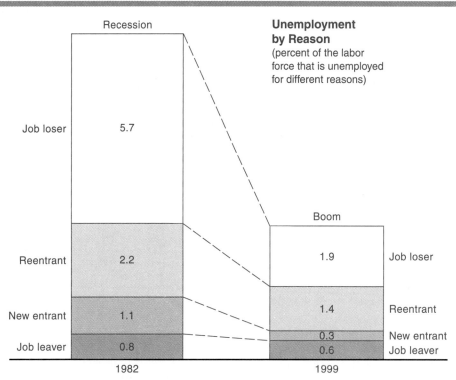

FIGURE 15-8. Distribution of Unemployment by Reason, 1982 and 1999

Why do people become unemployed? Very few were unemployed in 1999 because they left their jobs, and almost 2 percent were new entrants into the labor force (say, because they just graduated from college) or reentrants (people who earlier left the labor force and are back looking for a job). The major change in unemployment from boom to recession, however, is found in the number of job losers. From 1982 to 1999 the fraction of workers who became unemployed because they lost their jobs fell from 5.7 to 1.9 percent. (Source: U.S. Department of Labor, *Employment and Earnings.*)

ployment rates between 30 and 50 percent. Is this unemployment frictional, structural, or cyclical?

Recent evidence indicates that, particularly for whites, teenage unemployment has a large frictional component. Teenagers move in and out of the labor force very frequently. They get jobs quickly and change jobs often. The average duration of teenage unemployment is only half that of adult unemployment; by contrast, the average length of a typical job is 12 times greater for adults than teenagers. In most years, half the unemployed teenagers are "new entrants" who have never had a paying job before. All these factors suggest that teenage unemployment is largely frictional; that is, it represents the job search and turnover necessary for young people to discover their personal skills and to learn what working is all about.

But teenagers do eventually learn the skills and work habits of experienced workers. Table 15-4 shows the unemployment rates at different ages for blacks and whites in 1999. The acquisition of experience and training, along with a greater desire and need for full-time work, is the reason middle-aged workers have much lower unemployment rates than teenagers.

Teenage Unemployment of Minority Groups. While most evidence suggests that unemployment is largely

Age	Unemployment Rate (% of labor force)	
	White	**Black**
16–17	14.5	31.0
18–19	10.2	26.2
20–24	6.3	14.6
25–34	3.3	7.6
35–44	2.7	5.3
45–54	2.4	4.0
55–64	2.5	3.9
65 and older	2.9	5.0

TABLE 15-4. Unemployment Rates at Different Ages, 1999

As workers search for jobs and gain training, they settle on a particular occupation; they tend to stay in the labor force; and they find a preferred employer. As a result, the unemployment rates of older people fall to a fraction of those of teenagers. (Source: U.S. Department of Labor, *Employment and Earnings*, January 2000.)

frictional for white teenagers, the labor market for young African-American workers has behaved quite differently. For the first decade after World War II, the labor-force participation rates and unemployment rates of black and white teenagers were virtually identical. After that time, however, unemployment rates for black teenagers rose sharply relative to those of other groups while their labor-force participation rates have fallen. By 1999, 28 percent of black teenagers (16 to 19 years of age) were employed, compared to 49 percent of white teenagers. Figure 15-9 on page 332 compares the unemployment rates of black teenagers, white teenagers, and all white workers.

What accounts for this extraordinary divergence in the experience of minority teenagers from that of other groups? One explanation might be that labor market forces (such as the composition or location of jobs) have worked against black workers in general. This explanation does not tell the whole story. While adult black workers have always suffered higher unemployment rates than adult white workers—because of lower education attainment, fewer contacts with people who can provide jobs, less on-the-job training, and racial discrimination—the ratio of black to white adult unemployment rates has not increased since World War II.

Numerous studies of the sources of the rising black teenage unemployment rate have turned up no clear explanations for the trend. One possible source is discrimination, but a rise in the black-white unemployment differential would require an increase in racial discrimination—even in the face of increased legal protection for minority workers.

Another theory holds that a high minimum wage along with rising costs of fringe benefits tends to drive low-productivity black teenagers into unemployment. The change in the relation of the minimum wage to average wages allows a test of this hypothesis. From 1981 to 1989, the ratio of the minimum wage to average wages in nonfarm establishments fell from 46 to 34 percent, yet no improvement in the relative unemployment situation of black teenagers occurred. That no improvement took place casts doubt on the minimum wage as the prime suspect. Some conservative critics of the modern welfare state blame high unemployment of blacks on the culture of dependency that is nurtured by government aid to the poor, although there is little firm data to support this proposition.

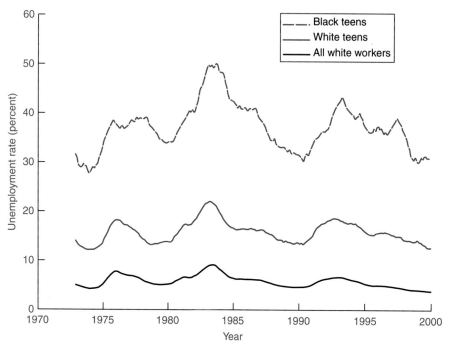

FIGURE 15-9. Unemployment Rates of Different Groups

Unemployment rates of teenagers, especially black teenagers, have been higher than those of adult workers. While the long expansion of the 1990s has cut into black teenage unemployment, it still remains high, with damaging effects on long-term wage and employment prospects. (Source: U.S. Department of Labor.)

Does high teenage unemployment lead to long-lasting labor market damage, with permanently lower levels of skills and wage rates? This question is a topic of intensive ongoing research, and the tentative answer is yes, particularly for minority teenagers. It appears that when youths are unable to develop on-the-job skills and work attitudes, they earn lower wages and experience higher unemployment when they are older. This finding suggests that public policy has an important stake in devising programs to reduce teenage unemployment among minority groups.

Unemployment: High in Europe, low in America

While American unemployment rates fell to unusually low levels in the late 1990s, European unemployment rose sharply over the last three decades. Figure 15-10 on page 333 shows the unemployment history in the two regions.

How can we explain the divergent labor markets of these two regions? Part of the reason probably lies in differences in macroeconomic policies. The United States has a single central bank, the Federal Reserve, that keeps careful watch over the American economy. When unemployment begins to rise, as it did in 1982 and again in 1991, the Fed loosened monetary policy to stimulate aggregate demand, increase output, and stem the unemployment increase.

Central banking in Europe was historically fragmented. Until 1999, Europe was a confederation of countries whose monetary policies were dominated by the German central bank, the Bundesbank. The Bundesbank was fiercely independent and aimed primarily at maintaining price stability *in Germany*. When unemployment rose in the rest of Europe and inflation rose in Germany—as happened after the reunification of Germany in 1990—the Bundesbank increased interest rates. This tended to depress output and raise unemployment in countries whose monetary policies were tied to Germany's. You can see this feature in the rise in unemployment in Europe after 1990.

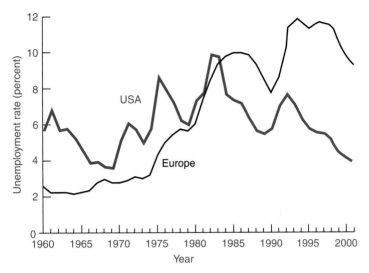

FIGURE 15-10. Unemployment in the United States and Europe

While unemployment has cycled without a marked trend in the United States, European unemployment has risen sharply over the last three decades. Some of the increase in European unemployment stems from the demand side, but the general trend stems from European labor market rigidities and social-welfare legislation. (Source: U.S. Department of Labor and OECD.)

A second feature of European unemployment relates to rising structural unemployment. Europe was the birthplace of the welfare state, and countries like Germany, France, and Sweden legislated generous welfare benefits, unemployment insurance, minimum wages, and job protection for workers. These policies tend to increase real wages because workers possess greater bargaining power and have more attractive alternative uses for their time. Persons who are collecting welfare or unemployment benefits might be voluntarily unemployed, but they are generally counted as unemployed in the actual statistics. The United States has been less generous in its unemployment and welfare benefits, and recent changes in welfare laws will make welfare even less attractive relative to work in the coming years.

We can understand the divergent economies in terms of our labor market supply-and-demand diagrams in Figure 15-6. American labor market institutions resemble the flexible-wage economy shown in part (*a*). A decline in the demand for labor will lead to an equilibrium at *E*. By contrast, the more rigid labor market institutions in Europe resemble Figure 15-6(*b*). In Europe, real wages have not declined as much as in the United States, but the number of the employed has grown slowly while unemployment has grown sharply.

What is the remedy for the high level of unemployment in Europe? Some economists believe that the new European central bank may maintain a better balance of aggregate supply and demand in that region. (Recall our discussion of the European Monetary Union in Chapter 14.) Demand-management policies will do little to cure Europe's structural unemployment, however. Many experts believe that it will be necessary to improve European labor market institutions by reducing the generosity of welfare and unemployment insurance and removing restrictions on hiring and firing practices of firms.

Slowly and painfully, reforms have been introduced in many countries. These reforms, along with monetary easing, a depreciating Euro, and the pull of the American economic locomotive, have begun to reduce the high unemployment in the European economy.

SUMMARY

A. The Foundations of Aggregate Supply

1. Aggregate supply describes the relationship between the output that businesses willingly produce and the overall price level, other things being constant. The factors underlying aggregate supply are (*a*) potential output, determined by the inputs of labor, capital, and natural resources available to an economy, along with the technology or efficiency with which these inputs are used, and (*b*) input costs, such as wages, energy prices, and import prices. Changes in these underlying factors will shift the *AS* curve.

2. Two major approaches to output determination are the classical and Keynesian views. The classical view holds that prices and wages are flexible; any excess supply or demand is quickly extinguished and full employment is established after *AD* or *AS* shocks. The classical view is represented by a vertical *AS* curve. The Keynesian view holds that prices and wages are sticky in the short run due to contractual rigidities such as labor-union agreements. In this kind of economy, output responds positively to higher levels of aggregate demand because the *AS* curve is relatively flat, particularly at low levels of output. In a Keynesian variant, the economy can experience long periods of persistent unemployment because wages and prices adjust slowly to shocks and equilibration toward full employment is slow.

3. A synthesis of classical and Keynesian views distinguishes the long run from the short run. In the short term, because wages and prices do not have time to adjust fully, the *AS* curve is upward-sloping, showing that businesses will supply more output at a higher price level. By contrast, in the long run, wages and prices have time to adjust fully to shocks, so we treat the long-run *AS* curve as vertical or classical. Hence, in the long run, output will be determined by a nation's potential output, and the evolution of aggregate demand will affect prices rather than output.

B. Unemployment

4. The government gathers monthly statistics on unemployment, employment, and the labor force in a sample survey of the population. People with jobs are categorized as employed; people without jobs who are looking for work are said to be unemployed; people without jobs who are not looking for work are considered outside the labor force. Over the last decade, 66 percent of the population over 16 was in the labor force, while 6 percent of the labor force was unemployed.

5. There is a clear connection between movements in output and the unemployment rate over the business cycle. According to Okun's Law, for every 2 percent that actual GDP declines relative to potential GDP, the unemployment rate rises 1 percentage point. This rule is useful in translating cyclical movements of GDP into their effects on unemployment.

6. Recessions and the associated high unemployment are extremely costly to the economy. Major periods of slack like the 1970s and early 1980s cost the nation hundreds of billions of dollars and have great social costs as well. Yet, even though unemployment has plagued capitalism since the Industrial Revolution, understanding its causes and costs has been possible only with the rise of modern macroeconomic theory.

7. Economists divide unemployment into three groups: (*a*) frictional unemployment, in which workers are between jobs or moving in and out of the labor force; (*b*) structural unemployment, consisting of workers who are in regions or industries that are in a persistent slump because of labor market imbalances or high real wages; and (*c*) cyclical unemployment, pertaining to workers laid off when the overall economy suffers a downturn.

8. Understanding the causes of unemployment has proved to be one of the major challenges of modern macroeconomics. Some unemployment (often called voluntary) would occur in a flexible-wage, perfectly competitive economy when qualified people chose not to work at the going wage rate. Voluntary unemployment might be the efficient outcome of competitive markets.

9. The theory of sticky wages and involuntary unemployment holds that the slow adjustment of wages produces surpluses and shortages in individual labor markets. This theory holds that the cyclical unemployment occurs because wages are inflexible, failing to adjust quickly to labor surpluses or shortages. If wages are above market-clearing levels, some workers are employed but other qualified workers cannot find jobs. Such unemployment is involuntary and also inefficient in that both workers and firms could benefit from an appropriate use of monetary and fiscal policies.

10. Labor markets fail to clear partly because of costs involved in administering the compensation system. Frequent adjustment of compensation for market conditions would command too large a share of management time, would upset workers' perceptions

of fairness, and would undermine worker morale and productivity. In the long run, wages tend to adjust and remove abnormal levels of unemployment or job vacancies. But the slow pace of wage adjustment means that societies may suffer prolonged periods of unemployment.

11. A careful look at the unemployment statistics reveals several regularities:

   a. Recessions hit all groups in roughly proportional fashion—that is, all groups see their unemployment rates go up and down in proportion to the overall unemployment rate.

   b. A very substantial part of U.S. unemployment is short term. In low-unemployment years (such as 1999) about 85 percent of unemployed workers are unemployed less than 26 weeks. The average duration of unemployment rises sharply in deep and prolonged recessions.

   c. In most years, a substantial amount of unemployment is due to simple turnover, or frictional causes, as people enter the labor force for the first time or reenter it. Only during recessions is the pool of unemployed composed primarily of job losers.

   d. The persistent unemployment in Europe appears to arise from a combination of weak aggregate demand and inflexible labor market institutions.

CONCEPTS FOR REVIEW

Foundations of Aggregate Supply

aggregate supply, *AS* curve
factors underlying and shifting aggregate supply
aggregate supply: role of potential output and production costs
short-run vs. long-run *AS*
classical vs. Keynesian view of aggregate supply
flexible vs. sticky wages and prices

Unemployment

population status:
   unemployed
   employed
   labor force
   not in labor force
unemployment rate
frictional, structural, and cyclical unemployment

Okun's Law

flexible-wage (market-clearing) unemployment vs. inflexible-wage (non-market-clearing) unemployment
voluntary vs. involuntary unemployment

FURTHER READING AND INTERNET WEBSITES

Further Reading

A recent study surveying many businesses about their employment practices to help understand cyclical wage behavior is Truman F. Bewley, *Why Wages Don't Fall During a Recession* (Harvard University Press, Cambridge, Mass., 2000).

Websites

Analysis of employment and unemployment for the United States comes from the Bureau of Labor Statistics, found at www.bls.gov. Statistics on unemployment in Europe and other OECD countries can be found at www.oecd.org/statlist.htm. The BLS site also has an online version of *The Monthly Labor Review* at www.bls.gov/opub/mlr/mlrhome.htm, which is an excellent source for studies about employment, labor issues, and compensation. For example, if you want to learn about trends in employment, you might consult "High-Technology Employment: A Broader View," *Monthly Labor Review*, June 1999, online at www.bls. gov/opub/ mlr/1999/06/art3full.pdf.

QUESTIONS FOR DISCUSSION

1. Explain carefully what is meant by the aggregate supply curve. Distinguish between movements along the curve and shifts of the curve. What might increase output by moving along the *AS* curve? What could increase output by shifting the *AS* curve?

2. Construct a table parallel to Table 15-1, illustrating events that would lead to a decrease in aggregate supply. (Be imaginative rather than simply using the same examples.)

3. What, if anything, would be the effect of each of the following on the *AS* curve in both the short run and the long run, other things being constant?
   a. Potential output increases by 25 percent.
   b. The threat of war leads the government to raise defense spending, and the central bank offsets the expansionary impact of this through tight money.
   c. Successful collusion among OPEC countries leads to a tripling of world oil prices.
   d. Environmentalists persuade governments to impose costly regulations on all new investments and energy use and to curb output in natural-resource sectors.

4. Assume that the unemployment rate is 7 percent and GDP is $4000 billion. What is a rough estimate of potential GDP if the NAIRU is 5 percent? Assume that potential GDP is growing at 3 percent annually. What will potential GDP be in 2 years? How fast will GDP have to grow to reach potential GDP in 2 years?

5. What is the labor-force status of each of the following?
   a. A teenager who sends out résumés in searching for a first job
   b. An autoworker who has been laid off and would like to work but has given up hope of finding work or being recalled
   c. A retired person who moved to Florida and answers advertisements for part-time positions
   d. A parent who works part-time, wants a full-time job, but doesn't have time to look
   e. A teacher who has a job but is too ill to work

6. In explaining its procedures, the Department of Labor gives the following examples:
   a. "Joan Howard told the interviewer that she has filed applications with three companies for summer jobs. However, it is only April and she doesn't wish to start work until at least June 15, because she is attending school. Although she has taken specific steps to find a job, Joan is classified as not in the labor force because she is not currently available for work."
   b. "James Kelly and Elyse Martin attend Jefferson High School. James works after school at the North Star Café, and Elyse is seeking a part-time job at the same establishment (also after school). James' job takes precedence over his non-labor force activity of going to school, as does Elyse's search for work; therefore, James is counted as employed and Elyse is counted as unemployed."
   Explain each of these examples. Take a survey of your classmates. Using the examples above, have people classify themselves in terms of their labor-force status into employed, unemployed, and not in the labor force.

7. Assume that Congress is considering a law that would set the minimum wage above the market-clearing wage for teenagers but below that for adult workers. Using supply-and-demand diagrams, show the impact of the minimum wage on the employment, unemployment, and incomes of both sets of workers. Is the unemployment voluntary or involuntary? What would you recommend to Congress if you were called to testify about the wisdom of this measure?

8. Do you think that the economic costs and personal stress of a teenager unemployed for 1 month of the summer might be less or more than those of a head-of-household unemployed for 1 year? Do you think that this suggests that public policy should have a different stance with respect to these two groups?

9. Make a list of reasons why unemployment looks so different in the United States as compared to Europe. Using the framework in Figure 15-6, show how a decrease in the demand for labor would lead to unchanged unemployment but lower wages in flexible-wage America, shown in (*a*), but to lower employment, higher unemployment, and unchanged wages in rigid-wage Europe, in (*b*).

In the late 1990s, the United States experienced a combination of low unemployment and minimal inflation that was virtually unique among high-income countries. A significant part of the low inflation was found in the restrained wage growth due to a decline in labor-union membership, a graying workforce, and greater worker docility in the face of aggressive management cost containment.

On the price side, oil and commodity prices declined through the end of 1999 as the world went through a pause in economic growth. When weak demand abroad was added to an appreciating dollar exchange rate, import prices into the United States actually fell. Additionally, labor productivity rebounded from two decades of sluggish growth and thereby reduced the growth of unit labor costs and prices for domestically produced goods and services.

One new factor in the inflation equation was the growing "globalization" of production. As the United States became more integrated in world markets, domestic firms found that their prices were constrained by the prices of international competitors. Even when domestic sales of automobiles were booming, domestic automakers could not raise their prices too much for fear of losing market share to Japanese and other foreign producers.

These were the forces at work in the American economy that kept inflation in check even as unemployment fell. Other countries were not so lucky, however. The present chapter will examine the meaning and determinants of inflation and describe the important public-policy issues that arise in this area. Figure 16-1 provides an overview of this chapter.

CHAPTER

16

Ensuring Price Stability

Lenin is said to have declared that the best way to destroy the capitalist system was to debauch the currency. By a continuing process of inflation, governments can confiscate, secretly and unobserved, an important part of the wealth of their citizens.

J. M. Keynes

A. DEFINITION AND IMPACT OF INFLATION

WHAT IS INFLATION?

We described the major price indexes and defined inflation in Chapter 5, but it will be useful to reiterate the basic definitions here:

Inflation occurs when the general level of prices is rising. Today, we calculate inflation by using price indexes—weighted averages of the prices of thousands of individual products. The consumer price index (CPI) measures the cost of a market basket of consumer goods and services relative to the cost of that bundle during a particular base year. The GDP deflator is the price of GDP.

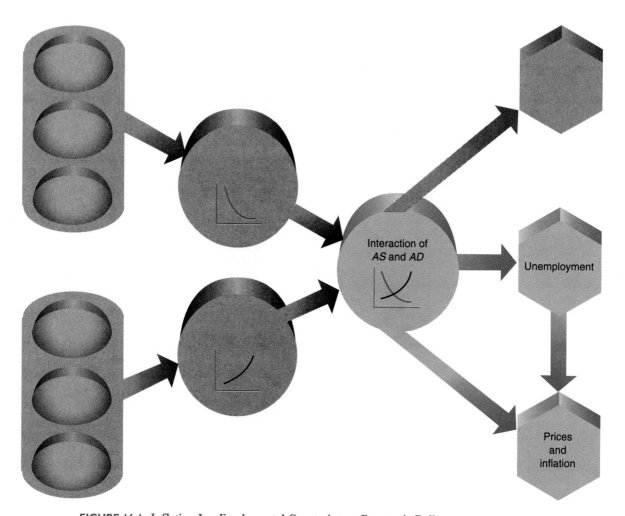

FIGURE 16-1. Inflation Is a Fundamental Constraint on Economic Policy

What are inflation's economic impacts? What forces lead to persistent inflation? How can governments slow inflation? These questions are central to macroeconomic theory and policy today.

The rate of inflation is the percentage change in the price level:

Rate of inflation (year t)

$$= \frac{\text{price level (year } t) - \text{price level (year } t-1)}{\text{price level (year } t-1)} \times 100$$

If you are unclear on the definitions, refresh your memory by reviewing Chapter 5.

The History of Inflation

Inflation is as old as market economies. Figure 16-2 depicts the history of prices in England since the thirteenth century. Over the long haul, prices have generally risen, as the blue line reveals. But examine also the black line, which plots the path of *real wages* (the wage rate divided by consumer prices). Real wages meandered along until the Industrial Revolution. Comparing the two lines shows that inflation is not necessarily accompanied by a decline in real income. You can see, too, that real wages have climbed steadily since around 1800, rising more than tenfold.

Figure 16-3 on page 340 focuses on the behavior of consumer prices in the United States since the Civil War. Until 1945, the pattern was regular: prices

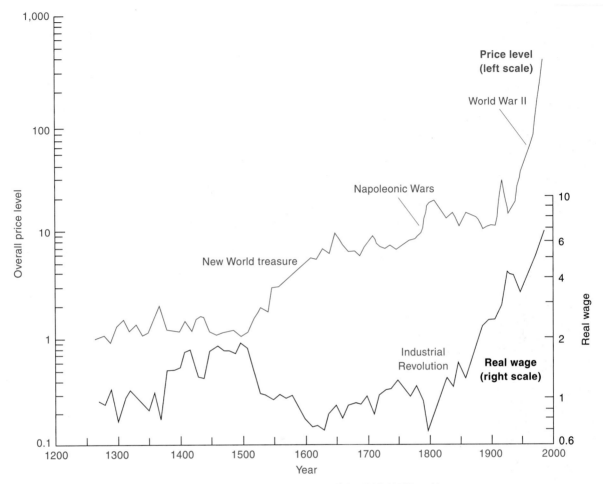

FIGURE 16-2. English Price Level and Real Wage, 1270–1999 (1270 = 1)

The graph shows England's history of prices and real wages since the Middle Ages. In early years, price increases were associated with increases in the money supply, such as from discoveries of New World treasure and the printing of money during the Napoleonic Wars. Note the meandering of the real wage prior to the Industrial Revolution. Since then, real wages have risen sharply and steadily. (Source: E. H. Phelps Brown and S. V. Hopkins, *Economica*, 1956, updated by the authors.)

would soar during wartime and then fall back during the postwar slump. But the pattern changed dramatically after World War II. Prices and wages now travel on a one-way street upward. They rise rapidly in periods of economic expansion; in recessions they do not fall but merely rise less rapidly.

Figure 16-4 on page 340 shows CPI inflation over the last half-century. You can see how unusual were the 1990s, with its low and stable inflation rate.

Three Strains of Inflation

Like diseases, inflations exhibit different levels of severity. It is useful to classify them into three categories: low inflation, galloping inflation, and hyperinflation.

Low Inflation. Low inflation is characterized by prices that rise slowly and predictably. We might define this as single-digit annual inflation rates. When

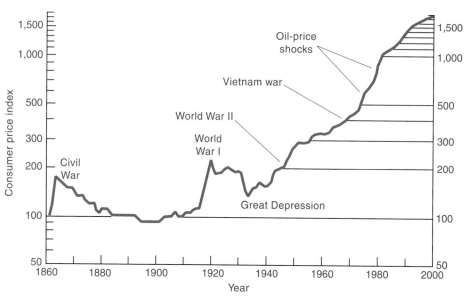

FIGURE 16-3. U.S. Prices since the Civil War

Until World War II, prices shot up with each war and then drifted down afterward. But since 1940, the trend has been upward, both here and abroad. (Source: U.S. Department of Labor, Bureau of Labor Statistics.)

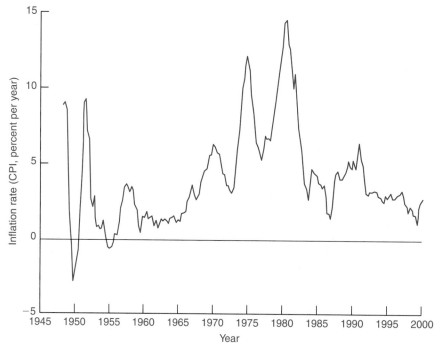

FIGURE 16-4. Inflation Has Remained Low and Stable in the 1990s

Historically, inflation in the United States was variable, and it reached unacceptably high rates in the early 1980s. In the 1990s, skillful management by the Federal Reserve along with favorable supply shocks led to low and stable inflation. (Source: Bureau of Labor Statistics, www. bls. gov. This graph shows the consumer price index.)

prices are relatively stable, *people trust money* because it retains its value from month to month and year to year. People are willing to write long-term contracts in money terms because they are confident that the relative prices of goods they buy and sell will not get too far out of line. Most industrial countries have experienced low inflation over the last decade.

Galloping Inflation. Inflation in the double- or triple-digit range of 20, 100, or 200 percent a year is called "galloping inflation." From time to time advanced industrial countries like Italy or Japan suffer from this syndrome. Many Latin American countries, such as Argentina and Brazil, had inflation rates of 50 to 700 percent per year in the 1970s and 1980s.

Once galloping inflation becomes entrenched, serious economic distortions arise. Generally, most contracts get indexed to a price index or to a foreign currency, like the dollar. In these conditions, money loses its value very quickly, so people hold only the bare-minimum amount of money needed for daily transactions. Financial markets wither away, as capital flees abroad. People hoard goods, buy houses, and never, never lend money at low nominal interest rates.

Hyperinflation. While economies seem to survive under galloping inflation, a third and deadly strain takes hold when the cancer of hyperinflation strikes. Nothing good can be said about a market economy in which prices are rising a million or even a trillion percent per year.

Hyperinflations are particularly interesting to students of inflation because they highlight its disastrous impacts. Consider this description of hyperinflation in the Confederacy during the Civil War:

> We used to go to the stores with money in our pockets and come back with food in our baskets. Now we go with money in baskets and return with food in our pockets. Everything is scarce except money! Prices are chaotic and production disorganized. A meal that used to cost the same amount as an opera ticket now costs twenty times as much. Everybody tends to hoard "things" and to try to get rid of the "bad" paper money, which drives the "good" metal money out of circulation. A partial return to barter inconvenience is the result.

The most thoroughly documented case of hyperinflation took place in the Weimar Republic of Germany in the 1920s. Figure 16-5 shows how the government unleashed the monetary printing presses, driving both money and prices to astronomical levels. From January 1922 to November 1923, the price index rose from 1 to 10,000,000,000. If a person had owned 300 million marks worth of German bonds in early 1922, this amount would not have bought a piece of candy 2 years later.

Studies have found several common features in hyperinflations. First, the real money stock (measured by the money stock divided by the price level) falls drastically. By the end of the German hyperinflation, real money demand was only one-thirtieth of its level 2 years earlier. People are in effect rushing around, dumping their money like hot potatoes before they get burned by money's loss of value. Second, relative prices become highly unstable. Under normal conditions, a person's real wages move only a percent or less from month to month. During 1923, German real wages changed on average one-third

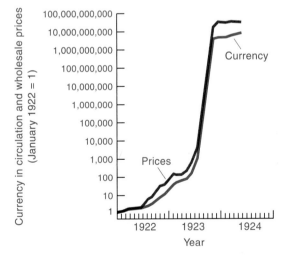

The German Hyperinflation

FIGURE 16-5. Money and Hyperinflation in Germany, 1922–1924

In the early 1920s, Germany could not raise enough taxes, so it used the monetary printing press to pay the government's bills. The stock of currency rose astronomically from early 1922 to December 1923, and prices spiraled upward as people frantically tried to spend their money before it lost all value.

(up or down) each month. This huge variation in relative prices and real wages—and the inequities and distortions caused by these fluctuations—took an enormous toll on workers and businesses, highlighting one of the major costs of inflation.

The impact of inflation was beautifully expressed by J. M. Keynes:

> As inflation proceeds and the real value of the currency fluctuates wildly from month to month, all permanent relations between debtors and creditors, which form the ultimate foundation of capitalism, become so utterly disordered as to be almost meaningless; and the process of wealth-getting degenerates into a game and a lottery.

Anticipated vs. Unanticipated Inflation

An important distinction in the analysis of inflation is whether the price increases are anticipated or unanticipated. Suppose that all prices are rising at 3 percent each year and everyone expects this trend to continue. Would there be any reason to get excited about inflation? Would it make any difference if both the actual and the expected inflation rates were 1 or 3 or 5 percent each year? Economists generally believe that anticipated inflation at low rates has little effect on economic efficiency or on the distribution of income and wealth. People would simply be adapting their behavior to a changing monetary yardstick.

But the reality is that inflation is usually unanticipated. For example, the Russian people had become accustomed to stable prices for many decades. When prices were liberalized in 1992, no one, not even the professional economists, guessed that prices would rise by 1000-fold over the next 5 years. People who were unlucky enough to hold their wealth in ruble assets saw their savings become worthless.

In more stable countries like the United States, the impact of unanticipated inflation is less dramatic, but the same general point applies. An unexpected jump in prices will impoverish some and enrich others. How costly is this redistribution? Perhaps "cost" does not describe the problem. The effects may be more social than economic. An epidemic of burglaries may not lower GDP, but it causes great distress. Similarly, randomly redistributing wealth by inflation is like forcing people to play a lottery they would prefer to avoid.

THE ECONOMIC IMPACTS OF INFLATION

Central bankers are united in their determination to contain inflation. During periods of high inflation, opinion polls often find that inflation is economic enemy number one. What is so dangerous and costly about inflation? We noted above that during periods of inflation all prices and wages do not move at the same rate; that is, changes in *relative prices* occur. As a result of the diverging relative prices, two definite effects of inflation are

- A *redistribution* of income and wealth among different groups
- *Distortions* in the relative prices and outputs of different goods, or sometimes in output and employment for the economy as a whole

Impacts on Income and Wealth Distribution

Inflation affects the distribution of income and wealth primarily because of differences in the assets and liabilities that people hold.[1] When people owe money, a sharp rise in prices is a windfall gain for them. Suppose you borrow $100,000 to buy a house and your annual fixed-interest-rate mortgage payments are $10,000. Suddenly, a great inflation doubles all wages and incomes. Your *nominal* mortgage payment is still $10,000 per year, but its real cost is halved. You will need to work only half as long as before to make your mortgage payment. The great inflation has increased your wealth by cutting in half the real value of your mortgage debt.

If you are a lender and have assets in fixed-interest-rate mortgages or long-term bonds, the shoe is on the other foot. An unexpected rise in prices will leave you the poorer because the dollars repaid to you are worth much less than the dollars you lent.

If an inflation persists for a long time, people come to anticipate it and markets begin to adapt. An allowance for inflation will gradually be built into the market interest rate. Say the economy starts out with interest rates of 3 percent and stable prices. Once people expect prices to rise at 9 percent per year, bonds and mortgages will tend to pay 12 percent

---

[1]The important elements of balance sheets were described in Chapters 9.

rather than 3 percent. The 12 percent nominal interest rate reflects a 3 percent real interest rate plus a 9 percent inflation premium. There are no further major redistributions of income and wealth once interest rates have adapted to the new inflation rate. The adjustment of interest rates to chronic inflation has been observed in all countries with a long history of rising prices.[2]

Because of institutional changes, some old myths no longer apply. It used to be thought that common stocks were a good inflation hedge, but stocks generally move inversely with inflation today. A common saying was that inflation hurts widows and orphans; today, they are insulated from inflation because social security benefits are indexed to consumer prices. Also, unanticipated inflation benefits debtors and hurts lenders less than before because many kinds of debt (like "floating-rate" mortgages) have interest rates that move up and down with market interest rates.

The major redistributive impact of inflation comes through its effect on the real value of people's wealth. In general, unanticipated inflation redistributes wealth from creditors to debtors, helping borrowers and hurting lenders. An unanticipated decline in inflation has the opposite effect. But inflation mostly churns income and assets, randomly redistributing wealth among the population with little significant impact on any single group.

Impacts on Economic Efficiency

In addition to redistributing incomes, inflation affects the real economy in two specific areas: It can harm economic efficiency, and it can affect total output. We begin with the efficiency impacts.

Inflation impairs economic efficiency because it *distorts prices and price signals*. In a low-inflation economy, if the market price of a good rises, both buyers and sellers know that there has been an actual change in the supply and/or demand conditions for that good, and they can react appropriately. For example, if the neighborhood supermarkets all boost their beef prices by 50 percent, perceptive consumers know that it's time to start eating more chicken. Similarly, if the prices of new computers fall by 90 percent, you may decide it's time to turn in your old model.

By contrast, in a high-inflation economy it's much harder to distinguish between changes in relative prices and changes in the overall price level. If inflation is running at 20 or 30 percent per month, price changes are so frequent that changes in relative prices get missed in the confusion.

Inflation also *distorts the use of money*. Currency is money that bears a zero nominal interest rate. If the inflation rate rises from 0 to 10 percent annually, the real interest rate on currency falls from 0 to -10 percent per year. There is no way to correct this distortion.

As a result of the negative real interest rate on money, people devote real resources to reducing their money holdings during inflationary times. They go to the bank more often—using up "shoe leather" and valuable time. Corporations set up elaborate cash-management schemes. Real resources are thereby consumed simply to adapt to a changing monetary yardstick rather than to make productive investments.

Many economists point to the *distortion of inflation on taxes*. Certain parts of the tax code are written in dollar terms. When prices rise, the real value of those provisions tends to decline. For example, you might be able to subtract a fixed-dollar "standard deduction" from your income in calculating your taxable income. With inflation, the real value of that standard deduction would decline and the real value of your taxes would rise. Such "taxation without legislation" has led many countries to index their tax laws to prevent inflation-induced tax increases. Parts of the U.S. tax code were indexed during the 1980s.

Indexing of tax brackets alone will not purge the tax system of the impacts of inflation because inflation distorts measures of income. For example, if you earned an interest rate of 6 percent on your funds in 1999, half of this return simply replaced your loss in the purchasing power of your funds from a 3 percent inflation rate. Yet the tax code does not distinguish between real return and the interest that just compensates for inflation. Many similar distortions of income and taxes are present in the tax code today. Recent studies by Martin Feldstein and others argue that the impact of inflation on taxes and thereby on saving and investment are the largest cost of inflation.[3]

---

[2] Fig. 9-3 shows movements in nominal and real interest rates for the United States in recent years.

[3] See Feldstein in the Further Reading section at the end of this chapter.

But these are not the only costs; some economists point to *menu costs* of inflation. The idea is that when prices are changed, firms must spend real resources adjusting their prices. For instance, restaurants reprint their menus, mail-order firms reprint their catalogs, taxi companies remeter their cabs, cities adjust parking meters, and stores change the price tags of goods. Sometimes, the costs are intangible, such as those involved in gathering people to make new pricing decisions.

Macroeconomic Impacts on Efficiency and Growth

In addition to the microeconomic and distributional impacts, are there effects of inflation on overall economic activity? This question is addressed in the next section, so we merely highlight the major points here. Until the 1970s, high inflation usually went hand in hand with high employment and output. In the United States, inflation tended to increase when investment was brisk and jobs were plentiful. Periods of deflation or declining inflation—the 1890s, the 1930s, 1954, 1958, 1982, and 1991—were times of high unemployment of labor and capital.

But a more careful examination of the historical record reveals an interesting fact: The positive association between output and inflation appears to be only a temporary relationship. Over the longer run, there seems to be an inverse-U-shaped relationship between inflation and output growth. Table 16-1 shows the results of a recent multicountry study of the association between inflation and growth. It indicates that economic growth is strongest in countries with low inflation, while countries with high inflation or deflation tend to grow more slowly. (But beware the *ex post* fallacy here, as explored in question 7 at the end of the chapter.)

Whatever the short-run or long-run impact of inflation on output and efficiency, there is no doubt about the reaction of the Federal Reserve when inflation threatens. Whenever inflation begins to rise, the Fed today takes forceful steps to stop inflation in its tracks—by reducing money growth, raising interest rates, and thereby restraining the growth of real output and raising unemployment. Indeed, the decision by central banks to contain inflation was the prime cause of the long and deep recession in North America that followed the 1979 oil-price increase as well as the profound downturn that persisted in West-

Inflation rate (% per year)	Growth of per capita GDP (% per year)
−20–0	0.7
0–10	2.4
10–20	1.8
20–40	0.4
100–200	−1.7
1,000+	−6.5

TABLE 16-1. Inflation and Economic Growth

The pooled experience of 127 countries shows that the most rapid growth is associated with low inflation rates. Deflation and moderate inflation accompany slow growth, while hyperinflations are associated with sharp downturns. (Source: Michael Bruno and William Easterly, "Inflation Crises and Long-Run Growth," World Bank Policy Research Working Paper 1517, September 1995.)

ern Europe in the first half of the 1990s. In late 1999 and early 2000, the Fed began to tighten monetary policy because the economy was operating at capacity and pressures for a price-wage-price spiral were building.

What Is the Optimal Rate of Inflation?

Most nations seek rapid economic growth, full employment, and price stability. But just what is meant by "price stability"? What is a desirable long-term trend for prices? Most macroeconomists point to the advantage of relatively low and stable inflation. In the 1991–2000 period in the United States, for example, consumer price inflation was stable at about 3 percent per year. During this period, output and price growth were relatively predictable, leading to a stable macroeconomic environment in the United States.

Some today argue that policy should go further and aim for absolutely stable prices or zero inflation. This school points to the value of having a predictable future price level when people make their investment decisions. If we are confident that the price level in 20 years will be very close to the price level today, we can make better long-term investment and saving decisions.

Many macroeconomists reply that, while a zero-inflation target might be sensible in an ideal economy, we do not live in a frictionless system. Perhaps the most important friction is the resistance of workers to declines in money wages. If the average wage level were stable, this would be the average of some wages that are rising and some that are falling. But workers and firms are extremely reluctant to cut money wages. Evidence for the downward rigidity of wages is found in a comprehensive government survey of wage changes in manufacturing over the period 1958–1978. During this period, on average less than 0.1 percent of workers received wage cuts, even in years when inflation was extremely low.

From a macroeconomic point of view, this suggests that zero inflation would be associated with a higher sustainable level of unemployment and a lower level of output than would be the case at an inflation rate of 2 to 4 percent. A recent study estimates that targeting stable prices would cost the United States between 1 and 3 percent lower output and employment *permanently* as compared with an inflation target of around 3 percent. The authors conclude:

> Downward rigidity [of wages] interferes with the ability of some firms to make adjustments in real wages, leading to inefficient reductions in employment. . . . The main implication for policymakers is that targeting zero inflation will lead to a large inefficiency in the allocation of resources, as reflected in an unemployment rate that is unnecessarily high.[4]

We can summarize our discussion in the following way:

> While economists may disagree on the exact target for inflation, most agree that a predictable and gently rising price level provides the best climate for healthy economic growth. A careful sifting of the evidence suggests that low inflation like that seen recently in the United States has little impact on productivity or real output. By contrast, galloping inflation or hyperinflation can cause serious harm to productivity and to individuals through the redistribution of income and wealth. Finally, even though the costs of inflation appear modest, central bankers will not long tolerate high inflation; they take measures to curb inflation by slowing output growth and raising unemployment.

---

[4] See the reference to Akerlof, Dickens, and Perry in this chapter's Further Reading section.

B. MODERN INFLATION THEORY

Can market economies simultaneously enjoy the blessings of full employment and price stability? Is there no way to control inflation other than by economic slowdowns that keep unemployment undesirably high? If recessions are too high a price to pay for the control of inflation, do we need "incomes policies" that can lower inflation without raising unemployment?

Questions, questions, questions. Yet answers to these are critical to the economic health of modern mixed economies. In the balance of this chapter we explore modern inflation theory and analyze the costs of lowering inflation.

PRICES IN THE *AS-AD* FRAMEWORK

There is no single source of inflation. Like illnesses, inflations occur for many reasons. Some inflations come from the demand side; others, from the supply side. But one key fact about modern inflations is that they develop an internal momentum and are costly to stop once under way.

Inertial Inflation

In modern industrial economies like the United States, inflation has great momentum and tends to persist at the same rate. Inertial inflation is like a lazy old dog. If the dog is not "shocked" by the push of a foot or the pull of a cat, it will stay put. Once disturbed, the dog may chase the cat, but then it eventually lies down in a new spot where it stays until the next shock.

During the 1990s, prices in the United States rose steadily at around 3 percent annually, and most people came to expect that inflation rate. This expected rate of inflation was built into the economy's institutions. Wage agreements between labor and management were designed around a 3 percent inflation rate; government monetary and fiscal plans assumed a 3 percent rate. During this period, the *inertial rate of inflation* was 3 percent per year. Other names sometimes heard for this concept are the *core, underlying,* or *expected* inflation rate.

While inflation can persist at the same rate for a while, history shows that shocks to the economy tend to push inflation up or down. The economy is constantly subject to changes in aggregate demand, sharp oil- and commodity-price changes, poor harvests, movements in the foreign exchange rate, productivity changes, and countless other economic events that push inflation away from its inertial rate.

The economy has an ongoing inertial rate of inflation to which people's expectations have adapted. This built-in inertial inflation rate tends to persist until a shock causes it to move up or down.

Demand-Pull Inflation

One of the major shocks to inflation is a change in aggregate demand. In earlier chapters we saw that changes in investment, government spending, or net exports can change aggregate demand and propel output beyond its potential. We also saw how a nation's central bank can affect economic activity. Whatever the reason, **demand-pull inflation** occurs when aggregate demand rises more rapidly than the economy's productive potential, pulling prices up to equilibrate aggregate supply and demand. In effect, demand dollars are competing for the limited supply of commodities and bid up their prices. As unemployment falls and workers become scarce, wages are bid up and the inflationary process accelerates.

One important factor behind demand inflation is rapid *money-supply growth.* Increases in the money supply increase aggregate demand, which in turn increases the price level. Thus, when the German central bank printed billions and billions of paper marks in 1922–1923 and they came into the marketplace in search of bread or housing, it was no wonder that the German price level rose a billionfold. This was demand-pull inflation with a vengeance. This scene was replayed when the Russian government financed its budget deficit by printing rubles in the early 1990s. The result was an inflation rate that averaged 25 percent *per month* [or $100 \times (1.25^{12} - 1) = 1355$ percent per year].[5]

---

[5] The next chapter's review of alternative approaches to macroeconomics examines "monetarist" theories, which hold that price changes depend principally on changes in the money supply.

Figure 16-6 illustrates the process of demand-pull inflation in terms of aggregate supply and demand. Starting from an initial equilibrium at point E, suppose there is an expansion of spending that pushes the AD curve up and to the right. The economy's equilibrium moves from E to E'. At this higher level of demand, prices have risen from P to P'. Demand-pull inflation has taken place.

Cost-Push Inflation

The rudiments of demand-pull inflation were understood by the classical economists and used by them to explain historical price movements. But a strange thing happened during the last half-century—the inflation process changed. Look back at the history of prices on page 340 and note that prices today travel a one-way street—up in recessions, up faster in booms. What differentiates modern inflation from the simple demand-pull variety is that prices and wages rise even in recessions when 30 percent of factory capacity lies idle and 10 percent of the labor force is unemployed. This phenomenon is known as *cost-push* or *supply-shock* inflation.

Inflation resulting from rising costs during periods of high unemployment and slack resource utilization is called **cost-push inflation.**

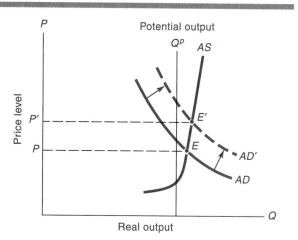

FIGURE 16-6. Demand-Pull Inflation Occurs When Too Much Spending Chases Too Few Goods

When aggregate demand increases, the rising spending is competing for limited goods. Prices rise from P to P' in demand-pull inflation. How would cost-push inflation be analyzed in this framework?

In looking for explanations of cost-push inflation, economists often start with wages. In 1982, for example, when the unemployment rate was almost 10 percent, wages rose 5 percent. Wages tend to rise even in recession because they are administered prices and because of the strong resistance to wage cuts.

Sometimes, cost-push shocks lead to an upward push to inflation. In 1973, in 1978, and again in late 1999 and early 2000, countries were minding their own macroeconomic business when severe shortages in oil markets occurred. Oil prices rose sharply, business costs of production increased, and a sharp burst of cost-push inflation followed. Sometimes, cost shocks are favorable. For example, during the 1990s, the United States enjoyed downward pressure on aggregate supply because of rapid productivity growth; falling energy, import, and commodity prices; and favorable trends in health costs.

Expectations and Inertial Inflation

Why, you might ask, does inflation have such strong inertia or momentum? The answer is that most prices and wages are set with an eye to future economic conditions. When prices and wages are rising rapidly and are expected to continue doing so, businesses and workers tend to build the rapid rate of inflation into their price and wage decisions. High or low inflation expectations tend to be self-fulfilling prophecies.

We can use a hypothetical example to illustrate the role of expectations in inertial inflation. Say that in 2000, Brass Mills Inc., a nonunionized light-manufacturing firm, was contemplating its annual wage and salary decisions for 2001. Its sales were growing well, and it was experiencing no major supply or demand shocks. Brass Mills' chief economist reported that no major inflationary or deflationary shocks were foreseen, and the major forecasting services were expecting national wage growth of 4 percent in 2001. Brass Mills had conducted a survey of local companies and found that most employers were planning on increases in compensation of 3 to 5 percent during the next year. All the signals, then, pointed to wage increases of around 4 percent for 2001 over 2000.

In examining its own internal labor market, Brass Mills determined that its wages were in line with the local labor market. Because the managers did not want to fall behind local wages, Brass Mills decided that it would try to match local wage increases. It therefore set wage increases at the expected market increase, an average 4 percent wage increase for 2001.

The process of setting wages and salaries with an eye to expected future economic conditions can be extended to virtually all employers. This kind of reasoning also applies to many product prices—such as college tuitions, automobile-model prices, and long-distance telephone rates—that cannot be easily changed after they have been set. Because of the length of time involved in modifying inflation expectations and in adjusting most wages and many prices, inertial inflation will yield only to major shocks or changes in economic policy.

Figure 16-7 illustrates the process of inertial inflation. Suppose that potential output is constant and that there are no supply or demand shocks. If everyone expects average costs and prices to rise at 3 percent each year, the *AS* curve will shift upward at 3 percent per year. If there are no demand shocks, the *AD* curve will also shift up at that rate. The intersection of the *AD* and *AS* curves will be 3 percent higher each year. Hence, the macroeconomic equilibrium moves from *E* to *E'* to *E''*. Prices are rising 3 percent from one year to the next: inertial inflation has set in at 3 percent.

Inertial inflation occurs when the *AS* and *AD* curves are moving steadily upward at the same rate.

Price Levels vs. Inflation

Using Figure 16-7 on the next page, we can make the useful distinction between movements in the price level and movements in inflation. In general, an increase in aggregate demand will raise prices, other things being equal. Similarly, an upward shift in the *AS* curve resulting from an increase in wages and other costs will raise prices, other things being equal.

But of course other things always change; in particular, *AD* and *AS* curves never sit still. Figure 16-7 shows, for example, the *AS* and *AD* curves marching up together.

What if there were an unexpected shift in the *AS* or *AD* curve during the third period? How would prices and inflation be affected? Suppose, for example, that the third period's *AD''* curve shifted to the left to *AD'''* because of a monetary contraction. This

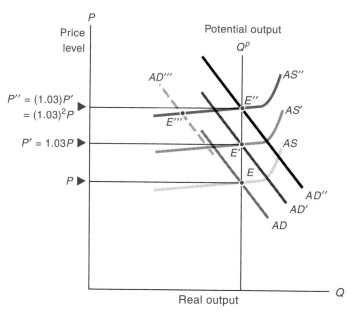

FIGURE 16-7. An Upward Spiral of Prices and Wages Occurs When Aggregate Supply and Demand Shift Up Together.

Suppose that production costs and *AD* rise by 3 percent each year. *AS* and *AD* curves would shift up 3 percent each year. As the equilibrium moves from *E* to *E′* to *E″*, prices march up steadily because of inertial inflation.

might cause a recession, with a new equilibrium at *E‴* on the *AS″* curve. At this point, output would have fallen below potential; prices and the inflation rate would be lower than at *E″*, but the economy would still be experiencing inflation because the price level at *E‴* is still above the previous period's equilibrium *E′* with price *P′*.

This example is a reminder that supply or demand shocks may reduce the price level below the level it would otherwise have attained. Nonetheless, because of inflation's momentum, the economy may continue to experience inflation.

THE PHILLIPS CURVE

A useful way of representing the process of inflation was developed by the economist A. W. Phillips, who quantified the determinants of wage inflation. After careful study of more than a century's worth of data on unemployment and money wages in the United Kingdom, Phillips found an inverse relationship between unemployment and the changes in money

wages. He found that wages tended to rise when unemployment was low and vice versa. Why might high unemployment lower the growth in money wages? The reason is that workers would press less strongly for wage increases when fewer alternative jobs were available, and, in addition, firms would resist wage demands more firmly when profits were low.

The Phillips curve is useful for analyzing short-run movements of unemployment and inflation. The simplest version is shown in Figure 16-8. On the diagram's horizontal axis is the unemployment rate. On the black left-hand vertical scale is the annual rate of price inflation. The blue right-hand vertical scale shows the rate of money-wage inflation. As you move leftward on the Phillips curve by reducing unemployment, the rate of price and wage increase indicated by the curve becomes higher.

An important piece of inflation arithmetic underlies this curve. Say that labor productivity (output per worker) rises at a steady rate of 1 percent each year. Further, assume that firms set prices on the basis of average labor costs, so prices always change just as much as average labor costs per unit of output. If wages are rising at 4 percent, and productivity is rising at 1 percent, then average labor costs will rise at 3 percent. Consequently, prices will also rise at 3 percent.

Using this inflation arithmetic, we can see the relation between wage and price increases in Figure 16-8. These two scales in the figure differ only by the assumed rate of productivity growth (so the price change of 4 percent per year would correspond to a wage change of 5 percent per year if productivity grew by 1 percent per year and if prices always rose as fast as average labor costs).

Interpretation

How does the Phillips curve fit into our model of aggregate supply and demand? The best way to think of the Phillips curve shown in Figure 16-8 is as a *short-run relationship between inflation and unemployment*

	Rate of CPI inflation(%)	Rate of wage growth(%)	Rate of productivity growth(%)
1959–1973	3.1	5.7	3.2
1973–1997	5.5	6.3	1.6
1998–1999	1.9	5.3	2.9

Source: Bureau of Labor Statistics. Note that these are geometric averages for the business sector.

when aggregate demand shifts but aggregate supply continues to change at its inertial rate. This can be understood by comparing Figures 16-6 and 16-7.

Assume that a 6 percent unemployment rate corresponds to potential output. Then, as long as output stays at its potential, unemployment stays at 6 percent and inflation continues to rise at 3 percent per year. Suppose, however, that a shift in aggregate demand occurs in the third period, so the equilibrium is at point E''' rather than E'' in Figure 16-7. Then output will be below potential, unemployment will rise above 6 percent, and inflation will fall. To

The logic of wage-price arithmetic

This relationship between prices, wages, and productivity can be formalized as follows: The fact that prices are based on average labor costs per unit of output implies that P is always proportional to WL/Q, where P is the price level, W is the wage rate, L is labor-hours, and Q is output. Further assume that average labor productivity (Q/L) is growing smoothly at 1 percent per year. Hence, if wages are growing at 4 percent annually, prices will grow at 3 percent annually (= 4 percent growth in wages − 1 percent growth in productivity). More generally,

$$\begin{pmatrix} \text{rate of} \\ \text{inflation} \end{pmatrix} = \begin{pmatrix} \text{rate of} \\ \text{wage growth} \end{pmatrix} - \begin{pmatrix} \text{rate of} \\ \text{productivity growth} \end{pmatrix}$$

This shows the relationship between price inflation and wage inflation.

We can illustrate how closely this relationship holds with actual numbers for a high-inflation period and for a low-inflation period. The following table shows the major long-run determinants of inflation to be wage growth and productivity change. From the first to the second period, inflation rose because wage growth increased slightly while productivity fell sharply. In the last 2 years, inflation was very low both because wage growth was restrained while productivity growth rebounded.

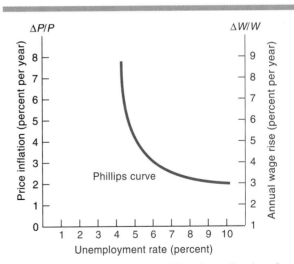

FIGURE 16-8. The Short-Run Phillips Curve Depicts the Trade-off between Inflation and Unemployment

A short-run Phillips curve shows the inverse relationship between inflation and unemployment. The blue wage-change scale on the right-hand vertical axis is higher than the black left-hand inflation scale by the assumed 1 percent rate of growth of average labor productivity.

cement your understanding of this point, pencil into Figure 16-8 the unemployment and inflation rates that correspond to points E'' and E''' in Figure 16-7.

It is important to note that the Phillips curve is not a fixed trade-off. When the inertial rate of inflation changes, the Phillips curve will also shift. Figure 16-9 shows the plot of inflation and unemployment over the period 1960–1999. The points circle clockwise, with some movement outward and inward. One of the major issues in modern macroeconomics has revolved around the interpretation of the clockwise movements in the Phillips curve.

THE NONACCELERATING INFLATION RATE OF UNEMPLOYMENT

To explain the strange looking "Phillips curl" in Figure 16-9, economists modified the original Phillips approach. Based on theoretical work of Edmund Phelps and Milton Friedman, along with statistical

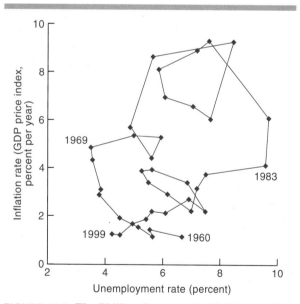

FIGURE 16-9. The Phillips Curve or the Phillips Curl?

Data on unemployment and inflation over the last three decades show a complicated relationship. Modern NAIRU theories explain the Phillips curl and the inward and outward drift by changes in the expected rate of inflation. (Source: *Economic Report of the President 2000;* the price index here is the chain-weighted price index for GDP.)

tests of the actual history, the modified theory distinguishes between the long-run Phillips curve and the short-run Phillips curve. In the current approach, the downward-sloping Phillips curve of Figure 16-8 holds only in the short run. In the long run, there is a minimum unemployment rate that is consistent with steady inflation. This is the *nonaccelerating inflation rate of unemployment* or *NAIRU* (pronounced "nay-rew").[6] In this updated view, the long-run Phillips curve is vertical at the NAIRU.

The ***nonaccelerating inflation rate of unemployment*** (or ***NAIRU***) is that unemployment rate consistent with a constant inflation rate. At the NAIRU, upward and downward forces on price and wage inflation are in balance, so there is no tendency for inflation to change. The NAIRU is the lowest unemployment rate that can be sustained without upward pressure on inflation.

Putting this differently, a stable inflation rate will occur when two conditions are met:

1. *No excess demand.* Inflation neither rises nor falls at the NAIRU because the upward wage pressures from job vacancies just match the downward wage pressure from unemployment.
2. *No supply shocks.* Inflation will stay on track if there are no supply shocks from oil or other commodity prices, from exchange rates, from productivity, or from other factors that affect the costs of production—that is, if there are no *AS* shocks.

In the absence of excess demand and supply shocks, actual inflation will continue at the inertial rate.

How would demand or cost shocks affect the economy? At very low unemployment, such as occurred during the Vietnam war, inflation would increase as the economy moves up along the short-run Phillips curve. On the other hand, if unemployment rises far above the NAIRU, as happened in the early 1980s, inflation would decline as the economy moves down the short-run Phillips curve.

But the story does not end here. Once actual inflation rises above its expected rate, people begin to

---

[6] Other terms will sometimes be encountered. The original name for the NAIRU was the "natural rate of unemployment." This term is unsatisfactory because there is nothing natural about the NAIRU.

adapt to the new level of inflation. They begin to expect higher inflation. The inertial rate of inflation then adjusts to the new reality, and the short-run Phillips curve shifts.

This brief narrative makes a crucial point about inflation: The trade-off between inflation and unemployment remains stable only as long as the inertial or expected inflation rate remains unchanged. But when the inertial inflation rate changes, the short-run Phillips curve will shift.

The Shifting Phillips Curve

This important idea—of a shifting Phillips curve—can be understood as a sequence of steps, illustrated by a "boom cycle" here and in Figure 16-10.

- *Period 1.* In the first period, unemployment is at the NAIRU. There are no demand or supply surprises, and the economy is at point A on the lower short-run Phillips curve (*SRPC*) in Figure 16-10.

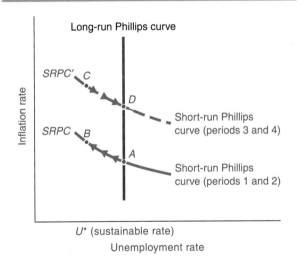

FIGURE 16-10. How Shocks Move the Phillips Curve

Period 1: The economy starts at point A. *Period 2:* The economy expands, with unemployment falling below the NAIRU and landing at point B. As a result, inflation rises above the inertial rate. *Period 3:* As time passes, the higher inflation becomes anticipated and gets built into the new short-run Phillips curve, *SRPC'*. *Period 4:* When the economy comes back to the NAIRU at point D, it is now saddled with higher inertial and actual inflation rates.

Connect points A, B, C, and D. The shifting curve has produced a clockwise loop like that seen in Fig. 16-9.

- *Period 2.* A rapid increase in output during an economic expansion lowers the unemployment rate. As unemployment declines, firms recruit workers more vigorously, giving larger wage increases than formerly. As output exceeds its potential, capacity utilization rises and price markups increase. Wages and prices begin to accelerate. In terms of our Phillips curve, the economy moves up and to the left to point B on its short-run Phillips curve (along *SRPC* in Figure 16-10). Inflation expectations have not yet changed, but the lower unemployment rate raises inflation during the second period.

- *Period 3.* With higher inflation, firms and workers begin to expect higher inflation. The higher expected rate of inflation is incorporated into wage and price decisions. The expected rate of inflation thus increases. The higher expected inflation shows up in the Phillips-curve framework when the short-run Phillips curve shifts upward and the new equilibrium is at point C. The new short-run Phillips curve (labeled *SRPC'* in Figure 16-10) lies above the original Phillips curve, reflecting the higher expected rate of inflation.

- *Period 4.* In the final period, as the economy slows, the contraction in economic activity brings output back to its potential, and the unemployment rate returns to the NAIRU at point D. Inflation declines because of the higher unemployment, but once the NAIRU is reached, the new expected rate of inflation is higher.

Note the surprising outcome. Because the expected inflation rate has increased, the rate of inflation is higher in period 4 than during period 1 even though the unemployment rate is the same. The economy will have the same *real* GDP and unemployment rate as it did in period 1, even though the *nominal* magnitudes (prices and nominal GDP) are now growing more rapidly than they did before the expansion raised the expected rate of inflation.

We sometimes also track an "austerity cycle" that occurs when unemployment rises and the actual inflation rate falls below the inertial rate. The inertial rate of inflation declines in recessions, and the economy enjoys a lower inflation rate when it returns to the NAIRU. This painful cycle of austerity occurred during the Carter-Volcker-Reagan wars against inflation during 1979–1984.

The Vertical Long-Run Phillips Curve

When the unemployment rate departs from the NAIRU, the inflation rate will tend to change. What happens if the gap between the actual unemployment rate and the NAIRU persists? For example, say that the NAIRU is 5 percent while the actual unemployment rate is 3 percent. Because of the gap, inflation will tend to rise from year to year. Inflation might be 3 percent in the first year, 4 percent in the second year, 5 percent in the third year—and might continue to move upward thereafter. When would this upward spiral stop? It stops only when unemployment moves back to the NAIRU. Put differently, as long as unemployment is below the NAIRU, wage inflation will tend to increase.

The opposite behavior will be seen at high unemployment. In that case, inflation will tend to fall as long as unemployment is above the NAIRU.

Only when unemployment is at the NAIRU will inflation stabilize; only then will the shifts of supply and demand in different labor markets be in balance; only then will inflation—at whatever is its inertial rate—tend neither to increase nor to decrease.

According to the NAIRU theory, the only level of unemployment consistent with a stable inflation rate is the NAIRU. The long-run Phillips curve is a vertical line, rising straight up at the NAIRU as shown by the vertical *DA* line in Figure 16-10.

The NAIRU theory of inflation has two important implications for economic policy. First, it implies that there is a minimum level of unemployment that an economy can sustain in the long run. According to this view, a nation cannot push unemployment below the NAIRU for long without igniting an upward spiral of wage and price inflation.

But even with this long-run constraint, there is much room in the short run for business cycles. A country might expand the economy and enjoy low unemployment for a period. But, eventually, this prosperity comes at the price of rising inflation. Conversely, when a nation thinks that its inertial inflation rate is too high, it can steel itself for a period of austerity, tighten money, induce a recession, and thereby reduce inflation.

Quantitative Estimates

Although the NAIRU is a crucial macroeconomic concept, precise numerical estimates of the NAIRU have proved elusive. Many macroeconomists, such as Robert J. Gordon, James Stock, and Mark Watson, have used advanced econometric techniques to estimate the NAIRU. For this text, we have adopted the consensus estimates prepared by the Congressional Budget Office (CBO), which estimates the NAIRU on the basis of scholarly studies. According to the CBO, the NAIRU rose gradually from the 1950s, peaked at 6.3 percent of the labor force around 1980, and declined to 5.2 percent by 2000. CBO estimates, along with the actual unemployment rate through the end of 1999, are shown in Figure 16-11.

Academic economists have produced a range of numbers, with informed opinion putting the NAIRU between 5 and $5^{1}/_{2}$ percent of the labor force for the late 1990s. Most economists hold that, given today's price- and wage-setting institutions, the United States could not maintain an unemployment rate below 5 percent without risking rising inflation.

The Declining NAIRU

The best evidence suggests that, after having risen in the 1970s and 1980s, the NAIRU in the United States has declined sharply over the last two decades. One reason for the decline has been the decrease in the power of labor unions. Labor unions controlled almost one-quarter of the labor force at their peak, but by 1999 that fraction had shrunk to about one-eighth of the workforce, with particularly sharp declines in the private sector. This weakening of labor's monopoly power means that labor market conditions, particularly high unemployment, are more quickly transmitted into wage changes.

Another important structural feature lowering the NAIRU is the strengthening of competition in the American economy. Over the last two decades, many industries have been deregulated, and foreign firms have invaded many previously sheltered domestic markets. In automobiles, telecommunications, and energy markets, stronger competition in the product market in effect increases competition in the labor market as well. With pressure from other, often foreign or nonunion, firms, wages tend to rise less during periods of strong demand, reducing the

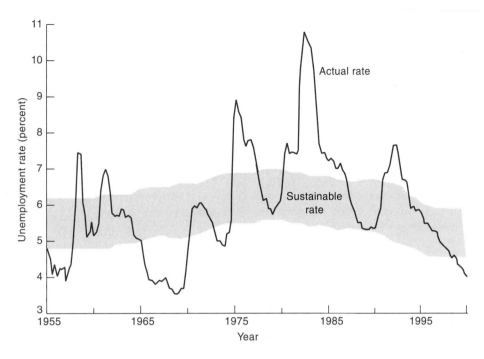

FIGURE 16-11. Actual Unemployment Rate and NAIRU, 1955–1999

The NAIRU comes where forces acting on inflation are in balance. Below that rate, inflation generally tends to rise; above it, inflation tends to subside. The NAIRU appears to have risen in the 1970s and 1980s and then declined over the last decade. The NAIRU is shown as a wide band to reflect the fact that it is difficult to estimate the NAIRU precisely. (Source: Actual unemployment rate from U.S. Department of Labor, *Employment and Earnings*; NAIRU from the Congressional Budget Office and research of private scholars.)

NAIRU. Some analysts believe that the pressure on labor markets from increased immigration reinforces the competitiveness of labor markets.

Yet a further source of decline in the NAIRU is demographic shifts. As the population aged in the 1990s, there were fewer high-unemployment-rate teenagers in the labor force. In addition, as women gained work experience, their unemployment rate declined relative to that of men. All these factors appear to have had a major impact on the NAIRU.

Some believe that the NAIRU has declined temporarily because of the recent upsurge in productivity growth. The productivity acceleration after 1995 has allowed firms to increase wages without the higher wages being reflected in higher inflation. As a result, inflation might temporarily stabilize at unemployment rates that are lower than would normally be the case.

After a few years, however, the high productivity growth and higher real wage growth will become expected, and the NAIRU will return to its long-run level.

Evidence of a decline in the NAIRU is seen in several labor market statistics. For example, the level of vacancies in 1999 was far below that in 1989 even though the unemployment rate was identical. With fewer vacancies, upward wage pressures tend to moderate. In addition, the fraction of workers who were "job leavers" was one-third lower in 1999 than in 1989 (see the discussion of this component of unemployment in Chapter 15). This indicates that fewer people are leaving their jobs to chase higher wages elsewhere. Economists will be sifting through the data carefully to see whether the apparent decline in the NAIRU is a durable feature of the American economy.

The inflation puzzle of the 1990s

The United States experienced a period of unusual macroeconomic stability and prosperity in the late 1990s. Output grew rapidly, unemployment fell sharply, and inflation was at its lowest rate for three decades.

While most Americans were satisfied with the robust economic growth, macroeconomists were puzzled about the unusual behavior of wages and prices. Economic studies from earlier periods suggested that wage and price inflation would begin to rise when unemployment fell below the NAIRU, which was generally thought to be around $5\frac{1}{2}$ percent of the labor force. Unemployment fell below 5 percent for 3 years running, starting in 1997. Yet inflation fell over this period.

The puzzle for inflation theorists is shown in Figure 16-12. The line marked "Actual" shows the actual inflation rate for the period 1995–1999. The line marked "Predicted" shows the predicted inflation rate based on the historical relationship between inflation and unemployment and assuming a NAIRU of $5\frac{1}{2}$ percent. Standard Phillips-curve theories would predict an inflation rate of over 4 percent for 1999, while the actual inflation rate was closer to 2 percent.

Many classical and supply-side economists see the 1990s as yet another nail in the Phillips-curve coffin. Others look to special factors as an explanation. What might have led to the restrained inflation in the 1990s? Here is the view of Fed Chairman Alan Greenspan:

The increasing availability of labor-displacing equipment and software, at declining prices and improving delivery lead times, is arguably at the root of the loss of business pricing power in recent years. To be sure, other inflation-suppressing forces have been at work as well. Marked increases in available global capacity were engendered as a number of countries that were previously members of the autarchic Soviet bloc opened to the West, and as many emerging-market economies blossomed. Reductions in Cold War spending in the United States and around the world also released resources to more productive private purposes. In addition, deregulation that removed bottlenecks and hence increased supply response in many economies, especially ours, has been a formidable force suppressing price increases as well. Finally, the global economic crisis of 1997 and 1998 reduced the prices of energy and other key inputs into production and consumption, helping to hold down inflation for several years.[7]

These forces have led to what Robert J. Gordon calls the "Goldilocks economy": an economy that was not too hot and not too cold but just right. But history cautions us that what goes down can go up. Many of the factors leading to the low inflation can easily be reversed. Two special factors that kept inflation down in the 1990s are already moving in the opposite direction in 2000: oil prices have risen sharply and medical-care prices have resumed their rapid increase. If these factors begin to take hold and spill over into wages, the Federal Reserve is likely to step on the brakes, raising unemployment and frightening investors.

Doubts about the NAIRU

The concept of the nonaccelerating inflation rate of unemployment, along with its output twin of potential GDP, is crucial for understanding inflation and the connection between the short run and the long run in macroeconomics. But the mainstream view remains controversial.

Critics wonder whether the NAIRU is a stable and reliable concept. The inflation experience of the United States has undermined faith about a stable NAIRU for that country. Another question is whether an extended period of high unemployment will lead to a deterioration of job skills, to loss of on-the-job training and experience, and thereby to a higher NAIRU. Might not slow growth of real GDP reduce investment and leave the country with a diminished capital stock? Might not that capacity shortage produce rising inflation even with unemployment rates above the NAIRU?

Experience in Europe over the last two decades confirms some of these worries (recall our discussion of the European unemployment puzzle at the end of the previous chapter). In the early 1960s, labor markets in Germany, France, and Britain appeared to be in equilibrium with unemployment

---

[7] See this chapter's Further Reading section for a reference to Greenspan's speech as well as for articles by Lawrence Katz, Alan Krueger, and Robert Gordon that discuss the inflation puzzle of the 1990s.

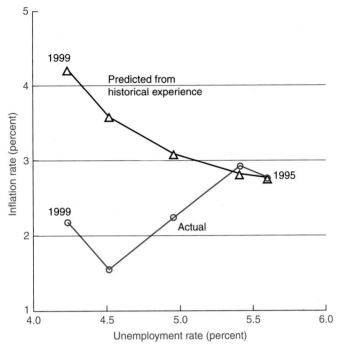

FIGURE 16-12. Actual and Predicted Inflation, 1995–1999

The late 1990s saw unusually moderate inflation for a period of rapid growth and low unemployment. This figure shows actual inflation for the late 1990s along with that predicted by a standard equation. Did this signal a "new era" in the American economy—or simply a coincidence of favorable price and wage surprises? (Source: Actual CPI and unemployment rate from Bureau of Labor Statistics. Predicted inflation assumes a NAIRU of 5.5 percent.)

rates between 1 and 2 percent. By the early 1990s, after a decade of stagnation and slow job growth, labor market equilibrium seemed to be in balance with unemployment rates in the 6 to 12 percent range. On the basis of recent European experience, many macroeconomists are looking for ways to explain the instability of the NAIRU and its dependence upon actual unemployment as well as labor market institutions.

Review

The major points to understand are the following:

- Inflation has great momentum and is highly inertial. It tends to persist until shocked either by demand or by costs.

- In the short run, an increase in aggregate demand which lowers the unemployment rate below the NAIRU will tend to increase the inflation rate. A demand decrease will tend to lower inflation. In the short run, there is a trade-off between inflation and unemployment.

- The Phillips curve tends to adapt to the ongoing rate of inflation. A period of low unemployment and increasing inflation will lead people to expect higher inflation and will tend to shift up the short-run Phillips curve.

- According to the NAIRU theory, the long-run Phillips curve is vertical at the nonaccelerating inflation rate of unemployment (NAIRU); as long as the unemployment rate is below the NAIRU, inflation will tend to rise continually.

⊛

C. DILEMMAS OF ANTI-INFLATION POLICY

The economy evolves in response to political forces and technological change. Our economic theories, designed to explain issues like inflation and unemployment, must also adapt. In this final section on inflation theory, we discuss the pressing issues that arise in combating inflation.

How Long Is the Long Run?

The NAIRU theory holds that the Phillips curve is vertical in the long run. Just how long is the long run for this purpose? The length of time that it takes the economy to adjust fully to a shock is not known with precision. Recent studies suggest that full adjustment takes at least 5 years or perhaps even a decade. The reason for the long delay is that it takes years for expectations to adjust, for labor and other long-term contracts to be renegotiated, and for all these effects to percolate through the economy.

How Much Does It Cost to Reduce Inflation?

Our analysis suggests that a nation can reduce the inertial rate of inflation by temporarily reducing output and raising unemployment. But policymakers may want to know just how much it costs to squeeze inflation out of the economy. How costly is *disinflation*, which denotes the policy of lowering the rate of inflation?

Studies of this subject find that the cost of reducing inflation varies depending upon the country, the initial inflation rate, and the policy used. Analyses for the United States give a reasonably consistent answer: Lowering the inertial inflation rate by 1 percentage point costs the nation about 4 percent of 1 year's GDP. In terms of the current level of GDP, this amounts to an output loss of about $360 billion (in 1999 prices) to reduce the inflation rate by 1 percentage point.

To understand the cost of disinflation, consider the Phillips curve. If the Phillips curve is relatively flat, reducing inflation will require much unemployment and loss in output; if the Phillips curve is steep, a small rise in unemployment will bring down inflation quickly and relatively painlessly. Statistical analyses indicate that when the unemployment rate rises 1 percentage point above the NAIRU for 1 year and then returns to the NAIRU, the inflation rate will decline about $1/2$ percentage point. Therefore, to reduce inflation by 1 full percentage point, unemployment must be held 2 percentage points above the NAIRU for 1 year.

Recall that Okun's Law (discussed in Chapter 15) holds that when the unemployment rate is 2 percentage points above the NAIRU, actual GDP is 4 percent below potential GDP. In 1999 terms, with a potential GDP (in 1999 prices) of $9000 billion, reducing inflation by 1 percentage point would require about a 2-percentage-point increase in the unemployment rate (U) for 1 year. In dollars, then, a disinflation of 1 percentage point would cost 2 U points × 2 percent of GDP per U point × $9000 billion of GDP = $360 billion. There is uncertainty here, however, and estimates of the cost range from $180 to $500 billion per point of inflation reduction.

This statistical estimate of the cost of reducing inflation can be compared to the American experience during the deep recession in the early 1980s. Table 16-2 shows a calculation of the estimated output loss from the recession (compared to producing at potential output), along with the estimated decline in the inertial inflation rate. This calculation indicates that the disinflation of the 1980–1984 period cost the nation approximately $250 billion of lost output (in 1999 prices) per percentage-point reduction in inflation. This episode corroborates statistical estimates of the cost of disinflation.

Credibility and Inflation

One of the most important questions in anti-inflation policy concerns the role of credibility of policy. Many economists argue that the Phillips-curve approach is too pessimistic. The dissenters hold that credible and publicly announced policies—for example, adopting fixed monetary rules or targeting nominal GDP—would allow anti-inflation policies to reduce inflation with lower output and unemployment costs.

The idea relies on the fact that inflation is an inertial process that depends on people's expectations of future inflation. A credible monetary policy—such as one that relentlessly targets a fixed, low inflation rate—might lead people to expect that inflation would be lower in the future, and this belief

The Cost of Disinflation, 1980–1984

Inertial rate of inflation:

1979	9%
1984	4%
Change:	−5 percentage points

Difference between potential and actual GDP(1999 prices):

1980	$120 billion
1981	170
1982	390
1983	390
1984	180

Total: $1,250 billion

Cost of disinflation = $1,250 billion/5 percentage points
= $250 billion per percentage point
= 26 percent of GDP = 5.2 percent of GDP per point of disinflation

TABLE 16-2. Illustration of the Cost of Disinflation

What was the cost of reducing inflation in the 1979–1984 period? Tight monetary policy produced a deep recession during which the economy produced $1250 billion less than its potential GDP. As a result, the inertial inflation rate declined by 5 percentage points. Dividing these two figures provides an estimate of $250 billion of output lost per percentage-point reduction in inflation. (Source: Authors' estimates. The calculation of potential output uses a NAIRU of 6 percent for 1979–1984.)

might in some measure be a self-fulfilling prophecy. Those emphasizing credibility backed their theories by citing "regime changes," such as monetary and fiscal reforms that ended Austrian and Bolivian hyperinflations at relatively low cost in terms of unemployment or lost GDP.

Many economists were skeptical about claims that credibility would significantly lower the output costs of disinflation. While such policies might work in countries torn by hyperinflation, war, or revolution, Draconian anti-inflation policies would be less credible in the United States. Congress and the president often lose heart when unemployment rises sharply to fight inflation, and farmers or construction workers storm the Capitol and circle the White House.

The bold U.S. experiment of 1980–1984 provided a good laboratory to test the credibility critique. During this period, monetary policy was tightened in a clear and forceful manner. Yet the price tag was extremely high, as Table 16-2 shows. Using tough, preannounced policies to enhance credibility

does not appear to have lowered the cost of disinflation in the United States. Economists have also examined the Argentinean experience of the late 1990s, during which Argentina adopted a currency board to enforce a hard fixed exchange rate with the U.S. dollar and thereby keep inflation in check. The government swore "death before devaluation," but the costs of disinflation still appear high even though firms and workers seem convinced of the credibility of the new monetary policy.

How Can We Lower the NAIRU?

Given the costs of high unemployment, we might ask: Is the NAIRU the optimal level of unemployment? If not, what can we do to lower it toward a more desirable level? Economists of a classical persuasion often argue that the NAIRU (or what they call the "natural rate") represents the economy's efficient unemployment level. They hold that it is the outcome of supply and demand grinding out an efficient pattern of jobs, job vacancies, and job search.

It would make no more sense to lower the NAIRU than to lower the vacancy rate for apartments or the number of spare tires we carry in our cars.

Other economists strongly disagree, holding that the NAIRU is likely to be above the optimal unemployment rate or the unemployment rate at which an economy's net economic welfare is maximized. This group argues that there are many spillovers or externalities in the labor market. For example, workers who have been laid off suffer from a variety of social and economic hardships. Yet employers do not pay the costs of unemployment; most of the costs (unemployment insurance, health costs, family distress, etc.) spill over as external costs and are absorbed by the worker or by the government. To the extent that unemployment has "external" costs, the NAIRU is likely to be higher than the optimal rate. Lowering the unemployment rate would raise the nation's net economic welfare.

An enormous social dividend, therefore, would reward the society that discovers how to reduce the NAIRU significantly. What measures might lower the NAIRU?

- *Improve labor market services.* Some unemployment occurs because job vacancies are not matched up with unemployed workers. Through better information, such as computerized job lists, the amount of frictional and structural unemployment can be reduced.
- *Bolster training programs.* If you read the help wanted section of your Sunday newspaper, you will find that most of the job vacancies call for skills held by few people. Conversely, most of the unemployed are unskilled or semiskilled workers or find themselves in the wrong job or in a depressed industry. Many believe that government or private training programs can help unemployed workers retool for better jobs in growing sectors. If successful, such programs provide the double bonus of allowing people to lead productive lives and of reducing the burden on government transfer programs.
- *Remove government obstacles.* We noted above that in protecting people from the hardships of unemployment and poverty, the government has at the same time removed the sting of unemployment and reduced incentives to seek work. Some economists call for reforming the unemployment-insurance system and for reducing the disincentives for work in health, disability, and so-

cial security programs. The United States has significantly reduced the generosity of its income-support programs in the last two decades, including a radical restructuring of welfare in 1996. While welfare reform is likely to increase the labor-force participation of low-income households, the impact on the NAIRU is unclear. If welfare cuts bring into the workforce unskilled and inexperienced workers who tend to have higher unemployment rates, these measures may well raise the NAIRU.

Having reviewed the options for reducing the NAIRU, we must add a cautionary note. Intensive research and labor market experiments on this subject have led objective analysts to be extremely modest in their claims. Few responsible scholars believe that realistic reforms would change the NAIRU by more than a few tenths of a percentage point. On the other hand, even such a change would have a major impact on the potential output of the economy.

Wanted: A Low-Cost Anti-inflation Policy

Mainstream macroeconomic theory holds that we can prevent rising inflation only by keeping unemployment from falling below the NAIRU. The economy pays a high price in terms of lost output and employment to maintain price stability. Some economists are troubled by this conclusion and are searching for less costly ways of containing inflation.

What are some approaches to anti-inflation policies? How successful have they been? Here are some examples:

- *Incomes policies* were popular in an earlier time. Incomes policies are government policies that attempt to moderate inflation directly, whether by verbal persuasion, legal controls, or other incentives. Such measures were used in Scandinavia, Britain, the United States, and elsewhere. Unfortunately, mandatory price controls tend to become ineffective because people evade them. Moreover, they are unlikely to slow price and wage increases unless they are accompanied by restrictive fiscal and monetary policies. There are today very few advocates of using wage-price controls to check inflation.
- A *market strategy* has been urged by many economists. This approach would rely on the disci-

pline of markets to restrain price and wage increases. Advocates emphasize strengthening market forces by deregulation of regulated industries; removing market impediments to competition in perverse antitrust laws and in retail-price maintenance; repealing government laws that inhibit competition such as foreign-trade quotas and minimum-wage laws; and banning labor-union monopolies. Particularly in open economies, one of the most important anti-inflation policies is *international competition*. Policies that strengthen market forces may increase the resistance to price and wage increases, particularly in imperfectly competitive labor and product markets.

- *Tax-based incomes policies* (sometimes dubbed "TIP") have been proposed as a way of using the market mechanism to attain macroeconomic objectives. TIP would use fiscal carrots and sticks to encourage anti-inflationary actions by taxing those whose wages and prices are rising rapidly and subsidizing those whose wages and prices are rising slowly. The TIP approach has been used in former socialist countries such as Hungary and Poland with some success, and has sometimes been proposed for the United States. Even the enthusiasts of TIP stress, however, that it is a complement and not a substitute for the discipline of the market mechanism and for the tight fiscal and monetary policies necessary to contain inflation.

- *Profit-sharing policies* have been proposed by Har-

vard's Martin Weitzman and Cambridge University's James Meade. The idea here is to devise new kinds of labor contracts that give workers a share of the profits or revenues rather than a straight wage. Under such an approach, the marginal cost of a worker would be less than the average compensation, so it would be less profitable for firms to lay off workers in recessions. The layoff "externality" we discussed above would be reduced, and, if successful, the NAIRU would consequently be reduced. Some believe the widespread use of stock options may keep down wage pressures.

What are the lessons about the relationship between unemployment and inflation? After reviewing the evidence on all sides, we conclude with the following cautious summary:

There appears to be a lowest sustainable unemployment rate, the NAIRU, below which our economies can operate only at the risk of spiraling inflation. Moreover, the lowest sustainable rate is inefficiently high. Critics of capitalism find the high unemployment that often prevails in North America and Europe to be a central flaw in modern capitalism. The need to keep unemployment above the optimal level to contain inflation is one of the cruelest dilemmas of modern macroeconomics. While the United States has avoided high unemployment and high inflation in the late 1990s, it is unlikely that these ailments have been banished from the modern market economy

SUMMARY

A. Definition and Impact of Inflation

1. Recall that inflation occurs when the general level of prices is rising. The rate of inflation is the percentage change in a price index from one period to the next. The major price indexes are the consumer price index (CPI) and the GDP deflator.

2. Like diseases, inflations come in different strains. We generally see low inflation in the United States (a few percentage points annually). Sometimes, galloping inflation produces price rises of 50 or 100 or 200 percent each year. Hyperinflation takes over when the printing presses spew out currency and prices start rising many times each month. Historically, hyperinfla-

tions have almost always been associated with war and revolution.

3. Inflation affects the economy by redistributing income and wealth and by impairing efficiency. Unanticipated inflation usually favors debtors, profit seekers, and risk-taking speculators. It hurts creditors, fixed-income classes, and timid investors. Inflation leads to distortions in relative prices, tax rates, and real interest rates. People take more trips to the bank, taxes may creep up, and measured income may become distorted. And when central banks take steps to lower inflation, the real costs of such steps in terms of lower output and employment can be painful.

B. Modern Inflation Theory

4. At any time, an economy has a given inertial or expected inflation rate. This is the rate that people have come to anticipate and that is built into labor contracts and other agreements. The inertial rate of inflation is a short-run equilibrium and persists until the economy is shocked.

5. In reality, the economy receives incessant price shocks. The major kinds of shocks that propel inflation away from its inertial rate are demand-pull and cost-push. Demand-pull inflation results from too much spending chasing too few goods, causing the aggregate demand curve to shift up and to the right. Wages and prices are then bid up in markets. Cost-push inflation is a new phenomenon of modern industrial economies and occurs when the costs of production rise even in periods of high unemployment and idle capacity.

6. The Phillips curve shows the relationship between inflation and unemployment. In the short run, lowering one rate means raising the other. But the short-run Phillips curve tends to shift over time as expected inflation and other factors change. If policymakers attempt to hold unemployment below the NAIRU for long periods, inflation will tend to spiral upward.

7. Modern inflation theory relies on the concept of the nonaccelerating inflation rate of unemployment, or NAIRU, which is the lowest sustainable unemployment rate that the nation can enjoy without risking an upward spiral of inflation. It represents the level of unemployment of resources at which labor and product markets are in inflationary balance. Under the NAIRU theory, there is no permanent trade-off between unemployment and inflation, and the long-run Phillips curve is vertical.

C. Dilemmas of Anti-inflation Policy

8. A central concern for policymakers is the cost of reducing inertial inflation. Current estimates indicate that a substantial recession is necessary to slow inertial inflation.

9. Economists have put forth many proposals for lowering the NAIRU; notable proposals include improving labor market information, improving education and training programs, and refashioning government programs so that workers have greater incentives to work. Sober analysis of politically viable proposals leads most economists to expect only small improvements from such labor market reforms.

10. Because of the high costs of reducing inflation through recessions, nations have often looked for other approaches. These are incomes policies such as wage-price controls and voluntary guidelines, tax-based approaches, and market-strengthening strategies.

CONCEPTS FOR REVIEW

History and Theories of Inflation

$$\text{Inflation}(t) = \frac{P(t) - P(t - 1)}{P(t - 1)} \times 100$$

strains of inflation:
  low
  galloping
  hyperinflation
impacts of inflation (redistributive, on output and employment)

anticipated and unanticipated
  inflation
costs of inflation:
  "shoe leather"
  menu costs
  income and tax distortions
  loss of information
inertial, demand-pull, and cost-push
  inflation
short-run and long-run Phillips
  curves

nonaccelerating inflation rate of unemployment (NAIRU) and the long-run Phillips curve

Anti-inflation Policy

costs of disinflation
measures to lower the NAIRU
alternative anti-inflation policies:
  incomes policies
  competition
  TIP
  profit sharing

FURTHER READING AND INTERNET WEBSITES

Further Reading

The source of the quote on low inflation is George A. Akerlof, William T. Dickens, and George L. Perry, "The Macroeconomics of Low Inflation," *Brookings Papers on Economic Activity*, no. 1, 1996, pp. 1–59. Martin Feldstein has argued that even low inflation has a large impact upon economic efficiency. See particularly, Martin Feldstein, ed., *The Costs and Benefits of Price Stability* (University of Chicago Press, 1999).

Interesting analyses of the inflation puzzle of the 1990s can be found in Lawrence F. Katz and Alan B. Krueger, "The High-Pressure U. S. Labor Market of the 1990s," *Brookings Papers on Economic Activity*, 1999:1, and Robert J. Gordon, "Foundations of the Goldilocks Economy," *Brookings Papers on Economic Activity*, 1998:2.

Websites

The quotes from Alan Greenspan are from a speech before the Economic Club of New York, New York, January 13, 2000, and is available at the Federal Reserve web page at www.bog.frb.fed.us/boarddocs/speeches/2000.

Analysis of the consumer price data for the United States comes from the Bureau of Labor Statistics, found at www.bls.gov.

❉ QUESTIONS FOR DISCUSSION

1. Consider the following impacts of inflation: tax distortions, income and wealth redistribution, shoe-leather costs, menu costs. For each, define the cost and provide an example.

2. "During periods of inflation, people use real resources to reduce their holdings of fiat money. Such activities produce a private benefit with no corresponding social gain, which illustrates the social cost of inflation." Explain this quotation and give an example.

3. Unanticipated deflation also produces serious social costs. For each of the following, describe the deflation and analyze the associated costs:

   a. During the Great Depression, prices of major crops fell along with the prices of other commodities. What would happen to farmers who had large mortgages?

   b. Japan experienced a mild deflation in the 1990s. Assume that Japanese students each borrowed 2,000,000 yen (about $20,000) to pay for their education, hoping that inflation would allow them to pay off their loans in inflated yen. What would happen to these students if wages and prices began to *fall* at 5 percent per year?

4. The data in Table 16-3 describe inflation and unemployment in the United States from 1979 to 1987. Note that the economy started out near the NAIRU in 1979 and ended near the NAIRU in 1987. Can you explain the decline of inflation over the intervening years? Do so by drawing the short-run and long-run Phillips curves for each of the years from 1979 to 1987.

5. Many economists argue as follows: "Because there is no long-run trade-off between unemployment and inflation, there is no point in trying to shave the peaks and troughs from the business cycle." This view suggests that we should not care whether the economy is stable or fluctuating widely as long as the average level of unemployment is the same. Discuss critically.

6. A leading economist has written: "If you think of the social costs of inflation, at least of moderate inflation, it is hard to avoid coming away with the impression that they are minor compared with the costs of unemployment and depressed production." Write a short essay describing your views on this issue.

7. Consider the data on annual inflation rates and growth of per capita GDP shown in Table 16-1. Can you see that low inflation is associated with the highest growth rates? What are the economic reasons why growth might be lower for deflation and for hyperinflation. Explain why the *ex post* fallacy might apply here (see the discussion in Chapter 1).

Year	Unemployment rate (%)	Inflation rate, CPI (% per year)
1979	5.8	11.3
1980	7.1	13.5
1981	7.6	10.3
1982	9.7	6.2
1983	9.6	3.2
1984	7.5	4.4
1985	7.2	3.6
1986	7.0	1.9
1987	6.2	3.6

TABLE 16-3. Unemployment and Inflation Data for the United States, 1979–1987

Source: *Economic Report of the President* 2000.

A. CLASSICAL STIRRINGS AND KEYNESIAN REVOLUTION

THE CLASSICAL TRADITION

Since the dawn of economics two centuries ago, economists have wondered whether or not a market economy has a tendency to move spontaneously toward a long-run, full-employment equilibrium without the need for government intervention. Using modern language, we label as **classical** those approaches that emphasize the self-correcting forces in an economy. The classical approach holds that prices and wages are flexible and the economy is stable, so the economy moves automatically and quickly to its full-employment equilibrium. Our discussion uses the aggregate supply-and-demand framework to explain the scientific foundations and the policy implications of the classical approach to macroeconomics.

Say's Law of Markets

Before Keynes developed his macroeconomic theories, the major economic thinkers generally adhered to the classical view of the economy, at least in good times. Early economists were fascinated by the Industrial Revolution, with its division of labor, accumulation of capital, and growing international trade. These economists knew about business cycles, but they viewed them as temporary and self-correcting aberrations.

Classical analysis revolved around **Say's Law of Markets.** This theory, propounded in 1803 by the French economist J. B. Say, states that overproduction is impossible by its very nature. This is sometimes expressed as "supply creates its own demand." What is the rationale for Say's Law? It rests on a view that there is no essential difference between a monetary economy and a barter economy—that whatever factories can produce, workers can afford to buy.

A long line of the most distinguished economists, including David Ricardo (1817), John Stuart Mill (1848), and Alfred Marshall (1890), subscribed to the classical macroeconomic view that overproduction is impossible. The classical view was stated clearly by the leading British economist A. C. Pigou, writing during the Great Depression:

With perfectly free competition there will always be a strong tendency toward full employment. Such unemployment as exists at any time is due wholly to the frictional resistances [that] prevent the appropriate wage and price adjustments being made instantaneously.[1]

The classical theory holds that wages and prices are flexible so that markets will very quickly "clear," or return to equilibrium. As a result, the economy operates at full employment.

The durable and valid core of Say's Law and of the classical approach is shown in Figure 17-1. This shows an economy where prices and real wages are determined in competitive markets, moving flexibly up and down to eliminate any excess demand or supply. In terms of our *AS-AD* analysis, it can be described by a standard, downward-sloping aggregate demand curve along with a vertical aggregate supply curve.

---

[1] See Pigou in the Further Reading section at the end of this chapter.

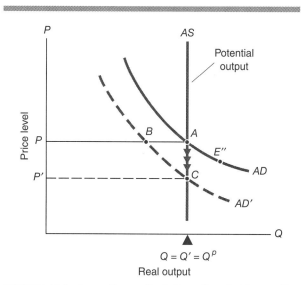

FIGURE 17-1. According to Say's Law, Supply Creates Its Own Demand as Prices Move to Balance Demand with Aggregate Supply

Classical economists thought that persistent periods of glut could not occur. If *AS* or *AD* shifted, prices would react flexibly to ensure that full-employment output was sold. Here we see how flexible prices move down enough to match real expenditures with full-employment output after a decline in aggregate demand.

Suppose that aggregate demand falls due to tight money, falling exports, or other exogenous forces. As a result, the *AD* curve shifts leftward to *AD'* in Figure 17-1. At the original price level of *P*, total spending would fall to point *B*. As a result of the excess supply, the overall price level falls from *P* to *P'*. As the price level falls, full employment is reestablished at point *C*.

In the classical view, changes in aggregate demand affect the price level but have no lasting impact upon output and employment. Price and wage flexibility ensures that the real level of spending is sufficient to maintain full employment.

Policy Consequences

The classical view has two conclusions that are vitally important for economic policy. To begin with, under the classical view the economy has only brief and temporary lapses from full employment and full utilization of capacity. There will be no long and sustained recessions or depressions, and qualified workers can quickly find work at the going market wage.

None of this implies that the classical economy is a nirvana of frictionless perfect competition. We may see frictional unemployment of people moving between jobs or structural unemployment of unionized workers who have bargained for above-equilibrium wage rates. Market power may produce *microeconomic* waste, distortions, and inefficiencies. But in the classical view, an economy has no pervasive and persistent *macroeconomic* waste in the sense of underutilized resources due to insufficient aggregate demand.

The second surprising element of the classical view is that aggregate demand policies cannot influence the level of unemployment and real output. Rather, monetary and fiscal policies can affect only the economy's price level, along with the composition of real GDP. This second classical proposition is easily seen in Figure 17-1. Consider an economy in equilibrium at point *A*. Suppose that the central bank decides to contract the money supply to reduce inflation. For a brief instant, at the initial price level *P*, there is excess supply. However, as prices and wages quickly begin to fall under the pressure of excess supply, the economy moves to the new equilibrium at point *C*. The contractionary economic policy has reduced the overall price level. But output and em-

ployment are essentially unchanged because price and wage flexibility has ensured a smooth transition between the old equilibrium and the new one.

At the heart of the classical view is the belief that prices and wages are flexible and that wage-price flexibility provides a self-correcting mechanism that quickly restores full employment. This approach is very much alive in the writings of today's new classical school, which we review later in this chapter. New classical economists move beyond the simplest classical approaches by allowing for imperfect information, the existence of technological shocks, and frictions from shifts of resources among industries. Although dressed in modern clothing, their policy conclusions are closely linked to those of the classical economists of an earlier age.

THE KEYNESIAN REVOLUTION

While classical economists were preaching the impossibility of persistent unemployment, economists of the 1930s could hardly ignore the vast army of unemployed workers begging for work and selling pencils on street corners. How could economics explain such massive and persistent idleness?

Keynes's *The General Theory of Employment, Interest and Money* (1936) offered an alternative macroeconomic theory, a new set of theoretical spectacles for looking at the impact of economic policies as well as external shocks. In fact, the Keynesian revolution combined two different elements. First, Keynes presented the concept of aggregate demand that was explored in depth in earlier chapters. A second and equally revolutionary feature was the Keynesian theory of aggregate supply. Whereas the classical approach assumed flexible prices and wages with the implication of a vertical classical *AS* curve, the Keynesian approach insisted on price and wage inflexibility and the flat or upward-sloping *AS* curve. In Keynes's approach, supply definitely does not create its own demand; demand can have a life of its own.

The Surprising Consequences

By combining these two new elements, Keynes brought a veritable revolution to macroeconomics. The essence of Keynes's argument is shown in Figure 17-2 on the next page. This now-familiar diagram combines an aggregate demand curve with a Keynesian, upward-sloping aggregate supply curve.

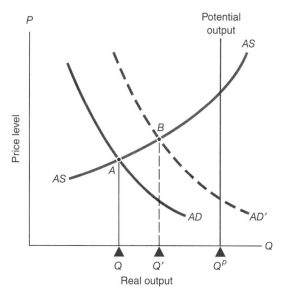

FIGURE 17-2. Aggregate Demand Helps Determine Output in the Keynesian Approach.

Keynesian aggregate supply slopes upward, implying that output will increase with higher aggregate demand as long as there are unused resources. With depressed demand, output will be in equilibrium at point *A*, with high unemployment.

If aggregate demand increases from *AD* to *AD'*, real output increases from *Q* to *Q'*. Keynesians emphasize that stimulating aggregate demand can succeed in increasing output and employment.

The first observation is that a modern market economy can get trapped in an underemployment equilibrium—a balance of aggregate supply and demand in which output is far below potential and a substantial fraction of the workforce is involuntarily unemployed. For example, if aggregate demand is depressed (shown as point *A* in Figure 17-2), the economy may get stuck in a high-unemployment equilibrium for a decade. A nation could remain in its low-output, high-misery condition for a long time because there is no self-correcting mechanism or invisible hand to guide the economy back to full employment.

Keynes's second observation follows from the first. Through monetary and fiscal policies, the government can stimulate the economy and help maintain high levels of output and employment. For ex-

ample, if the government were to increase its purchases, aggregate demand would increase, say, from *AD* to *AD'* in Figure 17-2. The impact would be an increase in output from *Q* to *Q'*, which reduces the gap between actual GDP and potential GDP.

Keynes's analysis created a revolution in macroeconomics, particularly among young economists who were living through the Great Depression of the 1930s and sensed something was terribly wrong with the classical model. Of course, the Great Depression was not the first event to reveal the flaws in the classical synthesis. Anyone with common sense could see the massive involuntary unemployment during depressions. But for the first time, the classical approach was confronted by a competing analysis. The Keynesian approach presented a new synthesis that swept through economics and fundamentally changed the way that economists and governments think about business cycles and economic policy.

THEORIES AND POLICY

In economics, what people see depends upon the theoretical spectacles they wear. Does a president, senator, or macroeconomist lean toward a classical or a Keynesian view? The answer to this question will often explain that person's view on many of the major economic-policy debates of the day.

Examples are legion. Economists who tend toward the classical view will often be skeptical about the need for government to stabilize business cycles. They argue that a government policy designed to increase aggregate demand will instead lead to escalating inflation. Even worse, Keynesian remedies will, in their view, slow long-run economic growth. Classical-type economists tend to worry about the long-run consequences of government actions on investment and economic growth. For example, in the classical view, government deficits may crowd out private investment. More public spending on health care or welfare will divert resources from private investment in factories and machinery.

Keynesian economists take a different tack. They think that the macroeconomy is prone to business cycles, with alternating periods of high unemployment followed by speculation and inflation. If the classical economist sees the economy as a temperate fellow who has the requisite glass of mineral water and vitamins every day, the Keynesian might picture the economy as a manic-depressive who periodically has a binge of irrational exuberance and shortly thereafter falls into a depressed hangover. Indeed, as one Fed chairman put it, the role of the Federal Reserve is to take the punch bowl away just when the party is getting lively.

Keynesians believe that the government can affect real economic activity by taking monetary or fiscal steps to change aggregate demand. A modern Keynesian economist would approve of steps to reduce aggregate demand when inflation is rising or to increase aggregate demand in recessions. Such economists in the United States increasingly lean toward using monetary policy to stabilize business cycles. But they also maintain the importance of fiscal automatic stabilizers that reduce the multiplier effect of unforeseen shocks, and they argue vehemently against policies, such as a constitutional amendment requiring a balanced budget, that would have fiscal policy exacerbate business fluctuations.

The debate between Keynesian and classical economists revolves fundamentally around whether the economy has strong self-correcting forces in flexible wages and prices that help maintain full employment. Classical approaches generally emphasize long-run economic growth and forgo business-cycle stabilization policies. Keynesian economists desire to supplement growth policies with appropriate monetary and fiscal policies to curb business-cycle excesses.

✳ B. THE MONETARIST APPROACH

Inflation is always and everywhere a monetary phenomenon in the sense that it is and can be produced only by a more rapid increase in the quantity of money than in output.

Milton Friedman, *The New Palgrave Dictionary of Economics* (1987)

Financial and monetary systems cannot manage themselves. The government, including the central bank, must make fundamental decisions about defin-

ing the monetary standard, determining the money supply, setting exchange-rate rules, governing international financial flows, and determining the ease or tightness of money and credit. Today, there are many different philosophies about the best way to manage monetary affairs. Some believe in an active policy that "leans against the wind" by slowing money growth when inflation threatens, and vice versa. Others are skeptical about the ability of policymakers to use monetary policy to "fine-tune" inflation and unemployment and would limit monetary policy to containing inflation. At the far end of the spectrum are the monetarists, who believe that discretionary monetary policy should be replaced by a fixed rule.

We can best understand monetarism if we first trace its history in the older quantity theory of money and prices (usually called the quantity theory of money). Then we can see that it has close linkages to both classical and Keynesian approaches.

THE ROOTS OF MONETARISM

Monetarism holds that the money supply is the primary determinant of short-run movements in nominal GDP and of long-run movements in prices. Of course, Keynesian macroeconomics also recognizes the key role of money in determining aggregate demand. The main difference between monetarists and Keynesians lies in the different approaches to the determination of aggregate demand. While Keynesian theories hold that many forces other than money affect aggregate demand, monetarists argue that changes in the money supply are the primary factor that determines output and price movements.

In order to understand monetarism, we need to introduce a new equation (the *equation of exchange*), a new concept (the *velocity of money*), and a new relationship (the *quantity theory of money*).

The Equation of Exchange and the Velocity of Money

Sometimes money turns over very slowly; it sits under the mattress or in bank accounts for long periods between transactions. At other times, particularly during rapid inflation, people get rid of money quickly and money circulates rapidly from hand to hand. The speed of turnover of money is described by the concept of the velocity of money, introduced at the turn of this century by Cambridge University's

Alfred Marshall and Yale's Irving Fisher. It measures the number of times per year that the average dollar in the money supply is spent for goods and services. When the quantity of money is large relative to the flow of expenditures, the velocity of circulation is low; when money turns over rapidly, money's velocity is high.

The concept of velocity is formally introduced in the **equation of exchange.** This equation states:

$$MV \equiv PQ \equiv (p_1 q_1 + p_2 q_2 + \cdots)$$

where M is the money supply, V is the velocity of money, P is the price level, and Q is real output. This can be restated as the *definition of the velocity of money* by dividing by M:

$$V \equiv \frac{PQ}{M}$$

We generally measure PQ as total income or output, GDP, and the associated velocity concept is the *income velocity of money.*

Velocity is the rate at which money circulates through the economy. The income velocity of money is measured as the ratio of nominal GDP to the stock of money.[2]

We can think of the income velocity of money intuitively as the speed at which money changes hands in the economy. As a simple example, assume that the economy produces only bread and that GDP consists of 48 million loaves of bread, each selling at a price of $1, so GDP = PQ = $48 million per year. If the money supply is $4 million, then by definition V = $48/$4 = 12 per year. This means that money turns over once a month as earnings are used to buy monthly bread.[3]

Figure 17-3 shows the recent history of the income velocity of transactions money (M_1). Note that nominal GDP has been rising faster than the money supply over the last four decades. We can thus conclude that the income velocity of money has been rising over time. The question of the stability and predictability of the velocity of money is central to macroeconomic policy.

The Quantity Theory of Prices

Having defined an interesting new variable called velocity, we now describe how early monetary specialists used the concept of velocity to explain movements in the overall price level. The key assumption is that *the velocity of money is relatively stable and predictable.* The reason for stability, according to monetarists, is that velocity mainly reflects underlying patterns in the timing of income and spending. If people get paid once a month and tend to spend all their incomes evenly over the course of the month, income velocity will be 12 per year. Incomes could double, prices might rise 20 percent, and total GDP may be up many times—yet with unchanged spending patterns the income velocity of money would remain unchanged. Only as people or businesses modify their spending patterns or the way they pay their bills does the velocity of income change.

On the basis of this insight about the relative stability of velocity, some early writers, particularly the classical economists, used velocity to explain changes in the price level. This approach, called the **quantity theory of money and prices,** rewrites the definition of velocity as follows:

$$P \equiv \frac{MV}{Q} \equiv \left(\frac{V}{Q}\right) M \equiv kM$$

This equation is obtained from the earlier definition of velocity by substituting the variable k as a shorthand for V/Q and solving for P. We write the equation this way because many classical economists believed that if transactions patterns were stable, k would be constant or relatively stable. In addition, they generally assumed full employment, which meant real output would grow smoothly and would equal potential GDP. Putting these two assumptions together, $k(= V/Q)$ would be near-constant in the short run and a smoothly growing trend in the long run.

What are the implications of the quantity theory? As we can see from the equation, if k were constant, the price level would then move proportionally with the supply of money. A stable money supply

---

[2] The definitional equations have been written with the three-bar identity symbol rather than with the more common two-bar equality symbol. This usage emphasizes that they are "identities"—statements which tell us nothing about reality but which hold true by definition even if the United States experienced a hyperinflation or were in a deep depression.

[3] The velocity of money is closely related to the demand for money. If we rewrite the equation of exchange, we have $M/(PQ) = 1/V$. The left-hand side is the demand for money per unit of GDP. Our earlier discussion of money demand applies equally well to an analysis of velocity.

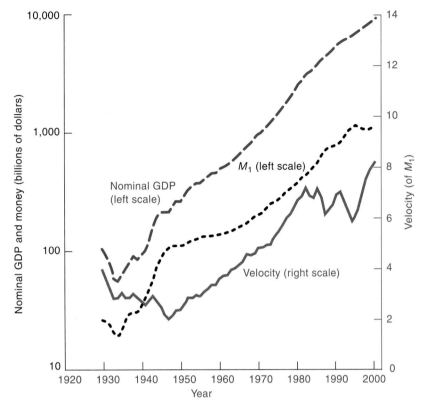

FIGURE 17-3 Velocity and Its Components, 1929–1995

Income velocity is the ratio of nominal GDP to M_1. One of the tenets of monetarism is that V is relatively stable and predictable. How stable does V appear? Can you think of some reasons why V has grown over time? *Hint:* How do interest rates affect velocity? (Source: V constructed by the authors from data from the Federal Reserve Board and the U.S. Department of Commerce.)

would produce stable prices; if the money supply grew rapidly, so would prices. Similarly, if the money supply was multiplied by 10 or 100, the economy would experience galloping inflation or hyperinflation. Indeed, the most vivid demonstrations of the quantity theory of money can be seen in hyperinflations. Turning back to Figure 16-5 (page 341), note how prices rose a billionfold in Weimar Germany after the central bank unleashed the monetary printing presses. This is the quantity theory with a vengeance.

To understand the quantity theory of money, it is essential to recall that money differs fundamentally from ordinary goods like bread or cars. We want bread to eat and cars to drive. But we want money only because it buys us bread or cars. If prices in Russia today are 1000 times what they were a few years ago, it is natural that people will need about 1000 times as much money to buy things as they did before. Here lies the core of the quantity theory of money: the demand for money rises proportionally with the price level.

The quantity theory of money and prices holds that prices move proportionally with the supply of money. Although the quantity theory of money and prices is only a rough approximation, it does help explain why countries with low money growth have moderate inflation while others with rapid money growth find their prices galloping along.

MODERN MONETARISM

Modern monetary economics was developed after World War II by Chicago's Milton Friedman and his numerous colleagues and followers. (You may want to reread the biography of Friedman in Chapter 2.) Under Friedman's leadership, monetarists challenged the Keynesian approach to macroeconomics and emphasized the importance of monetary policy in macroeconomic stabilization. About two decades ago, the monetarist approach branched. One fork continued the older tradition, which we will now describe. The younger offshoot became the influential new classical school, which is analyzed later in this chapter.

The monetarist approach postulates that the growth of money determines nominal GDP in the short run and prices in the long run. This analysis operates in the framework of the quantity theory of money and prices and relies on the analysis of trends in velocity. Monetarists argue that the velocity of money is stable (or, in extreme cases, constant). If correct, this is an important insight, for the quantity equation shows that if V is constant, movements in M will affect PQ (or nominal GDP) proportionally.

The Essence of Monetarism

Like all serious schools of thought, monetarism has differing emphases and degrees. The following points are central to monetarist thinking:

1. *Money-supply growth is the prime systematic determinant of nominal GDP growth.* Monetarism holds that nominal aggregate demand is affected primarily by changes in the money supply. Fiscal policy has no impact upon aggregate demand. This is put neatly in the following oversimplified way: "Only money matters."

   Two propositions are central to monetarist theories. First, as Friedman has stated, "There is an extraordinary empirical stability and regularity to such magnitudes as income velocity that cannot but impress anyone who works extensively with monetary data." Second, many monetarists used to argue that the demand for money is completely insensitive to interest rates.[4]

From the equation of exchange, if velocity V is stable, M will determine nominal GDP. Fiscal policy has no impact because, if V is stable, the only factor that can affect PQ is M. With constant V, there is simply no door by which taxes or government expenditures can enter the stage.

2. *Prices and wages are relatively flexible.* Recall that one of the precepts of Keynesian economics is that prices and wages are "sticky." While generally accepting the view that there is some inertia in wage-price setting, monetarists argue that the Phillips curve is relatively steep even in the short run and insist that the long-run Phillips curve is vertical. In the *AS-AD* framework, monetarists hold that the short-run *AS* curve is quite steep.

   The monetarists put points 1 and 2 together. Because (1) money is the prime determinant of nominal GDP and (2) prices and wages are fairly flexible around potential output, the implication is that money-supply changes have only small and temporary effects on real output. M mainly affects P.

   Accordingly, money can affect both output and prices in the short run. But within a few years, because the economy tends to operate near full employment, money's main impact is on the price level. Fiscal policy affects output and prices negligibly in both the short run and the long run. This is the essence of monetarist doctrine.

3. *The private sector is stable.* Finally, monetarists believe that the private economy, left to its own devices, is not prone to instability. Instead, most fluctuations in nominal GDP result from government action—in particular, changes in the money supply, which depend on the policies followed by the central bank.

Comparison of Monetarist and Keynesian Approaches

How do monetarist views compare with modern Keynesian approaches? In fact, there has been considerable convergence in views between these schools over the last three decades, and the disputes today are ones of emphasis rather than of fundamental beliefs.

We depict the major differences between monetarists and modern Keynesians in Figure 17-4. This figure shows both views in terms of the behavior of aggregate supply and demand. Two major differences stand out.

---

[4] If velocity is constant, then it is invariant to the interest rate. On the other hand, if velocity responds to the interest rate, this allows fiscal policy and other nonmonetary forces to affect output by changing velocity. The proposition that the demand for money is insensitive to the interest rate has fallen out of favor in recent years.

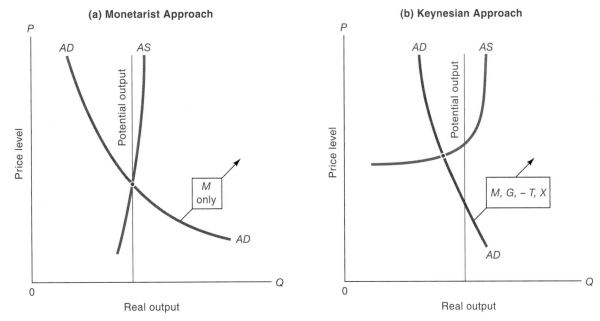

FIGURE 17-4. Comparison of Monetarist and Keynesian Views

In essence, monetarists say, "Only money matters for aggregate demand." Mainstream macro-economists reply, "Money matters, but so does fiscal policy." A second difference revolves around aggregate supply, where Keynesian economists stress that the *AS* curve is relatively flat. If prices and wages are relatively flexible, as monetarists believe, then output will generally be close to its potential.

First, the two schools disagree about the forces that operate on aggregate demand. Monetarists believe that aggregate demand is affected solely (or primarily) by the money supply and that the impact of money on aggregate demand is stable and reliable. They also believe that fiscal policy or autonomous changes in spending, unless accompanied by monetary changes, will have negligible effects upon output and prices.[5]

Keynesian economists, by contrast, hold that the world is more complex. While agreeing that money has an important effect upon aggregate demand, output, and prices, they argue that other factors also matter. Moreover, Keynesians point to conclusive

evidence that *V* rises systematically with interest rates, so keeping *M* constant is not enough to keep nominal or real GDP constant. In one of the most remarkable examples of convergence, both monetarists and Keynesians today tend to believe that stabilization policy in the United States should be conducted primarily through monetary policy.

The second major difference between monetarist and Keynesian economists concerns the behavior of aggregate supply. Keynesian economists emphasize the inertia in prices and wages. Monetarists think that Keynesian economists exaggerate the economy's wage-price stickiness and that the short-run *AS* curve is quite steep—not vertical, perhaps, but much steeper than a Keynesian economist would allow.

Because they hold differing views about the slope of the *AS* curve, Keynesian economists and monetarists disagree on the short-run impact of changes in aggregate demand. Keynesian economists believe that a change in (nominal) demand

---

[5] Note as well that the *AD* curve is drawn as a "rectangular hyperbola" under the monetarist assumptions. Recall that an equation $xy = constant$ describes a rectangular hyperbola in a graph of x and y. For given M and V, the aggregate demand curve is described by $PQ = constant$, so the *AD* curve is a rectangular hyperbola.

will significantly change output with little effect on prices in the short run. Monetarists hold that a shift in demand will primarily end up changing prices rather than quantities.

The essence of monetarism in macroeconomic thinking centers on the importance of money in determining aggregate demand and on the relative flexibility of wages and prices.

The Monetarist Platform: Constant Money Growth

Over the last four decades, monetarism has played a significant role in shaping economic policy. Monetarist economists often espouse free markets and laissez-faire microeconomic policies. But the foremost contribution to macroeconomic policy has been their advocacy of fixed monetary rules in preference to discretionary fiscal and monetary policies.

In principle, a monetarist might recommend using monetary policy to fine-tune the economy. But monetarists have taken a different tack, arguing that the private economy is stable and that the government tends to destabilize the economy. Moreover, monetarists believe that money affects output only after long and variable lags, so the design of effective stabilization policies is a formidable task.

Thus a cardinal part of the monetarist economic philosophy is a **monetary rule:** Optimal monetary policy sets the growth of the money supply at a fixed rate and holds to that rate through all economic conditions.

What is the rationale for this view? Monetarists believe that a fixed growth rate of money (at 3 to 5 percent annually) would eliminate the major source of instability in a modern economy—the capricious and unreliable shifts of monetary policy. If we replaced the Federal Reserve with a computer program that always produces a fixed M-growth rate, there would be no bursts in M growth. With stable velocity, nominal GDP would grow at a stable rate. And if M grew at about the growth rate of potential GDP, the economy would soon attain price stability.

The Monetarist Experiment

Monetarist views gained widespread influence in the late 1970s. In the United States, many thought that Keynesian stabilization policies had failed to contain inflation. When inflation moved up into the double-digit range in 1979, many economists and policymakers believed that monetary policy was the only hope for an effective anti-inflation policy.

In October 1979, the new Chairman of the Federal Reserve, Paul Volcker, launched a fierce counterattack against inflation in what has been called a *monetarist experiment.* In a dramatic change of its operating procedures, the Fed decided to stop focusing on interest rates and instead endeavored to keep bank reserves and the money supply on predetermined growth paths.[6]

The Fed hoped that a strict quantitative approach to monetary management would accomplish two things. First, it would allow interest rates to rise sharply enough to reduce aggregate demand, raise unemployment, and slow wage and price growth through the Phillips-curve mechanism. In addition, some believed that a tough and credible monetary policy would deflate inflationary expectations, particularly in labor contracts, and demonstrate that the high-inflation period was over. Once people's expectations were deflated, the economy could experience a relatively painless reduction in the underlying rate of inflation.

The experiment was clearly successful in slowing the economy and reducing inflation. As a result of the high interest rates induced by slow money growth, interest-sensitive spending slowed. Consequently, real GDP stagnated from 1979 to 1982, and the unemployment rate rose from under 6 percent to a peak of 10 percent in late 1982. Inflation fell sharply. Any lingering doubts about the effectiveness of monetary policy were killed. Money works. Money matters. But of course this is not the same thing as proving that *only* money matters!

But did this experiment validate the monetarist claim that a tough and credible monetary policy could reduce inflation relatively painlessly? Numerous economic studies of this question find that the tough monetarist policy worked—but at a high cost. In terms of unemployment and output losses, the economic sacrifices of the monetarist disinflation policy were about as large, per point of disinflation, as those of anti-inflation policies in earlier periods. Money works, but it does not work miracles. There is no free lunch on the monetarist menu.

---

[6] Recall the discussion of the monetarist experiment in Chapter 10.

The Decline of Monetarism

Paradoxically, just as the monetarist experiment succeeded in rooting inflation out of the American economy—indeed, perhaps *because* of the success —changes in financial markets led to shifts in behavior that undermined the monetarist approach. During and after the monetarist experiment, the behavior of velocity changed sharply. Recall that monetarists hold that velocity is relatively stable and predictable. Given stable velocity, changes in the money supply would get smoothly translated into changes in nominal GDP.

But just as the monetarist doctrine was adopted, velocity became extremely unstable. Figure 17-5 shows the rate of change in velocity over the period 1960–1999. It shows how M_1 velocity was relatively stable in the 1960–1980 period as monetarism became influential. Velocity became much more unstable after 1980, however, as the high interest rates of the 1979–1982 period spurred financial innovations and the spread of interest-bearing checking accounts. Some believe that the instability in velocity was actually produced by the heavy reliance on targeting monetary aggregates during this period.

As the velocity of money became increasingly unstable, the Federal Reserve gradually stopped using it as a guide for monetary policy. By the early 1990s, the Fed had turned primarily to trends in output, inflation, employment, and unemployment for its key indicators of the state of the economy. Indeed,

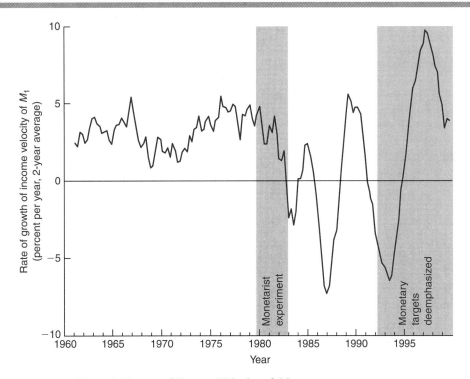

FIGURE 17-5. Rate of Change of Income Velocity of M_1

Monetarists rely upon stable velocity of money to argue for a constant rate of growth of the money supply. Velocity of money was relatively constant until the early 1980s. After that time, an active monetary policy, more volatile interest rates, and financial innovations led to extreme instability of velocity. (Source: Velocity defined as the ratio of GDP to M_1; money supply from the Federal Reserve Board and GDP from the Commerce Department.)

in 1999, the minutes of the Federal Open Market Committee contain not a single mention of the term "velocity" to describe the state of the economy or to explain the reasons for the committee's short-run policy actions.

None of these developments diminishes the importance of money in the conduct of macroeconomic policy. Indeed, monetary policy is currently the major macroeconomic policy tool used for business-cycle management in the United States and Europe. The velocity of money, and not money itself, was demoted among policymakers.

C. NEW CLASSICAL MACROECONOMICS

Existing Keynesian macroeconomic models cannot provide reliable guidance in the formulation of monetary, fiscal, or other types of policy.... [T]here is no hope that minor or even major modifications of these models will lead to significant improvements in their reliability.

Robert E. Lucas Jr. and Thomas J. Sargent, "After Keynesian Macroeconomics"

Although most macroeconomists agree that monetary policy can affect unemployment and output, at least in the short run, a new branch of the classical school challenges the standard approach. This theory, called **new classical macroeconomics,** was developed by Robert Lucas (Chicago), Thomas Sargent (Chicago and Stanford), and Robert Barro (Harvard). This approach is much in the spirit of the classical approach, discussed above, in emphasizing the role of flexible wages and prices, but it adds a new feature, called rational expectations, to explain observations such as the Phillips curve. For his contributions to developing the new classical approach, and particularly the modern view of rational expectations, Robert Lucas was awarded the Nobel Prize in economics in 1996.

FOUNDATIONS

New classical macroeconomics holds that (1) prices and wages are flexible and (2) people use all available information in making decisions. These two postulates are the essence of the new classical approach to macroeconomics.

The first part of the new classical approach draws on the classical assumption of price and wage flexibility. This familiar assumption simply means that prices and wages adjust rapidly to balance supply and demand.

The second and new assumption draws upon modern developments in areas such as statistics and behavior under uncertainty. This hypothesis holds that people form their expectations on the basis of all available information. Under this assumption, the government cannot "fool" the people, for people are well informed and have access to the same information as the government.

We discussed the significance of price and wage flexibility for macroeconomics earlier in this chapter. We now turn to the rational-expectations hypothesis.

Rational Expectations

Expectations are important in economic life. They influence how much investors will spend on investment goods and whether consumers spend or save for the future. But what is a sensible way to treat expectations in economics? New classical macroeconomists answer this question with the **rational-expectations hypothesis.** According to rational expectations, forecasts are unbiased and are based on all available information.[7]

What does all this mean? To begin with, the rational-expectations hypothesis holds that people make unbiased forecasts.[8] A more controversial as-

---

[7] Rational expectations is closely related to the efficient-market hypothesis concerning stock and other asset prices described in Chapter 9.

[8] A forecast is "unbiased" if it contains no systematic forecasting errors. Clearly a forecast cannot always be perfectly accurate—you cannot foresee how a coin flip will come up on a single toss. But you should not commit the statistical sin of *bias* by predicting that a fair coin would come up tails 10 or 90 percent of the time. You would be making an unbiased forecast if you predicted that the coin would come up tails 50 percent of the time or that one of the numbers on a die would, on average, come up one-sixth of the time.

sumption is that people use all available information and economic theory in making decisions. This implies that people understand how the economy works and what the government is doing. Thus, suppose that the government always boosts spending in election years. Rational-expectations theory assumes that people will anticipate this kind of behavior and act accordingly.

The key new assumption in new classical macroeconomics is that because of rational expectations the government cannot fool the people with systematic economic policies.

IMPLICATIONS FOR MACROECONOMICS

The approach of new classical macroeconomics can be fruitfully applied in many areas of economics. Here we concentrate on two implications: the nature of unemployment and the Phillips curve.

Unemployment

Is unemployment voluntary or involuntary? In our discussion in Chapter 15, we defined involuntary unemployment as a situation where qualified workers are unable to find jobs at the going wage. Refresh your memory with a glance back at Figure 15-6, which illustrates both voluntary and involuntary unemployment. Also recall that Keynesian economists think that in recessions a sizable fraction of unemployment is involuntary.

By contrast, new classical economists think that most unemployment is voluntary. In their view, labor markets adjust quickly after shocks as wages change to rebalance supply and demand. Unemployment, in this view, increases because more people are hunting for better jobs during recessions, not because they cannot find jobs. People are unemployed because they have quit their jobs to look for higher-paying ones rather than because wages are too high, as in the case of sticky-wage unemployment.

The Illusory Phillips Curve

One of the major challenges for any macroeconomic theory is to explain the business cycle in a way that is internally consistent and that conforms to the regularities of economic behavior. The classical approach to macroeconomics is attractive because it

conforms well to most of the microeconomics of supply and demand. But the challenge is to explain important features of business cycles, such as the Phillips curve or Okun's Law. If unemployment is high in recessions, it simply won't do to say that people have decided that it is a good year for longer vacations. How would such theories explain the long global depression of the 1930s or the more recent downturns in European economies?

Misperceptions Theories

The cyclical movements of unemployment are the greatest challenge for the new classical macroeconomics. One early approach (developed by Robert Lucas) pointed to *misperceptions* as the key to business cycles. Under this approach, high unemployment arises because workers are confused about economic conditions; workers voluntarily quit their jobs in the hope of getting better ones but are surprised to find themselves in the unemployment office. In the expansion phase of the business cycle, high output and low unemployment occur when people are fooled into working harder because they overestimate real wages.

The analysis can be illustrated using the Phillips curve of inflation theory. A classical economic approach would hold that the short-run Phillips curve is vertical at the equilibrium or natural unemployment rate. This conclusion is the Phillips-curve counterpart of the vertical classical aggregate supply curve in which output is unaffected by aggregate demand.

Where then do the actual downward-sloping Phillips curves come from? They come from a dynamic process in which people are temporarily confused about real wages. This line of reasoning leads to the *new classical Phillips curve*, shown in Figure 17-6 on page 376. Denote the expected rate of change of money wages as W^e, and assume prices rise as fast as wages. If the actual rate of increase of wages (W) is equal to the expected rate (so $W = W^e$), nobody is surprised or fooled, and unemployment is equal to the natural rate. Thus point A represents the no-surprise, natural-rate outcome.

The challenge is to generate points B and C. Each case arises from some kind of economic shock. To generate point B, assume that the Federal Reserve has unexpectedly increased the money supply, leading to an unexpected increase in wages and prices. Workers misperceive economic events, not knowing

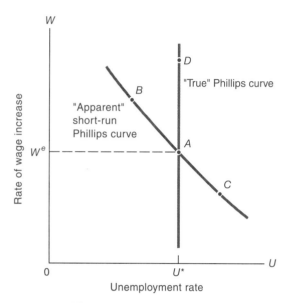

FIGURE 17-6. The New Classical Phillips Curve

According to new classical macroeconomics, the true Phillips curve is vertical. But we may observe an illusory or apparent downward-sloping short-run Phillips curve, drawn through points *B*, *A*, and *C*. Point *B* arises when an inflationary shock raises money wages above their expected levels. Confused workers, thinking that their real wages have increased, work more, and unemployment falls. Thus the economy moves from point *A* to point *B*. This produces what looks like a downward-sloping short-run Phillips curve.

---

that prices are rising as rapidly as wages. They supply more labor, unemployment falls, and the economy goes to point *B*. You should trace through how we can generate point *C* by an unexpected cut in wages and prices.

Surprisingly, if we connect points *B* and *C*, they trace out a downward-sloping line that resembles the Phillips curve. Thus, in new classical macroeconomics, the downward-sloping *apparent* or *illusory short-run Phillips curve* arises from misperceptions of real wages or relative prices.

Real Business Cycles

A closely related approach that has increasingly attracted classical macroeconomists, also relying on rational expectations and competitive markets but emphasizing different mechanisms, is **real-business-**

cycle (RBC) theory. This approach holds that business cycles are primarily due to changes in technology and does not invoke any monetary or demand-side forces.

In the RBC approach, shocks to technology, investment, or labor supply change the potential output of the economy. In other words, they shift a *vertical AS* curve. These supply shocks are transmitted into actual output by the fluctuations of aggregate supply and are completely independent of *AD*. Similarly, movements in the unemployment rate are the result of movements in the nonaccelerating inflation rate of unemployment (NAIRU) due to microeconomic forces such as the intensity of sectoral shocks or to tax and regulatory policies.

The Ricardian View of Fiscal Policy

One of the most influential criticisms of Keynesian macroeconomics was a new view of the role of fiscal policy. This view, known as the **Ricardian view of fiscal policy** and developed by Harvard's Robert Barro, argues that changes in tax rates have no impact upon consumption spending.

The idea is a logical extension of the life-cycle model of consumption introduced in Chapter 6. Under the Ricardian view, individuals are farsighted and form part of a succession of family members, like a dynasty. Parents care not only about their own consumption but also about the well-being of their children; the children, in turn, care about the well-being of their children; and so on. This structure, called "dynastic preferences," implies that the current generation's horizon stretches into the indefinite future through the overlapping concern of each generation about its offspring.

Here is where the surprising result comes: If the government cuts my taxes but leaves expenditures unchanged, this necessarily requires increased borrowing. But, with unchanged expenditures, the government will have to raise taxes to pay the interest on its new borrowing at some point in the future. In the Ricardian view, consumers have rational expectations about future policy, so when a tax cut occurs, they know they must plan for a future tax increase. They therefore will increase their saving by the amount of the tax cut, and consumption will remain unchanged. Moreover, even if the future tax increase comes after their lifetimes, people take into account the well-being of their children; they therefore cut current consumption so that they can increase their bequests to their children to pay the extra taxes.

The net result is that *in the Ricardian view tax changes have no impact upon consumption.* Moreover, government debt is not net debt from the point of view of households because they offset these assets in their mental calculations with the present value of taxes that must be paid to service the debt.

The Ricardian view of debt and deficits has stirred much controversy among macroeconomists. Critics point out that it requires that households be extremely farsighted, planning to give bequests to their children and constantly weighing their own interests against those of their descendants. The chain would be broken were there no children, no bequests, no concern for children, or poor foresight. The empirical evidence to date has not been kind to the Ricardian view, but it is a useful reminder of the logical limitations on fiscal policy.

Efficiency Wages

Another important recent development, fusing elements of both classical and Keynesian economics, is called **efficiency-wage theory.** This approach was developed by Columbia's Edmund Phelps, Joseph Stiglitz (chair of President Clinton's Council of Economic Advisers in 1995–1997), and Janet Yellen (a governor of the Fed and chair of the Clinton Council of Economic Advisers from 1997 to 1999). It explains the rigidity of real wages and the existence of involuntary unemployment in terms of firms' attempts to keep wages above the market-clearing level to increase productivity. According to this theory, higher wages lead to higher productivity because workers are healthier (particularly in poor countries), because workers will have higher morale or be less likely to goof off, because good workers are then less likely to quit and look for new jobs, or because higher wages may attract better workers.

As firms raise their wages to increase productivity, job seekers may be willing to stand in line for these high-paying jobs, thereby producing involuntary wait unemployment. *The startling feature of this theory is that the involuntary unemployment is an equilibrium feature and will not disappear over time.*

This approach was summarized in a thorough analysis by Columbia's Edmund Phelps. Phelps argued that much of the rise in unemployment in industrial countries came because efficiency-wage ele-

ments worsened, increasing the NAIRU. He presented statistical estimates showing that higher payroll taxes, increases in real interest rates, and energy-price shocks were responsible for the rising unemployment of the last two decades. The remedy for the future, according to Phelps, would be to reverse these trends, especially by reducing labor taxes and moving from labor taxes to consumption and value-added taxes.[9]

Supply-Side Economics

In the early 1980s, another loosely organized school joined the debate. This school, known as **supply-side economics,** emphasized incentives and tax cuts as a means of increasing economic growth. Supply-side economics was espoused forcefully by President Reagan in the United States (1981–1989) and by Prime Minister Thatcher in Great Britain (1979–1990).

A first theme of supply-side economics was the key role played by incentives, particularly adequate returns to working, saving, and entrepreneurship. Supply siders pointed to the miracles performed by unfettered free markets and sought to avoid the disincentives due to high tax rates; moreover, they argued that Keynesians, in their excessive concern with demand management, have ignored the impact of tax rates and incentives on aggregate supply.

The other strand of supply-side thinking was its advocacy of large tax cuts. We saw in our analysis of the multiplier model how taxes could affect aggregate demand and output. Supply-side economists argued that the demand-side impacts were overemphasized. Instead, in their view, high taxes lead people to reduce their labor and capital supply. Indeed, some supply-side economists, particularly Arthur Laffer, have suggested that high tax rates might actually lower tax revenues. This *Laffer-curve* proposition holds that high tax rates shrink the tax base because they reduce economic activity. Mainstream economists across the political spectrum, and even some supply-side economists, scoffed at the Laffer proposition that cutting tax rates would increase tax revenues.

To fix what they view as a defective tax system, supply-side economists proposed a radical restructuring of the tax system, through an approach some-

---

[9] See the Phelps reference in this chapter's Further Reading section.

times called "supply-side tax cuts." The philosophy underlying supply-side tax cuts was that the reforms should improve incentives by lowering tax rates on the last dollar of income (or marginal tax rates); that the tax system should be less progressive (that is, it should lower the tax burden on high-income individuals); and that the system should be designed to encourage productivity and supply rather than to manipulate aggregate demand.

After occupying center stage during the 1980s, the supply-side approach to economics gradually faded away after Ronald Reagan left office. While numerous questions remain, economists generally have found that many of the supply-side propositions were not supported by economic experience. Perhaps the most important legacy of the supply-side policies was the high budget deficits and growing government debt. Ironically, these were reversed only when a series of tax increases increased federal revenues enough to produce a budget surplus in 1998.

POLICY IMPLICATIONS

Policy Ineffectiveness

New classical macroeconomics has important policy implications. The most important is the ineffectiveness of systematic fiscal and monetary policies in combating unemployment. Say that the government tended to stimulate the economy whenever elections approached. After a couple of episodes of politically motivated fiscal policy, people would rationally come to expect that behavior. They would say to themselves, "Yes, elections are coming. From past experience, I know that the government always pumps up spending before elections. They can't fool me and get me to work any harder." In terms of the Phillips curve of Figure 17-6, the government tries to stimulate the economy and move it from point *A* to point *B*. But as people anticipate the government's economic stimulation, the economy ends up at point *D*, with unemployment equal to the NAIRU, but with higher inflation.

This is the **policy ineffectiveness theorem** of classical macroeconomics. With rational expectations and flexible prices and wages, anticipated government policy cannot affect real output or unemployment.

The policy ineffectiveness theorem depends on both rational expectations and flexible prices. The assumption of flexible prices implies that the only way that economic policy can affect output and unemployment is by surprising people and causing misperceptions. But you can hardly surprise people if your policies are predictable. Hence predictable policies cannot affect output and unemployment.

The Desirability of Fixed Rules

Earlier, we described the monetarist case for fixed rules. New classical macroeconomics puts this argument on a much firmer footing. An economic policy can be divided into two parts, a predictable part (the "rule") and an unpredictable part ("discretion").

New classical macroeconomists argue that discretion is a snare and a delusion. Policymakers, they contend, cannot forecast the economy any better than the private sector can. Therefore, by the time policymakers act on the news, flexibly moving prices in markets populated by well-informed buyers and sellers have already adapted to the news and reached their efficient supply-and-demand equilibria. There are no further *discretionary* steps the government can take to improve the outcome or prevent the unemployment that is caused by transient misperceptions or real-business-cycle shocks.

Although they cannot make things better, government policies can definitely make things worse. They can generate unpredictable discretionary policies that give misleading economic signals, confuse people, distort their economic behavior, and cause waste. According to new classical macroeconomists, governments should avoid any discretionary macroeconomic policies rather than risk such confusing "noise."

Monetarist Rules and the Lucas Critique

Although the new classical school has shown some pitfalls that face policy-making, it has also levied a devastating argument against a key monetarist assumption. Monetarists believe that the velocity of money has shown a remarkable stability. Thus, they conclude, we can stabilize $MV \equiv PQ \equiv$ nominal GDP by imposing a fixed-money rule.

But the *Lucas critique*, named after Chicago's Robert Lucas, argues that people may change their behavior when policy changes. Just as the apparent short-run Phillips curve might shift when Keynesian governments attempt to manipulate it, so might the apparently constant velocity change if the central bank adopts a fixed-money-growth rule.

This insight was borne out in the period from 1979 to 1982, when the United States conducted the monetarist experiment described in the previous section. Velocity became extremely unstable, and eventually the Fed downplayed the use of monetary aggregates in managing monetary policy. (Recall Figure 17-5 and the discussion of unstable velocity above.)

The Lucas critique is a stern warning that economic behavior can change when policymakers rely too heavily upon past regularities.

STATE OF THE DEBATE

The new classical macroeconomics remains at the center of macroeconomic controversies. In one sense, the debate is a replay of the earlier arguments between Keynes and the classical economists. As in earlier debates, one of the key issues revolves around the extent of price and wage flexibility. Keynesian economists point to much evidence suggesting that prices and particularly wages move slowly in response to shocks, and few economists believe that labor markets are in constant supply-demand equilibrium. When the assumption of perfectly flexible wages and prices is abandoned, policy will regain its power to affect the real economy in the short run.

Additionally, critics point to some of the counterfactual implications of new classical macroeconomics. The theory holds that business-cycle fluctuations are "equilibrium" situations where firms and workers are confused by price or money shocks. But can misperceptions about wages and prices really explain deep depressions and persistent bouts of unemployment? Did it really take people a full decade to learn how hard times were in the Great Depression? And can Europeans be unaware of the depressed job markets that have persisted in their countries since 1990?

Finally, how can we reconcile the theoretical prediction that cyclical unemployment is produced when workers quit to look for better jobs with the evidence showing that the fraction of job losers rises sharply in recessions (see Figure 15-8, page 330)? Be-

cause most classical theories have similar implausible implications, many mainstream economists are skeptical of the usefulness of new classical approaches for understanding business-cycle movements in output, employment, and goods prices.

A New Synthesis?

After two decades of digesting the new classical approach to macroeconomics, elements of a synthesis of old and new theories are beginning to appear. Economists now realize they must pay careful attention to expectations. A useful distinction is between the adaptive (or "backward-looking") approach and the rational (or "forward-looking") approach. The adaptive assumption holds that people form their expectations simply and mechanically on the basis of past information; the forward-looking or rational approach was described above. The importance of forward-looking expectations is crucial to understanding behavior, particularly in competitive auction markets like those in the financial sector.

Some macroeconomists have begun to fuse the new classical view of expectations with the Keynesian view of product and labor markets. This synthesis is embodied in macroeconomic models that assume (1) labor and goods markets display inflexible wages and prices, (2) the prices and quantities in financial auction markets adjust rapidly to economic shocks and expectations, and (3) the expectations in auction markets are formed in a forward-looking way.

A careful survey compares the behavior of macroeconomic models that incorporate different approaches to new classical macroeconomics, focusing particularly on expectations. One salient feature is that forward-looking models tend to have large "jumps" or discontinuous changes in interest rates, stock prices, or exchange rates when major changes in policy or external events occur. For example, an election of an expansionist president or prime minister might lead people to think that inflation is on the horizon. This perception could result in a sharp jump in interest rates along with a fall in the stock market and exchange rates. Or, when the central bank unexpectedly changes its stance on inflation, as occurred in the United States in February 1994, markets may get jittery and drive up long-term interest rates in anticipation of further interest-rate increases that may follow. The new classical prediction of "jumpy" prices replicates one realistic feature of auction markets and thus suggests where forward-looking expectations might be important in the real world.

Figure 17-7 compares another difference, the expenditure multipliers of four forward-looking models and of seven adaptive-expectations models. Note that the multipliers of the forward-looking models are significantly smaller than those of the adaptive models.

The smaller multipliers in the forward-looking models arise because of faster reactions in financial markets. One reason is that, after a fiscal expansion, interest rates generally rise more rapidly in forward-looking models because forward-looking market participants predict a future expansion of output after an increase in government spending. This higher ex-

pected future output tends to increase interest rates today, and investment therefore tends to decline rapidly in forward-looking models. In addition, as interest rates rise quickly in response to a fiscal stimulus in forward-looking models, the flexible and forward-looking exchange rate of the dollar tends to jump upward. A rise in the exchange rate of the dollar leads to a reduction in net exports and tends to reduce the size of the fiscal stimulus.

The new classical approach to macroeconomics has brought many fruitful insights. Most important, it reminds us that the economy is populated by intelligent information processors who react to and often anticipate policy. This reaction and counter-reaction can actually change the way the economy behaves.

* * *

AN INTERIM APPRAISAL

This chapter has surveyed the debates that have divided macroeconomists in recent years. After hearing the evidence, a jury of impartial economists might conclude as follows:

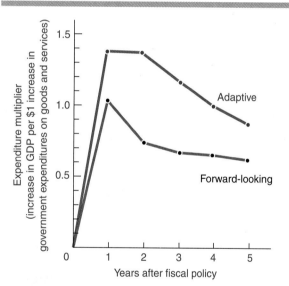

FIGURE 17-7. Comparison of Multipliers in Forward-Looking and Adaptive Models

What is the difference in the expenditure multipliers of models that are adaptive (backward-looking) and forward-looking (rational)? Because interest rates crowd out domestic investment and exchange rates affect net exports, adjustment takes place more rapidly in forward-looking models. Forward-looking expenditure multipliers are considerably smaller than those in adaptive models. [Source: Ralph C. Bryant, Gerald Holtham, and Peter Hooper, "Consensus and Diversity in the Model Simulations," in Ralph C. Bryant et al., eds., *Empirical Macroeconomics for Interdependent Economies* (Brookings Institution, Washington, D.C., 1988), Fig. 3-33.]

1. *Long-run economic growth.* Most macroeconomists agree that in the long run it is the potential output or capacity growth that determines the trend in living standards, real wages, and real incomes. Furthermore, potential output depends upon the quality and quantity of inputs like labor and capital as well as on the technology, entrepreneurship, and management skills in an economy. To improve long-run economic growth, economic policy must increase the growth of inputs or lead to improvements in efficiency and technology.

2. *Short-run output and employment.* In the short run, the picture is more controversial. Output and employment in the short run are determined by the interaction of aggregate supply and demand. The weight of evidence is that, at least for a few years, movements in aggregate demand (whether influenced by fiscal and monetary policies or by exogenous factors) can definitely influence the cyclical movements in output and employment. This implies that monetary and fiscal policies have the potential to stabilize business cycles.

Most economists today would call upon the Federal Reserve to take the lead in stabilization policy.

3. *Unemployment and inflation.* The preponderance of the evidence indicates that inflation is inertial and is affected by the pressure of demand in labor and product markets. If unemployment is pushed above the NAIRU, inflation tends to moderate, while high output and employment tend to lead to rising inflation. But the inflation-unemployment trade-off is unstable over time and space, so managing inflation is a complicated process. Moreover, there does not appear to be a permanent trade-off, so countries cannot buy permanently lower unemployment by allowing high inflation to persist.

Beyond these three major conclusions that emerge from our review of the warring factions in macroeconomics, there are many fine points and continuing controversies that must be left to advanced treatises. In the next chapter, we put these conclusions to work so that we can understand the major policy issues of today.

SUMMARY

A. Classical Stirrings and Keynesian Revolution

1. Classical economists relied upon Say's Law of Markets, which holds that "supply creates its own demand." In modern language, the classical approach means that flexible wages and prices quickly erase any excess supply or demand and quickly reestablish full employment and full utilization of capacity. In a classical system, macroeconomic policy has no role to play in stabilizing the real economy, although it will still determine the path of prices.

2. The Keynesian revolution postulated inflexibility of prices and wages, so output and unemployment are determined by the interaction of supply and demand forces. The Keynesian *AS* curve is upward-sloping rather than classically vertical, and monetary or fiscal policies therefore affect both prices and real output. There is no automatic self-correcting price mechanism, and the economy can therefore experience prolonged periods of depression or inflation.

3. In the modern Keynesian view, monetary and fiscal policies can substitute for flexible wages and prices, stimulating the economy during recessions and slowing aggregate demand during booms to forestall inflationary tendencies.

B. The Monetarist Approach

4. Monetarism holds that the money supply is the primary determinant of short-run movements in both real and nominal GDP as well as of long-run movements in nominal GDP.

5. Monetarism relies upon the analysis of trends in the velocity of money to understand the impact of money on the economy. The income velocity of circulation of money (V) is defined as the ratio of the dollar GDP flow to the stock of M:

$$V \equiv \frac{PQ}{M} \equiv \frac{GDP}{M}$$

While V is definitely not a constant—if only because it rises with interest rates—monetarists count on its movements being regular and predictable.

6. From velocity's definition comes the quantity theory of prices:

$$P \equiv kM \text{ where } k \equiv \frac{V}{Q}$$

The quantity theory of prices regards P as almost strictly proportional to M. This view is useful for understanding hyperinflations and certain long-term trends, but it should not be taken literally.

7. The monetarist school holds to three major propositions: (*a*) The growth of the money supply is the major systematic determinant of nominal GDP growth; (*b*) prices and wages are relatively flexible; and (*c*) the private economy is stable. These propositions suggest that macroeconomic fluctuations arise primarily from erratic money-supply growth.

8. Monetarism is generally associated with a laissez-faire and anti-big-government political philosophy. Because of a desire to avoid active government and a belief in the inherent stability of the private sector, monetarists often propose that the money supply grow at a fixed rate of 3 to 5 percent annually. Some monetarists believe that this will produce steady growth with stable prices in the long run.

9. The Federal Reserve conducted a full-scale monetarist experiment from 1979 to 1982. The experience during this period convinced remaining skeptics that money is a powerful determinant of aggregate demand and that most of the short-run effects of money changes are on output rather than on prices. However, as suggested by the Lucas critique, velocity may become quite unstable when a monetarist approach is followed.

C. New Classical Macroeconomics

10. New classical macroeconomics rests on two fundamental hypotheses: People's expectations are formed efficiently and rationally, and prices and wages are flexible. It follows from these assumptions in a new classical economy that unemployment is voluntary. Further, the Phillips curve is vertical in the short run, even though it may appear otherwise. The theory of the real business cycle points to supply-side technological disturbances and labor market shifts as the clue to business-cycle fluctuations.

11. The policy ineffectiveness theorem holds that predictable government policies cannot affect real output and unemployment. The new classical theory states that, while we may *observe* a downward-sloping short-run Phillips curve, we cannot *exploit* the slope for the purposes of lowering unemployment. If economic policymakers systematically attempt to increase output and decrease unemployment, people will soon come to understand and to anticipate the policy. Fixed policy rules will produce better economic outcomes.

12. Critics of new classical macroeconomics argue that prices and wages are inflexible in the short run. And the predictions—particularly that business cycles are caused by misperceptions and that cyclical unemployment comes when confused people quit their jobs—seem farfetched as an explanation of serious downturns, like those of the 1930s or early 1980s in the United States and of the 1990s in Europe.

13. Review the interim appraisal for the current mainstream synthesis of the warring schools of macroeconomics.

CONCEPTS FOR REVIEW

Classical Economists vs. Keynes

flexible vs. sticky wages and prices
Say's Law of Markets
alternative views of aggregate supply

Velocity and Monetarism

equation of exchange: $MV \equiv PQ$
velocity of circulation of money:
$\quad V \equiv PQ/M$

quantity theory of money and
$\quad$ prices: $P \equiv kM$
1979–1982 monetarist experiment

New Classical Macroeconomics

rational (forward-looking) expectations, adaptive (backward-looking) expectations
policy ineffectiveness theorem

real business cycle, efficiency wages
tenets of supply-side economics
key assumptions: rational expectations and flexible prices and wages
Lucas critique
Ricardian view of fiscal policy

FURTHER READING AND INTERNET WEBSITES

Further Reading

The quote from Alfred Pigou is from *The Theory of Unemployment* (London, Macmillan, 1933). The classic monetary history of the United States by Milton Friedman and Anna Jacobson Schwartz describes a monetarist interpretation of history. See their *Monetary History of the United States 1867–1960* (Princeton University Press, Princeton, N.J., 1963).

Many of the foundations of new classical economics were developed by Robert Lucas and republished in *Studies in Business-Cycle Theory* (MIT Press, Cambridge, Mass., 1990). A textbook presenting a classical point of view is Robert J. Barro, *Macroeconomics*, 5th ed. (MIT Press, Cambridge, Mass., 1997). Modern efficiency-wage theory is presented

in Edmund Phelps, *Structural Slumps: The Modern Equilibrium Theory of Unemployment, Interest, and Assets* (Harvard University Press, Cambridge, Mass., 1994).

A nontechnical review of the troops of the warring schools is given by Paul Krugman, *Peddling Prosperity: Economic Sense and Nonsense in the Age of Diminished Expectations* (Norton, New York, 1994).

Websites

Real-business-cycle theory has its own website at ideas. uqam.ca/QMRBC/index.html.

The Nobel Prize citations of Milton Friedman and Robert Lucas (one of the major pioneers of the new classical macroeconomics) can be found at www.nobel.se/laureates.

QUESTIONS FOR DISCUSSION

1. Monetarists say, "Only money matters." Keynesians answer, "Money matters, but other things, like fiscal policy, matter too." Explain and evaluate each position. Could you disagree with monetarists and still believe that monetary policy should be used to counter recessions? Explain.

2. Assume that nominal GDP was $1000 billion in year 0 while the GDP deflator was 1 in year 0. Furthermore, the money supply in years 0, 1, 2, 3 and 4 was (in billions) $50, $52, $55, $58 and $60.
   a. Give the level of nominal output in years 1, 2, 3, and 4 according to the strict quantity theory of money.
   b. If there was no growth in potential output and the level of the money supply was following a preannounced path, what would the level of real GDP be according to new classical macroeconomics?

3. If, in boom times, we printed and spent $100 trillion in new greenbacks, what would happen to prices? Is there some truth, then, to the quantity theory? What might happen to prices if M were increased 1 percent in a depression? Compare the two cases.

4. A Keynesian economist might recommend a tax cut to revive the economy. What would be the effect on the AD curve, on price, and on real output? Relate your answer to the monetarist theory. (*Hint*: What happens to velocity?)

5. Define income velocity (V). For the data in Table 17-1, calculate the annual growth rate of the money supply and the level and rate of change of velocity. Also draw or plot on a computer graphs of the variables.

6. What would monetarists, Keynesians, and new classical macroeconomists predict to be the impacts of each of the following on the course of prices, output, and employment (in each case, hold tax rates and the money supply constant unless specifically mentioned):
   a. A large tax cut
   b. A large increase in the money supply
   c. A wave of innovations that increase potential output by 10 percent
   d. A burst of exports

7. In the discussion of the demand for money, and in the demand-for-money schedule in Figure 10-4 it was shown that the demand for money would be sensitive to interest rates. What would be the impact of higher interest rates on velocity for a given level of nominal GDP? What are the implications of interest-sensitive demand for money on monetarist arguments that rely upon constant velocity of money?

8. State and explain Say's Law of Markets. Starting from a macroeconomic equilibrium, assume that potential output increases but aggregate demand is unchanged. Using a graphical extension of Figure 17-1, show how supply creates its own demand. Describe the process in words.

9. **Advanced problem** (on rational expectations): Consider the effect of rational expectations on consumption behavior.
   a. Say the government proposes a temporary tax cut of $20 billion, lasting for a year. Consumers with adaptive expectations might assume that their disposable incomes would be $20 billion higher every year. What would be the impact on consumption spending and GDP in the simple multiplier model of Chapter 8?
   b. Next suppose that consumers have rational expectations. They rationally forecast that the tax cut is for only 1 year. Being "life-cycle" consumers, they recognize that their average lifetime incomes will increase (say) only $2 billion per year, not $20 billion per year. What would be the reaction of such consumers? Analyze, then, the impact of rational expectations on the effectiveness of temporary tax cuts.
   c. Finally, assume that consumers behave according to the Ricardian view. What would be the impact of the tax cut on saving and consumption. Explain the difference between the different models.

Year	Nominal GDP ($, billion)	Money supply, M_1 ($, billion, lagged 12 months)
1981	3131.4	408.9
1982	3259.2	436.5
1983	3535.0	474.5
1984	3932.8	521.2
1985	4213.0	522.1
1986	4452.9	620.1
1987	4742.5	724.7
1988	5108.3	750.4
1989	5489.1	787.5
1990	5803.3	794.8

TABLE 17-1.

The U.S. economy has changed enormously over the last 50 years. Farmers are an endangered part of the population. Factory work has declined, and manufacturing involves more people at computers than on production lines. Taxes are higher, and government has become a permanent part of the economic landscape. Technology has revolutionized daily life. Advanced telecommunications systems enable businesses to control their operations across the country and around the world, and ever-more-powerful computers have eliminated many of the repetitive tasks which used to employ so many people. Goods and money flow easily across national boundaries.

Yet, after a half-century of change, the central goals of macroeconomic policy remain the same: good jobs, low unemployment, rising productivity and real incomes, and low and stable inflation. The challenge is to find a set of policies which can achieve these objectives as we enter the new millennium.

This chapter uses the tools of macroeconomics to examine some of today's major policy issues. We begin with an assessment of the consequences of government deficits and debt on economic activity and discuss the surprising turn toward surplus in the United States.

We then analyze controversies involving short-run economic stabilization, including current questions on the roles of monetary policy and fiscal policy. Should the government stop trying to smooth out business cycles and, instead, rely on fixed rules rather than discretion? We conclude with an analysis of the nagging worries posed by the slowdown in productivity and real wage growth over the last two decades and inquire into the policies that countries can pursue to improve their productivity and growth performance.

CHAPTER

18

Policies for Growth and Stability

The task of economic stabilization requires keeping the economy from straying too far above or below the path of steady high employment. One way lies inflation, and the other lies recession. Flexible and vigilant fiscal and monetary policy will allow us to hold the narrow middle course.

President John F. Kennedy (1962)

Productivity isn't everything, but in the long run it is almost everything.

Paul Krugman (1990)

A. THE ECONOMIC CONSEQUENCES OF THE GOVERNMENT DEBT

Like a monster rising from the deep, the budget deficit seemed to swallow up the nation's fiscal resources and terrify the populace in the 1980s and early 1990s. From $40 billion in 1979, the budget deficit grew to a peak of $290 billion in 1992. Then, after a long period of fiscal austerity, the deficit monster vanished from sight, and starting in 1998 the federal budget turned to a surplus.

How did the budget deficit get so high? Why did it turn to a surplus? What should the government do with the growing surplus? These important questions will be addressed in the present section. We will see that the popular concern with deficits has a firm economic foundation. A high deficit and government debt during periods of full employment carry serious consequences, including reduced national saving and investment and slower long-run economic growth.

Trends and Definitions

For the first two centuries after the American Revolution, the federal government of the United States generally balanced its fiscal budget. Heavy military spending during wartime was financed by borrowing, so the government debt—the total amount owed by the government—tended to soar in wartime. In peacetime, the government would pay off some of its debt, and the debt burden would shrink.

This pattern changed during the 1980s, when the Reagan administration's supply-side policies launched a major tax cut and defense buildup without an offsetting decrease in civilian spending. With less revenue and more spending, the government had to borrow to fill the gap. The federal budget deficit grew to over $200 billion a year by the mid-1980s, and the government debt during the Reagan-Bush years (1981–1992) increased from $660 billion to $3 trillion.

Governments use budgets to plan and control their fiscal affairs. A **budget** shows, for a given year, the planned expenditures of government programs and the expected revenues from tax systems. The budget typically contains a list of specific programs (education, welfare, defense, etc.), as well as tax sources (individual income tax, social-insurance taxes, etc.).

A **budget surplus** occurs when all taxes and other revenues exceed government expenditures for a year. A **budget deficit** is incurred when expenditures exceed taxes. When revenues and expenditures are equal during a given period—a rare event on the federal level—the government has a **balanced budget.**

When the government incurs a budget deficit, it must borrow from the public to pay its bills. To borrow, the government issues bonds, which are IOUs that promise to pay money in the future. The **government debt** (sometimes called the *public debt*) consists of the total or accumulated borrowings by the government; it is the total dollar value of government bonds.

It is useful to distinguish between the total debt and the net debt. The *net debt*, also called the *debt held by the public*, excludes debt held by the government itself. Net debt is owned by households, banks, businesses, foreigners, and other nonfederal entities. The *gross debt* equals the net debt plus bonds owned by the government, primarily by the social security trust fund. The social security trust fund is running a large surplus, so the difference between these two concepts is growing rapidly today.

Debt versus deficit

People often confuse the debt with the deficit. You can remember the difference as follows: The government debt is the *stock* of liabilities of the government. The deficit is a *flow* of new debt incurred when the government spends more than it raises in taxes. For example, when the government ran a deficit of $100 billion during 1995, it added that amount to the stock of government debt. By contrast, when the government enjoyed a surplus of $200 billion in 1999, this reduced the government debt by that amount.

GOVERNMENT BUDGET POLICY

The government budget serves two major economic functions. First, it is a device by which the government can set national priorities, allocating national output among private and public consumption and investment and providing incentives to increase or reduce output in particular sectors. From a macroeconomic point of view, it is through fiscal policy that the budget affects the key macroeconomic goals. More precisely, by **fiscal policy** we mean the setting of taxes and public expenditures to help dampen the swings of the business cycle and contribute to the maintenance of a growing, high-employment economy, free from high or volatile inflation.

Some early enthusiasts of the Keynesian approach believed that fiscal policy was like a knob they could turn to control or "fine-tune" the pace of the economy. A bigger budget deficit meant more stimulus for aggregate demand, which could lower unemployment and pull the economy out of recession. A budget surplus could slow down an overheated economy and dampen the threat of inflation.

Today, few believe that the business cycle can be quite so easily eliminated. Some 60 years after Keynes, recessions and inflations are still with us, and fiscal policy works better in theory than in practice. Moreover, monetary policy has become the preferred tool for moderating business-cycle swings. Still, whenever unemployment rises, there is usually strong public pressure for the government to boost spending. In this section, we will review the major ways in which government can employ fiscal policy,

and we will examine the practical shortcomings that have become apparent.

Actual, Structural, and Cyclical Budgets

Modern public finance distinguishes between structural and cyclical deficits. The idea is simple. The *structural* part of the budget is active—determined by discretionary policies such as those covering tax rates, public-works or education spending, or the size of defense purchases. In contrast, the *cyclical* part of the budget is determined passively by the state of the business cycle, that is, by the extent to which national income and output are high or low. The precise definitions follow:

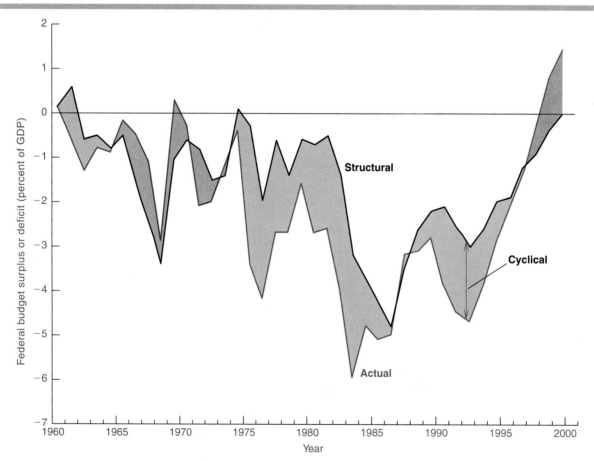

FIGURE 18-1. Actual, Structural, and Cyclical Budget Deficits

The blue line shows the actual budget deficit or surplus (as a percentage of potential GDP). The black curve depicts the structural component. The difference between the actual and the structural deficits or surpluses is the cyclical deficit or surplus. (Source: Congressional Budget Office.)

The **actual budget** records the actual dollar expenditures, revenues, and deficits in a given period.

The **structural budget** calculates what government revenues, expenditures, and deficits would be if the economy were operating at potential output.

The **cyclical budget** is the difference between the actual budget and the structural budget. It measures the impact of the business cycle on the budget, taking into account the effect of the cycle on revenues, expenditures, and the deficit.

The actual, structural, and cyclical budget deficits as a share of GDP are shown in Figure 18-1. The distinction between the actual and the structural budgets is important for policymakers who want to distinguish between long-term or trend budget changes and short-term changes that are primarily driven by the business cycle. Structural spending and revenues consist of the discretionary programs enacted by the legislature; cyclical spending and deficits consist of the taxes and spending that react automatically to the state of the economy.

The nation's saving and investment balance is primarily affected by the structural budget. Efforts to change government saving should focus on the structural budget because no durable change comes simply from increased taxes due to an economic boom.

Two Decades of Deficits

From 1980 until 1998, the most perplexing macro-economic controversies have revolved around the mounting federal budget deficit. Even though Congress passed laws attempting to stop the rising tide of red ink, the deficit continued throughout this period and the government debt climbed. Deficits were not new to the American economy, but a deficit of such magnitude during peacetime was unique, unusual, and disturbing.

Why did the deficit get so large? Republicans blamed the growing deficit on 50 years of Democratic "tax-and-spend" policies. Democrats counterattacked that Republican presidents were responsible and pointed to supply-side policies as the culprit in the mounting government debt.

What are the facts? No simple analysis can resolve this complex question, but Table 18-1 can help illuminate the major trends. This table lists the major federal budget categories and their shares

Federal budget component	Percent of GDP			
	1940	**1960**	**1980**	**2000**
Revenues	**6.7**	**17.9**	**18.9**	**20.2**
Individual and corporate income taxes	2.2	12.0	11.3	11.8
Social insurance	1.9	2.8	5.8	6.7
Other	2.8	3.0	1.8	1.7
Expenditures	**9.8**	**17.8**	**21.6**	**18.5**
Defense and international affairs	1.9	9.9	5.4	3.2
Health	0.1	0.2	2.0	3.7
Income Security	1.6	1.4	3.2	2.6
Social Security	0.0	2.2	4.3	4.2
Net Interest	0.9	1.3	1.9	2.3
Other	5.5	2.8	4.8	2.6
Surplus (+) or deficit (−)	**−3.0**	**0.1**	**−2.7**	**1.7**

TABLE 18-1. Federal Budget Trends, 1940–2000

The federal share of the economy grew sharply from 1940 to 1960 as the United States took an active military role in world affairs during hot and cold wars. After 1960, the federal share stabilized, but the composition of spending moved from military to health and other social spending. By 2000, the spending share was down and the government ran a significant budget surplus. [Source: Data are for fiscal years and come from the Department of the Treasury, Office of Management and Budget, and Department of Commerce.]

in GDP for the period from 1940 to 2000. The key features behind this change were the following:

- The share of federal spending and taxes grew sharply from 1940 to 1960 primarily because of the expansion of military spending. This growth was financed by a significant increase in individual and corporate taxation.
- From 1960 to 1980, the tax share stabilized, but this period marked the "New Society" programs for health, income security, and an expanded social security. As a result, the expenditure share grew sharply. The share of federal revenues in GDP stabilized over this period. The policy mix led to a budget deficit in 1980, and deficits continued for almost two decades.
- The period from 1980 to 2000 was a period in which both major political parties began to run against "big government." The supply-side tax cuts of the early 1980s produced a string of surging deficits. Public concern over the high deficits led to a series of controversial deficit-reduction measures, the most important being the 1990 and 1993 budget acts of the Bush and Clinton administrations. These put tight caps on expenditure growth and raised taxes, especially on high-income households. As a result, although health spending grew sharply, most other expenditure categories declined as a share of GDP. The net impact—as shown in the last column of Table 18-1—was that by 2000 the federal budget had turned to surplus. The government was therefore contributing positively to national saving.

ECONOMIC IMPACT OF DEFICITS AND DEBT

What are the various economic problems created by large deficits? What is the relationship between private saving and public saving? What are the opportunities afforded by a large budget surplus? Answering these questions is an important task for macroeconomics. At one extreme, we must avoid the customary practice of assuming that public deficits are bad because private debtors are punished. On the other hand, we must recognize the genuine problems associated with excessive government deficits and the advantages that come from a lower government debt.

Historical Trends

Long-run data for the United States appear in the figure on the front endpaper of this text, which shows the ratio of net federal debt to GDP since 1789. Notice how wars drove up the ratio of debt to GDP, while rapid output growth with roughly balanced budgets in peacetime normally reduced the ratio of debt to GDP. From 1980 until 1998, the historical pattern changed and government deficits climbed in a way not seen in earlier periods of peace and prosperity.

Most other industrialized countries today find themselves with rapidly growing government debt. Table 18-2 compares the United States with seven other large industrial countries. Japan's debt-GDP ratio has climbed sharply over the last decade because of aggressive fiscal policy and a prolonged recession. Japan's debt rating has been downgraded, and many economists worry that Japan is caught in a vicious cycle of high debt leading to high debt service which in turn increases the growth of the debt. The reversal of fiscal fortune in the United States, with a budget surplus and a shrinking debt-GDP ratio, is unique among major industrial countries today.

	Ratio of government debt to gross domestic product (%)			
	1970	1980	1990	1999
Italy	38	58	104	118
Japan	11	48	61	105
Sweden	31	43	43	68
France	—	30	40	65
Germany	18	30	42	63
United States	45	40	61	59
United Kingdom	78	55	39	54
South Korea	24	16	8	14

TABLE 18-2. Government Debt in Major Industrial Countries

Slow growth and rising entitlement programs led to rising deficits and a growing public debt in most industrial countries in the 1980s and 1990s. Only the United States managed to reduce its debt-GDP ratio in the last decade. (Source: OECD, *Analytical Database*, available on the web at http://www.oecd.org/puma/stats. Note these figures are gross debt and include holdings of government trust funds.)

To understand how government debt and deficits affect the economy, it is useful to analyze the short-run and the long-run outcomes separately. In the short run, the stock of government debt is given, and the deficit may affect the business cycle and the saving-investment balance. The short-run impact of budget deficits upon the economy is known as "crowding out," which we address first. In the long run, which is usefully analyzed as a full-employment economy, the government debt affects current capital formation and the consumption of future generations. This issue, known as the "burden of the debt," is considered at the end of this section.

THE CROWDING-OUT CONTROVERSY

Politicians and business leaders often argue that government spending undermines the economy, saying in effect, "Government spending saps our nation's vitality. When the government spends people's money on entitlement programs, these funds simply crowd out private investment."

This argument—that government spending reduces private investment—invokes the **crowding-out hypothesis.** In its extreme form, this hypothesis suggests that when the government purchases $100 in goods and services, private investment and other interest-sensitive spending falls by $100.

Crowding Out and the Money Market

What is the crowding-out mechanism? Suppose that the government spends money on school lunches or fuel for its ships. Our multiplier model says that in the short run, with no change in interest or exchange rates, GDP will rise by 2 or 3 times the increase in G. The same argument applies (with a smaller multiplier) to reductions in taxes.

This analysis is oversimplified because it must take into account the reaction of financial markets. As output and inflation rise, their increase is likely to provoke a monetary tightening, increasing interest rates and leading to an appreciation of the foreign exchange rate if the country has a floating exchange rate. The rising interest rates and appreciated currency will tend to choke off or "crowd out" domestic and foreign investment.[1] We showed the way a fiscal deficit would lead to lower domestic investment and lower net exports in Chapter 14's analysis of saving and investment (see particularly Figures 14-7 and 14-8).

An increase in the *structural* deficit, coming through tax cuts or higher government spending, will tend to raise interest rates, reduce domestic investment, and increase the trade deficit.

But be warned: Crowding out applies only to structural deficits. If the cyclical deficit rises because of a recession, the logic of crowding out simply does not apply. A recession causes a *decline* in the demand for money and leads to *lower* interest rates; the monetary authority tends to *loosen* monetary policy in a recession. The fact that crowding out does not apply in recessions is a reminder that there is no automatic link between deficits and investment.

Empirical Evidence

Does actual experience corroborate crowding-out theories? It depends on which period you are looking at. During the 1960s, fiscal expansions appear to have encouraged investment, partly because there were ample unutilized resources and partly because the Federal Reserve allowed the economy to expand without raising interest rates.

In the 1980s, by contrast, higher government deficits definitely did appear to discourage investment. The actual pattern of saving and investment for three periods before, during, and after the supply-side experiment of the 1980s is given in Table 18-3 on page 389. These data show that households and businesses reduced their saving as a share of GDP in the 1980s and early 1990s. This reduction was surprising because they were faced with lower tax rates and higher posttax real returns on saving.

Note that private domestic investment in housing and business plant and equipment fell as a share of GDP as the deficit increased—business investment was being crowded out by the higher interest rates of that period. Moreover, a significant part of the impact came in a decline in net foreign investment. As

---

[1] Recall that tight money leads to reduced spending in interest-sensitive sectors such as business investment, housing, consumption spending on consumer durables, net exports, and capital items of state and local governments. In the discussion that follows, we will examine the impact on investment, but keep in mind that the other components of spending are just as important.

	National Saving and Investment (percent of GDP)		
	Active fiscal stabilization policies (1961–1981)	Supply-side policies and high deficits (1982–1996)	Emerging government side surplus (1997–1999)
Net national saving	8.5%	4.1%	4.8%
Personal	5.7%	5.4%	3.2%
Business	4.7%	3.3%	1.7%
Government	−2.0%	−4.6%	−0.1%
Net national investment	8.5%	4.1%	4.8%
Private domestic(residential and business)	8.1%	5.6%	7.2%
Net foreign investment	0.4%	−1.5%	−2.4%

TABLE 18-3. Higher Government Deficit Produced Surprising Results

The increase in deficits of the 1980s provided a laboratory for different macroeconomic theories. During the supply-side years, the government deficits (or dissaving) grew sharply. Public dissaving was reinforced by lower personal and business saving. The impact was seen on both domestic and foreign investment. With the turn toward a balanced budget in the late 1990s, investment began to recover. (Source: U.S. Department of Commerce.)

we emphasized in our survey of open-economy macroeconomics, countries with flexible exchange rates and mobile capital will see some of their excess saving spill over into world financial markets. Without this inflow of foreign financial capital, the budget deficits would have crowded out even more private investment.

The events of the last two decades—particularly the decline in investment that accompanied the rising government deficit—lend support to the argument that structural government budget deficits do indeed crowd out private investment. But this link is not an absolute law which holds for all situations. The connection between deficit spending and investment depends on so many factors—including saving behavior, expectations, foreign exchange rates and foreign trade, financial markets, and monetary policy—that the exact impact of fiscal-policy changes is difficult to predict.

GOVERNMENT DEBT AND ECONOMIC GROWTH

We turn now from the short-run impact of government deficits to ask how the government debt affects living standards over the long run. To answer this, we need to analyze the difficulties of servicing a large external debt, the inefficiencies of levying taxes to pay interest on the debt, and the impact of the debt on capital accumulation.

External vs. Internal Debt

The first distinction to be made is between an internal debt and an external debt. *Internal debt* is owed by a nation to its own citizens. Many argue that an internal debt poses no burden because "we owe it all to ourselves." While this statement is oversimplified, it does represent a genuine insight. If each citizen owned $10,000 of government bonds and were liable for the taxes to service just that debt, it would make no sense to think of debt as a heavy load of rocks that each citizen must carry. People simply owe the debt to themselves.

An *external debt* is owed by a nation to foreigners. This debt does involve a net subtraction from the resources available to people in the debtor nation. In the 1980s, many nations experienced severe economic hardships after they incurred large external debts. They were forced to export more than they imported—to run trade surpluses—in order to service their external debts, that is, to pay the interest and principal on their past borrowings. Countries like Brazil and Mexico need to set aside one-fourth to one-third of their export earnings to service their external debts. The debt-service burden on an external debt represents a reduction in the consumption possibilities of a nation.

In the 1990s, the United States joined the list of debtor countries when large external deficits transformed America from a creditor nation into a debtor nation. By 2000, the United States owed more than $1500 billion to foreigners. While that seems like a large sum, it pales next to an annual output of $9000 billion. Still, the United States will need to export many billions of dollars more in aircraft, food, and other goods and services than it imports to pay the interest on its foreign loans.

Efficiency Losses from Taxation

An internal debt requires payments of interest to bondholders, and taxes must be levied for this purpose. But even if the same people were taxed to pay the same amounts they receive in interest, there would still be the *distorting effects on incentives* that are inescapably present in the case of any taxes. Taxing Paula's interest income or wages to pay Paula interest would introduce microeconomic distortions. Paula might work less and save less; either of these outcomes must be reckoned as a distortion of efficiency and well-being.

Displacement of Capital

Perhaps the most serious consequence of a large public debt is that it displaces capital from the nation's stock of private wealth. As a result, the pace of economic growth slows and future living standards will decline.

What is the mechanism by which debt affects capital? Recall from our earlier discussion that people accumulate wealth for a variety of purposes, such as retirement, education, and housing. We can separate the assets people hold into two groups: (1) government debt and (2) capital like houses and financial assets like corporate stocks that represent ownership of the stock of private capital.

The effect of government debt is that people will accumulate government debt instead of private capital, and the nation's private capital stock will be displaced by public debt.

To illustrate this point, suppose that people desire to hold exactly 1000 units of wealth for retirement and other purposes. As the government debt

increases, people's holdings of other assets will be reduced dollar for dollar. This occurs because as the government sells its bonds, other assets must be reduced, since total desired wealth holdings are fixed. But these other assets ultimately represent the stock of private capital; stocks, bonds, and mortgages are the counterparts of factories, equipment, and houses. In this example, if the government debt goes up 100 units, we would see that people's holdings of capital and other private assets fall by 100 units. This is the case of 100 percent displacement (which is the long-run analog of 100 percent crowding out).

Full displacement is unlikely to hold in practice. The higher debt may increase interest rates and stimulate domestic saving. In addition, the country may borrow abroad rather than reduce its domestic capital stock (as America did in the 1980s). The exact amount of capital displacement will depend on the conditions of production and on the saving behavior of domestic households and foreigners.

A Geometric Analysis. The process by which the stock of capital is displaced in the long run is illustrated in Figure 18-2 on page 392. The left panel shows the supply and demand for capital as a function of the real interest rate or return on capital. As interest rates rise, firms demand less capital, while individuals may want to supply more. The equilibrium shown is for a capital stock of 4000 units with a real interest rate of 4 percent.

Now say that the government debt rises from 0 to 1000—because of war, recession, supply-side fiscal policies, or some other reason. The impact of the increase in debt can be seen in the right-hand diagram of Figure 18-2. This figure shows the 1000-unit increase in debt as a shift in the supply-of-capital (or *SS*) curve. As depicted, the households' supply-of-capital schedule shifts 1000 units to the left, to *S'S'*.

We represent an increase in government debt as a leftward shift in the households' supply-of-capital schedule. Note that, because the *SS* curve represents the amount of private capital that people willingly hold at each interest rate, the capital holdings are equal to the total wealth holdings minus the holdings of government debt. Since the amount of government debt (or assets other than capital) rises by 1000, the amount of private capital that people can

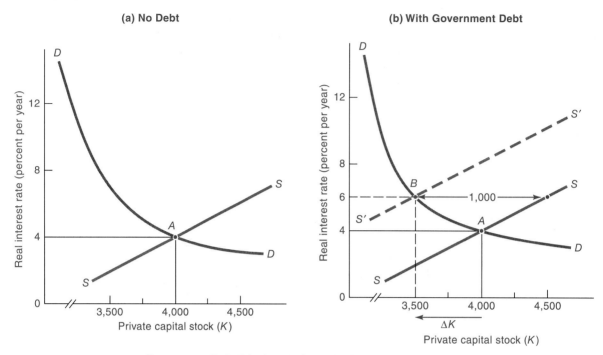

FIGURE 18-2. Government Debt Displaces Private Capital

Firms demand capital, while households supply capital by saving in private and public assets. The demand curve is the downward-sloping business demand for K, while the supply curve is the upward-sloping household supply of wealth.

Before-debt case in **(a)** shows the equilibrium without government debt: K is 4000 and the real interest rate is 4 percent.

After-debt case in **(b)** shows the impact of 1000 units of government debt. Debt shifts the net supply of K to the left by the 1000 units of the government debt. The new equilibrium arises northwest along the demand-for-K curve, moving from point A to point B. The interest rate is higher, firms are discouraged from holding K, and the capital stock falls.

buy after they own the 1000 units of government debt is 1000 less than total wealth at each interest rate. Therefore, if SS represents the total wealth held by people, $S'S'$ (equal to SS less 1000) represents the total amount of capital held by people. In short, after 1000 units of government debt are sold, the new supply-of-capital schedule is $S'S'$.

As the supply of capital dries up—with national saving going into government bonds rather than into housing or into companies' stocks and bonds—the market equilibrium moves northwest along the demand-for-K curve. Interest rates rise. Firms slow their purchases of new factories, trucks, and computers.

In the illustrative new long-run equilibrium, the capital stock falls from 4000 to 3500. Thus, in this example, 1000 units of government debt have dis-

placed 500 units of private capital. Such a reduction has significant economic effects, of course. With less capital, potential output, wages, and the nation's income are lower than they would otherwise be.

The diagrams in Figure 18-2 are illustrative. Economists do not have a firm estimate of the magnitude of the displacement effect. Looking at historical trends, the best evidence suggests that domestic capital is partially displaced by government debt but that some of the impact comes in higher foreign debt.

Debt and Growth

Considering all the effects of government debt on the economy, a large public debt is likely to reduce long-run economic growth. Figure 18-3 illustrates this connection. Say that an economy were to operate over time with no debt. According to the principles of economic growth outlined in Chapter 11, the capital stock and potential output would follow the hypothetical paths indicated by the solid black lines in Figure 18-3.

Next consider a situation with a growing national debt. As the debt accumulates over time, more and more capital is displaced, as shown by the dashed blue line for the capital stock in the bottom of Figure 18-3. As taxes are raised to pay interest on the debt, inefficiencies further lower output. Also, an increase in external debt lowers national income and raises the fraction of national output that has to be set aside for servicing the external debt. Taking all the effects together, output and consumption will grow more slowly than they would have had there been no large government debt and deficit, as can be seen by comparing the top lines in Figure 18-3.

What is the impact of a budget surplus and a *declining* government debt? Here, the argument works

in the other direction. A lower national debt means that more of national wealth is put into capital rather than government bonds. A higher capital stock increases the growth of output and increases wages and consumption per person.

This is the major point about the long-run impact of a large government debt on economic growth: A large government debt tends to reduce the growth in potential output because it displaces private capital, increases the inefficiency from taxation, and forces a nation to reduce consumption to service its foreign borrowing.

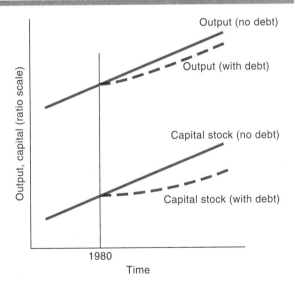

FIGURE 18-3. Impact of Government Debt on Economic Growth

The solid lines show the paths of capital and output if the government balances its books and has no debt. When the government incurs a debt, private capital is reduced. The dashed lines illustrate the impact on capital and output of the higher government debt.

The great budget debate of 1999–2000

Suppose that the nation discovered a trillion-dollar windfall. What would you do with the money? You might decide to improve education or the environment. Or build a high-speed rail network. Alternatively, you might think it important to raise the incomes of the poor or set up a fund for developing countries. Some would use the money to bolster social security and improve health care for the elderly. You might decide that the money belongs to the taxpayers and give a large tax cut. Or you might simply retain the funds and pay down the government debt.

Surprisingly, this is no academic question. It is exactly the happy dilemma that the United States faced in 2000. A decade of tight rules on spending and tax reductions, several tax increases (particularly those in 1990 and 1993), and a booming economy produced a sea change in the budget outlook. In early 2000, the Congressional Budget Office projected that the cumulative federal budget surplus over the next decade (with current programs growing with inflation) would be $3.1 trillion. This total was comprised of $2.3 trillion of social security surplus and $0.8 trillion of on-budget (non-social-security) surplus.

The emerging surplus provoked a fierce debate about the fiscal priorities of the nation. President Clinton and Democratic presidential candidate Al Gore proposed retaining most of the surplus and eventually eliminating the government debt. Republican presidential candidate George W. Bush countered with proposals to eliminate the $0.8 trillion on-budget surplus through large tax cuts.

What was the debate really about? In economics, we should always look behind the dollar numbers and analyze the impact on *real* variables. One important difference is whether *how*, *what*, and *for whom* would be determined by the federal government or by the private sector. Running a budget surplus gives the government discretion regarding whether to use the tax revenues for new programs such as expanded health care, more generous entitlement programs, or antimissile defense systems. Cutting taxes, by contrast, puts the decisions about resource allocation in the hands of individuals. The resources might go for food, clothing, and a used car if the tax cuts go to low-income people—or for yachts, BMWs, and vacation homes if the tax cuts go to the rich.

Second, the outcome of the debate has important implications for national saving. Recall that national saving has two components, private and public saving. Suppose that the government gives $1 trillion of tax cuts. Other things equal, this would reduce government saving by $1 trillion. But because the marginal propensity to save from tax cuts is likely to be far below unity, private saving is likely to increase by only a small fraction of the $1 trillion. Overall national saving over the decade might decline by $800 or $900 billion under the tax-cut approach.

A third difference involves the distribution of income. The large tax cuts are targeted primarily to the high-income households. For example, the congressional tax proposal in 1999 would cut taxes for the top 1 percent of households by an average of $54,000 per year. By contrast, households in the bottom 60 percent were to get an average tax cut of $175. And the lowest-income groups (who have no income taxes to be cut) would get no tax cuts at all.

Is the great fiscal debate of 1999–2000 simply sound and fury, signifying nothing? Absolutely not. There are big economic stakes in the outcome, affecting national saving, the distribution of income, and the division of national output between public and private uses.

✳ B. STABILIZING THE ECONOMY

While the United States has enjoyed a period of economic growth along with low unemployment and inflation that are the envy of the world, other nations have not been so fortunate. Europe and Japan were mired in a decade-long slump with high unemployment rates. East Asian economies saw their miracle turn temporarily to debacle by financial market tur-

moil. Russia's market economy has seen little more than inflation and declining output since 1990. While inflation has been stilled in most countries, few can forget the runaway price increases of the 1970s and early 1980s. No one can predict where or when a virulent business cycle will next strike.

It is therefore still critical to find policies which strike the proper balance between too high unemployment and unacceptable inflation. We have seen that the path of output and prices is determined by the interaction of aggregate supply and demand. *But policies to stabilize the business cycle must operate primarily through their impact on aggregate demand.* In other words, the primary way that government can counter recessions or slow inflation is by using its monetary and fiscal levers to affect the growth in aggregate demand.

These observations leave open two crucial questions: What is the best division of labor between monetary and fiscal policies for stabilizing the economy? Is it possible that monetary- and fiscal-policy makers do more harm than good by actively trying to stabilize the economy?

THE INTERACTION OF MONETARY AND FISCAL POLICIES

For large economies like the United States or Euroland, the best combination of monetary and fiscal policies will depend upon two factors: the need for demand management and the desired fiscal-monetary mix.

Demand Management

The top consideration in business-cycle management is the overall state of the economy and the need to adjust aggregate demand. When the economy is stagnating, fiscal and monetary policies can be used to stimulate the economy and promote economic recovery. When inflation threatens, monetary and fiscal policies can help slow the economy and dampen inflationary fires. These are examples of *demand management*, which refers to the active use of monetary and fiscal policies to affect the level of aggregate demand.

Suppose, for example, that the economy is entering a severe recession. Output is low relative to its potential. What can the government do to revive the lagging economy? It can increase aggregate demand by raising money growth or by boosting government spending or both. After the economy has responded to the monetary and fiscal stimulus, output growth and employment will increase and unemployment will fall. (What steps could the government take during inflationary periods?)

Let's review the relative strengths and weaknesses of monetary policy and fiscal policy.

Does Fiscal Policy Matter? Over the last three decades, fiscal policy has lost much of its attractiveness to policymakers and macroeconomists as a stabilization tool. In the early stages of the Keynesian revolution, macroeconomists emphasized fiscal policy as the most powerful and balanced remedy for demand management. Gradually, shortcomings of fiscal policy became apparent. The shortcomings stem from timing, politics, and macroeconomic theory.

One concern is that the time span between cyclical shock and effective response is long and growing longer. To begin with, it takes time before economists can recognize that a cyclical turning point has been reached. Then, in addition to the recognition lag, there is a response lag while the president decides what to do and Congress debates and passes the measure. Finally, even when taxation or spending is changed, there is an effectiveness lag before the economy responds.

While recognition, response, and effectiveness lags are present for both monetary policy and fiscal policy, the response lag for fiscal policy can be so long that it becomes useless for stabilization. The response lag in the United States has increased over the last few years as congressional budget procedures have become more complex, with almost a year's delay between presidential recommendations and final congressional action.

Another problem with fiscal policy is that it is easier to cut taxes than to raise them, and easier to raise spending than to cut it. During the 1960s, Congress was enthusiastic about passing the Kennedy-Johnson tax cuts. Two years later, when the Vietnam war expansion ignited inflationary pressures, contractionary policies were called for. But President Johnson and Congress delayed acting until inflation had already risen. Similarly, President Bush had to struggle mightily to get a relatively small tax increase through Congress as part of the 1990 deficit-reduction package, and even that small step badly damaged his standing within the Republican party and helped contribute to his defeat in 1992. President Clinton waged a mighty struggle in 1993 to reduce the deficit by raising taxes—this took nearly a year to accomplish and angered many whose taxes were increased.

In addition, even when put into action speedily, fiscal policy may not work as well as macroeconomists once thought. For example, many economists used to advocate temporary tax cuts during recessions and temporary tax increases when the economy becomes overheated and inflation looms. However, studies indicate that consumers realize that the tax changes are temporary and thus they do not change their spending patterns very much, since the temporary tax changes have little effect upon their permanent or lifetime incomes.

Effectiveness of Monetary Policy. Compared to fiscal policy, monetary policy operates much more indirectly on the economy. Whereas an expansive fiscal policy actually buys goods and services or puts income into the hands of consumers and businesses, monetary policy affects spending by altering interest rates, credit conditions, exchange rates, and asset prices. In the early years of the Keynesian revolution, some macroeconomists were skeptical about the effectiveness of monetary policy—some said "monetary policy was like pushing on a string." Over the last two decades, however, these concerns have been put to rest as the Federal Reserve has shown itself quite capable of slowing down, or speeding up, the economy.

The Federal Reserve is much better placed to conduct stabilization policy than are the fiscal-policy makers. Its staff of professional economists can recognize cyclical movements as well as anyone. And it can move quickly when the need arises. For example, on January 28, 1994, the Commerce Department announced that the economy was growing surprisingly rapidly at year-end 1993; only 1 week later, the Fed moved to slow down the economy by raising interest rates for the first time in half a decade. This episode stands in stark comparison to the 2-year tightening of fiscal policy during the Vietnam war. A key ingredient in Fed policy is its independence, and the Fed has proved that it can stand the heat of making politically unpopular decisions when they are necessary to slow inflation. Most important, as we noted above, is that from the point of view of demand management, monetary policy can do, or undo, anything that fiscal policy can accomplish.

Of course, to stabilize the economy, the central bank has to apply the right amount of monetary stimulus or restraint. Recent estimates of the quantitative impacts of monetary policy on the economy in different macroeconomic models are shown in Table 18-4. This study estimated the impact on the U.S. economy of increasing the money supply by 4 percent above the money supply of a baseline projection, with the money supply remaining 4 percent higher than the baseline for the indefinite future.

The results show a substantial initial response of real GDP to an increase in the money supply. By contrast, the increase in the price level builds up slowly over time, with less than one-fifth of the increase in nominal GDP in year 1 coming in prices. At the end of 5 years, according to the model simulations, most of the increase in nominal GDP shows up in prices rather than in real output. The models confirm the Keynesian prediction of a sluggish reaction of wages and prices to changes in the money supply but also indicate that the economy behaves increasingly like a classical economy in the long run.

How might the monetary authorities use these statistical results? Suppose, for example, that the Federal Reserve forecasts that real GDP will grow by 4 percent in the coming year; further, the Fed believes that a growth rate of 3 percent is the most that the economy can sustain without the risk of an unacceptable inflation. What change in the money supply would be needed to slow the rate of growth of real GDP by 1 percentage point? The answer is that the money-supply growth would have to be slowed by somewhat more than 4 percent to produce a 1-percentage-point decrease in real GDP.

Of course, the usefulness of such calculations depends on whether the statistical correlations which held in the past will still be true in the future. Monetary economists stress that the impacts of monetary policy are uncertain and may change over time as the economy evolves. For example, as the economy becomes increasingly exposed to foreign trade, the impact of monetary policy on net exports becomes more important at the same time that the impact upon housing and other domestic sectors is mitigated by financial deregulation.

We can summarize the current state of fiscal and monetary policy as follows:

	Money, Output, and Prices				
	Response of Affected Variable to 4 Percent Change in Money Supply (% change in affected variable from baseline path)				
Affected variable	Year 1	Year 2	Year 3	Year 4	Year 5
Real GDP	0.9	1.1	1.2	1.1	0.8
Consumer prices	0.2	0.7	1.1	1.5	1.8
Nominal GDP	1.1	1.8	2.3	2.5	2.7

TABLE 18-4. Estimated Effect of Monetary Policy on Output and Prices

A survey of eight econometric models examined the impact of monetary policy. In each case, a baseline run of the model was "shocked" by adding 4 percent to the money supply in year 1 and holding the money supply 4 percent above the baseline in all years thereafter. Estimates in the table show the average calculated response of the models.

Note the strong initial response of real output to a monetary-policy shift, with the peak response coming in year 3. The impact upon the price level builds up gradually because of the inertial response of price and wage behavior. Note that the impact on nominal GDP is less than proportional to the money growth even after 5 years. [Source: Ralph C. Bryant, Peter Hooper, and Gerald Holtham, "Consensus and Diversity in the Model Simulations," in Ralph Bryant et al., eds., *Empirical Macroeconomics for Interdependent Economies* (Brookings Institution, Washington, D.C., 1988).]

Stabilization policy is today primarily handled by the Federal Reserve in its monetary policy. Few doubt the effectiveness of monetary policy in determining aggregate demand, although the impacts have long and variable lags. Fiscal policy is currently little used for stabilization policy in the United States because of the long lags and political difficulties of successful implementation.

The Fiscal-Monetary Mix

The second factor affecting fiscal and monetary policy is the desired fiscal-monetary mix, which refers to the relative strength of fiscal and monetary policies and their effect on different sectors of the economy. A **change in the fiscal-monetary mix** is an approach which tightens one policy while easing the other in such a way that aggregate demand and therefore total output remain constant. The basic idea is that fiscal policy and monetary policy are substitutes in demand management. But while alternative combinations of monetary and fiscal policies can be used to stabilize the economy, they have different impacts upon the *composition* of output. By varying the mix of taxes, government spending, and monetary policy, the government can change the fraction of GDP devoted to business investment, consumption, net exports, and government purchases of goods and services.

Effect of Changing the Mix of Monetary and Fiscal Policies. To understand the impact of changing the fiscal-monetary mix, let's examine a specific set of policies. Suppose that the federal government reduces the federal budget deficit by $100 billion and that higher monetary growth exactly offsets the contractionary impact of the fiscal steps. This package is similar to the deficit-reduction measures enacted in 1993 along with a monetary policy that offset the drag from higher taxes and lower government spending.

We can estimate the impact using a quantitative economic model, such as the sophisticated DRI long-term model of the United States.[2] Table 18-5 shows

---

[2] This model was designed by the eminent Harvard macroeconomist Otto Eckstein. It contains a standard Keynesian structure for determining aggregate demand, and monetary and fiscal policies are both effective. Aggregate supply has endogenous potential output (determined by capital, labor, R&D, and energy), while prices and wages follow a Phillips-curve-type reaction to unemployment.

Sector		Change in output ($, billion, 1999 prices)
Investment sectors		132
Gross private domestic investment	48	
Housing	18	
Business fixed investment	30	
Net exports	83	
Consumption sectors		−106
Government purchases of goods and services	−68	
Personal consumption expenditures	−38	
Memoranda:		
Change in real GDP		26
Change in federal deficit		−100

TABLE 18-5. Changing the Fiscal-Monetary Mix

What would be the impact of a change in the fiscal-monetary mix for the United States? This simulation assumes that the federal deficit is cut by $100 billion through higher personal taxes and lower federal nondefense expenditures while the Federal Reserve uses monetary policy to keep unemployment on an unchanged trajectory. The simulation takes the average of the changes from the baseline path over the period 1990–1999. (Source: Simulation using the DRI model of the U.S. economy.)

the results of this experiment. Two interesting features emerge: First, the simulation indicates that a change in the fiscal-monetary mix would indeed change the composition of real GDP. While the deficit declines by $100 billion, business investment goes up by $30 billion. Investment in housing, too, increases as interest rates fall. At the same time, personal consumption declines, freeing up resources for investment. This simulation shows how a change in the fiscal-monetary mix might change the composition of output.

The simulation contains one particularly interesting result: Net exports rise far more than either housing or business fixed investment. This occurs because of the strong depreciation of the dollar which results from the lower interest rates. While this result is clearly sensitive to the reaction of financial markets and exchange rates to the deficit-reduction package, it suggests that some of the popular analyses of the impact of such a package may be misleading. Many analysts have argued that a deficit-reduction package would have a significant impact upon domestic business investment and upon productivity. However, to the extent that lower deficits mainly help net exports and housing, the nation is likely to experience relatively little increase in productivity growth. According to the DRI model, cutting the budget deficit by $100 billion will raise the growth rate of potential output from 2.3 percent per year to 2.6 percent per year over a 10-year period. Perhaps the small size of the payoff explains why it is so hard to muster the political will to cut the deficit.

Alternative mixes in practice

The fiscal-monetary mix has been sharply debated in American economic policy. Here are two major alternatives.

Loose fiscal–tight monetary policy. Assume that the economy begins in an initial situation with low inflation and output at its potential. A new president decides that it is necessary to increase defense spending sharply without raising taxes. By itself, this would increase the government deficit and increase aggregate demand. In this situation, the Federal Reserve would be inclined to tighten monetary policy to prevent the economy from overheating. The result would be higher real interest rates and an appreciation of the dollar exchange rate. The higher interest rates would squeeze investment while the appreciated dollar would reduce net exports. The net effect therefore would be that the higher defense spending would crowd out domestic investment and net exports. This policy was the one followed by the United States in the early 1980s.

Tight fiscal–loose monetary policy. Suppose that a country becomes concerned about a low national saving rate and desires to raise investment so as to increase the capital stock and boost the growth rate of potential output. To implement this approach, the country could raise consumption taxes and squeeze transfer payments so as to reduce disposable income and thereby lower consumption (tight fiscal policy). This would be accompanied by an expansionary monetary policy to lower interest rates and raise investment, lower the exchange rate, and expand net exports. This course would encourage private investment by increasing public saving. This was the economic philosophy of President Clinton which was embodied in the 1993 Budget Act and led to the budget surplus at decade's end.

RULES VS. DISCRETION

We have seen that fiscal and monetary policy can *in principle* stabilize the economy. Many economists believe that countries should *in practice* take steps to shave the peaks and troughs off the business cycle. Other economists are skeptical of our ability to forecast cycles and take the right steps at the right time for the right reasons; this second group concludes that government cannot be trusted to make good economic policy, so its freedom to act should be strictly limited.

For example, fiscal conservatives worry that it's easier for Congress to increase spending and cut taxes than to do the reverse. That means it's easy to increase the budget deficit during recessions but much harder to turn around and shrink the deficit again during booms, as a countercyclical fiscal policy would require. For that reason, conservatives have made several attempts to limit the ability of Congress to appropriate new funds or increase the deficit.

At the same time, monetary conservatives would like to tie the hands of central banks and force them to target money growth or inflation. This is designed to eliminate the uncertainty about policy and enhance the credibility of the central bank as an inflation fighter.

At the most general level, the debate about "rules versus discretion" boils down to whether the advantages of flexibility in decision making are outweighed by the uncertainties and potential abuse in unconstrained decisions. Those who believe that the economy is inherently unstable and complex and that governments generally make wise decisions are comfortable with giving policymakers wide discretion to react aggressively to stabilize the economy. Those who believe that the government is the major destabilizing force in the economy and that policymakers are prone to selfishness and misjudgments favor tying the hands of the fiscal and monetary authorities.

Budget Constraints on Legislatures?

As deficits began to grow during the 1980s, many people argued that Congress lacks the self-control to curb excessive spending and a burgeoning government debt. One proposal put forth by conservatives was a *constitutional amendment requiring a balanced budget.* Such an amendment was criticized by economists because it would make it difficult to use fiscal policy to fight recessions. To date, none of the proposed constitutional amendments has passed Congress.

Instead, Congress legislated a series of *budgetary rules to limit spending and tax reductions.* The first attempt was the Gramm-Rudman Act in 1985, which required that the deficit be reduced by a specified dollar amount each year and that the budget be balanced by 1991. If Congress was unable to meet the quantitative Gramm-Rudman target, expenditures would be automatically cut across the board.

The results fell far short of the congressional mandate. The Gramm-Rudman bill went into effect in late 1985, but the ambitious deficit targets were not met. The bill was amended in 1987, but the controls on the deficits proved unworkable and ineffective. In 1990 the targets were replaced by a set of spending limitations. These limitations were incorporated in the 1993 Budget Act and imposed stringent restrictions on the growth of discretionary programs (which include defense and nonentitlement civilian programs like education, science, and general government). The 1993 and 1997 Budget Acts required that discretionary programs decline by almost one-quarter in real terms over the 1993–1998 period.

The other important change introduced in the 1990 amendments and included in the 1993 and 1997 acts is a *pay-as-you-go budget rule.* This requires that Congress find the revenues to pay for any new spending program. The pay-as-you-go provision imposes a budget constraint on Congress, requiring that the costs of new programs be explicitly recognized either through higher taxes or lower expenditures in other areas.

What has been the impact of the budget constraints on Congress? Fiscal experts believe that the budget rules produced significant fiscal discipline, helped reduce the deficit over the 1990s, and eventually produced the surplus after 1998. But a rule legislated by Congress can be changed by Congress when circumstances change. When the deficit changed to surplus and the urgency of deficit reduction disappeared, policymakers began to evade the earlier budget caps with gimmicks like "emergency spending" for predictable items like the census. The role of budgetary rules in an era of surpluses is still an open issue.

Monetary Rules for the Fed?

In our discussion of monetarism in Chapter 17, we laid out the case for fixed policy rules. The traditional argument for fixed rules is that the private economy is relatively stable and active policy-making is likely to destabilize rather than stabilize the economy. Moreover, to the extent that a central bank under the thumb of the government may be tempted to expand the economy before elections and to create a political business cycle, fixed rules will tie its hands. In addition, modern macroeconomists point to the value of being able to commit to action in advance. If the central bank can commit to follow a noninflationary rule, people's expectations will adapt to this rule and inflationary expectations may be dampened.

Until recently, advocates of fixed monetary rules (particularly monetarists) recommended a fixed nominal growth of, say, 4 percent per year in the money supply. With a constant velocity and output growing at 3 percent a year, this would lead to steady annual inflation of 1 percent. But as the data on velocity show (see particularly Figure 17-3 in the previous chapter), velocity was never terribly stable and it has become much more unstable in the last two decades. Given the apparent instability of velocity, it would be hard to claim that a fixed monetary rule could have actually stabilized output during this period.

Targeting Inflation. Central banks have adopted many different approaches to monetary policy in recent decades. These range from highly discretionary approaches which coordinate monetary and fiscal policies under the direction of the government to highly mechanized approaches with fixed targets for the money supply or bank reserves.

One of the most important new developments in the last decade has been the trend toward inflation targeting in many countries. **Inflation targeting** is the announcement of official target ranges for the inflation rate along with an explicit statement that low and stable inflation is the overriding goal of monetary policy. Inflation targeting in hard or soft varieties has been adopted in recent years by many industrialized countries, including Canada, Britain, Australia, and New Zealand. Moreover, the treaty authorizing the new European central bank mandates that price stability be the ECB's primary objective, although it is not formally required to target inflation.[3] A number of economists and legislators are advocating this approach for the United States as well.

Inflation targeting involves the following:

- The government or central bank announces that monetary policy will strive to keep inflation near a numerically specified target.
- The target usually involves a range, such as 1 to 3 percent per year, rather than literal price stability. Generally, the government targets an inertial or core inflation rate such as the CPI excluding volatile food and energy prices and excluding price-raising taxes.
- Inflation is the primary or overriding target of policy in the medium run and long run. However, countries always make room for short-run stabilization objectives, particularly with respect to output, unemployment, financial stability, and the foreign exchange rate. These short-run ob-

jectives recognize that supply shocks can affect output and unemployment and that it may be desirable to have temporary departures from the inflation target to avoid excessive unemployment or output losses.

Proponents of inflation targeting point to many advantages. If there is no long-run trade-off between unemployment and inflation, a sensible inflation target is that rate which maximizes the efficiency of the price system. Our analysis of inflation in Chapter 16 suggested that a low and stable rate of inflation would promote efficiency and minimize unnecessary redistribution of income and wealth. In addition, some economists believe that a strong and credible commitment to low and stable inflation will improve the short-run inflation-unemployment trade-off. Finally, an explicit inflation target would increase the transparency of monetary policy.

Inflation targeting is a compromise between rule-based approaches and purely discretionary policies. The main disadvantage would come if the central bank began to rely too rigidly on the inflation rule and thereby allowed excessive unemployment in periods of severe supply shocks. Critics recall how the rigid rules of the 1979–1982 monetarist experiment led to highly volatile interest rates and a deep recession. Skeptics worry that the economy is too complex to be governed by fixed rules. Arguing by analogy, they ask whether one would advocate a fixed speed limit for cars or an automatic pilot for aircraft in all kinds of weather and emergencies.

Perhaps the most powerful argument against rigid targeting for the United States is the success of discretionary monetary policy over the last decade. Under the leadership of Alan Greenspan (Chairman of the Federal Reserve since 1987), monetary policy has helped produce the longest economic expansion in American history. Greenspan was clearly committed to keeping inflation low, yet policy was marked by discretionary policy changes when the need arose. The success of this period testifies to the wisdom of wise and disinterested discretionary policies aimed at clearly articulated goals.

The debate over rules versus discretion is one of the oldest debates of political economy. There is no single best approach for all times and places. Indeed, the dilemma reflects the difficulty that democratic societies have in making trade-offs between short-run

---

[3] European monetary union was discussed in Chapter 14.

policies intended to attract political support and long-run policies designed to enhance the general welfare.

✳ C. ECONOMIC PROSPECTS IN THE NEW CENTURY

THE HIGH STAKES IN ECONOMIC GROWTH

As we begin the twenty-first century, it is good to recall the striking words of MIT's Paul Krugman:

> Productivity isn't everything, but in the long run it is almost everything. A country's ability to improve its living standards over time depends almost entirely on its ability to raise its output per worker.[4]

Promoting a high and growing standard of living for the nation's residents is one of the fundamental goals of macroeconomic policy. Because the current *level* of real income reflects the history of the *growth* of productivity, we can measure the relative success of past growth by examining the per capita GDPs of different countries. A brief list is presented in Table 18-6. This table compares incomes by using *purchasing-power parity* exchange rates that measure the purchasing power of (or quantity of goods and services that can be bought by) different national currencies. Evidently, the United States has been successful in its past growth performance. Perhaps the most worri-

---

[4] See this chapter's Further Reading section.

Country	Per capita GNP, 1998
United States	$29,340
Japan	23,180
France	22,320
South Korea	12,270
Mexico	8,190
Russia	3,950
China	3,220
India	1,700
Nigeria	820

TABLE 18-6. Current Incomes Represent Effects of Past Growth

Those countries that have grown most rapidly in the past have reached the highest levels of per capita GNP. (Source: World Bank; data adjusted using purchasing-power parity exchange rates.)

some issue in recent years is that the growth in living standards has not been widely shared among the population.

In discussing growth rates, the numbers often seem tiny. A successful policy might increase a country's growth rate by only 1 percentage point per year (recall the estimated impact of the deficit-reduction package in the last section). But over long periods, this makes a big difference. Table 18-7 shows how tiny acorns grow into mighty oaks as small growth-rate differences cumulate and compound over time. A 4 percent-per-year growth difference leads to a 50-fold difference in income levels over a century.

How can public policy boost economic growth? As we emphasized in our chapters on economic

Growth rate (% per year)	Real Income per Capita (constant prices)		
	2000	2050	2100
0	$24,000	$ 24,000	$ 24,000
1	24,000	39,471	64,916
2	24,000	64,598	173,872
4	24,000	170,560	1,212,118

TABLE 18-7. Small Differences in Growth Rates Compound into Large Income Differentials over the Decades

growth, the growth of output per worker and of living standards depends upon a country's saving rate and upon its technological advance. Issues involving saving were discussed earlier in this chapter. Technological change includes not only new products and processes but also improvements in management as well as entrepreneurship and the spirit of enterprise—and we close our discussion with this topic.

THE SPIRIT OF ENTERPRISE

Although investment is a central factor in economic growth, technological advance is perhaps even more important. If we took the workers in 1900 and doubled or tripled their capital in mules, saddles, picks, and cow paths, their productivity still could not come close to that of today's workers using huge tractors, superhighways, and supercomputers.

Fostering Technological Advance

While it is easy to see how technological advance promotes growth in productivity and living standards, governments cannot simply command people to think longer or be smarter. Centrally planned socialist countries used "sticks" to promote science, technology, and innovation, but their efforts failed because neither the institutions nor the "carrots" were present to encourage both innovation and introduction of new technologies. Governments often promote rapid technological change best when they set a sound economic and legal framework with strong intellectual property rights and then allow great economic freedom within that framework. *Free markets in labor, capital, products, and ideas have proved to be the most fertile soil for innovation and technological change.*

Within the framework of free markets, governments can foster rapid technological change both by encouraging new ideas and by ensuring that technologies are effectively used. Policies can focus on both the supply side and the demand side.

Promoting Demand for Better Technologies. The

world is full of superior technologies that have not been adopted; otherwise, how could we explain the vast differences in productivity shown in Table 18-6? Before considering how to supply new technologies, therefore, governments must help ensure that firms

and industries are at the *technological frontier*, which is the best-practice technology anywhere.

The major lesson here is that "necessity is the mother of invention." In other words, vigorous competition among firms and industries is the ultimate discipline that ensures innovation. Just as athletes perform better when they are trying to outrun their competitors, so are firms spurred to improve their products and processes when the victors are given fame and fortune while the laggards may go bankrupt.

Vigorous competition involves both domestic and foreign competitors. For large countries on the technological frontier, domestic competition is necessary to promote innovation. The movement to deregulation over the last two decades has brought competition to airlines, energy, telecommunications, and finance, and the positive impact on innovation has been dramatic. For small or technologically backward countries, import competition is crucial to adopting advanced technologies and ensuring product market competition.

Promoting Supply of New Technologies. Rapid eco-

nomic growth requires pushing out the technological frontier by increasing the supply of inventions as well as ensuring that there is adequate demand for existing advanced technologies. There are three ways by which governments can encourage the supply of new technologies.

First, governments can ensure that the basic science, engineering, and technology are appropriately supported. In this respect, the world leader in the last half-century has been the United States, which combines company support for applied research with top-notch university basic research generously supported by government funding. Particularly outstanding have been the impressive improvements in biomedical technology in the form of new drugs and equipment that benefit consumers directly in daily life. The government's role in supporting for-profit research is accomplished by a strong patent system, predictable and cost-effective regulations, and fiscal incentives such as the current R&D tax credit.

Second, governments can advance technologies at home through encouraging investment by foreign firms. As foreign countries reach and pass the American technological frontier, they can also contribute to American know-how by establishing operations in the United States. The last decade has brought a number of Japanese automakers to the United States, and Japanese-owned plants have introduced new technologies and managerial practices to the benefit of both the profits of Japanese shareholders and the productivity of American workers.

Third, governments can promote new technologies by pursuing sound macroeconomic policies. These include low and stable taxes on capital income and a low cost of capital to firms. Indeed, the importance of the cost of capital brings us back full circle to the issue of the low saving rate and high real interest rate. American firms are sometimes accused of being myopic and being unwilling to invest for the long run. At least part of this myopia comes from being faced with high real interest rates—high real interest rates *force* rational American firms to look for quick payoffs in their investments. A change in economic policy that lowered real interest rates would change the "economic spectacles" through which firms look when considering their technological policies. If real interest rates were lower, firms would view long-term, high-risk projects such as investments in technology more favorably, and the increased investment in knowledge would lead to more rapid improvements in technology and productivity.

Valediction on economic growth

Following the Keynesian revolution, the capitalist democracies believed that they could flourish and grow rapidly while moderating the extremes of unemployment and inflation, poverty and wealth, privilege and deprivation. Many of these goals were met as the market economies experienced a period of output expansion and employment growth never before seen, and the last 15 years have been a period of unprecedented stability and low inflation in the United States. All the time, Marxists carped that capitalism was doomed to crash in a cataclysmic depression; ecologists fretted that market economies would choke in their own fumes; and libertarians worried that government planning was leading us down the road to serfdom. But the pessimists overlooked the spirit of enterprise which was nurtured by an open society and free markets and which led to a continuous stream of technological improvements.

A valediction from John Maynard Keynes, as timely today as it was in an earlier age, provides a fitting summary of our review of economic policy:

> It is Enterprise which builds and improves the world's possessions. If Enterprise is afoot, wealth accumulates whatever happens to Thrift; and if Enterprise is asleep, wealth decays whatever Thrift may be doing.

ECONOMIC PROGRESS AND POLITICAL FREEDOMS

One of the remarkable features of the twentieth century is the close association between economic progress and political freedoms. Philosophers of an earlier age believed that great wealth was the mark of aristocracies and monarchies. Yet a look at the world at the beginning of the twenty-first century reveals a striking fact: *While not every country with a market economy is democratic, every country with a democratic political system has a market economy. Moreover, virtually every high-income country is both a market economy and a political democracy.* The freedom of the marketplace goes hand in hand with political freedoms such as free and fair elections, the presence of a significant opposition, and self-determination for major minority groups; these go hand in hand with civil liberties such as freedom of expression and association, a free press, rule of law, and respect for human rights.

Why is a democratic political system hospitable to economic development? The link is described by Yale political scientist Robert Dahl as follows:

> Democratic systems foster the education of their people; and an educated workforce is helpful to innovation and economic growth. In addition, the rule of law is usually sustained more strongly in democratic countries; courts are more independent; property rights are more secure; contractual agreements are more effectively enforced; and arbitrary intervention in economic life by government and politicians is less likely. Finally, modern economies depend on communication, and in democratic countries the barriers to communication are much lower.[5]

Figure 18-4 shows how the march of freedoms generally goes alongside the growth of average incomes. The association between the two is clear, with

---
[5] See Dahl in the Further Reading section at the end of this chapter.

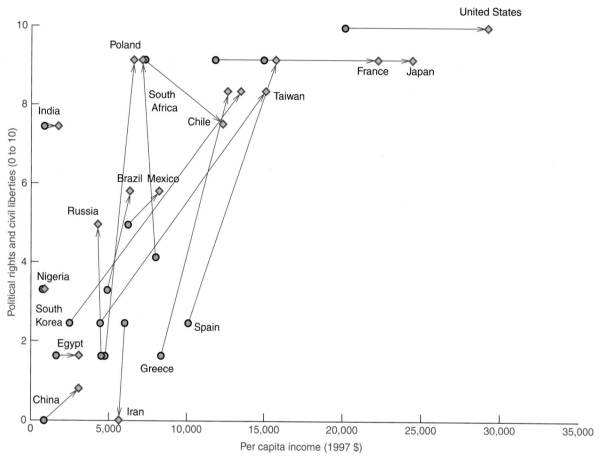

FIGURE 18-4. Economic Progress and Political Freedom, 1972 and 1998

High-income countries generally have the most political freedoms and civil liberties. As countries succeed in raising incomes, political freedoms often but not always go hand in hand. The arrows show the changes in per capita GDP and in political freedoms from 1972 to 1998. (Source: Freedom House for data on political rights and civil liberties. The index takes 0 to be the lowest and 10 to be the highest. Per capita income for 1997 comes from the World Bank and corrects for purchasing-power parities.)

the highest freedoms enjoyed by the richest countries while many poor countries suffer under the yoke of repression and curbs on speech, assembly, and the press. There are important exceptions, however, for a market economy is neither necessary nor sufficient for democracy. Some countries making the transition from traditional societies to advanced capitalism pass through a period of authoritarian rule—this was seen in the East Asian societies of Taiwan

and South Korea and in much of Latin America during this century. And during difficult economic times, countries sometimes experience democracy "fatigue" and allow strong leaders to overturn democratic institutions.

Additionally, we must not misinterpret the economic side of the coin. A modern market economy is not a laissez-faire society of anarchy plus the constable. The businesses in a free-enterprise system must pay taxes, meet health, safety and environmental standards, and obey the society's speed limits.

So, as we close our survey of economics, perhaps we can relax and speculate on what can never be proved scientifically. Our cautiously optimistic reading of history is this: A modern democracy, proceeding carefully and applying the best of accumulated wisdom, can have the best of both worlds. It can repair the worst flaws of a market economy. It can promote efficiency and fairness without excessive costs to either.

But at the same time it can preserve those precious things that can never be captured in our GDP: freedom to speak, freedom to change, and freedom to live as we choose.

✳ SUMMARY

A. The Economic Consequences of the Government Debt

1. Budgets are systems used by governments and organizations to plan and control expenditures and revenues. Budgets are in surplus (or deficit) when the government has revenues greater (or less) than its expenditures. Macroeconomic policy depends upon fiscal policy, which comprises the overall stance of spending and taxes.

2. Economists separate the actual budget into its structural and cyclical components. The structural budget calculates how much the government would collect and spend if the economy were operating at potential output. The cyclical budget accounts for the impact of the business cycle on tax revenues, expenditures, and the deficit. To assess fiscal policy, we should pay close attention to the structural deficit; changes in the cyclical deficit are a *result* of changes in the economy, while structural deficits are a *cause* of changes in the economy.

3. The government debt represents the accumulated borrowings from the public. It is the sum of past deficits. A useful measure of the size of the debt is the debt-GDP ratio, which for the United States has tended to rise during wartime and fall during peacetime. The 1980s were an exception, for the debt-GDP ratio rose sharply during this period.

4. In the short run, economists worry that structural government deficits crowd out investment. The extent of crowding out depends upon financial markets and international linkages, the determinants of investment, and how deficits are financed. The best bet today is that, outside of deep recessions, national investment (both domestic and foreign) will be significantly crowded out by government spending.

5. To the degree that we borrow from abroad for consumption and pledge posterity to pay back the interest and principal on such external debt, our descendants will indeed find themselves sacrificing consumption to service this debt. If we leave future generations an internal debt but no change in capital stock, there are various internal effects. The process of taxing Peter to pay Paula, or taxing Paula to pay Paula, can involve various microeconomic distortions of productivity and efficiency but should not be confused with owing money to another country.

6. Economic growth may slow if the public debt displaces capital. This syndrome occurs when people substitute public debt for capital or private assets, thereby reducing the economy's private capital stock. In the long run, a larger government debt may slow the growth of potential output and consumption because of the costs of servicing an external debt, the inefficiencies that arise from taxing to pay the interest on the debt, and the diminished capital accumulation that comes from capital displacement.

B. Stabilizing the Economy

7. Nations face two considerations in setting monetary and fiscal policies: the appropriate level of aggregate demand and the best monetary-fiscal mix. The mix of fiscal and monetary policies helps determine the composition of GDP. A high-investment strategy would call for a budget surplus along with low real interest rates.

8. After the Keynesian revolution, many economists had high hopes for countercyclical stabilization policy. In practice, fiscal policy has proved a cumbersome policy, particularly because of the difficulty of raising taxes and cutting expenditures during inflationary periods. Consequently, the United States today relies almost entirely upon monetary policy to stabilize the economy.

9. Should governments follow fixed rules or discretion? The answer involves both positive economics and normative values. Conservatives often espouse rules, while

liberals often advocate active fine-tuning to attain economic goals. More basic is the question of whether active and discretionary policies stabilize or destabilize the economy. Economists often stress the need for *credible* policies, whether credibility is generated by rigid rules or by wise leadership. A recent trend among countries is inflation targeting for monetary policy, which is a flexible rule-based system that sets a medium-term inflation target while allowing short-run flexibility when economic shocks make attaining a rigid inflation target too costly.

C. Economic Prospects in the New Century

10. Remember the dictum: "Productivity isn't everything, but in the long run it is almost everything." A country's ability to improve its living standards over time depends almost entirely on its ability to improve the technologies and capital used by the workforce.

11. Promoting economic growth entails advancing technology. The major role of government is to ensure free markets, protect strong intellectual property rights, promote vigorous competition, and support basic science and technology.

CONCEPTS FOR REVIEW

The Economics of Debt and Deficits

government budget
budget deficit, surplus, and balance
budget:
   actual
   structural
   cyclical
short-run impact: crowding out vs.
   investment encouragement

ratio of debt to GDP
long-run impacts on economic
   growth:
   internal vs. external debt
   distortions from taxation
   displacement of capital

Stabilization

demand management
fiscal-monetary mix

fixed rules vs. discretion
inflation targeting

Long-Run Growth and Productivity

reaching the technological frontier
   vs. moving it outward
the spirit of enterprise

FURTHER READING AND INTERNET WEBSITES

Further Reading

The Krugman quotation is from Paul Krugman, *The Age of Diminished Expectations* (MIT Press, Cambridge, Mass., 1990), p. 9. The source for Table 18-4 is Ralph C. Bryant, Peter Hooper, and Gerald Holtham, "Consensus and Diversity in the Model Simulations," in Ralph Bryant et al., eds., *Empirical Macroeconomics for Interdependent Economies* (Brookings Institution, Washington, D.C., 1988). The quote from Robert Dahl is from *On Democracy* (Yale University Press, New Haven, Conn., 1998), p. 59.

Websites

Economic issues and data on fiscal policy, budgets, and the debt are regularly provided by the nonpartisan Congressional Budget Office, which is staffed by professional economists. Recent documents are available at www.cbo.gov. The data on freedoms come from Freedom House's website at www.freedomhouse.org.

A survey of monetary discipline can be found in a January 2000 speech, "Inflation Targeting," by Federal Reserve governor Edward Gramlich at www.federal reserve.gov/boarddocs/speeches/2000.

QUESTIONS FOR DISCUSSION

1. A common confusion is that between the debt and the deficit. Explain each of the following:
   a. A budget deficit leads to a growing government debt.
   b. Reducing the deficit does not reduce the government debt.
   c. Reducing the government debt requires running a budget surplus.
   d. Even though the government deficit was reduced to zero in the 1993–1998 period, the government debt still rose significantly in these years.

2. Is it possible that government *promises* might have a displacement effect along with government debt? Thus, if the government were to promise large future social security benefits to workers, would workers feel richer? Might they reduce saving as a result? Could the capital stock end up smaller? Illustrate using Figure 18-2.

3. Trace the impact upon the government debt, the nation's capital stock, and real output of a government program that borrows abroad and spends the money on the following:
   a. Capital to drill for oil, which is exported (as did Mexico in the 1970s)
   b. Grain to feed its population (as did the Soviet Union in the 1980s)

4. Construct a graph like that in Figure 18-3 showing:
   a. The path of consumption and net exports with and without a large government debt
   b. The paths of consumption with a balanced budget and with a government fiscal surplus

5. Explain how a change in the mix of monetary and fiscal policies toward loose fiscal policy and tight money would increase the budget deficit, decrease domestic investment, and increase the trade or net-export deficit.

6. What are the various arguments for and against rigid inflation targeting in which the inflation target is required each year? Specifically, consider the difficulties of attaining a rigid inflation target after a sharp supply shock which shifted the Phillips curve up. Compare a rigid inflation target with a flexible inflation target in which the target would be attained on average over a 5-year period.

7. Political candidates have proposed the policies listed below to speed economic growth in recent years. For each, explain qualitatively the impact upon the growth of potential output and of per capita potential output. If possible, give a quantitative estimate of the increase in the growth of potential output and per capita potential output over the next decade.
   a. Cut the federal budget deficit (or raise the surplus) by 2 percent of GDP, increasing the ratio of investment to GDP by the same amount.
   b. Increase the federal subsidy to R&D by $1/4$ percent of GDP, assuming that this subsidy will increase private R&D by the same amount and that R&D has a social rate of return that is 4 times that of private investment.
   c. Decrease defense spending by 1 percent of GDP, with a multiplier of 2.
   d. Decrease the number of immigrants so that the labor force declines by 5 percent.
   e. Increase investments in human capital (or education and on-the-job training) by 1 percent of GDP.

8. J. M. Keynes wrote, "If the Treasury were to fill old bottles with banknotes, bury them in disused coal mines, and leave it to private enterprise to dig the notes up again, there need be no more unemployment and the real income of the community would probably become a good deal greater than it actually is" (*The General Theory*, p.129). Explain why Keynes's analysis of the utility of a discretionary public-works program might be correct during a depression. How could well-designed fiscal or monetary policies have the same impact on employment while producing a larger quantity of useful goods and services?

Valediction

We have now finished our tour of the exciting world of introductory economics. For us, the authors, this marks the first edition of the twenty-first century. Through seventeen editions, we have seen economics transformed into one of the most exciting and innovative of all the sciences.

For you, the introductory student, this marks the end of your first serious study of economics and the beginning of your life as a practicing economist. In this tour through the wonders of the world of economics you have discovered the realm of the qualified Invisible Hand, the promises and pitfalls of macroeconomic policy, the way that network economies and information are reshaping our lives, and the opportunities to use market tools to preserve our precious environment. The market economy has been our major focus, and we have seen how markets can be mighty engines of prosperity that also dish out great inequalities. One of the extraordinary results of a careful study of economic principles is that you view the world through different eyes. You see the *pattern* in economic life—instead of only the raw data of the upticks of the stock market and the downsizings of the labor market.

This new century provides the occasion for us to pause to reflect upon the evolution of economics and the economy. In designing this book, we continually ask ourselves; "What will the American and the global economies look like two or three decades from now? What vital problems and cruel dilemmas will arise when today's students are running tomorrow's businesses, governments, and central banks?"

One surprise about economics is how little the ailments change from decade to decade. As one old alum complained, "In economics, it's not the questions that change—it's the answers." The core problems of the 2000s differ little from those of the 1960s or the 1930s. We worry today as we did then about growth, stability, and distribution. Is our economic growth satisfactory? Are inflation and unemployment under control? Are the fruits of economic growth distributed fairly among the populace?

Central to all these questions is the perennial issue of how we should use our material gains to improve our personal and civic life. A striking analysis of this question was given by this century's greatest economist, John Maynard Keynes, in 1930. Keynes mused about the long-run prospects of the capitalist system and had these startling reflections:

> Suppose that a hundred years hence we are eight times better off than today. Assuming no important wars and no important increase in population, the *economic problem* may be solved. This means that the economic problem is not—if we look into the future—*the permanent problem of the human race.*
>
> Why, you may ask, is this so startling? It is startling because the economic problem, the struggle for subsistence, always has been hitherto the primary, most pressing problem of the human race—not only of the human race, but of the whole of the biological kingdom from the beginnings of life in its most primitive forms.
>
> Thus we have been expressly evolved by nature—with all our impulses and deepest instincts—for the purpose of solving the economic problem. If the economic problem is solved, mankind will be deprived of its traditional purpose. I think with dread of the readjustment of the habits and instincts of the ordinary man, bred into him for countless generations, which he may be asked to discard within a few decades.
>
> Must we not expect a general "nervous breakdown"? Thus for the first time since his creation man will be faced with his real, his permanent problem—how to use his freedom from pressing economic cares, how to occupy the leisure, which science and compound interest will have won for him, to live wisely and agreeably and well.
>
> There are changes in other spheres too which we must expect to come. When the accumulation of wealth is no longer of high social importance, there will be great changes in the code of morals. The love of money as a possession—as distinguished from the love of money as a means to the enjoyments and realities of life—will be recognized for what it is, a somewhat disgusting morbidity, one of those semi-criminal, semi-pathological propensities which one hands over with a shudder to the specialists in mental disease. . . .
>
> But beware! The time for all this is not yet. For at least another hundred years we must pretend to ourselves and to everyone that fair is foul and foul is fair; for foul is useful and fair is not. Avarice and usury and precaution must be our gods for a little longer still.[1]

---

[1] John Maynard Keynes, "Economic Possibilities for our Grandchildren," reprinted in his *Essays in Persuasion* (Macmillan, London, 1933), with minor editing.

We close with these fascinating thoughts because they remind us that great affluence has indeed not brought about a slackening of economic ambition in America. Even though our average incomes are more than 10 times those at the beginning of this century, our society has become more competitive in the struggle for profits and jobs and markets. Markets are more pervasive and more intrusive. The growing orientation toward the market has accompanied a widespread desire for smaller government, less regulation, and lower taxes.

Ours is the Ruthless Economy. People are increasingly judged on their current productivities rather than past contributions. Old-fashioned loyalty to firm or community counts for little. Suppose a firm finds it profitable to lay off 1000 workers, or moves from New England to the Sunbelt, or moves from the Sunbelt to Mexico. It is likely to move in the relentless pursuit of profits . . . and as a protection against another firm gaining a competitive advantage. Market-oriented economists will tell you that inequality is the price we pay for invention—that you can't make an omelette without breaking eggs. This hardheaded focus on efficiency pays no mind to the incomes of laid-off workers, of bankrupt firms, of crumbling cities, or of nations or regions which lose their comparative advantage.

A closer look finds a silver lining behind this ruthlessness of the marketplace. With increased foreign competition, deregulation of many industries, and labor unions at their weakest since the Great Depression, labor and product markets have nowadays become increasingly competitive. With more vigorous competition, America's macroeconomic performance has perceptibly improved. Compared to a decade ago, the U.S. produces $1½ trillion more output and has provided 17 million net new jobs. Money wage growth and price inflation have remained low and stable even as the unemployment rate fell below what most economists thought was its lowest sustainable rate. The labor force in our ruthless economy may feel cowed and anxious. But, from a macroeconomic point of view, meekness is a virtue because it keeps inflation low, allows a lower overall unemployment rate, and most significantly shields the least-skilled workers from being frozen out of any employment at all.

Europe—the cradle of the welfare state—models itself as the "compassionate economy" and is a stark contrast. European workers today are "protected" by strong unions, generous income-support systems, high minimum wages, and many restraints on hiring and firing. But weakening of market forces has led to hardening of the economic arteries as microeconomic generosity led to macroeconomic inefficiency. With growing inflexibility of its welfare and labor-market institutions, the unemployment rate in Europe climbed steadily over the last three decades. By 2000, the European unemployment rate was more than double that in the United States. Many European politicians are asking themselves whether they should in some degree emulate the ruthless competitiveness of the American model.

But before applauding the American successes too loudly, recall that competitive markets not only giveth much but also taketh away. Not everybody can be the Master of the Universe in the competitive Darwinian economy. The growing inequality of income in America—and the large numbers of people who are locked into dead-end jobs and living in run-down neighborhoods—is a sober reminder of the harsh inequalities possible in a market economy. Moreover, the incomes of the rich countries of North America, Western Europe, and East Asia are very unequally shared with the rest of the world. Indian villages, tropical Africa, and the Andean countries are far from markets, often torn by civil strife, crippled by disease, and largely forgotten by their affluent brothers and sisters.

So at the end, we render two cheers to the market, but not three. The last cheer is reserved for that day when people in all corners of our own country and in the globe have the opportunity for a good job, an adequate income, a healthy life, and a safe environment. These are worthy goals for economics and for economists in the century to come!

Glossary of Terms[1]

A

Ability-to-pay principle (of taxation). The principle that one's tax burden should depend upon the ability to pay as measured by income or wealth. This principle does not specify *how much* more those who are better off should pay.

Absolute advantage (in international trade). The ability of Country A to produce a commodity more efficiently (i.e., with greater output per unit of input) than Country B. Possession of such an absolute advantage does not necessarily mean that A can export this commodity to B successfully. Country B may still have the comparative advantage.

Accelerator principle. The theory that a change in the rate of output induces a change in the demand for investment in the same direction.

Actual, cyclical, and structural budget. The **actual budget** deficit or surplus is the amount recorded in a given year. This is composed of the **structural budget,** which calculates what government revenues, expenditures, and deficits would be if the economy were operating at potential output, and the **cyclical budget,** which measures the effect of the business cycle on the budget.

Adaptive expectations. See **expectations.**

Adjustable peg. An exchange-rate system in which countries maintain a fixed or "pegged" exchange rate with respect to other currencies. This exchange rate is subject to periodic adjustment, however, when it becomes too far out of line with fundamental forces. This system was used for major currencies during the Bretton Woods period from 1944 to 1971 and is called the **Bretton Woods system.**

Administered (or **inflexible**) **prices.** A term referring to prices which are set and kept constant for a period of time and over a series of transactions. (In contrast, refer to **price flexibility.**)

Adverse selection. A type of market failure in which those people with the highest risk are most likely to buy insurance. More broadly, adverse selection encompasses situations in which sellers and buyers have different information about a product, such as in the market for used cars.

Aggregate demand. Total planned or desired spending in the economy during a given period. It is determined by the aggregate price level and influenced by domestic investment, net exports, government spending, the consumption function, and the money supply.

Aggregate demand (*AD*) **curve.** The curve showing the relationship between the quantity of goods and services that people are willing to buy and the aggregate price level, other things equal. As with any demand curve, important variables lie behind the aggregate demand curve, e.g., government spending, exports, and the money supply.

Aggregate supply. The total value of goods and services that firms would willingly produce in a given time period. Aggregate supply is a function of available inputs, technology, and the price level.

Aggregate supply (*AS*) **curve.** The curve showing the relationship between the output firms would willingly supply and the aggregate price level, other things equal. The *AS* curve tends to be vertical at potential output in the very long run but may be relatively flat in the short run.

Allocative efficiency. A situation in which no reorganization or trade could raise the utility or satisfaction of one individual without lowering the utility or satisfaction of another individual. Under certain limited conditions, perfect competition leads to allocative efficiency. Also called **Pareto efficiency.**

Antitrust legislation. Laws prohibiting monopolization, restraints of trade, and collusion among firms to raise prices or inhibit competition.

Appreciation (of a currency). See **depreciation** (of a currency).

Appropriable. Describes a resource for which the owner can capture the full economic value. In a well-functioning competitive market, appropriable resources are usually priced and allocated efficiently. Also refer to **inappropriable.**

Arbitrage. The purchase of a good or asset in one market for immediate resale in another market in order to profit from a price discrepancy. Arbitrage is an important force in eliminating price discrepancies, thereby making markets function more efficiently.

Asset. A physical property or intangible right that has economic value. Important examples are plant, equipment, land, patents, copyrights, and financial instruments such as money or bonds.

Asset demand for money. See **demand for money.**

---

[1] Words in bold type within definitions appear as separate entries in the glossary. For a more detailed discussion of particular terms, the text will provide a useful starting point. More complete discussions are contained in Douglas Greenwald, ed., *The McGraw-Hill Encyclopedia of Economics* (McGraw-Hill, New York, 1994); David W. Pearce, *Macmillan Dictionary of Modern Economics,* rev. ed. (Macmillan, London, 1992); *International Encyclopedia of the Social Sciences* (Collier and Macmillan, New York, 1968); and John Eatwell, Murray Milgate, and Peter Newman, *The New Palgrave: A Dictionary of Economics* (Macmillan, London, 1987), four volumes.

Automatic (or built-in) stabilizers. The property of a government tax and spending system that cushions income changes in the private sector. Examples include unemployment compensation and progressive income taxes.

Average cost. Refer to **cost, average.**

Average cost curve, long-run (*LRAC*, or *LAC*). The graph of the minimum average cost of producing a commodity for each level of output, assuming that technology and input prices are given but that the producer is free to choose the optimal size of plants.

Average cost curve, short-run (*SRAC*, or *SAC*). The graph of the minimum average cost of producing a commodity, for each level of output, using the given state of technology, input prices, and existing plant.

Average fixed cost. Refer to **cost, average fixed.**

Average product. Total product or output divided by the quantity of one of the inputs. Hence, the average product of labor is defined as total product divided by the amount of labor input, and similarly for other inputs.

Average propensity to consume. See *marginal propensity to consume.*

Average revenue. Total revenue divided by total number of units sold—i.e., revenue per unit. Average revenue is generally equal to price.

Average tax rate. Total taxes divided by total income, also known as **effective tax rate.**

Average variable cost. Refer to **cost, average variable.**

B

Balance of international payments. A statement showing all of a nation's transactions with the rest of the world for a given period. It includes purchases and sales of goods and services, gifts, government transactions, and capital movements.

Balance of trade. The part of a nation's balance of payments that deals with merchandise (or visible) imports or exports, including such items as foodstuffs, capital goods, and automobiles. When services and other current items are included, this measures the **balance on current account.** In balance of payments accounting, the current account is financed by the **financial account.**

Balance on current account. See **balance of trade.**

Balance on financial account. See **balance of trade.**

Balance sheet. A statement of a firm's financial position as of a given date, listing **assets** in one column, **liabilities** plus **net worth** in the other. Each item is listed at its actual or estimated money value. Totals of the two columns must balance because net worth is defined as assets minus liabilities.

Balanced budget. Refer to **budget, balanced.**

Bank, commercial. A financial intermediary whose prime distinguishing feature until recently was that it accepts checkable deposits. All financial institutions that hold savings and checkable deposits are called depository institutions.

Bank money. Money created by banks, particularly the checking accounts (part of M_1) that are generated by a multiple expansion of bank reserves.

Bank reserves. Refer to **reserves, bank.**

Barriers to entry. Factors that impede entry into a market and thereby reduce the amount of competition or the number of producers in an industry. Important examples are legal barriers, regulation, and product differentiation.

Barter. The direct exchange of one good for another without using anything as money or as a medium of exchange.

Benefit principle (of taxation). The principle that people should be taxed in proportion to the benefits they receive from government programs.

Bond. An interest-bearing certificate issued by a government or corporation, promising to repay a sum of money (the principal) plus interest at specified dates in the future.

Break-even point (in macroeconomics). For an individual, family, or community, that level of income at which 100 percent is spent on consumption (i.e., the point where there is neither saving nor dissaving). Positive saving begins at higher income levels.

Bretton Woods system. See **adjustable peg.**

Broad money. A measure of the money supply (also known as M_2) that includes transactions money (or M_1) as well as savings accounts in banks and similar assets that are very close substitutes for transactions money.

Budget. An account, usually for a year, of the planned expenditures and the expected receipts. For a government, the receipts are tax revenues.

Budget, balanced. A budget in which total expenditures just equal total receipts (excluding any receipts from borrowing).

Budget constraint. See **budget line.**

Budget deficit. For a government, the excess of total expenditures over total receipts, with borrowing not included among receipts. This difference (the deficit) is ordinarily financed by borrowing.

Budget, government. A statement showing, for the government in question, planned expenditures and revenues for some period (typically 1 year).

Budget line. A line indicating the combination of commodities that a consumer can buy with a given income at a given set of prices. Also sometimes called the **budget constraint.**

Budget surplus. Excess of government revenues over government spending; the opposite of budget deficit.

Built-in stabilizers. See **automatic stabilizers.**

Business cycles. Fluctuations in total national output, income, and employment, usually lasting for a period of 2 to 10 years, marked by widespread and simultaneous expansion or contraction in many sectors of the economy. In modern macroeconomics, business cycles are said to occur when actual GDP rises relative to potential GDP (expansion) or falls relative to potential GDP (contraction or recession).

C

$C + I$, $C + I + G$, or $C + I + G + X$ schedule. A schedule showing the planned or desired levels of aggregate demand for each level of GDP, or the graph on which this schedule is depicted. The schedule includes consumption (C), investment (I), government spending on goods and services (G), and net exports (X).

Capital (capital goods, capital equipment). (1) In economic theory, one of the triad of productive inputs (land, labor, and capital). Capital consists of durable produced goods that are in turn used in production. (2) In accounting and finance, "capital" means the total amount of money subscribed by the shareholder-owners of a corporation, in return for which they receive shares of the company's stock.

Capital consumption allowance. See **depreciation** (of an asset).

Capital deepening. In economic-growth theory, an increase in the capital-labor ratio. (Contrast with **capital widening.**)

Capital gains. The rise in value of a capital asset, such as land or common stocks, the gain being the difference between the sales price and the purchase price of the asset.

Capital markets. Markets in which financial resources (money, bonds, stocks) are traded. These, along with **financial intermediaries,** are institutions through which saving in the economy is transferred to investors.

Capital-output ratio. In economic-growth theory, the ratio of the total capital stock to annual GDP.

Capital widening. A rate of growth in real capital stock just equal to the growth of the labor force (or of population), so that the ratio between total capital and total labor remains unchanged. (Contrast with **capital deepening.**)

Capitalism. An economic system in which most property (land and capital) is privately owned. In such an economy, private markets are the primary vehicles used to allocate resources and generate incomes.

Cardinal utility. See **ordinal utility.**

Cartel. An organization of independent firms producing similar products that work together to raise prices and restrict output. Cartels are illegal under U.S. antitrust laws.

Central bank. A government-established agency (in the United States, the Federal Reserve System) responsible for controlling the nation's money supply and credit conditions and for supervising the financial system, especially commercial banks and other depository institutions.

Change in demand vs. change in quantity demanded. A change in the quantity buyers want to purchase, prompted by any reason other than a change in price (e.g., increase in income, change in tastes, etc.), is a "change in demand." In graphical terms, it is a shift of the demand curve. If, in contrast, the decision to buy more or less is prompted by a change in the good's price, then it is a "change in quantity demanded." In graphical terms, a change in quantity demanded is a

movement along an unchanging demand curve.

Change in supply vs. change in quantity supplied. This distinction is the same for supply as for demand, so see **change in demand vs. change in quantity demanded.**

Checking accounts (or bank money). A deposit in a commercial bank or other financial intermediary upon which checks can be written and which is therefore transactions money (or M_1), also called "checkable deposits." Checkable deposits are the largest component of M_1.

Chicago School of Economics. A group of economists (among whom Henry Simons, F. A. von Hayek, and Milton Friedman have been the most prominent) who believe that competitive markets free of government intervention will lead to the most efficient operation of the economy.

Classical approach. See **classical economics.**

Classical economics. The predominant school of economic thought prior to the appearance of Keynes' work; founded by Adam Smith in 1776. Other major figures who followed him include David Ricardo, Thomas Malthus, and John Stuart Mill. By and large, this school believed that economic laws (particularly individual self-interest and competition) determine prices and factor rewards and that the price system is the best possible device for resource allocation.

Classical theories (in macroeconomics). Theories emphasizing the self-correcting forces in the economy. In the classical approach, there is generally full employment and policies to stimulate aggregate demand have no impact upon output.

Clearing market. A market in which prices are sufficiently flexible to equilibrate supply and demand very quickly. In markets that clear, there is no rationing, unemployed resources, or excess demand or supply. In practice, this is thought to apply to many commodity and financial markets but not to labor or many product markets.

Closed economy. See **open economy.**

Coase theorem. A view (not actually a theorem) put forth by Ronald Coase that externalities or economic inefficiencies will under certain conditions be corrected by bargaining between the affected parties.

Collective bargaining. The process of negotiations between a group of workers (usually a union) and their employer. Such bargaining leads to an agreement about wages, fringe benefits, and working conditions.

Collusion. Agreement between different firms to cooperate by raising prices, dividing markets, or otherwise restraining competition.

Collusive oligopoly. A market structure in which a small number of firms (i.e., a few oligopolists) collude and jointly make their decisions. When they succeed in maximizing their joint profits, the price and quantity in the market closely approach those prevailing under monopoly.

Command economy. A mode of economic organization in which the key economic functions—*what, how,* and *for whom*—are principally determined by government directive. Sometimes called a "centrally planned economy."

Commodity money. Money with **intrinsic value;** also, the use of some commodity (cattle, beads, etc.) as money.

Common currency. A situation where several countries form a monetary union with a single currency and a unified central bank. See especially the European Monetary Union (EMU) which introduced the Euro in 1999.

Common stock. The financial instrument representing ownership and, generally, voting rights in a corporation. A certain share of a company's stock gives the owner title to that fraction of the votes, net earnings, and assets of the corporation.

Communism. A communist economic system (also called Soviet-style central planning) is one in which the state owns and controls the means of production, particularly industrial capital. These economies are also characterized by extensive central planning, with the state setting many prices, output levels, and other important economic variables.

Comparative advantage (in international trade). The law of comparative advantage says that a nation should specialize in producing and exporting those commodities which it can produce at *relatively* lower cost, and that it should import those goods for which it is a *relatively* high-cost producer. Thus it is a comparative advantage, not an absolute advantage, that should dictate trade patterns.

Compensating differentials. Differences in wage rates among jobs that serve to offset or compensate for the nonmonetary differences of the jobs. For example, unpleasant jobs that require isolation for many months in Alaska pay wages much higher than those for similar jobs nearer to civilization.

Competition, imperfect. Refers to markets in which perfect competition does not hold because at least one seller (or buyer) is large enough to affect the market price and therefore faces a downward-sloping demand (or supply) curve. Imperfect competition refers to any kind of imperfection—pure **monopoly, oligopoly,** or **monopolistic competition.**

Competition, perfect. Refers to markets in which no firm or consumer is large enough to affect the market price. This situation arises where (1) the number of sellers and buyers is very large and (2) the products offered by sellers are homogeneous (or indistinguishable). Under such conditions, each firm faces a horizontal (or perfectly elastic) demand curve.

Competitive equilibrium. The balancing of supply and demand in a market or economy characterized by **perfect competition.** Because perfectly competitive sellers and buyers individually have no power to influence the market, price will move to the point at which it equals both marginal cost and marginal utility.

Competitive market. See **competition, perfect.**

Complements. Two goods which "go together" in the eyes of consumers (e.g., left shoes and right shoes). Goods are **substitutes** when they compete with each other (as do gloves and mittens).

Compound interest. Interest computed on the sum of all past interest earned as well as on the principal. For example, suppose $100 (the principal) is deposited in an account earning 10 percent interest compounded annually. At the end of year 1, interest of $10 is earned. At the end of year 2, the interest payment is $11, $10 on the original principal and $1 on the interest—and so on in future years.

Concentration ratio. The percentage of an industry's total output accounted for by the largest firms. A typical measure is the **four-firm concentration ratio,** which is the fraction of output accounted for by the four largest firms.

Conglomerate. A large corporation producing and selling a variety of unrelated goods (e.g., some cigarette companies have expanded into such unrelated areas as liquor, car rental, and movie production).

Conglomerate merger. See **merger.**

Constant returns to scale. See **returns to scale.**

Consumer price index (CPI). A price index that measures the cost of a fixed basket of consumer goods in which the weight assigned to each commodity is the share of expenditures on that commodity by urban consumers in 1982–1984.

Consumer surplus. The difference between the amount that a consumer would be willing to pay for a commodity and the amount actually paid. This difference arises because the marginal utilities (in dollar terms) of all but the last unit exceed the price. Under certain conditions, the money value of consumer surplus can be measured (using a demand-curve diagram) as the area under the demand curve but above the price line.

Consumption. In macroeconomics, the total spending, by individuals or a nation, on consumer goods during a given period. Strictly speaking, consumption should apply only to those goods totally used, enjoyed, or "eaten up" within that period. In practice, consumption expenditures include all consumer goods bought, many of which last well beyond the period in question—e.g., furniture, clothing, and automobiles.

Consumption function. A schedule relating total consumption to personal disposable income (**DI**). Total wealth and other variables are also frequently assumed to influence consumption.

Consumption-possibility line. See **budget line.**

Cooperative equilibrium. In game theory, an outcome in which the parties act in unison to find strategies that will optimize their joint payoffs.

Corporate income tax. A tax levied on the annual net income of a corporation.

Corporation. The dominant form of business organization in modern capitalist economies. A corporation is a firm owned by individuals or other corporations. It has the same rights to buy, sell, and make contracts as a person would have. It is legally separate from those who own it and has "limited liability."

Correlation. The degree to which two variables are systematically associated with each other.

Cost, average. Total cost (refer to **cost, total**) divided by the number of units produced.

Cost, average fixed. Fixed cost divided by the number of units produced.

Cost, average variable. Variable cost (refer to **cost, variable**) divided by the number of units produced.

Cost, fixed. The cost a firm would incur even if its output for the period in question were zero. Total fixed cost is made up of such individual contractual costs as interest payments, mortgage payments, and directors' fees.

Cost, marginal. The extra cost (or the increase in total cost) required to produce 1 extra unit of output (or the reduction in total cost from producing 1 unit less).

Cost, minimum. The lowest attainable cost per unit (whether average, variable, or marginal). Every point on an average cost curve is a minimum in the sense that it is the best the firm can do with respect to cost for the output which that point represents. Minimum average cost is the lowest point, or points, on that curve.

Cost-push inflation. Inflation originating on the supply side of markets from a sharp increase in costs. In the aggregate supply-and-demand framework, cost-push is illustrated as an upward shift of the *AS* curve. Also called **supply-shock** inflation.

Cost, total. The minimum attainable total cost, given a particular level of technology and set of input prices. Short-run total cost takes existing plant and other fixed costs as given. Long-run total cost is the cost that would be incurred if the firm had complete flexibility with respect to all inputs and decisions.

Cost, variable. A cost that varies with the level of output, such as raw materials, labor, and fuel costs. Variable costs equal total cost minus fixed cost.

Crawling (or sliding) peg. A technique for managing a nation's exchange rate that allows the exchange rate (or the bands around the rate) to "crawl" up or down by a small amount each day or week (say, 0.25 percent per week).

Credit. (1) In monetary theory, the use of someone else's funds in exchange for a promise to pay (usually with interest) at a later date. The major examples are short-term loans from a bank, credit extended by suppliers, and commercial paper. (2) In balance-of-payments accounting, an item such as exports that earns a country foreign currency.

Cross elasticity of demand. A measure of the influence of a change in one good's price on the demand for another good. More precisely, the cross elasticity of demand equals the percentage change in demand for good A when the price of good B changes by 1 percent, assuming other variables are held constant.

Crowding-out hypothesis. The proposition that government spending or government deficits reduce the amount of business investment.

Currency. Coins and paper money.

Currency appreciation (or depreciation). See **depreciation** (of a currency).

Currency board. A monetary institution operating like a central bank for a country that only issues currency that is fully backed by assets denominated in a key foreign currency, often the U.S. dollar.

Current account. See **balance of trade.**

Cyclical budget. See **actual, cyclical, and structural budget.**

Cyclical unemployment. See **frictional unemployment.**

D

Deadweight loss. The loss in real income or consumer and producer surplus that arises because of monopoly, tariffs and quotas, taxes, or other distortions. For example, when a monopolist raises its price, the loss in consumer satisfaction is more than the gain in the monopolist's revenue—the difference being the deadweight loss to society due to monopoly.

Debit. (1) An accounting term signifying an increase in assets or decrease in liabilities. (2) In balance-of-payments accounting, a debit is an item such as imports that reduces a country's stock of foreign currencies.

Decreasing returns to scale. See **returns to scale.**

Deficit spending. Government expenditures on goods and services and transfer payments in excess of its receipts from taxation and other revenue sources. The difference must be financed by borrowing from the public.

Deflating (of economic data). The process of converting "nominal" or current-dollar variables into "real" terms. This is accomplished by dividing current-dollar variables by a **price index.**

Deflation. A fall in the general level of prices.

Demand curve (or **demand schedule**). A schedule or curve showing the quantity of a good that buyers would purchase at each price, other things equal. Normally a demand curve has price on the vertical or Y axis and quantity demanded on the horizontal or X axis. Also see **change in demand vs. change in quantity demanded.**

Demand for money. A summary term used by economists to explain why individuals and businesses hold money balances. The major motivations for holding money are (1) **transactions demand,** signifying that people need money to purchase things, and (2) **asset demand,** relating to the desire to hold a very liquid, risk-free asset.

Demand-pull inflation. Price inflation caused by an excess demand for goods in general, caused, for example, by a major increase in aggregate demand. Often contrasted with **cost-push inflation.**

Demography. The study of the behavior of a population.

Depreciation (of an asset). A decline in the value of an asset. In both business and national accounts, depreciation is the dollar estimate of the extent to which capital has been "used up" or worn out over the period in question. Also termed **capital consumption allowance** in national-income accounting.

Depreciation (of a currency). A nation's currency is said to depreciate when it declines relative to other currencies. For example, if the foreign exchange rate of the dollar falls from 6 to 4 French francs per U.S. dollar, the dollar's value has fallen, and the dollar has undergone a depreciation. The opposite of a depreciation is an **appreciation,** which occurs when the foreign exchange rate of a currency rises.

Depression. A prolonged period characterized by high unemployment, low output and investment, depressed business confidence, falling prices, and widespread business failures. A milder form of business downturn is a **recession,** which has many of the features of a depression to a lesser extent; the precise definition of a recession today is a period in which real GNP declines for at least two consecutive calendar quarters.

Derived demand. The demand for a factor of production that results (is "derived") from the demand for the final good to which it contributes. Thus the demand for tires is derived from the demand for automobile transportation.

Devaluation. A decrease in the official price of a nation's currency, as expressed in the currencies of other nations or in terms of gold. Thus, when the official price of the dollar was lowered with respect to gold in 1971, the dollar was devalued. The opposite of devaluation is **revaluation,** which occurs when a nation raises its official foreign exchange rate relative to gold or other currencies.

Developing country. Same as **less-developed country.**

Differentiated products. Products which compete with each other and are close substitutes but are not identical. Differences may be manifest in the product's function, appearance, location, quality, or other attributes.

Diminishing marginal utility, law of. The law which says that, as more and more of any one commodity is consumed, its marginal utility declines.

Diminishing returns, law of. A law stating that the additional output from successive increases of one input will eventually diminish when other inputs are held constant. Technically, the law is equivalent to saying that the marginal product of the varying input declines after a point.

Direct taxes. Those levied directly on individuals or firms, including taxes on income, labor earnings, and profits. Direct taxes contrast with **indirect taxes,** which are those levied on goods and services and thus only indirectly on people, and which include sales taxes and taxes on property, alcohol, imports, and gasoline.

Discount rate. (1) The interest rate charged by a Federal Reserve Bank (the central bank) on a loan that it makes to a commercial bank.

(2) The rate used to calculate the present value of some asset.

Discounting (of future income). The process of converting future income into an equivalent present value. This process takes a future dollar amount and reduces it by a discount factor that reflects the appropriate interest rate. For example, if someone promises you $121 in 2 years, and the appropriate interest rate or discount rate is 10 percent per year, then we can calculate the present value by discounting the $121 by a discount factor of $(1.10)^2$. The rate at which future incomes are discounted is called the **discount rate.**

Discrimination. Differences in earnings that arise because of personal characteristics that are unrelated to job performance, especially those related to gender, race, ethnicity, sexual orientation, or religion.

Disequilibrium. The state in which an economy is not in **equilibrium.** This may arise when shocks (to income or prices) have shifted demand or supply schedules but the market price (or quantity) has not yet adjusted fully. In macroeconomics, unemployment is often thought to stem from market disequilibria.

Disinflation. The process of reducing a high inflation rate. For example, the deep recession of 1980–1983 led to a sharp disinflation over that period.

Disposable income (*DI***).** Roughly, take-home pay, or that part of the total national income that is available to households for consumption or saving. More precisely, it is equal to GNP less all taxes, business saving, and depreciation plus government and other transfer payments and government interest payments.

Disposable personal income. Same as **disposable income.**

Dissaving. Negative saving; spending more on consumption goods during a period than the disposable income available for that period (the difference being financed by borrowing or drawing on past saving).

Distribution. In economics, the manner in which total output and income is distributed among individuals or factors (e.g., the distribution of income between labor and capital).

Division of labor. A method of organizing production whereby each worker specializes in part of the productive process. Specialization of labor yields higher total output because labor can become more skilled at a particular task and because specialized machinery can be introduced to perform more carefully defined subtasks.

Dominant equilibrium. See **dominant strategy.**

Dominant strategy. In game theory, a situation where one player has a best strategy no matter what strategy the other player follows. When all players have a dominant strategy, we say that the outcome is a **dominant equilibrium.**

Downward-sloping demand, law of. The rule that says that when the price of some commodity falls, consumers will purchase more of that good when other things are held equal.

Duopoly. A market structure in which there are only two sellers. (Compare with **oligopoly.**)

Duopoly price game. A situation in game theory where the market is supplied by two firms who are deciding whether to engage in economic warfare by undercutting each others' prices.

E

Easy-money policy. The central-bank policy of increasing the money supply to reduce interest rates. The purpose of such a policy is to increase investment, thereby raising GDP. (Contrast with **tight-money policy.**)

Econometrics. The branch of economics that uses the methods of statistics to measure and estimate quantitative economic relationships.

Economic good. A good that is scarce relative to the total amount of it that is desired. It must therefore be rationed, usually by charging a positive price.

Economic growth. An increase in the total output of a nation over time. Economic growth is usually measured as the annual rate of increase in a nation's real GDP (or real potential GDP).

Economic regulation. See **regulation.**

Economic rent. Refer to **rent, economic.**

Economic surplus. A term denoting the excess in total satisfaction or utility over the costs of production. Equals the sum of consumer surplus (the excess of consumer satisfaction over total value of purchases) and producer surplus (the excess of producer revenues over costs).

Economics of information. Analysis of economic situations that involve information as a commodity. Because information is costly to produce but cheap to reproduce, market failures are common in markets for informational goods and services such as invention, publishing, and software.

Economies of scale. Increases in productivity, or decreases in average cost of production, that arise from increasing all the factors of production in the same proportion.

Economies of scope. Economies of producing multiple goods or services. Thus economies of scope exist if it is cheaper to produce good X and good Y together rather than separately.

Effective tax rate. Total taxes paid as a percentage of the total income or other tax base.

Efficiency. Absence of waste, or the use of economic resources that produces the maximum level of satisfaction possible with the given inputs and technology. A shorthand expression for **allocative efficiency.**

Efficiency-wage theory. According to this theory, higher wages lead to higher productivity. This occurs because with higher wages workers are healthier, have higher morale, or have lower turnover.

Efficient financial market. A financial market displaying the characteristics of an efficient market.

Efficient market (also **efficient-market theory**). A market or theory in which all new information is quickly understood by market participants and becomes immediately incorporated into market prices. In economics, efficient-market theory holds that all currently available information is already incorporated into the price of common stocks (or other assets).

Elasticity. A term widely used in economics to denote the responsiveness of one variable to changes in another. Thus the elasticity of X with respect to Y means the percentage change in X for every 1 percent change in Y. For especially important examples, see **price elasticity of demand** and **price elasticity of supply.**

Employed. According to official U.S. definitions, persons are employed if they perform any paid work, or if they hold jobs but are absent because of illness, strike, or vacations. Also see **unemployment.**

Equal-cost line. A line in a graph showing the various possible combinations of factor inputs that can be purchased with a given quantity of money.

Equal-product curve (or **isoquant**). A line in a graph showing the various possible combinations of factor inputs which will yield a given quantity of output.

Equation of exchange. A definitional equation which states that $MV \equiv$ PQ, or the money stock times velocity of money equals the price level times output. This equation forms the core of monetarism.

Equilibrium. The state in which an economic entity is at rest or in which the forces operating on the entity are in balance so that there is no tendency for change.

Equilibrium (for a business firm). That position or level of output in which the firm is maximizing its profit, subject to any constraints it may face, and therefore has no incentive to change its output or price level. In the standard theory of the firm, this means that the firm has chosen an output at which marginal revenue is just equal to marginal cost.

Equilibrium (for the individual consumer). That position in which the consumer is maximizing utility, i.e., has chosen the bundle of goods which, given income and prices, best satisfies the consumer's wants.

Equilibrium, competitive. Refer to **competitive equilibrium.**

Equilibrium, general. Refer to **general-equilibrium analysis.**

Equilibrium, macroeconomic. A GDP level at which intended aggregate demand equals intended aggregate supply. At the equilibrium, desired consumption (C), government expenditures (G), investment (I), and net exports (X) just equal the quantity that businesses wish to sell at the going price level.

Equimarginal principle. Principle for deciding the allocation of income among different consumption goods. Under this principle, a consumer's utility is maximized by choosing the consumption bundle such that the marginal utility per dollar spent is equal for all goods.

Exchange rate. See **foreign exchange rate.**

Exchange-rate system. The set of rules, arrangements, and institutions under which payments are made among nations. Historically, the most important exchange-rate systems have been the gold exchange standard, the Bretton Woods system, and today's flexible-exchange-rate system.

Excise tax vs. sales tax. An excise tax is one levied on the purchase of a specific commodity or group of commodities (e.g., alcohol or tobacco). A **sales tax** is one levied on all commodities with only a few specific exclusions (e.g., all purchases except food).

Exclusion principle. A criterion by which public goods are distinguished from private goods. When a producer sells a commodity to person A and can easily exclude B, C, D, etc., from enjoying the benefits of the commodity, the exclusion principle holds and the good is a private good. If, as in public health or national defense, people cannot easily be excluded from enjoying the benefits of the good's production, then the good has public-good characteristics.

Exogenous vs. induced variables. Exogenous variables are those determined by conditions outside the economy. They are contrasted with **induced variables,** which are determined by the internal workings of the economic system. Changes in the weather are exogenous; changes in consumption are often induced by changes in income.

Expectations. Views or beliefs about uncertain variables (such as future interest rates, prices, or tax rates). Expectations are said to be **rational** if they are not systematically wrong (or "biased") and use all available information. Expectations are said to be **adaptive** if people form their expectations on the basis of past behavior.

Expenditure multiplier. See **multiplier.**

Exports. Goods or services that are produced in the home country and sold to another country. These include merchandise trade (like cars), services (like transportation), and interest on loans and investments. **Imports** are simply flows in the opposite direction—into the home country from another country.

External diseconomies. Situations in which production or consumption imposes uncompensated costs on other parties. Steel factories that emit smoke and sulfurous fumes harm local property and public health, yet the injured parties are not paid for the damage. The pollution is an external diseconomy.

External economies. Situations in which production or consumption yields positive benefits to others without those others paying. A firm that hires a security guard scares thieves from the neighborhood, thus providing external security services. Together with external diseconomies, these are often referred to as **externalities.**

External variables. Same as **exogenous variables.**

Externalities. Activities that affect others for better or worse, without those others paying or being compensated for the activity. Externalities exist when private costs or benefits do not equal social costs or benefits. The two major species are **external economies** and **external diseconomies.**

F

Factors of production. Productive inputs, such as labor, land, and capital; the resources needed to produce goods and services. Also called **inputs.**

Fallacy of composition. The fallacy of assuming that what holds for individuals also holds for the group or the entire system.

Federal funds rate. The interest rate that banks pay each other for the overnight use of bank reserves.

Federal Reserve System. The **central bank** of the United States.

Fiat money. Money, like today's paper currency, without **intrinsic value** but decreed (by fiat) to be legal tender by the government. Fiat money is accepted only as long as people have confidence that it will be accepted.

Final good. A good that is produced for final use and not for resale or further manufacture. (Compare with **intermediate goods.**)

Financial assets. Monetary claims or obligations by one party against another party. Examples are bonds, mortgages, bank loans, and equities.

Financial economics. That branch of economics which analyzes how rational investors should invest their funds to attain their objectives in the best possible manner.

Financial intermediary. An institution that receives funds from savers and lends them to borrowers. These include depository institutions (such as commercial or savings banks) and nondepository institutions (such as money market mutual funds, brokerage houses, insurance companies, or pension funds).

Firm (business firm). The basic, private producing unit in an economy. It hires labor, rents or owns capital and land, and buys other inputs in order to make and sell goods and services.

Fiscal-monetary mix. Refers to the combination of fiscal and monetary policies used to influence macroeconomic activity. A tight-monetary-loose-fiscal policy will tend to encourage consumption and retard investment, while an easy-monetary-tight-fiscal policy will have the opposite effect.

Fiscal policy. A government's program with respect to (1) the purchase of goods and services and spending on transfer payments, and (2) the amount and type of taxes.

Fixed cost. Refer to **cost, fixed.**

Fixed exchange rate. See **foreign exchange rate.**

Flexible exchange rates. A system of foreign exchange rates among countries wherein the exchange rates are predominantly determined by private market forces (i.e., by supply and demand) without governments' setting and maintaining a particular pattern of exchange rates. Also sometimes called **floating exchange rates.** When the government refrains from any intervention in exchange markets, the system is called a pure flexible-exchange-rate system.

Floating exchange rates. See **flexible exchange rates.**

Flow vs. stock. A flow variable is one that has a time dimension or flows over time (like the flow through a stream). A stock variable is one that measures a quantity at a point of time (like the water in a lake). Income represents dollars per year and is thus a flow. Wealth as of December 2001 is a stock.

Foreign exchange. Currency (or other financial instruments) of different countries that allow one country to settle amounts owed to other countries.

Foreign exchange market. The market in which currencies of different countries are traded.

Foreign exchange rate. The rate, or price, at which one country's currency is exchanged for the currency of another country. For example, if you can buy 1.9 German marks for one U.S. dollar, then the exchange rate for the mark is 1.9. A country has a **fixed exchange rate** if it pegs its currency at a given exchange rate and stands ready to defend that rate. Exchange rates which are determined by market supply and demand are called **flexible exchange rates.**

Four-firm concentration ratio. See **concentration ratio.**

Fractional-reserve banking. A regulation in modern banking systems whereby financial institutions are legally required to keep a specified fraction of their deposits in the form of deposits with the central bank (or in vault cash).

Free goods. Those goods that are not **economic goods.** Like air or seawater, they exist in such large quantities that they need not be rationed out among those wishing to use them. Thus, their market price is zero.

Free trade. A policy whereby the government does not intervene in trading between nations by tariffs, quotas, or other means.

Frictional unemployment. Temporary unemployment caused by changes in individual markets. It takes time, for example, for new workers to search among different job possibilities; even experienced workers often spend a minimum period of unemployed time moving from one job to another. Frictional is thus distinct from **cyclical unemployment,** which results from a low level of aggregate demand in the context of sticky wages and prices.

Full employment. A term that is used in many senses. Historically, it was taken to be that level of employment at which no (or minimal) involuntary unemployment exists. Today, economists rely upon the concept of the **nonaccelerating inflation rate of unemployment** (*NAIRU*) to indicate the highest sustainable level of employment over the long run.

G

Gains from trade. Refers to the aggregate increase in welfare accruing from voluntary exchange. Equal to the sum of consumer surplus and gains in producer profits.

Galloping inflation. See **inflation.**

Game theory. An analysis of situations involving two or more decision makers with at least partially conflicting interests. It can be applied to the interaction of oligopolistic markets as well as to bargaining situations such as strikes or to conflicts such as games and war.

GDP deflator. The "price" of GDP, that is, the price index that measures the average price of the components in GDP relative to a base year.

GDP gap. The difference or gap between potential GDP and actual GDP.

General-equilibrium analysis. Analysis of the equilibrium state for the economy as a whole in which the markets for all goods and services are simultaneously in equilibrium. By contrast, **partial-equilibrium analysis** concerns the equilibrium in a single market.

GNP. See **gross national product.**

Gold standard. A system under which a nation (1) declares its currency unit to be equivalent to some fixed weight of gold, (2) holds gold reserves and will buy or sell gold freely at the price so proclaimed, and (3) puts no restriction on the export or import of gold.

Government debt. The total of government obligations in the form of bonds and shorter-term borrowings. Government debt held by the public excludes bonds held by quasi-governmental agencies such as the central bank.

Government expenditure multiplier. The increase in GDP resulting from an increase of $1 in government purchases.

Graduated income tax. See **income tax, personal.**

Gresham's Law. A law first attributed to Sir Thomas Gresham, adviser to Queen Elizabeth I of England, who stated in 1558 that "bad money drives out good"—i.e., if the public is suspicious of one component of the money supply, it will hoard the "good money" and try to pass off the "bad money" to someone else.

Gross domestic product, nominal (or **nominal GDP).** The value, at current market prices, of the total final output produced inside a country during a given year.

Gross domestic product, real (or **real GDP).** Nominal GDP corrected for inflation, i.e., real GDP = nominal GDP divided by the GDP deflator.

Gross national product, nominal (or **nominal GNP).** The value, at current market prices, of all final goods and services produced during a year by the factors owned by a nation.

Gross national product, real (or **real GNP).** Nominal GNP corrected for inflation, i.e., real GNP = nominal GNP divided by the GNP deflator.

Growth accounting. A technique for estimating the contribution of different factors to economic growth. Using marginal productivity theory, growth accounting decomposes the growth of output into the growth in labor, land, capital, education, technical knowledge, and other miscellaneous sources.

H

Hedging. A technique for avoiding a risk by making a counteracting transaction. For example, if a farmer produces wheat that will be harvested in the fall, the risk of price fluctuations can be offset, or hedged, by selling in the spring or summer the quantity of wheat that will be produced.

Herfindahl-Hirschman Index (HHI). A measure of market power often used in analysis of market structure. It is calculated by summing the squares of the percentage market shares of all participants in a market. Perfect competition would have an HHI of near zero, while complete monopoly has an HHI of 10,000.

High-powered money. Same as **monetary base.**

Horizontal equity vs. vertical equity. **Horizontal equity** refers to the fairness or equity in treatment of persons in similar situations; the principle of horizontal equity states that those who are essentially equal should receive equal treatment. **Vertical equity** refers to the equitable treatment of those who are in different circumstances.

Horizontal integration. See **integration, vertical vs. horizontal.**

Horizontal merger. See **merger.**

Human capital. The stock of technical knowledge and skill embodied in a nation's work force, resulting from investments in formal education and on-the-job training.

Hyperinflation. See **inflation.**

I

Imperfect competition. Refer to **competition, imperfect.**

Imperfect competitor. Any firm that buys or sells a good in large enough quantities to be able to affect the price of that good.

Implicit-cost elements. Costs that do not show up as explicit money costs but nevertheless should be counted as such (such as the labor cost of the owner of a small store). Sometimes called **opportunity cost,** although "opportunity cost" has a broader meaning.

Imports. See **exports.**

Inappropriability. See **inappropriable.**

Inappropriable. Describes resources for which the individual cost of use is free, or less than the full social costs. These resources are characterized by the presence of externalities, and thus markets will allocate their use inefficiently from a social point of view.

Incidence (or tax incidence). The ultimate economic effect of a tax on the real incomes of producers or consumers (as opposed to the legal requirement for payment). Thus a sales tax may be paid by a retailer, but it is likely that the incidence falls upon the consumer. The exact incidence of a tax depends on the price elasticities of supply and demand.

Income. The flow of wages, interest payments, dividends, and other receipts accruing to an individual or nation during a period of time (usually a year).

Income effect (of a price change). Change in the quantity demanded of a commodity because the change in its price has the effect of changing a consumer's real income. Thus it supplements the **substitution effect** of a price change.

Income elasticity of demand. The demand for any given good is influenced not only by the good's price but by buyers' incomes. Income elasticity measures this responsiveness. Its precise definition is percentage change in quantity demanded divided by percentage change in income. (Compare with **price elasticity of demand.**)

Income statement. A company's statement, covering a specified time period (usually a year), showing sales or revenue earned during that period, all costs properly charged against the goods sold, and the profit (net income) remaining after deduction of such costs. Also called a **profit-and-loss statement.**

Income tax, negative. Refer to **negative income tax.**

Income tax, personal. Tax levied on the income received by individuals in the form either of wages and salaries or income from property, such as rents, dividends, or interest. In the United States, personal income tax is **graduated,** meaning that people with higher incomes pay taxes at a higher average rate than people with lower incomes.

Income velocity of money. See **velocity of money.**

Incomes policy. A government policy that attempts directly to restrict wage and price changes in an effort to slow inflation. Such policies range from voluntary wage-price guidelines to outright legal control over wages, salaries, and prices.

Increasing returns to scale. See **returns to scale.**

Independent goods. Goods whose demands are relatively separate from each other. More precisely, goods A and B are independent when a change in the price of good A has no effect on the quantity demanded of good B, other things equal.

Indexing (or **indexation**). A mechanism by which wages, prices, and contracts are partially or wholly adjusted to compensate for changes in the general price level.

Indifference curve. A curve drawn on a graph whose two axes measure amounts of different goods consumed. Each point on one curve (indicating different combinations of the two goods) yields exactly the same level of satisfaction for a given consumer.

Indifference map. A graph showing a family of indifference curves for a consumer. In general, curves that lie farther northeast from the graph's origin represent higher levels of satisfaction.

Indirect taxes. See **direct taxes.**

Induced variables. See **exogenous vs. induced variables.**

Industry. A group of firms producing similar or identical products.

Inertial rate of inflation. A process of steady inflation that occurs when inflation is expected to persist and the ongoing rate of inflation is built into contracts and people's expectations.

Infant industry. In foreign-trade theory, an industry that has not had sufficient time to develop the experience or expertise to exploit the economies of scale needed to compete successfully with more mature industries producing the same commodity in other countries. Infant industries are often thought to need tariffs or quotas to protect them while they develop.

Inferior good. A good whose consumption goes down as income rises.

Inflation (or **inflation rate**). The inflation rate is the percentage of annual increase in a general price level. **Hyperinflation** is inflation at extremely high rates (say, 1000, 1 million, or even 1 billion percent a year). **Galloping inflation** is a rate of 50 or 100 or 200 percent annually. **Moderate inflation** is a price-level rise that does not distort relative prices or incomes severely.

Inflation targeting. The announcement of official target ranges for the inflation rate along with an explicit statement that low and stable inflation is the overriding goal of monetary policy. Inflation targeting in hard or soft varieties has been adopted in recent years by many industrial countries.

Innovation. A term particularly associated with Joseph Schumpeter, who meant by it (1) the bringing to market of a new and significantly different product, (2) the introduction of a new production technique, or (3) the opening up of a new market. (Contrast with **invention.**)

Inputs. Inputs (or **factors of production**) are commodities or services used by firms in their production processes.

Insurance. A system by which individuals can reduce their exposure to risk of large losses by spreading the risks among a large number of persons.

Integration, vertical vs. horizontal. The production process is one of stages-e.g., iron ore into steel ingots, steel ingots into rolled steel sheets, rolled steel sheets into an automobile body. **Vertical integration** is the combination in a single firm of two or more different stages of this process (e.g., iron ore with steel ingots). **Horizontal integration** is the combination in a single firm of different units that operate at the same stage of production.

Intellectual property rights. Laws governing patents, copyrights, trade secrets, electronic media, and other commodities comprised primarily of information. These laws generally provide the original creator the right to control and be compensated for reproduction of the work.

Interest. The return paid to those who lend money.

Interest rate. The price paid for borrowing money for a period of time, usually expressed as a percentage of the principal per year. Thus, if the interest rate is 10 percent per year, then $100 would be paid for a loan of $1000 for 1 year.

Intermediate goods. Goods that have undergone some manufacturing or processing but have not yet reached the stage of becoming final products. For example, steel and cotton yarn are intermediate goods.

International monetary system (also **international financial system**). The institutions under which payments are made for transactions that reach across national boundaries. A central policy issue concerns the arrangement for determining how foreign exchange rates are set and how governments can affect exchange rates.

Intervention. An activity in which a government buys or sells its currency in the foreign exchange market in order to affect its currency's exchange rate.

Intrinsic value (of money). The commodity value of a piece of money (e.g., the market value of the weight of copper in a copper coin).

Invention. The creation of a new product or discovery of a new production technique. (Distinguish from innovation.)

Investment. (1) Economic activity that forgoes consumption today with an eye to increasing output in the future. It includes tangible capital such as houses and intangible investments such as education. Net investment is the value of total investment after an allowance has been made for depreciation. Gross investment is investment without allowance for depreciation. (2) In finance terms, investment has an altogether different meaning and denotes the purchase of a security, such as a stock or a bond.

Investment demand (or **investment demand curve**). The schedule showing the relationship between the level of investment and the cost of capital (or, more specifically, the real interest rate); also, the graph of that relationship.

Invisible hand. A concept introduced by Adam Smith in 1776 to describe the paradox of a laissez-faire market economy. The invisible-hand doctrine holds that, with each participant pursuing his or her own private interest, a market system nevertheless works to the benefit of all as though a benevolent invisible hand were directing the whole process.

Involuntarily unemployed. See **unemployment.**

Iron law of wages. In the economic theories of Malthus and Marx, the theory that there is an inevitable tendency in capitalism for wages to be driven down to a subsistence level.

Isoquant. See **equal product curve.**

K

Keynesian economics. The body of thought developed by John Maynard Keynes holding that a capitalist system does not automatically tend toward a full-employment equilibrium. According to Keynes, the resulting underemployment equilibrium could be cured by fiscal or monetary policies to raise aggregate demand.

Keynesian school. See **Keynesian economics.**

L

Labor force. In official U.S. statistics, that group of people 16 years of age and older who are either employed or unemployed.

Labor-force participation rate. Ratio of those in the labor force to the entire population 16 years of age or older.

Labor productivity. See **productivity.**

Labor supply. The number of workers (or, more generally, the number of labor-hours) available to an economy. The principal determinants of labor supply are population, real wages, and social traditions.

Labor theory of value. The view, often associated with Karl Marx, that every commodity should be valued solely according to the quantity of labor required for its production.

Laissez-faire ("Leave us alone"). The view that government should interfere as little as possible in economic activity and leave decisions to the marketplace. As expressed by classical economists like Adam Smith, this view held that the role of government should be limited to maintenance of law and order, national defense, and provision of certain public goods that private business would not undertake (e.g., public health and sanitation).

Land. In classical and neoclassical economics, one of the three basic factors of production (along with labor and capital). More generally, land is taken to include land used for agricultural or industrial purposes as well as natural resources taken from above or below the soil.

Law of downward-sloping demand. The nearly universal observation that when the price of a commodity is raised (and other things are held constant), buyers buy less of the commodity. Similarly, when the price is lowered, other things being constant, quantity demanded increases.

Law of diminishing marginal utility. See **diminishing marginal utility, law of.**

Law of diminishing returns. See **diminishing returns, law of.**

Least-cost rule (of production). The rule that the cost of producing a specific level of output is minimized when the ratio of the marginal revenue product of each input to the price of that input is the same for all inputs.

Legal tender. Money that by law must be accepted as payment for debts. All U.S. coins and currency are legal tender, but checks are not.

Less-developed country (LDC). A country with a per capita income far below that of "developed" nations (the latter usually includes most nations of North America and Western Europe).

Liabilities. In accounting, debts or financial obligations owed to other firms or persons.

Libertarianism. An economic philosophy that emphasizes the importance of personal freedom in economic and political affairs; also sometimes called "liberalism." Libertarian writers, including Adam Smith in an earlier age and Milton Friedman and James Buchanan today, hold that people should be able to follow their own interests and desires and that government activities should be limited to guaranteeing contracts and to providing police and national defense, thereby allowing maximum personal freedom.

Limited liability. The restriction of an owner's loss in a business to the amount of capital that the owner has contributed to the company. Limited liability was an important factor in the rise of large corporations. By contrast, owners in partnerships and individual proprietorships generally have **unlimited liability** for the debts of those firms.

Long run. A term used to denote a period over which full adjustment to changes can take place. In microeconomics, it denotes the time over which firms can enter or leave an industry and the capital stock can be replaced. In macroeconomics, it is often used to mean the period over which all prices, wage contracts, tax rates, and expectations can fully adjust.

Long-run aggregate supply schedule. A schedule showing the relationship between output and the price level after all price and wage adjustments have taken place, and the AS curve is therefore vertical.

Lorenz curve. A graph used to show the extent of inequality of income or wealth.

Lump-of-labor fallacy. The mistaken idea that the total amount of work to be done in a society is fixed. It is false because labor markets can adjust through wage changes or migration to accommodate changes in the supply and demand for labor.

M

M_1, M_2. See **money supply.**

Macroeconomic equilibrium. Refer to **equilibrium, macroeconomic.**

Macroeconomics. Analysis dealing with the behavior of the economy as a whole with respect to output, income, the price level, foreign trade, unemployment, and other aggregate economic variables. (Contrast with **microeconomics.**)

Malthusian theory of population growth. The hypothesis, first expressed by Thomas Malthus, that the "natural" tendency of population is to grow more rapidly than the food supply. Per capita food production would thus decline over time, thereby putting a check on population. In general, a view that population tends to grow more rapidly as incomes or living standards of the population rise.

Managed exchange rate. The most prevalent exchange-rate system today. In this system, a country occasionally intervenes to stabilize its currency but there is no fixed or announced parity.

Marginal cost. Refer to **cost, marginal.**

Marginal principle. The fundamental notion that people will maximize their income or profits when the marginal costs and marginal benefits of their actions are equal.

Marginal product (*MP*). The extra output resulting from 1 extra unit of a specified input when all other inputs are held constant. Sometimes called marginal physical product.

Marginal product theory of distribution. A theory of the distribution of income proposed by John B. Clark, according to which each productive input is paid according to its **marginal product.**

Marginal propensity to consume (*MPC*). The extra amount that people consume when they receive an extra dollar of disposable income. To be distinguished from the **average propensity to consume,** which is the ratio of total consumption to total disposable income.

Marginal propensity to import (*MPm*). In macroeconomics, the increase in the dollar value of imports resulting from each dollar increase in the value of GDP.

Marginal propensity to save (*MPS*). That fraction of an additional dollar of disposable income that is saved. Note that, by definition, $MPC + MPS = 1$.

Marginal revenue (*MR*). The additional revenue a firm would earn if it sold 1 extra unit of output. In perfect competition, *MR* equals price. Under imperfect competition, *MR* is less than price because, in order to sell the extra unit, the price must be reduced on all prior units sold.

Marginal revenue product (*MRP*) (of an input). Marginal revenue multiplied by marginal product. It is the extra revenue that would be brought in if a firm were to buy 1 extra unit of an input, put it to work, and sell the extra product it produced.

Marginal tax rate. For an income tax, the percentage of the last dollar of income paid in taxes. If a tax system is progressive, the marginal tax rate is higher than the average tax rate.

Marginal utility (*MU*). The additional or extra satisfaction yielded from consuming 1 additional unit of a commodity, with amounts of all other goods consumed held constant.

Market. An arrangement whereby buyers and sellers interact to determine the prices and quantities of a commodity. Some markets (such as the stock market or a flea market) take place in physical locations; other markets are conducted over the telephone or are organized by computers, and some markets now are organized on the Internet.

Market-clearing price. The price in a supply and demand equilibrium. This denotes that all supply and demand orders are filled at that price, so that the books are "cleared" of orders.

Market economy. An economy in which the *what, how,* and *for whom* questions concerning resource allocation are primarily determined by supply and demand in markets. In this form of economic organization, firms, motivated by the desire to maximize profits, buy inputs and produce and sell outputs. Households, armed with their factor incomes, go to markets and determine the demand for commodities. The interaction of firms' supply and households' demand then determines the prices and quantities of goods.

Market equilibrium. Same as **competitive equilibrium.**

Market failure. An imperfection in a price system that prevents an effi-

cient allocation of resources. Important examples are **externalities and imperfect competition.**

Market power. The degree of control that a firm or group of firms has over the price and production decisions in an industry. In a monopoly, the firm has a high degree of market power; firms in perfectly competitive industries have no market power. **Concentration ratios** are the most widely used measures of market power.

Market share. That fraction of an industry's output accounted for by an individual firm or group of firms.

Markup pricing. The pricing method used by many firms in situations of imperfect competition; under this method they estimate average cost and then add some fixed percentage to that cost in order to reach the price they charge.

Marxism. The set of social, political, and economic doctrines developed by Karl Marx in the nineteenth century. As an economic theory, Marxism predicted that capitalism would collapse as a result of its own internal contradictions, especially its tendency to exploit the working classes. The conviction that workers would inevitably be oppressed under capitalism was based on the **iron law of wages,** which holds that wages would decline to subsistence levels.

Mean. In statistics, the same thing as "average." Thus for the numbers 1, 3, 6, 10, 20, the mean is 8.

Median. In statistics, the figure exactly in the middle of a series of numbers ordered or ranked from lowest to highest (e.g., incomes or examination grades). Thus for the numbers 1, 3, 6, 10, 20, the median is 6.

Mercantilism. A political doctrine emphasizing the importance of balance-of-payments surpluses as a device to accumulate gold. Proponents therefore advocated tight government control of economic policies, believing that laissez-faire policies might lead to a loss of gold.

Merchandise trade balance. See **trade balance.**

Merger. The acquisition of one corporation by another, which usually occurs when one firm buys the stock of another. Important examples are (1) **vertical mergers,** which occur when the two firms are at different stages of a production process (e.g., iron ore and steel), (2) **horizontal mergers,** which occur when the two firms produce in the same market (e.g., two automobile manufacturers), and (3) **conglomerate mergers,** which occur when the two firms operate in unrelated markets (e.g., shoelaces and oil refining).

Microeconomics. Analysis dealing with the behavior of individual elements in an economy—such as the determination of the price of a single product or the behavior of a single consumer or business firm. (Contrast with **macroeconomics.**)

Minimum cost. Refer to **cost, minimum.**

Mixed economy. The dominant form of economic organization in noncommunist countries. Mixed economies rely primarily on the price system for their economic organization but use a variety of government interventions (such as taxes, spending, and regulation) to handle macroeconomic instability and market failures.

Model. A formal framework for representing the basic features of a complex system by a few central relationships. Models take the form of graphs, mathematical equations, and computer programs.

Moderate inflation. See **inflation.**

Momentary run. A period of time that is so short that production is fixed.

Monetarism. A school of thought holding that changes in the money supply are the major cause of macroeconomic fluctuations. For the short run, this view holds that changes in the money supply are the primary determinant of changes in both real output and the price level. For the longer run, this holds that prices tend to move proportionally with the money supply. Monetarists often conclude that the best macroeconomic policy is one with a stable growth in the money supply.

Monetary base. The net monetary liabilities of the government that are held by the public. In the United States, the monetary base is equal to currency and bank reserves. Sometimes called **high-powered money.**

Monetary economy. An economy in which the trade takes place through a commonly accepted medium of exchange.

Monetary policy. The objectives of the central bank in exercising its control over money, interest rates, and credit conditions. The instruments of monetary policy are primarily open-market operations, reserve requirements, and the discount rate.

Monetary rule. The cardinal tenet of monetarist economic philosophy is the monetary rule which asserts that optimal monetary policy sets the growth of money supply at a fixed rate and holds to that rate through thick and thin.

Monetary transmission mechanism. In macroeconomics, the route by which changes in the supply of money are translated into changes in output, employment, prices, and inflation.

Monetary union. An arrangement by which several nations adopt a common currency as a unit of account and medium of exchange. The European Monetary Union is scheduled to adopt the "Euro" as the common currency in 1999.

Money. The means of payment or medium of exchange. For the items constituting money, see **money supply.**

Money demand schedule. The relationship between holdings of money and interest rates. As interest rates rise, bonds and other securities become more attractive, lowering the quantity of money demanded. See also **demand for money.**

Money funds. Shorthand expression for very liquid short-term financial instruments whose interst rates are not regulated. The major examples are money market mutual funds and commercial bank money market deposit accounts.

Money market. A term denoting the set of institutions that handle the purchase or sale of short-term credit instruments like Treasury bills and commercial paper.

Money supply. The narrowly defined money supply, or narrow money, (M_1) consists of coins, paper currency, plus all demand or checking deposits; this is narrow, or transactions, money. The broadly defined supply (M_2) includes all items in M_1 plus certain liquid assets or near-monies—savings deposits, money market funds, and the like.

Money-supply effect. The relationship whereby a price rise operating on a fixed nominal money supply produces tight money and lowers aggregate spending.

Money-supply multiplier. The ratio of the increase in the money supply (or in deposits) to the increase in bank reserves. Generally, the money-supply multiplier is equal to the inverse of the required reserve ratio. For example, if the required reserve ratio is 0.125, then the money-supply multiplier is 8.

Money, velocity of. Refer to **velocity of money.**

Monopolistic competition. A market structure in which there are many sellers who are supplying goods that are close, but not perfect, substitutes. In such a market, each firm can exercise some effect on its product's price.

Monopoly. A market structure in which a commodity is supplied by a single firm. Also see **natural monopoly.**

Monopsony. The mirror image of monopoly: a market in which there is a single buyer; a "buyer's monopoly."

Moral hazard. A type of market failure in which the presence of insurance against an insured risk increases the likelihood of the risky event occurring. For example, a car owner insured against auto theft may be careless about locking the car because the presence of insurance reduces the incentive to prevent the theft.

MPC. See **marginal propensity to consume.**

MPS. See **marginal propensity to save.**

Multiplier. A term in macroeconomics denoting the change in an induced variable (such as GDP or money supply) per unit of change in an external variable (such as government spending or bank reserves). The **expenditure multiplier** refers to the increase in GDP that would result from a $1 increase in expenditure (say, on investment).

Multiplier model. In macroeconomics, a theory developed by J. M. Keynes that emphasizes the importance of changes in autonomous expenditures (especially investment, government spending, and net exports) in determining changes in output and employment. Also see **multiplier.**

N

NAIRU. See **nonaccelerating inflation rate of unemployment**

Narrow money. See **money supply.**

Nash equilibrium. In game theory, a set of strategies for the players where no player can improve his or her payoff given the other player's strategy. That is, given player A's strategy, player B can do no better, and given B's strategy, A can do no better. The Nash equilibrium is also sometimes called the **noncooperative equilibrium.**

National debt. Same as **government debt.**

National income and product accounts (NIPA). A set of accounts that measures the spending, income, and output of the entire nation for a quarter or a year.

National saving rate. Total saving, private and public, divided by net domestic product.

Natural monopoly. A firm or industry whose average cost per unit of production falls sharply over the entire range of its output, as for example in local electricity distribution. Thus a single firm, a monopoly, can supply the industry output more efficiently than can multiple firms.

"Near-money." Financial assets that are risk-free and so readily convertible into money that they are close to actually being money. Examples are money funds and Treasury bills.

Negative income tax. A plan for replacing current income-support programs (welfare, food stamps, etc.) with a unified program. Under such a plan, poor families would receive an income supplement and would have benefits reduced as their earnings increase.

Neoclassical model of growth. A theory or model used to explain long-term trends in economic growth of industrial economies. This model emphasizes the importance of capital deepening (i.e., a growing capital-labor ratio) and technological change in explaining the growth of potential real GDP.

Net domestic product (NDP). GDP less an allowance for depreciation of capital goods.

Net economic welfare (NEW). A measure of national output that corrects several limitations of the GDP measure.

Net exports. In the national product accounts, the value of exports of goods and services minus the value of imports of goods and services.

Net foreign investment. Net saving by a country abroad, also approximately equal to net exports.

Net investment. Gross investment minus depreciation of capital goods.

Net national product (NNP). GNP less an allowance for depreciation of capital goods.

Net worth. In accounting, total assets minus total liabilities.

New classical macroeconomics. This theory holds that (1) prices and wages are flexible and (2) people make forecasts in accordance with the rational expectations hypothesis. The main implication of this theory is the policy ineffectiveness theorem. See **rational expectations hypothesis** and **policy ineffectiveness theorem.**

NNP. See **net national product.**

Nominal GDP. See **gross domestic product, nominal.**

Nominal GNP. See **gross national product, nominal.**

Nominal (or **money**) **interest rate.** The **interest rate** paid on different assets. This represents a dollar return per year per dollar invested. Compare with the **real interest rate,** which represents the return per year in goods per unit of goods invested.

Nonaccelerating inflation rate of unemployment (or **NAIRU**). That unemployment rate consistent with a constant inflation rate. At the NAIRU, upward and downward forces on price and wage inflation are in balance so there is no tendency for inflation to change. The NAIRU is the lowest unemployment rate that can be sustained without upward pressure on inflation. The NAIRU is the unemployment rate at which the long-run Phillips curve is vertical.

Noncooperative equilibrium. See **Nash equilibrium.**

Nonrenewable resources. Those natural resources, like oil and gas, that are essentially fixed in supply and whose regeneration is not quick enough to be economically relevant.

Normative vs. positive economics. Normative economics considers "what ought to be"—value judgments, or goals, of public policy. Positive economics, by contrast, is the analysis of facts and behavior in an economy, or "the way things are."

Not in the labor force. That part of the adult population that is neither working nor looking for work.

O

Okun's Law. The empirical relationship, discovered by Arthur Okun, between cyclical movements in GDP and unemployment. The law states that when actual GDP declines 2 percent relative to potential GDP, the unemployment rate increases by about 1 percentage point. (Earlier estimates placed the ratio at 3 to 1.)

Oligopoly. A situation of imperfect competition in which an industry is dominated by a small number of suppliers.

Open economy. An economy that engages in international trade (i.e., imports and exports) of goods and capital with other countries. A **closed economy** is one that has no imports or exports.

Open-economy multiplier. In an open economy, income leaks into imports as well as into saving. Therefore, the open-economy multiplier for investment or government expenditure is given by

Open-economy multiplier =
$$1/(MPS + MPm)$$

where MPS = marginal propensity to save and MPm = marginal propensity to import.

Open-market operations. The activity of a central bank in buying or selling government bonds to influence bank reserves, the money supply, and interest rates. If securities are bought, the money paid out by the central bank increases commercial-bank reserves, and the money supply increases. If securities are sold, the money supply contracts.

Opportunity cost. The value of the next best use (or opportunity) for an economic good, or the value of the sacrificed alternative. Thus, say that the best alternative use of the inputs employed to mine a ton of coal was to grow 10 bushels of wheat. The opportunity cost of a ton of coal is thus the 10 bushels of wheat that *could* have been produced but were not. Opportunity cost is particularly useful for valuing nonmarketed goods such as environmental health or safety.

Optimal currency area. A grouping of regions or countries which have high labor mobility or have common and synchronous aggregate supply or demand shocks. Under such conditions, significant changes in exchange rates are not necessary to ensure rapid macroeconomic adjustment and the countries can have fixed exchange rates or a common currency.

Ordinal utility. A dimensionless utility measure used in demand theory. Ordinal utility enables one to state that A is preferred to B, but we cannot say by how much. That is, any two bundles of goods can be ranked relative to each other, but the absolute difference between bundles cannot be measured. This contrasts with **cardinal utility,** or dimensional utility, which is sometimes used in the analysis of behavior toward risk. An example of a cardinal measure comes when we say that a substance at 100 K (kelvin) is twice as hot as one at 50 K.

Other things constant. A phrase (sometimes stated "ceteris paribus") that signifies that a factor under consideration is changed while all other factors are held constant or unchanged. For example, a downward-sloping demand curve shows that the quantity demanded will decline as the price rises, as long as other things (such as incomes) are held constant.

Outputs. These are the various useful goods or services that are either consumed or used in further production.

P

Paradox of thrift. The principle, first proposed by John Maynard Keynes, that an attempt by a society to increase its saving may result in a reduction in the amount which it actually saves.

Paradox of value. The paradox that many necessities of life (e.g., water) have a low "market" value, while many luxuries (e.g., diamonds) with little "use" value have a high market price. It is explained by the fact that a price reflects not the total utility of a commodity but its marginal utility.

Pareto efficiency (or **Pareto optimality**). See **allocative efficiency.**

Partial-equilibrium analysis. Analysis concentrating on the effect of changes in an individual market, holding other things equal (e.g., disregarding changes in income).

Partnership. An association of two or more persons to conduct a business which is not in corporate form and does not enjoy limited liability.

Patent. An exclusive right granted to an inventor to control the use of an invention for, in the United States, a period of 20 years. Patents create temporary monopolies as a way of rewarding inventive activity and, like other intellectual property rights, are a tool for promoting invention among individuals or small firms.

Payoff table. In game theory, a table used to describe the strategies and payoffs of a game with two or more players. The profits or utilities of the different players are the **payoffs.**

Payoffs. See **payoff table.**

Perfect competition. Refer to **competition, perfect.**

Personal income. A measure of income before taxes have been deducted. More precisely, it equals disposable personal income plus net taxes.

Personal saving. That part of income which is not consumed; in other words, the difference between disposable income and consumption.

Personal saving rate. The ratio of personal saving to personal disposable income, in percent.

Phillips curve. A graph first devised by A. W. Phillips, showing the tradeoff between unemployment and inflation. In modern mainstream macroeconomics, the downward-sloping "tradeoff" Phillips curve is generally held to be valid only in the short run; in the long run, the Phillips curve is usually thought to be vertical at the nonaccelerating inflation rate of unemployment (or NAIRU).

Policy ineffectiveness theorem. A theorem which asserts that, with rational expectations and flexible prices and wages, anticipated government monetary or fiscal policy cannot affect real output or unemployment.

Portfolio theory. An economic theory that describes how rational investors allocate their wealth among different financial asset—that is, how they put their wealth into a "portfolio."

Positive economics. See **normative vs. positive economics.**

Post hoc fallacy. From the Latin, *post hoc, ergo propter hoc,* which translates as "after this, therefore because of this." This fallacy arises when it is assumed that because event A precedes event B, it follows that A *causes* B.

Potential GDP. High-employment GDP; more precisely, the maximum level of GDP that can be sustained with a given state of technology and population size without accelerating inflation. Today, it is generally taken to be equivalent to the level of output corresponding to the **nonaccelerating inflation rate of unemployment** (or **NAIRU**). Potential output is not necessarily maximum output.

Potential output. Same as **potential GDP.**

Poverty. Today, the U.S. government defines the "poverty line" to be the minimum adequate standard of living.

PPF. See **production-possibility frontier.**

Present value (of an asset). Today's value for an asset that yields a stream of income over time. Valuation of such time streams of returns requires calculating the present worth of each component of the income, which is done by applying a discount rate (or interest rate) to future incomes.

Price. The money cost of a good, service, or asset. Price is measured in monetary units per unit of the good (as in 3 dollars per 1 hamburger).

Price discrimination. A situation where the same product is sold to different consumers for different prices.

Price-elastic demand (or **elastic demand**). The situation in which price elasticity of demand exceeds 1 in absolute value. This signifies that the percentage change in quantity demanded is greater than the percentage change in price. In addition, elastic demand implies that total revenue (price times quantity) rises when price falls because the increase in quantity demanded is so large. (Contrast with **price-inelastic demand.**)

Price elasticity of demand. A measure of the extent to which quantity demanded responds to a price change. The elasticity coefficient (price elasticity of demand E_P) is percentage change in quantity demanded divided by percentage change in price. In figuring percentages, use the averages of old and new quantities in the numerator and of old and new prices in the denominator; disregard the minus sign. Refer also to **price-elastic demand, price-inelastic demand, unit-elastic demand.**

Price elasticity of supply. Conceptually similar to **price elasticity of demand,** except that it measures the supply responsiveness to a price change. More precisely, the price elasticity of supply measures the percentage change in quantity supplied divided by the percentage change in price. Supply elasticities are most useful in perfect competition.

Price flexibility. Price behavior in "auction" markets (e.g., for many raw commodities or the stock market), in which prices immediately respond to changes in demand or in supply. (In contrast, refer to **administered prices.**)

Price index. An index number that shows how the average price of a bundle of goods has changed over a period of time. In computing the average, the prices of the different goods are generally weighted by their economic importance (e.g., by each commodity's share of total consumer expenditures in the **consumer price index**).

Price-inelastic demand (or **inelastic demand**). The situation in which price elasticity of demand is below 1 in absolute value. In this case, when price declines, total revenue declines, and when price is increased, total revenue goes up. Perfectly inelastic demand means that there is no change at all in quantity demanded when price goes up or down. (Contrast with **price-elastic demand** and **unit-elastic demand.**)

Prisoner's dilemma. A famous game in which the non-cooperative equilibrium is inefficient.

Private good.   See **public good.**

Producer price index.   The price index of goods sold at the wholesale level (such as steel, wheat, oil).

Producer surplus.   The difference between the producer sales revenue and the producer cost. The producer surplus is generally measured as the area above the supply curve but under the price line up to the amount sold.

Product, average.   Refer to **average product.**

Product differentiation.   The existence of characteristics that make similar goods less-than-perfect substitutes. Thus locational differences make similar types of gasoline sold at separate points imperfect substitutes. Firms enjoying product differentiation face a downward-sloping demand curve instead of the horizontal demand curve of the perfect competitor.

Product, marginal.   Refer to **marginal product.**

Production function.   A relation (or mathematical function) specifying the maximum output that can be produced with given inputs for a given level of technology. Applies to a firm or, as an aggregate production function, to the economy as a whole.

Production-possibility frontier (*PPF*).   A graph showing the menu of goods that can be produced by an economy. In a frequently cited case, the choice is reduced to two goods, guns and butter. Points outside the *PPF* (to the northeast of it) are unattainable. Points inside it are inefficient since resources are not being fully employed, resources are not being used properly, or outdated production techniques are being utilized.

Productive efficiency.   A situation in which an economy cannot produce more of one good without producing less of another good; this implies that the economy is on its production-possibility frontier.

Productivity.   A term referring to the ratio of output to inputs (total output divided by labor inputs is **labor productivity**). Productivity increases if the same quantity of inputs produces more output. Labor productivity increases because of improved technology, improvements in labor skills, or capital deepening.

Productivity growth.   The rate of increase in **productivity** from one period to another. For example, if an index of labor productivity is 100 in 1990 and 101.7 in 1991, the rate of productivity growth is 1.7 percent per year for 1991 over 1990.

Productivity of capital, net.   See **rate of return.**

Profit.   (1) In accounting terms, total revenue minus costs properly chargeable against the goods sold (see income statement). (2) In economic theory, the difference between sales revenue and the full opportunity cost of resources involved in producing the goods.

Profit-and-loss statement.   See **income statement.**

Progressive, proportional, and regressive taxes.   A progressive tax weighs more heavily upon the rich; a regressive tax does the opposite. More precisely, a tax is progressive if the average tax rate (i.e., taxes divided by income) is higher for those with higher incomes; it is a regressive tax if the average tax rate declines with higher incomes; it is a proportional tax if the average tax rate is equal at all income levels.

Property rights.   Property rights define the ability of individuals or firms to own, buy, sell, and use the capital goods and other property in a market economy.

Proportional tax.   See **progressive, proportional, and regressive taxes.**

Proprietorship, individual.   A business firm owned and operated by one person.

Protectionism.   Any policy adopted by a country to protect domestic industries against competition from imports (most commonly, a tariff or quota imposed on such imports).

Public choice (also **public-choice theory**).   Branch of economics and political science dealing with the way that governments make choices and direct the economy. This theory differs from the theory of markets in emphasizing the influence of vote maximizing for politicians, which contrasts to profit maximizing by firms.

Public debt.   See **government debt.**

Public good.   A commodity whose benefits are indivisibly spread among the entire community, whether or not particular individuals desire to consume the public good. For example, a public-health measure that eradicates smallpox protects all, not just those paying for the vaccinations. To be contrasted with **private goods,** such as bread, which, if consumed by one person, cannot be consumed by another person.

Pure economic rent.   See **rent, economic.**

Q

Quantity demanded.   See **change in demand vs. change in quantity demanded.**

Quantity equation of exchange.   A tautology, $MV \equiv PQ$, where M is the money supply, V is the income velocity of money, and PQ (price times quantity) is the money value of total output (nominal GDP). The equation must always hold exactly since V is defined as PQ/M.

Quantity supplied.   See **change in supply vs. change in quantity supplied.**

Quantity theory of money.   A theory of the determination of output and the overall price level holding that prices move proportionately with the money supply. A more cautious approach put forth by monetarists holds that the money supply is the most important determinant of changes in nominal GDP (see **monetarism**).

Quota. A form of import protectionism in which the total quantity of imports of a particular commodity (e.g., sugar or cars) during a given period is limited.

R

Random-walk theory (of stock market prices). See the **efficient-market theory.**

Rate of inflation. See **inflation.**

Rate of return (or **return**) **on capital.** The yield on an investment or on a capital good. Thus, an investment costing $100 and yielding $12 annually has a rate of return of 12 percent per year.

Rational expectations. See **expectations.**

Rational-expectations hypothesis. This hypothesis holds that people make unbiased forecasts and further that people use all available information and economic theory to make these forecasts.

Rational-expectations macroeconomics. A school, led by Robert Lucas, Robert Barro, and Thomas Sargent, holding that markets clear quickly and that expectations are rational. Under these and other conditions it can be shown that predictable macroeconomic policies have no effect on real output or unemployment. Sometimes called **new classical macroeconomics.**

Real-business-cycle theory. A theory that explains business cycles purely as shifts in aggregate supply, primarily due to technological disturbances, without any reference to monetary or other demand-side forces.

Real GDP. See **gross domestic product, real.**

Real interest rate. The interest rate measured in terms of goods rather than money. It is thus equal to the money (or nominal) interest rate less the rate of inflation.

Real wages. The purchasing power of a worker's wages in terms of goods and services. It is measured by the ratio of the money wage rate to the consumer price index.

Recession. A downturn in real GDP for two or more successive quarters. See also **depression.**

Regressive tax. See **progressive, proportional, and regressive taxes.**

Regulation. Government laws or rules designed to control the behavior of firms. The major kinds are **economic regulation** (which affects the prices, entry, or service of a single industry, such as telephone service) and **social regulation** (which attempts to correct externalities that prevail across a number of industries, such as air or water pollution).

Renewable resources. Natural resources (like agricultural land) whose services replenish regularly and which, if properly managed, can yield useful services indefinitely.

Rent, economic (or **pure economic rent**). This term was applied to income earned from land. The total supply of land available is (with minor qualifications) fixed, and the return paid to the landowner is rent. The term is often extended to the return paid to any factor in fixed supply—i.e., to any input having a perfectly inelastic or vertical supply curve.

Required reserves. See **reserves, bank.**

Reserves, bank. That portion of deposits that a bank sets aside in the form of vault cash or non-interest-earning deposits with Federal Reserve Banks. In the United States, banks are required to hold 12 percent of checking deposits (or transactions accounts) in the form of reserves.

Reserves, international. Every nation holds at least some reserves, in such forms as gold, currencies of other nations, and special drawing rights. International reserves serve as "international money," to be used when a country encounters balance-of-payments difficulties. If a nation were prepared to allow its exchange rate to float freely, it would need minimal reserves.

Resource allocation. The manner in which an economy distributes its resources (its factors of production) among the potential uses so as to produce a particular set of final goods.

Returns to scale. The rate at which output increases when all inputs are increased proportionately. For example, if all the inputs double and output is exactly doubled, that process is said to exhibit **constant returns to scale.** If, however, output grows by less than 100 percent when all inputs are doubled, the process shows **decreasing returns to scale;** if output more than doubles, the process demonstrates **increasing returns to scale.**

Revaluation. An increase in the official foreign exchange rate of a currency. See also **devaluation.**

Ricardian view of fiscal policy. A theory developed by Harvard's Robert Barro which holds that changes in tax rates have no impact upon consumption spending.

Risk. In financial economics, refers to the variability of the returns on an investment.

Risk averse. A person is risk averse when, faced with an uncertain situation, the displeasure from losing a given amount of income is greater than the pleasure from gaining the same amount of income.

Risk spreading. The process of taking large risks and spreading them around so that they are but small risks for a large number of people. The major form of risk spreading is **insurance,** which is a kind of gambling in reverse.

Rule of 70. A useful shortcut for approximating compound interest. A quantity that grows at r percent per year will double in about $70/r$ years.

S

Sales tax. See **excise tax vs. sales tax.**

Saving function. The schedule showing the amount of saving that households or a nation will undertake at each level of income.

Say's Law of Markets. The theory that "supply creates its own demand." J. B. Say argued in 1803 that, because total purchasing power is exactly equal to total incomes and outputs, excess demand or supply is impossible. Keynes attacked Say's Law, pointing out that an extra dollar of income need not be spent entirely (i.e., the marginal propensity to spend is not necessarily unity).

Scarcity. Scarcity is the distinguishing characteristic of an economic good. That an economic good is scarce does not mean that it is rare, but only that it is not freely available for the taking. To obtain such a good, one must either produce it or offer other economic goods in exchange.

Scarcity, law of. The principle that most things that people want are available only in limited supply (the exception being **free goods**). Thus goods are generally scarce and must somehow be rationed, whether by price or some other means.

Schedule (demand, supply, aggregate demand, aggregate supply). Term used interchangably with curve, as in demand curve, supply curve, etc.

Securities. A term used to designate a wide variety of financial assets, such as stocks, bonds, options, and notes; more precisely, the documents used to establish ownership of these assets.

Short run. A period in which not all factors can adjust fully. In microeconomics, the capital stock and other "fixed" inputs cannot be adjusted and entry is not free in the short run. In macroeconomics, prices, wage contracts, tax rates, and expectations may not fully adjust in the short run.

Short-run aggregate supply schedule. The schedule showing the relationship between output and prices in the short run wherein changes in aggregate demand can affect output. Also represented by an upward-sloping or horizontal *AS* curve.

Shutdown price (or point, or rule). In the theory of the firm, the shutdown point comes at that point where the market price is just sufficient to cover average variable cost and no more. Hence, the firm's losses per period just equal its fixed costs; it might as well shut down.

Single-tax movement. A nineteenth-century movement, originated by Henry George, holding that continued poverty in the midst of steady economic progress was attributable to the scarcity of land and the large rents flowing to landowners. The "single tax" was to be a tax on economic rent earned from landownership.

Slope. In a graph, the change in the variable on the vertical axis per unit of change in the variable on the horizontal axis. Upward-sloping lines have positive slopes, downward-sloping curves (like demand curves) have negative slopes, and horizontal lines have slopes of zero.

Social insurance. Mandatory insurance provided by government to improve social welfare by preventing the losses created by market failures such as moral hazard or adverse selection.

Social overhead capital. The essential investments on which economic development depends, particularly for sanitation and drinking water, transportation, and communications. Sometimes called "infrastructure."

Social regulation. See **regulation.**

Socialism. A political theory that holds that all (or almost all) the means of production, other than labor, should be owned by the community. This allows the return on capital to be shared more equally than under capitalism.

Speculator. Someone engaged in speculation, i.e., someone who buys (or sells) a commodity or financial asset with the aim of profiting from later selling (or buying) the item at a higher (or lower) price.

Spillovers. Same as **externalities.**

Stagflation. A term, coined in the early 1970s, describing the coexistence of high unemployment, or *stag*nation, with persistent in*flation*. Its explanation lies primarily in the inertial nature of the inflationary process.

Statistical discrimination. Treatment of individuals on the basis of the average behavior or characteristics of members of the group to which they belong. Statistical discrimination can be self-fulfilling by reducing incentives for individuals to overcome the stereotype.

Stock, common. Refer to **common stock.**

Stock market. An organized marketplace in which common stocks are traded. In the United States, the largest stock market is the New York Stock Exchange, on which are traded the stocks of the largest U.S. companies.

Stock vs. flow. See **flow vs. stock.**

Strategic interaction. A situation in oligopolistic markets in which each firm's business strategies depend upon its rival's plans. A formal analysis of strategic interaction is given in **game theory.**

Structural budget. See **actual, cyclical, and structural budget.**

Structural unemployment. Unemployment resulting because the regional or occupational pattern of job vacancies does not match the pattern of worker availability. There may be jobs available, but unemployed workers may not have the required skill; or the jobs may be in different regions from where the unemployed workers live.

Subsidy. A payment by a government to a firm or household that provides or consumes a commodity. For example, governments often subsidize food by paying for part of the food expenditures of low-income households.

Substitutes. Goods that compete with each other (as with gloves and mittens). By contrast, goods that go together in the eyes of consumers (such as left shoes and right shoes) are **complements.**

Substitution effect (of a price change). The tendency of consumers is to consume more of a good when its relative price falls (to "substitute" in favor of that good) and to consume less of the good when its relative price increases (to "substitute" away from that good). This substitution effect of a price change leads to a downward-sloping demand curve. (Compare with **income effect.**)

Substitution rule. This asserts that if the price of one factor falls while all other factor prices remain the same, firms will profit by substituting the now-cheaper factor for all the other factors. The rule is a corollary of the **least-cost rule.**

Supply curve (or **supply schedule**). A schedule showing the quantity of a good that suppliers in a given market desire to sell at each price, holding other things equal.

Supply shock. In macroeconomics, a sudden change in production costs or productivity that has a large and unexpected impact upon aggregate supply. As a result of a supply shock, real GNP and the price level change unexpectedly.

Supply-side economics. A view emphasizing policy measures to affect aggregate supply or potential output. This approach holds that high marginal tax rates on labor and capital incomes reduce work effort and saving.

T

Tangible assets. Those assets, such as land or capital goods like computers, buildings, and automobiles, that are used to produce further goods and services.

Tariff. A levy or tax imposed upon each unit of a commodity imported into a country.

Tax incidence. See **incidence.**

Technological change. A change in the process of production or introduction of new products such that more or improved output can be obtained from the same bundle of inputs. It results in an outward shift in the production-possibility curve.

Technological progress. See **technological change.**

Terms of trade (in international trade). The "real" terms at which a nation sells its export products and buys its import products. It equals the ratio of an index of export prices to an index of import prices.

Theory of income distribution. A theory explaining the manner in which personal income and wealth are distributed in a society.

Tight-money policy. A central-bank policy of restraining or reducing the money supply and of raising interest rates. This policy has the effect of slowing the growth of real GDP, reducing the rate of inflation, or raising the nation's foreign exchange rate. (Contrast with **easy-money policy.**)

Time deposit. Funds, held in a bank, that have a minimum "time of withdrawal." Included in broad money (M_2) but not in M_1 because they are not accepted as a means of payment.

Token money. Money with little or no intrinsic value.

Total cost. Refer to **cost, total.**

Total factor productivity (also sometimes call multifactor productivity). An index of productivity that measures total output per unit of total input. The numerator of the index is total output (say, GDP), while the denominator is a weighted average of inputs of capital, labor, and resources. The growth of total factor productivity is often taken as an index of the rate of technological progress.

Total product (or **output**). The total amount of a commodity produced, measured in physical units such as bushels of wheat, tons of steel, or number of haircuts.

Total revenue. Price times quantity, or total sales.

Trade balance or merchandise trade balance. See **balance of trade.**

Trade barrier. Any of a number of protectionist devices by which nations discourage imports. Tariffs and quotas are the most visible barriers, but in recent years nontariff barriers (or NTBs), such as burdensome regulatory proceedings, have replaced more traditional measures.

Transactions demand for money. See **demand for money.**

Transactions money. A measure of money supply (also known as M_1) which consists of items that are actually for transactions, namely, currency and checking accounts.

Transfer payments, government. Payments made by a government to individuals, for which the individual performs no current service in return. Examples are social security payments and unemployment insurance.

Treasury bills (T-bills). Short-term bonds or securities issued by the federal government.

U

Underground economy. Unreported economic activity. The underground economy includes otherwise legal activities not reported to the taxing authorities (such as garage sales or services "bartered" among friends) and illegal activities (such as the drug trade, gambling, and prostitution).

Unemployed. People who are not employed but are actively looking for work or waiting to return to work.

Unemployment. (1) In economic terms, **involuntary unemployment** occurs if there are qualified workers who would be willing to work at prevailing wages but cannot find jobs. (2) In the official (U.S. Bureau of Labor Statistics) definition, a worker is unemployed if he or she (*a*) is not working and (*b*) either is waiting for recall from layoff or has actively looked for work in the last 4 weeks.

Unemployment, frictional. Refer to **frictional unemployment.**

Unemployment rate. The percentage of the labor force that is unemployed.

Unit-elastic demand. The situation, between **price-elastic demand** and **price-inelastic demand,** in which price elasticity is just equal to 1 in absolute value. See also **price elasticity of demand.**

Unlimited liability. See **limited liability.**

Usury. The charging of an interest rate above a legal maximum on borrowed money.

Utility (also **total utility**). The total satisfaction derived from the consumption of goods or services. To be contrasted with **marginal utility,** which is the additional utility arising from consumption of an additional unit of the commodity.

Utility-possibility frontier. Analogous to the **production-possibility frontier;** a graph showing the utility or satisfaction of two consumers (or groups), one on each axis. It is downward-sloping to indicate that redistributing income from A to B will lower the utility of A and raise that of B. Points on the utility-possibility frontier display **allocative** (or **Pareto**) **efficiency.** For Pareto-efficient allocations, it is impossible to find feasible outcomes that would make one person better off without making someone else worse off.

V

Value added. The difference between the value of goods produced and the cost of materials and supplies used in producing them. In a $1 loaf of bread embodying $0.60 worth of wheat and other materials, the value added is $0.40. Value added consists of the wages, interest, and profit components added to the output by a firm or industry.

Value-added tax (or **VAT**). A tax levied upon a firm as a percentage of its value added.

Value, paradox of. Refer to **paradox of value.**

Variable. A magnitude of interest that can be defined and measured. Important variables in economics include prices, quantities, interest rates, exchange rates, dollars of wealth, and so forth.

Variable cost. Refer to **cost, variable.**

Velocity of money. In serving its function as a medium of exchange, money moves from buyer to seller to new buyer and so on. Its "velocity" refers to the "speed" of this movement. The **income velocity of money** is defined as nominal GNP divided by the total money supply $V \equiv P \times Q/M \equiv \text{GNP}/M$.

Vertical equity. See **horizontal equity vs. vertical equity.**

Vertical integration. See **integration, vertical vs. horizontal.**

Vertical merger. See **merger.**

Voluntarily unemployed. Describes an individual who is unemployed because she perceives the value of wages to be less than the opportunity use of time, say in leisure.

W

Wealth. The net value of tangible and financial items owned by a nation or person at a point of time. It equals all assets less all liabilities.

Welfare economics. The normative analysis of economic systems, i.e., the study of what is "wrong" or "right" about the economy's functioning.

Welfare state. A concept of the mixed economy arising in Europe in the late nineteenth century and introduced in the United States in the 1930s. In the modern conception of the welfare state, markets direct the detailed activities of day to day economic life while governments regulate social conditions and provide pensions, health care, and other aspects of the social safety net.

What, how,* and *for whom. The three fundamental problems of economic organization. *What* is the problem of how much of each possible good and service will be produced with the society's limited stock of resources or inputs. *How* is the choice of the particular technique by which each good of the what shall be produced. *For whom* refers to the distribution of consumption goods among the members of that society.

Winner-take-all games. Situations in which payoffs are determined by merit relative to other competitors/players rather than by absolute merit. These contests generally are characterized by rewards heavily or entirely concentrated among the very best competitors.

Y

Yield. Same as the **interest rate or rate of return** on an asset.

Z

Zero-profit point. For a business firm, that level of price at which the firm breaks even, covering all costs but earning zero profit.

Index

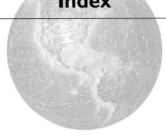